Psychopathy and Criminal Behavior

Psychopathy and Criminal Behavior

Current Trends and Challenges

Edited by

Paulo Barbosa Marques
Immigration and Borders Service (SEF), Porto, Portugal

Mauro Paulino
Mind – Institute of Clinical and Forensic Psychology, Lisbon, Portugal

Laura Alho
Laura Alho – Clinical and Forensic Psychology, Mind – Institute of Clinical and Forensic Psychology, and WPO, Aveiro, Portugal

ELSEVIER

ACADEMIC PRESS
An imprint of Elsevier

Academic Press is an imprint of Elsevier
125 London Wall, London EC2Y 5AS, United Kingdom
525 B Street, Suite 1650, San Diego, CA 92101, United States
50 Hampshire Street, 5th Floor, Cambridge, MA 02139, United States
The Boulevard, Langford Lane, Kidlington, Oxford OX5 1GB, United Kingdom

Library of Congress Cataloging-in-Publication Data
A catalog record for this book is available from the Library of Congress

British Library Cataloguing-in-Publication Data
A catalogue record for this book is available from the British Library

ISBN 978-0-12-811419-3

For information on all Academic Press publications
visit our website at https://www.elsevier.com/books-and-journals

Publisher: Stacy Masucci
Acquisitions Editor: Elizabeth Brown
Editorial Project Manager: Fernanda A. Oliveira
Production Project Manager: Selvaraj Raviraj
Cover Designer: Mark Rogers
Cover Artwork: Emanuel de Castro Dias

Typeset by STRAIVE, India

Dedication

The editors would like to dedicate this book to their families.

In loving memory of Professor Scott Lilienfeld[a]
1960–2020

Over the course of more than three decades, Scott Lilienfeld provided the psychopathy field lenses through which to see its problems, instruments to provide solutions to those problems, and theoretical rigor to challenge the field's thinking. Throughout his career Scott highlighted the importance of skeptical thinking and willingness to critically examine assumptions in the face of new data. We have been fortunate to have such an intellectual giant shaping our field.

Some of Scott's initial papers highlighted why self-reports of psychopathy correlated weakly with each other: They covered various features of psychopathy incompletely, often focusing on antisocial behaviors rather than the personality dispositions underpinning psychopathy. His Psychopathic Personality Inventory (PPI) wove together the strands of decades of theorizing on psychopathy into a comprehensive measure of the psychopathic personality. Beyond developing the PPI, his work demonstrated how psychopathy, psychopathology, and personality are manifestations of the same fundamental processes; separated key features of psychopathy into their constituent and mechanistic parts; and sought to examine psychopathy's manifestations in real-world contexts. The numerous honors and awards he received, including the Society for Scientific Study of Psychopathy Robert D. Hare Lifetime Achievement Award, all reflect the importance and impact of his work.

Perhaps even greater than Scott's intellectual impact was his kindness and mentorship for those in the field. He guided his students on their professional paths, helping them attain success along their own tracks. He frequently gave of his time and good company to those who sought it. He generously provided career advice, letters of recommendation, and perspectives on the field and its history to those who asked. He also graciously served our society as board member and as president. He has helped guide the society's path, growth, and promise to provide a home to vigorous and respectful scholarly debate. And with his vivid and fascinating stories about the roots of psychopathy research, he made sure that we would learn to imagine the future of psychopathy research by remembering its past.

Scott Lilienfeld's light has brightened our field, which examines the darkest aspects of humanity. May his example continue to illuminate those who seek truth about psychopathy and so many other scholarly and human matters.

Society for the Scientific Study of Psychopathy, 2020

[a] See also notes of appreciation for Scott at: https://www.kudoboard.com/boards/WI8hPMQ3.

In loving memory of Dr. Lieke Nentjes
1986–2020

The chapter on "Emotional functioning in psychopathy" is a posthumous work led by Dr. Lieke Nentjes. Lieke, Carlo, and Dave began this work in 2016, inspired and led by Lieke's initiative to clarify the complex literature on emotion and psychopathy, in an attempt to better our understanding and treatment hopes for psychopathic individuals. Lieke's work was always driven by a genuine passion for science and for making a concrete impact on society. Already before defending her dissertation, she had started a position as Assistant Professor and began what would have certainly been a career of excellence. Most importantly, Lieke was so generous and collegial to favor collaboration over individual achievements. When she realized that she was already too sick to continue her academic work, one of her priorities became to ensure that the fruit of her work would not remain hidden in a shelf. She made sure to pass on all of her materials and progress to colleagues and friends around her who could ensure that her contribution would see the light, without requests of any sort. Her altruism and selflessness were so outstanding and humbling, in stark contrast with a culture of individualism and prestige that too often plagues academia. The chapter is the first, but not the last, example that Lieke is still with us and that her work will continue to inspire new generations of scholars. It is extremely saddening and heartbreaking that she will not be able to hold the fruit of her work in her hands, but her contribution to science and society will be everlasting, and her proud husband and family will treasure these printed pages. Not only her professional qualities but also her personal qualities that enriched the lives of everyone who has crossed paths with her are missed and irreplaceable. For her, we can only and must pay it forward, following her example of generosity, selflessness, and passion in our work as well as in our professional relationships.

Carlo Garofalo, 2021

Contents

About the editors

Paulo Barbosa Marques is a chartered clinical and forensic psychologist and a law enforcement officer. He began his law enforcement career serving as a frontline police officer in the Polícia de Segurança Pública (PSP) and later as a criminal investigator at the Criminal Investigation Department—Organized Crime Brigade. Paulo is now an inspector at the Serviço de Estrangeiros e Fronteiras (SEF), the Portuguese Immigration and Borders Service. He holds a master's degree in law and security from the Faculty of Law—NOVA University of Lisbon, a postgraduate diploma in Internal Security, and specialized training in forensic psychological assessment and criminal investigation. Over the past years, his research has focused on the police officers', prosecutors', and judges' perceptions of investigative interviewing operational practices and training needs in Portugal. Paulo is a founding member and a former Secretary-General of the Portuguese Society of Psychiatry and Psychology of Justice and an International Investigative Interviewing Research Group (iIIRG) Regional Champion for Portugal. He regularly presents at conferences to both academics and practitioners. He is a coeditor of *Police Psychology: New Trends in Forensic Psychological Science*.

Mauro Paulino is currently a coordinator at Mind, Institute of Clinical and Forensic Psychology (Lisbon, Portugal). He is also a forensic psychologist consultant at the Instituto Nacional de Medicina Legal e Ciências Forenses, I.P. (Gabinete Médico-Legal e Forense Península Setúbal). Mauro received his master's degree in legal medicine and forensic sciences at the University of Lisbon, Faculty of Medicine, completing his research in the field of spousal violence. He is a PhD student of Forensic Psychology at the Faculty of Psychology and Education Sciences, University of Coimbra (Portugal). He is also a member of the Center for Research in Neuropsychology and Cognitive Behavioral Intervention (CINEICC) and the Psychological Assessment and Psychometrics Laboratory (PsyAssessmentLab). He is an author and coordinator of several books and is a guest lecturer at various national and international universities.

Laura Alho is a clinical and forensic psychologist and holds a PhD in psychology, a master's degree in forensic psychology, and a postgraduate degree in criminology. She has specialized training in criminal profiling, victimology, psychology of justice, and criminal investigation. Her line of research is psychology of testimony. She was assistant professor at Lusófona University of Humanities and Technologies and she is now an independent psychology professor, consultant and researcher at some educational and training entities. She is also an author and coordinator of some books and a guest lecturer at national and international conferences.

About the authors

Jonathan T. Alicchio is a recent alumnus of Marymount University with an MA in forensic and legal psychology with a concentration in intelligence studies. Under Dr. Holly Hargreaves Cormany's mentorship, Jonathan has had continued participation in her team's research throughout his graduate career and postgraduation. Prior to his graduate career, he had graduated from Montclair State University in 2018 with a Bachelor of Arts degree in psychology with a minor in criminal justice. Jonathan is currently employed in the field of education and is working toward a career within the criminal justice system.

James Beasley is an adjunct faculty member at Marymount University in Arlington, Virginia. He served for more than 30 years as a special agent in the FBI. For the latter half of his career, he was assigned to the Behavioral Analysis Unit in Quantico, VA, where he conducted behavioral assessments of offenders in violent crime investigations, including crimes against children, serial murder, serial rape, threats, and online criminal activities. He also conducted research through interviews with dozens of incarcerated offenders. He holds a B.S. degree in psychology from Central Missouri State University, and a master's degree in public administration from the University of Missouri at Kansas City.

Henriette Bergstrøm is a senior lecturer in forensic psychology at the University of Derby in Derby, United Kingdom. Her main research interest is the study of psychopathy within a developmental and life-course (DLC) criminology perspective.

Ana Seara Cardoso is a researcher and lecturer at the Psychological Neuroscience Lab in the School of Psychology, University of Minho, Portugal. She holds a PhD from University College London and has been the recipient of doctoral and postdoctoral fellowships and research grants from the Foundation for Science and Technology (Fundação para a Ciência e Tecnologia, FCT). Her research interests focus on the neurobiological basis of complex social cognitive processes and how dysfunction in these processes may be linked to persistent antisocial behavior. She is interested in understanding how neurocognitive correlates of empathy and morality develop from childhood to adulthood and of how variability in these neurocognitive correlates is linked to antisocial behavior in general, and to the development of psychopathy and antisocial personality disorder in particular.

Emily Corner is a senior lecturer of criminology at the Centre for Social Research and Methods at the Australian National University (ANU). Prior to joining the ANU, Emily was a research associate at the department of Security and Crime Science at

University College London, working on projects examining lone and group-based terrorism, radicalization, mass murderers, and fixated individuals. Her doctoral research focused on examining mental disorders and terrorist behavior, and won her the Terrorism Research Initiative's Thesis award in 2016. She has published in leading psychology, forensic science, criminology, threat assessment, and political science journals. She has worked on research projects funded by the Defence Science and Technology Laboratory, the European Union, the National Institute of Justice, the US Department of Defense, and the Department of Home Affairs. Prior to her doctoral research, she worked across step-down, low-, and medium- secure psychiatric hospitals, in both inpatient and outpatient settings.

Raymond Corrado is a professor in the School of Criminology at Simon Fraser University. He has published more than 100 articles and book chapters on various policy issues, including juvenile justice, violent young offenders, mental health, adolescent psychopathy, victimization, child/adolescent case management strategies, and terrorism.

Ted B. Cunliffe, PhD, is a clinical and forensic psychologist licensed to practice in the State of Florida and is the current Associate Director of Clinical Training at Albizu University in Miami, Florida. For many years in addition to his academic work, he has provided expert witness services in various jurisdictions and courts within Florida and beyond on a full-time and part-time basis. He has provided assessment services and worked with forensic populations in a wide variety of settings, including juvenile detention centers, adult prisons, juvenile probation, and outreach programs in the community for more than 30 years. Specifically, he has served as Staff Psychologist and Mental Health Director at a wide number of correctional facilities in Florida, California, and Canada. Further, he has provided expert witness services to the Florida, California, and Virginia courts in the areas of competency to stand trial, not guilty by reason of insanity, dangerousness, death penalty, wrongful death, dependency, mitigation, and civil litigation.

Matt DeLisi is Distinguished Professor, College of Liberal Arts and Sciences Dean's Professor, Coordinator of Criminal Justice, and Faculty Affiliate of the Center for the Study of Violence at Iowa State University. A renowned scholar, Professor DeLisi is one of the most influential and prolific criminologists in the world with more than 400 scholarly publications on an array of topics in the social, behavioral, and forensic sciences. He is the only scientist in the world who is Fellow of the Academy of Criminal Justice Sciences and the Association for Psychological Science.

Wyatt D'Emilia, PhD, graduated from the clinical psychology PhD program at Long Island University-Brooklyn. He is currently completing his postdoctoral residency in the PTSD clinic at the Albany Stratton VA Medical Center. His research is focused on coping and perceptions of control among individuals living in adverse or oppressive environments. His dissertation focused on identifying the efficacy of secondary control as a method for helping young adult women in the United States cope with experiences of sexist discrimination without incurring additional negative mental health outcomes.

John Edens, PhD, is a professor and former Director of Clinical Training in the Department of Psychological and Brain Sciences at Texas A&M University. He has published approximately 200 journal articles and book chapters, focused primarily on the interface between mental health, psychological assessment, and law and, per *Essential Science Indicators*, is among the top 1% of cited scientific researchers in psychology and psychiatry. Dr. Edens is a former recipient of the Saleem Shah Award for Early Career Contributions to Law and Psychology (*American Psychology—Law Society*) and the Theodore Millon Award in Personality Psychology (*Society of Clinical Psychology*). He is a fellow of the *Association for Psychological Science* and the *American Psychological Association* and a former associate editor of the journals *Psychological Assessment*, the *Journal of Personality Assessment*, and *Assessment*. He is also the lead author of the *Personality Assessment Inventory Computerized Interpretive Report for Correctional Settings*.

Jacob Eikenberry, MSW, is a social work PhD candidate focused on creating sustainable alternatives to incarceration and improving systems that interact with incarcerated populations. His research interests include exploring the intersection of trauma, mental health and substance abuse among justice-involved individuals, and peer mentorship/support as an activator of domains that support healthy transitions for individuals exiting the criminal justice system.

David P. Farrington, OBE, is Emeritus Professor of Psychological Criminology at Cambridge University. He has been President of the American Society of Criminology, President of the European Association of Psychology and Law, and President of the British Society of Criminology. He has received many prizes and awards, including the Stockholm Prize in Criminology. His major research interest is in developmental criminology, and he is Director of the Cambridge Study in Delinquent Development, which is a prospective longitudinal survey of more than 400 London males from age 8 to age 61. In addition to 866 published journal articles and book chapters on criminological and psychological topics, he has published 117 books, monographs, and government publications and 163 shorter publications (total = 1146). According to Google Scholar on March 10, 2021, his publications have been cited a total of 113,271 times, and 750 of his works have been cited at least 10 times each.

Bryanna Fox is Associate Professor of Criminology at the University of South Florida. Dr. Fox earned her PhD from Cambridge University and is a former FBI special agent. Dr. Fox's research on psychological risk factors for criminal behavior and evidence-based policing has been recognized with the 2014 Excellence in Law Enforcement Research Award from the International Association of Chiefs of Police and 2017 Early Career Award from the ASC Division of Developmental and Life-Course Criminology.

Carl B. Gacono, PhD, ABAP, formerly the Assessment Center Director (Atascadero State Hospital, CA), and a chief psychologist (FCI Bastrop, TX), worked more than 20 years in correctional and forensic psychiatric facilities. He is the coauthor of *The Rorschach Assessment of Aggressive & Psychopathic Personalities*, senior editor of the *Handbook of Forensic Rorschach Assessment,* author of *The Clinical & Forensic*

Interview Schedule for The Hare PCL: Revised & Screening Version, editor of *the Clinical & Forensic Assessment of Psychopathy: A Practitioner's Guide*, coauthor of *Understanding Female Offenders*, and author or coauthor of more than 100 articles and book chapters (https://www.researchgate.net/profile/Carl_Gacono). He is the recipient of the 1994 Beck Award and 2000 W. Klopfer Award. He is a member of the American Board of Assessment Psychology and a fellow of SPA. A noted artist, his paintings (carlgaconoart.com & carlgaconoart [Instagram]) have been exhibited and appeared on book covers. Dr. Gacono maintains a consulting practice in Asheville, NC, where he lives with his son, Jackson. Please visit maverickpsychology.com for webinar training.

Carlo Garofalo, PhD, graduated from Sapienza University of Rome (Italy) and is currently an assistant professor at Tilburg University, the Netherlands. He is a licensed clinical psychologist and his clinical and research interests are mainly focused on the relevance of emotion and personality pathology (especially psychopathy) for aggression and antisocial behavior, from a developmental psychopathology perspective. He serves as Associate Editor for the *Journal of Criminal Justice* and the *International Journal of Offender Therapy and Comparative Criminology*. He is currently a member of the European Association of Psychology and Law, member and part of the communication committee for the Society for the Scientific Study of Psychopathy, and founding member and cochair (together with Dr. Luna Centifanti) of the Section for the study and treatment of antisocial personality disorder and psychopathy for the European Society for the Study of Personality Disorders.

Nathanael Gaspar is a 2019 graduate from Marymount University's Forensic and Legal Psychology Master's Program. Nathanael helped conduct a research study that was presented at the American Psychology-Law Society's 2019 Conference on the effectiveness of a Court Diversion program for juveniles. The research study examined the effectiveness of the program's ability to decrease antisocial behavior and increase empathic response from juvenile participants. Nathanael previously worked in the field of threat assessment as a research analyst with Kiernan Group Holdings where they specialized in data analysis trends in digital behaviors and warning signs for active shooters since 1999. He currently works in the field of crime detection and prevention as an analyst for the National Center for Missing and Exploited Children's Electronic Crimes Division.

Paul Gill is Professor of Security and Crime Science at University College London. He has more than 90 publications on the topic of terrorist behavior. He has conducted research funded by the Office for Naval Research, the Department of Homeland Security, DSTL, the European Union, the National Institute of Justice, CREST, Public Safety Canada, and MINERVA. He currently manages European Research Council Starter Grant project entitled GRIEVANCE. Collectively these grants have been worth over 9 million euro. These projects focused upon various aspects of terrorist behavior, including the IED development, creativity, terrorist network structures, risk assessment and management, and lone-actor terrorism. His doctoral research focused on the underlying individual and organizational motivations behind suicide bombing. This piece of research won the Jean Blondel Prize for the best PhD thesis in political science in Europe for 2010. He has published in leading psychology, criminology, and political science journals.

James Lynn Greenstone, EdD, JD, DABECI, CDM, has been in private practice for more than 55 years and is Diplomate of the Society for Police and Criminal Psychology. He serves as a professor in the Disaster and Emergency Management Program at Nova Southeastern University, College of Osteopathic Medicine. He is a supervisory mental health specialist with the NDMS Disaster Medical Assistance Team. Dr. Greenstone served as the Director of Psychological Services for the Fort Worth Police Department and has been a licensed and commissioned Peace Officer for more than 40 years. He is a trained hostage negotiator and has trained negotiators around the world. He recently retired as a colonel with the Texas Medical Brigade, Texas Military Forces. His current books include *The Elements of Police Hostage and Crisis Negotiations, The Elements of Crisis Intervention: Crises and How to Respond to Them*, 3rd edition, and *The Elements of Disaster Psychology: Managing Psychosocial Trauma.* Dr. Greenstone is also the Editor-in-Chief Emeritus of *The Journal of Police Crisis Negotiations*, and current editor of the *Journal of Police Emergency Response: International Journal of Hostage Negotiations and Crisis Intervention.* Additionally, he served on the editorial boards of *Military Medicine* and the *International Journal of Emergency Mental Health.*

Sara Chiara Haden, PhD, is an associate professor at Long Island University, Brooklyn. She completed her doctoral degree in clinical psychology at Virginia Polytechnic Institute and State University (Virginia Tech) after receiving her MA in psychology from the University of Massachusetts. Dr. Haden's research focuses on the effects of exposure to community violence as well as risk and protective factors involved in the development of aggressive behavior in children. She is a licensed psychologist in New York. Her clinical experience includes work with sex offenders, survivors of torture and war trauma, psychiatric emergency patients, pediatric HIV clinic clients, primary care patients, mentally ill offenders, and adult male prisoners.

Robert D. Hare, CM, PhD, is Emeritus Professor of Psychology, University of British Columbia. He has devoted most of his academic career to investigating psychopathy, its nature, assessment, and implications for mental health, criminal justice, and society. Although retired, he continues his research with international colleagues. He is the author of several books, including *Psychopathy: Theory and Research, Without Conscience*, and (with Paul Babiak) *Snakes in Suits*, 2nd edition. In addition, he has authored or coauthored more than 300 chapters and scientific articles on psychopathy, is the developer of the *Psychopathy Checklist-Revised* (PCL-R), and a coauthor of its derivatives, the *Psychopathy Checklist: Screening Version*, the *Psychopathy Checklist: Youth Version*, the *Antisocial Process Screening Device*, and *Self-Report Psychopathy Scale* (SRP-4). He has consulted with criminal justice agencies in many countries, and received many national and international awards and honors, including induction into the Order of Canada.

Holly Hargreaves-Cormany is Assistant Professor of Forensic and Legal Psychology at Marymount University. She previously served as a research fellow with the Oak

Ridge Institute for Science and Education. She is a licensed clinical professional counselor with a PhD in counseling and master's degrees in forensic psychology and community counseling. She has published and conducted research studies on the sex trafficking of juveniles, the association between animal cruelty and interpersonal violence, humane education, and animal-assisted therapy/intervention programs and has presented such research at national and international conferences. Dr. Hargreaves-Cormany uses her clinical experience practicing as a psychotherapist in private practice to inform her teaching and research.

Katie Holzer is a research instructor in the Division of Clinical and Translational Research at Washington University School of Medicine in St. Louis and a licensed clinical social worker in the State of Missouri. She is also the Director of the Center for Perioperative Mental Health. Her research has contributed to the understanding of the applicability of diagnostic criteria for older adults with investigations into the diagnosis of personality disorders. Her recent work in this area focuses on antisocial personality disorder among older adults and the exclusion of this population from evaluations of the psychometric properties of personality disorder assessments.

Aaron J. Kivisto, PhD, is a forensic and clinical psychologist and Associate Professor of Clinical Psychology at the University of Indianapolis. His research focuses on a range of forensic issues, including violence risk assessment and management with individuals with serious mental illness, suicide prevention, the motivations and psychiatric characteristics of fatal and nonfatal intimate partner violence perpetrators, risk management of those who stalk and threaten mental health professionals, evaluation of competency to stand trial, and the admissibility of psychological testing in legal contexts. He maintains a private practice specializing in forensic psychological evaluation in Indianapolis, Indiana.

Dave Kosson is Professor of Psychology at Rosalind Franklin University of Medicine and Science. His research focuses on the cognitive, emotional, interpersonal, and developmental mechanisms underlying psychopathy and other personality disorders. He has authored more than 100 articles in peer-reviewed journals and coauthored the Psychopathy Checklist: Youth Version. He also developed the Interpersonal Measure of Psychopathy along with interpersonal measures of several other personality disorders. He is a past president of the Society for the Scientific Study of Psychopathy and has served as President of the Aftermath Foundation since 2006.

Scott O. Lilienfeld was born and raised in New York City. He received his BA in psychology from Cornell University in 1982 and his PhD in psychology (clinical) from the University of Minnesota in 1990. He completed his clinical internship at Western Psychiatric Institute and Clinic in Pittsburgh, Pennsylvania, from 1986 to 1987. He was Assistant Professor in the Department of Psychology at State University of New York (SUNY) at Albany from 1990 to 1994, and was a faculty member in the Department of Psychology at Emory since 1994. He was also a visiting fellow at the University of Melbourne in Australia. Dr. Lilienfeld was a Samuel Candler Dobbs Professor of Psychology at Emory. He was Editor-in-Chief of the APS journal *Clinical Psychological Science* and Associate Editor of the APA journal *Archives of*

Scientific Psychology; he also sat on the editorial boards of several journals, including *American Psychologist*. He was a president of the Society for a Science of Clinical Psychology (Section 3 of APA Division 12) and the Society for the Scientific Study of Psychopathy. He was a fellow of, and Executive Board Member of, the Committee for Skeptical Inquiry and a Consulting Editor for *Skeptical Inquirer* magazine. He was also a member of the Executive Committee of the Heterodox Academy.

Patrick Lussier is Professor of criminology at the School of Social Work and Criminology at Université Laval, Canada. In 2005, Professor Lussier received the Academic Gold Medal from the Governor General of Canada for the excellence of his PhD dissertation. Since 2019, he is the Editor of the *Canadian Journal of Criminology and Criminal Justice*. His field of expertise is at the intersection of criminology and criminal justice and includes, among other things, the etiology of criminal conduct, sexual offending, risk assessment and management, and quantitative research methods.

Evita March, PhD, is a senior lecturer and researcher of psychology and is currently employed at Federation University Australia, Victoria, Berwick Campus. Evita's areas of research expertise include cyberpsychology, personality, and interpersonal relationships.

Cynthia Mathieu, PhD, is Professor of Organizational Behavior, Université du Québec à Trois-Rivières, Canada. She consults with organizations, teaches, and actively engages in research and publications on employee selection and well-being, organizational fraud, leadership, narcissism, and psychopathy in the workplace. She is the author of the book *Dark Personalities in the Workplace*. Additional information on her work and on dark personalities in the workplace can be found at cynthiamathieu.com.

Evan McCuish is an assistant professor at Simon Fraser University and is the Principal Investigator of the Incarcerated Serious and Violent Young Offender Study. He is the recipient of the Simon Fraser University Dean's Convocation Medal for Academic Excellence, the American Psychology-Law Society Outstanding Dissertation Award, and the American Society of Criminology Division of Developmental and Life Course Criminology Early Career Award. His research interests include criminal careers, desistance, developmental criminology, foster care, gang involvement, psychopathy, sexual offending, and violence.

Shelby E. McDonald, PhD, is Director of the Children, Families, and Animals Research (CFAR) Group, LLC, in Richmond, Virginia, and a faculty affiliate of the Virginia Commonwealth University (VCU) Department of Psychology and VCU School of Social Work. She is also Director of Research in the Department of Strategy and Research at the American Society for the Prevention of Cruelty to Animals®. Her research centers on the role of human-animal interaction in human health and wellbeing, particularly during the developmental periods of childhood and emerging adulthood.

Kara Meadows studied psychology and criminology at The Pennsylvania State University. She then became a research assistant at The George Washington University in the Early Childhood & Development Lab examining callous-unemotional traits and behaviors. She went on to earn a master's degree in forensic and legal psychology from Marymount University, where she collaborated with Dr. Hargreaves-Cormany and her colleagues on the present publication, *Psychopathy and Criminal Behavior: Current Trends and Challenges*. Kara currently works for the federal government as an analyst at The United States Sentencing Commission in Washington, DC.

J. Reid Meloy, PhD, ABPP, is a clinical professor of psychiatry at the University of California, San Diego, School of Medicine, and a faculty member of the San Diego Psychoanalytic Center. He has been a consultant to the FBI Behavioral Analysis Units for the past two decades. His most recent coedited book (with Dr. Jens Hoffmann) is the *International Handbook of Threat Assessment*, 2nd edition (Oxford University Press, 2021).

Princess-Kasharáe Middleton has graduated *Magna Cum Laude* with a degree in political science at Spelman College, United States. In 2017, she was accredited a *Juris Doctor* degree from North Carolina Central University School of Law. She is attending the forensic psychology program at Marymount University. Although she has been quite busy with her schooling, over the past 15 years, she has dedicated her life to researching the laws, politics, and policies surrounding international and domestic criminal justice reform.

Leslie C. Morey is Professor of Psychology at Texas A&M University. He received his PhD in clinical psychology from the University of Florida, and has served on the faculty at Vanderbilt University, Harvard Medical School, the Yale University School of Medicine, and the University of Tulsa. He has published more than 200 articles, books, and chapters on the assessment and diagnosis of mental disorders, and his work has been cited in the scientific literature more than 5000 times. He is the author of the *Personality Assessment Inventory* (1991), *Personality Assessment Screener* (1997), the *Personality Assessment Inventory-Adolescent* (2007), the *Interpretive Guide to the Personality Assessment Inventory* (1996), and *Essentials of PAI Assessment* (2003).

Lieke Nentjes, PhD, graduated from the University of Maastricht, the Netherlands, and subsequently held a position of Assistant Professor of Clinical Forensic Psychology at the University of Amsterdam, the Netherlands. Her research work lay at the intersection of experimental, clinical, and forensic psychology, with special interest in the role of emotional functioning for psychopathy and other personality disorders in offenders. Her work has been published in top-tier journals in the fields of psychiatry, clinical psychology, and criminology/forensic psychology. She was a member of the Society for the Scientific Study of Psychopathy. She was coauthor (with Prof. Dr. David Bernstein) of the manual for the adaptation of Schema Therapy for forensic patients with personality disorders. Lieke passed away on March 5, 2020, at the age of 33, after fighting with a terminal illness.

Craig S. Neumann is Distinguished Research Professor at the University of North Texas (UNT) and has been actively teaching, supervising, and conducting research in the Clinical Psychology Graduate Training Program at UNT for more than 20 years. He has been consistently funded by The William H. Donner Foundation, has published more than 130 peer-reviewed journal articles and dozens of book chapters, and has given invited talks throughout North America and Europe. His research on personality and personality pathology had made substantial international impact. His latest research explores the motivational nature of light (vs dark) personality traits and processes that build resilience.

James R.P. Ogloff, AM, JD, PhD, is trained as clinical and forensic psychologist and lawyer. He is the University Distinguished Professor and Director of the Centre for Forensic Behavioural Science at Swinburne University and Executive Director of Psychological Services and Research at Forensicare. He has worked in the field for more than 35 years and began studying and working with psychopaths in the 1980s. He has published 18 books and more than 300 articles and chapters in forensic psychology and forensic mental health. His research has been very influential in the fields of forensic psychology and forensic mental health. He has held many editorial and professional leadership roles and has received numerous awards for his work, including distinguished contribution awards in forensic psychology from peak bodies in Australia, Canada, and the United States.

Mark Olver, PhD, is Professor and Registered Doctoral Psychologist in the Clinical Psychology Program at the University of Saskatchewan, Canada, where he is involved in graduate and undergraduate research supervision, teaching, administration, clinical training, and applied forensic research. Prior to his academic appointment, Mark worked as a clinical psychologist in various capacities, including providing assessment, treatment, and consultation services for young offenders in the Saskatoon Health Region and for adult federal offenders in the Correctional Service of Canada. He has published more than 150 journal articles and book chapters and his research interests include offender risk assessment and treatment, young offenders, psychopathy, and the evaluation of therapeutic change. He is the codeveloper of the Violence Risk Scale-Sexual Offense version (VRS-SO) and the Violence Risk Scale-Youth Sexual Offense version (VRS-YSO), and he provides training and consultation services internationally in the assessment and treatment of high psychopathy, sexual, and violent offending populations.

Terri Patterson is a principal in the Washington, DC, office of Control Risks, a global crisis and risk consultancy. A recently retired special agent with the Federal Bureau of Investigation (FBI), Terri has over two decades of experience leading law enforcement operations, strategic programs, and critical incident preparedness. She is a recognized expert in behavioral assessment and risk mitigation, with a specialization in global security solutions to combat criminal and national security threat actors. Terri holds a PhD in legal psychology from Florida International University in Miami, Florida, and is a member of the American Psychological Association (APA) and American Psychology and Law Society (APLS).

David C. Pyrooz is an Associate Professor of Sociology and faculty associate of Prevention Science Program at the Institute of Behavioral Science at the University of Colorado Boulder. His research interests are in the areas of gangs and criminal networks, incarceration and prisoner reentry, and developmental and life-course criminology. He is the coauthor of Competing for Control: Gangs and the Social Order of Prisons (Cambridge University Press) and On Gangs (Temple University Press).

David Rowlands has a background in clinical practice, working for 15 years in the substance misuse field. After leaving clinical practice in 2016, he completed his PhD at the University of Huddersfield, studying identity processes in addiction recovery. His research interests include narrative and social identity processes. He currently works as a postdoctoral research fellow at Keele University.

Adriana Sampaio, MD, PhD, is the lab director of the Psychological Neuroscience Lab (https://psychologicalneurosciencelab.weebly.com/) in the School of Psychology, University of Minho, Portugal. Her main research is in the field of developmental cognitive neuroscience, namely in the structural and neurofunctional and genetic basis of (ab)normal cognitive and emotional processes. In particular, using cutting-edge technologies that combine morphometric with functional neuroimaging measures, her work aims to map specific neurodevelopmental processes associated with normal higher cognitive function and their age-related trajectories, by looking at the dynamic interplay between genetic, biological, and environmental factors that shape brain development. As part of her work, Adriana Sampaio has published more than a hundred articles in ISI journals, collaborating with several research teams (Spain, France, the United Kingdom, Brazil, and the United States). She is the principal investigator of several projects funded by FCT and Fundação Bial. She was also awarded for her work in the area of research in psychology.

Mário R. Simões is Full Professor at the University of Coimbra—Faculty of Psychology and Educational Sciences (FPCEUC), Director of PsyAssessmentLab, PI of the Research Group *Neuropsychological Assessment and Ageing Processes* of the Center for Research in Neuropsychology and Cognitive Behavioral Intervention of the University of Coimbra, and responsible for the FPCEUC Neuropsychological Assessment Consultation, which responds to requests from the Courts. He participated actively as a principal investigator of projects with external funding and/or as a supervisor of doctoral theses and master's dissertations in research that led to the adaptation and/or validation of tests and other (neuro) psychological assessment instruments for the Portuguese population in forensic, educational, and clinical contexts. His teaching activities include the following courses: Psychological Assessment and Forensic Expertise, Neuropsychological Assessment, and Assessment Instruments and Psychological Reports.

Jason M. Smith, PsyD, ABPP, since 2014, has worked as a licensed clinical psychologist (currently Chief Psychologist) for a Correctional Prison in West Virginia, United States, where he has continued treating, assessing, and managing incarcerated women. With his coauthors, he has published on female offenders/psychopathy as well as theoretical Rorschach articles. He is on the Board of Assessors for Rorschachiana and has received board certification from the American Board of Professional Psychology (ABPP) in clinical psychology. Dr. Smith has presented his research and workshops on assessing and treating female offenders both nationally and internationally. He is the senior author of *Understanding Female Offenders: Psychopathy, Criminal Behavior, Assessment, and Treatment*. He was awarded the APA Division 18 Criminal Justice Section Outstanding Dissertation Award (2014) and the SPA John E. Exner Scholar Award (2019). Please visit maverickpsychology.com for our webinar trainings.

Michel St-Yves is a forensic psychologist working with the Behavioural Analysis Unit of the *Sûreté du Québec* (Quebec's provincial police force), offering support in criminal investigations, both by profiling suspects and by preparing police interrogations. He also teaches the psychology of investigative interviews at the *École nationale de police du Québec* (Quebec Police Academy) and is a lecturer at the Department of Criminology of *Université de Montréal*. He has participated in the creation of the first continuing education training program in matters of investigative interviews in Switzerland, where he has been a training instructor since 2007. He also acts as Deputy Chair of the Scientific Committee of the International investigative interviewing research group (iIIRG). His publications, in both French and English, deal mainly with the psychology of criminal investigations, crisis negotiation, and investigative interviews.

Jeff Thompson, PhD, is Adjunct Associate Research Scientist at the Molecular Imaging and Neuropathology Division of the New York State Psychiatric Institute at the Columbia University Irving Medical Center. He is a 16-year law enforcement veteran detective with the New York City Police Department (NYPD) and a former hostage negotiator. In his current role at the NYPD, Detective Thompson is currently the first-ever Mental Health and Wellness Coordinator. He is also a professor at Lipscomb University and New York University, researcher, and trainer.

Sophia Tkazky, PhD, MBPsS, CPsychol, is a lecturer in forensic psychology in the School of Health, Psychology and Social Care, University of Derby. Before she joined this university in 2019, she was a PhD candidate and a research associate at the International Centre for Investigative Psychology and Offender Profiling. Sophia also works as a consultant in the Agis Consultancy Ltd. and as an assistant editor of the *Journal for Investigative Psychology and Offender Profiling*. Her main research interests are offenders' narratives and the methods of elicitation and interpretation of these narratives, the narrative manifestations of the Dark Triad, and psychology of persuasion and manipulation. Her research activities currently are primarily focused on the offenders' characteristics and crime scene behaviors and on the narratives of crime (e.g., crime descriptions) and life personal experiences (e.g., general life narratives or neutral episodes).

Jennifer J. Tostlebe is a doctoral candidate in the Department of Sociology at the University of Colorado Boulder. She received her BA in interdisciplinary studies in criminology and criminal justice and her MS in sociology from Iowa State University. Her research interests are in the areas of incarceration and prisoner reentry, mental and physical health, and gangs and criminal networks. Currently, her work investigates the intersection of social influences and individual characteristics and how they independently and interactively impact illicit activity during incarceration and postrelease.

Tiffany N. Truong is a 4th-year PhD student in clinical psychology at Texas A&M University. Her research primarily focuses on psychological assessment in forensic and correctional settings. She is particularly interested in the use of personality testing to predict maladaptive behaviors among justice-involved individuals, as well as the potentially stigmatizing effects of the label "psychopath" and its associated personality traits on legal decision-making.

Margarida Vasconcelos is a postdoctoral researcher at the Psychological Neuroscience Lab in the School of Psychology, University of Minho, Braga, Portugal. Margarida has a doctoral degree in basic psychology and has developed research in the main area of cognitive neuroscience. Her research has been dedicated to investigate the effects of musical expertise on neuroplasticity, particularly the transfer effects from music to language. In this realm, Margarida has investigated the electrophysiological correlates of auditory statistical learning in both children and adults. More recently, her research focus turned to social cognition, namely to the investigation of the neural bases of moral judgment and emotions, and social decision-making, in collaboration with Ana Seara-Cardoso, PhD. Currently, she also investigates the mechanisms of memory suppression in binge drinkers and alcohol-dependent individuals using behavioral measures and neuroimaging techniques.

Michael G. Vaughn, PhD, is Professor and Director of the PhD program in the School of Social Work, College for Public Health and Social Justice, Saint Louis University. He is the author of 8 books and more than 500 scholarly papers. He is a fellow of the American Academy of Social Work and Social Welfare and Fellow of the Society for Social Work and Research. His agenda comprises several interrelated foci such as temperament and psychopathy, drug use, violence, school dropout, biosocial interplay in human behavior, and epidemiologic studies of health and criminal justice.

Ryan Veal is a sessional academic with the Centre for Forensic Behavioural Science at Swinburne University of Technology and psychologist (clinical and forensic registrar) with Forensicare. He has an interest in the area of personality assessment relative to violent behavior and recidivism, having recently completed his Doctorate of Psychology (Clinical and Forensic) at the Centre for Forensic Behavioural Science in which he contributed to the research on the reliability and validity of the Psychopathy Checklist measures in Australia.

Ellen Wood is a recent alumna of Marymount University where she served as the student leader for Dr. Holly Hargreaves-Cormany's research team. She graduated in 2020 with an MA in forensic and legal psychology, following the completion of her BSc from Bluefield College in criminal justice, psychology, and forensic science in 2018. She is currently employed as a forensic interviewer and family advocate at a Children's Advocacy Center in Virginia.

Donna Youngs is a senior lecturer at the University of Kingston, London, specializing in investigative psychology. Her research interests include the modeling of psychological styles of criminal action and the analysis of underlying criminal narratives. She coauthored the first text on investigative psychology (with David Canter) in 2009 and currently edits the *Journal of Investigative Psychology*.

Foreword

The usual purpose of a Foreword is to comment on the nature and contents of a book or, in this case, an edited volume, which I will do. However, the authors uniformly have produced chapters that are highly informative, self-contained, and "speak for themselves," thus providing me with the opportunity to comment on several issues I consider relevant to the topics contained herein. I thank the editors for giving me the latitude to take this route. In a sense, they have allowed me to write a mini-chapter, one that supplements rather than summarizes what already is an excellent compendium of essential reading for those involved in the criminal justice system. Parenthetically, I first met Paulo Marques at the inaugural conference of the Portuguese Society of Psychiatry and Psychology of Justice in Porto, 2007, and the following PCL-R Workshop organized by him and Rui Abrunhosa Gonçalves.

I begin with some words in memory of Scott Lilienfeld, the author of the Afterword for this book. Scott passed away on September 30, 2020, several months after completing his contribution to this volume. He was a prominent and outstanding psychologist with a vast impact on behavioral science and a commentator on public awareness of science and pseudoscience. Articles he co-authored during his illness are making their way through the publication process. Before his death, friends and colleagues posted an E-Card with comments, pictures, anecdotes, and expressions of deep appreciation and respect for him and his extraordinary works. A large number of posts to the E-Card is a testament to the esteem and affection in which so many people held him. My post noted that Scott's remarkable body of theory and research had become enduring contributions to psychological science and society. His intellect and insights into the human condition were inspirational, far-reaching, and wonderfully expressed in his writings and warm interactions with colleagues, students, and scholars. I was pleased to be a co-author with him on an article detailing Hervey Cleckley's influence on current conceptualizations of psychopathy (Lilienfeld, Watts, Smith, Patrick, & Hare, 2018). The link to the E-Card is https://www.kudoboard.com/boards/WI8hPMQ3.

When I began research on "psychopathy" more than five decades ago, only a few dozen published empirical articles on the topic appeared each year. I could complete a literature search in a few hours, even though it meant a walk through the library stacks—endless rows of bookshelves, thankfully unfamiliar to recent generations—to find and make "xerox" copies of the latest articles. Correspondence with other researchers was by mail and slow; there was no internet. Researchers and commentators used several measures of psychopathy, mainly construct ratings, psychiatric diagnoses, and self-report scales. However, these instruments did not measure the same construct (Hare, 1985), an example of the jingle fallacy in which instruments with the same name (e.g., psychopathy) measure different or weakly related constructs.

In their discussion of this fallacy, along with the jangle fallacy (different terms, same construct), Larsen and Bong (2016, p. 529) stated, "The problem of detecting whether two behavioral constructs reference the same real-world phenomenon has existed for over 100 years. Discordant naming of constructs is here termed the construct identity fallacy." Compounding the problem, at least in my view, was the uncertain connection between various measures and the traditional clinical construct of psychopathy, as exemplified by Cleckley's (1941, 1976) writings and other influential clinicians.

The situation began to change in the 1970s, with the development of a research scale based on clinical tradition, the extensive experience my students and I had working with offenders at a prison near Vancouver, and concern about what we were trying to measure. The result was a 22-item construct rating scale, first described at a 1979 meeting in Europe attended by Hans Eysenck. He asked me to submit an article to his new journal, *Personality and Individual Differences*. The scale, now commonly referred to as the Psychopathy Checklist (PCL; Hare, 1980), was the predecessor to the PCL-R (Hare, 1991, 2003). Direct clinical/forensic derivatives of the PCL-R included the *Psychopathy Checklist: Screening Version* (PCL: SV; Hart, Cox, & Hare, 1995) and the *Psychopathy Checklist: Youth Version* (PCL: YV; Forth, Kosson, & Hare, 2003). Collectively, these PCL instruments began to facilitate communications among clinicians and researchers by providing them with a standard metric. Even if some were not in agreement with our formulations, they knew what we meant when we referred to psychopathy. Sleep, Weiss, Lynam, and Miller (2019, p. 1) noted, "Hare's theoretical and empirical work, especially the development of the Psychopathy Checklist and its revision (PCL/PCL-R; Hare, 1980, 2003), allowed a robust empirical literature on psychopathy to develop." This sharp expansion in research also owes much to the introduction and widespread use of self-report measures of psychopathy, some based on the PCL-R and others on general personality theory or as part of an omnibus inventory (Sleep et al., 2019). Together, they helped to extend and broaden interest and research on psychopathy and to illustrate its enormous implications for all segments of society. A significant development was the Society for the Scientific Study of Psychopathy (SSSP), which held its first meeting in Vancouver in 2005. SSSP has become a vibrant, multidisciplinary, and multinational organization that strongly values active student participation, The latter is apparent in students' high proportion of conference presentations and their joint authorship of chapters and journal articles. By the end of 2020, the cumulative total of psychopathy articles exceeded 8000, with a yearly rate of over 600 (Web of Science).

The PCL-R is an integral part of the nomological network of psychopathy and an international standard for clinicians and researchers. Nevertheless, it is by no means the only instrument in wide use. As Miller and Lynam (2015, p. 585) noted: "In general, the modern literature on psychopathy is impressive for the varied nature of assessment methods used." Indeed, this is good for science, but only if the tools have well-established theoretical and psychometric properties and empirical correlates relevant to the construct they purport to measure. They form part of a frame of reference for delineating the construct and guiding its use in basic and applied settings. Unfortunately, not all measures of psychopathy meet scientific and psychometric standards. Their positions in the nomological network (or networks) are uncertain, raising again the possibility of construct identity fallacy. As stated by Larsen and Bong (2016,

p. 552), failure to appreciate the consequences of this fallacy may contribute to "(1) confusion, misunderstandings, and conceptual messes in research; (2) waste of scientific time; and (3) difficulty in theory unification and knowledge cumulation."

Additionally, early research, including my own, treated psychopathy as a unidimensional construct. Although I had reported that the PCL comprised several factors, some were difficult to interpret (Hare, 1980). Later, Harpur, Hakstian, and Hare (1988), using more sophisticated analyses, determined that two correlated factors underpinned the PCL: Factor 1, *A selfish, callous, and remorseless use of others*: and Factor 2, *A chronically unstable and antisocial lifestyle* (p. 745). Harpur, Hare, and Hakstian (1989) replicated this finding and demonstrated that the factors, or dimensions, had different patterns of correlations with a variety of clinical, self-report, demographic, and experimental data. Lilienfeld (2018, p. 80) said of the latter, "This seminal publication was the first to highlight the dual points that (a) psychopathy comprises more than one dimension, and (b) these subfactors often display psychologically important differential correlates." Most measures of psychopathy now are multifaceted (Miller & Lynam, 2015), although a researcher may find it helpful to treat the score on a particular scale as unidimensional. This procedure provides interpretative problems. As noted by Smith, McCarthy, and Zapolski (2009, p. 273), the use of a single score to represent a multidimensional scale "is likely to have reduced scientific value."

The structures of psychopathy scales differ from one another, often following the conceptual views and experiences of a particular investigator or group. As indicated in this volume and elsewhere, some scales include positive attributes or exclude overt antisocial features, whereas others do not (see DeLisi, 2019; Felthous & Sass, 2021; Gacono, 2016; Patrick, 2018). In many cases, researchers use the PCL-R and its factor structure to validate these other scales. Modern item-level modeling procedures have provided strong evidence for a correlated *four-factor model* of the PCL-R and its derivatives (Hare, 2003; Hare, Neumann, & Mokros, 2018; Higgs, Tully, & Browne, 2018; Neumann, Hare, & Pardini, 2015; Roy, Hare, Pardini, & Neumann, 2021). Further, structural equation modeling (SEM) indicates that these first-order dimensions (Interpersonal, Affective, Lifestyle, and Antisocial) underpin a single superordinate psychopathy factor (Hare et al., 2018; Neumann, Hare, & Newman, 2007). It is also possible to use these four factors to model a higher-order two-factor model consistent with the original two-factor model described above.

We can also subject the four-factor scores to latent profile analysis (LPA), a *person-centered* method that reveals homogenous subgroups of individuals that vary in expressions of psychopathic features (Mokros, Hare, Neumann, & Habermeyer, 2021; Neumann, Vitacco, & Mokros, 2016). For example, in the first LPA study of the PCL-R factors, Mokros et al. (2015) identified two profiles among offenders with a PCL-R score of 30 or higher. We labeled the profiles *Manipulative* and *Aggressive*, respectively, and considered each a "variation on the theme" of psychopathy. When we lowered the cut score to 27, a third profile emerged, consistent with Antisocial Personality Disorder (ASPD). When applied to the full range of PCL-R scores, four latent classes typically appeared, labeled *Prototypic Psychopathic*, *Callous-Conning*, *Externalizing*, and *General* offenders (Mokros et al., 2021; Neumann et al., 2016; Roy et al., 2021). Importantly, these latent profiles have theoretically meaningful associations with various external variables (Hare et al., 2018; Krstic et al., 2018; Neumann et al., 2016; Roy et al., 2021; Vitacco, Neumann, & Jackson, 2005). The LPA of the PCL factors can provide valuable information about subtypes of the individuals described in several chapters in this volume.

The current volume consists of uniformly excellent chapters written by a stellar group of clinicians, researchers, and experts with a strong background in law enforcement. Many authors have produced or edited similar volumes of their own. Some authors deal with issues concerning the assessment of psychopathy and its many roles in the criminal justice system, including risk assessment, sentencing, release decisions, and management/treatment issues. Others discuss etiological, neurobiological, and developmental factors and processes relevant to understanding the nature of psychopathy. Of particular interest is incorporating psychopathy into the realms of criminology, corporate behavior, hostage taking, cybercrime, violent extremism, gang dynamics, human trafficking, and communication/interview techniques. These latter areas are under-researched but of enormous practical value for the well-being of society.

As several chapters make clear, law enforcement personnel have long been aware of the importance of psychopathy in understanding and managing the people with whom they deal (Hare & Logan, 2009; Meloy & Hoffmann, 2014). My interactions with these personnel invariably have been enlightening, for they often were ahead of me in their practical awareness of the strategies and tactics used by psychopaths. A gratifying period was the decade when I was a member of the Federal Bureau of Investigation (FBI) Research Advisory Panel for the Child Abduction and Serial Murder Investigative Resources Center (CASMIRC). I made many presentations at the FBI Academy and worked closely with Special Supervisory Agent Mary Ellen O'Toole. In 2007, Adelle Forth and I conducted the first of several PCL-R Workshops and seminars at the FBI's Behavioral Analysis Unit (BAU) in Quantico. A particularly satisfying event was the publication of a special edition of the *FBI Law Enforcement Bulletin* in 2012, devoted entirely to psychopathy. In the Introduction to this edition of the LEB, I noted that it fulfilled a dream that Supervisory Special Agent Mary Ellen O'Toole, Special Agent George De Shazor, and I had years before (https://www.hsdl.org/?view&did=718311).

I finish with two points, one important and the other reactive. First, as my colleagues and I have stated many times, antisociality is central to the PCL scales and the construct they measure, but criminality is not (Hare, 2003; Hare & Neumann, 2010; Roy et al., 2021). Claims that we consider criminality essential to the conceptualization of psychopathy and its measurement with the PCL-R are patently false, and made with a curious disregard for our published statements and the empirical literature. I developed the PCL-R in forensic settings because the prevalence of psychopathy is high, and the information needed for assessment is readily available. As I have said elsewhere, I might have started my research in a different context, say, financial or political, but there were too many practical difficulties in doing so. As it is, the PCL-R discriminates psychopathic criminals from other criminals. In the PCL-R Manual (Hare, 2003), I pointed out that this does not mean that criminality is essential to the construct of psychopathy, just as studentship is not critical to constructs tapped by self-report measures developed with college students. Further, the PCL-R includes several forensic-related items, "not as measures of criminality per se, but as indicators of more general predispositions to violate a range of societal standards, in this case, formal and legal in nature" (Hare, 2003, p. 2). Researchers and clinicians who assess noncriminals know that they should omit PCL-R items designed to differentiate among offenders and prorate the resulting score to a 20-item scale. Individuals without indications of criminal activity can and do obtain PCL-R scores high enough to meet the research threshold (30/40) for psychopathy.

The second point is that I find it increasingly more challenging to make sense of the deluge of new journal articles, chapters, and conference presentations that appear every day. Things now are dramatically different from when I trudged through the library stacks decades ago. My age aside, we now have powerful computers, rapid and unlimited access to just about everything, and new generations of researchers. When I do a literature search, I always find an interesting article that cites other articles, which in turn cite other articles, and so on. Unfortunately, until I track them down, I usually have no idea about the methodologies the cited articles used to assess psychopathy. This important information is missing from the title, abstract, and keywords, and often buried in the text, seemingly as an afterthought. I fear that my early concerns about the construct identity fallacy are re-emerging. Part of the problem is the increasing use of self-reports, some with dubious psychometric properties, and validation that relies heavily on their associations with similar scales. The pool of items used in these scales is limited and scale redundancy is inevitable, with correlations among them being moderate to high. Moreover, there may be a growing trend toward the development of two (potentially diverging) lines of theory and research: one based on construct rating scales tied to clinical tradition and the other on self-reports derived from general personality theory. This is not a problem if researchers use multiple measures of psychopathy and can integrate the results in meaningful ways. Theory and research derived from construct rating and self-report tools certainly can have a symbiotic, enabling relationship, with one providing insights and hypotheses to the other. However, the correlations between self-reports and construct rating scales are small to moderate, at best. This is not surprising, for those skilled at impression management and deception are unlikely to respond to scale items in a manner that accurately reflects who they are (Gillard & Rogers, 2015; Harris, Rice, & Cormier, 2013). Most researchers and practitioners no doubt are cognizant of the strengths and limitations of each type of assessment. Still, my reading of the literature suggests that some authors and commentators take it for granted that theory and evidence from self-reports and construct ratings are in part interchangeable. Their assumption may be valid, but we should use caution when using such reciprocal extrapolations of theory and data to understand what we presume is a common construct. Problems arise if different assessment methods lead to different and conceptually incompatible results. In any case, it would be helpful for authors and commentators to be precise about their working definition of psychopathy, and for editors and reviewers to insist that they do so.

I thank Paulo Barbosa Marques, Mauro Paulino, and Laura Alho for their work in putting together this fine volume and for tolerating my meanderings.

Robert D. Hare

References

Cleckley, H. (1941). *The mask of sanity*. St. Louis, MO: Mosby.
Cleckley, H. (1976). *The mask of sanity* (5th ed.). St. Louis, MO: Mosby.
DeLisi, M. (2019). *Routledge international handbook of psychopathy and crime*. Routledge.
Felthous, A. R., & Sass, H. (Eds.). (2021). *Vol. I and II. The Wiley international handbook on psychopathic disorders and the law* Wiley & Sons.
Forth, A. E., Kosson, D., & Hare, R. D. (2003). *The hare psychopathy checklist: Youth version (PCL: YV)*. Multi-Health Systems.
Gacono, C. B. (Ed.). (2016). *The clinical and forensic assessment of psychopathy: A practitioner's guide* (2nd ed.). Routledge.
Gillard, N. D., & Rogers, R. (2015). Denial of risk: The effects of positive impression management on risk assessments for psychopathic and nonpsychopathic offenders. *International Journal of Law and Psychiatry, 42–43*, 106–113. https://doi.org/10.1016/j.ijlp.2015.08.014.
Hare, R. D. (1980). A research scale for the assessment of psychopathy in criminal populations. *Personality and Individual Differences, 1*, 111–119. https://doi.org/10.1016/0191-8869(80)90028-8.
Hare, R. D. (1985). Comparison of the procedures for the assessment of psychopathy. *Journal of Consulting and Clinical Psychology, 53*, 7–16. https://psycnet.apa.org/doi/10.1037/0022-006X.53.1.7.
Hare, R. D. (1991). *The hare psychopathy checklist-revised*. Multi-Health Systems.
Hare, R. D. (2003). *The hare psychopathy checklist-revised* (2nd ed.). Multi-Health Systems.
Hare, R. D., & Logan, M. H. (2009). Criminal psychopathy: An introduction for police. In M. St-Yves, & M. Tanguay (Eds.), *The psychology of criminal investigations: The search for the truth* (pp. 393–442). Editions Yvon Blais.
Hare, R. D., Neumann, C. S., & Mokros, A. (2018). The PCL-R assessment of psychopathy: Development, structural properties, and new directions. In C. Patrick (Ed.), *Handbook of psychopathy* (2nd ed., pp. 39–79). The Guilford Press.
Hare, R. D., & Neumann, C. S. (2010). The role of antisociality in the psychopathy construct: Comment on Skeem and Cooke (2010). *Psychological Assessment, 22*(2), 446–454. https://doi.org/10.1037/a0013635.
Harpur, T. J., Hakstian, R., & Hare, R. D. (1988). Factor structure of the psychopathy checklist. *Journal of Consulting and Clinical Psychology, 56*, 741–747. https://doi.org/10.1037/0022-006X.56.5.741.
Harpur, T. J., Hare, R. D., & Hakstian, R. (1989). A two-factor conceptualization of psychopathy: Construct validity and implications for assessment. *Psychological Assessment: A Journal of Consulting and Clinical Psychology, 1*, 6–17. https://psycnet.apa.org/doi/10.1037/1040-3590.1.1.6.
Harris, G. T., Rice, M. E., & Cormier, C. A. (2013). Research and clinical scoring of the psychopathy checklist can show good agreement. *Criminal Justice and Behavior, 40*, 1349–1362. https://doi.org/10.1177/0093854813492959.
Hart, S. D., Cox, D. N., & Hare, R. D. (1995). *The hare psychopathy checklist: Screening version (PCL: SV)*. Multi-Health Systems.
Higgs, T., Tully, R. J., & Browne, K. D. (2018). Psychometric properties in forensic application of the screening version of the psychopathy checklist. *International Journal of Offender Therapy and Comparative Criminology, 62*, 1869–1887. https://doi.org/10.1177/0306624X17719289.
Krstic, S., Neumann, C. S., Roy, S., Robertson, C., Knight, R. A., & Hare, R. D. (2018). Using latent variable- and person-centered approaches to examine the role of psychopathic traits in sex offenders. *Personality Disorders, Theory, Research, and Treatment, 9*, 207–216. https://doi.org/10.1037/per0000249.

Larsen, K. R., & Bong, C. H. (2016). A tool for addressing construct identity in literature reviews and meta-analyses. *MIS Quarterly*, *40*, 529–551. https://doi.org/10.25300/MISQ/2016/40.3.01.

Lilienfeld, S. O. (2018). The multidimensional nature of psychopathy: Five recommendations for research. *Journal of Psychopathology and Behavioral Assessment*, *40*, 79–85. https://doi.org/10.1007/s10862-018-9657-7.

Lilienfeld, S. O., Watts, A. L., Smith, S. F., Patrick, C. J., & Hare, R. D. (2018). Hervey Cleckley (1903-1984): Contributions to the study of psychopathy. *Personality Disorders, Theory, Research, and Treatment*, *9*, 520. https://doi.org/10.1037/per0000306.

Meloy, J. R., & Hoffmann, J. (Eds.). (2014). *International handbook of threat assessment* Oxford University Press.

Miller, J. D., & Lynam, D. R. (2015). Psychopathy and personality: Advances and debates. *Journal of Personality*, *83*, 585–592. https://doi.org/10.1111/jopy.12145.

Mokros, A., Hare, R. D., Neumann, C. S., & Habermeyer, E. (2021). Subtypes and variations of psychopathic disorders. In A. R. Felthous, & H. Saß (Eds.), *The Wiley international handbook on psychopathic disorders and the law: Vol. I. Diagnosis and treatment* (2nd ed., pp. 107–144). Wiley & Sons.

Mokros, A., Hare, R. D., Neumann, C. S., Santtila, P., Habermeyer, E., & Nitschke, J. (2015). Variants of psychopathy in adult male offenders: A latent profile analysis. *Journal of Abnormal Psychology*, *124*, 372–386. https://doi.org/10.1037/abn0000042.

Neumann, C. S., Hare, R. D., & Newman, J. P. (2007). The superordinate nature of the psychopathy checklist-revised. *Journal of Personality Disorders*, *21*, 102–117. https://doi.org/10.1521/pedi.2007.21.2.102.

Neumann, C. S., Hare, R. D., & Pardini, D. A. (2015). Antisociality and the construct of psychopathy: Data from across the globe. *Journal of Personality*, *83*, 678–692. https://doi.org/10.1111/jopy.12127.

Neumann, C. S., Vitacco, M. J., & Mokros, A. S. (2016). Using both variable-centered and person-centered approaches to understanding psychopathic personality. In C. B. Gacono (Ed.), *The clinical and forensic assessment of psychopathy: A practitioner's guide* (2nd ed., pp. 14–31). Routledge.

Patrick, C. J. (2018). Psychopathy as masked pathology. In C. Patrick (Ed.), *Handbook of psychopathy* (2nd ed., pp. 3–21). The Guilford Press.

Roy, S., Hare, R. D., Pardini, D. A., & Neumann, C. S. (2021). *The centrality of antisociality in the assessment of psychopathy: Evidence from large sample latent variable and longitudinal analyses*. (Manuscript under review).

Sleep, C. E., Weiss, B., Lynam, D. R., & Miller, J. D. (2019). An examination of the triarchic model of psychopathy's nomological network: A meta-analytic review. *Clinical Psychology Review*, *71*, 1–26. https://doi.org/10.1016/j.cpr.2019.04.005.

Smith, G. T., McCarthy, D. M., & Zapolski, T. C. B. (2009). On the value of homogeneous constructs for construct validation, theory testing, and the description of psychopathology. *Psychological Assessment*, *21*, 272–284. https://doi.org/10.1037/a0016699.

Vitacco, M. J., Neumann, C. S., & Jackson, R. (2005). Testing a four-factor model of psychopathy and its association with ethnicity, gender, intelligence, and violence. *Journal of Consulting and Clinical Psychology*, *73*, 466–478. https://doi.org/10.1037/0022-006X.73.3.466.

Practical considerations for the clinical and forensic use of psychopathy

1

Jason M. Smith, Carl B. Gacono, Ted B. Cunliffe, and Aaron Kivisto

Introduction

Psychopaths have been reported in most societies throughout time (Cleckley, 1941/1976; Cooke, 1998; Gacono, 2016). Cleckley (1941/1976) identified the Athenian general of the 5th century BC—Alcibiades—as a prototypical psychopath whom he described as charming and manipulative, reckless, impulsive, and violent (Cooke, 1998). Hermann Goring's psychosocial history is consistent with a diagnosis of psychopathy as well. Many of the infamous cult leaders exhibit histories consistent with psychopathy. As noted by Robins, Tipp, and Przybeck (1991), "it [antisocial personality disorder] occurs and is recognized by every society, no matter what its economic system, and in all eras, showing that it is not purely an indication of a modern 'sick' society" (p. 259).

Consequently, labels for psychopaths exist in most cultures (Cooke, 1998; Murphy, 1976). In fact, the abundance of terms used for psychopathy can be quite confusing (Gacono, 1988). It is often incorrectly assumed that terms such as antisocial, psychopathic, and sociopathic are synonymous. These terms, however, have different origins and meanings, with associated measurable and clinically relevant differences (Gacono, 2016; Gacono & Meloy, 1994).

Sociopathy (American Psychiatric Association [APA], 1952) and Antisocial Personality Disorder (American Psychiatric Association, 1994, 2013) are terms used in various editions of the Diagnostic and Statistical Manual of Mental Disorders (DSM). Lacking contemporary clinical meaning, Sociopathy was used in the first DSM (American Psychiatric Association, 1952) to describe a variety of conditions such as sexual deviation, alcoholism, and "dissocial" and "antisocial" reactions. Characteristics of the Cleckley (1941/1976) psychopath were most visible in the "antisocial reaction" criteria (Gacono, 1988). Antisocial Personality Disorder (ASPD) replaced Sociopathy in the DSM-II (American Psychiatric Association, 1968), and many of the traditional personality-based characteristics of psychopathy disappeared from ASPD in the DSM-III in an effort to enhance interrater reliability through an increased emphasis on observable behavioral criteria (American Psychiatric Association, 1980). Subsequent versions of the DSM (American Psychiatric Association, 1980, 1987, 1994, 2013) have reflected the influence of a social deviancy model (Robins, 1966) through their continued reliance on behavioral criteria. Unlike ASPD, psychopathy is comprised of both trait and behavioral criteria (Cleckley, 1941/1976; Hare, 1996;

Psychopathy and Criminal Behavior. https://doi.org/10.1016/B978-0-12-811419-3.00009-1

Meloy, 1988). While most criminal psychopaths meet criteria for ASPD, the majority of ASPD individuals are not psychopaths. This remains the case for the most recent version of the DSM (DSM-5; American Psychiatric Association, 2013).

Hervey Cleckley's (1941/1976) *The Mask of Sanity* is widely considered to provide the most seminal description of the psychopath whereby he emphasized the psychopath's inability to feel and experience emotions as a central and definitive feature. He described 16 criteria that defined psychopathy, including: (1) Superficial charm and good intelligence; (2) Absence of delusions and other signs of irrational thinking; (3) Absence of "nervousness" or psychoneurotic manifestations; (4) Unreliability; (5) Untruthfulness and insincerity; (6) Lack of remorse or shame; (7) Inadequately motivated antisocial behavior; (8) Poor judgment and failure to learn by experience; (9) Pathologic egocentricity and incapacity for love; (10) General poverty in affective reactions; (11) Specific loss of insight; (12) Unresponsiveness in general interpersonal relations; (13) Fantastic and uninviting behavior with or without drink; (14) Suicide rarely carried out; (15) Sex life impersonal, trivial, and poorly integrated; (16) Failure to follow any life plan (Table 1).

Using Cleckley's criteria, Robert Hare's research led to the development of a semistructured interview schedule for differentiating among individuals based on their psychopathy level. Throughout the 1990s and beyond, the Psychopathy Checklist-Revised (PCL-R) became a promising research-based diagnostic tool based on its well-established reliability and validity and, in part, due to the limitations of standardized testing and extant structured interviews in identifying psychopathy.

Hare and colleagues began initial work on a psychopathy screening instrument in the 1970s in the form of a simple 7-point global rating scale anchored in Cleckley's model of psychopathy. Although high interrater reliability could be achieved through this method, the "test" existed within the clinician's head; that is, it relied too heavily on implicit knowledge of expert raters. Consequently, in order to increase its applicability to clinical practice, criteria were operationalized in the form of the 22-item Psychopathy Checklist (PCL; Hare, 1980). Two items were eliminated from the PCL, due to very low factor loadings, to form the Psychopathy Checklist-Revised (PCL-R; Hare, 2003; see Richards et al., 2016).

Like most test developers working after the 1980s, Hare employed factor analysis to refine the PCL-R from rationally deduced constructs to empirically derived factors. Through subsequent research with the PCL-R over the past 25 years, the structure of the measure is now generally agreed to consist of a four-facet solution subsumed within two higher-order factors, known as the four facet/two factor model (4f/2F; see Neumann, Vitacco, & Mokros, 2016). Psychopathy studies are so variegated that some convention is needed to make it clear if the Hare (2003) model is used or only implicated. For instance, publications may cite a four-factor model of the PCL-R, but the model referred to may not include all 20 PCL-R items. Other studies may describe a "four factor psychopathy," but their methods consist entirely of measures other than the PCL-R and its variants that are purportedly related to the psychopathy construct. It is important to be aware of these inconsistencies in the psychopathy literature to avoid reaching erroneous conclusions due to inadvertently comparing orthogonal or unrelated factors (i.e., comparing apples to oranges).

Table 1 Cleckley (1941/1976), ASPD (American Psychiatric Association, 2013), and PCL-R (Hare, 2003) criteria.

Cleckley	ASPD	PCL-R
1. Superficial charm and good intelligence	1. Failure to conform to social norms	1. Glibness/superficial charm
2. Absence of delusions and other signs of irrational thinking	2. Deceitfulness, lying	2. Grandiose sense of self-worth
3. Absence of "nervousness" or psychoneurotic manifestations	3. Impulsivity	3. Need for stimulation/ proneness to boredom
4. Unreliability	4. Irritability and aggressiveness, fights and assaults	4. Pathological lying
5. Untruthfulness and insincerity	5. Reckless disregard for safety of self or others	5. Conning/manipulative
6. Lack of remorse or shame	6. Irresponsibility	6. Lack of remorse or guilt
7. Inadequately motivated antisocial behavior	7. Lacks remorse	7. Shallow affect
8. Poor judgment and failure to learn by experience		8. Callous/lack of empathy
9. Pathologic egocentricity and incapacity for love		9. Parasitic lifestyle
10. General poverty in affective reactions		10. Poor behavioral controls
11. Specific loss of insight		11. Promiscuous sexual behavior
12. Unresponsiveness in general interpersonal relations		12. Early behavior problems
13. Fantastic and uninviting behavior with or without drink		13. Lack of realistic long-term goals
14. Suicide rarely carried out		14. Impulsivity
15. Sex life impersonal, trivial, and poorly integrated		15. Irresponsibility
16. Failure to follow any life plan		16. Failure to accept responsibility for own actions
		17. Many short-term marital relationships
		18. Juvenile delinquency
		19. Revocation of conditional release
		20. Criminal versatility

The 4f/2F model was preceded by a model articulating two global oblique factors, Factor 1 and Factor 2. Factor 1 is described in the test manual as "Selfish, callous, and remorseless use of others" (Hare, 2003, p. 202). Not surprisingly, PCL-R Factor 1 scores are negatively correlated with avoidant and dependent personalities, intensity of affect, and anxiety, while positively correlated with narcissistic and histrionic disorder personality diagnoses (Hare, 1991). Self-report measures of trait machiavellianism and narcissism also correlate highly with Factor 1 and similar scores from self-report measures derived from the PCL-R. Although Factor 1 does not appear to correlate very highly with antisocial behavior and overt violence overall, some authors have suggested that this factor is uniquely implicated in certain types of violence, such as sexual violence and coercion (Harris, Rice, Hilton, Lalumiére, & Quinsey, 2007) and nonsexual sadism (Porter & Porter, 2007).

Factor 2 (items 3, 9–10, 12–15, and 18–20) relates to a construct described in the manual as a "Chronically unstable and antisocial lifestyle" (Hare, 2003, p. 202), characterized by an irresponsible, impulsive, thrill-seeking, and antisocial lifestyle and social deviance. Factor 2 correlates more highly than Factor 1 with contemporary definitions of ASPD and measures of social deviance. Factor 2 is also more strongly associated with lower socioeconomic status (SES), IQ, education, and higher criminal recidivism and self-reported diversity of antisocial behavior (Hare, 1991). Most self-report measures of antisociality (such as the PAI Antisocial Features scale, MMPI-2 Pd Scale, MMPI-2 RF Antisocial Behavior Scale, or MCMI-III Antisocial Scale) correlate more strongly with PCL-R Factor 2 than Factor 1.

The 4f/2F model further delineates Factor 1 and Factor 2 such that each is comprised of two distinct underlying facets. Factor 1 is comprised of the Interpersonal and Affective facets while Factor 2 is comprised of the Lifestyle and Antisocial facets. Beginning with the facets underlying Factor 1, the PCL-R items *glibness, superficial charm, grandiose sense of self-worth, pathological deception*, and *conning manipulative* cohere to form an Interpersonal facet (Facet 1). The Affective facet (Facet 2) consists of PCL-R items relating to lack *of remorse or guilt, shallow affect, callous lack of empathy*, and *failure to accept responsibility for actions*.

Correspondingly, Factor 2, the Lifestyle Antisocial factor, encompasses the two remaining facets: the Lifestyle facet (Facet 3: *need for stimulation proneness to boredom, parasitic lifestyle, lack of realistic long-term goals, impulsivity, irresponsibility*) and the Antisocial facet (Facet 4: *poor behavioral controls, early behavior problems, juvenile delinquency, revocation of conditional release, criminal versatility*). Two items (*promiscuity and marital relations*), although nonetheless integral to the PCL-R construct of psychopathy, do not load onto any facet. These two items can be treated in tandem as an item duplet, or test-let, which assesses behaviors stemming from opportunistic sexuality and a penchant for pseudo-intimate, exploitative pairing.

Using the Hare Psychopathy Checklist-Revised (PCL-R), those who score ≥ 30 (two standard deviations above the mean) have higher rates of violent and nonviolent offending, commit a greater variety of offenses, reoffend more often, demonstrate a poorer treatment response (Ogloff, Wong, & Greenwood, 1990; Rice, Harris, & Cormier, 1992), and exhibit more institutional misbehavior than those with lower scores (Gacono, Meloy, Sheppard, Speth, & Roske, 1995; Gacono, Meloy, Speth, &

Roske, 1997; Richards et al., 2016). These differences remain stable even when culture, gender, and the presence or absence of a major mental disorder is controlled (Cooke, 1998).

While the PCL-R is considered the gold standard for designating psychopathy, the construct is more than a sum of traits and behaviors. Rorschach findings have elucidated the dynamics of the psychopath's "inner world" (Cunliffe et al., 2012; Gacono, Evans, Kaser-Boyd, & Gacono, 2008; Gacono & Meloy, 1994; Meloy & Gacono, 1998). Consistent with Kernberg's (1975) formulations, male psychopathy emerged as a highly aggressive and emotionally detached variant of a narcissistic personality organized at a borderline level of functioning (Gacono, 1990; Gacono & Meloy, 1991; Gacono, Meloy, & Heaven, 1990). By contrast, the female psychopath has been identified as malignant form of hysteria organized at a borderline level (Cunliffe, 2002; Cunliffe & Gacono, 2005, 2008; Cunliffe, Gacono, Meloy, & Taylor, 2013; Smith, 2013; Smith, Gacono, & Cunliffe, 2018, 2021; Smith, Gacono, Cunliffe, Kivisto, & Taylor, 2014). Equally important, the PCL-R is also much more that a tool for assessing psychopathy or risk assessment and is also useful for making diagnostic formulations and facilitating treatment planning (Gacono, Jumes, & Gray, 2016).

Understanding psychopathy research

Understanding that "psychopathy" can be conceptualized in both a dimensional and categorical (taxon; PCL-R ≥ 30) manner is essential to understanding research findings (Gacono, 2013, 2016; Gacono & Gacono, 2006; Gacono, Loving, & Bodholdt, 2001). Empirical results can be obscured when authors make categorical inferences (discuss psychopathy; PCL-R ≥ 30) from studies utilizing dimensional research designs (e.g., correlations of behavior with total PCL-R scores; and/or absence of a psychopathic group, ≥ 30 scorers). Dimensional uses of psychopathy are particularly relevant to clinical applications. Clinically, determining what ranges of PCL-R scores are the best predictors of behavior is of most interest compared to whether the individual meets the threshold score for a designation of psychopathy (Bodholdt, Richards, & Gacono, 2000; Gacono & Bodholdt, 2001). For research purposes, our understanding of psychopathy (category) is enhanced when groups of psychopaths (PCL-R ≥ 30) are compared to groups of nonpsychopaths (PCL-R ≤ 24) to highlight key aspects of the construct. Surprisingly, some studies have examined the construct based on data where there were not enough numbers of PCL-R ≥ 30 scorers present. What might seem obvious—to make inferences about psychopathy a study must have psychopaths in it—is frequently overlooked (Gacono, 2016; Gacono & Gacono, 2006).

Two common research procedures that can create samples without psychopaths involve using the Psychopathy Checklist-Screening Version (PCL:SV), using a self-report measure for creating a "psychopathic group," and/or lowering PCL-R cutoff scores to form a "psychopathic" group (Gacono, 2016; Gacono & Gacono, 2006; Smith et al., 2018, 2021). Another common methodological misstep occurs when the PCL:SV is used to designate a subject as psychopathic. Since the PCL:SV, unlike the PCL-R, does not allow for a categorical designation of psychopathy (PCL-R ≥ 30), it is not a substitute for the PCL-R. Although the PCL:SV is appropriate for screening research or therapy participants and examining relative differences within a given sample, when used as the independent measure for forming "psychopathy groups," it may tarnish findings because it can be difficult—or impossible—to determine how many actual psychopaths were in the study (Gacono, 2016; Gacono & Gacono, 2006).

A similar, yet stronger, argument can be made against the use of self-report measures (i.e., Psychopathic Personality Inventory-Revised [PPI-R]; Lilienfeld & Widows, 2005). These instruments suggest that individual traits (dimensional—inherent in any one of several disorders and nondisorders) are individually psychopathic (category). However, these results do not hold up to clinical or statistical scrutiny (Gacono, 2016; Gacono & Gacono, 2006). For example, one can obtain a score on a single PCL-R item and still produce a low total PCL-R score (not be psychopathic). A designation of psychopathy is appropriate only when enough individual traits are fully present. Thus it is the aggregate of traits, rather than the presence of any individual trait, that determines psychopathy. With some exceptions, self-report measures assess traits or dimensions, as opposed to categories (presence of a psychopath). Mislabeling traits such as self-centeredness, impulsivity, impaired empathy, and irresponsibility as inherently "psychopathic" returns psychology to the pre-1900s nosology of including all personality disorders under the rubric of psychopathy (Gacono, 2016; Gacono & Gacono, 2006).

Even established self-report measures, such as the MMPI-2, are not appropriate for establishing psychopathic groups (Gacono, 2016; Hare, 1991, 2003). A related concern involves lowering PCL-R cut-off scores to form a "psychopathic" group (a common finding with female psychopathy research; see Smith, 2013). Researchers do this for one reason—their samples do not contain enough numbers of actual psychopaths (PCL-R $\geq$ 30). While this can be part of an acceptable research design, the author(s) must refrain from making inferences about psychopaths (category) when they have few, if any, established psychopaths in their sample. When lowered PCL-R cutoff scores are used to establish groups, the best that can be inferred is relative differences among high versus low scorers only within that sample (Gacono, 2016; Gacono & Gacono, 2006).

Clearly, the methods used for creating a psychopathy group have direct bearing on the types of inferences that can be made, including evaluating the study's generalizability to other findings. Results across studies can only be compared appropriately when psychopathy has been defined by a PCL-R score $\geq$ 30 (measurement error notwithstanding), and other relevant confounds are controlled (Bolt, Hare, & Neumann, 2007; Bolt, Hare, Vitale, & Newman, 2004; Gacono, 2016; Gacono & Gacono, 2006; Hare, 1991, 2003; Hare & Neumann, 2009). Divergent research findings can frequently be explained not by true differences but by the simple fact the study has few or no psychopaths in it, and/or no differences would be expected due to uncontrolled confounds (factors such as gender, IQ, presence of a mental illness which may affect the dependent measure). Additionally, statistical approaches that use simple correlational methods to compare dependent variables to individual PCL-R scores (dimensional application) fail to capture true between-group differences (Bolt et al., 2004, 2007; Gacono, 2016; Gacono & Gacono, 2006; Hare, 1991, 2003; Hare & Neumann,

2009). The results of such findings provide minimal guidance for clinicians as clinical decision-making is facilitated most directly by comparisons of groups based upon clearly defined cut-scores.

When evaluating research findings that present conclusions about psychopathy, the reviewer must always examine the mean, standard deviation, frequencies, and ranges of PCL-R scores for the sample. This data should always be provided by the researcher. Given an acceptable methodology, this data will allow a determination of whether there were enough psychopathic subjects (PCL-R ≥ 30) to justify the study's conclusions (Gacono, 2016; Gacono & Gacono, 2006). For inferences to be made regarding psychopathy (category), the PCL-R must be used as the independent measure, and there must be enough numbers of ≥ 30 scorers in the sample(s).

PCL-R usage

Use of the PCL-R requires specialized training, most often found in clinical and forensic psychologists with considerable experience assessing and treating individuals seen in correctional or other forensic settings (Gacono, 2000, 2016; Gacono & Hutton, 1994; Hare, 1991, 2003; Neumann et al., 2016). Clinicians must be acutely aware of the potential scoring biases that can develop when learning to use the PCL-R (see Murrie, Boccaccini, Guarnera, & Rufino, 2013). They must also be aware of methods for cross checking their scoring (see Gacono, 2016). Gacono (2013, 2016) provided the following PCL-R administration steps:

1. Establishing a basis for use of the instrument. Evaluate the purpose of referral, use of findings, and whether the prospective interviewee is well represented in normative studies.
2. Review of collateral records, including automated criminal records ("rap sheets") offense reports (i.e., Presentence investigation (PSI), hospital and treatment records before the interview).
3. Notation of events and situations to be queried or probed during interviews and tentative prescoring of items from record information.
4. Interview(s) with persons with significant knowledge and experience of the subject, such as family members, friends, clinicians, and institutional staff.
5. Clinical interview of the subject.
6. Integration of information through an item-by-item scoring.
7. Calculation of scale scores and total score. Cross check scoring for consistency.
8. Comparison of scores to relevant normative samples.
9. Interpretation of scores.
10. Integration of psychopathy-related findings with other assessment data.

The step-by-step approach suggested by Gacono (2013, 2016) cannot be overstated. For example, it is imperative to conduct the review of relevant records ***before*** the individual is interviewed. Although it may be temporally expedient to do the interview or several interviews first (as was suggested to one of the authors [TBC] by a psychopathy researcher), this approach is extremely problematic and significantly affects PCL-R scores. Since, as Hare (1991, 2003) highlighted in the PCL-R manual, a central feature of psychopathy is manipulativeness and pathological lying, it is essential for the clinician or interviewer to come to the assessment session "armed" with independently verified information to confront evaluatee's statements. This is also important since their responses to these types of challenges from the interviewer can provide important information to score other items such as Glib/Superficial Charm, Grandiose Sense of Self, Poor Behavioral Controls, and Shallow of Affect, to name just a few. Therefore this fluid, semistructured and data-based approach is important to guard against clinical and assessment errors which arise since evaluatees, particularly ≥ 30 PCL-R scorers, can provide very convincing yet incorrect or skewed descriptions and statements.

The Rorschach

The Rorschach is ideally suited for contributing to the assessment of psychopathy. It avoids the face validity of self-report measures yet provides reliable and valid information about the individual's personality structure and function (Exner, 2003). Although we hesitate to state that the Rorschach cannot be malingered, research has shown that even individuals coached about the test are unable to successfully simulate healthy psychological functioning on the Rorschach (Hartmann & Hartmann, 2014; Nørbech, Fodstad, Kuisma, Lunde, & Hartmann, 2016). Consistent with these studies, we have found that the test is usually only beaten by the psychopathic patient who sufficiently constricts his response frequency (Gacono & Meloy, 1994). Such a psychometrically invalid protocol, however, may still yield worthwhile psychodiagnostic information (Weiner, 2003).

We have found that ASPD males, in general, produce normative response frequencies (Gacono & Meloy, 1994), at least in research settings. Rorschach protocols taken for forensic purposes in pretrial criminal cases may be constricted, but the examiner should aggressively pursue a valid protocol ($R \geq 14$) according to Exner's guidelines. Through a series of studies (Cunliffe, 2002; Cunliffe et al., 2016; Cunliffe & Gacono, 2005, 2008; Gacono, 1990; Gacono et al., 1990; Gacono & Meloy, 1991, 1994; Smith et al., 2014, 2018, 2021) we validated the use of the Rorschach as a sensitive instrument to discriminate between male and female psychopathic and nonpsychopathic subjects (see Table 2 for gender differences among male and female psychopaths on the Rorschach). Specifically, female psychopaths tend to display more emotional difficulties on the Rorschach. Females presented with a pathological self-focus and self-criticism (EGOI without Reflections & SumV), dependency ($T > 2$, ROD), and reality testing problems (X-%). Thus unlike male psychopaths who exalt in their self-perceptions (grandiosity and narcissism), the females were bothered by negative emotion and critical and negative self-attributions.

Interpersonally, the finding with SumT (attachment; more for females than males) appears to signify that male psychopaths are more detached while female psychopaths prefer interpersonal contact. Further, both males and females have a pathological self-focus (EGOI); however, the lack of reflections and increased SumV among females suggest a damaged sense of self rather than the grandiose sense of self normally expressed by the male psychopaths.

Table 2 Select comprehensive system Rorschach variables for male and female psychopaths (Smith et al., 2018).

	Male psychopaths			Female psychopaths					
	M	*SD*	Freq (%)	*M*	*SD*	Freq (%)	Statistic	*P*	*es (r)*
Variable									
Sum V > 1			3 (7%)			12 (26%)	6.01**	.01	0.26
Sum V > 2			2 (5%)			10 (22%)	5.75**	.02	0.25
EGOI ≥ 0.44 & Fr + rF = 0			3 (7%)			10 (22%)	4.05**	.04	0.21
Sum Y ≥ 2			12 (27%)			24 (52%)	5.81**	.02	0.25
Sum T	0.11	0.49	3 (7%)	0.89	1.46	21 (46%)	617.50*	< .001	0.34
Sum T = 0			41 (93%)			25 (54%)	17.34**	< .001	0.44
Sum T = 1			2 (5%)			13 (28%)	9.11**	.003	0.32
Sum T > 1			1 (2%)			8 (17%)	5.71**	.02	0.25
Pairs > 10			3 (7%)			12 (26%)	6.01**	.01	0.26

Notes: M = mean; SD = standard deviation; Freq = frequency; es = effect size; * = Mann-Whitney *U*; ** = Chi-square.

The psychopathy checklists (PCL-R; Hare, 2003) were developed, normed, and validated exclusively on males. Although recent data has suggested that some of the PCL-R items may be accurate for use with females (Bolt et al., 2004), some investigators have suggested that some of the item descriptions do not sufficiently capture the syndrome in women (Cunliffe et al., 2013, 2016; Cunliffe & Gacono, 2005; Grann, 2000). Although male and female psychopaths display many similar behaviors and share a comparable interpersonal style, both Rorschach research and other findings suggest that the syndrome is not equivalent across gender (Cunliffe, 2002; Cunliffe & Gacono, 2005, 2008; Forouzan & Cooke, 2005; Gacono & Meloy, 1994; Kreis & Cooke, 2011, 2012; Smith et al., 2014, 2018; Verona & Vitale, 2006). Biological, behavioral, developmental, and personality findings suggest that some of the items would be expected to manifest differently in female populations and, as a result, measures such as the PCL-R may require revisions to adequately capture these distinctions (Cunliffe et al., 2013, 2016).

Female psychopathy appears to be characterized by a need for increased contact and approval from others rather than the arrogant, solitary detachment, and isolation described for male psychopaths (Gacono & Meloy, 1994; Hare, 2003). These findings are consistent with expected gender differences and are reflected in their criminal and interpersonal behaviors. For example, it is common for female psychopaths to enlist the assistance of an aggressive male ally or codefendant to accomplish her criminal or antisocial goals; to offend against those in their immediate social milieu (intimates, children, and associates); and to present with a friendly, fragile, and seemingly less malevolent interpersonal style than males. However, when her claims are checked or her actions are scrutinized, she is likely to be found to be every bit as dangerous and lacking in empathy and remorse as her male counterpart despite her outward appearance.

Contrary to previous suggestions (see Peaslee, 1993), female psychopaths can and should be identified by a PCL-R cut-score ≥ 30 (also see Cunliffe, 2002; Cunliffe et al., 2012, 2013, 2016; Smith, 2013; Smith et al., 2014, 2018, 2021) for creating psychopathic groups (Gacono & Gacono, 2006) and identifying female psychopathy clinically. Several caveats are suggested by our work with female psychopaths (Cunliffe et al., 2016; Smith et al., 2014, 2018, 2021):

1. Although eliminating or minimizing sources of bias are important in any assessment, the clinician should be particularly on guard against the effects of several different types of bias when evaluating females.
2. The female psychopath's experience of dysphoric affect and chronic self-criticism should be carefully evaluated and not necessarily be interpreted as evidence of a deeper, longer lasting depression or remorse.
3. Given the female psychopath's heightened needs for approval and attention from others (particularly other women), an empathic and supportive interview style is recommended.
4. Meticulous review of records is an important aspect of the assessment of psychopathy in women.
5. A consideration of counter-transference is a key aspect of the assessment of female offenders in order to guard against errors of clinical judgment.

The knowledge base for understanding female psychopaths has been growing. Based on our empirical and clinical work with female offenders (Cunliffe, 2002; Cunliffe et al., 2013, 2016; Cunliffe & Gacono, 2005, 2008; Gacono & Meloy, 1994; Smith, 2013; Smith et al., 2014, 2018, 2021), the presentation of female psychopathic offenders is different than that described by Hare (2003) and others (Gacono & Meloy, 1994; Meloy, 1988) for males. Although a well-informed knowledge of base rates for behavior is necessary to assess symptoms present in any clinical population, the assessment of psychopathy in women is complicated by the paucity of well-designed and methodologically sound studies, less developed scientific literature, several sources of bias, and a lack of knowledge or clinical exposure to the female offender population by many evaluators.

Conclusions

Assessment forms the cornerstone of the "forensic mind-set"—one that is data-based, utilizes test data, observation, interviewing, and multiple sources of substantiated historical information in forming, testing, and modifying hypotheses (Gacono & Bodholdt, 2001). Ultimately, true or valid assessment allows the clinician to articulate the steps that led to their clinical and forensic opinions. Administering the PCL-R is an essential component of adult psychopathy assessment (Gacono, 2013, 2016). At a time when assessment is being devalued at large, it may be difficult to introduce the PCL-R or any instrument to an organization or choose to include it within one's practice. At the same time, when we have a tool of considerable value, but fail to educate about it, then we risk a false conclusion, that "nobody is interested" and/or "there is nothing that works" (Gacono, 2016).

Often, institutions that manage violent offenders prolong the introduction of the PCL-R as part of their assessment protocol. The psychologist holds a special responsibility, to see that well-rounded, unbiased education be provided about the benefits and costs of using an instrument such as the PCL-R as part of an assessment protocol (Gacono, 2013, 2016). One frequent concern is that the PCL-R is too "time-intensive" (not cost effective). As psychopathy assessment constitutes an essential component to risk assessment, the practice of not using the PCL-R cannot be defended ethically or legally. The time needed to administer the PCL-R should be weighed against the routine use of "empty" assessment protocols filled with paper and pencil tests that have little relationship to the forensic issue and, consequently, are less useful than the PCL-R. When understood in this manner, PCL-R usage is extremely cost effective (Gacono, 2013, 2016).

For institutions that manage violent patients or inmates, it is essential to develop policy and procedures that guide violence management and ensure the safety of staff and patients. In this area, psychologists can embrace an assessment role that distinguishes them from other mental health professionals; allows them to walk "hand in hand" in clinical respectability with other staff; and provides, in certain cases, essential information that cannot be obtained with similar efficacy by other methods.

Assessment should not be an afterthought, but, rather, the process should begin at admissions with standardized triage procedures (see Gacono, 2013, 2016).

Psychopathy assessment plays an integral role in the management of institutional violence, as a guide to treatment planning, as an aid in release decisions, and as part of an assessment battery designed to answer specific forensic questions (Gacono, 2013, 2016). Community psychologists, in certain cases, are required to use the PCL-R, and, if they never administer a PCL-R, an understanding of psychopathy is necessary for screening and referral. With appropriate training/supervision, implementation of standardized procedures, and continued study of clinical utility/validity, the Psychopathy Checklists have become invaluable to the assessment of psychopathy (Rice et al., 1992). For those who may encounter a psychopath outside of a clinical/forensic setting, as noted by Kosson, Gacono, Klipfel, & Bodholdt (2016, p. 271):

1. Never ignore or deny gross inconsistencies in a person's behavior. Avoid making rationalizations and excuses for behaviors that do not seem to make sense.
2. Do not settle for a personal history with significant gaps.
3. Do not get caught up in curiosity about inconsistencies and an apparent lack of empathy, remorse, and compassion. Trying to figure something out that is beyond the comprehension for one who considers relationships to be based on give and take and compassion rather than power and control, becomes part of getting entangled in his or her web.
4. Do not gloss over what seem like unusual emotional reactions that occur when involved with a psychopath.
5. Do not be naïve or gullible about what human beings are capable of. If you begin from the premise that "all" people are basically good and tend to "put your faith in the kindness of strangers" you are at considerable risk should you be unfortunate enough to cross paths with a psychopath.
6. If you have experienced a recent loss or setback you may be at additional risk.
7. Clinical conditions and personal history, such as having Posttraumatic Stress Disorder (PTSD) or being raised in an alcoholic family, can increase a person's vulnerability to being victimized.

An additional caution concerns the importance of maintaining an independent or impartial orientation related to the process of forensic assessment. Melton et al. (2018) and other researchers have highlighted the tendency or temptation for forensic psychologists to view themselves as "part of the defense or prosecution team" rather than an independent evaluator. In private practice, the practicing psychologist must balance concerns related to providing quality clinical work that will be useful and capable of withstanding scrutiny in court with remaining independent. In the most severe cases, this is manifested in situations whereby forensic psychologists sacrifice their clinical objectivity and integrity in the interests of "giving the client what they want" (the referring lawyer, defense, or prosecution team).

This is reflected in PCL-R research whereby PCL-R scores have been found to vary depending on which side (defense or prosecution) of a legal case requested the evaluation (Murrie et al., 2009). Although some have suggested that this is an indictment of the use of the PCL-R in court, we suggest that it highlights the importance of ensuring that PCL-R assessment involves a data-driven, fact-based approach and methodology.

We believe the future clinical/forensic use of the PCL-R rests not on the psychometric properties nor the utility of the instrument, but rather on ethical and thoughtful integration of psychopathy assessment into public policy, careful implementation regulating its usage within institutional settings, and the ability of practitioners to use it in reliable, professional manner (Gacono, 2016). Regarding the latter, the poor interrater agreement for PCL-R scores administered in the community suggests that this has not occurred. For the PCL-R to be useful, practitioners must be challenged to receive the adequate supervision necessary to use the PCL-R and understand that a single PCL-R workshop or certification process is not enough to ensure competency with the instrument (Gacono, 2016). It is the hope of the authors that steps will be taken to ensure the ethical and competent use of this invaluable forensic tool.

References

American Psychiatric Association. (1952). *Diagnostic and statistical manual of mental disorders*. Washington, DC: American Psychiatric Association.

American Psychiatric Association. (1968). *Diagnostic and statistical manual of mental disorders* (2nd ed.). Washington, DC: American Psychiatric Association.

American Psychiatric Association. (1980). *Diagnostic and statistical manual of mental disorders* (3rd ed.). Washington, DC: American Psychiatric Association.

American Psychiatric Association. (1987). *Diagnostic and statistical manual of mental disorders* (3rd ed. revised). Washington, DC: American Psychiatric Association.

American Psychiatric Association. (1994). *Diagnostic and statistical manual of mental disorders* (4th ed.). Washington, DC: American Psychiatric Association.

American Psychiatric Association. (2013). *Diagnostic and statistical manual of mental disorders* (5th ed.). Washington, DC: American Psychiatric Association.

Bodholdt, R. H., Richards, H. R., & Gacono, C. B. (2000). Assessing psychopathy in adults: The psychopathy checklists, revised and screening version. In C. B. Gacono (Ed.), *The clinical and forensic assessment of psychopathy: A practitioner's guide* (pp. 55–86). Mahwah, NJ: Lawrence Erlbaum Associates.

Bolt, D. M., Hare, R. D., & Neumann, C. S. (2007). Score metric equivalence of the psychopathy checklist–revised (PCL-R) across criminal offenders in North America and the United Kingdom: A critique of Cooke, Michie, Hart, and Clark (2005) and new analyses. *Assessment*, *14*(1), 44–56. https://doi.org/10.1177/1073191106293505.

Bolt, D. M., Hare, R. D., Vitale, J. E., & Newman, J. P. (2004). A multigroup item response theory analysis of the psychopathy checklist-revised. *Psychological Assessment*, *16*(2), 155–168.

Cleckley, H. (1941/1976). *The mask of sanity* (5th ed.). St. Louis, MO: Mosby.

Cooke, D. J. (1998). Cross-cultural aspects of psychopathy. In T. Millon, E. Simonsen, M. Birket-Smith, & R. Davis (Eds.), *Psychopathy: Antisocial, criminal, and violent behavior* (pp. 260–276). New York: The Guilford Press.

Cunliffe, T. B. (2002). *A Rorschach investigation of incarcerated female psychopaths* (unpublished doctoral dissertation). Palo Alto, CA: Pacific Graduate School of Psychology.

Cunliffe, T. B., & Gacono, C. B. (2005). A Rorschach investigation of incarcerated antisocial personality disordered female offenders. *International Journal of Offender Therapy and Comparative Criminology*, *49*, 530–547.

Cunliffe, T. B., & Gacono, C. B. (2008). A Rorschach understanding of antisocial and psychopathic women. In C. B. Gacono, F. B. Evans, N. Kaser-Boyd, & L. A. Gacono (Eds.), *The handbook of forensic Rorschach assessment* (pp. 361–378). New York, NY: Routledge.

Cunliffe, T. B., Gacono, C. B., Meloy, J. R., Smith, J. M., Taylor, E. E., & Landry, D. (2012). Psychopathy and the Rorschach: A response to Wood et al. (2010). *Archives of Assessment Psychology*, *2*(1), 1–31.

Cunliffe, T. B., Gacono, C. B., Meloy, J. R., & Taylor, E. E. (2013). Are male and female psychopaths equivalent? A Rorschach study. In J. Helfgott (Ed.), *Vol. 2. Criminal psychology* (pp. 423–460). Westport, CT: Praeger Publishers.

Cunliffe, T. B., Gacono, C. B., Smith, J. M., Kivisto, A. J., Meloy, J. R., & Taylor, E. E. (2016). Assessing psychopathy in women. In C. B. Gacono (Ed.), *The clinical and forensic assessment of psychopathy: A practitioner's guide* (2nd ed., pp. 167–190). New York, NY: Routledge/Taylor & Francis Group.

Exner, J. E. (2003). *The Rorschach: A comprehensive system* (4th ed.). New York: Wiley.

Forouzan, E., & Cooke, D. J. (2005). Figuring out la femme fatale: Conceptual and assessment issues concerning psychopathy in females. *Behavioral Sciences & the Law*, *23*, 765–778.

Gacono, C. B. (1988). *A Rorschach interpretation of object relations and defensive structure and their relationship to narcissism and psychopathy in a group of antisocial offenders (Unpublished doctoral dissertation).* San Diego, CA: United States International University.

Gacono, C. B. (1990). An empirical study of object relations and defensive operations in antisocial personality. *Journal of Personality Assessment*, *54*, 589–600.

Gacono, C. B. (2013). Guidelines for the evaluation and interpretation of psychopathy research findings. In J. Helfgott (Ed.), *Vol. 2. Criminal psychology* (pp. 341–353). Westport, CT: Praeger Publishers.

Gacono, C. B. (2016). Introduction. In C. B. Gacono (Ed.), *The clinical and forensic assessment of psychopathy: A practitioner's guide* (pp. 3–13). New York, NY: Routledge/Taylor & Francis Group.

Gacono, C. B., & Bodholdt, R. (2001). The role of the psychopathy checklist-revised (PCL-R) in risk assessment. *Journal of Threat Assessment*, *1*(4), 65–79.

Gacono, C. B. (Ed.). (2000). *The clinical and forensic assessment of psychopathy: A practitioner's guide*. Mahwah, NJ: Erlbaum.

Gacono, C. B., Evans, F. B., Kaser-Boyd, N., & Gacono, L. A. (Eds.). (2008). *The handbook of forensic Rorschach assessment*. Mahwah, NJ: Lawrence Erlbaum Associates.

Gacono, C. B., & Gacono, L. A. (2006). Some caveats for evaluating the research of psychopathy. *The Correctional Psychologist*, *38*(2), 7–9.

Gacono, C. B., & Hutton, H. E. (1994). Suggestions for the clinical and forensic use of the Hare psychopathy checklist-revised (PCL-R). *International Journal of Law and Psychiatry*, *17*(3), 303–317.

Gacono, C. B., Jumes, M. T, & Gray, B. T. (2016). Using the PCL-R and Rorschach in forensic treatment planning. *The clinical and forensic assessment of psychopathy: A practitioner's guide* (2nd, pp. 311–332). New York, NY: Routledge/Taylor & Francis Group.

Gacono, C. B., Loving, J. L., & Bodholdt, R. H. (2001). The Rorschach and psychopathy: Toward a more accurate understanding of the research findings. *Journal of Personality Assessment*, *77*, 16–38.

Gacono, C. B., & Meloy, J. R. (1991). A Rorschach investigation of attachment and anxiety in antisocial personality. *Journal of Nervous and Mental Disease*, *179*, 546–552.

Gacono, C. B., & Meloy, J. R. (1994). *The Rorschach assessment of aggressive and psychopathic personalities*. Hillsdale, NJ: Erlbaum.

Gacono, C. B., Meloy, J. R., & Heaven, T. (1990). A Rorschach investigation of narcissism and hysteria in antisocial personality disorder. *Journal of Personality Assessment*, *55*, 270–279.
Gacono, C., Meloy, R., Sheppard, K., Speth, E., & Roske, A. (1995). A clinical investigation of malingering and psychopathy in hospitalized insanity acquittees. *Bulletin of the American Academy of Psychiatry and the Law*, *23*, 387–397.
Gacono, C. B., Meloy, J. R., Speth, E., & Roske, A. (1997). Above the law: Escapes from a maximum security forensic hospital and psychopathy. *The Journal of the American Academy of Psychiatry and the Law*, *25*, 547–550.
Grann, M. (2000). The PCL–R and gender. *European Journal of Psychological Assessment*, *16*(3), 147–149.
Hare, R. D. (1980). A research scale for the assessment of psychopathy in criminal populations. *Personality and Individual Differences*, *1*, 111–119.
Hare, R. D. (1991). *The Hare psychopathy checklist-revised manual*. Toronto: Multi-Health Systems.
Hare, R. D. (1996). Psychopathy: A clinical construct whose time has come. *Criminal Justice and Behavior*, *23*(1), 25–54.
Hare, R. D. (2003). *The Hare psychopathy checklist-revised manual*. Toronto: Multi-Health Systems.
Hare, R. D., & Neumann, C. S. (2009). Psychopathy: Assessment and forensic implications. *The Canadian Journal of Psychiatry*, *54*(12), 791–802. https://doi.org/10.1177/070674370905401202.
Harris, G. T., Rice, M. E., Hilton, N., Lalumiére, M. L., & Quinsey, V. L. (2007). Coercive and precocious sexuality as a fundamental aspect of psychopathy. *Journal of Personality Disorders*, *21*(1), 1–27.
Hartmann, E., & Hartmann, T. (2014). The impact of exposure to internet-based information about the Rorschach and the MMPI-2 on psychiatric outpatients' ability to simulate mentally healthy test performance. *Journal of Personality Assessment*, *96*, 432–444.
Kernberg, O. (1975). *Borderline conditions and pathological narcissism*. New York: Aronson.
Kosson, D. S., Gacono, C. B., Klipfel, K. M., & Bodholdt, R. (2016). Understanding and assessing psychopathy: Interpersonal aspects and clinical interviewing. In C. B. Gacono (Ed.), *Personality and clinical psychology series. The clinical and forensic assessment of psychopathy: A practitioner's guide* (pp. 252–275). New York, NY: Routledge/Taylor & Francis Group.
Kreis, M. K. F., & Cooke, D. J. (2011). Capturing the psychopathic female: A prototypicality analysis of the Comprehensive Assessment of Psychopathic Personality (CAPP) across gender. *Behavioral Sciences & the Law*, *29*(5), 634–648.
Kreis, M. K. F., & Cooke, D. J. (2012). The manifestation of psychopathic traits in women: An exploration using case examples. *International Journal of Forensic Mental Health*, *11*(4), 267–279.
Lilienfeld, S. O., & Widows, M. R. (2005). *Psychopathic personality inventory-revised (PPI-R) professional manual*. Odessa, FL: Psychological Assessment Resources.
Meloy, J. R. (1988). *The psychopathic mind: Origins, dynamics, and treatment*. Northvale, NJ: Aronson.
Meloy, J. R., & Gacono, C. B. (1998). The internal world of the psychopath: A Rorschach investigation. In T. Millon, E. Simonsen, & M. Birket-Smith (Eds.), *Psychopathy: Antisocial, criminal, and violent behaviors*. New York: Guilford Press.
Melton, G. B., Petrila, J., Poythress, N. G., Slobogin, C., Otto, R. K., Mossman, D., et al. (2018). *Psychological evaluations for the courts: A handbook for mental health professionals and lawyers* (4th ed.). New York, NY: Guilford Press.

Murphy, J. (1976). Psychiatric labeling in cross-cultural perspective. *Science, 191*, 1019–1028.

Murrie, D. C., Boccaccini, M. T., Guarnera, L. A., & Rufino, K. A. (2013). Are forensic experts biased by the side that retained them? *Psychological Science, 24*, 1889–1897.

Murrie, D. C., Boccaccini, M. T., Turner, D. B., Meeks, M., Woods, C., & Tussey, C. (2009). Rater (dis)agreement on risk assessment measures in sexually violent predator proceedings: Evidence of adversarial allegiance in forensic evaluation? *Psychology, Public Policy, and Law*, *15*(1), 19–53. https://doi.org/10.1037/a0014897.

Neumann, C. S., Vitacco, M. J., & Mokros, A. S. (2016). Using both variable-centered and person-centered approaches to understanding psychopathic personality. In C. B. Gacono (Ed.), *Personality and clinical psychology series. The clinical and forensic assessment of psychopathy: A practitioner's guide* (pp. 14–31). New York, NY: Routledge/Taylor & Francis Group.

Nørbech, P. C. B., Fodstad, L., Kuisma, I., Lunde, K. B., & Hartmann, E. (2016). Incarcerated violent offenders' ability to avoid revealing their potential for violence on the Rorschach and MMPI-2. *Journal of Personality Assessment, 98*, 419–429.

Ogloff, J., Wong, S., & Greenwood, A. (1990). Treating criminal psychopaths in a therapeutic community program. *Behavioral Sciences & the Law*, *8*, 81–90.

Peaslee, D. (1993). *An investigation of incarcerated females: Rorschach indices and psychopathy checklist scores* (unpublished doctoral dissertation). Fresno, CA: California School of Professional Psychology.

Porter, S., Porter, S., Herv'e, H., & Yuille, J. C. (2007). Psychopathy and violent crime. In *The psychopath: Theory, research, and practice* (pp. 287–300). Mahwah, NJ: Lawrence Erlbaum Associates.

Rice, M. E., Harris, G. T., & Cormier, C. A. (1992). An evaluation of a maximum security therapeutic community for psychopaths and other mentally disordered offenders. *Law and Human Behavior*, *16*(4), 399–412.

Richards, H. J., Gacono, C. B., Cunliffe, T. B., Kivisto, A. J., Smith, J. M., & Bodholdt, R. (2016). Assessing psychopathy in adults: The Hare psychopathy checklist—Revised and psychopathy checklist screening version. In C. B. Gacono (Ed.), *Personality and clinical psychology series. The clinical and forensic assessment of psychopathy: A practitioner's guide* (pp. 137–166). New York, NY: Routledge/Taylor & Francis Group.

Robins, L. N. (1966). *Deviant children grown up: A sociological and psychiatric study of sociopathic personality*. Baltimore: Williams & Wilkins.

Robins, L. N., Tipp, J., & Przybeck, T. (1991). Psychiatric disorders in America. In L. N. Robins, & D. A. Reger (Eds.), *Antisocial personality disorder* (pp. 258–290). Free Press.

Smith, J. M. (2013). *Female psychopathy: A Rorschach investigation of personality structure* (unpublished doctoral project). Miami, FL: Carlos Albizu University.

Smith, J. M., Gacono, C. B., & Cunliffe, T. B. (2018). Comparison of male and female psychopaths on select CS Rorschach variables. *SIS Journal of Projective Psychology and Mental Health*, *25*(2), 138–155.

Smith, J. M., Gacono, C. B., & Cunliffe, T. B. (2021). *Understanding female offenders: Psychopathy, criminal behavior, assessment, & treatment*. San Diego, CA: Elsevier.

Smith, J. M., Gacono, C. B., Cunliffe, T. B., Kivisto, A. J., & Taylor, E. E. (2014). Psychodynamics in the female psychopath: A PCL-R/Rorschach investigation. *Violence and Gender*, *1*(4), 176–187.

Verona, E., & Vitale, J. (2006). Psychopathy in women. In C. Patrick (Ed.), *Handbook of psychopathy* (pp. 415–436). New York: Guilford.

Weiner, I. B. (2003). *Principles of Rorschach interpretation* (2nd ed.). Mahwah, NJ: Lawrence Erlbaum Associates.

The emergence and development of psychopathy

2

Laura Alho, Mauro Paulino, Paulo Barbosa Marques, and J. Reid Meloy

Introduction

Psychopathic individuals are characterized by antisocial deviance and premeditated violent behavior, lack of empathy, remorse, or guilt, shallow affect, and poor emotional regulation and behavioral control (Hare, 1998; Hare & Neumann, 2008; Meloy, 1988, 2001; Salekin, 2017). Defined as a personality disorder, psychopathy is estimated to be between 0.6% and 4% in the general population and approximately in 20% of criminal violent offenders (Hare, 1991; Patrick, 2005), with a higher proportion of males (Thompson, Ramos, & Willett, 2014). Furthermore, it is considered a strong predictor of both nonviolent and violent recidivism (Hare, 2006; Skilling, Harris, Rice, & Quinsey, 2002).

The etiology of psychopathy, according to some, seems to be founded on an impaired emotional response that is manifest in the absence of fear and empathy, promoting the risk of antisocial behavior and hindering the development of moral conscience (e.g., Blair, 1995; Skeem, Johansson, Andershed, Kerr, & Louden, 2007; Skeem, Poythress, Edens, Lilienfeld, & Cale, 2003). In a more general sense, limbic anomalies, centered on the amygdala and its connective pathways to higher cortical centers, are the focus of research attention. Many studies have also shown strong correlations between psychopathic traits and genetic factors in childhood and adulthood (Vernon, Villani, Vickers, & Harris, 2008; Viding, Jones, Paul, Moffitt, & Plomin, 2008), such work predicting antisocial behaviors in children (Viding et al., 2008; Viding, Blair, Moffitt, & Plomin, 2005), adolescents (Frick, Stickle, Dandreaux, Farrell, & Kimonis, 2005), and also in adults (Blonigen, Hicks, Krueger, Patrick, & Iacono, 2006). A variation in antisocial behavior is explained by genetic factors when psychopathic traits are present, suggesting that antisocial behaviors in psychopathic individuals are somewhat rooted and stronger (Viding et al., 2005).

There are the two subtypes of psychopathy: primary and secondary. While primary psychopathy is mostly related to genetic features, associated with reduced neural activation to others' emotions, secondary psychopathy—what used to be called sociopathy—develops mostly from environmental causes, such as parental abuse or rejection, resulting in neuroticism, aggression, impulsivity, and emotional reactivity (e.g., Blackburn & Maybury, 1985; Sethi et al., 2018).

It is not perfectly understood how the personality of a psychopath develops, but there are certain events in early life that may act as risk factors or predictors of psychopathy in adult life. The literature suggests an integrative approach between cognitive neuroscience and genetics to understand the development of psychopathy. We

Psychopathy and Criminal Behavior. https://doi.org/10.1016/B978-0-12-811419-3.00020-0

intend to explore some aspects of the development of psychopathy by reviewing genetic, environmental, neurobiological, cognitive, and behavioral studies, enlightening how and why this disorder emerges and develops. Nevertheless, it is important to bear in mind that although we divided this chapter into different areas of research regarding possible psychopathy etiologies—for the sake of the organization—they are interconnected and related to each other.

Genetic and environmental research

The trajectory of each individual is determined by an interplay between genetic, social, and cognitive factors and even though the genome is quite important to the phenotypic expression, it is not a *sine qua non* condition of how an individual will be as an adult. The research on genetic influences in psychopathy requires the investigation of the interactions between genes and the social and contextual environment in order to improve the understanding of how genetic risks are associated with the disorder.

Although some psychopathic traits are observed in childhood, including the emotional impairment known as callous-unemotional (CU) traits, the *psychopath* label is not used to describe children. CU traits, however, do provide information for the comprehension of psychopathy during an individual's life. They are related to a lack of empathy, guilt, or remorse, and are reported to be a developmental precursor to psychopathy (Frick & White, 2008). High CU traits are associated with lower levels of fear (Frick, Lilienfeld, Ellis, Loney, & Silverthorn, 1999; Petitclerc et al., 2019), and with a decrease in the response to negative emotional stimuli (Dadds et al., 2006), which are characteristics of psychopathic individuals.

Gene-association studies have focused on CU traits in children or adolescents that present some disruptive behavior (e.g., Fontaine, Rijsdijk, McCrory, & Viding, 2010; Moore et al., 2019; Muratori et al., 2016). Studies with twins have shown that individual differences in CU are estimated to be moderately to strongly heritable (e.g., Flom & Saudino, 2017; Viding & McCrory, 2015). In fact, recent genetic research suggests modest to high heritability of psychopathic traits (see Dhanani et al., 2018). Disruptive behaviors associated with high levels of CU traits appear to be strongly heritable, whereas disruptive behaviors with low levels of CU traits seem to have a major influence from environmental factors (Viding et al., 2005, 2008). For instance, negative parenting has been associated with higher levels of CU traits and disruptive behaviors, and a positive parental style has been associated with lower levels of CU traits and disruptive behaviors in children (see Waller, Gardner, & Hyde, 2013).

Longitudinal studies focusing on genetics have also investigated parenting and development of CU traits (Hyde et al., 2016; Waller, Shaw, & Hyde, 2016), and results have shown that the level of antisocial behavior and fearlessness in the biological mother predicted early CU behaviors in adopted children. Moreover, positive reinforcement provided by an adoptive mother was a protective factor against the development of CU traits even in the presence of significant biological risks, such as a biological mother with antisocial traits. Nonetheless, an adoptive mother with positive reinforcement buffered the effects of heritable risk for CU behaviors; this may be explained by the high motivation levels and financial resources that adoptive parents habitually have, contrary to biological families, wherein parents of children with CU traits are more likely to have genetic and social risk factors involved.

Concerning the empathy and love from parents with children with high levels of CU traits, Dadds et al. (2012, 2014) found that compared with other children with disruptive behaviors, those with high levels of CU traits were less prone to establish eye contact with their mothers. The mothers of children with high levels of CU traits, on the other hand, did not differ from mothers of non-CU children with disruptive behaviors in terms of the amount of eye contact they had with their children. Furthermore, a recent cross-sectional study from Loney, Huntenburg, Counts-Allan, and Schmeelk (2007) found a significant association between maternal affective features of psychopathy and the CU traits of their children, wherein parenting dysfunction fully mediated the relationship.

Research has consistently revealed a significant overlap in genes that influence CU traits (Bezdjian, Raine, Baker, & Lynam, 2011; Forsman, Lichtenstein, Andershed, & Larsson, 2008) with the stability in CU traits being driven by genetics (Flom & Saudino, 2017; Fontaine et al., 2010). In order to explore the genetic and environmental overlap between psychopathic traits and antisocial behavior, Larsson et al. (2007) did a study with a longitudinal population based on 1480 twin adolescents. Multivariate twin methods were performed to analyze how genetic and environmental factors contributed to the associations between the psychopathic personality and antisocial behavior. Interestingly, a common genetic factor loaded substantially on both psychopathic personality traits and antisocial behavior, but a common shared environmental factor loaded solely on antisocial behavior. These observed shared environmental influences only in antisocial behavior may suggest a distinction between psychopathic personality dimensions and antisocial behavior etiologies (Larsson et al., 2007).

To further explore genetic influences, several authors (Beitchman et al., 2012; Dadds et al., 2014) have focused on variants of genes related to the serotonin and oxytocin systems. For example, Sadeh et al. (2010) found that the long allele of a serotonin transporter polymorphism—that was found to be related to a decreased amygdala reactivity—represented a genotype risk for elevated CU traits, but only in the context of lower socioeconomic backgrounds. This result demonstrates and reinforces the idea that the genetic vulnerability to CU traits is highly dependent on the deprived social environment in which the child is developing.

Besides serotonin, it has been theorized that there is a role for depleted oxytocin (OXT) in psychopathy (Bora, Yucel, & Allen, 2009; Dadds & Rhodes, 2008). Oxytocin is a neuropeptide, often called the "cuddly chemical," and is strongly linked to prosocial behavior, empathy, and affiliation/attachment. Beitchman et al. (2012) have shown that common polymorphisms of common OXTR (oxytocin-receptor) single-nucleotide polymorphisms are associated with high levels of CU traits in samples that presented conduct problems. Subsequent studies have found that higher CU traits are associated with greater methylation of the oxytocin receptor gene (Cecil et al., 2014; Dadds et al., 2014).

More recently, Verona, Murphy, and Bresin (2018) suggested that oxytocin dysfunction may be related to the absence of loving and empathy in psychopathy. The authors examined the associations between three oxytocin-related single-nucleotide polymorphisms (SNP) and results showed that the rs53576 SNP on the oxytocin receptor and cumulative risk alleles across the 3 SNPs were associated with psychopathic traits. Moreover, the interaction between cumulative risk factors and a poor emotional environment was associated with affective deficits of psychopathy.

Tuvblad, Fanti, Andershed, Colins, and Larsson (2017) investigated the genetic and environmental sources among three psychopathic personality dimensions (grandiose-deceitful, callous-unemotional, and impulsive-need for stimulation) in 5-year-old children. The authors found that genetic and/or shared environment explained the majority of variance in all dimensions, and the proportions of the phenotypic correlations among these dimensions were mediated by genetic and shared environmental influences. Their results exhibited a moderate genetic influence (25%) and higher shared environmental influence (48%) on the callous-unemotional dimension, which goes in a contrary direction to what Viding et al. (2005) have found (i.e., high heritability [67%] for antisocial behavior in the presence of CU traits in a sample of 7-year-old twins, and no influence from shared environment).

A recent review of literature (Moore et al., 2019) presented 39 quantitative and/or molecular genetic studies on CU traits. Some of them included quantitative components, and the range of heritability was 25%–80%, depending on the study. Nevertheless, it is important to highlight that the percentage of heritability of CU traits in the general population of individuals in middle childhood, adolescence, and adulthood (between 36% and 67%) is not so different than most other temperament and personality traits of childhood and adolescence (see Polderman et al., 2015), a fact which maintains the debate concerning the genetic and environmental influences on CU traits.

Altogether, these findings provide support for the importance and interplay of both genetic and shared environmental risk factors (e.g., heritability, parenting style, social and contextual environment) in psychopathic personality traits. While Antisocial Personality Disorder (APD) shares a common genetic base with psychopathy (Larsson et al., 2007), environmental factors seem only to influence the development of APD, suggesting that APD is related to behavioral adaptations, whereas psychopathy may be innate (e.g., Freedman & Verdun-Jones, 2010). Further longitudinal and epigenetic research is needed, particularly with larger samples, in order to increase the understanding of psychopathy genetic and environmental etiology. Antisocial personality disorder may represent the phenotypic expression of the psychopathic genotype (Meloy, 2001).

Family dynamics associated with intergenerational transmission of psychopathy

Many theorists have examined the interaction between victimization at an early age and future offending, suggesting that victims have higher risk of future criminal behavior (CB) (e.g., Miley, Fox, Muniz, Perkins, & DeLisi, 2020). Adverse childhood experiences (ACEs), such as abuse and neglect during development, tend to promote negative behaviors as well as mental health problems throughout the lifespan (e.g., Baglivio & Epps, 2016; Craig, Piquero, Farrington, & Ttofi, 2017). In fact, data demonstrate that a large percentage of juvenile offenders have experienced trauma, abuse, neglect, or maltreatment in childhood, and the consequences of such increase significantly the chances of violence (see review Bland, Lambie, & Best, 2018).

A significant amount of research has studied both genetic and environmental risks involved in the transmission of CU traits in youth populations (e.g., Frogner, Gibson, Andershed, & Andershed, 2018). However, it is valuable to also examine the intergenerational similarity of these traits between parents and their children.

Intergenerational transmission (IT) can be explained by a combination of processes, such as social learning, criminogenic environments, biological proneness, and parenting dynamics that may result in disadvantage for the children. Literature in IT can be wide ranging, pointing to variables such as socioeconomic status (e.g., Bailey, Hill, Oesterle, & Hawkins, 2009), educational attainment (e.g., Wertz et al., 2018), substance use (Bailey et al., 2009), mental health (e.g., Serbin & Stack, 1998), parenting behaviors (e.g., Farrington, Coid, & Murray, 2009), and criminal behavior (e.g., Thornberry, 2005). The effects of parenting behaviors have been the most widely studied.

For instance, Kahn, Deater-Deckard, King-Casas, and Kim-Spoon (2016) have examined whether the association between parents and children, both with CU traits, was mediated by parenting behavior. The authors also assessed whether this association was moderated by household environment. Results showed that negative parenting mediated the association between parents and adolescents with CU traits in a high household chaos context. Additionally, household chaos intensified the effects of hostile parenting on CU traits in adolescents, resulting in susceptibility to IT of CU traits.

Other studies have shown that physical abuse, emotional neglect, and household violence or substance abuse predicted externalizing outcomes (e.g., Bonner, DeLisi, Jones-Johnson, Caudill, & Trulson, 2019; Muniz et al., 2019). Other problems experienced by the parents (e.g., unemployment, poverty, unsafe neighborhoods) may also impact children's criminal behavior in the future.

Thornberry (2005, 2009) recognized a direct effect of antisocial behavior on one generation from the previous generation through genetic and social learning influences. He observed that delinquent adolescents confront more difficulties in transitioning into adulthood, and that criminal parents seem to use more severe parenting skills with their children, resulting in an increased children's tendency for criminal behavior. Moreover, children with two criminal parents have an incremental risk of exhibiting antisocial behavior (Frick & Loney, 2002). However, criminal behavior is not directly conveyed from parents to offspring, but rather through a continuous pattern of criminogenic and antisocial features (e.g., Berti & Pivetti, 2019).

A systematic review made by Besemer, Ahmad, Hinshaw, and Farrington (2017) showed that children with criminal parents have about 2.4 times greater probability of criminal behavior in the future compared to children without criminal parents; the transmission seems strongest from mothers to daughters, followed by mothers to sons, fathers to daughters, and fathers to sons. In this regard, another interesting finding highlighted from the literature is that a punitive environment (e.g., long incarceration sentences) might impact IT (see Besemer & Bui, 2019 for a meta-analysis).

Parental gender seems to be a critical factor in IT, since men and women typically do not engage in criminal behavior to the same degree and in the same way (e.g., Auty, Farrington, & Coid, 2015, 2017). Men are more likely to be involved in CB than women, and women who engage in criminal behavior might be more deviant compared with men, and are more likely to be the main caretakers of their children (Glaze & Maruschak, 2016). Similarly, young men and women tend to react differently to stressful life events such as parental criminal behavior. In general, young men show more externalizing problems (e.g., delinquency, antisocial behavior, aggression) while girls display more internalizing problems, such as depression and anxiety (Besemer et al., 2017; Glenn, 2019; Vieno, Nation, Pastore, & Santinello, 2009).

Studies have suggested that at least some of the origins of psychopathic traits are present in infancy and early childhood. But there is limited evidence about the relationship between parental and offspring psychopathy. A cross-sectional study by Loney et al. (2007) found a significant association between maternal affective features of psychopathy and the CU traits of their children, with parenting dysfunction fully mediating the relationship.

Auty et al. (2015) examined two consecutive generations in a large community sample in order to observe whether psychosocial risk factors can explain intergenerational transmission. Their findings provided the first evidence that the psychopathic personality traits of a community sample of men have a significant association with the psychopathic personality traits of their male and female offspring. This study also suggested that employment problems of the fathers played an important role in explaining the intergenerational transmission of psychopathic personality traits (Factor 1 scores) to both male and female offspring.

Schimmenti, Di Carlo, Passanisi, and Caretti (2015) reported a very high prevalence of emotional abuse among psychopathic offenders, and found a positive relationship between PCL-R Factor 1 and Factor 2 scores and emotional abuse history. The authors suggest that experiencing frequent emotionally abusive relationships in childhood may result in extreme levels of distress among children that ultimately reduce the ability of the child to relate to others. These experiences, in combination with other environmental risk factors, may emphasize dysfunctional affective and impulsive behavioral profile that typifies psychopathy.

Regarding the history of child abuse or neglect and its impact on psychopathy, Poythress, Skeem, and Lilienfeld (2006) proposed that both are positively but weakly related to global psychopathic features. Their findings revealed that abuse is unrelated to the core affective and interpersonal traits of psychopathy (Factor 1), but relates moderately to the impulsive and irresponsible lifestyle (Factor 2) or externalizing psychopathic features. Their findings suggest that early abuse and neglect may shut off affective responses, thereby resulting in individuals who possess the cold and callous features of primary psychopathy.

Gao, Raine, Chan, Venables, and Mednick (2010) demonstrated that poor parental bonding (lack of maternal care and low paternal overprotection) and childhood physical abuse were both associated with psychopathic personality. Those subjects separated from parents in the first three years of life were particularly characterized by low parental bonding and a psychopathic personality in adulthood; and the deviant behavior factor of psychopathy was related to lack of maternal care, whereas the emotional detachment factor was related to both lack of maternal care and paternal overprotection.

Dargis and Koenigs (2018) demonstrated that one subgroup of psychopathic offenders is characterized by a more extensive history of childhood maltreatment. More recently, it has been shown that men who experienced childhood abuse of any kind were more likely to demonstrate a fearful or preoccupied attachment style. Those who were securely attached were less likely to engage in antisocial behavior, and those who were more anxiously attached were less arrogant and deceptive in interpersonal relations (Grady, Looman, & Abracen, 2019).

Current evidence suggests that psychopathic tendencies in children are related to negative parenting styles that may have long-term effects on children's future behaviors (Krupić, Ručević, & Vučković, 2020). Since children may develop psychopathic tendencies by imitating their parents, this suggests that parents with psychopathic tendencies have a greater chance of raising children with propensities to psychopathy. However, it is worthy to mention that there are protective factors that decrease the effects of risk factors on later offending. Research indicates that early childhood interventions may not only help reduce future offending, but also increase the child's chances of doing well in other life domains (Craig, Piquero, & Farrington, 2020).

Neurobiological research

Psychopathic traits are present in childhood, with psychological, behavioral, and temperamental differences detectable at an early age in individuals who develop psychopathic traits in adulthood (e.g., Frick, O'Brien, Wootton, & McBurnett, 1994; Glenn, Raine, Venables, & Mednick, 2007; Loney, Frick, Clements, Ellis, & Kerlin, 2003; Lynam, Caspi, Moffitt, Loeber, & Stouthamer-Loeber, 2007).

Studies through the years have also been conducted to determine the psychophysiological functioning of the psychopathic individual (e.g., Hare, 1970). For instance, electroencephalography (EEG) studies have been performed in order to comprehend the neural network and the specific dynamics of individuals with psychopathic traits (e.g., Gao et al., 2018; Hare & Quinn, 1971). Clark, Bontemps, Batky, Watts, and Salekin (2019) reviewed 68 studies that focused on psychopathy and several components of EEG. Results show that psychopathic individuals have robust early selection processes paired with reduced or elaborative sustained processing of emotional information. This may suggest the existence of automatic and strategic aspects related to the information processing of the psychopathic individual. Those with higher psychopathic traits spend less time processing distress stimuli, which meets the idea that the LPP (Late Positive Potential) amplitude can be attenuated by voluntary top-down control (see Hajcak, MacNamara, & Olvet, 2010). Thus the psychopathic individual decides which stimuli to ignore or follow (Meloy, Book, Hosker-Field, Methot-Jones, & Roters, 2018).

We addressed in the previous section of this chapter that children with disruptive behaviors and CU traits show a lack of empathy, guilt, or remorse, and they engage in instrumental aggression (Viding & McCrory, 2015). The literature on children with disruptive behaviors and CU traits has focused mainly on the processing of emotions and in the relationship between children and their caregivers. In this regard, functional magnetic resonance imaging (fMRI) studies of children and adolescents with disruptive behaviors and CU traits have tried to understand the functioning of brain areas that are implicated in affective and reward processing (see Puzzo, Smaragdi, Gonzalez, Martin-Key, & Fairchild, 2016). These studies revealed that children with disruptive behaviors and high levels of CU traits display a reduced activity and altered connectivity in brain areas that are associated with empathy for others seen in healthy individuals.

Blair, Leibenluft, and Pine (2014) have shown a neural activity profile consistent with low emotional responsiveness to others suffering, and a weak ability to learn from reinforcement. It has been shown that dysfunction in the amygdala assumes a great importance in psychopathy (Blair, 2005; Waller et al., 2019). Specifically, reduced volume of the amygdala has been consistently reported with psychopathic individuals (Boccardi et al., 2011; Yang, Raine, Narr, Colletti, & Toga, 2009). These impairments likely occur early in life (Blair, Peschardt, Budhani, Mitchell, & Pine, 2006), although it is not perfectly clear how and why this happens.

The amygdala is a neural structure implicated in aversive conditioning, necessary for enhancing attention to emotional stimuli, facilitating empathy for others, and the detection of threats (Blair, 2006; Flor, Birbaumer, Hermann, Ziegler, & Patrick, 2002). It is also significant for the recognition of fearful facial expressions (Blair, Colledge, Murray, & Mitchell, 2001) and the augmentation of the startle reflex by visual threat stimuli (Levenston, Patrick, Bradley, & Lang, 2000). White et al. (2012) found unusually low amygdala activation to fear stimuli in children with disruptive behaviors and CU traits under low attentional load conditions, while fear stimuli elicited amygdala activation in healthy participants. Furthermore, reduced amygdala and insula activity have been observed in children with disruptive behaviors and high CU traits. These children engage in more complex forms of behaviors, such as social judgment regarding other people's distress, making decisions about whether they will benefit themselves by harming others, or making decisions about appropriate responses to the distress of others (Marsh et al., 2011; Sakai et al., 2017; Sebastian et al., 2012, respectively). Other studies of children exhibiting disruptive behaviors and varying levels of CU traits have consistently reported atypical neural reactivity to the pain of others (Michalska, Zeffiro, & Decety, 2016; Yoder, Lahey, & Decety, 2016).

Since the amygdala represents a binding site for steroid hormones, one possible explanation for its impairment is that hormones imbalances, before birth or in early childhood, affect the development of subcortical structures, and may continue to influence functioning into adulthood (van Honk & Schutter, 2006). Because it also affects gene transcription, hormones have the ability to change functioning by increasing or decreasing the probability of certain behaviors in response to threat (Schulkin, 2003).

Likewise, there are other genetic and neurotransmitter features that may affect amygdala functioning. The amygdala has numerous serotonergic inputs and may be sensitive to changes in serotonin transmission. In this context, Blair (2007) performed a study demonstrating that individuals who are homozygous for the long version of the serotonin transporter gene (5-HTTLPR) show significantly reduced amygdala responses to emotional expressions relative to those with the short-form polymorphism (Brown & Hariri, 2006), and behavioral impairment of emotional learning tasks that depend on the amygdala (Finger et al., 2007).

Serotonin neurotransmission has an effect on the hypothalamic-pituitary-adrenal (HPA) axis. Increased activity at serotonin receptor sites in the hypothalamus raise the production of cortisol, which is important since it mobilizes the resources in the body and provides energy in stressful times (Kudielka & Kirschbaum, 2005). Cortisol is also involved in potentiating the state of fear (Schulkin, Gold, & McEwen, 1998), sensitivity to punishment, and withdrawal behavior (Schulkin, 2003). When a disruption of serotonin neurotransmission happens, it will trigger off cortisol reactivity to a stress-inducing task (e.g., Sobczak, Honig, Nicolson, & Riedel, 2001). Hence, dysregulation of serotonin in the brain may contribute to the low cortisol levels observed in psychopathy.

Serotonin may also interact with testosterone levels to increase the probability of violent aggression (Birger et al., 2003). van Honk and Schutter (2006) propose that the underlying source of emotional deficits observed in psychopathy is a result of an imbalance of cortisol and testosterone. Testosterone is a product of the hypothalamic-pituitary-gonadal (HPG) axis and is associated with approach-related behavior, as well as reward sensitivity and fear reduction (Boissy & Bouissou, 1994). Testosterone and cortisol have antagonistic properties. On one hand, low serotonin levels combined with high testosterone levels increase the rates and intensity of aggression (Birger et al., 2003; Higley et al., 1996). On the other hand, cortisol suppresses the activity of the hypothalamic-pituitary-gonadal (HPG) axis on all levels, decreasing testosterone and inhibiting its effects (Tilbrook, Turner, & Clarke, 2000). And in turn, testosterone inhibits activity of the HPA axis (Viau, 2002). van Honk and colleagues have found that injections of testosterone reduce fearfulness (van Honk, Peper, & Schutter, 2005), promoting the response to angry faces (van Honk, Tuiten, et al., 2001), and shifting the balance from punishment to reward sensitivity (van Honk et al., 2004).

It has been hypothesized that deficits in the fronto-temporal neural circuit, particularly the ventromedial prefrontal cortex, dorsolateral prefrontal cortex, medial temporal regions, and cingulate cortex, may play important roles in the neurobiology of psychopathy (Kiehl, 2006). Indeed, abnormalities have also been observed in other subcortical regions such as the hippocampus. Raine et al. (2004) found asymmetries within the hippocampus in imprisoned psychopaths. Atypical brain asymmetries are thought in part to reflect disrupted neurodevelopmental processes (Best, 1988), thus structural asymmetries in psychopaths may reflect an interruption to the normal developmental process. Laakso et al. (2001) found psychopathy to be negatively correlated with the volume of the posterior hippocampus. The hippocampus has solid interconnections to the amygdala and prefrontal cortex, which are also implicated in psychopathy.

Prefrontal impairments have been linked to poor decision making, while deficits in the temporal regions seem to contribute to the lack of emotion and social dysfunction in psychopathic individuals. Raine, Lencz, Bihrle, LaCasse, and Colletti (2000) observed a reduction in prefrontal gray matter volume in a group of individuals with antisocial personality disorder (11%) compared to normal and psychiatric control groups. The individuals with APD also showed reduced skin conductance activity during a social stress test, and those with low prefrontal gray showed particularly reduced stress reactivity. These results support evidence that prefrontal regions are involved in generating somatic states. In this regard, van Honk, Schutter, et al. (2001) provided further empirical evidence by using repeated transcranial magnetic stimulation (rTMS) to inhibit the activity of the orbitofrontal cortex and found significant reductions in skin conductance responses. In a study by Yang et al. (2005), reduced (22%) prefrontal gray matter was observed in a group of unsuccessful psychopaths.

Yang, Raine, Colletti, Toga, and Narr (2009) also identified differences in cortical gray matter thickness in psychopaths compared with nonpsychopathic controls. Psychopaths showed significant cortical gray matter thinning in the right frontal and temporal cortices compared with a nonpsychopathic control group. The orbitofrontal cortex is associated with the anticipation of punishment and reward, as well as with the response reversal during changing reinforcement contingencies, and social cognition (Mitchell, Colledge, Leonard, & Blair, 2002). Functional imaging studies have shown reduced activity associated with psychopathy in the orbitofrontal cortex during fear conditioning (Birbaumer et al., 2005; Veit et al., 2002), and during a socially interactive game (Rilling et al., 2007). Older research demonstrated that damage to the orbitofrontal cortex often resulted in pathological lying, promiscuous sexual behavior, shallow affect, lack of guilt or remorse, and irresponsibility (Anderson, Bechara, Damasio, Tranel, & Damasio, 1999), all characteristics of psychopathy personality.

The orbital frontal cortex and the parietal lobes are responsible for working memory, the ability to plan and organize behavior, and behavioral inhibition. These structures also aid in the capacity to learn from experience (a deficit characteristic of psychopathic individuals) and are deeply entangled with the limbic system. In an fMRI study, Raine et al. (2000) found that individuals with APD had less gray matter within the prefrontal cortex compared to individuals who were not diagnosed with APD. Several studies have observed increased activation in higher cognitive areas such as the dorsolateral prefrontal cortex during emotional tasks in psychopaths compared to controls (Gordon, Baird, & End, 2004; Intrator et al., 1997; Rilling et al., 2007). In sum, significant gray matter thinning suggests that the structural correlates of psychopathy may be linked to the emotional deficits portraying psychopaths.

Psychopathy has also been associated with abnormalities in other regions. For example, reduced functioning in the anterior cingulate (connected with the amygdala and involved in emotional processing) has been observed during experimental conditioning (Birbaumer et al., 2005; Veit et al., 2002) in criminal psychopaths in the processing of emotional information (Müller et al., 2003). Deficits in the angular gyrus (posterior superior temporal gyrus) have been found in psychopathic and antisocial individuals, and deficits in functioning of the posterior cingulate may be involved in self-referencing and experiencing emotion (Kiehl et al., 2004). Reduced functioning of the insula has also been observed during fear conditioning (Birbaumer et al., 2005; Veit et al., 2002). Kiehl (2006) argued for a paralimbic system dysfunction of psychopathy, but in reality, it is quite difficult to determine whether each region associated with psychopathy makes an exceptional and exclusive contribution to the disorder.

In addition to the abnormal functioning observed in certain brain areas of psychopathic individuals, some studies have also explored the connectivity between areas. van Honk and Schutter (2006) hypothesize that disruptions in the connectivity between subcortical and cortical regions may contribute to psychopathy. Such connectivity, according to Damasio (1994), allows emotional information from subcortical regions to provide input to cortical regions, which is important for decision making and cognitive evaluation. Connectivity between the amygdala and orbitofrontal cortex may be important in the generation of somatic markers.

The orbitofrontal cortex receives emotional information from the amygdala and stores representations of certain stimuli that can be later retrieved. If an individual recalls or anticipates these stimuli, the orbitofrontal cortex triggers the somatic state, and if the connections between the amygdala and orbitofrontal cortex are disrupted, the orbitofrontal cortex will be unable to form representations, and anticipatory fear of aversive events will not be produced (Bechara, Damasio, & Damasio, 2003). Indeed, reduced connectivity between the orbitofrontal cortex and the amygdala has been associated with lower sensitivity to threat cues (Buckholtz et al., 2008). Thus poor connectivity between these areas would result in reduced regulation of subcortical structures by prefrontal areas, contributing to the disinhibition and reactive aggression observed in psychopathy. Psychopaths also display impaired connectivity between the two hemispheres. Hiatt and Newman (2007) found that the time required to transfer information from one hemisphere to the other is significantly lengthier in criminal psychopaths compared to criminal nonpsychopaths.

Lead (Pb) exposure has also been linked to behaviors that are related to psychopathy (Braun, Kahn, Froehlich, Auinger, & Lanphear, 2006; Needleman, Riess, Tobin, Biesecker, & Greenhouse, 1996). Lead exposure has been found to be associated with deficits in frontal lobe functioning. For instance, Trope, Lopez-Villegas, Cecil, and Lenkinski (2001), in a study with magnetic resonance spectroscopy, found that lead-exposed youths had a higher level of neuronal loss and damage within the frontal cortex than healthy participants. Meng, Zhu, Ruan, She, and Luo (2005) also found that lead exposure was associated with a lower density of neurons in the frontal lobe and hippocampus. An additional investigation with magnetic resonance imaging data from the Cincinnati Lead Study (Cecil et al., 2008) revealed that childhood lead exposure corresponded to significantly lower levels of adult gray matter within the frontal lobe. Thus results from brain imaging studies (e.g., Bellinger, 2008) demonstrate that lead exposure is related to deficits in brain structure and functioning, especially within the frontal lobe.

A longitudinal study (Dietrich, Ris, Succop, Berger, & Bornschein, 2001) revealed that prenatal and postnatal blood lead levels were related to both parent-reported and child-reported delinquent behaviors. In a follow-up investigation of these youths, results showed that prenatal and postnatal blood lead levels were associated with the number of criminal arrests in adulthood (Wright, Dietrich, Ris, Hornung, & Wessel, 2008). To further explore these effects and transpose to psychopathy, Wright, Boisvert, and Vaske (2009) investigated whether childhood blood lead concentrations were related to psychopathy in adulthood. Results revealed that higher blood lead concentrations in early childhood were indeed associated with higher levels of psychopathic traits in adulthood, controlling for the effects of gender, race, mother's intelligence quotient, child's intellectual achievement, and the quality of the home environment. The authors also concluded that childhood lead levels predicted variation in Machiavellian Egocentricity, Social Potency, Impulsive Nonconformity, and Blame Externalization, dimensions that represent an individual with CU traits. Overall, these studies associate lead exposure to the etiology of psychopathy.

Cognitive and behavioral research

The increased amount of research in psychopathy has provided important advances in the understanding of this disorder. We started this chapter by pointing to some of the personality traits present in psychopathic individuals, taking the previous psychopathy definition and research work of Cleckley (1941, 1976) and Hare (1991, 2003). Research has continually yielded insights into personality traits in psychopathic individuals associated with proneness to impulse-related disorders and to recidivism (Hare, 2006).

According to Lilienfeld and Fowler (2006), individuals with clinical and/or criminal levels of psychopathy have the same personality profiles as their subclinical counterparts (nonclinical). Thus what really seem to differentiate one from another is the frequency, degree, and intensity with which the individuals engage in the deviant behaviors (LeBreton, Binning, & Adorno, 2006), suggesting that psychopathy is a continuum construct in which individuals can vary from low, moderate, to high levels of psychopathy (Lilienfeld & Fowler, 2006).

As mentioned earlier in this chapter, psychopathic personality traits include affective deficits (e.g., shallow affect, lack of remorse and empathy, callousness), as well as dysfunctional personality features associated with social functioning (e.g., manipulativeness, egocentricity, insincerity; Cleckley, 1941, 1976; Hare, 2003). Although distinct, it is important to keep in mind that psychopathy shares many traits similar to other personality disorders, in particular with APD.

As discussed earlier, CU traits have been studied as a symptomatic component of psychopathy. However, it cannot be considered a singular trait that predicts psychopathy. A recent study (Salekin, Andershed, Batky, & Bontemps, 2018) argued that psychopathy is more predictive of negative outcomes than CU traits by themselves, or CU traits + Conduct Problems (CP, such as breaking of norms, rules, or laws resorting or not to violence). Severe CP in childhood are associated with CU personality traits. Children with both CP and CU traits constitute a subgroup of CP children who exhibit a more severe and stable form of CP, more emotional and cognitive deficits, and also more psychiatric morbidity compared to children with CP without co-occurring CU traits (Frick, Ray, Thornton, & Kahn, 2014).

Salekin (2017) has emphasized the utility of considering interpersonal, affective, and lifestyle/antisocial dimensions of psychopathic traits when assessing youth with CD. It is well known that prosocial judgments and regulation capacities become more developed in middle childhood (McKown & Weinstein, 2003). Children who are characterized by psychopathic traits have more difficulties in prosocial reasoning and self-regulation during middle childhood (Poythress et al., 2006).

The most common and widely used instrument to assess psychopathy in adults is the PCL-R (Hare, 1991, 2003), a 20-item rating scale that comprises two correlated factors: Factor 1 and Factor 2, described earlier. There is considerable empirical evidence linking psychopathy assessed by the PCL-R with criminality and violence (see Edens, Campbell, & Weir, 2007). Others have proposed a three-factor model (Cooke & Michie, 2001); however, cross-cultural research and the aggregation of large samples from various countries support a two-factor model with both factors (1 and 2) subdivided into two facets (Mokros et al., 2015; Neumann, Hare, & Pardini, 2015). There are also other instruments to assess the development risk for psychopathy in children and adolescents, particularly the risk of persistent antisocial behavior:

- *Antisocial Process Screening Device* (Frick & Hare, 2001),
- *Youth Psychopathic Traits Inventory* (Andershed, Gustafson, Kerr, & Stattin, 2002),
- *Inventory of Callous Unemotional Traits* (Essau, Sasagawa, & Frick, 2006),
- *Child Problematic Traits Inventory* (Colins et al., 2014).

None of the instruments would be relevant if there were no models and theories of personality to support them. The acknowledgment of the value and usefulness of models of personality such as the Five-Factor Model (FFM, McCrae & Costa, 1990), whereby personality disorders have been conceptualized, is also a major advance in the research of psychopathy.

FFM comprises five domains and thirty facets assessed by NEO PI-R. Although McCrae and Costa (2013) have noticed that there are traits that are not included within the FFM facets, the NEO PI-R is the most validated instrument to evaluate the personality profiles of normals cross-culturally.

In light of the FFM, psychopathy has been reliably described as the convergence of low agreeableness and low conscientiousness (Lynam, Leukefeld, & Clayton, 2003), regardless of the approach used to create the psychopathic profile (for translation of psychopathy measures into FFM traits, see Lynam & Derefinko, 2006). Some studies supported that Factor 1 and Factor 2 were related to low agreeableness, but differed in Factor 2, which was more strongly related to low conscientiousness and high neuroticism (Lynam & Derefinko, 2006).

Follow-up studies have shown fluctuating relations between Factor 1 measures and agreeableness and the other FFM dimensions (e.g., Seibert, Miller, Few, Zeichner, & Lynam, 2011). Relatedly, higher-order factors of Constraint and Negative Emotionality from Tellegen's temperament-oriented personality model (Patrick, Curtin, & Tellegen, 2002; Tellegen & Waller, 2008) were associated with antisocial personality disorder and substance dependence, and both predict the occurrence of these situations (Krueger, 1999) and delinquency (Caspi et al., 1994).

Research on the stability of psychopathic traits during the life course of an individual has shown consistency in the structure and correlates of psychopathic traits as assessed with clinical measures of psychopathic traits in adolescence and in adulthood. Nevertheless, there is less agreement about the nature of psychopathic traits in childhood. As we presented in a previous section of this chapter, some studies suggest that psychopathic traits begin in early age and they are partly heritable and undeniably manifested in childhood (e.g., Viding & McCrory, 2018). According to Kosson et al. (2013), psychopathy in adolescence and in adulthood is underpinned by four correlated dimensions consisting of interpersonal traits, affective, lifestyle, and antisocial traits—the four-facet theory of Hare (Neumann et al., 2015). Psychopathy is characterized by several dimensions that can be identified in children as young as two or three years of age (e.g., Flom & Saudino, 2017). The combined research findings also suggest that psychopathic traits in youth may imply the development of the homogeneous disorder of psychopathy identified in adults.

Recently, Gorin et al. (2019) performed a study that aimed to understand the nature of psychopathic traits in youth by examining the fit of one-, two-, three-, and four-factor models of psychopathic traits during middle childhood (in the ages of 6, 7, and 8 years old). Additionally, they intended to examine the stability of the factor structure of psychopathic traits over time. The main results showed that a hierarchical three-factor model of psychopathic traits, consisting of interpersonal, affective, and lifestyle/antisocial factors, was the best fit to the data at all ages, thus providing evidence that the internal structure for psychopathic traits in middle childhood is similar but slightly less differentiated than the factor structure identified during adolescence. This study strongly suggests that psychopathy is a homogeneous syndrome with observed traits as early as six years of age.

Conclusions

This chapter aimed to explore the different etiologies of psychopathy, illustrated by scientific evidence throughout the decades. We presented several risk factors that underlie psychopathy related to genetic, social environment, family dynamics, neurobiological, and cognitive variables, which are all interconnected.

Inheritance of CU traits and the influence from environmental factors are well established. Research has consistently revealed a significant overlap in genes that influence CU traits (Bezdjian et al., 2011), with the stability in CU traits being driven by genetics. Moreover, studies have demonstrated the idea that genetic vulnerability to CU traits is highly dependent on the deprived social environment within which the child is developing. In a real sense, the environment shapes the expression of CU traits in the child.

Family dynamics also are extremely important as predictors of antisocial and criminal behavior in their offspring. Risk factors such as a poor lifestyle (poverty, unemployment, substance abuse, unsafe neighborhood), parent's background, parenting styles, and their psychological structure have an enormous negative impact. The presented findings provide support for the importance and interaction of genetic and environmental risk factors (e.g., heritability, parenting style, social and contextual environment) in the development of psychopathic traits.

Psychopathy is a complex syndrome. Despite popular interest in the topic and the substantial body of new scientific research published each year, it remains unclear how genetic and environmental/social risk factors contribute to the development of a pattern of neurocognitive processing that increases the risk for psychopathy. Likewise, we still do not know how that particular processing may influence the environmental and contextual settings of the individual's life course.

There are more than 85,000 publications on psychopathy, and despite the continued writing and research, there is yet much to learn and to be discovered. In fact, what we already know about the different etiologies and expressions of this disorder are important markers that guide new research pathways in which new answers will be given and new questions will arise.

References

Andershed, H., Gustafson, S. B., Kerr, M., & Stattin, H. (2002). The usefulness of self-reported psychopathy-like traits in the study of antisocial behaviour among non-referred adolescents. *European Journal of Personality*, *16*(5), 383–402. https://doi.org/10.1002/per.455.

Anderson, S. W., Bechara, A., Damasio, H., Tranel, D., & Damasio, A. R. (1999). Impairment of social and moral behavior related to early damage in human prefrontal cortex. *Nature Neuroscience*, *2*(11), 1032–1037. https://doi.org/10.1038/14833.

Auty, K. M., Farrington, D. P., & Coid, J. W. (2015). Intergenerational transmission of psychopathy and mediation via psychosocial risk factors. *The British Journal of Psychiatry*, *206*(1), 26–31. https://doi.org/10.1192/bjp.bp.114.151050.

Auty, K. M., Farrington, D. P., & Coid, J. W. (2017). The intergenerational transmission of criminal offending: Exploring gender-specific mechanisms. *British Journal of Criminology*, *57*(1), 215–237. https://doi.org/10.1093/bjc/azv115.

Baglivio, M. T., & Epps, N. (2016). The interrelatedness of adverse childhood experiences among high-risk juvenile offenders. *Youth Violence and Juvenile Justice*, *14*(3), 179–198. https://doi.org/10.1177/1541204014566286.

Bailey, J. A., Hill, K. G., Oesterle, S., & Hawkins, J. D. (2009). Parenting practices and problem behavior across three generations: Monitoring, harsh discipline, and drug use in the intergenerational transmission of externalizing behavior. *Developmental Psychology*, *45*(5), 1214–1226. https://doi.org/10.1037/a0016129.

Bechara, A., Damasio, H., & Damasio, A. R. (2003). Role of the amygdala in decision-making. *Annals of the New York Academy of Sciences*, *985*(1), 356–369. https://doi.org/10.1111/j.1749-6632.2003.tb07094.x.

Beitchman, J. H., Zai, C. C., Muir, K., Berall, L., Nowrouzi, B., Choi, E., & Kennedy, J. L. (2012). Childhood aggression, callous-unemotional traits and oxytocin genes. *European Child & Adolescent Psychiatry*, *21*(3), 125–132. https://doi.org/10.1111/j.1601-183X.2012.00776.x.

Bellinger, D. (2008). Neurological and behavioral consequences of childhood lead exposure. *PLoS Medicine*, *5*(5), e115. https://doi.org/10.1371/journal.pmed.0050112.

Berti, C., & Pivetti, M. (2019). Childhood economic disadvantage and antisocial behavior: Intervening factors and pathways. *Children and Youth Services Review*, *97*, 120–126. https://doi.org/10.1016/j.childyouth.2017.06.007.

Besemer, S., Ahmad, S. I., Hinshaw, S. P., & Farrington, D. P. (2017). A systematic review and meta-analysis of the intergenerational transmission of criminal behavior. *Aggression and Violent Behavior*, *37*, 161–178. https://doi.org/10.1016/j.avb.2017.10.004.

Besemer, S., & Bui, L. (2019). Intergenerational transmission of criminal behaviour. In M. Hutton, & D. Moran (Eds.), *The Palgrave handbook of prison and the family* (pp. 457–478). Cham: Palgrave Macmillan.

Best, C. T. (1988). The emergence of cerebral asymmetries in early human development: A literature review and a neuroembryological model. In D. L. Molfese, & S. J. Segalowitz (Eds.), *Brain lateralization in children: Developmental implications* (pp. 5–34). NY: Guilford Press.

Bezdjian, S., Raine, A., Baker, L. A., & Lynam, D. R. (2011). Psychopathic personality in children: Genetic and environmental contributions. *Psychological Medicine*, *41*(3), 589–600. https://doi.org/10.1017/S0033291710000966.

Birbaumer, N., Veit, R., Lotze, M., Erb, M., Hermann, C., Grodd, W., & Flor, H. (2005). Deficient fear conditioning in psychopathy: A functional magnetic resonance imaging study. *Archives of General Psychiatry*, *62*(7), 799–805. https://doi.org/10.1001/archpsyc.62.7.799.

Birger, M., Swartz, M., Cohen, D., Alesh, Y. A., Grishpan, C., & Kotelr, M. (2003). Aggression: The testosterone-serotonin link. *Israel Medical Association Journal*, *5*(9), 653–658.

Blackburn, R., & Maybury, C. (1985). Identifying the psychopath: The relation of Cleckley's criteria to the interpersonal domain. *Personality and Individual Differences*, *6*, 375–386. https://doi.org/10.1016/0191-8869(85)90062-5.

Blair, R. J. R. (1995). A cognitive developmental approach to morality: Investigating the psychopath. *Cognition*, *57*(1), 1–29. https://doi.org/10.1016/0010-0277(95)00676-P.

Blair, R. J. R. (2005). Applying a cognitive neuroscience perspective to the disorder of psychopathy. *Development and Psychopathology*, *17*(3), 865–891. https://doi.org/10.1017/S0954579405050418.

Blair, R. J. R. (2006). Subcortical brain systems in psychopathy. In C. J. Patrick (Ed.), *Handbook of psychopathy* (pp. 296–312). New York: Guilford Press.

Blair, R. J. R. (2007). The amygdala and ventromedial prefrontal cortex in morality and psychopathy. *Trends in Cognitive Science*, *11*(9), 387–392. https://doi.org/10.1016/j.tics.2007.07.003.

Blair, R. J. R., Colledge, E., Murray, L., & Mitchell, D. G. V. (2001). A selective impairment in the processing of sad and fearful expressions in children with psychopathic tendencies. *Journal of Abnormal Child Psychology*, *29*(6), 491–498. https://doi.org/10.1023/A:1012225108281.

Blair, R. J. R., Leibenluft, E., & Pine, D. S. (2014). Conduct disorder and callous–unemotional traits in youth. *New England Journal of Medicine*, *371*(23), 2207–2216. https://doi.org/10.1056/NEJMra1315612.

Blair, R. J. R., Peschardt, K. S., Budhani, S., Mitchell, D. G. V., & Pine, D. S. (2006). The development of psychopathy. *Journal of Child Psychology and Psychiatry*, *47*(3–4), 262–276. https://doi.org/10.1111/j.1469-7610.2006.01596.x.

Bland, V. J., Lambie, I., & Best, C. (2018). Does childhood neglect contribute to violent behavior in adulthood? A review of possible links. *Clinical Psychology Review*, *60*, 126–135. https://doi.org/10.1016/j.cpr.2018.02.001.

Blonigen, D. M., Hicks, B. M., Krueger, R. F., Patrick, C. J., & Iacono, W. G. (2006). Continuity and change in psychopathic traits as measured via normal-range personality: A longitudinal-biometric study. *Journal of Abnormal Psychology*, *115*(1), 85. https://doi.org/10.1037/0021-843X.115.1.85.

Boccardi, M., Frisoni, G. B., Hare, R. D., Cavedo, E., Najt, P., Pievani, M., … Vaurio, O. (2011). Cortex and amygdala morphology in psychopathy. *Psychiatry Research: Neuroimaging*, *193*(2), 85–92. https://doi.org/10.1016/j.pscychresns.2010.12.013.

Boissy, A., & Bouissou, M. F. (1994). Effects of androgen treatment on behavioral and physiological responses of heifers to fear-eliciting situations. *Hormones and Behavior*, *28*(1), 66–83. https://doi.org/10.1006/hbeh.1994.1006.

Bonner, T., DeLisi, M., Jones-Johnson, G., Caudill, J. W., & Trulson, C. (2019). Chaotic homes, adverse childhood experiences, and serious delinquency: Differential effects by race and ethnicity. *Justice Quarterly*, 1–18. https://doi.org/10.1080/07418825.2019.1688852.

Bora, E., Yucel, M., & Allen, N. B. (2009). Neurobiology of human affiliative behaviour: Implications for psychiatric disorders. *Current Opinion in Psychiatry*, *22*(3), 320–325. https://doi.org/10.1097/YCO.0b013e328329e970.

Braun, J. M., Kahn, R. S., Froehlich, T., Auinger, P., & Lanphear, B. P. (2006). Exposures to environmental toxicants and attention deficit hyperactivity disorder in US children. *Environmental Health Perspectives*, *114*(12), 1904–1909. https://doi.org/10.1289/ehp.9478.

Brown, S. M., & Hariri, A. R. (2006). Neuroimaging studies of serotonin gene polymorphisms: Exploring the interplay of genes, brain, and behavior. *Cognitive, Affective, & Behavioral Neuroscience*, *6*(1), 44–52. https://doi.org/10.3758/CABN.6.1.44.

Buckholtz, J. W., Callicott, J. H., Kolachana, B., Hariri, A. R., Goldberg, T. E., Genderson, M., … Meyer-Lindenberg, A. (2008). Genetic variation in MAOA modulates ventromedial prefrontal circuitry mediating individual differences in human personality. *Molecular Psychiatry*, *13*(3), 313–324. https://doi.org/10.1038/sj.mp.4002020.

Caspi, A., Moffitt, T. E., Silva, P. A., Stouthamer-Loeber, M., Krueger, R. F., & Schmutte, P. S. (1994). Are some people crime-prone? Replications of the personality-crime relationship across countries, genders, races, and methods. *Criminology*, *32*(2), 163–196. https://doi.org/10.1111/j.1745-9125.1994.tb01151.x.

Cecil, C. A., Lysenko, L. J., Jaffee, S. R., Pingault, J. B., Smith, R. G., Relton, C. L., … Barker, E. D. (2014). Environmental risk, Oxytocin Receptor Gene (OXTR) methylation and youth callous-unemotional traits: A 13-year longitudinal study. *Molecular Psychiatry*, *19*(10), 1071. https://doi.org/10.1038/mp.2014.95.

Cecil, K. M., Brubaker, C. J., Adler, C. M., Dietrich, K. N., Altaye, M., Egeloff, J. C., … Lanphear, B. P. (2008). Decreased brain volume in adults with childhood lead exposure. *PLoS Medicine*, *5*(5), e112. https://doi.org/10.1371/journal.pmed.0050112.

Clark, A. P., Bontemps, A. P., Batky, B. D., Watts, E. K., & Salekin, R. T. (2019). Psychopathy and neurodynamic brain functioning: A review of EEG research. *Neuroscience and Biobehavioral Reviews*, *103*, 352–373. https://doi.org/10.1016/j.neubiorev.2019.05.025.

Cleckley, H. (1941). *The mask of sanity: An attempt to reinterpret the so-called psychopathic personality*. Oxford, England: Mosby.

Cleckley, H. M. (1976). *The mask of sanity* (5th ed.). St. Louis, MO: Mosby.

Colins, O. F., Andershed, H., Frogner, L., Lopez-Romero, L., Veen, V., & Andershed, A. K. (2014). A new measure to assess psychopathic personality in children: The child problematic traits inventory. *Journal of Psychopathology and Behavioral Assessment*, *36*(1), 4–21. https://doi.org/10.1007/s10862-013-9385-y.

Cooke, D. J., & Michie, C. (2001). Refining the construct of psychopathy: Towards a hierarchical model. *Psychological Assessment*, *13*(2), 171–188. https://doi.org/10.1037/1040-3590.13.2.171.

Craig, J. M., Piquero, A. R., & Farrington, D. P. (2020). Not all at-risk boys have bad outcomes: Predictors of later life success. *Crime & Delinquency*, *66*(3), 392–419. https://doi.org/10.1177/0011128719854344.

Craig, J. M., Piquero, A. R., Farrington, D. P., & Ttofi, M. M. (2017). A little early risk goes a long bad way: Adverse childhood experiences and life-course offending in the Cambridge study. *Journal of Criminal Justice*, *53*, 34–45. https://doi.org/10.1016/j.jcrimjus.2017.09.005.

Dadds, M. R., Allen, J. L., Oliver, B. R., Faulkner, N., Legge, K., Moul, C., … Scott, S. (2012). Love, eye contact and the developmental origins of empathy v. psychopathy. *The British Journal of Psychiatry*, *200*(3), 191–196. https://doi.org/10.1192/bjp.bp.110.085720.

Dadds, M. R., Moul, C., Cauchi, A., Dobson-Stone, C., Hawes, D. J., Brennan, J., & Ebstein, R. E. (2014). Methylation of the oxytocin receptor gene and oxytocin blood levels in the development of psychopathy. *Development and Psychopathology*, *26*(1), 33–40. https://doi.org/10.1017/S0954579413000497.

Dadds, M. R., Perry, Y., Hawes, D. J., Merz, S., Riddell, A. C., Haines, D. J., … Abeygunawardane, A. I. (2006). Attention to the eyes and fear-recognition deficits in child psychopathy. *The British Journal of Psychiatry*, *189*(3), 280–281. https://doi.org/10.1192/bjp.bp.105.018150.

Dadds, M. R., & Rhodes, T. (2008). Aggression in young children with concurrent callous–unemotional traits: Can the neurosciences inform progress and innovation in treatment approaches? *Philosophical Transactions of the Royal Society B: Biological Sciences*, *363*(1503), 2567–2576. https://doi.org/10.1098/rstb.2008.0029.

Damasio, A. R. (1994). *Descartes' error: Emotion, reason, and the human brain*. New York: GP Putnam's Sons.

Dargis, M., & Koenigs, M. (2018). Two subtypes of psychopathic criminals differ in negative affect and history of childhood abuse. *Psychological Trauma: Theory, Research, Practice, and Policy*, *10*(4), 444–451. https://doi.org/10.1037/tra0000328.

Dhanani, S., Kumari, V., Puri, B. K., Tresaden, I., Houng, S., & Sen, P. (2018). A systematic review of the heritability of specific psychopathic traits using Hare's two-factor model of psychopathy. *CNS Spectrums*, *23*(1), 29–38. https://doi.org/10.1017/S109285291700027X.

Dietrich, K. N., Ris, M. D., Succop, P. A., Berger, O. G., & Bornschein, R. L. (2001). Early exposure to lead and juvenile delinquency. *Neurotoxicology Teratology*, *23*(6), 511–518. https://doi.org/10.1016/S0892-0362(01)00184-2.

Edens, J. F., Campbell, J. S., & Weir, J. M. (2007). Youth psychopathy and criminal recidivism: A meta-analysis of the psychopathy checklist measures. *Law and Human Behavior*, *31*(1), 53–75. https://doi.org/10.1007/s10979-006-9019-y.

Essau, C. A., Sasagawa, S., & Frick, P. J. (2006). Callous-unemotional traits in a community sample of adolescents. *Assessment*, *13*(4), 454–469. https://doi.org/10.1177/1073191106287354.

Farrington, D. P., Coid, J. W., & Murray, J. (2009). Family factors in the intergenerational transmission of offending. *Criminal Behaviour and Mental Health*, *19*(2), 109–124. https://doi.org/10.1002/cbm.717.

Finger, E. C., Marsh, A. A., Buzas, B., Kamel, N., Rhodes, R., Vythilingham, M., … Blair, J. R. (2007). The impact of tryptophan depletion and 5-HTTLPR genotype on passive avoidance and response reversal instrumental learning tasks. *Neuropsychopharmacology*, *32*(1), 206–215. https://doi.org/10.1038/sj.npp.1301182.

Flom, M., & Saudino, K. J. (2017). Callous–unemotional behaviors in early childhood: Genetic and environmental contributions to stability and change. *Development and Psychopathology*, *29*(4), 1227–1234. https://doi.org/10.1017/S0954579416001267.

Flor, H., Birbaumer, N., Hermann, C., Ziegler, S., & Patrick, C. J. (2002). Aversive Pavlovian conditioning in psychopaths: Peripheral and central correlates. *Psychophysiology*, *39*(4), 505–518. https://doi.org/10.1017/S0048577202394046.

Fontaine, N. M., Rijsdijk, F. V., McCrory, E. J., & Viding, E. (2010). Etiology of different developmental trajectories of callous-unemotional traits. *Journal of the American Academy of Child & Adolescent Psychiatry*, *49*(7), 656–664. https://doi.org/10.1016/j.jaac.2010.03.014.

Forsman, M., Lichtenstein, P., Andershed, H., & Larsson, H. (2008). Genetic effects explain the stability of psychopathic personality from mid-to late adolescence. *Journal of Abnormal Psychology*, *117*(3), 606. https://doi.org/10.1037/0021-843X.117.3.606.

Freedman, L. F., & Verdun-Jones, S. N. (2010). Blaming the parts instead of the person: Understanding and applying neurobiological factors associated with psychopathy. *Canadian Journal of Criminology and Criminal Justice*, *52*(1), 29–53. https://doi.org/10.3138/cjccj.52.1.29.

Frick, P. J., & Hare, R. D. (2001). *The antisocial process screening device*. Toronto: Multi-Health Systems.

Frick, P. J., Lilienfeld, S. O., Ellis, M., Loney, B., & Silverthorn, P. (1999). The association between anxiety and psychopathy dimensions in children. *Journal of Abnormal Child Psychology*, *27*(5), 383–392. https://doi.org/10.1023/A:102192801.

Frick, P. J., & Loney, B. R. (2002). Understanding the association between parent and child antisocial behavior. In R. J. McMahon, & R. D. Peters (Eds.), *The effects of parental dysfunction on children*. Boston, MA: Springer. https://doi.org/10.1007/978-1-4615-1739-9_6.

Frick, P. J., O'Brien, B. S., Wootton, J. M., & McBurnett, K. (1994). Psychopathy and conduct problems in children. *Journal of Abnormal Psychology*, *103*(4), 700–707. https://doi.org/10.1037/0021-843X.103.4.700.

Frick, P. J., Ray, J. V., Thornton, L. C., & Kahn, R. E. (2014). Can callous-unemotional traits enhance the understanding, diagnosis, and treatment of serious conduct problems in children and adolescents? A comprehensive review. *Psychological Bulletin*, *140*(1), 1–57. https://doi.org/10.1037/a0033076.

Frick, P. J., Stickle, T. R., Dandreaux, D. M., Farrell, J. M., & Kimonis, E. R. (2005). Callous–unemotional traits in predicting the severity and stability of conduct problems and delinquency. *Journal of Abnormal Child Psychology*, *33*(4), 471–487. https://doi.org/10.1007/s10648-005-5728-9.

Frick, P. J., & White, S. F. (2008). Research review: The importance of callous-unemotional traits for developmental models of aggressive and antisocial behavior. *Journal of Child Psychology and Psychiatry*, *49*(4), 359–375. https://doi.org/10.1111/j.1469-7610.2007.01862.x.

Frogner, L., Gibson, C. L., Andershed, A. K., & Andershed, H. (2018). Childhood psychopathic personality and callous–unemotional traits in the prediction of conduct problems. *American Journal of Orthopsychiatry*, *88*(2), 211–225. https://doi.org/10.1037/ort0000205.

Gao, Y., Raine, A., Chan, F., Venables, P. H., & Mednick, S. A. (2010). Early maternal and paternal bonding, childhood physical abuse and adult psychopathic personality. *Psychological Medicine*, *40*(6), 1007–1016. https://doi.org/10.1017/S0033291709991279.

Gao, Y., Zhang, W., Eisenbarth, H., Fung, A. L. C., Lu, M., Raine, A., … Li, X. (2018). P3 amplitude and psychopathic traits in youths: Distinct contributions of the grandiose-manipulative and daring-impulsivity traits. *Personality and Individual Differences*, *120*, 87–94. https://doi.org/10.1016/j.paid.2017.08.017.

Glaze, L. E., & Maruschak, L. M. (2016). Parents in prison and their minor children. *Bureau of Justice Statistics*, 1–25. Retrieved from: http://biblioteca.cejamericas.org/bitstream/handle/2015/2976/Parents_Prison_Minor_Children.pdf?sequence=1&isAllowed=y.

Glenn, A. L. (2019). Early life predictors of callous—Unemotional and psychopathic traits. *Infant Mental Health Journal*, *40*(1), 39–53. https://doi.org/10.1002/imhj.21757.

Glenn, A. L., Raine, A., Venables, P. H., & Mednick, S. A. (2007). Early temperamental and psychophysiological precursors of adult psychopathic personality. *Journal of Abnormal Psychology*, *116*(3), 508–518. https://doi.org/10.1037/0021-843x.116.3.508.

Gordon, H. L., Baird, A. A., & End, A. (2004). Functional differences among those high and low on a trait measure of psychopathy. *Biological Psychiatry*, *56*(7), 516–521. https://doi.org/10.1016/j.biopsych.2004.06.030.

Gorin, H. M., Kosson, D. S., Miller, S. A., Fontaine, N. M., Vitaro, F., Séguin, J. R., … Tremblay, R. E. (2019). Psychopathic traits in middle childhood: Evidence of a hierarchical three-factor structure. *Journal of Psychopathology and Behavioral Assessment*, *41*(3), 341–352. https://doi.org/10.1007/s10862-019-09733-2.

Grady, M. D., Looman, J., & Abracen, J. (2019). Childhood abuse, attachment, and psychopathy among individuals who commit sexual offenses. *Sexual Addiction & Compulsivity*, *26*(1–2), 77–102. https://doi.org/10.1080/10720162.2019.1620660.

Hajcak, G., MacNamara, A., & Olvet, D. M. (2010). Event-related potentials, emotion, and emotion regulation: An integrative review. *Developmental Neuropsychology*, *35*(2), 129–155. https://doi.org/10.1080/87565640903526504.

Hare, R. D. (1970). *Psychopathy: Theory and research*. New York: Wiley.

Hare, R. D. (1991). *Manual for the Hare psychopathy checklist-revised*. Multi-Health Systems.

Hare, R. D. (1998). Psychopaths and their nature: Implications for the mental health and criminal justice systems. In T. Millon, E. Simonsen, M. Birket-Smith, & R. D. Davis (Eds.), *Psychopathy: Antisocial, criminal and violent behavior* (pp. 188–212). New York: Guilford Press.

Hare, R. D. (2003). *The Hare psychopathy checklist—Revised* (2nd ed.). Toronto: Multi-Health Systems.

Hare, R. D. (2006). Psychopathy: A clinical and forensic overview. *Psychiatric Clinics*, *29*(3), 709–724. https://doi.org/10.1016/j.psc.2006.04.007.

Hare, R. D., & Neumann, C. S. (2008). Psychopathy as a clinical and empirical construct. *Annual Review of Clinical Psychology*, *4*, 217–246. https://doi.org/10.1146/annurev.clinpsy.3.022806.091452.

Hare, R. D., & Quinn, M. J. (1971). Psychopathy and autonomic conditioning. *Journal of Abnormal Psychology*, *77*(3), 223–235. https://doi.org/10.1037/h0031012.

Hiatt, K. D., & Newman, J. P. (2007). Behavioral evidence of prolonged interhemispheric transfer time among psychopathic offenders. *Neuropsychology*, *21*(3), 313–318. https://doi.org/10.1037/0894-4105.21.3.313.

Higley, J. D., Mehlman, P. T., Poland, R. E., Taub, D. M., Vickers, J., Suomi, S. J., & Linnoila, M. (1996). CSF testosterone and 5-HIAA correlate with different types of aggressive behaviors. *Biological Psychiatry*, *40*(11), 1067–1082. https://doi.org/10.1016/S0006-3223(95)00675-3.

Hyde, L. W., Waller, R., Trentacosta, C. J., Shaw, D. S., Neiderhiser, J. M., Ganiban, J. M., … Leve, L. D. (2016). Heritable and nonheritable pathways to early callous-unemotional behaviors. *American Journal of Psychiatry*, *173*(9), 903–910. https://doi.org/10.1176/appi.ajp.2016.15111381.

Intrator, J., Hare, R., Stritzke, P., Brichtswein, K., Dorfman, D., Harpur, T., … Rosen, J. (1997). A brain imaging (single photon emission computerized tomography) study of semantic and affective processing in psychopaths. *Biological Psychiatry*, *42*(2), 96–103. https://doi.org/10.1016/S0006-3223(96)00290-9.

Kahn, R. E., Deater-Deckard, K., King-Casas, B., & Kim-Spoon, J. (2016). Intergenerational similarity in callous-unemotional traits: Contributions of hostile parenting and household chaos during adolescence. *Psychiatry Research*, *246*, 815–820. https://doi.org/10.1016/j.psychres.2016.10.023.

Kiehl, K. A. (2006). A cognitive neuroscience perspective on psychopathy: Evidence for paralimbic system dysfunction. *Psychiatry Research*, *142*(2–3), 107–128. https://doi.org/10.1016/j.psychres.2005.09.013.

Kiehl, K. A., Smith, A. M., Mendrek, A., Forster, B. B., Hare, R. D., & Liddle, P. F. (2004). Temporal lobe abnormalities in semantic processing by criminal psychopaths as revealed by functional magnetic resonance imaging. *Psychiatry Research: Neuroimaging*, *130*(1), 27–42. https://doi.org/10.1016/S0925-4927(03)00106-9.

Kosson, D. S., Neumann, C. S., Forth, A. E., Salekin, R. T., Hare, R. D., Krischer, M. K., & Sevecke, K. (2013). Factor structure of the Hare psychopathy checklist: Youth version (PCL: YV) in adolescent females. *Psychological Assessment*, *25*(1), 71–83. https://doi.org/10.1037/a0028986.

Krueger, R. F. (1999). Personality traits in late adolescence predict mental disorders in early adulthood: A perspective-epidemiological study. *Journal of Personality*, *67*(1), 39–65. https://doi.org/10.1111/1467-6494.00047.

Krupić, D., Ručević, S., & Vučković, S. (2020). From parental personality over parental styles to children psychopathic tendencies. *Current Psychology*, 1–10. https://doi.org/10.1007/s12144-020-00676-6.

Kudielka, B. M., & Kirschbaum, C. (2005). Sex differences in HPA axis responses to stress: A review. *Biological Psychology*, *69*(1), 113–132. https://doi.org/10.1016/j.biopsycho.2004.11.009.

Laakso, M. P., Vaurio, O., Koivisto, E., Savolainen, L., Eronen, M., Aronen, H. J., … Tiihonen, J. (2001). Psychopathy and the posterior hippocampus. *Behavioural Brain Research*, *118*(2), 187–193. https://doi.org/10.1016/S0166-4328(00)00324-7.

Larsson, H., Tuvblad, C., Rijsdijk, F. V., Andershed, H., Grann, M., & Lichtenstein, P. (2007). A common genetic factor explains the association between psychopathic personality and antisocial behavior. *Psychological Medicine*, *37*(1), 15–26. https://doi.org/10.1017/S003329170600907X.

LeBreton, J. M., Binning, J. F., & Adorno, A. J. (2006). Subclinical psychopaths. In J. C. Thomas, & D. L. Segal (Eds.), *Vol. 1. Comprehensive handbook of personality and psychopathology* (pp. 388–411). New Jersey: John Wiley & Sons, Inc.

Levenston, G. K., Patrick, C. J., Bradley, M. M., & Lang, P. J. (2000). The psychopath as observer: Emotion and attention in picture processing. *Journal of Abnormal Psychology*, *109*(3), 373. https://doi.org/10.1037/0021-843X.109.3.373.

Lilienfeld, S. O., & Fowler, K. A. (2006). The self-report assessment of psychopathy: Problems, pitfalls, and promises. In C. J. Patrick (Ed.), *Handbook of psychopath* (pp. 107–132). New York, NY: The Guilford Press.

Loney, B. R., Frick, P. J., Clements, C. B., Ellis, M. L., & Kerlin, K. (2003). Emotional reactivity and callous unemotional traits in adolescents. *Journal of Clinical Child and Adolescent Psychology*, *32*(1), 66–80.

Loney, B. R., Huntenburg, A., Counts-Allan, C., & Schmeelk, K. M. (2007). A preliminary examination of the intergenerational continuity of maternal psychopathic features. *Aggressive Behavior*, *33*(1), 14–25. https://doi.org/10.1002/ab.20163.

Lynam, D. R., Caspi, A., Moffitt, T. E., Loeber, R., & Stouthamer-Loeber, M. (2007). Longitudinal evidence that psychopathy scores in early adolescence predict adult psychopathy. *Journal of Abnormal Psychology*, *116*(1), 155–165. https://doi.org/10.1037/0021-843X.116.1.155.

Lynam, D. R., & Derefinko, K. J. (2006). Psychopathy and personality. In C. J. Patrick (Ed.), *Handbook of psychopathy* (pp. 133–155). New York: Guilford.

Lynam, D. R., Leukefeld, C., & Clayton, R. R. (2003). The contribution of personality to the overlap between antisocial behavior and substance use/misuse. *Aggressive Behavior*, *29*(4), 316–331. https://doi.org/10.1002/ab.10073.

Marsh, A. A., Finger, E. C., Schechter, J. C., Jurkowitz, I. T. N., Reid, M. E., & Blair, R. J. R. (2011). Adolescents with psychopathic traits report reductions in physiological responses to fear. *Journal of Child Psychology and Psychiatry*, *52*(8), 834–841. https://doi.org/10.1111/j.1469-7610.2010.02353.x.

McCrae, R. R., & Costa, P. T. (1990). *Personality in adulthood*. New York: Guilford.

McCrae, R. R., & Costa, P. T. (2013). Introduction to the empirical and theoretical status of the five-factor model of personality traits. In T. A. Widiger, & P. T. Costa (Eds.), *Personality disorders and the five-factor model of personality* (3rd ed., pp. 15–27). Washington, DC: American Psychological Association.

McKown, C., & Weinstein, R. S. (2003). The development and consequences of stereotype consciousness in middle childhood. *Child Development*, *74*(2), 498–515. https://doi.org/10.1111/1467-8624.7402012.

Meloy, J. R. (1988). *The psychopathic mind: Origins, dynamics, and treatment*. Northvale, NJ: Aronson.

Meloy, J. R. (2001). *The mark of Cain: Psychoanalytic insight and the psychopath*. Hillsdale, NJ: The Analytic Press.

Meloy, J. R., Book, A., Hosker-Field, A., Methot-Jones, T., & Roters, J. (2018). Social, sexual, and violent predation: Are psychopathic traits evolutionarily adaptive? *Violence and Gender*, *5*(3), 153–165. https://doi.org/10.1089/vio.2018.0012.

Meng, X. M., Zhu, D. M., Ruan, D. Y., She, J. Q., & Luo, L. (2005). Effects of chronic lead exposure on 1H MRS of hippocampus and frontal lobes in children. *Neurology*, *64*(4), 1644–1647. https://doi.org/10.1212/01.WNL.0000160391.58004.D4.

Michalska, K. J., Zeffiro, T. A., & Decety, J. (2016). Brain response to viewing others being harmed in children with conduct disorder symptoms. *Journal of Child Psychology and Psychiatry*, *57*(4), 510–519. https://doi.org/10.1111/jcpp.12474.

Miley, L. N., Fox, B., Muniz, C. N., Perkins, R., & DeLisi, M. (2020). Does childhood victimization predict specific adolescent offending? An analysis of generality versus specificity in the victim-offender overlap. *Child Abuse & Neglect*, *101*. https://doi.org/10.1016/j.chiabu.2019.104328, 104328.

Mitchell, D. G., Colledge, E., Leonard, A., & Blair, R. J. R. (2002). Risky decisions and response reversal: Is there evidence of orbitofrontal cortex dysfunction in psychopathic individuals? *Neuropsychologia*, *40*(12), 2013–2022. https://doi.org/10.1016/S0028-3932(02)00056-8.

Mokros, A., Neumann, C., Habermeyer, E., Hare, R., Santtila, P., & Nitschke, J. (2015). Variants of psychopathy in adult male offenders: A latent profile analysis. *Journal of Abnormal Psychology*, *124*, 372–386.

Moore, A. A., Rappaport, L. M., Blair, R. J., Pine, D. S., Leibenluft, E., Brotman, M. A., … Roberson-Nay, R. (2019). Genetic underpinnings of callous-unemotional traits and emotion recognition in children, adolescents, and emerging adults. *Journal of Child Psychology and Psychiatry*, *60*(6), 638–645. https://doi.org/10.1111/jcpp.13018.

Müller, J. L., Sommer, M., Wagner, V., Lange, K., Taschler, H., Röder, C. H., … Hajak, G. (2003). Abnormalities in emotion processing within cortical and subcortical regions in criminal psychopaths: Evidence from a functional magnetic resonance imaging study using pictures with emotional content. *Biological Psychiatry*, *54*(2), 152–162. https://doi.org/10.1016/S0006-3223(02)01749-3.

Muniz, C. N., Fox, B., Miley, L. N., DeLisi, M., Cigarran, G. P., & Birnbaum, A. (2019). The effects of adverse childhood experiences on internalizing versus externalizing outcomes. *Criminal Justice and Behavior*, *46*(4), 568–589. https://doi.org/10.1177/0093854819826213.

Muratori, P., Lochman, J. E., Manfredi, A., Milone, A., Nocentini, A., Pisano, S., & Masi, G. (2016). Callous unemotional traits in children with disruptive behavior disorder: Predictors of developmental trajectories and adolescent outcomes. *Psychiatry Research*, *236*, 35–41. https://doi.org/10.1016/j.psychres.2016.01.003.

Needleman, H. L., Riess, J. A., Tobin, M. J., Biesecker, G. E., & Greenhouse, J. B. (1996). Bone lead levels and delinquent behavior. *JAMA*, *275*(5), 363–369. https://doi.org/10.1001/jama.1996.03530290033034.

Neumann, C., Hare, R., & Pardini, D. (2015). Antisociality and the construct of psychopathy: Data from across the globe. *Journal of Personality*, *83*, 678–692.

Patrick, C. J. (Ed.). (2005). *Handbook of psychopathy*. New York: Guilford.

Patrick, C. J., Curtin, J. J., & Tellegen, A. (2002). Development and validation of a brief form of the Multidimensional Personality Questionnaire. *Psychological Assessment*, *14*(2), 150–163. https://doi.org/10.1037/1040-3590.14.2.150.

Petitclerc, A., Henry, J., Feng, B., Poliakova, N., Brendgen, M., Dionne, G., ... Boivin, M. (2019). Genetic correlation between child callous-unemotional behaviors and fear recognition deficit: Evidence for a neurocognitive Endophenotype. *Journal of Abnormal Child Psychology*, *47*(9), 1483–1493. https://doi.org/10.1007/s10802-019-00529-2.

Polderman, T. J., Benyamin, B., De Leeuw, C. A., Sullivan, P. F., Van Bochoven, A., Visscher, P. M., & Posthuma, D. (2015). Meta-analysis of the heritability of human traits based on fifty years of twin studies. *Nature Genetics*, *47*(7), 702–709. https://doi.org/10.1038/ng.3285.

Poythress, N. G., Skeem, J. L., & Lilienfeld, S. O. (2006). Associations among early abuse, dissociation, and psychopathy in an offender sample. *Journal of Abnormal Psychology*, *115*(2), 288–297. https://doi.org/10.1037/0021-843X.115.2.288.

Puzzo, I., Smaragdi, A., Gonzalez, K., Martin-Key, N., & Fairchild, G. (2016). Neurobiological, neuroimaging, and neuropsychological studies of children and adolescents with disruptive behavior disorders. *Family Relations*, *65*(1), 134–150. https://doi.org/10.1111/fare.12182.

Raine, A., Ishikawa, S. S., Arce, E., Lencz, T., Knuth, K. H., Bihrle, S., ... Colletti, P. (2004). Hippocampal structural asymmetry in unsuccessful psychopaths. *Biological Psychiatry*, *55*(2), 185–191. https://doi.org/10.1016/S0006-3223(03)00727-3.

Raine, A., Lencz, T., Bihrle, S., LaCasse, L., & Colletti, P. (2000). Reduced prefrontal gray matter volume and reduced autonomic activity in antisocial personality disorder. *Archives of General Psychiatry*, *57*(2), 119–127. https://doi.org/10.1001/archpsyc.57.2.119.

Rilling, J. K., Glenn, A. L., Jairam, M. R., Pagnoni, G., Goldsmith, D. R., Elfenbein, H. A., & Lilienfeld, S. O. (2007). Neural correlates of social cooperation and non-cooperation as a function of psychopathy. *Biological Psychiatry*, *61*(11), 1260–1271. https://doi.org/10.1016/j.biopsych.2006.07.021.

Sadeh, N., Javdani, S., Jackson, J. J., Reynolds, E. K., Potenza, M. N., Gelernter, J., ... Verona, E. (2010). Serotonin transporter gene associations with psychopathic traits in youth vary as a function of socioeconomic resources. *Journal of Abnormal Psychology*, *119*(3), 604–609. https://doi.org/10.1037/a0019709.

Sakai, J. T., Dalwani, M. S., Mikulich-Gilbertson, S. K., Raymond, K., McWilliams, S., Tanabe, J., ... Crowley, T. J. (2017). Imaging decision about whether to benefit self by harming others: Adolescents with conduct and substance problems, with or without callous-unemotionality, or developing typically. *Psychiatry Research: Neuroimaging*, *263*, 103–112. https://doi.org/10.1016/j.pscychresns.2017.03.004.

Salekin, R. T. (2017). Research review: What do we know about psychopathic traits in children? *Journal of Child Psychology and Psychiatry*, *58*(11), 1180–1200. https://doi.org/10.1111/jcpp.12738.

Salekin, R. T., Andershed, H., Batky, B. D., & Bontemps, A. P. (2018). Are callous unemotional (CU) traits enough? *Journal of Psychopathology and Behavioral Assessment*, *40*(1), 1–5. https://doi.org/10.1007/s10862-018-9663-9.

Schimmenti, A., Di Carlo, G., Passanisi, A., & Caretti, V. (2015). Abuse in childhood and psychopathic traits in a sample of violent offenders. *Psychological Trauma: Theory, Research, Practice, and Policy*, *7*(4), 340–347. https://doi.org/10.1037/tra0000023.

Schulkin, J. (2003). Allostasis: A neural behavioral perspective. *Hormones and Behavior*, *43*(1), 21–27. https://doi.org/10.1016/S0018-506X(02)00035-1.

Schulkin, J., Gold, P. W., & McEwen, B. S. (1998). Induction of corticotropin-releasing hormone gene expression by glucocorticoids: Implication for understanding the states of fear and anxiety and allostatic load. *Psychoneuroendocrinology*, *23*(3), 219–243. https://doi.org/10.1016/S0306-4530(97)00099-1.

Sebastian, C. L., McCrory, E. J., Cecil, C. A., Lockwood, P. L., De Brito, S. A., Fontaine, N. M., & Viding, E. (2012). Neural responses to affective and cognitive theory of mind in children with conduct problems and varying levels of callous-unemotional traits. *Archives of General Psychiatry*, *69*, 814–822. https://doi.org/10.1001/archgenpsychiatry.2011.2070.

Seibert, L. A., Miller, J. D., Few, L. R., Zeichner, A., & Lynam, D. R. (2011). An examination of the structure of self-report psychopathy measures and their relations with general traits and externalizing behaviors. *Personality Disorders: Theory, Research, and Treatment*, *2*(3), 193–208. https://doi.org/10.1037/a0019232.

Serbin, L. A., & Stack, D. M. (1998). Introduction to the special section: Studying intergenerational continuity and the transfer of risk. *Developmental Psychology*, *34*(6), 1159–1161. https://doi.org/10.1037/0012-1649.34.6.1159.

Sethi, A., McCrory, E., Puetz, V., Hoffmann, F., Knodt, A. R., Radtke, S. R., … Viding, E. (2018). Primary and secondary variants of psychopathy in a volunteer sample are associated with different neurocognitive mechanisms. *Biological Psychiatry: Cognitive Neuroscience and Neuroimaging*, *3*(12), 1013–1021. https://doi.org/10.1016/j.bpsc.2018.04.002.

Skeem, J., Johansson, P., Andershed, H., Kerr, M., & Louden, J. E. (2007). Two subtypes of psychopathic violent offenders that parallel primary and secondary variants. *Journal of Abnormal Psychology*, *116*(2), 395–409. https://doi.org/10.1037/0021-843x.116.2.395.

Skeem, J. L., Poythress, N., Edens, J. F., Lilienfeld, S. O., & Cale, E. M. (2003). Psychopathic personality or personalities? Exploring potential variants of psychopathy and their implications for risk assessment. *Aggression and Violent Behavior*, *8*(5), 513–546. https://doi.org/10.1016/S1359-1789(02)00098-8.

Skilling, T. A., Harris, G. T., Rice, M. E., & Quinsey, V. L. (2002). Identifying persistently antisocial offenders using the Hare Psychopathy Checklist and DSM antisocial personality disorder criteria. *Psychological Assessment*, *14*(1), 27–38. https://doi.org/10.1037/1040-3590.14.1.27.

Sobczak, S., Honig, A., Nicolson, N. A., & Riedel, W. J. (2001). Effects of acute tryptophan depletion on mood and cortisol release in first-degree relatives of type I and type II bipolar patients and healthy matched controls. *Neuropsychopharmacology*, *27*(5), 834. https://doi.org/10.1016/S0893-133X(02)00345-7.

Tellegen, A., & Waller, N. G. (2008). Exploring personality through test construction: Development of the multidimensional personality questionnaire. In G. J. Boyle, G. Matthews, & D. H. Saklofske (Eds.), *Vol. 2. The SAGE handbook of personality theory and assessment* (pp. 261–292). London: Sage.

Thompson, D. F., Ramos, C. L., & Willett, J. K. (2014). Psychopathy: Clinical features, developmental basis and therapeutic challenges. *Journal of Clinical Pharmacy and Therapeutics*, *39*(5), 485–495. https://doi.org/10.1111/jcpt.12182.

Thornberry, T. P. (2005). Explaining multiple patterns of offending across the life course and across generations. *The Annals of the American Academy of Political and Social Science*, *602*(1), 156–195. https://doi.org/10.1177/0002716205280641.

Thornberry, T. P. (2009). The apple doesn't fall far from the tree (or does it?): Intergenerational patterns of antisocial behavior—The American Society of Criminology 2008 Sutherland address. *Criminology*, *47*(2), 297–325. https://doi.org/10.1111/j.1745-9125.2009.00153.x.

Tilbrook, A. J., Turner, A. I., & Clarke, I. J. (2000). Effects of stress on reproduction in non-rodent mammals: The role of glucocorticoids and sex differences. *Reviews of Reproduction*, *5*(2), 105–113. https://doi.org/10.1530/ror.0.0050105.

Trope, I., Lopez-Villegas, D., Cecil, K. M., & Lenkinski, R. E. (2001). Exposure to lead appears to selectively alter metabolism of cortical gray matter. *Pediatrics*, *107*(6), 1437–1442. https://doi.org/10.1542/peds.107.6.1437.

Tuvblad, C., Fanti, K. A., Andershed, H., Colins, O. F., & Larsson, H. (2017). Psychopathic personality traits in 5-year-old twins: The importance of genetic and shared environmental influences. *European Child & Adolescent Psychiatry*, *26*(4), 469–479. https://doi.org/10.1007/s00787-016-0899-1.

van Honk, J., Peper, J. S., & Schutter, D. J. (2005). Testosterone reduces unconscious fear but not consciously experienced anxiety: Implications for the disorders of fear and anxiety. *Biological Psychiatry*, *58*(3), 218–225. https://doi.org/10.1016/j.biopsych.2005.04.003.

van Honk, J., Schutter, D. J., d'Alfonso, A., Kessels, R. P., Postma, A., & de Haan, E. H. (2001). Repetitive transcranial magnetic stimulation at the frontopolar cortex reduces skin conductance but not heart rate: Reduced gray matter excitability in orbitofrontal regions. *Archives of General Psychiatry*, *58*(10), 973–974. https://doi.org/10.1080/13546800500233728.

van Honk, J., Schutter, D. J., Hermans, E. J., Putman, P., Tuiten, A., & Koppeschaar, H. (2004). Testosterone shifts the balance between sensitivity for punishment and reward in healthy young women. *Psychoneuroendocrinology*, *29*(7), 937–943. https://doi.org/10.1016/j.psyneuen.2003.08.007.

van Honk, J., & Schutter, D. J. L. G. (2006). Unmasking feigned sanity: A neurobiological model of emotion processing in primary psychopathy. *Cognitive Neuropsychiatry*, *11*(3), 285–306. https://doi.org/10.1080/13546800500233728.

van Honk, J., Tuiten, A., Hermans, E., Putnam, P., Koppeschaar, H., Thijssen, J., … van Doornen, L. (2001). A single administration of testosterone induces cardiac accelerative responses to angry faces in healthy young women. *Behavioral Neuroscience*, *115*(1), 238–242. https://doi.org/10.1037/0735-7044.115.1.238.

Veit, R., Flor, H., Erb, M., Hermann, C., Lotze, M., Grodd, W., & Birbaumer, N. (2002). Brain circuits involved in emotional learning in antisocial behavior and social phobia in humans. *Neuroscience Letters*, *328*(3), 233–236. https://doi.org/10.1016/S0304-3940(02)00519-0.

Vernon, P. A., Villani, V. C., Vickers, L. C., & Harris, J. A. (2008). A behavioral genetic investigation of the Dark Triad and the Big 5. *Personality and Individual Differences*, *44*(2), 445–452. https://doi.org/10.1016/j.paid.2007.09.007.

Verona, E., Murphy, B., & Bresin, K. (2018). Oxytocin-related single-nucleotide polymorphisms, family environment, and psychopathic traits. *Personality Disorders, Theory, Research, and Treatment*, *9*(6), 584–589. https://doi.org/10.1037/per0000290.

Viau, V. (2002). Functional cross-talk between the hypothalamic-pituitary-gonadal and-adrenal axes. *Journal of Neuroendocrinology*, *14*(6), 506–513. https://doi.org/10.1046/j.1365-2826.2002.00798.x.

Viding, E., Blair, R. J. R., Moffitt, T. E., & Plomin, R. (2005). Evidence for substantial genetic risk for psychopathy in 7-year-olds. *Journal of Child Psychology and Psychiatry*, *46*(6), 592–597. https://doi.org/10.1111/j.1469-7610.2004.00393.x.

Viding, E., Jones, A. P., Paul, J. F., Moffitt, T. E., & Plomin, R. (2008). Heritability of antisocial behaviour at 9: Do callous-unemotional traits matter? *Developmental Science*, *11*(1), 17–22. https://doi.org/10.1111/j.1467-7687.2007.00648.x.

Viding, E., & McCrory, E. J. (2015). Developmental risk for psychopathy. In A. Thapar, D. S. Pine, J. F. Leckman, S. Scott, M. J. Snowling, & E. Taylor (Eds.), *Rutter's child and adolescent psychiatry* (6th ed., pp. 966–980). John Wiley & Sons.

Viding, E., & McCrory, E. J. (2018). Understanding the development of psychopathy: Progress and challenges. *Psychological Medicine*, *48*(4), 566–577. https://doi.org/10.1017/S0033291717002847.

Vieno, A., Nation, M., Pastore, M., & Santinello, M. (2009). Parenting and antisocial behavior: A model of the relationship between adolescent self-disclosure, parental closeness, parental control, and adolescent antisocial behavior. *Developmental Psychology*, *45*(6), 1509–1519. https://doi.org/10.1037/a0016929.

Waller, R., Gard, A. M., Shaw, D. S., Forbes, E. E., Neumann, C. S., & Hyde, L. W. (2019). Weakened functional connectivity between the amygdala and the ventromedial prefrontal cortex is longitudinally related to psychopathic traits in low-income males during early adulthood. *Clinical Psychological Science*, *7*(3), 628–635. https://doi.org/10.1177/2167702618810231.

Waller, R., Gardner, F., & Hyde, L. W. (2013). What are the associations between parenting, callous–unemotional traits, and antisocial behavior in youth? A systematic review of evidence. *Clinical Psychology Review*, *33*(4), 593–608. https://doi.org/10.1016/j.cpr.2013.03.001.

Waller, R., Shaw, D. S., & Hyde, L. W. (2016). Observed fearlessness and positive parenting interact to predict childhood callous-unemotional behaviors among low-income boys. *Journal of Child Psychology and Psychiatry*, *58*(3), 282–291. https://doi.org/10.1111/jcpp.12666.

Wertz, J., Caspi, A., Belsky, D. W., Beckley, A. L., Arseneault, L., Barnes, J. C., … Odgers, C. L. (2018). Genetics and crime: Integrating new genomic discoveries into psychological research about antisocial behavior. *Psychological Science*, *29*(5), 791–803. https://doi.org/10.1177/0956797617744542.

White, S. F., Marsh, A. A., Fowler, K. A., Schechter, J. C., Adalio, C., Pope, K., … Blair, R. J. R. (2012). Reduced amygdala response in youths with disruptive behavior disorders and psychopathic traits: Decreased emotional response versus increased top-down attention to nonemotional features. *American Journal of Psychiatry*, *169*(7), 750–758. https://doi.org/10.1017/s0033291717002847.

Wright, J. P., Boisvert, D., & Vaske, J. (2009). Blood lead levels in early childhood predict adulthood psychopathy. *Youth Violence and Juvenile Justice*, *7*(3), 208–222. https://doi.org/10.1177/1541204009333827.

Wright, J. P., Dietrich, K. N., Ris, M. D., Hornung, R. W., & Wessel, S. D. (2008). Association of prenatal and childhood blood lead concentrations with criminal arrests in early adulthood. *PLoS Medicine*, *5*, 732–740. https://doi.org/10.1371/journal.pmed.0050101.

Yang, Y., Raine, A., Colletti, P., Toga, A. W., & Narr, K. L. (2009). Abnormal temporal and prefrontal cortical gray matter thinning in psychopaths. *Molecular Psychiatry*, *14*(6), 561–562. https://doi.org/10.1038/mp.2009.12.

Yang, Y., Raine, A., Lencz, T., Bihrle, S., LaCasse, L., & Colletti, P. (2005). Volume reduction in prefrontal gray matter in unsuccessful criminal psychopaths. *Biological Psychiatry*, *57*(10), 1103–1108. https://doi.org/10.1016/j.biopsych.2005.01.021.

Yang, Y., Raine, A., Narr, K. L., Colletti, P., & Toga, A. W. (2009). Localization of deformations within the amygdala in individuals with psychopathy. *Archives of General Psychiatry*, *66*(9), 986–994. https://doi.org/10.1001/archgenpsychiatry.2009.110.

Yoder, K. J., Lahey, B. B., & Decety, J. (2016). Callous traits in children with and without conduct problems predict reduced connectivity when viewing harm to others. *Scientific Reports*, *6*, 20216. https://doi.org/10.1038/srep20216.

Neural correlates of psychopathy: A comprehensive review

3

Ana Seara-Cardoso, Margarida Vasconcelos, Adriana Sampaio, and Craig S. Neumann

Introduction

Psychopathy is a personality disorder characterized by abnormal affective-interpersonal traits, such as lack of empathy and manipulativeness, and by deviant lifestyle-antisocial characteristics, such as impulsiveness and repeated antisocial behavior (e.g., Blair, Mitchell, & Blair, 2005; Hare, 2003; Hare & Neumann, 2008; Viding, McCrory, & Seara-Cardoso, 2014). The extreme profile of criminals with psychopathy has long intrigued and captured the attention of both laymen and academics. In the past two decades, with the development and increased availability of neuroimaging techniques such as functional magnetic resonance imaging (fMRI), research to probe the neural correlates that underlie this personality disorder has vastly grown. fMRI is a noninvasive neuroimaging technique that provides indirect measure of brain activity with excellent spatial and good temporal resolution; it measures the changes in brain blood oxygenation and flow that occur while individuals perform experimental tasks. Those changes—reflected in blood oxygenation level dependent (BOLD) signal alterations—allow for the estimation of the neural activity associated with a specific psychological process.

As with many forms of mental disorder, evidence indicates that the structure of psychopathic personality is dimensional rather than categorical. Psychopathic traits are continuously distributed in the general population (Neumann, Hare, & Pardini, 2015), and individuals with a diagnosis of psychopathy represent an extreme end of that distribution (see Hare & Neumann, 2008 for a review). Traditionally, the psychopathy domains were thought of in terms of Factor 1 (interpersonal-affective) or Factor 2 (lifestyle-antisocial). More recent perspectives consider psychopathy to be represented by four unidimensional correlated factors reflecting interpersonal, affective, lifestyle, and antisocial features (Hare & Neumann, 2008). The Psychopathy Checklist-Revised (PCL-R; Hare, 2003), the standard tool for assessment of psychopathy in adult offenders, contains 20 items, each of which are rated by an experienced examiner on a scale of 0 to 2, and thus has a maximum score of 40; a score of 30 or above is often used as a cutoff for cases of severely psychopathic individuals, though as noted, psychopathy is dimensional in nature, and therefore 30 is a somewhat arbitrary cut-point (Hare, 2003). Based on the same mathematically modeling approach used to solidify the structure of the PCL-R, Neumann and colleagues have provided a wealth of empirical findings to demonstrate that the same four factors can be used to represent psychopathic personality features in general population, corporate, and youth samples,

Psychopathy and Criminal Behavior. https://doi.org/10.1016/B978-0-12-811419-3.00019-4

across an array of cultures and different types of assessments (Neumann et al., 2015). The identification of coherent factors that can be used to assess psychopathic features across the full spectrum of personality pathology is a critically important aspect of research on psychopathy, given that psychopathy is a multifarious construct, and it appears that its underlying neurobiology is also complex.

In this up-to-date comprehensive review, we will first review fMRI findings on samples of individuals who qualify for the diagnosis of criminal psychopathy as assessed using the PCL-R (Hare, 2003) and then findings from studies that inspect neural correlates of the continuum of psychopathic personality traits on samples from the community.

Neuroimaging studies with forensic samples

At the time of writing this chapter, we conducted a PubMed and Scopus search using the following search terms: ("functional magnetic resonance" or "MR" or "MRI" or "fMRI" or "neuroimaging") and ("psychopathy"). The search brought up 356 articles. Exclusion criteria for this review were: (1) studies which did not include a formal assessment with the PCL-R; (2) studies of children and youth; (3) studies with psychiatric populations; (4) studies reporting structural, resting-state, or exclusively connectivity MRI analyses. Twenty-nine articles fulfilled our criteria (see Table 1). The reported studies varied substantially in terms of sample size (ranging from 12 to 245 participants) and fMRI paradigms used. The range of fMRI paradigms, from tasks assessing basic processing of salient/affective stimuli to more complex tasks indexing neural correlates of moral and economic decision-making, reflects attempts to understand the neural underpinnings of the unemotional, unempathetic, amoral, and impulsive behavior that characterizes psychopathy in both naturalistic and experimental settings.

Processing of emotional/salient stimuli

Emotional dysfunction is one of the hallmarks of psychopathy (Blair et al., 2005) and early fMRI studies have focused on whether individuals with psychopathy presented differential brain activity when processing affective content. One of the first fMRI studies on psychopathy was conducted by Kiehl and colleagues (Kiehl et al., 2001). Kiehl and colleagues compared criminal psychopaths ($N=8$) with criminal nonpsychopaths ($N=8$) and noncriminal controls ($N=8$) while performing a task where they had to recognize previously encountered affective (i.e., negatively valenced) or nonaffective words among a list. Compared to the other groups, criminal psychopaths presented significantly less differential activity between affective and neutral conditions in the amygdala/hippocampal formation, parahippocampal gyrus, ventral striatum, and anterior and posterior cingulate gyrus. Although the size of the psychopathic group was small ($N=8$), the sample was well characterized, all individuals in the psychopathic group had high PCL-R scores (above 28), and the groups were carefully matched. Two early studies by Muller and colleagues investigated neural responses to affective-laden

Table 1 fMRI studies in high-risk samples diagnosed with psychopathy checklist—revised (PCL-R).

Study	Sample	Tasks	Compared to controls, High PP presented:
Abe, Greene, and Kiehl (2018)	18 high (PCL-*R* > 30), 17 mid (21 < PCL-*R* > 29), and 32 low PP (PCL-*R* < 20) incarcerated males	Incentivized Prediction task (deception)	- Less ACC response during opportunity to lie to win money (vs. nonopportunity to lie); - ACC response mediated the association between PCL-R scores and faster reaction times during opportunity to lie to win trials.
Anderson, Maurer, Steele, and Kiehl (2018)	168 incarcerated males	Auditory Oddball task	- Less mPFC, dACC, anterior temporal cortex, TPJ, and PCC response to unexpected sounds (vs. an implicit baseline).
Anderson et al. (2017)	120 incarcerated males	Emotional/ attentional task	- F1 and F2 positively associated with insula and prefrontal response when classifying the valence of emotional stimuli (vs. of nonemotional stimuli); - F1 negatively associated with cuneus and occipital response when classifying a contextual aspect of emotional stimuli (vs. of nonemotional stimuli); - F2 positively associated with AMY, subgenual cingulate, and frontal regions response when classifying a contextual aspect of emotional stimuli (vs. of nonemotional stimuli).
Birbaumer et al. (2005)	10 offenders (PCL-*R* > 15); 10 controls	Emotional learning	- Less AMY, AI, ACC, and OFC response to conditioned stimulus (neutral faces paired with painful pressure).
Decety, Chen, Harenski, and Kiehl (2013)	37 high (PCL-R > 30); 44 mid (PCL-R: 21–29); 40 low PP (PCL-R < 20) offenders	Perspective taking/ Empathy for pain	- More AI, ACC, and IFG response to body parts in pain when instructed to imagine themselves in that situation; - Less AI, AMY, OFC, vmPFC response to body parts in pain when instructed to imagine other in that situation.
Decety, Skelly, and Kiehl (2013)	27 high (PCL-R > 30); 28 mid (PCL-R: 21–29); 25 low PP (PCL-R < 20) offenders	Empathy for pain	- Less vmPFC, lOFC, and periaqueductal gray response to body parts in pain; - More AI, dACC, DS, IFG, mPFC, pSTS, SMG response to body parts in pain; - Less IFG, midCC, pSTS, SMG, dACC, dmPFC response to pain facial expressions; - More AI, postcentral gyrus, IPL, and precentral gyrus response to pain facial expressions.

Continued

Table 1 Continued

Study	Sample	Tasks	Compared to controls, High PP presented:
Decety, Chen, Harenski, and Kiehl (2015)	38 high (PCL-R > 30), 67 mid (21 < PCL-*R* < 29) and 50 low PP (PCL-R < 20) incarcerated males	Emotional recognition task	- Less AI, dlPFC, and pSTS/TPJ response when inferring emotional states of agents of interpersonal harm/assistance (vs. low PCL-R scorers); - More AI, dlPFC, pSTS/TPJ, AMY, and ACC response when inferring emotional states of a victim of harm (vs. low PCL-R scorers).
Decety, Skelly, Yoder, and Kiehl (2014)	27 high (PCL-R > 30); 25 mid (PCL-R: 21–29); 28 low PP (PCL-R < 20) offenders	Passive viewing of dynamic facial expressions	- Less IFG, OFC, inferior occipital gyrus, fusiform gyrus, and STS response to emotional facial expressions; - More AI response to negative facial expressions.
Deeley et al. (2006)	10 high PP offenders (PCL-*R* > 25); 9 controls	Implicit facial emotion	- Less fusiform gyrus and extrastriate cortex response to emotional (i.e., happy and fearful) faces (vs. neutral faces).
Deming et al. (2018)	57 male inmates (8.4 < PCL-*R* > 27);	Personality trait judgment task	- F2 scores negatively associated with bilateral precuneus, right TPJ and right precentral gyrus response when performing self vs. other personality judgments.
Fede et al. (2016)	245 incarcerated men (PCL-R: 20.73 ± 6.81 [Mean ± SD])	Controversial vs. Uncontroversial moral stimuli	- Less response in ACC when processing wrong (vs. not wrong) uncontroversial words; - Less response in TPJ and DLPFC when processing controversial (vs. noncontroversial) words.
Geurts et al. (2016)	14 offenders (PCL-*R* > 26; 10 controls with high (> 146) and 10 with low PPI IA scores (< 146)	Monetary incentive delay task	- More VS response during reward expectation (vs. no-reward expectation) relative to low PPI IA controls.
Gregory et al. (2015)	12 offenders with ASPD and PP (PCL-R > 25), 20 offenders with ASPD and 18 healthy nonoffenders	Probabilistic response-reversal (decision-making)	- More PCC response during punished reversal error trials (vs. rewarded correct responses); - Less right STG and anterior MTG response during rewarded correct trials.
Harenski, Harenski, Shane, and Kiehl (2010)	16 high (PCL-R > 30); 16 low PP (PCL-*R* < 18) offenders	Moral judgment of pictures	- Less vmPFC and anterior temporal cortex response to moral violations (vs. nonmoral); - Weaker association between AMY response and severity of moral violation ratings; - Stronger association between posterior temporal and severity of moral violation ratings.

Hosking et al. (2017)	45 incarcerated male offenders	Delay discounting task	- Increased subjective value related BOLD signal in ventral striatum.
Kiehl et al. (2001)	8 high (PCL-*R* > 28); 8 low PP offenders (PCL-*R* < 23); 8 controls	Affective recognition memory task	- Less AMY/hippocampal formation, parahippocampal gyrus, VS, ACC, and PCC response to affective—i.e., negative—words (vs. neutral words); - More bilateral fronto-temporal cortex response to affective words.
Meffert, Gazzola, Den Boer, Bartels, & Keysers, 2013	18 high PP offenders (PCL-R > 28); 26 controls	Empathy for pain	- Less AI, IFG, dACC, and AMY response during the observation of clips depicting emotional hand interactions; - Group differences reduced when individuals were instructed to "empathize."
Mier et al. (2014)	11 high PP offenders (PCL-R > 25); 18 controls	Facial emotion recognition and ToM task	- Less fusiform gyrus response during face processing; - Less STS, IFG, and AMY response to increasing demands of the task (gender < emotion recognition < ToM).
Müller et al. (2003)	6 high PP offenders (PCL-R > 30); 6 controls	Mood induction	- More fusiform, temporal, precentral, cerebellum, and IFG response to positive pictures; - Less occipital, MFG, and MTG response to positive pictures; - More occipital, MTG, STG, IFG and MFG, ACC, and AMY response to negative pictures; - Less ACC, MTG, fusiform, and parahippocampal gyrus response to negative pictures.
Müller, Sommer, Phil, and Weber (2008)	10 high PP offenders (PCL-R > 28); 12 controls	Attentional paradigm after mood induction	- Significant Task x Emotion interaction in right insula (controls presented a significant Task x Emotion interaction in MFG, IFG, SMG, and precuneus).
Prehn et al. (2013)	11 high PP (PCL-*R* > 23); 12 borderline and antisocial offenders; 13 controls	Economic decision-making	- Less ACC and left precentral gyrus response to high uncertainty trials; - Less IFG response when making low-risk options during high uncertainty; - More IFG response when making high-risk options during high uncertainty.
Pujara, Motzkin, Newman, Kiehl, and Koenigs (2013)	18 high (PCL-R > 30); 23 low PP (PCL-R < 20) offenders	Passive monetary reward	- Positive association between VS response to reward and PCL-R scores in high PP group.
Pujol et al. (2012)	22 high PP offenders (PCL-*R* > 20); 22 controls	Moral dilemmas	- Less mPFC, PCC, and HIPP response to highly emotional moral dilemmas.
Rodman et al. (2016)	49 incarcerated males	Modified Erikson flanker test	- More left OFC, left dlPFC, anterior MPFC, and left TPJ interference suppression-related activity (i.e., Incongruent > Congruent trials); - More left TPJ and left dlPFC inhibition-related activity (NO-Go vs Congruent trials).

Continued

Table 1 Continued

Study	Sample	Tasks	Compared to controls, High PP presented:
Schultz, Balderston, Baskin-Sommers, Larson, and Helmstetter (2016)	19 high (PCL-R > 30); 31 low PP (PCL-R < 20) offenders	Fear learning	- More left AMY, right FG, left parahippocampal gyrus, and right MFG response to the conditioned stimulus (vs. unpaired fractal images) during acquisition.
Schneider et al. (2000)	12 high PP offenders (PCL-*R* > 24); 12 controls	Emotional learning	- Less AMY response to unconditioned stimulus (unpleasant odor); - More AMY and dlPFC response to conditioned stimuli (neutral faces paired with UC).
Shane and Groat (2018)	23 low (PCL-R ≤ 20), 29 mid (21 < PCL-R < 29) and 15 high (PCL-*R* ≥ 30) PCL-R scores	Emotional/ attentional task	- Less bilateral ventromedial/ventrolateral, left AC and left OC response (vs. low and mid groups) when passively watching negative images; - No group differences when individuals were instructed to up-regulate their emotional response toward negative stimuli.
Sommer et al. (2010)	14 high (PCL-R > 28); 14 low PP (PCL-*R* < 15) offenders	ToM/Emotion attribution	- More OFC, MFG, and left TPJ response during emotion attribution.
Yoder, Harenski, Kiehl, and Decety (2015)	28 high (PCL-R ≥ 30) and 32 low (PCL-R < 20) PP incarcerated males.	Implicit and explicit moral evaluation	- Less DLPFC and the right caudate responses when processing morally bad (vs. good) scenes implicitly (i.e., evaluating if the scenes occurred indoors); - More left insula, right temporal pole, and subgenual ACC responses when processing morally bad (vs. good) scenes implicitly; - Less amygdala/hippocampal gyri, dorsal ACC, and supramarginal gyrus response when processing morally bad (vs. good) scenes explicitly (i.e., evaluating whether the scene was morally wrong); - More left putamen and right thalamus responses when processing morally bad (vs. good) scenes explicitly.

Notes: ACC, anterior cingulate cortex; *AC*, angular cortex; *AI*, anterior insula; *AMY*, amygdala; *dACC*, dorsal anterior cingulate cortex; *dlPFC*, dorsolateral prefrontal cortex; *dmPFC*, dorsomedial prefrontal cortex; *DS*, dorsal striatum; *F1*, Factor 1; *F2*, Factor 2; *FG*, fusiform gyrus; *IA*, impulsive/antisocial; *HIPP*, hippocampus; *IFG*, inferior frontal cortex; *IPL*, inferior parietal lobe; *LA*, lifestyle-antisocial; *lOFC*, lateral orbitofrontal cortex; *MFG*, middle frontal gyrus; *midCC*, midcingulate cortex; *mPFC*, medial prefrontal cortex; *mOFC*, medial orbitofrontal cortex; *MTG*, middle temporal gyrus; *NAc*, nucleus accumbens; *PP*, psychopathy; *OFC*, orbitofrontal cortex; *OC*, occipital cortex; *PCC*, posterior cingulate cortex; *pSTS*, posterior superior temporal sulcus; *SMG*, supramarginal gyrus; *STG*, superior temporal gyrus; *STS*, superior temporal sulcus; *TPJ*, temporoparietal junction; *vmPFC*, ventromedial prefrontal cortex; *VS*, ventral striatum.

pictures in criminal psychopaths. In the first study, criminal psychopaths ($N=6$) and a group of controls ($N=6$) were scanned while observing positive, negative, or neutral photos from the IAPS (Müller et al., 2003); in the second study, criminal psychopaths ($N=10$) and controls ($N=12$) observed pictures from the IAPS and then did a simple attentional task (Müller et al., 2008). The authors report attenuated BOLD response in individuals with psychopathy (relative to healthy controls) in affective brain areas such as amygdala, hippocampal gyrus, and anterior cingulate cortex (ACC) after observing affective-laden pictures. Yet, reduced sample sizes (High PCL-R $N<10$) and ambiguity in the psychological processes in which the statistical analyses tap into make these findings difficult to interpret.

A prominent theory in psychopathy is that psychopathic individuals have difficulties in diverting (or modulating) attention away from task-relevant stimuli toward salient but task-irrelevant stimuli, and that these attentional deficits may explain the emotional processing impairments observed in psychopaths (e.g., Patterson & Newman, 1993). Based on this response modulation theory, Anderson et al. (2018) scanned incarcerated psychopaths ($N=168$) with varying levels of PCL-R scores (between 7 and 37.9) while doing an auditory oddball task. PCL-R Factor 1 scores were negatively associated with neural response in areas of the default mode and salience networks, such as the medial prefrontal cortex (MPFC), dorsal ACC, anterior temporal cortex, temporoparietal junction (TPJ), and posterior cingulate cortex (PCC), when hearing unexpected sounds (contrasted against an implicit baseline). In another study, Anderson and colleagues (Anderson et al., 2017) investigated implicit and explicit emotional processing among incarcerated individuals ($N=120$: PCL-R range between 3.2 and 36). Both Factor 1 and Factor 2 scores were positively associated with response in insula and prefrontal regions when processing emotional content explicitly (i.e., when instructed to classify the emotional valence of emotional vs. nonemotional stimuli). When processing emotional content implicitly (i.e., when instructed to classify a contextual aspect of emotional vs. nonemotional stimuli), PCL-R Factor 1 scores were negatively associated with responses in the cuneus and occipital regions, which the authors suggest resulted from diminished feedback from the amygdala, while Factor 2 scores were positively associated with response in amygdala, subgenual cingulate, and frontal regions. Interestingly, Factor 2 scores were also positively associated with amygdala response when processing nonemotional stimuli explicitly vs. implicitly, which might indicate amygdala *hyper*-responsivity regardless of emotional content. In a similar task, Shane and colleagues (Shane & Groat, 2018) also compared incarcerated individuals with relatively low PCL-R scores ($N=23$; PCL-$R\leq 20$), mid-range ($N=29$; $21<$PCL-$R<29$), and high ($N=15$; PCL-$R\geq 30$) when watching neutral and negative emotional images under implicit and explicit conditions. When passively watching negative images, individuals with high psychopathy revealed blunted neural responses in bilateral ventromedial/ventrolateral PFC, left angular and left occipital cortices comparatively with low/mid psychopathy groups. However, when instructed to up-regulate their emotional response toward the negative stimuli, all individuals showed similar neural responses, including increased activity in ACC/MPFC, orbitofrontal cortex (OFC), and insula. These studies are important in that they suggest that (1) attentional focus is critical for understanding the nature of the brain responses in psychopathic individuals, and (2) that attenuated affective neural responses often seen in psychopathic individuals may depend on the precise content of the instruction given. These considerations will be elaborated upon later with respect to emotion dysregulation in psychopathy.

In sum, these studies show that individuals with psychopathy have atypical brain response to emotional and salient stimuli. An extended set of cortical and subcortical brain regions has been implicated, with the most commonly reported functional atypicalities found in amygdala, ACC, and portions of the PFC. Interestingly, when inspecting Factor 1 and Factor 2 scores separately, atypical responses in these regions are sometimes found in opposing directions. Of particular note, affective-interpersonal traits are frequently linked to amygdala *hypo*-responsivity while impulsive lifestyle and antisocial characteristics, which are also present in individuals with antisocial personality disorder without psychopathy, have been linked to amygdala *hyper*-responsivity, suggesting distinct aspects of emotion dysregulation in psychopathy (Hoppenbrouwers, Neumann, Lewis, & Johansson, 2015). These findings also add to previous interpretations about the hypo-responsivity to negative stimuli in psychopaths by highlighting (1) the potential role of emotion-attention interactions in psychopaths' emotional disturbance and (2) suggesting that under specific contexts, individuals exhibiting high psychopathic traits might be capable of compensatory neural responses.

Emotional learning

Intact emotional processing is critical for emotional learning, a form of classic conditioning that results from the association of a neutral stimulus with an emotional unconditioned stimulus. Early fMRI studies thus have focused on whether individuals with psychopathy presented differential brain activity when learning emotional associations through classic conditioning. Schneider and colleagues (Schneider et al., 2000) used unpleasant olfactory stimulus and Birbaumer and collaborators (Birbaumer et al., 2005) painful pressure as unconditioned stimuli (US). The conditioned stimuli (CS) for both these studies were neutral faces. Schneider et al. (2000) reported that, contrary to healthy controls ($N=12$), individuals with psychopathy ($N=12$; $24 \leq \text{PCL-}R \leq 35$) showed decreased activity in amygdala in response to the US and increased amygdala and dorsolateral prefrontal cortex (DLPFC) activity in response to the CS during the acquisition phase. On the other hand, Birbaumer et al. (2005) reported no group differences in response to the US and decreased activity in amygdala, anterior insula, ACC, and OFC in the psychopathic group ($N=10$; $15 \leq \text{PCL-}R \leq 31$) (relative to healthy controls [$N=10$]) in response to the CS during the acquisition phase. More recently, Schulz and colleagues (Schultz et al., 2016) used electric shocks as the US and fractal images as CS. In comparison to incarcerated nonpsychopaths ($N=19$; $\text{PCL-}R \leq 20$), psychopaths ($N=31$; $\text{PCL-}R \geq 30$) showed greater response to the CS in left amygdala, left parahippocampal gyrus, and right middle frontal gyrus during acquisition. These studies show that the deficient conditioning typically observed in individuals with psychopathy seems to be accompanied by atypical response in cortical and subcortical regions, in particular in the amygdala (albeit in distinct directions). It should be noted though that two of these studies (Birbaumer et al., 2005; Schneider et al., 2000) had relatively small groups of individuals with psychopathy ($N < 12$), used rather different ranges for defining individuals with elevated levels of psychopathic traits and, finally, Schulz and colleagues did not include a neurotypical group. Further research is necessary to clarify putative amygdala mediated deficits in emotional learning in individuals with psychopathy.

Empathy and related constructs

Callous, unempathic behavior is one of the central hallmarks of individuals with psychopathic personality. It has been proposed that the absence of a robust empathic response to other people's distress explains why these individuals have a propensity to harm others (Blair, 2013; Blair et al., 2005). Empathy comprises a number of dissociable components, subserved by distinct, but interacting, neural networks (e.g., Bird & Viding, 2014; Decety & Jackson, 2004). Two critical components are affective and cognitive empathy. The first encompasses the ability to vicariously experience other people's emotional experience while the later refers to the ability to comprehend other peoples' experience (e.g., Bird & Viding, 2014; Decety & Jackson, 2004). Bearing on this idea, a number of studies have inspected neural correlates of empathy-related processes in individuals with psychopathy. These studies have used different types of paradigms to probe these processes—from the simple observation of emotional facial expressions and of others' experiences of pain, to more complex paradigms where participants are asked to infer others' affective states.

Emotional facial expressions

Three studies to date have investigated neural responses to facial emotions in individuals with psychopathy. The first of these studies (Deeley et al., 2006) investigated emotional-facial processing implicitly by asking participants to name the gender of neutral and affective faces (i.e., happy and fearful expressions). The authors compared healthy controls ($N=9$) with individuals scoring high in psychopathy ($N=6$; High PCL-R range: 25–34). Compared to controls, the latter group presented reduced activity to emotional faces in fusiform gyrus and extrastriate cortex. The authors speculated that this could be a reflection of a deficient feedback modulation from the amygdala to these regions (Vuilleumier, Richardson, Armony, Driver, & Dolan, 2004).

More recently, Decety et al. (2014) scanned a large group of inmates ($N=80$) with varying levels of PCL-R scores while observing dynamic facial expressions of fear, sadness, happiness, and pain. Compared to those with low ($N=28$; PCL-$R \leq 20$) and medium ($N=25$; $21 <$ PCL-$R < 29$) PCL scores, inmates scoring high in psychopathy ($N=27$; PCL-$R \geq 30$) presented reduced activity in the fusiform gyrus, inferior frontal gyrus (IFG), and OFC, when passively viewing the faces (contrasted against scrambled baseline). Interestingly, high psychopathy inmates showed the highest response in anterior insula to negative expressions. This was unexpected considering the putative involvement of this region in affective processing (Craig, 2009; Critchley & Harrison, 2013; Critchley, Wiens, Rotshtein, Öhman, & Dolan, 2004).

Using a more complex facial processing task, Mier et al. (2014) compared a group of 11 incarcerated males with psychopathy (PCL-R range: 25–29) to a group of 18 controls from the general population. Participants had to either recognize the gender of neutral faces (neutral condition), the emotion portrayed by emotional expressions (emotional recognition condition), or their intentions (Theory of Mind condition). The psychopathy group did not differ from the control group in their behavioral responses. However, the psychopathy group did not present an increase in BOLD response in the fusiform gyrus when processing faces nor in in STS, IFG, and amygdala with increasing demands of the task (i.e., BOLD response during theory of mind > emotion recognition > neutral) which corroborates previous findings from Deeley and cols (Deeley et al., 2006). These results suggest that, despite high psychopathy individuals being able to make accurate judgments about mental and emotional states, they show atypical underlying brain activity in affective processing areas.

Empathy for pain

Decety, Skelly, and Kiehl (2013) found that, when observing facial expressions of pain, male inmates with high levels of psychopathy ($N=27$; PCL-$R \geq 30$) (compared with inmates with low levels of psychopathy—$N=28$; PCL-$R \leq 20$) showed greater activity in anterior insula and reduced responses in IFG and dorsal ACC, regions that have been found to be robustly activated during the observation of others' experiences of pain (Fan, Duncan, de Greck, & Northoff, 2011; Lamm, Decety, & Singer, 2011). Similarly, these individuals presented increased activity in these regions when observing body parts in pain. In a follow-up study, Decety, Chen, et al. (2013) reported that changing the instruction given to participants changed the patterns of activation observed. When high psychopathy inmates (N=27; PCL-R≥30) (vs. low psychopathy inmates [$N=40$; PCL-R≤20]) were told to imagine themselves in the pictures, they presented enhanced responses in anterior insula, dorsal ACC, and IFG; but, when told to imagine others in the same scenarios, weaker responses and connectivity were observed in OFC, amygdala, and anterior insula. Additionally, there was a negative association between Factor 1 scores and response in anterior insula and amygdala. In the same line, Meffert et al. (2013) studied the patterns of brain activation in response to video interactions depicting hands being caressed or hit by another hand, for example. Similarly to Decety, Chen, et al. (2013), the authors found that, relative to nonoffenders ($N=26$), male offenders with psychopathy ($N=20$; PCL-$R \geq 26$) presented reduced response in affective processing brain regions (i.e., anterior insula, IFG, dorsal ACC, and amygdala). Plus, they found that these reduced responses were attenuated when the individuals were instructed to "empathize" with the video characters. Although this suggests that top-down instruction can modulate neural responses to affective stimuli in individuals with psychopathy, it is still unclear whether their experience of empathy is itself altered.

Cognitive empathy/theory of mind

Sommer et al. (2010) investigated how the brains of low (PCL-$R < 15$, $N=14$) and high (PCL-$R > 28$, $N=14$) psychopathy criminal patients responded during a task in which they were asked to attribute an emotional state to the main character of a story. Although the difference between groups was not statistically significant, while the low psychopathy group showed augmented response in STS, supramarginal gyrus and frontal gyrus, the high psychopathy group did not. Psychopathic criminals rather presented higher activation in the OFC, MPFC, and left TPJ. Interestingly, despite evidencing distinct patterns of brain activations, the groups showed similar behavioral responses to the task (as also found in Mier et al., 2014). The authors interpreted these findings as evidence that individuals with psychopathy engage different computational strategies to infer the mental states of others; the engagement of OFC and TPJ, brain regions typically involved in mentalizing (Amodio & Frith, 2006), reflecting an enhanced effort to infer the mental states of others in order to compensate for an inability to automatically simulate these states.

Decety et al. (2015) examined the attribution of affective states in clips depicting interpersonal harm or assistance in criminal male offenders with high ($N=38$, PCL-$R>30$), mid ($N=67$, $21<$PCL-$R<29$), and low ($N=50$, PCL-$R<20$) psychopathy. High PCL-R scorers were more accurate at identifying the emotional state of the recipients of both harm and helpful actions but were less accurate to identify the emotions of the agents of such actions. Compared to low PCL-R scorers, high PCL-R individuals presented increased activity in a network of regions typically involved in both affective and cognitive empathy—including pSTS/TPJ, amygdala, and ACC—when inferring emotional states of agents and recipients of both helpful and harmful actions (contrasted with the viewing phase). However, when the authors inspected inference of the emotional states of agents and victims separately, distinct patterns of differential response were observed. Compared to low PCL-R group, when inferring emotional states of agents high PCL-R scorers presented lower activation in anterior insula, DLPFC, and pSTS/TPJ; when inferring emotional states of a victim of harm, they showed increased response in these regions as well as in the amygdala and ACC. These results are difficult to interpret and it is possible that this differential pattern of atypical brain responses might not be related to inference of emotional states (i.e., cognitive empathy) per se, but to other cognitive processes or affective content that were not equated across conditions. Finally, Deming et al. (2018) examined male inmates ($N=57$; PCL-R range: 8.4–37) during personality trait judgments about oneself and a familiar subject. The authors found reduced self vs. other responses in bilateral precuneus, right TPJ, and right precentral gyrus in individuals with high PCL-R Factor 2 scores but no other significant associations with other PCL-R scores (Factor 1 or distinct facets).

Existing evidence thus suggests atypical engagement of amygdala, anterior insula, ACC, and temporoparietal junction, brain areas typically associated with emotional salience, emotional resonance, and emotional understanding, in individuals with high levels of psychopathic traits during emotional recognition, empathic processing, and when inferring others' emotional states. Plus, they further add to the notion that the two PCL-R factors present distinct neurocognitive correlates and, more tentatively, to the notion that individuals with high Factor 1 scores do not necessarily display difficulties in inferring others' internal states when these do not include affective content.

Moral processing

Behavioral evidence suggests that psychopaths might be able to correctly distinguish between morally wrong and correct situations but they show abnormal emotional processing while doing it (Cima, Tonnaer, & Hauser, 2010; Raine & Yang, 2006). Four studies have now inspected moral judgment in psychopathy and, more recently, one has inspected moral behavior.

Glenn, Raine, and Schug (2009) investigated the associations between psychopathy and moral judgment by assessing 17 individuals from the community (PCL-R scores range: 7.4–32). Participants viewed a set of classical moral dilemmas that included both nonmoral situations (e.g., taking the bus) and dilemmas with varying emotional intensity (e.g., killing a baby, keeping someone else's money). Individuals scoring high in psychopathy showed reduced response in amygdala, posterior cingulate, angular gyrus, and MPFC when assessing extreme vs. less extreme moral dilemmas. Moreover, the higher the psychopathy scores (and all its facets), the lower the activity in the amygdala. Response in the remaining regions was negatively correlated with the interpersonal factor only. Conversely, higher response in the dorsolateral PFC (when contrasting more vs. less extreme dilemmas) was found in individuals scoring high in the antisocial and lifestyle facets. Besides, Glenn et al. (2009) found no association between psychopathy and behavioral answers to the dilemmas. Similar results were found in a study by Pujol et al. (2012) in which the response to identical moral dilemmas was assessed in a sample of male inmates ($N=22$; PCL-$R>20$) and controls ($N=22$). This bulk of research on moral judgment suggests that psychopathy is associated with greater recruitment of brain regions implicated in cognitive control and less involvement of regions related to evaluative and affective processing during judgment of extreme moral situations.

Harenski et al. (2010) asked two groups of incarcerated men (high PCL-$R>30$, $N=16$; low PCL-$R<18$, $N=16$) to evaluate the presence of moral violations in different scenarios and to rate its severity. The scenarios could be neutral scenes (i.e., with no moral content or emotional arousal), moral transgressions, or emotional arousing situations without moral content. The authors found no group differences in behavioral responses. However, observing moral scenes (as opposed to neutral or nonmoral but emotional stimuli) elicited reduced response in anterior temporal cortex and ventromedial PFC in inmates with high psychopathic traits comparatively to those with low traits. Similarly, Decety et al. (2015) found that PCL-R Factor 1 scores were associated with reduced activity in the right superior temporal sulcus (STS)/TPJ and in the dorsomedial PFC while subjects viewed morally laden situations. In addition, Harenski et al. (2010) found that, contrary to incarcerated controls, psychopathic individuals did not show a positive modulation of the severity of moral content in the amygdala. That is, in psychopathic individuals, amygdala response to moral transgressions did not vary as a function of its perceived moral wrongness, while posterior temporal cortex response decreased as a function of moral ratings.

Yoder et al. (2015) tested implicit and explicit moral evaluation in a sample of high ($N=28$; PCL-$R\geq 30$) and low ($N=32$; PCL-$R<20$) psychopathy incarcerated males. Individuals were presented with visual scenes that depicted interpersonal harm (i.e., morally bad) or assistance (i.e., morally good). Participants were first asked about a physical aspect of the task (i.e., implicit task) and later about the wrongness of the action (i.e., explicit task). Thus the explicit task required individuals to actively rely on moral relevant cues to answer the tasks' question. When contrasting the responses to morally bad vs. good scenes during the implicit task, the authors found high PCL-R individuals to show reduced responses in DLPFC and the right caudate but increased responses in left insula, right temporal pole, and subgenual ACC. During the explicit task, high psychopathic traits were associated with blunted responses in amygdala/hippocampal gyri, dorsal ACC, and supramarginal gyrus, and increased responses in the left putamen and right thalamus. These findings provide new evidence on the neural abnormalities associated with psychopathic traits that occur during moral evaluations depending on attentional demands. Fede et al. (2016) extended these findings and investigated how incarcerated men ($N=245$; PCL-R: Mean = 20.73 ± 6.81) process negative (e.g., stealing) but also positive (e.g., charity) and controversial (e.g., euthanasia) moral stimuli. Participants were asked to rate each stimulus as wrong or not wrong. PCL-R scores were negatively associated with response in ACC when processing wrong (vs. not wrong) uncontroversial stimuli (i.e., both positive and negative). When contrasting "wrong" > "not wrong" conditions, the authors found that individuals scoring high in PCL-R showed reduced response in the ACC. Additionally, PCL-R scores were negatively associated with response in TPJ and DLPFC.

Recently, Abe et al. (2018) used an interesting design to investigate neural correlates of dishonest behavior in incarcerated males with high ($N=18$; PCL-$R>30$), mid ($N=17$; $21<$PCL-$R>29$), and low (control group, $N=32$; PCL-$R<20$) psychopathy. The authors used an incentivized prediction task where participants had the opportunity to gain money dishonestly by lying about the accuracy of their predictions. PCL-R total score, Factor 1 and 2 were negatively associated activity in the left ACC in trials where they had the opportunity to behave dishonestly (compared with trials without such opportunity). There were no significant differences between individuals in self-reported accuracy (i.e., those with high psychopathy did not seem to have behaved more dishonestly) or reaction times, which could have been explained by the lack of a healthy control group. However, activity in the ACC mediated the association between PCL-R scores and faster reaction times during trials with the opportunity for dishonest behavior.

Overall, these results seem to suggest: (1) less involvement of regions typically involved in affective processing ; (2) moral judgment ability may be spared in individuals with psychopathy but that they may use different strategies, and engage different brain regions, to compute their judgments; (3) alterations in neural processing of moral stimuli related to psychopathic traits might not be circumscribed to negative stimuli but might also extend to positive and controversial moral content; and (4) lower levels of decision conflict might underlie dishonest behavior when faced with the opportunity to achieve personal gains.

Punishment, reward, and decision-making

Prehn et al. (2013) tested decision-making with a task involving low- and high-risk economic choices, in which high-risk decisions could have different levels of uncertainty. They compared three groups of individuals: high psychopathy offenders ($N=11$; $23<$PCL-$R<29$), offenders with antisocial and borderline personality disorder ($N=12$), and a group of healthy controls ($N=13$). There were no behavioral differences between the groups in risk-seeking behavior; all groups were equally likely to opt for low-risk options under high uncertainty. However, subjects with high levels of psychopathy presented attenuated responses in rostral ACC in trials with high uncertainty. Plus, during high uncertainty trials, they showed reduced response in IFG before choosing the low-risk option and increased response before choosing the high-risk option. This pattern of results suggests atypical neural processing during financial decision-making for those with high levels of psychopathy. This pattern of atypical responses was interpreted by the authors as reflecting diminished ability to emotionally represent uncertainty (thought to be underpinned by the rostral ACC), as well as atypical emotional and behavioral regulation (thought to be underpinned by the IFG).

Gregory et al. (2015) used a reversal learning task, a task that involves the capacity to learn and change stimulus-response associations (i.e., images associated with gain/loss of points) depending on reward and punishment contingencies, in a sample of offenders with antisocial personality disorder (ASPD) and psychopathy ($N=12$; PCL-$R>25$), offenders with ASPD but not psychopathy ($N=20$; $10\leq$PCL-$R\leq24$), and healthy nonoffenders ($N=18$; PCL-$R\leq8$). Compared with other offenders and healthy controls, those with ASPD and psychopathy presented increased response to punishment in PCC and anterior insula and reduced responses to reward in right superior temporal gyrus and anterior middle temporal gyrus. Pujara et al. (2013) administered a passive monetary reward and loss task to male inmates with low and high levels of psychopathy (low: $N=23$, PCL-$R<20$; high: $N=18$, PCL-$R>32$). Although the authors did not observe any group differences in neural response to reward in the ventral striatum, a region considered to be crucial in the brain reward circuitry, they did observe a significant positive association between levels of psychopathy and neural response in this region in the high psychopathy group. Geurts et al. (2016) examined reward-related neural activity during a monetary incentive delay task in psychopathic criminals ($N=14$; PCL-$R>30$) and two groups of noncriminals with either high ($N=10$) or low ($N=10$) impulsive/antisocial traits (measured with the Psychopathic Personality Inventory; PPI[a]; Lilienfeld & Andrews, 1996). Participants had to respond as quickly as possibly to a target that appeared after a cue signaling a reward/no-reward trial. Psychopathic criminals showed increased reward-related signal in the ventral striatum relatively to low impulsive/antisocial traits noncriminals. Interestingly, reward-related activity was similar across groups with high impulsive/

[a] The PPI contains eight subscales thought to measure psychopathic features. The PPI is often described in terms of a model with 2 higher-order factors, one indexing "Fearless dominance" (consisting of the social potency, stress immunity, and fearlessness scales), the other indexing "Impulsive antisociality" (consisting of the carefree nonplanfulness, blame externalization, machiavellian egocentricity, and impulsive nonconformity scales), along with a remaining subscale, coldheartedness, which does not load on any factor (Benning, Patrick, Hicks, Blonigen, & Krueger, 2003). The PPI was not originally designed to mirror the traditional two-factor structure of the PCL-R in the general population and, although the PPI does share some variance with the features measured by the PCL-R, its factors do not neatly map onto the PCL-R factors (Malterer, Lilienfeld, Neumann, & Newman, 2010).

antisocial traits (criminals and noncriminals), supporting the notion of a link between aberrant striatal function and impulsivity. Hosking et al. (2017) also found a positive association between subjective-value related BOLD signal in ventral striatum and PCL-R total score during choice in a task that involved choosing between larger-but-later and smaller-but-sooner monetary rewards in male incarcerated offenders with varying levels of psychopathy ($N=45$; $8 \leq \text{PCL-}R \leq 35$).

Altogether, these findings point to increased striatum and cingulate cortex responses to reward in individuals with psychopathy and tentatively suggest that this altered response might be linked to variance in impulsive-lifestyle and antisocial traits. It is possible that altered activity might underlie the suboptimal choice options performed during decisions involving cost-benefits that are frequently observed in individuals with high levels of psychopathy but also in individuals with high levels of antisocial behavior in general.

Executive functioning/inhibitory control

Studies have been consistent in reporting disturbances in executive function among individuals with antisocial behavior (Dolan, 2012; Dolan & Park, 2002; Morgan & Lilienfeld, 2000). At the same time, recent research suggests that the PCL-R factors may have differential associations with executive functioning. In particular, Baskin-Sommers et al. (2015) found in a large sample ($N=377$) of male offenders (PCL-R range 3–36) that the interpersonal factor positively and the affective factor negatively predicted executive functioning. Psychopathy and externalizing features of antisocial behavior seem to be related to distinct alterations in executive function. Rodman et al. (2016) attempted to clarify this issue by investigating 49 incarcerated males (PCL-R scores were not reported), using a modified Erikson flanker test task—a Go-No-go task—that allowed selective evaluation of interference suppression and response inhibition. At the neural level, the authors reported enhanced interference suppression-related activity in several regions (i.e., OFC, DLPFC, MPFC, and TPJ) to be associated with higher PCL-R scores. Higher psychopathy scores were also positively associated with inhibition-related BOLD signal within the TPJ and DLPFC. On the contrary, lower DLPFC inhibition-related activity was associated with higher externalizing scores. Thus while individuals scoring high in psychopathy presented greater recruitment of fronto-parietal areas during response inhibition, high externalizing individuals show blunted response in similar areas. These findings add further evidence of a neurobiological dissociation between psychopathy and externalizing behavior and contribute to clarify inhibitory control alterations in antisocial individuals. At the same time, the findings from Baskin-Sommers et al. (2015) suggest there may be differential links between specific psychopathic domains and executive functioning, which corresponds to some of the findings of fMRI studies highlighting increased prefrontal engagement and decreased limbic system activation for certain tasks.

Summary

In sum, studies on high-risk offender samples diagnosed with the PCL-R have reported atypical function in an extensive set of brain regions—from cortical prefrontal and temporal regions to subcortical regions such as the amygdala and ventral striatum—in response to a wide range of tasks probing different cognitive processes (from tasks involving simple viewing of emotional stimuli to tasks requiring complex moral judgment and economic decision-making). Although the direction of the findings is not unequivocally consistent across studies, overall they point to: (1) reduced response in regions typically associated with affective processing, such as amygdala, insula, and OFC during processing of emotional content, irrespective of type of task, which might explain psychopaths' unemotional and uncaring profile; (2) increased activity in prefrontal regions in tasks involving decisions, which might reflect the use of different cognitive strategies to compensate for lack of affective input important for such decisions; and (3) increased striatum response to reward, which might be related to high levels of impulsivity characteristic of the disorder.

It should be noted though, that some of these studies have only included a comparison group of individuals with antisocial behavior with low levels of psychopathy while others have only included a group of healthy controls. The lack of a healthy adult comparison group precludes the establishment of a neurotypical baseline making it difficult to know whether a significant group difference equates departure from healthy functioning and for which group. On the other hand, the lack of a control group of individuals with high levels of antisocial behavior but low levels of psychopathy makes it difficult to disambiguate whether the differential activations found between groups are driven by high levels of psychopathy per se or are due to other characteristics present in individuals with extreme antisocial behavior. Finally, equivalent paradigms have not been replicated across different laboratories, which hinder the assessment of the robustness and consistency of the findings.

Neuroimaging studies with community samples

Recent evidence indicates that the structure of psychopathic personality is dimensional rather than categorical; psychopathic traits are continuously distributed in the general population (Neumann & Hare, 2008), and individuals with a diagnosis of psychopathy represent an extreme end of that distribution (see Hare & Neumann, 2008 for a review). This dimensional perspective of psychopathy has led to a growing interest in the correlates of psychopathic traits in the general population (e.g., Carré, Hyde, Neumann, Viding, & Hariri, 2013; Lilienfeld, Fowler, & Patrick, 2006). Not surprisingly, extant findings from behavioral studies with community samples mostly mirror those from forensic samples, pointing to the existence of continuities in the mechanisms underlying psychopathic traits in community and forensic samples. Akin to forensic samples, higher levels of psychopathic traits in the general population have been found to be associated with reduced startle potentiation (Benning, Patrick, & Iacono, 2005; Justus & Finn, 2007) and autonomic responses to aversive images (Benning et al., 2005; Osumi, Shimazaki, Imai, Sugiura, & Ohira, 2007), blunted affective responses to others' emotions (Ali, Amorim, & Chamorro-Premuzic, 2009; Seara-Cardoso, Dolberg, Neumann, Roiser, & Viding, 2013; Seara-Cardoso, Neumann, Roiser, McCrory, & Viding, 2012), atypical responses during moral processing (Cima et al., 2010; Seara-Cardoso et al.,

2013, 2012), and poor decision-making during gambling tasks (Mahmut, Homewood, & Stevenson, 2008).

Our PubMed and Scopus search brought up 18 fMRI studies that included participants from the general population assessed with a self-report measure of psychopathic traits. Search terms were ("functional magnetic resonance" or "MR" or "MRI" or "fMRI" or "neuroimaging") and ("psychopathy" or "psychopathic traits"). Exclusion criteria were (1) studies which did not include assessment with psychopathy measures; (2) studies of children and youth; (3) studies with psychiatric populations; (4) studies reporting structural, resting-state, or exclusively connectivity MRI analyses. Similar to studies of clinical/forensic samples, studies with community samples also varied in their sample size (ranging from 10 to 232) as well as the paradigms used. In this review we concentrate on describing those studies ($N=12$) that used paradigms that can be reasonably compared with paradigms used in the clinical/forensic/offender samples (see Table 2).

Empathy and related constructs

Emotional facial expressions

Gordon et al. (2004) were the first to investigate the neural correlates of psychopathic traits in a community sample. The authors assessed twenty male college students while performing a facial recognition task. Gordon et al. (2004) used the PPI (Lilienfeld & Andrews, 1996) to measure psychopathic traits. Inside the scanner, participants were asked to identify pictures that either depicted a previously seen person—identity condition—or the emotional expression—emotional condition. When performing the emotion condition (contrasted against rest), the group with high levels of fearless dominance (defined by a median split of participants' scores) presented significantly less activation in amygdala, IFG, and MPFC than the group with low levels of psychopathic traits. Gordon et al. (2004) also found that, when dividing groups on basis of scores of the second factor of the PPI, "Impulsive antisociality," the group with high scores presented increased amygdala response during emotional recognition in comparison to the low group.

Using a different psychopathy measure, the Self-Report Psychopathy questionnaire (SRP; Paulhus, Neumann, & Hare, 2015),[b] and a robust sample of 200 healthy individuals, Carré et al. (2013) found that individuals scoring higher in interpersonal traits presented weaker amygdala responses to fearful facial expressions. Further in line with the findings of Gordon et al. (2004), Carré et al. (2013) also found that lifestyle traits of psychopathy were associated with increased amygdala response to angry faces. Interestingly, using the same task as Carré et al. (2013) in a sample of 103 participants (53 females), and deriving PCL-R and antisocial personality scores

[b] The SRP, developed by Hare and colleagues as an extension of PCL-R to measure psychopathic traits in the general population, mirrors the latent structure of the PCL-R (Paulhus et al., 2015). Like the PCL-R, the SRP assesses four facets of psychopathic traits—interpersonal, affective, lifestyle, and antisocial—which can also be modeled in terms of the traditional two-factor dimensions.

Table 2 fMRI studies in community samples.

Study	Sample/instrument	Tasks	Higher PP scores were associated with:
Bjork, Chen, and Hommer (2012)	$N=31$; PPI	Factorial reward anticipation	- More VS and ACC response during the instrumental (i.e., an active motor response for trial success) anticipation of rewards (vs. no rewards); - More mFC response during the passive anticipation of rewards (vs. no rewards).
Buckholtz et al. (2010)	$N=24$; PPI-R	Monetary incentive delay	- Impulsive-antisocial traits positively associated with VS (right NAc, specifically) response during the anticipation of monetary rewards (vs. no-rewards).
Carré et al. (2013)	$N=200$; SRP	Face-matching	- Interpersonal traits negatively associated with right dorsal AMY response to fearful faces; - Lifestyle traits scores positively associated with right dorsal AMY response to angry faces and negatively associated with left VS response to positive feedback.
Gordon, Baird, and End (2004)	$N=20$; PPI	Facial recognition	- Emotional-interpersonal factor scores negatively associated with AMY, IFG, and mPFC response when participants matched the emotion of facial expressions presented in subsequent pictures—emotion recognition (vs. rest); - Socially deviant factor scores positively associated with rAMY response during emotion recognition.
Glenn et al. (2009)	17 participants from community (PCL-R: 7.2–32)	Moral dilemmas	- Less left AMY response to highly emotional moral dilemmas (vs. impersonal—less emotional—moral dilemmas); - F1 scores negatively associated with mPFC, PCC, and angular gyrus response to emotional dilemmas; - F2 scores positively associated with dlPFC response to emotional dilemmas.
Harenski, Kim, and Hamann (2009)	$N=10$; $100 \leq PPI \leq 140$	Moral judgment of visual stimuli	- Less anterior mPFC response to moral pictures (vs. unpleasant pictures without moral content); - Coldheartedness scores negatively associated with left AMY response to moral pictures (vs. odd-even baseline task) and total PP scores were also negatively associated with mPFC response to the same contrast.

Hyde, Byrd, Votruba-drzal, Hariri, and Manuck (2014)	$N=103$; PCL-R	Face-matching	- Less AMY reactivity to angry faces (vs. shapes) (when accounting for Antisocial Personality Disorder scores).
Seara-Cardoso et al. (2015)	$N=30$; $31 \leq$ SRP-SF ≤ 109	Affective resonance task with facial expressions	- Less bilateral aINS response while subjectively evaluating the affective response to emotional faces (vs. baseline); - Affective-interpersonal traits and total PP scores negatively associated with rAMY response; - Lifestyle-antisocial traits negatively associated with aINS response;
Seara-Cardoso et al. (2015)	$N=46$; SRP-SF; Affective-interpersonal scores: 15–61; Lifestyle-antisocial scores: 15–47	Implicit pain processing	- Affective-interpersonal traits (when controlling for lifestyle-antisocial traits) negatively associated with aINS, midCC, and IFG responses when participants viewed painful pictures (vs. nonpainful); - Lifestyle-antisocial traits (when controlling for affective-interpersonal traits) positively associated with aINS, midCC, and IFG responses.
Seara-Cardoso et al. (2016)	$N=28$; $31 \leq$ SRP-SF ≤ 80	Everyday moral transgressions	- Interpersonal traits negatively associated with the modulation of guilt in response to everyday moral transgressions in aINS.
Sethi et al. (2018)	3 groups: primary (↑ SRP Factor 1 and ↓ anxiety; $N=50$), secondary (↑ SRP Factor 1 and ↑ anxiety; $N=100$) and comparison (scoring ↓ on both measures; $N=82$)	Face processing	- Less AMY and bilateral INS response to fearful faces (vs. shapes) in the primary group comparatively to the comparison group; - No differences between the secondary and comparison groups in the abovementioned regions in response to fearful faces (vs. shapes).
Vieira, Tavares, Marsh, and Mitchell (2017)	$N=23$; PPI-R = Coldheartedness range: 33–67	Interpersonal distance task with emotional and neutral faces	- Coldheartedness scores negatively associated with AMY response to approaching sad faces.

Notes: ACC, anterior cingulate cortex; *AC*, angular cortex; *aINS*, anterior insula; *AMY*, amygdala; *dACC*, dorsal anterior cingulate cortex; *CC*, cingulate cortex; *dlPFC*, dorsolateral prefrontal cortex; *dmPFC*, dorsomedial prefrontal cortex; *DS*, dorsal striatum; *F1*, Factor 1; *F2*, Factor 2; *FD*, fearless dominance; *FG*, fusiform gyrus; *IFC*, inferior frontal cortex; *IPL*, inferior parietal lobe; *lOFC*, lateral orbitofrontal cortex; *MFG*, middle frontal gyrus; *midCC*, midcingulate cortex; *mFC*, mesial frontal cortex; *mPFC*, medial prefrontal cortex; *mOFC*, medial orbitofrontal cortex; *MTG*, middle temporal gyrus; *NAc*, nucleus accumbens; *PP*, psychopathy; *OFC*, orbitofrontal cortex; *OC*, occipital cortex; *PCC*, posterior cingulate cortex; *pSTS*, posterior superior temporal sulcus; *SMG*, supramarginal gyrus; *STG*, superior temporal gyrus; *STS*, superior temporal sulcus; *TPJ*, temporo-parietal junction; *vmPFC*, ventromedial prefrontal cortex; *VS*, ventral striatum; ↑, high; ↓, low.

from a measure of general personality,[c] Hyde et al. (2014) found a suppressor effect on amygdala reactivity to angry faces. That is, psychopathy scores presented a negative association with amygdala reactivity to angry faces, but only accounting for the shared variance with antisociality. Sethi et al. (2018) compared three groups of community volunteers according to their levels of psychopathy (as measured by a short form of the SRP, the SRP-SF (Paulhus et al., 2015)) and anxiety: (1) primary psychopathy (i.e., high SRP Factor 1 and low anxiety scores; $N=50$), (2) secondary psychopathy (i.e., high SRP Factor 1 and high anxiety scores; $N=100$), and (3) comparison (i.e., scoring low on both measures; $N=82$) groups. Similar to previous studies, the primary group exhibited a blunted response to fearful faces in amygdala and bilateral insula whereas the secondary psychopathy group did not.

To date, only one study has tried to probe subjective emotional responses to emotional faces. Seara-Cardoso et al. (2015) scanned male participants ($N=30$) while they performed an affective resonance task where, instead of observing or recognizing emotional expressions, participants were asked to rate their own affective responses to emotional facial expressions. The authors found that neural responses in amygdala and anterior insula varied as a function of the intensity of participants' affective ratings, strengthening the notion that these regions play important roles in the elicitation of an affective response to others' emotional displays. Critically, affective-interpersonal and lifestyle-antisocial psychopathic traits (as measured by the SRP-SF) were negatively correlated with neural response in both these regions. Finally, Vieira et al. (2017) scanned individuals with distinct levels of coldheartedness ($N=23$) while they were presented with angry, fearful, happy, sad, and neutral facial expressions that could either appear to move toward (i.e., increase in size/approach) or away (i.e., decrease in size/withdraw) from them. Higher scores of coldheartedness were associated with reduced amygdala response to approaching sad expressions.

Empathy for pain

To date, only one study inspected neural correlates of empathy for pain and their association with psychopathic traits in the general population. Seara-Cardoso et al. (2015) scanned 46 men from the community (psychopathic traits were measured with the SRP-SF) were shown pictures of hands and feet in painful/no-painful situations and were asked to indicate whether they were visualizing hands or feet. Interestingly, variation in response to painful (vs. nonpainful) images in regions typically involved in empathy for pain (i.e., anterior insula, midcingulate cortex, and IFG) presented distinct associations with the two dimensions of psychopathy. When holding lifestyle-antisocial traits constant, response in these regions was negatively associated with

[c] Lynam and colleagues (Miller, Lyman, Widiger, & Leukefeld, 2001; Miller & Lynam, 2003; Widiger & Lynam, 1998) have made substantial contributions to investigating psychopathy from the perspective of the Five-Factor Model of personality and propose that psychopathy can be understood as an extreme variant of common dimensions of personality. Factor 1 psychopathic traits map onto low agreeableness (e.g., low altruism, compliance, modesty) and low neuroticism (e.g., low anxiety, depression, vulnerability to stress), whereas Factor 2 psychopathic traits map onto low agreeableness, low conscientiousness (low dutifulness, self-discipline, deliberation), and high neuroticism (high angry hostility, impulsiveness).

high levels of affective-interpersonal traits. The opposite pattern of associations was found for the lifestyle-antisocial dimension when holding affective-interpersonal traits constant.

Moral processing

The first study inspecting moral processing and psychopathic traits in the general population was conducted by Harenski et al. (2009). Hresnki and colleagues scanned a small sample of 10 females while performing the same paradigm reported in the previous section in Harenski et al. (2010). The authors found that psychopathic traits, as measured by the PPI, were negatively associated with activity in MPFC when presented with moral stimuli (vs. unpleasant but nonmoral stimuli). Additionally, coldheartedness traits were negatively associated with amygdala response to moral stimuli (in comparison to a baseline task where participants had to judge if numbers were odd or even). These results are in line with the findings that the same authors report for their forensic sample. It should be noted, though, that the sample size might constitute a constraint to correlational statistics and that it is unclear whether the negative association found between coldheartedness and amygdala response relates to moral processing specifically, or whether it is driven by differences between stimuli type (social stimuli vs. numbers) or even by differences between the computational demands of the two tasks.

Seara-Cardoso et al. (2016) used a moral transgressions paradigm where participants ($N=28$) were asked to rate how guilty they would feel in scenarios depicting everyday harm-to-others. The authors found that response in anterior insula, an important region for interoception, varied as a function of anticipated guilt. This modulation of guilt in the anterior insula was negatively associated with levels of interpersonal traits (as measured by the SRP-SF). That is, for those with high levels of these traits, anterior insula response did not vary as a function of guilt. In a follow-up study, the authors used the same stimuli and asked participants ($N=28$) to judge the wrongness of the scenarios. No interaction, nor any other associations with psychopathic traits were found. This study contributes to disambiguate the functional underpinnings of the affective and judgment dimensions of atypical moral processing in those with high levels of psychopathic traits. It provides further evidence that psychopaths' (a)moral behavior appears to be driven by dysfunctional affective/motivational processes rather than by an incapacity to judge the correctness of a situation. Due to the nature of the task used (everyday scenarios), these results are difficult to directly compare with those from clinical/forensic samples. Nonetheless, they are in line with the hypothesis that atypical moral processing in individuals with high levels of psychopathic traits is circumscribed to affective and motivational components rather than to an inability to compute moral judgments per se (Buon, Seara-Cardoso, & Viding, 2016; Cima et al., 2010; Raine, Yang, Narr, & Toga, 2011).

Reward

To date, three studies have inspected the neural correlates of reward in relation to psychopathic traits in community samples (Bjork et al., 2012; Buckholtz et al., 2010;

Carré et al., 2013). Buckholtz et al. (2010) scanned 24 males during a monetary incentive delay task. Psychopathic traits (as measured by the PPI-R) were positively associated with activity in ventral striatum during monetary reward anticipation (contrasted to anticipation in no-reward trials). Interestingly, this association was specific to impulsive antisocial features of psychopathic traits. Bjork et al. (2012) reported similar findings. In a larger sample of 200 participants, Carré et al. (2013) also found that psychopathic traits, as measured by the SRP, presented a positive correlation with ventral striatum response during reward (positive feedback) in a card guessing game. Additionally, they found divergent associations between the unique variance of different facets of psychopathy and ventral striatum response to reward. More specifically, after removing shared variance with all other facets, lifestyle traits presented a negative association with ventral striatum response, while antisocial traits presented a positive association. This suggests that hyperreactivity to reward in ventral striatum may be specifically associated to antisocial traits and not to other characteristics of the psychopathic personality. It should be noted, however, that the Carré et al. (2013) used a block design paradigm. This prevents a direct comparison with previous studies since it rules out the possibility of assessing different phases of reward processing and, furthermore, the extent to which associations of psychopathic traits with ventral striatum response were related to the anticipation of receiving a reward or to indeed receiving a reward.

Summary

Extant findings from fMRI research with samples from the general population mostly mirror those observed in forensic/clinical samples and add support the notion that psychopathy is a dimensional construct. The bulk of fMRI research on the neural correlates of psychopathic traits in the general population suggests an overall negative association between variance in these traits and brain response in regions typically involved in affective processing, such as the amygdala and anterior insula. From research on the neural correlates of basic emotional recognition to research on more complex forms of social cognition, the evidence points to increasingly poorer responses in these regions to affective content as psychopathic traits increase, in particular when blunt affect and callous interpersonal characteristics increase. Moreover, research in samples from the community has been consistent in pointing to an association between increased striatum response to reward and levels of inmpulsive lifestyle and antisocial behavior, though less so in relation to affective and interpersonal characteristics.

It is relevant to mention that the literature brought up distinct, and sometimes opposing, findings relatively to the associations between the different facets of psychopathy and amygdala response to emotional stimuli. This is in line with the idea that the two dimensions of psychopathy may tap into somewhat separable constructs which may exert suppressor effects on each other (e.g., Hicks & Patrick, 2006; Uzieblo, Verschuere, Van den Bussche, & Crombez, 2009). Behavioral studies have shown that after partialling out the shared variance between the two dimensions, the affective-interpersonal dimension is negatively associated with emotion-related variables such as fearfulness, emotional reactivity, and empathic concern, while the lifestyle-antisocial dimension is positively associated with these variables (e.g., Hicks & Patrick, 2006;

Seara-Cardoso et al., 2012; Uzieblo et al., 2009). At the neural level, this pattern has also been reported in children with variable levels of callous-unemotional traits (akin to psychopathic traits in adults) in response to emotional stimuli in children with conduct problems (Lockwood et al., 2013; Lozier, Cardinale, VanMeter, & Marsh, 2014; Sebastian et al., 2012). This suggests that, although affective-interpersonal and lifestyle-antisocial features can co-occur, the unique aspects of each dimension (i.e., those not shared with the other dimension) may reflect distinct underlying biological vulnerabilities: one corresponding to low emotional reactivity and the other to increased emotional reactivity and a basic weakness in inhibitory control systems (Patrick, Hicks, Nichol, & Krueger, 2007). It should be noted though that suppressor effects have not been yet reported in adult forensic samples. Furthermore, although the use of partial correlations is a powerful and informative technique to identify associations between different variables, it also poses some difficulties in the interpretation of results (Lynam, Hoyle, & Newman, 2006). The most important one is the difficulty in knowing exactly what construct is left once the variance of another correlated construct is removed (Lynam et al., 2006). For variable-centred studies, the use of semi-partial as opposed to partial correlations may help address interpretation difficulties regarding the latter (The replication of these findings using a group comparison approach, with groups defined by high and low levels on the two dimensions, would provide important further validation of these results.

Conclusions

The existent data, stemming from the study of different populations with varying paradigms and measurement tools, reveal that response to emotional/salient stimuli in affect processing areas, such as amygdala and anterior insula, is blunted in individuals with high levels of psychopathy (but see exceptions: Decety, Chen, et al., 2013; Müller et al., 2003; Schneider et al., 2000). But care is needed when interpreting these findings since, in some cases, attenuated responses to emotional/salient stimuli may depend on the specificities of the experimental paradigm (e.g., the type of salient stimuli used and instructions given to participants). In contrast, response in regions such as the ventral striatum and dorsolateral PFC—which are known to be involved in reward processing and cognitive control—shows augmented activity when high psychopathy individuals have to process moral stimuli, make decisions, and respond to rewards.

Research also suggests that the two dimensions of psychopathy are associated with different patterns of atypical neural activity, and thus with distinct underlying biological vulnerabilities. For example, attenuated activity to emotional stimuli has been more commonly found to be associated with affective-interpersonal features of psychopathy, whereas exaggerated activity to reward appears to be mostly associated with lifestyle-antisocial features. At the same time, new findings are emerging which suggest it may be productive to also parse the traditional two psychopathy domains (Factor 1 & 2) in terms of the more nuanced four-factor model (Hare & Neumann, 2008), given that the four psychopathy domains are differentially associated with executive functioning (Baskin-Sommers et al., 2015) and the behavior activation/inhibition systems (Hoppenbrouwers et al., 2015). Moreover, the four-factor model provides an optimal basis for subtyping offenders based on PCL-R profile and these profiles have been linked to risk for violence (Krstic, Neumann, Roy, Robertson, & Hare, 2018). Such profiles may be productive to use in future fMRI research.

In addition to specific limitations approached in the previous sections, there are a number of limitations to the present research that need to be addressed in future studies. First, different laboratories have used different stimuli and paradigms with variable control conditions. This prevents a comprehensive evaluation of the contradictory findings in the field. In addition, many tasks have relied on multiple cognitive operations with contrast conditions that do not allow parsing apart specific processes. Future research should consider the need of carefully designed (and, ideally, more ecologically valid) tasks that isolate the distinct processes and components that comprise complex phenomena such as empathy, moral processing, and decision-making. Only with such tasks researchers are able to systematically identify and characterize the precise neurocognitive deficits associated with psychopathy. Second, many of the early studies presented here have been underpowered, a common problem in fMRI research due to its high costs. Underpowered studies are likely to produce unreliable findings; they have reduced chances of detecting true effects and are less likely to detect statistically significant results that reflect true effects (Button et al., 2013). Recent research has highlighted the benefit of using either large samples (e.g., Baskin-Sommers et al., 2015) or meta-analytic data (e.g., Poeppl et al., 2019) to model the links between neurobiology and psychopathic features.

Finally, it is reasonable to suggest that the scope of many neurobiological studies (e.g., fear recognition, moral processing) is influenced, at least in part, by the strong association that psychopathy has with violence (Neumann & Hare, 2008). This is understandable, but research on more basic processes that are empirically related to personality pathology in general may be profitable. For example, emerging research suggests that psychopathy might be associated with emotion dysregulation, not just deficient affect per se, in line with a wealth of research on other personality disorders (Garofalo et al., 2018; Garofalo & Neumann, 2018). Furthermore, new research has demonstrated that psychopathic individuals can modulate their affective experience (Shane & Groat, 2018). In sum, the field would benefit from collaborative efforts to precisely specify those cognitive-affective processes that should be investigated with regard to psychopathic personality and the best fMRI paradigms to do that, which ideally would be tested in reasonably sized samples (from clinical/forensic and community settings and with appropriate control groups), and replicated across different laboratories.

Acknowledgments

The preparation of this manuscript was supported by Portuguese Foundation for Science and Technology (FCT) grants awarded to ASC (PTDC/MHC-PCN/2296/2014; SFRH/BPD/94970/2013), at the Psychology Research Centre, University of Minho (UID/PSI/01662/2013), co-financed by FEDER through COMPETE2020 under the PT2020 Partnership Agreement (POCI-01-0145-FEDER-016747; POCI-01-0145-FEDER-007653).

References

Abe, N., Greene, J. D., & Kiehl, K. A. (2018). Reduced engagement of the anterior cingulate cortex in the dishonest decision-making of incarcerated psychopaths. *Social Cognitive and Affective Neuroscience*, *13*(8), 797–807. https://doi.org/10.1093/scan/nsy050.

Ali, F., Amorim, I. S., & Chamorro-Premuzic, T. (2009). Empathy deficits and trait emotional intelligence in psychopathy and Machiavellianism. *Personality and Individual Differences*, *47*(7), 758–762. https://doi.org/10.1016/j.paid.2009.06.016.

Amodio, D. M., & Frith, C. D. (2006). Meeting of minds: The medial frontal cortex and social cognition. *Nature Reviews Neuroscience*, *7*(4), 268–277. https://doi.org/10.1038/nrn1884.

Anderson, N. E., Steele, V. R., Maurer, J. M., Rao, V., Koenigs, M. R., Decety, J., … Kiehl, K. A. (2017). Differentiating emotional processing and attention in psychopathy with functional neuroimaging. *Cognitive, Affective, & Behavioral Neuroscience*, *17*(3), 491–515. https://doi.org/10.3758/s13415-016-0493-5.

Anderson, N. E., Maurer, J. M., Steele, V. R., & Kiehl, K. A. (2018). Psychopathic traits associated with abnormal hemodynamic activity in salience and default mode networks during auditory oddball task. *Cognitive, Affective, & Behavioral Neuroscience*, *18*(3), 564–580. https://doi.org/10.3758/s13415-018-0588-2.

Baskin-Sommers, A. R., Brazil, I. A., Ryan, J., Kohlenberg, N. J., Neumann, C. S., & Newman, J. P. (2015). Mapping the association of global executive functioning onto diverse measures of psychopathic traits. *Personality Disorders: Theory, Research, and Treatment*, *6*(4), 336–346. https://doi.org/10.1037/per0000125.

Benning, S., Patrick, C., Hicks, B., Blonigen, D., & Krueger, R. (2003). Factor structure of the Psychopathic Personality Inventory: Validity and implications for clinical assessment. *Psychological Assessment*, *15*, 340–350. https://doi.org/10.1037/1040-3590.15.3.340.

Benning, S. D., Patrick, C. J., & Iacono, W. G. (2005). Psychopathy, startle blink modulation, and electrodermal reactivity in twin men. *Psychophysiology*, *42*(6), 753–762. https://doi.org/10.1111/j.1469-8986.2005.00353.x.

Birbaumer, N., Veit, R., Lotze, M., Erb, M., Hermann, C., Grodd, W., & Flor, H. (2005). Deficient fear conditioning in psychopathy. *Archives of General Psychiatry*, *62*(7), 799. https://doi.org/10.1001/archpsyc.62.7.799.

Bird, G., & Viding, E. (2014). Neuroscience and biobehavioral reviews the self to other model of empathy: Providing a new framework for understanding empathy impairments in psychopathy, autism, and alexithymia. *Neuroscience and Biobehavioral Reviews*, *47*, 520–532. https://doi.org/10.1016/j.neubiorev.2014.09.021.

Bjork, J. M., Chen, G., & Hommer, D. W. (2012). Psychopathic tendencies and mesolimbic recruitment by cues for instrumental and passively obtained rewards. *Biological Psychology*, *89*(2), 408–415. https://doi.org/10.1016/j.biopsycho.2011.12.003.

Blair, J., Mitchell, D., & Blair, K. (2005). *The psychopath: Emotion and the brain*. Blackwell Publishing.

Blair, R. J. R. (2013). The neurobiology of psychopathic traits in youths. *Nature Reviews Neuroscience*, *14*(11), 786–799. https://doi.org/10.1038/nrn3577.

Buckholtz, J. W., Treadway, M. T., Cowan, R. L., Woodward, N. D., Benning, S. D., Li, R., … Zald, D. H. (2010). Mesolimbic dopamine reward system hypersensitivity in individuals with psychopathic traits. *Nature Publishing Group*, *13*(4), 419–421. https://doi.org/10.1038/nn.2510.

Buon, M., Seara-Cardoso, A., & Viding, E. (2016). Why (and how) should we study the interplay between emotional arousal, Theory of Mind, and inhibitory control to understand moral cognition? *Psychonomic Bulletin and Review*, *23*(6), 1660–1680. https://doi.org/10.3758/s13423-016-1042-5.

Button, K. S., Ioannidis, J. P. A., Mokrysz, C., Nosek, B. A., Flint, J., Robinson, E. S. J., & Munafò, M. R. (2013). Erratum: Power failure: Why small sample size undermines the reliability of neuroscience. *Nature Reviews Neuroscience*, *14*(6), 451. https://doi.org/10.1038/nrn3502.

Carré, J. M., Hyde, L. W., Neumann, C. S., Viding, E., & Hariri, A. R. (2013). The neural signatures of distinct psychopathic traits. *Social Neuroscience*, *8*(2), 122–135. https://doi.org/10.1080/17470919.2012.703623.

Cima, M., Tonnaer, F., & Hauser, M. D. (2010). Psychopaths know right from wrong but don't care. *Social Cognitive and Affective Neuroscience*, *5*(1), 59–67. https://doi.org/10.1093/scan/nsp051.

Craig, A. D. (2009). How do you feel—Now? The anterior insula and human awareness. *Nature Reviews Neuroscience*, *10*(1), 59–70. https://doi.org/10.1038/nrn2555.

Critchley, H. D., & Harrison, N. A. (2013). Visceral influences on brain and behavior. *Neuron*, *77*(4), 624–638. https://doi.org/10.1016/j.neuron.2013.02.008.

Critchley, H. D., Wiens, S., Rotshtein, P., Öhman, A., & Dolan, R. J. (2004). Neural systems supporting interoceptive awareness. *Nature Neuroscience*, *7*(2), 189–195. https://doi.org/10.1038/nn1176.

Decety, J., Chen, C., Harenski, C., & Kiehl, K. A. (2013). An fMRI study of affective perspective taking in individuals with psychopathy: Imagining another in pain does not evoke empathy. *Frontiers in Human Neuroscience*, *7*. https://doi.org/10.3389/fnhum.2013.00489.

Decety, J., Chen, C., Harenski, C. L., & Kiehl, K. A. (2015). Socioemotional processing of morally-laden behavior and their consequences on others in forensic psychopaths. *Human Brain Mapping*, *36*(6), 2015–2026. https://doi.org/10.1002/hbm.22752.

Decety, J., & Jackson, P. L. (2004). The functional architecture of human empathy. *Behavioral and Cognitive Neuroscience Reviews*, *3*(2), 71–100. https://doi.org/10.1177/1534582304267187.

Decety, J., Skelly, L., Yoder, K. J., & Kiehl, K. A. (2014). Neural processing of dynamic emotional facial expressions in psychopaths. *Social Neuroscience*, (9), 37–41. https://doi.org/10.1080/17470919.2013.866905.

Decety, J., Skelly, L. R., & Kiehl, K. A. (2013). Brain response to empathy-eliciting scenarios involving pain in incarcerated individuals with psychopathy. *JAMA Psychiatry*, *70*(6), 638–645. https://doi.org/10.1001/jamapsychiatry.2013.27.

Deeley, Q., Daly, E., Surguladze, S., Tunstall, N., Mezey, G., Beer, D., … Murphy, D. G. (2006). Facial emotion processing in criminal psychopathy. *British Journal of Psychiatry*, *189*(6), 533–539. https://doi.org/10.1192/bjp.bp.106.021410.

Deming, P., Philippi, C. L., Wolf, R. C., Dargis, M., Kiehl, K. A., & Koenigs, M. (2018). Psychopathic traits linked to alterations in neural activity during personality judgments of self and others. *NeuroImage*, *18*, 575–581. https://doi.org/10.1016/j.nicl.2018.02.029.

Dolan, M. (2012). The neuropsychology of prefrontal function in antisocial personality disordered offenders with varying degrees of psychopathy. *Psychological Medicine*, *42*(8), 1715–1725. https://doi.org/10.1017/s0033291711002686.

Dolan, M., & Park, I. (2002). The neuropsychology of antisocial personality disorder. *Psychological Medicine*, *32*(3). https://doi.org/10.1017/s0033291702005378.

Fan, Y., Duncan, N. W., de Greck, M., & Northoff, G. (2011). Is there a core neural network in empathy? An fMRI based quantitative meta-analysis. *Neuroscience & Biobehavioral Reviews*, *35*(3), 903–911. https://doi.org/10.1016/j.neubiorev.2010.10.009.

Fede, S. J., Borg, J. S., Nyalakanti, P. K., Harenski, C. L., Cope, L. M., Sinnott-Armstrong, W., … Kiehl, K. A. (2016). Distinct neuronal patterns of positive and negative moral processing in psychopathy. *Cognitive, Affective, & Behavioral Neuroscience*, *16*(6), 1074–1085. https://doi.org/10.3758/s13415-016-0454-z.

Garofalo, C., & Neumann, C. S. (2018). Psychopathy and emotion regulation: Taking stock and moving forward. In M. DeLisi (Ed.), *Routledge international handbook of psychopathy and crime* (pp. 76–97). Routledge.

Garofalo, C., Velotti, P., Callea, A., Popolo, R., Salvatore, G., Cavallo, F., & Dimaggio, G. (2018). Emotion dysregulation, impulsivity and personality disorder traits: A community sample study. *Psychiatry Research*, *266*, 186–192. https://doi.org/10.1016/j.psychres.2018.05.067.

Geurts, D. E. M., von Borries, K., Volman, I., Bulten, B. H., Cools, R., & Verkes, R.-J. (2016). Neural connectivity during reward expectation dissociates psychopathic criminals from non-criminal individuals with high impulsive/antisocial psychopathic traits. *Social Cognitive and Affective Neuroscience*, *11*(8), 1326–1334. https://doi.org/10.1093/scan/nsw040.

Glenn, A. L., Raine, A., & Schug, R. A. (2009). The neural correlates of moral decision-making in psychopathy. *Molecular Psychiatry*, *14*(1), 5–6. https://doi.org/10.1038/mp.2008.104.

Gordon, H. L., Baird, A. A., & End, A. (2004). Functional differences among those high and low on a trait measure of psychopathy. *Biological Psychiatry*, *56*(1), 516–521. https://doi.org/10.1016/j.biopsych.2004.06.030.

Gregory, S., Blair, R. J., ffytche, D., Simmons, A., Kumari, V., Hodgins, S., & Blackwood, N. (2015). Punishment and psychopathy: A case-control functional MRI investigation of reinforcement learning in violent antisocial personality disordered men. *The Lancet Psychiatry*, *2*(2), 153–160. https://doi.org/10.1016/S2215-0366(14)00071-6.

Hare, R. D. (2003). *The psychopathy checklist–revised*. Toronto, ON: Multi-Health Systems.

Hare, R. D., & Neumann, C. S. (2008). Psychopathy as a clinical and empirical construct. *Annual Review of Clinical Psychology*, *4*(1), 217–246. https://doi.org/10.1146/annurev.clinpsy.3.022806.091452.

Harenski, C. L., Harenski, K. A., Shane, M. S., & Kiehl, K. A. (2010). Aberrant neural processing of moral violations in criminal psychopaths. *Journal of Abnormal Psychology*, *119*(4), 863–874. https://doi.org/10.1037/a0020979.

Harenski, C. L., Kim, S. H., & Hamann, S. (2009). Neuroticism and psychopathy predict brain activation during moral and nonmoral emotion regulation. *Cognitive, Affective, & Behavioral Neuroscience*, *9*(1), 1–15. https://doi.org/10.3758/cabn.9.1.1.

Hicks, B. M., & Patrick, C. J. (2006). Psychopathy and negative emotionality: Analyses of suppressor effects reveal distinct relations with emotional distress, fearfulness, and anger-hostility. *Journal of Abnormal Psychology*, *115*(2), 276–287. https://doi.org/10.1037/0021-843x.115.2.276.

Hoppenbrouwers, S. S., Neumann, C. S., Lewis, J., & Johansson, P. (2015). A latent variable analysis of the Psychopathy Checklist-Revised and behavioral inhibition system/behavioral activation system factors in North American and Swedish offenders. *Personality Disorders: Theory, Research, and Treatment*, *6*(3), 251–260. https://doi.org/10.1037/per0000115.

Hosking, J. G., Kastman, E. K., Dorfman, H. M., Samanez-Larkin, G. R., Baskin-Sommers, A., Kiehl, K. A., … Buckholtz, J. W. (2017). Disrupted prefrontal regulation of striatal subjective value signals in psychopathy. *Neuron*, *95*(1), 221–231.e4. https://doi.org/10.1016/j.neuron.2017.06.030.

Hyde, L. W., Byrd, A. L., Votruba-drzal, E., Hariri, A. R., & Manuck, S. B. (2014). Amygdala reactivity and negative emotionality: Divergent correlates of antisocial personality and psychopathy traits in a community sample. *Journal of Abnormal Psychology*, *123*(1), 214–224. https://doi.org/10.1037/a0035467.

Justus, A. N., & Finn, P. R. (2007). Startle modulation in non-incarcerated men and women with psychopathic traits. *Personality and Individual Differences*, *43*(8), 2057–2071. https://doi.org/10.1016/j.paid.2007.06.020.

Kiehl, K. A., Smith, A. M., Hare, R. D., Mendrek, A., Forster, B. B., Brink, J., & Liddle, P. F. (2001). Limbic abnormalities in affective processing by criminal psychopaths as revealed by functional magnetic resonance imaging. *Biological Psychiatry*, *50*(9), 677–684. https://doi.org/10.1016/s0006-3223(01)01222-7.

Krstic, S., Neumann, C. S., Roy, S., Robertson, C. A., & Hare, R. D. (2018). Using latent variable- and person-centered approaches to examine the role of psychopathic traits in sex offenders. *Personality Disorders: Theory, Research, and Treatment*, *9*(3), 207–216. https://doi.org/10.1037/per0000249.Using.

Lamm, C., Decety, J., & Singer, T. (2011). Meta-analytic evidence for common and distinct neural networks associated with directly experienced pain and empathy for pain. *NeuroImage*, *54*(3), 2492–2502. https://doi.org/10.1016/j.neuroimage.2010.10.014.

Lilienfeld, S. O., & Andrews, B. P. (1996). Development and preliminary validation of a self-report measure of psychopathic personality traits in noncriminal population. *Journal of Personality Assessment*, *66*(3), 488–524. https://doi.org/10.1207/s15327752jpa6603_3.

Lilienfeld, S. O., Fowler, K. A., & Patrick, C. (2006). The self-report assessment of psychopathy. In *Handbook of psychopathy* (pp. 107–132). Guilford Press.

Lockwood, P. L., Sebastian, C. L., McCrory, E. J., Hyde, Z. H., Gu, X., De Brito, S. A., & Viding, E. (2013). Association of Callous Traits with reduced neural response to others' pain in children with conduct problems. *Current Biology*, *23*(10), 901–905. https://doi.org/10.1016/j.cub.2013.04.018.

Lozier, L. M., Cardinale, E. M., VanMeter, J. W., & Marsh, A. A. (2014). Mediation of the relationship between callous-unemotional traits and proactive aggression by amygdala response to fear among children with conduct problems. *JAMA Psychiatry*, *71*(6), 627. https://doi.org/10.1001/jamapsychiatry.2013.4540.

Lynam, D. R., Hoyle, R. H., & Newman, J. P. (2006). The perils of Partialling: Cautionary tales from aggression and psychopathy. *Assessment*, *13*(2), 328–341. https://doi.org/10.1177/1073191106290562.

Mahmut, M. K., Homewood, J., & Stevenson, R. J. (2008). The characteristics of non-criminals with high psychopathy traits: Are they similar to criminal psychopaths? *Journal of Research in Personality*, *42*(3), 679–692. https://doi.org/10.1016/j.jrp.2007.09.002.

Malterer, M. B., Lilienfeld, S. O., Neumann, C. S., & Newman, J. P. (2010). Concurrent validity of the Psychopathic Personality Inventory with offender and community samples. *Assessment*, *17*(1), 3–15. https://doi.org/10.1177/1073191109349743.

Meffert, H., Gazzola, V., Den Boer, J. A., Bartels, A. A. J., & Keysers, C. (2013). Reduced spontaneous but relatively normal deliberate vicarious representations in psychopathy. *Brain*, *136*(Pt 8), 2550–2562. https://doi.org/10.1093/brain/awt190.

Mier, D., Haddad, L., Diers, K., Dressing, H., Meyer-lindenberg, A., & Kirsch, P. (2014). Reduced embodied simulation in psychopathy. *The World Journal of Biological Psychiatry*, *15*(6), 479–487. https://doi.org/10.3109/15622975.2014.902541.

Miller, J. D., Lyman, D. R., Widiger, T. A., & Leukefeld, C. (2001). Personality disorders as extreme variants of common personality dimensions: Can the five factor model adequately represent psychopathy? *Journal of Personality*, *69*(2), 253–276. https://doi.org/10.1111/1467-6494.00144.

Miller, J. D., & Lynam, D. R. (2003). Psychopathy and the five-factor model of personality: A replication and extension. *Journal of Personality Assessment*, *81*(2), 168–178. https://doi.org/10.1207/S15327752JPA8102_08.

Morgan, A. B., & Lilienfeld, S. O. (2000). A meta-analytic review of the relation between antisocial behavior and neuropsychological measures of executive function. *Clinical Psychology Review*, *20*(1), 113–136. https://doi.org/10.1016/s0272-7358(98)00096-8.

Müller, J., Sommer, M., Phil, D., & Weber, T. (2008). Disturbed prefrontal and temporal brain function during emotion and cognition interaction in criminal psychopathy. *Behavioural Sciences and the Law*, *150*, 131–150. https://doi.org/10.1002/bsl.

Müller, J., Sommer, M., Wagner, V., Lange, K., Taschler, H., Ro, C. H., … Klein, H. E. (2003). Abnormalities in emotion processing within cortical and subcortical regions in criminal psychopaths : Evidence from a functional magnetic resonance imaging study using pictures with emotional content. *Biological Psychiatry*, *54*(2), 152–162. https://doi.org/10.1016/s0006-3223(02)01749-3.

Neumann, C. S., & Hare, R. D. (2008). Psychopathic traits in a large community sample: Links to violence, alcohol use, and intelligence. *Journal of Consulting and Clinical Psychology*, *76*(5), 893–899. https://doi.org/10.1037/0022-006X.76.5.893.

Neumann, C. S., Hare, R. D., & Pardini, D. A. (2015). Antisociality and the construct of psychopathy: Data from across the globe. *Journal of Personality*, *83*(6), 678–692. https://doi.org/10.1111/jopy.12127.

Osumi, T., Shimazaki, H., Imai, A., Sugiura, Y., & Ohira, H. (2007). Psychopathic traits and cardiovascular responses to emotional stimuli. *Personality and Individual Differences*, *42*(7), 1391–1402. https://doi.org/10.1016/j.paid.2006.10.016.

Patrick, C. J., Hicks, B. M., Nichol, P. E., & Krueger, R. F. (2007). A Bifactor approach to modeling the structure of the psychopathy checklist-revised. *Journal of Personality Disorders*, *21*(2), 118–141. https://doi.org/10.1521/pedi.2007.21.2.118.

Patterson, C. M., & Newman, J. P. (1993). Reflectivity and learning from aversive events: Toward a psychological mechanism for the syndromes of disinhibition. *Psychological Review*, *100*(4), 716–736. https://doi.org/10.1037/0033-295x.100.4.716.

Paulhus, D. L., Neumann, C. S., & Hare, R. D. (2015). *Manual for the self-report psychopathy scale* (4th ed.). Toronto: Multi-Health Systems.

Poeppl, T. B., Donges, M. R., Mokros, A., Rupprecht, R., Fox, P. T., Laird, A. R., … Eickhoff, S. B. (2019). A view behind the mask of sanity: Meta-analysis of aberrant brain activity in psychopaths. *Molecular Psychiatry*, *24*(3), 463–470. https://doi.org/10.1038/s41380-018-0122-5.

Prehn, K., Schlagenhauf, F., Schulze, L., Berger, C., Vohs, K., Fleischer, M., … Herpertz, S. C. (2013). Neural correlates of risk taking in violent criminal offenders characterized by emotional hypo- and hyper-reactivity. *Social Neuroscience*, *8*(2), 136–147. https://doi.org/10.1080/17470919.2012.686923.

Pujara, M., Motzkin, J. C., Newman, J. P., Kiehl, K. A., & Koenigs, M. (2013). Neural correlates of reward and loss sensitivity in psychopathy. *Social Cognitive and Affective Neuroscience*, *9*(6), 794–801. https://doi.org/10.1093/scan/nst054.

Pujol, J., Batalla, I., Contreras-Rodríguez, O., Harrison, B. J., Pera, V., Hernández-Ribas, R., … Cardoner, N. (2012). Breakdown in the brain network subserving moral judgment in criminal psychopathy. *Social Cognitive and Affective Neuroscience*, *7*(8), 917–923. https://doi.org/10.1093/scan/nsr075.

Raine, A., Yang, Y., Narr, K. L., & Toga, A. W. (2011). Sex differences in orbitofrontal gray as a partial explanation for sex differences in antisocial personality. *Molecular Psychiatry*, *16*(2), 227–236. https://doi.org/10.1038/mp.2009.136.

Raine, A., & Yang, Y. (2006). Neural foundations to moral reasoning and antisocial behavior. *Social Cognitive and Affective Neuroscience*, *1*(2), 203–213. https://doi.org/10.1093/scan/nsl033.

Rodman, A. M., Kastman, E. K., Dorfman, H. M., Baskin-Sommers, A. R., Kiehl, K. A., Newman, J. P., & Buckholtz, J. W. (2016). Selective mapping of psychopathy and externalizing to dissociable circuits for inhibitory self-control. *Clinical Psychological Science*, *4*(3), 559–571. https://doi.org/10.1177/2167702616631495.

Schneider, F., Habel, U., Kessler, C., Posse, S., Grodd, W., & Müller-Gärtner, H.-W. (2000). Functional imaging of conditioned aversive emotional responses in antisocial personality disorder. *Neuropsychobiology*, *42*(4), 192–201. https://doi.org/10.1159/000026693.

Schultz, D. H., Balderston, N. L., Baskin-Sommers, A. R., Larson, C. L., & Helmstetter, F. J. (2016). Psychopaths show enhanced amygdala activation during fear conditioning. *Frontiers in Psychology*, *7*. https://doi.org/10.3389/fpsyg.2016.00348.

Seara-Cardoso, A., Dolberg, H., Neumann, C., Roiser, J. P., & Viding, E. (2013). Empathy, morality and psychopathic traits in women. *Personality and Individual Differences*, *55*(3), 328–333. https://doi.org/10.1016/j.paid.2013.03.011.

Seara-Cardoso, A., Neumann, C., Roiser, J., McCrory, E., & Viding, E. (2012). Investigating associations between empathy, morality and psychopathic personality traits in the general population. *Personality and Individual Differences*, *52*(1), 67–71. https://doi.org/10.1016/j.paid.2011.08.029.

Seara-Cardoso, A., Sebastian, C. L., McCrory, E., Foulkes, L., Buon, M., Roiser, J. P., & Viding, E. (2016). Anticipation of guilt for everyday moral transgressions: The role of the anterior insula and the influence of interpersonal psychopathic traits. *Scientific Reports*, *6*, 1–10. https://doi.org/10.1038/srep36273.

Seara-Cardoso, A., Sebastian, C. L., Viding, E., Roiser, J. P., Sebastian, C. L., Viding, E., … Viding, E. (2015). Affective resonance in response to others ' emotional faces varies with affective ratings and psychopathic traits in amygdala and anterior insula. *Social Neuroscience*, *11*, 140–152. https://doi.org/10.1080/17470919.2015.1044672.

Sebastian, C. L., McCrory, E. J. P., Cecil, C. A. M., Lockwood, P. L., De Brito, S. A., Fontaine, N. M. G., & Viding, E. (2012). Neural responses to affective and cognitive theory of mind in children with conduct problems and varying levels of callous-unemotional traits. *Archives of General Psychiatry*, *69*(8), 814. https://doi.org/10.1001/archgenpsychiatry.2011.20.

Sethi, A., McCrory, E., Puetz, V., Hoffmann, F., Knodt, A. R., Radtke, S. R., … Viding, E. (2018). Primary and secondary variants of psychopathy in a volunteer sample are associated with different neurocognitive mechanisms. *Biological Psychiatry*, *3*(12), 1013–1021. https://doi.org/10.1016/j.bpsc.2018.04.002.

Shane, M. S., & Groat, L. L. (2018). Capacity for upregulation of emotional processing in psychopathy: All you have to do is ask. *Social Cognitive and Affective Neuroscience*, *13*(11), 1163–1176. https://doi.org/10.1093/scan/nsy088.

Sommer, M., Sodian, B., Döhnel, K., Schwerdtner, J., Meinhardt, J., & Hajak, G. (2010). In psychopathic patients emotion attribution modulates activity in outcome-related brain areas. *Psychiatry Research: Neuroimaging*, *182*(2), 88–95. https://doi.org/10.1016/j.pscychresns.2010.01.007.

Uzieblo, K., Verschuere, B., Van den Bussche, E., & Crombez, G. (2009). The validity of the psychopathic personality inventory—Revised in a community sample. *Assessment*, *17*(3), 334–346. https://doi.org/10.1177/1073191109356544.

Viding, E., McCrory, E., & Seara-Cardoso, A. (2014). Psychopathy. *Current Biology*, *24*(18), R871–R874. https://doi.org/10.1016/j.cub.2014.06.055.

Vieira, J. B., Tavares, T. P., Marsh, A. A., & Mitchell, D. G. V. (2017). Emotion and personal space: Neural correlates of approach-avoidance tendencies to different facial expressions as a function of coldhearted psychopathic traits. *Human Brain Mapping*, *38*(3), 1492–1506. https://doi.org/10.1002/hbm.23467.

Vuilleumier, P., Richardson, M. P., Armony, J. L., Driver, J., & Dolan, R. J. (2004). Distant influences of amygdala lesion on visual cortical activation during emotional face processing. *Nature Neuroscience*, *7*(11), 1271–1278. https://doi.org/10.1038/nn1341.

Widiger, T. A., & Lynam, D. R. (1998). Psychopathy and the five-factor model of personality. In *Psychopathy: Antisocial, criminal, and violent behavior* (pp. 171–187). Guilford Press.
Yoder, K. J., Harenski, C., Kiehl, K. A., & Decety, J. (2015). Neural networks underlying implicit and explicit moral evaluations in psychopathy. *Translational Psychiatry*, *5*(8). https://doi.org/10.1038/tp.2015.117.

Emotional functioning in psychopathy: A critical review and integration with general emotion theories

4

Lieke Nentjes[†]*, Carlo Garofalo, and David S. Kosson*

For Lieke and Jan

Introduction

In essence, human beings are social creatures. Our social adaptation is deeply rooted in a remarkable capacity to show love and compassion, to form attachment relationships with one another, and to display acts of altruism and self-sacrifice. A relatively small number of individuals with high levels of psychopathic traits deviate fundamentally from these norms. While displaying a callous lack of empathy toward others, psychopathic individuals seem to have profound difficulties in showing loyalty to even their closest relatives, and engage in conduct that seems primarily driven by self-benefiting, egocentric motives (Hare, 1993; Meloy, 1988). Not surprisingly, psychopathy is associated with a considerable societal burden in both financial costs and emotional consequences for the people who are victimized by those who have psychopathic features (Reidy et al., 2015).

Deficiencies in affective functioning are widely accepted as one of the core aspects of psychopathy. These deficiencies, in turn, are allegedly linked to the display of antisocial behavior (Brook, Brieman, & Kosson, 2013; Herpertz et al., 2001). The nature of such emotional abnormalities in psychopathy, however, remains to be elucidated. One aspect that seems to hinder a comprehensive understanding of emotional functioning in psychopathy is that different theories tend to vary greatly in their conceptualizations of emotion, and to focus on different aspects of the broader emotional functioning domain. The goal of the current review is to provide an overview of the main approaches that have been adopted to conceptualize the emotional disturbances that characterize psychopathy. Subsequently, the applicability of these perspectives to explain the full range of emotional and behavioral features that have been clinically and empirically linked to psychopathy is critically discussed. A more comprehensive, contemporary perspective on emotion is then provided, outlining a number of components that appear crucial for a precise understanding of psychopathy. For each of these components, we briefly describe the potential relevance to psychopathy, and we summarize the state-of-the-art of empirical research, focusing in particular on studies

[†] Deceased 5 March 2020

Psychopathy and Criminal Behavior. https://doi.org/10.1016/B978-0-12-811419-3.00006-6

with adult forensic populations. This analysis allows us to provide a more comprehensive perspective on the emotional functioning that characterizes psychopathy than is commonly provided. Finally, we propose avenues for further research to achieve a more sophisticated understanding of psychopathic individuals' emotional functioning across multiple components.

Although modern conceptualizations and methods of operationalization differ in defining the necessary components and the boundaries of this disorder, there is general agreement that psychopathy is multidimensional in nature and characterized by traits that span the interpersonal, affective, and behavioral domains. Importantly, empirical research highlights the importance of distinguishing between different psychopathy dimensions as they reveal differential associations with a range of external correlates (Fowles & Dindo, 2009; Hare & Neumann, 2008; Patrick, Cuthbert, & Lang, 1994). Contemporary conceptualizations of psychopathy draw heavily on Cleckley's (1941) description of the disorder. In his work "The Mask of Sanity," Cleckley (1941) described the prototypical psychopath as a slick and deceitful individual, whose life was characterized by a lack of long-term planning and whose antisocial behaviors were often reckless and poorly motivated. Of note, according to Cleckley, psychopathic symptoms could be traced to a general poverty in affective responding, and a related profound deficiency in the ability or propensity to relate to others. However, it should be noted that, in Cleckley's writing, what was abnormal was more the *depth* of emotions that are experienced and expressed, as well as their integration with other functions (e.g., cognition, behavior), rather than a complete absence of emotionality. Cleckley posited that the psychopath can become "vexed and rebellious and frets in lively and constant impatience when confined, but he does not grieve as others grieve" (pp. 348–349). Overall, Cleckley connected the reduced range, maturity, and depth of emotions in the psychopath to an incapacity (or lack of propensity) for love, rather than describing the psychopath as completely devoid of emotion (Garofalo & Neumann, 2018).

Focus on emotion in theories of adult psychopathy

The low-fear hypothesis

For a long time, theories have predominantly traced psychopathic dysfunction back to an innate deficit in the neurophysiological systems regulating fear. According to Lykken's influential low-fear hypothesis (Lykken, 1995), for example, children with a fearless temperament are prone to developing psychopathy due to their weak responsiveness to punishment, which would impede moral socialization. This low-fear account has been corroborated by several kinds of evidence over the years, including documented relations between psychopathy and reduced startle potentiation (Patrick, Bradley, & Lang, 1993), attenuated anticipatory responsivity to threat (Gao, Raine, & Schug, 2012), reduced electrodermal fear conditioning (Veit et al., 2013), and reductions in physiological reactivity to fear-inducing stimuli (Marsh et al., 2010).

The low-fear hypothesis has contributed greatly to our understanding of psychopathy. However, a number of problems have been raised with this theoretical framework, including limited compatibility with more recent accounts that indicate that moral socialization is generally achieved through empathy induction rather than through the use of fear-inducing strategies like punishment (Blair, Mitchell, & Blair, 2005; Hoffman, 2000). Furthermore, recent meta-analyses aimed at parsing the broader constructs of fear and anxiety into their subcomponents have revealed that psychopathy shows a robust negative association with threat detection as well as with constraint, whereas findings linking psychopathy with the subjective experience of fear and anxiety are far less consistent (Derefinko, 2015; Hoppenbrouwers, Bulten, & Brazil, 2016).

The violence inhibition mechanism model

Another account of the emotional dysfunctions that characterize psychopathy is Blair's (1995) violence inhibition mechanism (VIM) model. According to this model, most humans are biologically predisposed to experience others' distress as aversive. Signals of discomfort, such as expressions of fear or sadness, activate the VIM that gives rise to a "freeze" response (inhibiting ongoing behavior) and an increase in attention and arousal. This physiological arousal is subsequently experienced as aversive and results in moral affect (e.g., guilt, the vicarious experience of distress). Through classical conditioning, transgressions (and eventually thoughts of transgressions) become triggers for the VIM, thereby inhibiting future antisocial behavior. Blair posits that children prone to psychopathy show deficiencies in the VIM. This account complements the low fear-dysfunction hypothesis by explaining psychopathy-specific deficiencies in the experience of guilt and empathy (Hare, 2003). It also provides a framework for understanding psychopathic individuals' reduced capacity to recognize fearful and sad expressions (Marsh & Blair, 2008) and attenuated physiological responsiveness to others' pain and distress (Blair et al., 2005; Blair, Jones, Clark, & Smith, 1997; Decety, Skelly, & Kiehl, 2013). It does not, however, explain why several studies have found psychopathic offenders' dysfunction to extend to a wider range of emotions (e.g., happiness, surprise), together with inconsistent findings regarding sadness and fear in particular (e.g., Blair et al., 2006; Brook et al., 2013; Dawel, O'Kearney, McKone, & Palermo, 2012; Verona, Patrick, Curtin, Bradley, & Lang, 2004). In addition, it does not explain why such attenuation in emotional responsiveness does not always occur, as psychopathic individuals' emotional responses appear intact under some conditions (e.g., Shane & Groat, 2018).

The integrated emotion systems model

More recently, the VIM model was extended with the formulation of the integrated emotion systems (IES) model (Blair et al., 2005), which proposes that a genetically based dysfunction in the amygdala and its connections with other brain systems constitute the major cause of the interpersonal/affective traits of psychopathy. In addition, this amygdala deficiency is only believed to contribute to the development of lifestyle/antisocial traits when combined with certain social environmental influences (e.g., an antisocial learning history). The IES model provides an elaboration of the VIM model by clarifying the nature of the emotional dysfunctions that are central to psychopathy. That is, deficits in the amygdala can explain the dysfunctions described in the VIM model, including deficits in responding to others' distress cues, as well as deficits in the formation of associations between signals of such distress and transgressions, as the amygdala is involved in these processes. The IES model differs from the low-fear hypothesis by stating that fearlessness is not necessarily the first causal factor in the etiology of psychopathy but rather is the result of reductions in amygdala functioning. In addition, it helps to explain some findings that are inconsistent with the low-fear account, such as evidence of intact learning from monetary punishment in psychopathic offenders (e.g., Newman & Kosson, 1986). In short, the IES model suggests that all processes that depend upon the amygdala, and only processes that depend upon the amygdala, and only processes that depend upon the amygdala are impaired in psychopathy.

Substantial empirical evidence is consistent with the IES model. Psychopathy is related to deficiencies in a number of processes that rely on intact amygdala functioning, such as emotion-facilitated word processing (Reidy, Zeichner, Hunnicutt-Ferguson, & Lilienfeld, 2008), emotional memory (Christianson et al., 1996), and augmentation of the startle reflex in the context of aversive stimuli (Levenston, Patrick, Bradley, & Lang, 2000). There are, however, also a number of psychopathic characteristics that fall outside the scope of the IES. Although this model recognizes that social influences contribute to the development of psychopathy as a whole, the nature of these environmental factors and the way in which they interact with genetic predispositions remain highly underspecified, and limited largely to the lifestyle and antisocial traits of psychopathy, rather than also impacting its other core interpersonal and affective features. Furthermore, the IES does not provide explanations for processes that are sometimes considered central to psychopathic individuals' interpersonal behavior, such as the tendency to dominate and control others (Vitacco & Kosson, 2010) or their hostile and antagonistic interpersonal style (Garofalo, Neumann, Zeigler-Hill, & Meloy, 2019; Hicks & Patrick, 2006; Lynam & Widiger, 2007; Miller & Lynam, 2015). Lastly, although the IES model posits that psychopathy also reflects dysfunction in orbital/ventrolateral frontal cortex functioning (Blair et al., 2005), it does not account for the wider range of brain abnormalities that has been empirically and theoretically linked to psychopathy (see, Kiehl 2006) for an overview of this neuroscientific literature). Finally, the IES model cannot explain why, under some conditions, psychopathic traits are associated with enhanced—rather than reduced—activation in response to emotional stimuli in certain areas of the amygdala (Moul, Killcross, & Dadds, 2012; Schultz, Balderston, Baskin-Sommers, Larson, & Helmstetter, 2016), or why associations between psychopathy and amygdala activation appear to be moderated by attention (Larson et al., 2013).

The response modulation hypothesis

The theories described earlier place direct emphasis on affective disturbances as a primary deficit in psychopathy. Newman and colleagues, however, claim that these emotional abnormalities are the result of an attentional problem, rather than being reflective of a fundamental incapacity for processing emotional material (Newman, 1998; Newman & Baskin-Sommers, 2011). According to the response modulation hypothesis (RMH), psychopathic symptomatology arises from a deficit in the relatively automatic shift of attention to process important information that is outside the current dominant response set. Normally, such reallocation of attention enables an individual to use peripheral, yet goal-relevant information (e.g., negative feedback) to adjust behavior resulting in more adaptive choices. The RMH posits that psychopathic individuals, due to their reduced attention to peripheral cues (including emotional information), have difficulty altering maladaptive behavior in the face of changing contingencies. This hypothesis explains a range of behavioral dysfunctions seen in psychopathic individuals, including deficits also explained by the IES, such as difficulties in response reversal (Mitchell, Colledge, Leonard, & Blair, 2002) and decreased interference of emotion in semantic processing (Lorenz & Newman, 2002; Mitchell, Richell, Leonard, & Blair, 2006). However, a variety of evidence that emotional deficits are moderated by instructional manipulations that alter participants' focus of attention corroborates the RMH but is relatively difficult to explain with perspectives such as the low-fear and IES models.[a] At the same time, the predictions of the RMH about the specific mechanisms linking attentional anomalies to the development and expression of psychopathic traits in daily life, such as interpersonal callousness and decreased moral emotion, have not been comprehensively examined in empirical studies to date. Furthermore, the origin of these attentional abnormalities remains unclear (Smith & Lilienfeld, 2015; see also Newman & Baskin-Sommers, 2016).

The affect regulation theory

Recently, a very different perspective on emotional dysfunction in psychopathy has been advanced. According to Penney and Kosson (2014) (see also Kosson, Vitacco, Swogger, & Steuerwald, 2016), the development of psychopathic traits reflects an interaction between genetic predisposition, environmental adversity, and negative emotional experience early in life. More precisely, among children with the genetic predisposition for psychopathy, those who encounter early abuse, neglect, or more subtle forms of rejection or hostility are said to be prone to experience substantial negative emotion early in life, including substantial fear, sadness, and anger. All these experiences interact to contribute to the development of maladaptive methods of regulating emotion that in turn contribute to the development of the core affective and interpersonal traits of psychopathy.

The affect regulation theory (ART) specifies three forms that maladaptive emotion regulation take in youth who develop psychopathic traits: (1) negative preception, that is, the tuning out or attenuation of negative emotional experiences; (2) a resistance to processing emotion that results from the eventual automatization of the tuning out of emotion; and (3) a tendency to chronic expression of the anger that is experienced. According to this theory, these maladaptive mechanisms lead such youth to develop

[a] There is also evidence of both deficits and advantages associated with psychopathy outside of the realm of emotional processing that are consistent with the RMH but difficult to explain with most traditional emotion perspectives on psychopathy (for a review, see Hamilton & Newman, 2018).

into people who appear not to experience very much emotion and who are generally not good at processing emotion but who are capable of processing emotion to some extent when they attempt to do so. In addition, this theory posits that the development of an affective style of chronic anger expression may help account, at least in part, for the relationships between psychopathy and aggression or violent behavior.

Explaining emotion in psychopathy: An evaluation of current theories

The theories outlined earlier have been of tremendous value in advancing our understanding of psychopathy. However, it may be noted that there are several apparent conflicts among the different theories when considering emotional dysfunction in psychopathy. A first issue concerns the range of emotions involved in the affective disturbances that characterize psychopathy, with some perspectives emphasizing more general dysfunction and others pointing to more specific dysfunctions for some emotions (low-fear hypothesis, VIM, IES) or dynamic changes in emotional function over the course of development (ART) or across different situations or contexts (RMH, ART). A second issue regards the focus on different specific components in the broader domain of emotional functioning that might be impaired in psychopathy. Overall, most emotion-focused accounts describe psychopathic features (especially interpersonal and affective traits) as resulting from an innate unresponsiveness to cues that would normally elicit emotional reactions. This assumption has been based on a variety of studies that demonstrate psychopathic individuals to show deficient processing and physiological responses in the context of emotion (for a review, see Brook et al., 2013). Furthermore, a deficit in the recognition of others' emotional states has been theoretically linked to the empathic deficiencies that characterize psychopathy (Blair et al., 2005).

These clusters of findings have been extended to hypotheses that psychopaths also manifest a (general or specific) deficiency in the subjective experience of emotions. As a consequence of being fundamentally devoid of (some) emotions, the affective and interpersonal traits of psychopathy should be unrelated to difficulties in the regulation of emotions, because in the absence of emotional experiences, emotion regulation would not be necessary. One exception is the ART, which suggests that the specific form of maladaptive emotion regulation is a mechanism designed to attenuate some emotional experiences. Yet, the majority of studies remain largely silent on the role of several of these other aspects of emotional functioning, even though there are well-grounded theoretical and empirical reasons to assume that they might be, in fact, relevant to deepen our understanding of the disorder. Cleckley (1941), for example, emphasized the relationship between psychopathy and the incapacity to *experience* emotions. Furthermore, with the mere title of his work ("*The mask of sanity*"), he stressed the importance of certain facial *expressive* behaviors (a heightened readiness for emotional expression) as one of the hallmarks of this disorder. However, surprisingly little research has been dedicated to the study of facial displays of affect or the subjective experience of emotion. Likewise, only in recent years has the study of emotion regulation gained traction in the psychopathy field (e.g., Penney & Kosson, 2014; for a review, see Garofalo & Neumann, 2018). In order to broaden the breadth of our understanding of emotional functioning in psychopathy, it is necessary to take theories of normal affective functioning into account. Therefore we next summarize a contemporary, general theoretical framework of emotion, which is followed by a discussion of the implications of current evidence on psychopathy for our understanding of psychopathic individuals' emotional functioning in light of this framework.

The nature of emotion: A multicomponential framework for studying emotional functioning in psychopathy

From a functionalist perspective, emotions are broadly defined as short-lived, affective (i.e., positive or negative) responses to internal or external instigating stimuli in the service of adaptive behavior (Frijda, 2008). Providing more detailed accounts of emotion has proven to be exceptionally challenging. As a result, a great number of theoretical perspectives have historically been adopted to explain different affective processes. Somatic approaches, for example, focus largely on patterns of bodily reactions as crucial to emotion (James, 1884; Larsen, Berntson, Poehlmann, Ito, & Cacioppo, 2008), with some theorists identifying emotion as the activation of largely innate physiological systems with different adaptive functions (Bradley, Codispoti, Cuthbert, & Lang, 2001; Damasio, Everitt, & Bishop, 1996). Cognitively oriented accounts, on the other hand, stress the necessity of interpretative processes for the emergence of affect (e.g., Lazarus, 1991). The definition of emotion has further been complicated by different attempts to distinguish between specific types of emotions. Ekman (1993), for example, considered emotion to be best conceptualized in discrete terms, with distinct patterns of facial expression providing indications of qualitatively distinct emotional response profiles associated with different emotional states. Other theorists, conversely, consider emotion to be more fluid in nature and describe affective states by mapping them onto a small number of different dimensions (e.g., dominance, arousal, and valence) (Bradley & Lang, 1994).

According to recent emotion theories, these different accounts are not necessarily mutually exclusive; rather, it has been suggested that the distinct theories emphasize different aspects of emotion. In contrast, contemporary perspectives provide an integration of theoretical approaches by describing emotion as a complex response pattern involving the activation and interaction of various components (Frijda, 2008; Plutchik, 2001; Power & Dalgleish, 2008; Scherer, 2000). The components that are considered to constitute an emotional response (i.e., a specific episode of emotion) vary slightly across theories, but generally include appraisal (or perception), physiological arousal, action potential (or tendency), subjective experience, and expression of emotion. Furthermore, emotion regulation is widely considered to play a central role in affective processes, as it pertains to the ability to monitor, evaluate, and manage the experience and expression of emotions to achieve a desired (emotional) end state

(Frijda, 2008; Gross, 2002; Power & Dalgleish, 2008). Despite their mutual relatedness, each of these elements or components of an emotion may have a different degree and course of activation as affective processes unfold (Scherer, 2000). For an emotion to occur, it might thus not be necessary that all of the different components are involved at the same time in a particular context. Whether the various constituent mechanisms in an emotional response are activated and influence each other may depend on a variety of contextual factors including an individual's general mood, motivation, personality, and (interpersonal) environment (Frijda, 2008; Power & Dalgleish, 2008). Such a dynamic, pan-theoretical view reconciles disparities between unidimensional emotion theories and explains why emotional responses in different domains (e.g., bodily responses vs. facial expressions) do not always show identical patterns (Larsen et al., 2008). In addition, this perspective stresses the importance of taking all these components into account when trying to fully understand the emotional abnormalities associated with psychopathological constructs. Therefore we now turn to an evaluation of the existing literature regarding the distinct components of emotional function in psychopathy.

The role of different emotion components in psychopathy

Psychopathy and the appraisal of emotional cues

Appraisal processes give meaning and affective value to incoming stimulus information in the light of an individual's goals and well-being and provide a means to evaluate the personal relevance of an event (Frijda, 2008; Lazarus, 1991; Scherer, 2000). There is compelling evidence that it is the appraisal of a stimulus that gives rise to emotion, rather than an event itself: as a result, a similar situation or stimulus can result in a range of different emotions across individuals (Power & Dalgleish, 2008; Scherer, 2000). Distortions in appraisal have been empirically linked to the etiology of a wide range of mental disorders (Crocker et al., 2013). In addition, the capacity to functionally appraise the emotional meaning of interpersonal stimuli is considered crucial for the establishment of close, nonhostile interactions (Frijda, 2008). Consequently, it is important to consider these evaluative processes when studying psychopathy.

The appraisal of emotional stimuli is believed to be modulated by dissociable neurocognitive pathways that differ in level and speed of information processing. A subcortical pathway (depending on limbic structures like the amygdala) provides an intuitive and reflexive impression, whereas a slower, cortical route that relies on higher-order processes results in a more fine-grained interpretation of information (Adolphs, 2002; LeDoux, 1996). Research suggests that psychopathy is associated with processing deficiencies when this processing requires the integrity of the first, automatic pathway. Psychopathic individuals show, for example, difficulties in processing the affective value of words in priming paradigms (e.g., Blair et al., 2006), as well as in the identification of various vocal and facial expressions of emotion (Dawel et al., 2012). One influential theory suggests that social information processing occurs in the following temporal stages: (1) encoding cues, (2) interpreting those cues, (3) clarifying a goal, (4) generating a goal, (5) selecting a response and evaluating its possible effects, and (6) enacting the behavioral response (Crick & Dodge, 1994). Notably, evidence for abnormalities in the early stages of social information processing emerges from studies linking psychopathy and hostile attribution bias (Doninger & Kosson, 2001; Vitale, Newman, Serin, & Bolt, 2005). Specifically, Vitale et al. (2005) documented associations between psychopathy and an increased probability of attributing hostile intentions to story characters.[b] Further, Nentjes, Bernstein, Arntz, van Breukelen, and Slaats (2015) found that psychopathic offenders more accurately detected hostility in others' eyes than did nonpsychopathic offenders. As the tendency for hostile appraisal increases the likelihood of anger and aggression (Power & Dalgleish, 2008), these results illustrate the necessity of elaborating on the handful of studies that have previously investigated the emotional meaning that psychopaths give to their interpersonal world.

Notably, psychopathic individuals do not seem to be characterized by global deficiencies in the slower, cognitive appraisal of emotional stimuli. Indeed, reviewing the literature that had used clinical measures of psychopathy, Brook et al. (2013) concluded that there were no differences associated with psychopathy in the subjective appraisal of emotional stimuli. Further, psychopathic individuals show an intact capacity to identify other individuals' mental states (like thoughts and intentions), even when these mental states are emotional in nature (i.e., psychopathic individuals have a relatively intact Theory of Mind; Dolan & Fullam, 2004; Nentjes et al., 2015). However, it should be emphasized that psychopaths could make a distorted use of such knowledge about others' mental states. Specifically, it has been argued that individuals with psychopathic traits activate their Theory of Mind skills primarily as a means to control and manipulate others (Bateman, Bolton, & Fonagy, 2013). This pattern of findings suggests that their understanding of others' mental states relies primarily on the effortful pathway to appraisal and is likely to be somewhat simplistic. On the other hand, some studies have provided indications that psychopathic offenders present with more specific abnormalities in higher-order appraisal and metacognitive (or mentalizing) processes (Viding & McCrory, 2012). Similarly, in the same study in which Dolan and Fullam (2004) found psychopathic offenders to have intact Theory of Mind abilities, they also observed associations between psychopathy and mentalizing deficits. In addition, a recent study has reported that mentalizing deficits were not only related to psychopathic traits but also moderated the link between psychopathy and proactive aggression. Specifically, the greater the extent of mentalizing deficits, the stronger the link between psychopathic traits and proactive aggression (Taubner, White, Zimmermann, Fonagy, & Nolte, 2013).

Studies that have looked at more comprehensive and sophisticated metacognitive skills have reported that psychopathy was strongly associated with impairments in metacognition, with a major deficit in the mastery domain, which refers to the

[b] In addition, in one study, the interpersonal traits of psychopathy have been related to heightened attention to negative emotional stimuli, and specifically toward pictures depicting others' distress (Muñoz Centifanti, Kimonis, Frick, & Aucoin, 2013). However, in this study, the interpersonal features were linked to proactive, but not reactive aggression.

ability to use knowledge about one's own and others' mental states to solve social and psychological dilemmas (Abu-Akel, Heinke, Gillespie, Mitchell, & Bo, 2015). Taking a closer look at specific metacognitive domains impaired in psychopathy, Bo, Abu-Akel, Kongerslev, Haahr, and Bateman (2014) found that psychopathy was unrelated to metacognitive deficits in the cognitive domain, but was related to impairments in emotional metacognitive skills, and that such deficits mediated the link between psychopathy and aggression. Overall, it appears that psychopathic individuals may have relatively intact basic Theory of Mind skills, but lack more sophisticated skills. Two studies that may help explain the different findings across studies are those by Anastassiou-Hadjicharalambous and Warden (2008) and Shamay-Tsoory, Harari, Aharon-Peretz, and Levkovitz (2010), both of which reported deficits for individuals with psychopathic traits in affective perspective-taking (i.e., cognitive empathy) but not in cognitive perspective-taking (i.e., not in other components of Theory of Mind). Using a novel paradigm to assess empathic accuracy, Brook and Kosson (2013) provided additional evidence for impairments in cognitive empathy in psychopathic offenders. Similarly, de Wied, van Boxtel, Matthys, and Meeus (2012) and Georgiou, Kimonis, and Fanti (2018) reported evidence that deficits in cognitive empathy are important in explaining the antisocial behavior of youth with callous-unemotional traits, a developmental precursor of the core affective features of adult psychopathy.

There is also evidence that these deficits do not generalize to all domains of emotional response. Brook et al. (2013) reported that the majority of studies of subjective ratings of affective stimuli point to no relationship between psychopathic traits and subjective self-reports of emotional experience although they acknowledged isolated studies suggesting that psychopathic traits were associated with less negative ratings of conditioned aversive stimuli (CS+'s) during aversive conditioning in one study (Flor, Birbaumer, Hermann, Ziegler, & Patrick, 2002) and with more negative ratings of nonreinforced conditioned stimuli (CS−'s) in another study (Birbaumer et al., 2005).

Psychopathy and physiological responsiveness to emotional stimuli

An appreciably large number of studies has focused on the physiological substrates of emotional reactivity in psychopathy. Psychophysiological assessments provide information about emotional arousal that is considered to be less susceptible to voluntary control than subjective appraisals. Moreover, unlike self-reported emotion, individuals do not need insight into their own responsiveness in order to yield reliable physiological evidence of emotional responses (Larsen et al., 2008). Especially in forensic contexts, where concerns about truthful self-presentation and introspection are pertinent, physiological research thus provides a valuable means of complementing evidence from other assessment domains. Indices that have frequently been used in physiological studies on psychopathy concern skin conductance (SC) and heart rate (HR), which are both robustly associated with emotion-induced autonomic nervous system activity (Larsen et al., 2008; see later for reviews of findings on the startle reflex and facial behavior).

Several studies have examined physiological responses to aversive or noxious stimuli. Seminal studies reported that psychopathic offenders showed larger HR increase and smaller increases in SC responses in anticipation of an electric shock (Hare, 1978; Lykken, 1957). Although studies are less consistent about physiological responses after the shock, some studies also provide evidence of autonomic hyporeactivity (both HR and SC) after the shock (e.g., Hare, 1978) whereas others do not (e.g., Dindo & Fowles, 2011; Gao et al., 2012; Ogloff & Wong, 1990). Overall, research shows that psychopathy is generally related to reduced electrodermal responsiveness but normal or heightened cardiovascular responsiveness in the anticipation of signaled (or predictable) stressors (e.g., Brook et al., 2013). In response to the actual aversive events themselves, however, psychopaths often exhibit normal autonomic arousal.

Other studies have investigated aversive conditioning to evaluate whether psychopathic traits are associated with impairments in learning from aversive stimuli. Several authors have reported that psychopathic traits were associated with reduced aversive conditioning (e.g., Schmauk, 1970). Birbaumer et al. (2005) observed less differentiation between CS+ and CS− for psychopathic participants both electrodermally, subjectively, and in activity in multiple brain regions. Flor et al. (2002) also reported reduced evidence of aversive conditioning during acquisition in multiple response measures (including electrodermal, event-related potentials, corrugator muscle activity) but reported greater heart rate differentiation between CS+ and CS− for controls only during extinction.[c] More recently, López, Poy, Patrick, and Moltó (2013) and Rothemund et al. (2012) have replicated these findings with independent samples and, in one case (López et al., 2013) with a self-report measure of psychopathic traits.

Studies that have examined the effects of other kinds of emotional material (e.g., pictures or film clips) on HR and SC activity have yielded more complex results. In a recent review, Brook et al. (2013) concluded that, in the majority of such investigations, psychopathic individuals and their nonpsychopathic counterparts exhibited similar physiological responsivity to a range of different emotional stimuli (e.g., joy, fear, sadness, disgust; e.g., Pham, Philippot, & Rime, 2000). Brook et al. (2013) did reveal some emotion-specific effects for individuals with psychopathic traits, such as increased SC reactivity in the context of anger and thrill scenes in one study, along with reduced responsivity when looking at others in distress and during fearful imagery (e.g., Blair et al., 1997; Levenston et al., 2000).

In addition, Casey, Rogers, Burns, and Yiend (2013) found that psychopathy was associated with greater cardiovascular reactivity in response to negative images than positive ones but lower physiological activity when participants were asked to "get into the feeling" of the character in the picture, suggesting that it may be the sharing of an emotional experience that is selectively impaired in psychopathy. More recently, Shane and Groat (2018) reported that psychopathic offenders were able to increase their responsiveness to emotion-eliciting cues when explicitly asked to do so. Similarly, as noted earlier, psychopathic offenders have been reported to display normal activity in the amygdala and

[c] Their findings (Fig. 5 in Flor et al.'s [2005] paper) appear to indicate greater HR responding among psychopathic participants than among healthy controls for both kinds of stimuli (CS+s and CS−s) during both acquisition and extinction, although the significance of these group differences was not addressed explicitly in the article.

normal startle potentiation when asked to focus on threat cues but deficient amygdala responsiveness when instructed to attend to other stimuli or tasks (e.g., Larson et al., 2013; Newman, Curtin, Bertsch, & Baskin-Sommers, 2010; see also Baskin-Sommers, Curtin, & Newman, 2013). Based on these findings, Shane and Groat (2018) advanced the intriguing possibility that psychopathic individuals lack the *motivation* to react to emotion-eliciting stimuli rather than the *capacity* for doing so. This interpretation is also consistent with the ART prediction that psychopathic individuals are able to process emotion cues to some extent when asked to do so but that this processing requires heightened effort for them to overcome an automatic resistance to emotional content.

With specific regard to response to provocation, Lobbestael, Arntz, Cima, and Chakhssi (2009) found nonsignificant associations between total psychopathy scores and reactivity to provocation. However, in this study, the affective traits of psychopathy were associated with smaller increases in self-reported negative emotion and smaller increases in diastolic blood pressure. Steuerwald, Brown, Mneimne, and Kosson (2017) published evidence that, in response to anger induction (i.e., following unjust criticism about participants' performance on a computer-based affective lexical decision task and the denial of a performance bonus they had reason to expect) individuals with psychopathic traits showed similar increases in several measures of anger that were similar to those exhibited by individuals without psychopathic traits, including increases in blood pressure, pulse, and self-reported anger, as well as similar levels of retaliation toward the confederate, but, at the same time, smaller increases in facial muscle activity associated with anger. These findings are consistent with the possibility that psychopathic individuals do experience anger, but they also suggest the possibility that there may be a disconnect between the experience and the expression of this emotion (and arguably other emotions as well). In another study, callous-unemotional traits were related to lower SC in conditions of low provocation, but not when level of competitive/aggressive provocation was high (Muñoz, Frick, Kimonis, & Aucoin, 2008). Further, among male juvenile offenders, self-reported interpersonal traits of psychopathy have been linked to the perpetration of proactive aggression among boys who also had lower physiological reactivity, whereas the same interpersonal traits of psychopathy were linked to the perpetration of reactive aggression among those boys who also showed a pattern of coactivation (i.e., greater sympathetic and parasympathetic response; Muñoz Centifanti et al., 2013).

Taken together, this pattern of findings does not corroborate predictions of the absence of emotional reactivity in psychopathic individuals. Rather, such findings suggest that emotional reactivity may be relevant to understand the aggressive tendencies of individual with psychopathic traits. Current research suggests that psychopaths are physiologically hyporesponsive *under certain conditions*. However, psychopaths are not consistently unresponsive to provocative stimuli, and they appear to be less responsive to aversive stimuli electrodermally than cardiovascularly. Moreover, there have been relatively few studies examining responsiveness to other kinds of emotion inductions (but see Kosson et al., 2016, for a recent review). Consequently, studies are far from conclusive about the exact physiological correlates of emotional functioning in psychopathic individuals, or about the specific contexts or motives that alter psychopathic individuals' emotional functioning.

Psychopathy and action potentials

One important function of emotion is to prompt a state of physiological and mental readiness that enables an individual to carry out the behavior that is most adaptive in the context of a particular emotion-eliciting event (Bradley et al., 2001; Frijda, 2008; Lazarus, 1991; Scherer, 2000). According to some theories, discrete emotions are characterized by more or less fixed patterns of physiology and action tendencies that result in specific behaviors (Plutchik, 2001). Disgust, for example, prevents us from consuming harmful substances, whereas anger prepares us for confrontation. Although this account is intuitively appealing, research has yielded mixed results on whether action potentials differ for specific emotions and seems to provide stronger support for the value of valence in predicting action tendencies (Larsen et al., 2008). That is, the experience of positive emotions tends to be robustly associated with approach tendencies, whereas negative emotions more readily result in avoidance. One exception is the experience of anger, which is a negative emotion associated with approach tendencies (Carver & Harmon-Jones, 2009; Krieglmeyer, Deutsch, de Houwer, & de Raedt, 2010). Thus investigating the experience of anger and its expression may constitute an important avenue for future research aimed at examining the emotional correlates of psychopathy, as well as their impact on some of the correlates of psychopathy (e.g., aggression).

Lang and colleagues have formulated a theory that has been relatively influential in psychopathy research. This account states that emotion is fundamentally organized around two motivational neural systems that regulate action tendencies: a defensive system that governs avoidance behaviors (e.g., escape, withdrawal) and an appetitive system that modulates approach tendencies (e.g., exploration; Bradley et al., 2001; Lang, Bradley, & Cuthbert, 1990). In this context, the modulation of startle reactivity (e.g., eye blink responsivity elicited by a loud noise) by emotional stimuli is believed to be an index of the activity of these two motivational systems. In healthy individuals, the startle reflex is reduced when individuals are primed with positive material and is enhanced when they are primed by the presentation of negative material. Psychopathy (and especially its interpersonal and affective traits) has been related to a decreased enhancement of the startle reflex when viewing negative material (e.g., victim scenes, threatening material) when compared to neutral pictures (Levenston et al., 2000; Pastor, Moltó, Vila, & Lang, 2003). This finding has been interpreted as reflecting a diminished activation in the defensive system that governs avoidance potential (Levenston et al., 2000). Notably, however, these findings do not describe a pattern of reactivity to negative stimuli that is comparable to neutral stimuli. Rather, psychopathic individuals tend to react to negative stimuli in a similar manner to the way they react to positive stimuli. Thus these findings do not seem suggestive of an absence of emotion processing but may actually be indicative of an abnormal processing of negative cues (see also Newman et al., 2010, for evidence that such abnormalities do not appear when participants are asked to focus on the negative stimuli). Recent investigations have expanded on this interpretation, by showing that psychopathic offenders do not display the behavioral avoidance tendencies that healthy controls show when being confronted with angry facial stimuli (Von Borries et al., 2012).

Interestingly, a reduced reflexive tendency to avoid angry faces has also been linked to interpersonal dominance (Terburg, Hooiveld, Aarts, Kenemans, & van Honk, 2011), a well-established feature of psychopathy.

Psychopathy and the subjective experience of emotion

The experience of emotion has been described as the conscious awareness of the other components that constitute emotion (Frijda, 2008; Power & Dalgleish, 2008). Theories of emotional experience have mainly focused on the importance of bodily symptoms in the *feeling* component of emotion. Several perspectives posit that emotional experience results from the apperception of changes in visceral activity in the context of emotion-eliciting stimuli (Damasio et al., 1996; James, 1884; Larsen et al., 2008; Schachter & Singer, 1962). In line with this account, research has shown emotional experience to be partly mediated by the sensitivity for symptoms arising in the body (also called *interoceptive awareness*). Wiens, Mezzacappa, and Katkin (2000), for example, showed that the capacity to detect one's own heartbeat was positively related to the self-reported intensity of emotional experience. Further, extensive overlap has been found in the neural mechanisms underlying subjective emotion experience and interoception (Terasawa, Fukushima, & Umeda, 2013).

Subjective emotional experience is commonly assessed using self-report measures, or ideally, with combination of self-report and other indices (Givon, Itzhak-Raz, Karmon-Presser, Danieli, & Meiran, 2019; Lieberman, 2019). Studies on the emotional experience of psychopathic individuals have revealed an intriguing paradox. Indeed, psychopathic individuals seem to report normal affective experiences on self-report measures assessing a wide range of different emotional experiences (e.g., Casey et al., 2013; Pham et al., 2000; Verona et al., 2004; for reviews, see Derefinko, 2015; Hoppenbrouwers et al., 2016; Kosson et al., 2016). Using a counterfactual decision-making paradigm, Baskin-Sommers, Stuppy-Sullivan, and Buckholtz (2016) reported that individuals with high levels of psychopathic traits reported as much or more negative affect in response to regret-inducing counterfactual outcomes. They interpreted this finding as evidence that psychopathic individuals may have intact affective regret sensitivity, but they are unable to use prospective regret signals to guide adaptive behavior.

Results consistent with intact emotional experience in psychopathy were reported in a meta-analysis. Brook et al. (2013), reviewing only PCL-assessed psychopathy studies, reported that the majority of studies of self-reported emotional state following an affective manipulation reported no relationship between psychopathic traits and subjective self-reports of emotional experience. However, they noted that two prior studies have reported negative relationships between psychopathic traits and subjective ratings of negative affect. As noted earlier, Lobbestael et al. (2009) reported that overall levels of psychopathic traits were unrelated to self-ratings of emotion after an anger induction, but higher levels of affective traits were associated with reduced increases in several negative emotions after the induction. In addition, Levenston et al. (2000) reported that overall levels of psychopathic traits were associated with reduced self-ratings of negative emotion while viewing negative affective slides and with increased self-ratings of positive emotion while viewing positive affective slides.

The studies reviewed earlier addressed the state-like subjective experience of emotions (i.e., in response to stimuli presented in laboratory tasks). Another group of studies has approached the investigation of the subjective emotional experience in psychopathy focusing on the trait-like emotional experience, that is, the habitual tendency to experience a given emotion (or a group of emotions) as assessed with self-report measures. In contrast to emotion deficit perspectives, which place strong emphasis on the reduction in the experience of (some) emotions, or in their complete absence, recent meta-analyses have documented negative associations between psychopathic traits and happiness but null associations between psychopathy and anxiety, and positive associations between psychopathy and anger (Derefinko, 2015; Hoppenbrouwers et al., 2016). Accordingly, it has been argued that the experience of other-directed negative emotions (e.g., anger) may be central to the affective features of psychopathy (Benning, 2013; Lynam & Widiger, 2007). Further, taking into consideration low-arousal negative emotions that are other-directed and share an interpersonal component (e.g., spite, contempt) may help increase our understanding of the emotional experiences of psychopathic individuals (Garofalo et al., 2019).

If psychopathic individuals self-report the experience of discrete emotions to different degrees, it is worth noting that psychopathy is also related to a reduced intensity of some self-reported bodily sensations in response to emotional induction (Gao et al., 2012; Marsh et al., 2010; Pham et al., 2000). In addition, the impulsive-antisocial traits of psychopathy have been experimentally linked to reduced heartbeat detection capacities (Nentjes, Meijer, Bernstein, Arntz, & Medendorp, 2013). Affective experience in psychopathy thus seems to be less "embodied," which resembles Cleckley's (1941) descriptions of psychopathic individuals being very well capable of giving verbal descriptions of emotion, while at the same time lacking the full appreciation of affective experience (so-called semantic aphasia). However, the studies reviewed earlier addressing impairments in higher-order metacognitive functions (especially related to understanding of and reasoning about emotions) seem to suggest that psychopathy could be related to both deficits in the ability to identify emotions and deficits in connecting emotions to bodily sensations. This is consistent with studies reporting negative associations between psychopathy and emotional awareness, according to which, when upset, psychopathic individuals would pay little attention to their emotional reactions (Garofalo, Neumann, & Velotti, 2018; Gori et al., 2014; Ridings & Lutz-Zois, 2014). This perspective is also in line with predictions of the ART, as well as with Cleckley's (1941) original conceptualization of psychopathy, which included as one of the 16 criteria a specific lack of true insight, that is, an inability to see oneself as others do. However, there are, to our knowledge, few published studies of psychopathy and insight (but see Maples-Keller & Miller, 2018 for a study on self- and metaperceptions of psychopathic traits).

Psychopathy and the expression of emotion

Besides mobilizing autonomic and mental resources for action, emotion also serves an important communicative function (Ekman, 1993; Frijda, 2008; Matsumoto, Keltner, Shiota, O'Sullivan, & Frank, 2008; Scherer, 2000). The behavioral signs of emotion (or emotion expression) can become apparent in, for example, body language, tone of voice, and facial expressive behavior. Such overt affective displays almost always accompany emotional experiences (Scherer, 2000) and show robust associations with other emotional components (such as the appraisal and subjective experience of emotion; Matsumoto et al., 2008). Psychological research on affective expressiveness has focused primarily on facial displays of emotion, drawing on studies like those of Ekman (1993) whose cross-cultural research indicates that certain basic emotional states (e.g., anger, happiness, fear) are accompanied by a discrete pattern of facial musculature across diverse cultures.

Studies on facial expressiveness in psychopathy have yielded mixed results. In some studies, psychopathic individuals have exhibited reduced frowning, as indexed by reduced electromyographic [EMG] activity in the corrugator supercilii muscle while watching (un)pleasant pictures when compared to neutral pictures (e.g., Herpertz et al., 2001), whereas other research has failed to demonstrate such EMG hyporesponsiveness in psychopathy (e.g., Levenston et al., 2000; for a review, see Brook et al., 2013). In addition, the study by Steuerwald et al. (2017) mentioned earlier, suggested that individuals with psychopathic traits exhibit reduced facial expressions of anger in the presence of intact physiological and subjective anger responses. This finding also raises the possibility that psychopathic individuals could also demonstrate discrepancies between subjective and physiological activity and expression of other emotions. The complexity of the findings on expression of emotion in psychopathy highlights the need for research that adopts more differentiated assessment methods.

In one such study, Künecke, Mokros, Olderbak, and Wilhelm (2018) assessed emotional expression (measuring facial muscle activity in the corrugator supercilii with electromyography) in response to the facial emotion expression of others in offenders with high levels of psychopathic traits, and compared them with offenders with low levels of psychopathic traits and nonoffenders. Controlling for general facial responsiveness, and modeling three emotion-specific factors for the expression of anger, happiness, and sadness stimuli in response to the categorization of angry, happy, and sad faces dynamically presented, respectively, they found no significant differences across the three groups. Similarly, Nentjes, Bernstein, Meijer, Arntz, and Wiers (2016) investigated facial expressiveness in psychopathy using a multirater approach to assess a wide range of facial emotions in offenders. In this research, psychopathic offenders, nonpsychopathic offenders, and nonoffender controls were all equally able to adopt a *poker face* (i.e., inhibiting all outward signs of facial expressiveness), while watching a series of emotional film clips with different valences (happy, fear, sad). All participants also showed content-appropriate facial affect in response to a series of similarly valenced emotional fragments in a condition in which they were asked to express their emotions. Psychopaths did not differ from the other two groups in the capacity to display or inhibit facial emotions, challenging the view that psychopathy is characterized by a generalized impairment in showing facial affect.

Taken together with findings on the subjective experience of emotions, these findings raise questions that are in need of further investigation, such as whether the facial displays of psychopathic individuals generally reflect social mimicry or actual emotional experience, and whether psychopaths may show low propensity or motivation, but not low ability, for the subjective experience of at least certain emotions and their expression (Keysers & Gazzola, 2014; Shane & Groat, 2018). Indeed, prior research had shown that deficits in brain activation typically seen in psychopaths when witnessing others' distress were reduced when participants were explicitly asked to empathize with the target, indicating that psychopathy may be related to selective impairments in the spontaneous—but not deliberate—vicarious experience of emotions (i.e., Meffert, Gazzola, den Boer, Bartels, & Keysers, 2013; see also Shane & Groat, 2018).

Psychopathy and emotion regulation

Emotion regulation is defined as the process through which people influence the experience and expression of emotions (Gross, 2002). Although the regulation of emotion has gained interest only relatively recently, contemporary theorists agree that the processes by which emotions are controlled and possibly adjusted are crucial to understanding emotional function (Frijda, 2008; Power & Dalgleish, 2008; Scherer, 2000). Regulatory attempts can change the course of emotion at a variety of different stages. We can, for example, exert control over the emotion-eliciting events to which we are exposed, or we can modify a situation so that it will be less affect-provoking. Furthermore, we can change the meaning of a given stimulus so that its emotional significance changes (i.e., "reappraisal"). Last, the experience of emotion, as well as its psychophysiological and behavioral correlates can be changed through response modulation (e.g., the modulation of facial affect; Gross, 2002).

As difficulties in the regulation of impulses figure prominently in various conceptualizations of psychopathy (Fowles & Dindo, 2009; Hare, 2003; Patrick, Fowles, & Krueger, 2009), abnormalities in emotion regulation seem crucial to the understanding of this disorder. However, the kind of emotion regulation that is most commonly applied to psychopathy focuses on an inability to control behavior when upset, especially in response to anger (Hare, 2003). Accordingly, there is evidence that psychopathy is associated with dysfunction of the ventromedial prefrontal cortex (Finger et al., 2008; Kiehl, 2006), a brain structure implicated in the down-regulation of frustration (Harenski & Kiehl, 2010). It is noteworthy that some preliminary evidence appears to suggest that such emotion regulation problems associated to psychopathy may extend to other emotions, such as shame (i.e., based on findings linking psychopathic traits and maladaptive shame-coping styles; Campbell & Elison, 2005; Ribeiro da Silva, Vagos, & Rijo, 2019; Velotti, Elison, & Garofalo, 2014), yet few studies have examined behavioral control of emotions other than anger, and more research is needed.

Of import, these emotion regulation difficulties have traditionally been linked exclusively to the antisocial and lifestyle traits of psychopathy. In contrast, the core affective and interpersonal features have been conceptualized as related to intact—or even superior—emotion regulation skills (Fowles & Dindo, 2009; Patrick et al., 2009). However, recent studies have shown that broad difficulties in emotion regulation are more broadly related to psychopathic traits, including its callous-affective components (Garofalo et al., 2018; for a review, see Garofalo & Neumann, 2018). In line with these perspectives, other scholars have suggested that not only is psychopathy related to more pervasive problems with emotion regulation, but these problems in regulating emotions account for some of the associations between psychopathy and aggressive behavior (Harenski & Kiehl, 2010). Accordingly, studies in adult samples have reported links between both the over- and underregulation of emotion and aggression (Roberton, Daffern, & Bucks, 2012), and have demonstrated that emotion dysregulation predicts aggression above and beyond the effect of other well-established correlates, like anger control (Roberton, Daffern, & Bucks, 2015) and impulsivity (Garofalo et al., 2018).

When considering these findings, there has been surprisingly little research on the ways in which psychopathic individuals regulate emotions. This lack of research is even more surprising if we consider that most of the findings reviewed earlier with regard to the physiological experience and the expression of emotions appear to suggest that individuals with psychopathic traits make use of emotional suppression mechanisms. Of note, whereas emotional suppression may be related to greater subjective well-being in the short term (e.g., not thinking of a sad recent event while working on a task), a chronic and inflexible reliance on emotional suppression mechanisms has consistently been linked with poor psychological well-being and a range of maladaptive outcomes, including aggression (Roberton et al., 2012). However, we are aware of no studies that have comprehensively examined associations between psychopathy and emotion regulation strategies. Thus little is known about the ability of psychopathic individuals to flexibly rely on effective and contextually appropriate emotion regulation strategies.

To our knowledge, only a few studies have adopted an experimental paradigm in examining the use of emotion regulation strategy in psychopathy. In the study described earlier by Casey et al. (2013), prisoners were presented with neutral, negative, and positive pictures and were instructed to either just look at each picture, suppress their emotional response, or "get into the feeling" of the target person. Results showed that the interpersonal and affective traits of psychopathy were related to reduced HR reactivity when instructed to experience the feeling of negative pictures when compared to the "just look" condition, potentially reflecting a reduced capacity for upregulating emotion. Recently, Nentjes et al. (2016) investigated the physiological correlates of inhibiting and expressing emotion in psychopathy. In this study, psychopathic offenders did not differ from nonpsychopaths in their capacity to inhibit or express facial emotions in response to emotion induction. Furthermore, in this study, emotion inhibition was associated with a decrease in HR, an effect that has previously been described as the cardiovascular cost of emotion suppression (Gross, 2002). This effect was not dependent on psychopathy, implying emotion suppression to be an effortful process in psychopaths as well.

Regarding the use of specific emotion regulation strategies, the negative preception hypothesis of the ART, Kosson, McBride, Miller, Riser, and Whitman (2018) predicted that individuals with psychopathic traits would display an attentional bias away from some negative emotional stimuli following affectively charged experiences. They assessed attentional bias using an affective dot probe paradigm in a sample of detained adolescent offenders following a frustration experience, and they reported an interaction between age and the core interpersonal and affective traits of psychopathy. Among younger youth, these interpersonal and affective traits were associated with an attentional bias toward sadness words; however, as age increased, these traits predicted an increasing attentional bias away from sadness words.

Based on the considerations presented earlier regarding the experience of emotions and the mixed findings concerning the regulation of emotions in psychopathy across studies and methods, future studies are needed that attempt to pinpoint regulation processes for specific emotions (e.g., anger versus fear), and to tap the motivational aspects of emotion regulation. For example, it is plausible that research may find that certain motivationally salient contexts elicit stronger emotional reactions in psychopathic individuals compared to contexts or stimuli that are not motivationally salient for them. In addition, a recent study has advanced the possibility that psychopathy may be related to different motivations to experience and regulate emotions (i.e., increased motivation to experience anger and decreased motivation to experience happiness; Spantidaki-Kyriazi, Bogaerts, Tamir, Denissen, & Garofalo, 2021).

Conclusions

In the current review, a number of theoretical approaches were outlined that have been used to explain psychopathy, a disorder that is generally believed to be characterized by gross emotional deficiencies in a number of domains (Hare, 2003). From this overview, it became clearer that the focus of several theories is on decreased fear responsivity as one of the main risk factors for the development of psychopathy (Blair et al., 2005; Lykken, 1995). Further, insensitivity to others' feelings (Blair et al., 2005; Fowles & Dindo, 2009; Patrick et al., 2009) as well as poor control of emotional and behavioral impulses have been included in several recent accounts of psychopathy (Fowles & Dindo, 2009; Hare, 2003; Patrick et al., 2009)—although, in these accounts, these two mechanisms have been selectively linked to different clusters of psychopathic features (the interpersonal-affective and antisocial-lifestyle features of psychopathy, respectively). In order to examine whether current theories and research provide a full appreciation of emotional functioning in psychopathy, we evaluated this literature in light of a more integrative framework of emotion (e.g., Frijda, 2008; Power & Dalgleish, 2008).

Departing from this pan-theoretical background, the present chapter reviewed the literature that has focused separately within multiple domains of emotional function, and highlighted that some aspects of emotion have been studied quite extensively in psychopathy (e.g., physiological responsiveness, facial affect recognition). At the same time, the relative scarcity of studies in many other affective domains is striking (e.g., the interpretative processes that underlie emotional appraisal, facial expressiveness, action potential, emotion regulation). Some of the most recent studies have also challenged some of the earlier assumptions posited by theories on the emotional functioning in psychopathy. For instance, links between psychopathy and reduced subjective experience of emotions are not compelling (e.g., Hoppenbrouwers et al., 2016), and preliminary but increasing evidence suggests that associations between psychopathy and emotion dysregulation may extend to the core affective traits of psychopathy (e.g., Garofalo & Neumann, 2018). Further, an integration of motivational processes in the experience and regulation of emotional states in psychopathic individuals has only recently been proposed, and holds promise for further theoretical and empirical developments (e.g., Kosson et al., 2016, 2018; Shane & Groat, 2018). Finally, in addition to including a wider variety of emotional domains, psychopathy research would also benefit from a broader focus that explains the role of different emotion "families" (e.g., guilt, shame, hostility, compassion, love, grief), beyond the more widely studied basic emotions such as fear and sadness.

In conclusion, we suggest two important and related avenues for future research on psychopathy. First, the time has come to realize that psychopathy in adult offenders might be more dynamic than is commonly believed. Recent research has provided increasing evidence that environmental factors are related to the development of psychopathic traits over the course of childhood (e.g., Christian, Meltzer, Thede, & Kosson, 2017; Hyde et al., 2016; Waller, Shaw, Forbes, & Hyde, 2015). Recent research indicates, for example, that psychopathic traits in children are inversely related to factors like parental warmth (Kimonis, Centifanti, Allen, & Frick, 2014). Although psychopathy in children is thus believed to interact with the environment to a certain degree, the majority of theories reviewed implicitly assume that the features of psychopathy and the impairments in emotional function are relatively stable throughout an individual's life and across different contexts, as well as largely innate. Additional investigations are needed to examine how psychopathic features change over time during childhood and adolescence and in how the nomological network surrounding psychopathic features in childhood differs from the nomological network surrounding adult psychopathy. Relatively recent research also challenges the view that the emotional dysfunction in adult psychopathic individuals is static (i.e., invariant across situations), indicating that some of the emotional capacities that are considered deficient in psychopathy (e.g., emotional startle reflex, amygdala responsiveness to threat and others' pain) are dynamic: they are present in some contexts and absent following some specific manipulations of participants' attention, cognitive load, or motivation (e.g., Baskin-Sommers, Curtin, & Newman, 2011; Larson et al., 2013; Meffert et al., 2013). Future research should further investigate this potential state dependency of affective dysfunction in psychopathy and examine under which circumstances and in which emotional domains psychopathic individuals are capable of showing normal emotional functioning.

Second, theory and research should focus more extensively on the interpersonal factors that interact with psychopathic features. In most influential theories of personality pathology, biological predispositions are believed to interact with the environment in the development and maintenance of personality disorders. It is often suggested that the stability of such pathology is moderated by processes such as interpersonal events and their interpretation, including the ways in which someone feels related to others, and the ways in which someone behaves toward others (including relationship behaviors; e.g., Millon & Strack, 2015). To date, research has largely overlooked these interactional processes in psychopathic adults, even though promising therapeutic interventions for personality disorders (including psychopathy) recognize the interpersonal nature of these disorders. Forensic Schema Therapy, for example, places substantial emphasis on the importance of developing a strong patient-therapist attachment relationship in order to provide corrective interpersonal and emotional experiences for patients with psychopathic traits (Bernstein et al., 2012). In light of evidence that interpersonal factors sometimes impact the antisocial behavior of youth with psychopathic traits (e.g., Edens, Skopp, & Cahill, 2008; Pasalich, Dadds, Hawes, & Brennan, 2011), additional research should be conducted to elucidate the interpersonal influences that impact the nature and stability of psychopathic traits, which strategies psychopathic offenders adopt to control their interpersonal environment, and how these processes interact (e.g., see Waller et al., 2014). Ideally, such research will not overlook temperamental predispositions and the early emotional function of youth who later exhibit psychopathic traits (e.g., Mills-Koonce et al., 2015) but will consider their influence within a more dynamic framework in order to provide a more fine-grained understanding of this costly disorder.

References

Abu-Akel, A., Heinke, D., Gillespie, S. M., Mitchell, I. J., & Bo, S. (2015). Metacognitive impairments in schizophrenia are arrested at extreme levels of psychopathy: The cut-off effect. *Journal of Abnormal Psychology*, *124*(4), 1102–1109. https://doi.org/10.1037/abn0000096.

Adolphs, R. (2002). Neural systems for recognizing emotion. *Current Opinion in Neurobiology*, *12*, 169–177. https://doi.org/10.1016/S0959-4388(02)00301-X.

Anastassiou-Hadjicharalambous, X., & Warden, D. (2008). Cognitive and affective perspective-taking in conduct-disordered children high and low on callous-unemotional traits. *Child and Adolescent Psychiatry and Mental Health*, *2*, 16. https://doi.org/10.1186/1753-2000-2-16.

Baskin-Sommers, A. R., Curtin, J. J., & Newman, J. P. (2011). Specifying the attentional selection that moderates the fearlessness of psychopathic offenders. *Psychological Science*, *22*, 226–234. https://doi.org/10.1177/0956797610396227.

Baskin-Sommers, A. R., Curtin, J. J., & Newman, J. P. (2013). Emotion-modulated startle in psychopathy: Clarifying familiar effects. *Journal of Abnormal Psychology*, *122*(2), 458–468. https://doi.org/10.1037/a0030958.

Baskin-Sommers, A. R., Stuppy-Sullivan, A. M., & Buckholtz, J. (2016). Psychopathic individuals exhibit but do not avoid regret during counterfactual decision making. *Proceedings of the National Academy of Sciences of the United States of America*, *113*, 14438–14443. https://doi.org/10.1073/pnas.1609985113.

Bateman, A., Bolton, R., & Fonagy, P. (2013). Antisocial personality disorder: A mentalizing framework. *Focus: Journal of Lifelong Learning in Psychiatry*, *XI*, 1–9. https://doi.org/10.1176/appi.focus.11.2.178.

Benning, S. D. (2013). Heterogeneity in content and psychopathies: Comment on marcus et al. *Personality Disorders, Theory, Research, and Treatment*, *4*, 83–84. https://doi.org/10.1037/a0027451.

Bernstein, D. P., Nijman, H., Karos, K., Keulen-de Vos, M., de Vogel, V., & Lucker, T. (2012). Schema therapy for forensic patients with personality disorders: Design and preliminary findings of a multicenter randomized clinical trial in the Netherlands. *International Journal of Forensic Mental Health*, *11*, 312–324. https://doi.org/10.1080/14999013.2012.746757.

Birbaumer, N., Veit, R., Lotze, M., Erb, M., Hermann, C., Grodd, W., & Flor, H. (2005). Deficient fear conditioning in psychopathy: A functional magnetic resonance imaging study. *Archives of General Psychiatry*, *62*(7), 799–805.

Blair, K. S., Richell, R. A., Mitchell, D. G. V., Leonard, A., Morton, J., & Blair, R. J. R. (2006). They know the words, but not the music: Affective and semantic priming in individuals with psychopathy. *Biological Psychology*, *73*, 114–123. https://doi.org/10.1016/j.biopsycho.2005.12.006.

Blair, R. J. R. (1995). A cognitive developmental approach to morality: Investigating the psychopathy. *Cognition*, *57*, 1–29. https://doi.org/10.1016/0010-0277(95)00676-P.

Blair, R. J. R., Jones, L., Clark, F., & Smith, M. (1997). The psychopathic individual: A lack of responsiveness to distress cues? *Psychophysiology*, *34*, 192–198. https://doi.org/10.1111/j.1469-8986.1997.tb02131.x.

Blair, R. J. R., Mitchell, D. G. V., & Blair, K. S. (2005). *The psychopath: Emotion and the brain*. Oxford, UK: Blackwell.

Bo, S., Abu-Akel, A., Kongerslev, M., Haahr, U. H., & Bateman, A. (2014). Mentalizing mediates the relationship between psychopathy and type of aggression in schizophrenia. *The Journal of Nervous and Mental Disease*, *202*(1), 55–63. https://doi.org/10.1097/NMD.0000000000000067.

Bradley, M. M., Codispoti, M., Cuthbert, B. N., & Lang, P. J. (2001). Emotion and motivation I: Defensive and appetitive reactions in picture processing. *Emotion*, *1*, 276–298.

Bradley, M. M., & Lang, P. J. (1994). Measuring emotion: The self-assessment manikin and the semantic differential. *Journal of Behavior Therapy and Experimental Psychiatry*, *25*, 49–59. https://doi.org/10.1037/1528-3542.1.3.276.

Brook, M., Brieman, C. L., & Kosson, D. S. (2013). Emotion processing in psychopathy checklist-assessed psychopathy: A review of the literature. *Clinical Psychology Review*, *33*, 979–995. https://doi.org/10.1016/j.cpr.2013.07.008.

Brook, M., & Kosson, D. S. (2013). Impaired cognitive empathy in criminal psychopathy: Evidence from a laboratory measure of empathic accuracy. *Journal of Abnormal Psychology*, *122*(1), 156–166. https://doi.org/10.1037/a0030261.

Campbell, J. S., & Elison, J. (2005). Shame coping styles and psychopathic personality traits. *Journal of Personality Assessment*, *84*(1), 96–104. https://doi.org/10.1207/s15327752jpa8401_16.

Carver, C., & Harmon-Jones, E. (2009). Anger is an approach-related affect: Evidence and implications. *Psychological Bulletin*, *135*(2), 183–204. https://doi.org/10.1037/a0013965.

Casey, H., Rogers, R. D., Burns, T., & Yiend, J. (2013). Emotion regulation in psychopathy. *Biological Psychology*, *92*, 541–548. https://doi.org/10.1016/j.biopsycho.2012.06.011.

Christian, E. J., Meltzer, C. L., Thede, L. L., & Kosson, D. S. (2017). The relationship between early life events, parental attachment, and psychopathic tendencies in adolescent detainees. *Child Psychiatry and Human Development*, *48*(2), 260–269. https://doi.org/10.1007/s10578-016-0638-3.

Christianson, S.-Å., Forth, A. E., Hare, R. D., Strachan, C., Lidberg, L., & Thorell, L.-H. (1996). Remembering details of emotional events: A comparison between psychopathic and nonpsychopathic offenders. *Personality and Individual Differences*, *20*, 437–443. https://doi.org/10.1016/0191-8869(95)00220-0.

Cleckley, H. M. (1941). *The mask of sanity*. St Louis, MO: Mosby.

Crick, N. R., & Dodge, K. A. (1994). A review and reformulation of social information-processing mechanisms in children's social adjustment. *Psychological Bulletin*, *115*(1), 74–101. https://doi.org/10.1037/0033-2909.115.1.74.

Crocker, L. D., Heller, W., Warren, S. L., O'Hare, A. J., Infantolino, Z. P., & Miller, G. A. (2013). Relationships among cognition, emotion, and motivation: Implications for intervention and neuroplasticty in psychopathology. *Frontiers in Human Neuroscience*, *7*, 1–19. https://doi.org/10.3389/fnhum.2013.00261.

Damasio, A. R., Everitt, B. J., & Bishop, D. (1996). The somatic marker hypothesis and the possible functions of the prefrontal cortex [and discussion]. *Philosophical Transactions of the Royal Society, B: Biological Sciences, 351*(1346), 1413–1420. https://doi.org/10.1098/rstb.1996.0125.

Dawel, A., O'Kearney, R., McKone, E., & Palermo, R. (2012). Not just fear and sadness: Meta-analytic evidence of pervasive emotion recognition deficits for facial and vocal expressions in psychopathy. *Neuroscience and Biobehavioral Reviews, 36*, 2288–2304. https://doi.org/10.1016/j.neubiorev.2012.08.006.

de Wied, M., van Boxtel, A., Matthys, W., & Meeus, W. (2012). Verbal, facial and autonomic responses to empathy-eliciting film clips by disruptive male adolescents with high versus low callous-unemotional traits. *Journal of Abnormal Child Psychology, 40*, 211–223. https://doi.org/10.1007/s10802-011-9557-8.

Decety, J., Skelly, L. R., & Kiehl, K. A. (2013). Brain response to empathy-eliciting scenarios involving pain in incarcerated individuals with psychopathy. *JAMA Psychiatry, 70*, 638–645. https://doi.org/10.1001/jamapsychiatry.2013.27.

Derefinko, K. J. (2015). Psychopathy and low anxiety: Meta-analytic evidence for the absence of inhibition, not affect. *Journal of Personality, 83*(6), 693–709. https://doi.org/10.1111/jopy.12124.

Dindo, L., & Fowles, D. (2011). Dual temperamental risk factors for psychopathic personality: Evidence from self-report and skin conductance. *Journal of Personality and Social Psychology, 100*, 557–566. https://doi.org/10.1037/a0021848.

Dolan, M., & Fullam, R. (2004). Theory of mind and mentalizing ability in antisocial personality disorders with and without psychopathy. *Psychological Medicine, 34*, 1093–1102. https://doi.org/10.1017/S0033291704002028.

Doninger, N. A., & Kosson, D. S. (2001). Interpersonal construct systems among psychopaths. *Personality and Individual Differences, 30*(8), 1263–1281. https://doi.org/10.1016/S0191-8869(00)00109-4.

Edens, J. F., Skopp, N. A., & Cahill, M. A. (2008). Psychopathic features moderate the relationship between harsh and inconsistent parental discipline and adolescent antisocial behavior. *Journal of Clinical Child and Adolescent Psychology, 37*(2), 472–476. https://doi.org/10.1080/15374410801955938.

Ekman, P. (1993). Facial expression and emotion. *The American Psychologist, 48*, 384–392. https://doi.org/10.1037/0003-066X.48.4.384.

Finger, E. C., Marsh, A. A., Mitchell, D. G., Reid, M. E., Sims, C., Budhani, S., … Blair, J. R. (2008). Abnormal ventromedial prefrontal cortex function in children with psychopathic traits during reversal learning. *Archives of General Psychiatry, 65*(5), 586–594. https://doi.org/10.1001/archpsyc.65.5.586.

Flor, H., Birbaumer, N., Hermann, C., Ziegler, S., & Patrick, C. J. (2002). Aversive Pavlovian conditioning in psychopaths: Peripheral and central correlates. *Psychophysiology, 39*(4), 505–518. https://doi.org/10.1017/S0048577202394046.

Fowles, D. C., & Dindo, L. (2009). Temperament and psychopathy: A dual-pathway model. *Current Directions in Psychological Science, 18*, 179–183. https://doi.org/10.1111/j.1467-8721.2009.01632.x.

Frijda, N. H. (2008). The psychologists' point of view. In M. Lewis, J. M. Haviland-Jones, & L. Feldman Barrett (Eds.), *Handbook of emotions* (pp. 68–87). New York, NY: Guilford Press.

Gao, Y., Raine, A., & Schug, R. A. (2012). Somatic aphasia: Mismatch of body sensations with autonomic stress reactivity in psychopathy. *Biological Psychology, 90*, 228–233. https://doi.org/10.1016/j.biopsycho.2012.03.015.

Garofalo, C., & Neumann, C. S. (2018). Psychopathy and emotion regulation: Taking stock and moving forward. In M. DeLisi (Ed.), *Routledge international handbook of psychopathy and crime* (pp. 76–97). London, UK: Routledge.

Garofalo, C., Neumann, C. S., & Velotti, P. (2018). Difficulties in emotion regulation and psychopathic traits in violent offenders. *Journal of Criminal Justice*, *57*, 116–125. https://doi.org/10.1016/j.jcrimjus.2018.05.013.

Garofalo, C., Neumann, C. S., Zeigler-Hill, V., & Meloy, J. R. (2019). Spiteful and contemptuous: A new look at the emotional experiences related to psychopathy. *Personality Disorders, Theory, Research, and Treatment*, *10*(2), 173–184. https://doi.org/10.1037/per0000310.

Georgiou, G., Kimonis, E. R., & Fanti, K. A. (2018). What do others feel? Cognitive empathy deficits explain the association between callous-unemotional traits and conduct problems among preschool children. *European Journal of Developmental Psychology*. https://doi.org/10.1080/17405629.2018.1478810.

Givon, E., Itzhak-Raz, A., Karmon-Presser, A., Danieli, G., & Meiran, N. (2019). How does the emotional experience evolve? Feeling generation as evidence accumulation. *Emotion*. https://doi.org/10.1037/emo0000537.

Gori, A., Craparo, G., Sareri, G. I., Caretti, V., Giannini, M., & Meringolo, P. (2014). Antisocial and psychopathic personalities in a sample of addicted subjects: Differences in psychological resources, symptoms, alexithymia and impulsivity. *Comprehensive Psychiatry*, *55*(7), 1580–1586. https://doi.org/10.1016/j.comppsych.2014.05.023.

Gross, J. J. (2002). Emotion regulation: Affective, cognitive, and social consequences. *Psychophysiology*, *39*, 281–291. https://doi.org/10.1017/S0048577201393198.

Hamilton, R. B., & Newman, J. P. (2018). The response modulation hypothesis: Formulation, development, and implications for psychopathy. In C. J. Patrick (Ed.), *Handbook of psychopathy* (pp. 80–93). New York, NY: The Guilford Press.

Hare, R. D. (1978). Psychopathy and electrodermal responses to nonsignal stimulation. *Biological Psychology*, *6*(4), 237–246. https://doi.org/10.1016/0301-0511(78)90026-1.

Hare, R. D. (1993). *Without conscience: The disturbing world of the psychopaths among us*. New York, NY: Simon & Schuster (Pocket Books).

Hare, R. D. (2003). *Manual for the revised psychopathy checklist-revised* (2nd ed.). Toronto, ON: Multi-Health Systems.

Hare, R. D., & Neumann, C. S. (2008). Psychopathy as a clinical and empirical construct. *Annual Review of Clinical Psychology*, *4*, 217–246. https://doi.org/10.1146/annurev.clinpsy.3.022806.091452.

Harenski, C. L., & Kiehl, K. A. (2010). Reactive aggression in psychopathy and the role of frustration: Susceptibility, experience, and control. *British Journal of Psychology*, *101*, 401–406. https://doi.org/10.1348/000712609X471067.

Herpertz, S. C., Werth, U., Lucas, G., Qunaibi, M., Schuerkens, A., Kunert, H., … Sass, H. (2001). Emotion in criminal offenders with psychopathy and borderline personality disorders. *Archives of General Psychiatry*, *58*, 737–745. https://doi.org/10.1001/archpsyc.58.8.737.

Hicks, B. M., & Patrick, C. J. (2006). Psychopathy and negative emotionality: Analyses of suppressor effects reveal distinct relations with emotional distress, fearfulness, and anger-hostility. *Journal of Abnormal Psychology*, *115*, 276–287. https://doi.org/10.1037/0021-843X.115.2.276.

Hoffman, M. L. (2000). *Empathy and moral development: Implications for caring and justice*. Cambridge, UK: Cambridge University Press.

Hoppenbrouwers, S. S., Bulten, B. H., & Brazil, I. A. (2016). Parsing fear: A reassessment of the evidence for fear deficits in psychopathy. *Psychological Bulletin*, *142*(6), 573–600. https://doi.org/10.1037/bul0000040.

Hyde, L. W., Waller, R., Trentacosta, C. J., Shaw, D. S., Neiderhiser, J. M., Ganiban, J. M., … Leve, L. D. (2016). Heritable and non-heritable pathways to early callous-unemotional behaviors. *The American Journal of Psychiatry*, *173*(9), 903–910. https://doi.org/10.1176/appi.ajp.2016.15111381.

James, W. (1884). What is an emotion? *Mind*, *9*, 188–205.

Keysers, C., & Gazzola, V. (2014). Dissociating the ability and propensity for empathy. *Trends in Cognitive Sciences*, *18*(4), 163–166. https://doi.org/10.1016/j.tics.2013.12.011.

Kiehl, K. A. (2006). A cognitive neuroscience perspective on psychopathy: Evidence for paralimbic system dysfunction. *Psychiatry Research*, *142*, 107–128. https://doi.org/10.1016/j.psychres.2005.09.013.

Kimonis, E. R., Centifanti, L. C. M., Allen, J. L., & Frick, P. J. (2014). Reciprocal influences between negative life events and callous-unemotional traits. *Journal of Abnormal Child Psychology*, *42*, 1287–1298. https://doi.org/10.1007/s10802-014-9882-9.

Kosson, D. S., McBride, C. K., Miller, S. A., Riser, N. R. E., & Whitman, L. A. (2018). Attentional bias following frustration in youth with psychopathic traits: Emotional deficit versus negative preception. *Journal of Experimental Psychopathology*. https://doi.org/10.5127/jep.060116.

Kosson, D. S., Vitacco, M. J., Swogger, M. T., & Steuerwald, B. L. (2016). Emotional experiences of the psychopath. In C. B. Gacono (Ed.), *The clinical and forensic assessment of psychopathy* (2nd ed.). New York: Routledge, Taylor & Francis Group.

Krieglmeyer, R., Deutsch, R., de Houwer, J., & de Raedt, R. (2010). Being moved: Valence activates approach-avoidance behavior independently of evaluation and approach-avoidance intentions. *Psychological Science*, *21*, 607–613. https://doi.org/10.1177/0956797610365131.

Künecke, J., Mokros, A., Olderbak, S., & Wilhelm, O. (2018). Facial responsiveness of psychopaths to the emotional expressions of others. *PLoS ONE*, *13*(1). https://doi.org/10.1371/journal.pone.0190714, e0190714.

Lang, P. J., Bradley, M. M., & Cuthbert, B. (1990). Emotion, attention, and the startle reflex. *Psychological Review*, *97*, 377–395. https://doi.org/10.1037/0033-295X.97.3.377.

Larsen, J. T., Berntson, G. G., Poehlmann, K. M., Ito, T. A., & Cacioppo, J. T. (2008). The psychophysiology of emotion. In M. Lewis, J. M. Haviland-Jones, & L. Feldman Barrett (Eds.), *Handbook of emotions* (pp. 180–195). New York, NY: Guilford Press.

Larson, C. L., Baskin-Sommers, A. R., Stout, D. M., Balderston, N. L., Curtin, J. J., Schultz, D. H., … Newman, J. P. (2013). The interplay of attention and emotion: Top-down attention modulates amygdala activation in psychopathy. *Cognitive, Affective, & Behavioral Neuroscience*, *13*, 757–770. https://doi.org/10.3758/s13415-013-0172-8.

Lazarus, R. S. (1991). Progress on a cognitive–motivational–relational theory of emotion. *The American Psychologist*, *46*, 819–834. https://doi.org/10.1037/0003-066X.46.8.819.

LeDoux, J. (1996). *The emotional brain*. New York: Simon & Schuster.

Levenston, G. K., Patrick, C. J., Bradley, M. M., & Lang, P. J. (2000). The psychopath as observer: Emotion and attention in picture processing. *Journal of Abnormal Psychology*, *109*, 373–385. https://doi.org/10.1037/0021-843X.109.3.373.

Lieberman, M. D. (2019). Boo! The consciousness problem in emotion. *Cognition & Emotion*, *33*(1), 24–30. https://doi.org/10.1080/02699931.2018.1515726.

Lobbestael, J., Arntz, A., Cima, M., & Chakhssi, F. (2009). Effects of induced anger in patients with antisocial personality disorder. *Psychological Medicine*, *39*(4), 557–568. https://doi.org/10.1017/S0033291708005102.

López, R., Poy, R., Patrick, C. J., & Moltó, J. (2013). Deficient fear conditioning and self-reported psychopathy: The role of fearless dominance. *Psychophysiology*, *50*, 210–218. https://doi.org/10.1111/j.1469-8986.2012.01493.x.

Lorenz, A. R., & Newman, J. P. (2002). Deficient response modulation and emotion processing in low-anxious Caucasian psychopathic offenders: Results from a lexical decision task. *Emotion*, *2*, 91–104. https://doi.org/10.1037/1528-3542.2.2.91.

Lykken, D. T. (1957). A study of anxiety in the sociopathic personality. *Journal of Abnormal and Social Psychology*, *55*, 6–10. https://doi.org/10.1037/h0047232.

Lykken, D. T. (1995). *The antisocial personalities*. Mahwah, NJ: Erlbaum.

Lynam, D. R., & Widiger, T. A. (2007). Using a general model of personality to identify the basic elements of psychopathy. *Journal of Personality Disorders*, *21*, 160–178. https://doi.org/10.1521/pedi.2007.21.2.160.

Maples-Keller, J. L., & Miller, J. D. (2018). Insight and the Dark Triad: Comparing self- and meta-perceptions in relation to psychopathy, narcissism, and Machiavellianism. *Personality Disorders, Theory, Research, and Treatment*, *9*(1), 30–39. https://doi.org/10.1037/per0000207.

Marsh, A. A., & Blair, R. J. R. (2008). Deficits in facial affect recognition among antisocial populations: A meta-analysis. *Neuroscience and Biobehavioral Reviews*, *32*, 454–465. https://doi.org/10.1016/j.neubiorev.2007.08.003.

Marsh, A. A., Finger, E. C., Schechter, J. C., Jurkowitz, I. T. N., Reid, M. E., & Blair, R. J. R. (2010). Adolescents with psychopathic traits report reductions in physiological responses to fear. *Journal of Child Psychology and Psychiatry*, *52*, 834–841. https://doi.org/10.1111/j.1469-7610.2010.02353.x.

Matsumoto, D., Keltner, D., Shiota, M. N., O'Sullivan, M., & Frank, M. (2008). Facial expressions of emotion. In M. Lewis, J. M. Haviland-Jones, & L. Feldman Barrett (Eds.), *Handbook of emotions* (pp. 211–234). New York, NY: Guilford Press.

Meffert, H., Gazzola, V., den Boer, J. A., Bartels, A. A., & Keysers, C. (2013). Reduced spontaneous but relatively normal deliberate vicarious representations in psychopathy. *Brain*, *136*, 2550–2562. https://doi.org/10.1093/brain/awt190.

Meloy, J. R. (1988). *The psychopathic mind: Origins, dynamics, and treatment*. Northvale, NJ: Jason Aronson.

Miller, J. D., & Lynam, D. R. (2015). Psychopathy and personality: Advances and debates. *Journal of Personality*, *83*, 585–592. https://doi.org/10.1111/jopy.12145.

Millon, T., & Strack, S. (2015). An integrating and comprehensive model of personality pathology based on evolutionary theory. In S. K. Huprich (Ed.), *Personality disorders: Toward theoretical and empirical integration in diagnosis and assessment* (pp. 367–393). Washington, DC: American Psychological Association.

Mills-Koonce, W. R., Wagner, N. J., Willoughby, M. T., Stifter, C., Blair, C., Granger, D. A., & Family Life Project Key Investigators. (2015). Greater fear reactivity and psychophysiological hyperactivity among infants with later conduct problems and callous-unemotional traits. *Journal of Child Psychology and Psychiatry, and Allied Disciplines*, *56*(2), 147–154. https://doi.org/10.1111/jcpp.12289.

Mitchell, D. G. V., Colledge, E., Leonard, A., & Blair, R. J. R. (2002). Risky decisions and response reversal: Is there evidence of orbito-frontal cortex dysfunction in psychopathic individuals? *Neuropsychologia*, *40*, 2013–2022. https://doi.org/10.1016/S0028-3932(02)00056-8.

Mitchell, D. G. V., Richell, R. A., Leonard, A., & Blair, R. J. R. (2006). Emotion at the expense of cognition: Psychopathic individuals outperform controls on an operant response task. *Journal of Abnormal Psychology*, *115*, 559–566. https://doi.org/10.1037/0021-843X.115.3.559.

Moul, C., Killcross, S., & Dadds, M. R. (2012). A model of differential amygdala activation in psychopathy. *Psychological Review*, *119*(4), 789–806. https://doi.org/10.1037/a0029342.

Muñoz Centifanti, L. C., Kimonis, E. R., Frick, P. J., & Aucoin, K. J. (2013). Emotional reactivity and the association between psychopathy-linked narcissism and aggression in detained adolescent boys. *Development and Psychopathology*, *25*(2), 473–485. https://doi.org/10.1017/S0954579412001186.

Muñoz, L. C., Frick, P. J., Kimonis, E. R., & Aucoin, K. J. (2008). Types of aggression, responsiveness to provocation, and callous-unemotional traits in detained adolescents. *Journal of Abnormal Child Psychology*, *36*(1), 15–28. https://doi.org/10.1007/s10802-007-9137-0.

Nentjes, L., Bernstein, D. P., Arntz, A., van Breukelen, G., & Slaats, M. (2015). Examining the influence of psychopathy, hostility biases, and automatic processing on criminal offenders' theory of mind. *Journal of International Law and Psychiatry*, *38*, 92–99. https://doi.org/10.1016/j.ijlp.2015.01.012.

Nentjes, L., Bernstein, D. P., Meijer, E., Arntz, A., & Wiers, R. W. (2016). The mask of sanity: Facial expressive, self-reported, and physiological consequences of emotion regulation in psychopathic offenders. *Journal of Personality Disorders*, *30*, 235–263. https://doi.org/10.1521/pedi_2016_30_235.

Nentjes, L., Meijer, E. H., Bernstein, D. P., Arntz, A., & Medendorp, W. N. (2013). Investigating the relationship between psychopathy and interoceptive awareness. *Journal of Personality Disorders*, *27*, 617–624. https://doi.org/10.1521/pedi_2013_27_105.

Newman, J., & Baskin-Sommers, A. (2016). Smith and lilienfeld's meta-analysis of the response modulation hypothesis: Important theoretical and quantitative clarifications. *Psychological Bulletin*, *142*(12), 1384–1393. https://doi.org/10.1037/bul0000056.

Newman, J. P. (1998). Psychopathy: An information processing perspective. In D. J. Cooke, A. E. Forth, & R. D. Hare (Eds.), *Psychopathy: Theory, research, and implications for society* (pp. 81–104). London, UK: Kluwer Academic Press.

Newman, J. P., & Baskin-Sommers, A. (2011). Early selective attention abnormalities in psychopathy: Implications for self-regulation. In M. Posner (Ed.), *Cognitive neuroscience of attention*. New York, NY: Guilford Press.

Newman, J. P., Curtin, J. J., Bertsch, J. D., & Baskin-Sommers, A. R. (2010). Attention moderates the fearlessness of psychopathic offenders. *Biological Psychiatry*, *67*(1), 66–70. https://doi.org/10.1016/j.biopsych.2009.07.035.

Newman, J. P., & Kosson, D. S. (1986). Passive avoidance learning in psychopathic and nonpsychopathic offenders. *Journal of Abnormal Psychology*, *95*(3), 252–256. https://doi.org/10.1037/0021-843X.95.3.252.

Ogloff, J. R. P., & Wong, S. (1990). Electrodermal and cardiovascular evidence of a coping response in psychopaths. *Criminal Justice and Behavior*, *17*, 231–245. https://doi.org/10.1177/0093854890017002006.

Pasalich, D. S., Dadds, M. R., Hawes, D. J., & Brennan, J. (2011). Do callous-unemotional traits moderate the relative importance of parental coercion versus warmth in child conduct problems? An observational study. *Journal of Child Psychology and Psychiatry*, *52*(12), 1308–1315. https://doi.org/10.1111/j.1469-7610.2011.02435.x.

Pastor, M. C., Moltó, J., Vila, J., & Lang, P. J. (2003). Startle reflex modulation, affective ratings and autonomic reactivity in incarcerated Spanish psychopaths. *Psychophysiology*, *40*(6), 934–938. https://doi.org/10.1111/1469-8986.00111.

Patrick, C. J., Bradley, M. M., & Lang, P. J. (1993). Emotion in the criminal psychopath: Startle reflex modulation. *Journal of Abnormal Psychology*, *102*(1), 82–92. https://doi.org/10.1037/0021-843X.102.1.82.

Patrick, C. J., Cuthbert, B. N., & Lang, P. J. (1994). Emotion in the criminal psychopath: Fear image processing. *Journal of Abnormal Psychology*, *103*, 523–534. https://doi.org/10.1037/0021-843X.103.3.523.

Patrick, C. J., Fowles, D. C., & Krueger, R. F. (2009). Triarchic conceptualization of psychopathy: Developmental origins of disinhibition, boldness, and meanness. *Development and Psychopathology*, *21*, 913–938. https://doi.org/10.1017/S0954579409000492.

Penney, S. R., & Kosson, D. S. (2014). *Affect regulation and psychopathy: How developmental theory can inform the etiology and manifestation of psychopathic features in youth.* (Manuscript submitted for publication).

Pham, T. H., Philippot, P., & Rime, B. (2000). Subjective and autonomic responses to emotion induction in psychopaths. *L'Encéphale*, *26*, 45–51.

Plutchik, R. (2001). The nature of emotions. *American Scientist*, *89*, 344–350.

Power, M. J., & Dalgleish, T. (2008). *Cognition and emotion: From order to disorder* (2nd ed.). Hove, UK: Taylor Francis.

Reidy, D. E., Kearns, M. C., DeGuea, S., Lilienfeld, S. O., Massetti, G., & Kiehl, K. A. (2015). Why psychopathy matters: Implications for public health and violence prevention. *Aggression and Violent Behavior*, *24*, 214–225. https://doi.org/10.1016/j.avb.2015.05.018.

Reidy, D. E., Zeichner, A., Hunnicutt-Ferguson, K., & Lilienfeld, S. O. (2008). Psychopathy traits and the processing of emotion words: Results of a lexical decision task. *Cognition & Emotion*, *22*, 1174–1186. https://doi.org/10.1080/02699930701745663.

Ribeiro da Silva, D., Vagos, P., & Rijo, D. (2019). An evolutionary model to conceptualize psychopathic traits across community and forensic male youth. *International Journal of Offender Therapy and Comparative Criminology*, *63*(4), 574–596. https://doi.org/10.1177/0306624X18823624.

Ridings, L. E., & Lutz-Zois, C. J. (2014). Emotional dysregulation and borderline personality disorder: Explaining the link between secondary psychopathy and alexithymia. *Personality and Individual Differences*, *57*, 14–19. https://doi.org/10.1016/j.paid.2013.09.008.

Roberton, T., Daffern, M., & Bucks, R. S. (2012). Emotion regulation and aggression. *Aggression and Violent Behavior*, *17*, 72–82. https://doi.org/10.1016/j.avb.2011.09.006.

Roberton, T., Daffern, M., & Bucks, R. S. (2015). Beyond anger control: Difficulty attending to emotions also predicts aggression in offenders. *Psychology of Violence*, *5*, 74–83. https://doi.org/10.1037/a0037214.

Rothemund, Y., Ziegler, S., Hermann, C., Gruesser, S. M., Foell, J., Patrick, C. J., & Flor, H. (2012). Fear conditioning in psychopaths: Event-related potentials and peripheral measures. *Biological Psychology*, *90*, 50–59. https://doi.org/10.1016/j.biopsycho.2012.02.011.

Schachter, S., & Singer, J. E. (1962). Cognitive, social, and physiological determinants of emotional state. *Psychological Review*, *69*, 379–399. https://doi.org/10.1037/h0046234.

Scherer, K. R. (2000). Psychological models of emotion. In J. C. Borod (Ed.), *The neuropsychology of emotion* (pp. 137–162). New York, NY: Oxford University Press.

Schmauk, F. J. (1970). Punishment, arousal, and avoidance learning in sociopaths. *Journal of Abnormal Psychology*, *76*(3, Pt.1), 325–335. https://doi.org/10.1037/h0030398.

Schultz, D. H., Balderston, N. L., Baskin-Sommers, A. R., Larson, C. L., & Helmstetter, F. J. (2016). Psychopaths show enhanced amygdala activation during fear conditioning. *Frontiers in Psychology*, *7*. https://doi.org/10.3389/fpsyg.2016.00348.

Shamay-Tsoory, S. G., Harari, H., Aharon-Peretz, J., & Levkovitz, Y. (2010). The role of the orbitofrontal cortex in affective theory of mind deficits in criminal offenders with psychopathic tendencies. *Cortex*, *46*(5), 668–677. https://doi.org/10.1016/j.cortex.2009.04.008.

Shane, M. S., & Groat, L. L. (2018). Capacity for upregulation of emotional processing in psychopathy: All you have to do is ask. *Social Cognitive and Affective Neuroscience*, *13*(11), 1163–1176. https://doi.org/10.1093/scan/nsy088.

Smith, S. F., & Lilienfeld, S. O. (2015). The response modulation hypothesis of psychopathy: A meta-analytic and narrative analysis. *Psychological Bulletin*, *141*(6), 1145–1177. https://doi.org/10.1037/bul0000024.

Spantidaki-Kyriazi, S., Bogaerts, S., Tamir, M., Denissen, J. J. A., & Garofalo, C. (2021). Emotion goals: A missing piece in research on psychopathy and emotion regulation. *Journal of Personality Disorders*, *35*(A), 57–82. https://doi.org/10.1521/pedi_2020_34_488.

Steuerwald, B. L., Brown, A. R., Mneimne, M., & Kosson, D. (2017). Anger following provocation in individuals with psychopathic traits. *Journal of Criminal Psychology*, *7*(4), 244–261. https://doi.org/10.1108/JCP-02-2017-0007.

Taubner, S., White, L. O., Zimmermann, J., Fonagy, P., & Nolte, T. (2013). Attachment-related mentalization moderates the relationship between psychopathic traits and proactive aggression in adolescence. *Journal of Abnormal Child Psychology*, *41*(6), 929–938. https://doi.org/10.1007/s10802-013-9736-x.

Terasawa, Y., Fukushima, H., & Umeda, S. (2013). How does interoceptive awareness interact with the subjective experience of emotion? An fMRI study. *Human Brain Mapping*, *34*, 598–612. https://doi.org/10.1002/hbm.21458.

Terburg, D., Hooiveld, N., Aarts, H., Kenemans, J. L., & van Honk, J. (2011). Eye tracking unconscious face-to-face confrontations: Dominance motives prolong gaze to masked angry faces. *Psychological Science*, *22*, 314–319. https://doi.org/10.1177/0956797611398492.

Veit, R., Konicar, L., Klinzing, J. G., Barth, B., Yilmaz, Ö., & Birbaumer, N. (2013). Deficient fear conditioning in psychopathy as a function of interpersonal and affective disturbances. *Frontiers in Human Neuroscience*, *7*, 706. https://doi.org/10.3389/fnhum.2013.00706.

Velotti, P., Elison, J., & Garofalo, C. (2014). Shame and aggression: Different trajectories and implications. *Aggression and Violent Behavior*, *19*(4), 454–461. https://doi.org/10.1016/j.avb.2014.04.011.

Verona, E., Patrick, C. J., Curtin, J. J., Bradley, M. M., & Lang, P. J. (2004). Psychopathy and physiological response to emotionally evocative sounds. *Journal of Abnormal Psychology*, *113*, 99–108. https://doi.org/10.1037/0021-843X.113.1.99.

Viding, E., & McCrory, E. J. (2012). Genetic and neurocognitive contributions to the development of psychopathy. *Development and Psychopathology*, *24*, 969–983. https://doi.org/10.1017/S095457941200048X.

Vitacco, M. J., & Kosson, D. S. (2010). Understanding psychopathy through an evaluation of interpersonal behavior: Testing the factor structure of the interpersonal measure of psychopathy in a large sample of jail detainees. *Psychological Assessment*, *22*, 638–649. https://doi.org/10.1037/a0019780.

Vitale, J. E., Newman, J. P., Serin, R. C., & Bolt, D. M. (2005). Hostile attributions in incarcerated adult male offenders: An exploration of diverse pathways. *Aggressive Behavior*, *31*, 99–115. https://doi.org/10.1002/ab.20050.

Von Borries, A. K. L., Volman, I., de Bruijn, E. R. A., Bulten, B. H., Verkse, R. J., & Roelofs, K. (2012). Psychopaths lack the automatic avoidance of social threat: Relation to instrumental aggression. *Psychiatry Research*, *200*, 761–766. https://doi.org/10.1016/j.psychres.2012.06.026.

Waller, R., Gardner, F., Viding, E., Shaw, D. S., Dishion, T. J., Wilson, M. N., & Hyde, L. W. (2014). Bidirectional associations between parental warmth, callous unemotional behavior, and behavior problems in high-risk preschoolers. *Journal of Abnormal Child Psychology*, *42*(8), 1275–1285. https://doi.org/10.1007/s10802-014-9871-z.

Waller, R., Shaw, D. S., Forbes, E. E., & Hyde, L. W. (2015). Understanding early contextual and parental risk factors for the development of limited prosocial emotions. *Journal of Abnormal Child Psychology*, *43*(6), 1025–1039. https://doi.org/10.1007/s10802-014-9965-7.

Wiens, S., Mezzacappa, E. S., & Katkin, E. S. (2000). Heartbeat detection and the experience of emotions. *Cognition & Emotion*, *14*, 417–427. https://doi.org/10.1080/026999300378905.

The development of psychopathy through the lifespan and its relation to offending

5

David P. Farrington and Henriette Bergstrøm

Introduction

Psychopathy within a developmental and life-course criminology perspective

The current chapter takes a Developmental and Life-Course (DLC) Criminology perspective on the relationship between psychopathy and offending. DLC Criminology is an established and very productive field within the larger discipline of Criminology (Carlsson & Sarnecki, 2015; Kazemian, Farrington, & Piquero, 2019). Research in this field has informed knowledge and practice in areas such as why people commit crime (e.g., Choy et al., 2019; Fagan & Benedini, 2019; Farrington, 2005a; Jolliffe & Farrington, 2019), specialization and versatility in offending (e.g., Mazerolle & McPhedran, 2019), the intergenerational transmission of offending (e.g., Farrington, Ttofi, & Crago, 2017, Farrington, Ttofi, & Crago, 2018), what works in rehabilitation (e.g., Zara, 2019), and what factors encourage desistance (e.g., Liu & Bushway, 2019).

As we will show throughout this chapter, DLC Criminology is a useful framework for understanding the relationship between psychopathy and criminal behavior and delinquency (Fox, Jennings, & Farrington, 2015). Based on results from longitudinal studies, we have learned much about the development of psychopathy and criminality. Unique for this chapter is that, instead of focusing on differences *between* people on psychopathy and offending, we will here look at *within-individual* relationships over time. This is central to the DLC Criminology perspective (Carlsson & Sarnecki, 2015; Farrington, 2005b; Kazemian et al., 2019).

Definition and measurement

Psychopathy is most commonly understood as a personality disorder with traits or symptoms that load on to four facets named interpersonal (facet 1), affective (facet 2), lifestyle (facet 3), and antisocial (facet 4). These four facets load on to two higher order factors referred to as interpersonal/affective (Factor 1) and lifestyle/antisocial (social deviance) (Factor 2) (Hare, 2003). The most common way of measuring psychopathy has been through the Hare Psychopathy Checklist tradition (Hare, 2003), which has prompted the development of multiple derivatives allowing for investigations across the life-course (e.g., for youth, the Hare Psychopathy Checklist: Youth Version; Forth, Kosson, & Hare, 2003; for children/youth, Antisocial Process Screening

Psychopathy and Criminal Behavior. https://doi.org/10.1016/B978-0-12-811419-3.00014-5

Device; Frick & Hare, 2001) and across contexts (e.g., correctional settings: Hare P-SCAN; Hare & Herve, 1999; self-report in nonforensic settings, the SRP-4: Paulhus, Neumann, Hare, Williams, & Hemphill, 2017; screening for traits in forensic samples and in the community, the Hare Psychopathy Screening Version, PCL:SV; Hart, Cox, & Hare, 1995). For a more thorough discussion of measurement issues, please see Morey et al. (Chapter 6) and Ryan Veal and Ogloff (Chapter 7).

Psychopathy and offending

Ever since the early historical conceptualizations of psychopathy, the role of offending, delinquency, and antisocial behavior has been central to this construct (Hare, 1980, 1991, 2003; Hare & Neumann, 2010; Millon, Simonsen, & Birket-Smith, 1998). Cleckley (1988) included "inadequately motivated antisocial behavior" in the psychopath's clinical profile: "*He will commit theft, forgery, adultery, fraud and other deeds for astonishingly small stakes and under much greater risks of being discovered than will the ordinary scoundrel. He will in fact, commit such deeds in the absence of any apparent goal at all*" (Cleckley, 1988, p. 343). The emphasis on antisociality was continued within the Hare PCL tradition (Hare, 1980, 1991, 2003), which has been described earlier and discussed elsewhere (e.g., see Cooke, 2014).

Much research has shown that psychopathy is predictive of antisocial and criminal behavior in adolescence and adulthood (e.g., Boddy, 2011; Boduszek, Debowska, & Willmott, 2017; Dembo et al., 2007; Firestone, Bradford, Greenberg, & Serran, 2000; Forth, Hart, & Hare, 1990; Myers, Chan, Vo, & Lazarou, 2010; Porter et al., 2000; Ragatz, Fremouw, & Baker, 2012).

As highlighted in Bergstrøm, Larmour, and Farrington (2018) the relationship between psychopathy and violence is especially strong. Psychopathy is, however, related to other crimes as well, such as being implicated in sexual offenses (e.g., McCuish, Lussier, & Corrado, Chapter 15), and especially in sexual homicides (DeLisi & Fox, Chapter 16). For a more in-depth discussion of how psychopathy is related to offending style, please see Youngs and Tkazky (Chapter 12). Of more recent interest has been how psychopathy is related to more "modern" crimes (e.g., white-collar crime and corporate misdeeds, Mathieu, Chapter 19; cybercrime; March, Chapter 20; human trafficking, Hargreaves-Cormany and colleagues, Chapter 17; violent extremism, Gill & Corner, Chapter 18).

There is a major issue of tautology in comparing the PCL measures of psychopathy with antisocial behavior, because the PCL includes antisocial behavior. A critic might complain that this is merely showing that antisocial behavior predicts antisocial behavior (see Bergstrøm et al., 2018; Cooke, 2014; Hare & Neumann, 2010; Skeem & Cooke, 2010a, 2010b). It would be desirable to study the more personality-oriented Factor 1 separately from the more behavior-oriented Factor 2 in investigating the relation between psychopathic personality and offending.

Psychopathy and offending within theoretical frameworks

Previous reviews (e.g., Bergstrøm et al., 2018; Cooke, 2014) have discussed the importance of understanding the mechanisms underlying the relationship between psychopathy and criminal behavior. Why are psychopathic traits and symptoms related to criminal behavior and offending? While we try to avoid rhetorical questions, in this context they facilitate a review of theoretical underpinnings that can explain the relationship (see also Bergstrøm et al., 2018).

From an evolutionary psychology standpoint, the psychopathic traits, symptoms, and behaviors appear to be adaptive in securing human and genetic survival (Glenn & Raine, 2009; Hare, 1993). Evolutionary psychology has been increasing in popularity as an explanatory framework for psychopathy (Da Silva, Rijo, & Salekin, 2015; Glenn, Kurzban, & Raine, 2011). Within this framework, the antisocial and criminal behavior, committed by people who are high on psychopathic traits, is a strategy across the life-course that has led to effective natural selection (Glenn & Raine, 2009; Walsh & Wu, 2008). There is research showing that there is both intergenerational transmission of criminal behavior (Besemer & Farrington, 2012; Farrington, Coid, & Murray, 2009; Farrington, Ttofi, & Crago, 2017; Långström, Babchishin, Fazel, Lichtenstein, & Frisell, 2015) and of psychopathy (Auty, Farrington, & Coid, 2015), indicating that antisociality and delinquency are working tactics that are transmitted across generations.

From a criminological perspective, DeLisi (2009, 2016) and Fox et al. (2015) are the most noted examples of how psychopathy has been included in criminological theories. DeLisi (2009, 2016) took this integration further and suggested that psychopathy is the core explanatory variable for a wide range of antisocial and criminal activity. DeLisi (2016) also showed how psychopathic traits might contribute to such behavior from adolescence to adulthood—taking a developmental and life-course perspective on the relationship between psychopathy and offending.

Fox et al. (2015) took a somewhat different approach to the theoretical understanding of how psychopathy is related to criminal behavior and delinquency. As highlighted in the introduction to this chapter, DLC Criminology has spurred great interest in theory generation (Carlsson & Sarnecki, 2015; Farrington, 2005b; Kazemian et al., 2019), and Fox et al. (2015) successfully showed how psychopathy as a clinical construct can be a valuable addition to many DLC theories and increase their explanatory power in the understanding of offending behavior. We will here refer to how psychopathy is related to delinquency in some of the most central DLC theories. Fox et al. (2015) have shown how psychopathy can increase different types of antisocial potential (AP) across the life-course in the renowned Integrated Cognitive Antisocial Potential (ICAP) theory (Farrington, 2005a; Farrington & McGee, 2019); that psychopathic youths are more likely to follow a life-course persistent (LCP) pathway in Moffitt's (McGee & Moffitt, 2019; Moffitt, 1993) prominent developmental taxonomy; that they show delinquent behavior in accordance with the Overt pathway in Loeber's (Loeber, 2019) Developmental Pathways model; that they have a high degree of intergenerational transmission in traits and behavior in Thornberry and Krohn's interactional theory (Thornberry & Krohn, 2019); and that psychopathy increases criminal propensity in Wikström's Situational Action Theory (Wikström, 2005; Wikström & Treiber, 2019). For a more thorough overview, we recommend the reader to consult Fox et al. (2015) directly.

It is unfortunate that the study of psychopathy tends to have been divorced from the study of normative personality. Miller, Lynam, Widiger, and Leukefeld (2001) argued that psychopathy could be understood within the five-factor model of personality and measured using the NEO-PI-R (Costa & McCrae, 1992). For example, Kavish, Bergstrøm, Piquero, Farrington, and Boutwell (2020) measured psychopathy using both the PCL:SV and the NEO-PI-R and showed that low resting heart rate in adolescence predicted both measures of psychopathy at age 48. It would be desirable for the study of psychopathy to be integrated more with mainstream psychology and criminology.

Longitudinal studies and psychopathy

What these theoretical perspectives, ranging from evolutionary psychology to psychopathy to DLC criminology theories, suggest is that the relationship between psychopathy and antisocial and criminal behavior is likely to co-occur across the life-course. Uniquely for the DLC Criminological theories is their emphasis on, and their foundation in, longitudinal studies (Farrington, 2005b). Farrington has repeatedly called for more prospective longitudinal studies on psychopathy (e.g., Bergstrøm et al., 2018; Farrington & Bergstrøm, 2018).

Surprisingly, there are very few prospective longitudinal studies that have included measures of psychopathy, and there are several potential explanations for this. Some of the most prominent longitudinal studies started years before there were widely accepted measures in place for the assessment of psychopathic personality (e.g., the original Hare PCL was not published until 1980) (Salekin & Lynam, 2010), while other criminological studies might not have been that interested in a clinical "psychological" construct such as psychopathy. Also, inspired by Hare's focus on adult prisoners, psychopathy researchers have been more interested in biological correlates of psychopathy than in the development of psychopathy from childhood. There has been some reluctance even to accept the idea of childhood psychopathy (see e.g., Farrington, 2005c).

The following section presents some longitudinal studies that have psychopathy measures available that are relevant to the current context.

Social and physical development, intervention, and adaptation

The social and physical development, intervention, and adaptation (SOFIA) study is a Swedish prospective longitudinal study that is unique in research on psychopathy because of the young age of the participants at the start of the study. The sample was selected from a representative town in Sweden, and all the children born in a 2-year period (2005–07) in this town were eligible to participate. The researchers were able to secure cooperation from a high percentage of the eligible children (response rate: 85.7%; $N=2121$). At the first data collection in 2010, the youngest children were age 3, and the oldest children were age 5 (Klingzell, Fanti, Colins, Andershed, & Andershed, 2016). A novel measure of psychopathic symptoms in children was developed and tested on this sample; namely the Child Problematic Traits Inventory (CPTI; Colins et al., 2014), which allowed for the assessment of psychopathic traits in early childhood (age 3 and onwards). The emerging empirical research available from this study indicates that psychopathic traits are mainly stable during this developmental period (Klingzell et al., 2016) and predict conduct problems (Frogner, Gibson, Andershed, & Andershed, 2018). Since these children are too young for official criminal records, the latter result is perhaps the best indication of later antisociality, since conduct problems are related to later criminality (e.g., Farrington, Loeber, & van Kammen, 1990; Satterfield et al., 2007).

Pittsburgh Youth Study

The Pittsburgh Youth Study (PYS) has not only contributed to knowledge on general delinquency (Jennings, Loeber, Pardini, Piquero, & Farrington, 2015), but also to the understanding of psychopathy (e.g., Lynam, 1997, 1998). The Pittsburgh Youth Study (PYS) is a prospective longitudinal study consisting of three cohorts (oldest, middle, and youngest) that was started in 1987 (Loeber, Farrington, Stouthamer-Loeber, & van Kammen, 1998; Loeber et al., 2001). The follow-up period differed depending on the cohort. The oldest cohort was in the seventh grade at the start of the study, the middle cohort was in the fourth grade, and the youngest cohort was in the first grade (Loeber et al., 2001). The PYS has been central in understanding development, as the widely used Child Psychopathy Scale (CPS; Lynam, 1997) was created and validated on data from this study. Studies using the CPS on data from the PYS have found that psychopathic traits in youth are predictive of delinquency and antisocial behavior (Lynam, 1997, 1998; Lynam, Miller, Vachon, Loeber, & Stouthamer-Loeber, 2009), and this has also been replicated using other measures of psychopathic symptoms (e.g., Neumann & Pardini, 2014; Vize, Lynam, Lamkin, Miller, & Pardini, 2016).

Incarcerated Serious and Violent Young Offender Study (ISVYOS)

The Incarcerated Serious and Violent Young Offender Study (ISVYOS) is unique in the current context as it is not based on a community sample like the other prospective longitudinal studies discussed here. Instead, the sample consists of high-risk delinquent youth in Canada in the province of British Columbia (B.C.) (Corrado, McCuish, Hart, & DeLisi, 2015; McCuish, Lussier, & Corrado, 2021). The ISVYOS duration is more than 20 years (Corrado et al., 2015), and the ages of the participants ranged from early adolescence (age 12) to emerging adulthood (age 19) (Lussier, McCuish, & Corrado, 2015). The main inclusion criteria were that the youths were incarcerated in young offender institutions (closed or open) (Corrado, Cohen, Glackman, & Odgers, 2003; Corrado et al., 2015; Lussier et al., 2015).

Research from this study has informed the relationship between psychopathy and offending. For example, psychopathy in youths has been found to be robustly related to offending (Corrado et al., 2015; McCuish, Corrado, Hart, & DeLisi, 2015; McCuish, Corrado, Lussier, & Hart, 2014). Because of the time that had passed since the start of the ISVYOS, these three studies were able to assess the relationship over a longer time period (age 12–28). All of these studies utilized subsamples of over 300 males and females (the majority were males), and as such they provide a very good understanding of psychopathy and offending over time. We recommend the reader to access Chapter 15 for more information about the work of McCuish, Lussier, and Corrado, and to read an upcoming book summarizing the first 20 years of ISVYOS (McCuish et al., 2021).

MacArthur Violence Risk Assessment Study

The MacArthur Violence Risk Assessment Study is a comprehensive clinical study of more than 1000 psychiatric patients in the United States (Monahan et al., 2001). According to Monahan et al. (2001) no children were included in the study as all participants were over the age of 18 at the initial data collection. There was however also a maximum age of 40, and as a result, middle age and old age patients were not represented in this study. The data collection started when the participants were in-patients on one of the hospital sites included in the study, and they were then followed up in the community after release from the hospital (Monahan et al., 2001). Compared to the other studies mentioned in this section, this is a longitudinal study of shorter duration (1 year after discharge), but there were multiple assessment waves across this year. Participants were interviewed (mainly in person) a total of five times (Monahan et al., 2001).

Skeem and Mulvey (2001) assessed the relationship between psychopathy as measured by the PCL:SV and violence using data from the MacArthur Violence Risk Assessment Study, and found that psychopathic symptoms were indeed related to violence. It should however be noted that other factors (e.g., criminal history and substance abuse) appeared to impact this relationship and should be taken into consideration when critically evaluating the relationship between psychopathy and violence. Edens, Skeem, and Douglas (2006) did however find, in another study using this sample that the psychopathy construct was central to predicting violence when it was compared with a widely used violence risk assessment tool. Furthermore, using a smaller subsample from this study, Neumann and Hare (2008) also found significant relationships between all of the components of psychopathy (interpersonal, affective, lifestyle, and antisocial) and violence. In this study, the strongest relationships were found between the affective features ($r=0.40$) and the antisocial features ($r=0.46$) and violence.

Cambridge Study in Delinquent Development

The Cambridge Study in Delinquent Development (CSDD) is perhaps the most important prospective longitudinal study within the field of DLC Criminology because of its longevity, its real-world policy impact (e.g., Rock, 1994), and its large volume of empirical research (e.g., Farrington, 2003, 2019a, 2019b; Farrington, Coid, & West, 2009; Farrington et al., 2018; Farrington, Ttofi, & Crago, 2017). The CSDD has been a template for other influential criminological studies, as well as influencing theory development and refinement (Farrington, 2005a; Farrington & McGee, 2019). This chapter will present new results from the CSDD and describe it in more detail. To summarize for the current paragraph, the CSDD followed 411 males from childhood across the life-course (Generation 2, "G2"). Data was also obtained from Generation 2's parents (Generation 1, "G1") and Generation 2's biological children

(Generation 3, "G3"). The CSDD has contributed to the knowledge base about psychopathy in several ways; for example, how early risk factors (i.e., at individual, family, and socioenvironmental levels) are predictive of later psychopathy (e.g., Farrington & Bergstrøm, 2018).

Some notable findings on the relationship between psychopathy and offending have also come from this study. Farrington and Bergstrøm (2018) found that the higher the score on the PCL:SV, the more convictions the males had. Piquero et al. (2012) conducted an interesting study, where different offending trajectories were investigated in relation to psychopathy at age 48. The results indicated that males who engaged in chronic offending ("high-rate chronics") from the age of 10 until 40 had higher psychopathy scores than nonoffenders and other offending trajectories (e.g., "low-adolescence peak"). More recently, Theobald, Farrington, Coid, and Piquero (2016) investigated how psychopathy was related to intimate partner violence (IPV) in the G2 males. The authors found that based on all facets and factors of psychopathy, those who had engaged in IPV were higher on psychopathic traits at age 48 than those who had not engaged in such violence.

What do we know from these prospective longitudinal studies?

The current section ("Longitudinal studies and psychopathy" section) has provided an overview of some long-running and some more recent prospective longitudinal studies spanning multiple developmental periods. Based on the SOFIA study, we know that psychopathic traits in early childhood are related to antisocial behavior (Frogner et al., 2018). Results from the PYS indicate that psychopathy is predictive of offending behavior in adolescence (e.g., Lynam et al., 2009), and the CSDD shows how psychopathic traits are related to delinquency across the life-course (e.g., Farrington & Bergstrøm, 2018; Piquero et al., 2012; Theobald et al., 2016). In addition, it appears that these relationships are found for samples in the community (e.g., results from SOFIA, PYS, and the CSDD), for incarcerated samples (e.g., the ISVYOS), as well as in former psychiatric patients (e.g., MacArthur Violence Risk Assessment Study). However, there are still important gaps in knowledge that need to be addressed.

The current study: What do we need to know?

The current chapter has reviewed the relationship between psychopathy and offending within a Developmental and Life-Course (DLC) Criminology perspective. This criminological framework allows for a better understanding of criminal behavior than traditional criminological theories (Farrington, 2005a, 2005b). To study the relationship between psychopathy and offending in-depth, it is necessary to carry out prospective longitudinal studies so that one can follow the same individuals across time—the focus is relationships *within* individuals, not *between* individuals (see e.g., Farrington, 2005a; Farrington & Bergstrøm, 2018).

As highlighted in this chapter, there are strong theoretical bases for psychopathy to be related to criminal behavior, and the emerging knowledge base from prominent prospective longitudinal studies indicates that this relationship may be consistent across the life-course and across contexts. There are however still some research gaps as most of the studies have only focused on one or two developmental periods (usually childhood and adolescence). As a result, this limits our understanding of the relationship between psychopathy and offending. The current chapter attempts to provide a more comprehensive understanding of the relationship by not just looking at whether or not individuals have been convicted, but also how psychopathy is related to the number of convictions (and offenses), the duration of criminal careers, and the length of incarceration during criminal careers.

The Cambridge Study in Delinquent Development

Past and more recent results from the CSDD have been referred to earlier in this chapter. The current section will provide a broader overview, before presenting new results from this study.

Design and sample

The CSDD is a prospective longitudinal study that was started in the early 1960s by Professor Donald West. The original aim of the study was to follow the development of delinquency from late childhood and onwards. The sample consisted of 411 males from South London (G2); they were living in a relatively deprived area at the time. Since the aim was to establish explanations of delinquency and criminal careers, the sample selection was influenced by a need to increase the likelihood of delinquent cases developing. The sample is unique as it is a community sample, but at the same time, it is of higher risk than the "typical" community sample (Farrington, 2003; Farrington & Bergstrøm, 2018). For example, Farrington (2019a) found that by the age of 61, 44% of the original G2 males had at least one conviction throughout their life-course. Recent research by Zara and Farrington (2019, 2020) showed that 54 offenders were considered life-course persistent offenders according to official conviction records, and 56 qualified as life-course persistent offenders based on self-reported offending. For an in-depth description of some of these chronic offenders, please see Zara and Farrington (2016). Later, the biological children of the G2 males who were at least 18 at the time of assessment were interviewed (Generation 3; "G3") (Farrington & Bergstrøm, 2018).

Procedure

The CSDD started interviewing the G2 boys when they were 8 years old. The interviews were carried out regularly until the age of 18 by social workers. A total of nine interviews have been conducted across the life-course; the last interview was at age 48. Across childhood and adolescence, a wide range of variables were measured based on tests in schools and interviews with the boys, their parents, peers, and teachers. The social interview at age 48 included a psychopathy assessment. Criminal convictions and self-reported offenses were assessed on a regular basis across the life-course (for more information, please see Farrington & Bergstrøm, 2018).

Variables

In the current study we focused on psychopathy measures as predictors and convictions and self-reported offenses as outcome variables.

Psychopathy

Psychopathy was measured at different time points in the life-course. As highlighted earlier in this chapter, validated measures of psychopathy were not available when the G2 males were adolescents. However, retrospective coding of the data at age 12–14 was carried out using the Antisocial Process Screening Device (APSD; Frick & Hare, 2001). The coding was endorsed by two other scholars who were familiar with the measure, and the 12–14 and 16–18 APSD scores have been used in prior publications (Bergstrøm & Farrington, 2018; Bergstrøm, Forth, & Farrington, 2016). The APSD measures psychopathic symptoms in childhood and adolescence (Frick & Hare, 2001), and the score ranges between 0 and 40 (20 items were each measured on an ordinal scale ranging from 0 to 2). For the current study, the total APSD scores were used in the analyses.

Psychopathy in adulthood was measured at age 48 using the Hare Psychopathy Checklist: Screening Version (PCL:SV; Hart et al., 1995) which consists of 12 items with a total score of 24 (each item scored on an ordinal scale ranging from 0 to 2). The PCL:SV is a shorter version (i.e., a screening tool) of the more comprehensive Hare Psychopathy Checklist-Revised (PCL-R; Hare, 2003). The PCL:SV measures psychopathy as an overarching psychopathy score with two underlying factors (Factor 1: Interpersonal/Affective; Factor 2: Lifestyle/Antisocial), and four facets (facet 1: Interpersonal; facet 2: Affective; facet 3: Lifestyle, facet 4: Antisocial).

Offending

Convictions were measured from age 10 to age 61 in the CSDD (the age of criminal responsibility is 10 in the United Kingdom). For information about the conviction data in the CSDD, please see Farrington (2019a, 2019b). Convictions are here treated both as a continuous variable (the number of convictions) and whether individuals have been convicted (1 means that they have not been convicted across the life-course, while 2 means that they had a criminal conviction). The duration of the criminal career (age of most recent criminal conviction minus age of first criminal conviction), the number of criminal convictions and offenses (one conviction could be for multiple offenses), and the time spent in incarceration during the criminal career were also included. The time spent incarcerated was estimated from the sentence length (it was generally between half and two-thirds of the sentence). It was added up over all sentences.

Analytical approach

There are many ways of assessing relationships between variables in this context, and there is much debate on this topic (e.g., Farrington & Loeber, 2000; Hanson, 2009; Helmus & Babchishin, 2017). The current study will initially investigate whether there are group differences in average levels of psychopathy between those that have engaged in criminal behavior and those who have not. We will then calculate Cohen's *d* to measure effect sizes (e.g., Hanson, 2009; Helmus & Babchishin, 2017). Bivariate correlations were calculated between psychopathy and criminal career duration, number of convictions (and offenses), and time spent incarcerated (during criminal careers).

Results

Group differences

The results from Table 1 show that there are group differences in the average level of psychopathic traits, and independent *t*-tests indicated that nearly all of the differences were significant at $P<.001$. Table 1 shows that those who have been convicted of a criminal offense at some point during their life-time score higher on psychopathy overall than those who have not been convicted. The calculated effect sizes (Cohen's *d*'s) show that the strongest effect is for the total score of the PCL:SV, Factor 2 (Lifestyle/Antisocial), and facet 4 (Antisocial). Using Cohen's (1988) guidelines, the effects range from medium to big effects. This indicates that there are quite large differences between those who have been convicted and those who have not been convicted in terms of psychopathy. The large effects for Factor 2 and Facet 4 are not surprising since these measure antisocial behavior directly (also see Bergstrøm et al., 2018 for a discussion of tautology). It should however be noted that the effect sizes for Factor 1,

Table 1 Psychopathic symptoms versus conviction status.

	Not convicted Mean (SD)	Convicted Mean (SD)	Cohen's *d*
APSD total age 12–14	10.04 (3.07)	12.09 (4.51)	0.53**
APSD total age 16–18	11.83 (3.04)	13.04 (3.70)	0.36*
PCL:SV total age 48	1.65 (2.19)	5.88 (4.19)	1.27**
Factor 1 interpersonal/affective	0.69 (1.16)	1.79 (1.83)	0.72**
Facet 1 interpersonal	0.29 (0.64)	0.81 (0.98)	0.63**
Facet 2 affective	0.40 (0.77)	0.98 (1.24)	0.56**
Factor 2 lifestyle/antisocial	0.96 (1.35)	4.09 (2.80)	1.42**
Facet 3 lifestyle	0.29 (0.59)	1.04 (1.34)	0.72**
Facet 4 antisocial	0.67 (1.34)	3.05 (1.73)	1.54**

* Significant at $P<.05$.
** Significant at $P<.001$.

Facet 1, and Facet 2 are in the medium to large range (Cohen, 1988), showing the importance of these symptoms' relationship with offending. Furthermore, Cohen's guidelines for effect sizes should be adjusted down because data from social science studies rarely conform to the mathematical requirements (e.g., equal-interval scales, normally distributed, linearly related, error-free) (Bergstrøm et al., 2016).

Bivariate correlations

While Table 1 highlights that those who have been convicted for criminal behavior are overall higher on psychopathic traits than those who have not, these findings have limited utility in understanding how psychopathy is related to offending across the life-course (partly because of the issue of tautology). Table 2 elucidates the relationship in a more comprehensive manner through investigating how psychopathic traits are related to the duration of criminal careers, the number of convictions across the life-course, as well as the time spent incarcerated. Following Farrington's (2019a) study on the duration of criminal careers, the current chapter shows that there are significant positive relationships between psychopathic symptoms and criminal career duration. It appears that the higher someone is on psychopathy, the longer their criminal career is (e.g., $r=0.36$ between psychopathy at age 12–14 and criminal career duration and $r=0.55$ between psychopathy at age 48 and criminal career duration). Following the adjusted recommendations for effect sizes by Bergstrøm et al. (2016), these are sizeable effects that should not be ignored. In light of these results, it is not surprising that psychopathy is similarly related to number of convictions/offenses. The positive relationships between psychopathy and time spent in incarceration are also not surprising in light of these initial findings. Psychopathic symptoms are also typically higher among prisoners (Hare, 2003).

Table 2 Bivariate correlations (Pearson's ***r***).

	Duration of criminal career	**Number of convictions**	**Number of offenses**	**Time in incarceration**
APSD age 12–14	0.36**	0.41**	0.41**	0.24**
APSD age 16–18	0.26**	0.30**	0.31**	0.13**
PCL:SV total age 48	0.55**	0.73**	0.72**	0.34**
Factor 1 interpersonal/ affective	0.38**	0.53**	0.53**	0.23**
Facet 1 interpersonal	0.29*	0.42**	0.41*	0.06
Facet 2 affective	0.34**	0.46**	0.47**	0.29**
Factor 2 lifestyle/ antisocial	0.57**	0.75**	0.74**	0.36**
Facet 3 lifestyle	0.48**	0.62**	0.61**	0.38**
Facet 4 antisocial	0.55**	0.72**	0.71**	0.30**

* $P<.05$.
** $P<.01$.

Conclusions

Psychopathy and life-course offending

A developmental and life-course perspective on the relationship between psychopathy and offending has been lacking in the literature. Even the available criminological prospective longitudinal studies tend to focus on the earlier stages of life. This is however not surprising, since many of the longitudinal studies are recently started studies (e.g., SOFIA), which limits the long-term study of this relationship. The CSDD, because of its longevity and rigorous methodology, is therefore unique among its peers in its ability to follow offending from age 10 to 61.

The results indicate that not only does it appear that psychopathy is related to convictions across the life-course, but being high on psychopathic symptoms is also related to longer criminal careers, more convictions (and offenses), as well as time incarcerated during the criminal career. The results are consistent for psychopathic symptoms measured both in adolescence and in middle age. The consistency of the relationship across the life-course is in accordance with the DLC Criminology literature.

These results suggest that psychopathic personality should be incorporated into DLC theories. For example, in the ICAP theory (Farrington, 2005b, 2020), it could be incorporated as an additional factor that influences antisocial potential (AP). Based on the results of Farrington and Bergstrøm (2018), it could be suggested that a convicted parent, poor child-rearing, low family income, low IQ/attainment, and high impulsiveness all contribute to the development of psychopathic personality, which in turn influences long-term antisocial potential. Alternatively, psychopathic personality could be used as an empirical measure of the underlying theoretical construct of antisocial potential, rather than antisocial attitude (which was used by Farrington & McGee, 2017, 2019). Future research on the ICAP theory should compare and contrast these two ways in which psychopathic personality could be incorporated. Also, we plan to measure psychopathy in the CSDD at age 32, so that we will be better able to track the development of psychopathy from ages 12–14 to age 48.

Implications for criminal justice interventions

There are several important implications for criminal justice interventions. The results indicate that those who score high on psychopathic symptoms are antisocial across the life-course, indicating the need for developmental interventions across different developmental periods. While some have argued ardently against the successful treatment of psychopathy (e.g., Harris & Rice, 2006), Farrington and Bergstrøm (2018) reviewed early interventions, and argued that the best approach to reducing psychopathic symptoms and antisocial behavior is to target childhood risk factors associated with later psychopathy. Other reviews have come to similar conclusions. For example, Hawes, Price, and Dadds (2014) reviewed methodologically sound studies on interventions and found that targeting parental behaviors (i.e., targeting socioenvironmental risk factors) was quite successful in reducing callous-unemotional traits.

Since risk factors for psychopathy seem to mirror risk factors for general offending (see for example Farrington, 2015; Farrington & Bergstrøm, 2018), it is arguably useful to draw on the general best-practices literature of risk-focused prevention. Programs that are targeted at multiple interconnected levels around the individual child are likely to increase success rates (Farrington, 2000, 2015; Farrington, Gaffney, Lösel, & Ttofi, 2017). These could take place in the home, at school, and/or in the community and should involve the most central people in the child's life such as parents (Farrington, 2015). Some examples of programs that were discussed in Farrington and Bergstrøm (2018) that could be used with youths high on psychopathic symptoms are David Olds' nurse-family partnership program (e.g., Bilukha et al., 2005; Eckenrode et al., 2010), the Perry Pre-School Program (e.g., Schweinhart et al., 2005), and the Triple-P Positive Parenting Programme (e.g., Thomas & Zimmer-Gembeck, 2007).

A program that shows great potential in reducing delinquency is the SNAP program (Augimeri, Walsh, Kivlenieks, & Pepler, 2017; Burke & Loeber, 2015; Koegl, Farrington, Augimeri, & Day, 2008), and we argue that this program should be evaluated on children with psychopathic traits. The SNAP program was developed in Canada, and SNAP stands for "Stop Now and Plan" and targets children from the age of 6–11 (Augimeri et al., 2017; Burke & Loeber, 2015). The children enrolled in the program are taught how to stop when they are about to do something impulsively, snap their fingers, and consider alternative actions (Augimeri, Walsh, Donato, Blackman, & Piquero, 2018). The program is a form of cognitive behavioral therapy at an individual level but includes important additional components for both the children and parents (Augimeri et al., 2017, 2018; Koegl et al., 2008). The goal of the program, across the span of 12 weeks, is to facilitate skill development in both the at-risk child as well as their parents (Burke & Loeber, 2015; Koegl et al., 2008). The SNAP program has been found to not only reduce offending, but also to be cost effective (Farrington & Koegl, 2015). Since the current study shows that psychopathic symptoms are associated with duration of criminal careers, convictions, and time spent incarcerated, children at risk should be targeted as early as possible. The use of the Child Problematic Traits Inventory (CPTI; Colins et al., 2014) that allows for the measurement of such symptoms in children in early childhood would be beneficial in this context.

Taking a DLC Criminology perspective also allows for a longer time-frame across multiple developmental periods (Carlsson & Sarnecki, 2015; Kazemian et al., 2019). As Loeber and Farrington (1998) argued, evidence-based interventions can be successful later in life. The results presented in the current chapter indicate that scoring high on psychopathy is related to spending more time incarcerated across the life-course, which means that programs for adults in prisons might be fruitful. In the United Kingdom, the Chromis program is offered to offenders who score high on psychopathic symptoms. Chromis is an accredited program in the Her Majesty's Prison and Probation Service (HMPPS) where the main focus is on individual level cognitive treatment targets (Tew & Atkinson, 2013). There are some promising results (e.g., Tew, Bennett, & Dixon, 2016; Tew, Dixon, Harkins, & Bennett, 2012). Also, Henfrey (2018) describes Kaizen as a program that might work well with this group of offenders. Kaizen not only takes account of individual level treatment targets but considers that the offender's behavior is influenced by social factors as well, so the program takes a broader biopsychosocial approach. Long-term, methodologically sound evaluations are however needed to assess the effect that these programs might have on reducing both offending and psychopathic symptoms in this group of offenders.

By the time a person is justice-involved to the point of incarceration in adulthood, their life opportunities would have been severely reduced and they would have incurred great costs to society (Farrington & Welsh, 2008; Moffitt, 1993). There are also questions about whether treatment in adulthood will truly be effective (Polaschek & Skeem, 2018). We strongly recommend that policy makers should focus their resources on programs that target childhood socioenvironmental risk factors, as these are likely to be most effective and to save most money at both individual and society levels (Caspi et al., 2016; Farrington & Welsh, 2008; Olds et al., 2010) and this approach has been shown to be successful with delinquency and psychopathic symptoms (e.g., Farrington & Bergstrøm, 2018; Farrington & Welsh, 2008). However, more research is needed on early intervention programs and their effect on psychopathic symptoms. There is also a great need for prospective longitudinal studies following the effects of programs on individuals across multiple developmental periods (Farrington & Bergstrøm, 2018), and evaluations of programs should be replicated in multiple longitudinal samples; for more on the need for replication, please see Farrington et al. (2019) and Lösel (2018).

Acknowledgments

For funding the CSDD, we are very grateful to the Home Office, the Department of Health, the Department for Education, the Rayne foundation, the Barrow Cadbury Trust, and the Smith-Richardson Foundation. For carrying out criminal record searches, we are very grateful to Gwen Gundry in the 1960s and 1970s, Lynda Morley in the 1980s, Sandra Lambert in the 1990s, Debbie Wilson in the 2000s, Owen Thomas in 2011–12, and Lisa Robinson in 2017.

References

Augimeri, L. K., Walsh, M., Donato, A., Blackman, A., & Piquero, A. R. (2018). SNAP (Stop Now And Plan): Helping children improve their self-control and externalizing behavior problems. *Journal of Criminal Justice*, *56*, 43–49.

Augimeri, L. K., Walsh, M., Kivlenieks, M., & Pepler, D. (2017). Addressing children's disruptive behavior problems: A thirty-year journey with SNAP (stop now and plan). In P. Sturmey (Ed.), *Handbook of violence and aggression, Volume 2: Assessment, prevention, and treatment of individuals*. U.S.: Wiley-Blackwell (Chapter 28).

Auty, K. M., Farrington, D. P., & Coid, J. W. (2015). Intergenerational transmission of psychopathy and mediation via psychosocial risk factors. *British Journal of Psychiatry*, *206*, 26–31.

Bergstrøm, H., & Farrington, D. P. (2018). Grandiose-manipulative, callous-unemotional, and daring-impulsive: The prediction of psychopathic traits in adolescence and their outcomes in adulthood. *Journal of Psychopathology and Behavioral Assessment*, *40*, 149–158.

Bergstrøm, H., Forth, A. E., & Farrington, D. P. (2016). The psychopath: Continuity or change? In A. Kapardis, & D. P. Farrington (Eds.), *The psychology of crime, policing, and courts* (pp. 94–115). Abingdon: Routledge.

Bergstrøm, H., Larmour, S. R., & Farrington, D. P. (2018). The usefulness of psychopathy in explaining and predicting violence: Discussing the utility of competing perspectives. *Aggression and Violent Behavior*, *42*, 84–95.

Besemer, S., & Farrington, D. P. (2012). Intergenerational transmission of criminal behaviour: Conviction trajectories of fathers and their children. *European Journal of Criminology*, *9*, 120–141.

Bilukha, O., Hahn, R. A., Crosby, A., Fullilove, M. T., Liberman, A., Moscicki, E., et al. (2005). The effectiveness of early childhood home visitation in preventing violence. *American Journal of Preventive Medicine*, *28*, 11–39.

Boddy, C. R. (2011). The corporate psychopaths theory of the global financial crisis. *Journal of Business Ethics*, *102*, 255–259.

Boduszek, D., Debowska, A., & Willmott, D. (2017). Latent profile analysis of psychopathic traits among homicide, general violent, property, and white-collar offenders. *Journal of Criminal Justice*, *51*, 17–23.

Burke, J. D., & Loeber, R. (2015). The effectiveness of the stop now and plan (SNAP) program for boys at risk for violence and delinquency. *Prevention Science*, *16*, 242–253.

Carlsson, C., & Sarnecki, J. (2015). *An introduction to life-course criminology*. London: Sage.

Caspi, A., Houts, R. M., Belsky, D. W., Harrington, H., Hogan, S., Ramrakha, S., et al. (2016). Childhood forecasting of a small segment of the population with large economic burden. *Nature Human Behaviour*, *1*, 0005.

Choy, O., Portnoy, J., Raine, A., Remmel, R. J., Schug, R., Tuvblad, C., et al. (2019). Biosocial influences on offending across the life course. In D. P. Farrington, L. Kazemian, & A. R. Piquero (Eds.), *The Oxford handbook of developmental and life-course criminology* (pp. 325–354). Oxford: Oxford University Press.

Cleckley. (1988). *The mask of sanity. An attempt to clarify some issues about the so called psychopathic personality* (5th ed.). Augusta, GA: Emily Cleckley.

Cohen, J. (1988). *Statistical power analysis for the behavioral sciences* (2nd ed.). Hillsdale: Erlbaum.

Colins, O. F., Andershed, H., Frogner, L., Lopez-Romero, L., Veen, V., & Andershed, A.-K. (2014). A new measure to assess psychopathic personality in children: The child problematic traits inventory. *Journal of Psychopathology and Behavioral Assessment*, *36*, 4–21.

Cooke, D. J. (2014). Psychopathy and offending. In G. Bruinsma, & D. Weisburd (Eds.), *Encyclopedia of criminology and criminal justice* (pp. 4126–4134). New York: Springer.

Corrado, R. R., Cohen, I. M., Glackman, W., & Odgers, C. (2003). Serious and violent young offenders' decisions to recidivate: An assessment of five sentencing models. *Crime and Delinquency*, *49*, 179–200.

Corrado, R. R., McCuish, E. C., Hart, S. D., & DeLisi, M. (2015). The role of psychopathic traits and developmental risk factors on offending trajectories from early adolescence to adulthood: A prospective study of incarcerated youth. *Journal of Criminal Justice*, *43*, 357–368.

Costa, P. T., & McCrae, R. R. (1992). The five-factor model of personality and its relevance to personality disorders. *Journal of Personality Disorders*, *6*(4), 343–359.

Da Silva, D. R., Rijo, D., & Salekin, R. T. (2015). The evolutionary roots of psychopathy. *Aggression and Violent Behavior*, *21*, 85–96.

DeLisi, M. (2009). Psychopathy is the unified theory of crime. *Youth Violence and Juvenile Justice*, *7*, 256–273.

DeLisi, M. (2016). *Psychopathy as unified theory of crime*. New York: Palgrave Macmillan.

Dembo, R., Jainchill, N., Turner, C., Fong, C., Farkas, S., & Childs, K. (2007). Levels of psychopathy and its correlates: A study of incarcerated youths in three states. *Behavioral Sciences & the Law*, *25*, 717–738.

Eckenrode, J., Campa, M., Luckey, D. W., Henderson, C. R., Cole, R., Kitzman, H., et al. (2010). Long-term effects of prenatal and infancy nurse home visitation on the life course of youths. *Archives of Pediatrics and Adolescent Medicine*, *164*, 9–15.

Edens, J. F., Skeem, J. L., & Douglas, K. S. (2006). Incremental validity analyses of the violence risk appraisal guide and the psychopathy checklist: Screening version in a civil psychiatric sample. *Assessment*, *13*, 368–374.

Fagan, A. A., & Benedini, K. M. (2019). Family influences on youth offending. In D. P. Farrington, L. Kazemian, & A. R. Piquero (Eds.), *The Oxford handbook of developmental and life-course criminology* (pp. 378–403). Oxford: Oxford University Press.

Farrington, D. P. (2000). Explaining and preventing crime: The globalization of knowledge—The American Society of Criminology 1999 presidential address. *Criminology*, *38*, 1–24.

Farrington, D. P. (2003). Key results from the first 40 years of the Cambridge study in delinquent development. In T. P. Thornberry, & M. D. Krohn (Eds.), *Taking stock of delinquency: An overview of findings from contemporary longitudinal studies* (pp. 137–183). New York: Kluwer/Plenum.

Farrington, D. P. (2005a). The integrated cognitive antisocial potential (ICAP) theory. In D. P. Farrington (Ed.), *Advances in criminological theory: Vol. 14. Integrated developmental and life-course theories of offending* (pp. 73–92). New York: Routledge.

Farrington, D. P. (2005b). Introduction to integrated developmental and life-course theories of offending. In D. P. Farrington (Ed.), *Advances in criminological theory: Vol. 14. Integrated developmental and life-course theories offending* (pp. 1–14). New York: Routledge.

Farrington, D. P. (2005c). The importance of child and adolescent psychopathy. *Journal of Abnormal Child Psychology*, *33*, 489–497.

Farrington, D. P. (2015). The developmental evidence base: The prevention base. In D. A. Crighton, & G. J. Towl (Eds.), *Forensic psychology* (2nd ed., pp. 141–159). Chichester: John Wiley & Sons.

Farrington, D. P. (2019a). The duration of criminal careers: How many offenders do not desist up to age 61? *Journal of Developmental and Life-Course Criminology*, *5*, 4–21.

Farrington, D. P. (2019b). The Cambridge study in delinquent development. In D. Eaves, C. D. Webster, Q. Haque, & J. Eaves-Thalken (Eds.), *Risk rules: A practical guide to structured professional judgment and violence prevention* (pp. 225–233). Hove, East Sussex: Pavilion Publishing.

Farrington, D. P. (2020). The integrated cognitive antisocial potential (ICAP) theory: Past, present, and future. *Journal of Developmental and Life-Course Criminology*, *6*, 172–187.

Farrington, D. P., & Bergstrøm, H. (2018). Family background and psychopathy. In C. J. Patrick (Ed.), *Handbook of psychopathy* (2nd ed., pp. 354–379). New York: Guilford Publications.

Farrington, D. P., Coid, J. W., & Murray, J. (2009). Family factors in the intergenerational transmission of offending. *Criminal Behavior and Mental Health*, *19*, 109–124.

Farrington, D. P., Coid, J. W., & West, D. J. (2009). The development of offending from age 8 to age 50: Recent results from the Cambridge Study in Delinquent Development. *Monatsschrift fur Kriminologie und Strafrechtsreform (Journal of Criminology and Penal Reform)*, *92*, 160–173.

Farrington, D. P., Gaffney, H., Lösel, F., & Ttofi, M. M. (2017). Systematic reviews of the effectiveness of developmental prevention programs in reducing delinquency, aggression and bullying. *Aggression and Violent Behavior*, *33*, 91–106.

Farrington, D. P., & Koegl, C. J. (2015). Monetary benefits and costs of the stop now and plan program for boys aged 6-11, based on the prevention of later offending. *Journal of Quantitative Criminology*, *31*, 263–287.

Farrington, D. P., & Loeber, R. (2000). Some benefits of dichotomization in psychiatric and criminological research. *Criminal Behavior and Mental Health*, *10*, 100–122.

Farrington, D. P., Loeber, R., & van Kammen, W. B. (1990). Long term criminal outcomes of hyperactivity-impulsivity-attention deficit and conduct problems in childhood. In L. N. Robins, & M. Rutter (Eds.), *Straight and devious pathways from childhood to adulthood* (pp. 62–81). Cambridge: Cambridge University Press.

Farrington, D. P., Lösel, F., Boruch, R. F., Gottfredson, D. C., Mazerolle, L., Sherman, L. W., et al. (2019). Advancing knowledge about replication in criminology. *Journal of Experimental Criminology*, *15*, 373–396.

Farrington, D. P., & McGee, T. R. (2017). The integrated cognitive antisocial potential (ICAP) theory: Empirical testing. In A. Blokland, & V. van der Geest (Eds.), *The Routledge handbook of life-course criminology* (pp. 11–28). Abingdon: Routledge.

Farrington, D. P., & McGee, T. R. (2019). The integrated cognitive antisocial potential (ICAP) theory: New empirical tests. In D. P. Farrington, L. Kazemian, & A. R. Piquero (Eds.), *The Oxford handbook of developmental and life-course criminology* (pp. 173–192). Oxford: Oxford University Press.

Farrington, D. P., Ttofi, M., & Crago, R. V. (2017). Intergenerational transmission of convictions for different types of offenses. *Victims and Offenders*, *12*, 1–20.

Farrington, D. P., Ttofi, M. M., & Crago, R. V. (2018). Intergenerational transmission of self reported offending in the Cambridge Study in Delinquent Development. In V. I. Eichelsheim, & S. G. A. Van de Weijer (Eds.), *Intergenerational continuity of criminal and antisocial behaviour: An international overview of studies* (pp. 115–136). Abingdon: Routledge.

Farrington, D. P., & Welsh, B. C. (2008). *Saving children from a life of crime: Early risk factors and effective interventions*. Oxford: Oxford University Press.

Firestone, P., Bradford, J. M., Greenberg, D. M., & Serran, G. A. (2000). The relationship of deviant sexual arousal and psychopathy in incest offenders, extrafamilial child molesters, and rapists. *Journal of the American Academy of Psychiatry and the Law*, *28*(3), 303–308.

Forth, A. E., Hart, S. D., & Hare, R. D. (1990). Assessment of psychopathy in male young offenders. *Psychological Assessment: A Journal of Consulting and Clinical Psychology*, *2*, 342–344.

Forth, A. E., Kosson, D. S., & Hare, R. D. (2003). *Hare psychopathy checklist: Youth version*. Toronto: Multi Health Systems.

Fox, B. H., Jennings, W. G., & Farrington, D. P. (2015). Bringing psychopathy into developmental and life-course criminology theories and research. *Journal of Criminal Justice*, *43*, 274–289.

Frick, P. J., & Hare, R. D. (2001). *Antisocial process screening device*. Toronto: Multi Health Systems.

Frogner, L., Gibson, C. L., Andershed, A.-K., & Andershed, H. (2018). Childhood psychopathic personality and callous-unemotional traits in the prediction of conduct problems. *American Journal of Orthopsychiatry*, *88*, 211–225.

Glenn, A. L., Kurzban, R., & Raine, A. (2011). Evolutionary theory and psychopathy. *Aggression and Violent Behavior*, *16*, 371–380.

Glenn, A. L., & Raine, A. (2009). Psychopathy and instrumental aggression: Evolutionary, neurobiological, and legal perspectives. *International Journal of Law and Psychiatry*, *32*, 253–258.

Hanson, R. K. (2009). The psychological assessment of risk for crime and violence. *Canadian Psychology*, *50*, 172–182.

Hare, R. D. (1980). A research scale for the assessment of psychopathy in criminal populations. *Personality and Individual Differences*, *1*, 111–119.

Hare, R. D. (1991). *Hare psychopathy checklist-revised.* Toronto: Multi Health Systems.

Hare, R. D. (1993). *Without conscience: The disturbing world of the psychopaths among us.* New York: Guilford Press.

Hare, R. D. (2003). *Hare psychopathy checklist-revised* (2nd ed.). Toronto: Multi Health Systems.

Hare, R. D., & Herve, H. F. (1999). *Hare P-SCAN*. Toronto: Multi Health Systems.

Hare, R. D., & Neumann, C. S. (2010). The role of antisociality in the psychopathy construct: Comment on Skeem and Cooke. *Psychological Assessment*, *22*, 446–454.

Harris, G. T., & Rice, M. E. (2006). Treatment of psychopathy. A review of empirical findings. In C. J. Patrick (Ed.), *Handbook of psychopathy* (pp. 555–572). New York: Guilford Press.

Hart, S. D., Cox, D. N., & Hare, R. D. (1995). *Psychopathy checklist: Screening version (PCL:SV)*. Toronto: Multi Health Systems.

Hawes, D. J., Price, M. J., & Dadds, M. R. (2014). Callous-unemotional traits and the treatment of conduct problems in childhood and adolescence: A comprehensive review. *Clinical Child and Family Psychology Review*, *17*, 248–267.

Helmus, L. M., & Babchishin, K. M. (2017). Primer on risk assessment and the statistics used to evaluate its accuracy. *Criminal Justice and Behavior*, *44*, 8–25.

Henfrey, S. A. (2018). Kaizen: Working responsively with psychopathic traits. *Journal of Criminological Research, Policy and Practice*, *4*, 199–211.

Jennings, W. G., Loeber, R., Pardini, D. A., Piquero, A. R., & Farrington, D. P. (2015). *Offending from childhood to young adulthood. Recent results from the Pittsburgh Youth Study*. New York: Springer.

Jolliffe, D., & Farrington, D. P. (2019). Personality and other individual influences on offending. In D. P. Farrington, L. Kazemian, & A. R. Piquero (Eds.), *The Oxford handbook of developmental and life-course criminology* (pp. 355–377). Oxford: Oxford University Press.

Kavish, N., Bergstrøm, H., Piquero, A. R., Farrington, D. P., & Boutwell, B. B. (2020). The longitudinal association between resting heart rate and psychopathic traits from a normative personality perspective. *American Journal of Criminal Justice*, *45*, 410–425.

Kazemian, L., Farrington, D. P., & Piquero, A. R. (2019). Developmental and life-course criminology. In D. P. Farrington, L. Kazemian, & A. R. Piquero (Eds.), *The Oxford handbook of developmental and life-course criminology* (pp. 3–10). Oxford: Oxford University Press.

Klingzell, I., Fanti, K. A., Colins, O. F., Andershed, A.-K., & Andershed, H. (2016). Early childhood trajectories of conduct problems and callous-unemotional traits: The role of fearlessness and psychopathic personality dimensions. *Child Psychiatry and Human Development*, *47*, 236–247.

Koegl, C. J., Farrington, D. P., Augimeri, L. K., & Day, D. M. (2008). Evaluation of a targeted cognitive-behavioral program for children with conduct problems—The SNAP® under 12 outreach project: Service intensity, age, and gender effects on short- and long-term outcomes. *Clinical Child Psychology and Psychiatry*, *13*, 419–434.

Långström, N., Babchishin, K. M., Fazel, S., Lichtenstein, P., & Frisell, T. (2015). Sexual offending runs in families: A 37-year nationwide study. *International Journal of Epidemiology*, *44*, 713–720.

Liu, S., & Bushway, S. D. (2019). Persistence and desistance. In D. P. Farrington, L. Kazemian, & A. R. Piquero (Eds.), *The Oxford handbook of developmental and life-course criminology* (pp. 81–96). Oxford: Oxford University Press.

Loeber, R. (2019). Developmental pathways to conduct problems and serious forms of delinquency. In D. P. Farrington, L. Kazemian, & A. R. Piquero (Eds.), *The Oxford handbook of developmental and life-course criminology* (pp. 159–172). Oxford: Oxford University Press.

Loeber, R., & Farrington, D. P. (1998). Never too early, never too late: Risk factors and successful interventions for serious and violent juvenile offenders. *Studies on Crime and Crime Prevention*, *7*, 7–30.

Loeber, R., Farrington, D. P., Stouthamer-Loeber, M., Moffitt, T. E., Caspi, A., & Lynam, D. (2001). Male mental health problems, psychopathy, and personality traits: Key findings from the first 14 years of the Pittsburgh Youth Study. *Clinical Child and Family Psychology Review*, *4*, 273–297.

Loeber, R., Farrington, D. P., Stouthamer-Loeber, M., & van Kammen, W. B. (1998). *Antisocial behavior and mental health problems: Explanatory factors in childhood and adolescence*. Mahwah, NJ: Lawrence Erlbaum.

Lösel, F. (2018). Evidence comes by replication, but needs differentiation: The reproducibility issue in science and its relevance for criminology. *Journal of Experimental Criminology*, *14*, 257–278.

Lussier, P., McCuish, E., & Corrado, R. R. (2015). The adolescence-adulthood transition and desistance from crime: Examining the underlying structure of desistance. *Journal of Developmental and Life-Course Criminology*, *1*, 87–117.

Lynam, D. R. (1997). Pursuing the psychopath: Capturing the fledgling psychopath in a nomological net. *Journal of Abnormal Psychology*, *106*, 425–438.

Lynam, D. R. (1998). Early identification of the fledgling psychopath: Locating the psychopathic child in the current nomenclature. *Journal of Abnormal Psychology*, *107*, 566–575.

Lynam, D. R., Miller, D. J., Vachon, D., Loeber, R., & Stouthamer-Loeber, M. (2009). Psychopathy in adolescence predicts official reports of offending in adulthood. *Youth Violence and Juvenile Justice*, *7*, 189–207.

Mazerolle, P., & McPhedran, S. (2019). Specialization and versatility in offending. In D. P. Farrington, L. Kazemian, & A. R. Piquero (Eds.), *The Oxford handbook of developmental and life-course criminology* (pp. 49–69). Oxford: Oxford University Press.

McCuish, E. C., Corrado, R. R., Hart, S. D., & DeLisi, M. (2015). The role of symptoms of psychopathy in persistent violence over the criminal career into full adulthood. *Journal of Criminal Justice*, *43*, 345–356.

McCuish, E. C., Corrado, R. R., Lussier, P., & Hart, S. D. (2014). Psychopathic traits and offending trajectories from early adolescence to adulthood. *Journal of Criminal Justice*, *42*, 66–76.

McCuish, E. C., Lussier, P., & Corrado, R. R. (2021). *The life course of serious and violent youth grown up: A twenty-year longitudinal study*. Abingdon: Routledge.

McGee, T. R., & Moffitt, T. E. (2019). The developmental taxonomy. In D. P. Farrington, L. Kazemian, & A. R. Piquero (Eds.), *The Oxford handbook of developmental and life-course criminology* (pp. 149–158). Oxford: Oxford University Press.

Miller, J. D., Lynam, D. R., Widiger, T. A., & Leukefeld, C. (2001). Personality disorders as extreme variants of common personality dimensions: Can the five-factor model of personality adequately represent psychopathy? *Journal of Personality*, *69*, 253–276.

Millon, T., Simonsen, E., & Birket-Smith, M. (1998). Historical conceptions of psychopathy in the United States and Europe. In T. Millon, E. Simonsen, M. Birket-Smith, & R. D. Davis (Eds.), *Psychopathy: Antisocial, criminal, and violent behavior* (pp. 3–31). New York: Guildford Press.

Moffitt, T. E. (1993). Adolescence-limited and life-course persistent antisocial behavior: A developmental taxonomy. *Psychological Review, 100*, 674–701.

Monahan, J., Steadman, H. J., Silver, E., Appelbaum, P. S., Robbins, P. C., Mulvey, E. P., et al. (2001). *Rethinking risk assessment. The Macarthur study of mental disorder and violence.* Oxford: Oxford University Press.

Myers, W. C., Chan, H. C. C., Vo, E. J., & Lazarou, E. (2010). Sexual sadism, psychopathy, and recidivism in juvenile sexual murderers. *Journal of Investigative Psychology and Offender Profiling, 7*, 49–58.

Neumann, C. S., & Hare, R. D. (2008). Psychopathic traits in a large community sample: Links to violence, alcohol use, and intelligence. *Journal of Consulting and Clinical Psychology, 76*(5), 893–899.

Neumann, C. S., & Pardini, D. (2014). Factor structure and construct validity of the self report psychopathy (SRP) scale and the youth psychopathic traits inventory (YPI) in young men. *Journal of Personality Disorders, 28*, 419–433.

Olds, D. L., Kitzman, H. J., Cole, R. E., Hanks, C. A., Arcoleo, K. J., Anson, E. A., et al. (2010). Enduring effects of prenatal and infancy home visiting by nurses on maternal life course and government spending. *Archives of Pediatrics & Adolescent Medicine, 164*, 419–424.

Paulhus, D. L., Neumann, C. S., Hare, R. D., Williams, K. M., & Hemphill, J. F. (2017). *Self-report psychopathy scale. (SRP-4) manual* (4th ed.). Toronto: Multi Health Systems.

Piquero, A. R., Farrington, D. P., Fontaine, N. M. G., Vincent, G., Coid, J., & Ullrich, S. (2012). Childhood risk, offending trajectories, and psychopathy at age 48 years in the Cambridge Study in Delinquent Development. *Psychology, Public Policy, and Law, 18*, 577–598.

Polaschek, D. L. L., & Skeem, J. L. (2018). Treatment of adults and juveniles with psychopathy. In C. J. Patrick (Ed.), *Handbook of psychopathy* (2nd ed., pp. 710–731). New York: Guildford Publications.

Porter, S., Fairweather, D., Drugge, J., Herve, H., Birt, A., & Boer, D. P. (2000). Profiles of psychopathy in incarcerated sexual offenders. *Criminal Justice and Behavior, 27*, 216–233.

Ragatz, L. L., Fremouw, W., & Baker, E. (2012). The psychological profile of white-collar offenders: Demographics, criminal thinking, psychopathic traits, and psychopathology. *Criminal Justice and Behavior, 39*, 978–997.

Rock, P. (1994). The social organization of a Home Office initiative. *European Journal of Crime, Criminal Law and Criminal Justice, 2*, 141–167.

Salekin, R. T., & Lynam, D. R. (2010). Child and adolescent psychopathy. An introduction. In R. T. Salekin, & D. R. Lynam (Eds.), *Handbook of child and adolescent psychopathy* (pp. 1–14). New York: Guilford Press.

Satterfield, J. H., Faller, K. J., Crinella, F. M., Schell, A. M., Swanson, J. M., & Homer, L. D. (2007). A 30-year prospective follow-up study of hyperactive boys with conduct problems: Adult criminality. *Journal of the American Academy of Child and Adolescent Psychiatry, 46*, 601–610.

Schweinhart, L. J., Montie, J., Xiang, Z., Barnett, S. W., Belfield, C. R., & Nores, M. (2005). *Lifetime effects: The high/scope Perry preschool study through age 40.* Ypsilanti: High/Scope Press.

Skeem, J. L., & Cooke, D. J. (2010a). Is criminal behavior a central component of psychopathy? Conceptual directions for resolving the debate. *Psychological Assessment, 22*, 433–445.

Skeem, J. L., & Cooke, D. J. (2010b). One measure does not a construct make: Directions toward reinvigorating psychopathy research—Reply to Hare and Neumann (2010). *Psychological Assessment, 22*, 455–459.

Skeem, J. L., & Mulvey, E. P. (2001). Psychopathy and community violence among civil psychiatric patients: Results from the MacArthur violence risk assessment study. *Journal of Consulting and Clinical Psychology, 69*, 358–374.

Tew, J., & Atkinson, R. (2013). The Chromis programme: From conception to evaluation. *Psychology, Crime & Law*, *19*, 415–431.

Tew, J., Bennett, A., & Dixon, L. (2016). The Chromis experience: An interpretative phenomenological analysis of participants' experiences of the Chromis programme. *International Journal of Offender Therapy and Comparative Criminology*, *60*, 1669–1689.

Tew, J., Dixon, L., Harkins, L., & Bennett, A. (2012). Investigating changes in anger and aggression in offenders with high levels of psychopathic traits attending the Chromis violence reduction programme. *Criminal Behaviour and Mental Health*, *22*, 191–201.

Theobald, D., Farrington, D. P., Coid, J. W., & Piquero, A. (2016). Are male perpetrators of intimate partner violence different from convicted violent offenders? Examination of psychopathic traits and life success in males from a community survey. *Journal of Interpersonal Violence*, *31*, 1687–1718.

Thomas, R., & Zimmer-Gembeck, M. J. (2007). Behavioral outcomes of parent-child interaction therapy and triple p-positive parenting program: A review and meta-analysis. *Journal of Abnormal Child Psychology*, *35*, 475–495.

Thornberry, T. P., & Krohn, M. D. (2019). Interactional theory. In D. P. Farrington, L. Kazemian, & A. R. Piquero (Eds.), *The Oxford handbook of developmental and life-course criminology*. New York: Oxford University Press.

Vize, C. E., Lynam, D. R., Lamkin, J., Miller, J. D., & Pardini, D. (2016). Identifying essential features of juvenile psychopathy in the prediction of later antisocial behaviour: Is there an additive, synergistic, or curvilinear role for fearless dominance? *Clinical Psychological Science*, *4*, 572–590.

Walsh, A., & Wu, H.-H. (2008). Differentiating antisocial personality disorder, psychopathy and sociopathy: Evolutionary, genetic, neurological, and sociological considerations. *Criminal Justice Studies*, *21*, 135–152.

Wikström, P.-O. (2005). The social origins of pathways in crime: Towards a developmental ecological action theory of crime involvement and its changes. In D. P. Farrington (Ed.), *Advances in criminological theory: Vol. 14. Integrated developmental and life-course theories offending* (pp. 211–246). New York: Routledge.

Wikström, P.-O. H., & Treiber, K. (2019). The dynamics of change: Criminogenic interactions and life-course patterns in crime. In D. P. Farrington, L. Kazemian, & A. R. Piquero (Eds.), *The Oxford handbook of developmental and life-course criminology* (pp. 272–294). Oxford: Oxford University Press.

Zara, G. (2019). Cognitive-behavioral treatment to prevent offending and rehabilitate offenders. In D. P. Farrington, L. Kazemian, & A. R. Piquero (Eds.), *The Oxford handbook of developmental and life-course criminology* (pp. 673–693). Oxford: Oxford University Press.

Zara, G., & Farrington, D. P. (2016). *Criminal recidivism: Explanation, prediction and prevention*. Abingdon: Routledge.

Zara, G., & Farrington, D. P. (2019). Unsuccessful life style in middle-aged official and self reported types of offenders. *Journal of Criminal Justice*, *64*, 34–42.

Zara, G., & Farrington, D. P. (2020). Childhood risk factors for self-reported versus official life-course-persistent, adolescence-limited and late onset offending. *Criminal Justice and Behavior*, *47*, 352–368.

Assessment of psychopathy and antisocial behavior

6

Mauro Paulino, Mário R. Simões, Leslie Morey, Brittany Penson, Paulo Barbosa Marques, and Laura Alho

Introduction

The construct of psychopathy has been discussed in the literature in recent centuries (e.g., Pinel, 1806, cited by Hyatt, Crowe, Lynam, & Miller, 2020), by different disciplines such as psychology, neuroscience, and criminology (Kavish, Schiafo, Sellbom, & Anderson, 2020) and in different populations such as the clinical and forensic community (Gao & Raine, 2010; Neumann & Hare, 2008; Vitacco, Neumann, Welch, & Buckley, 2016; Yang et al., 2019).

Rigorous assessment, using appropriate tools for the specificities of this pathology, is imperative for the evolution of research on etiology, risk assessment, prevention, and intervention (Sellbom, 2011).

The main factors that define the importance of evaluating psychopathy include, on the one hand, the possibility of predicting and, in some way, explaining criminal behavior and the high risk of recidivism associated with this pathology (Rice & Harris, 2013; Vitacco et al., 2016), including violent behavior and sexual assault (e.g., Hare & Neumann, 2008). On the other hand, the association of this pathology with a range of antisocial behaviors such as substance abuse, domestic violence, and gambling problems (Few, Miller, & Lynam, 2013; Seibert, Miller, Few, Zeichner, & Lynam, 2011; Wilson, Miller, Zeichner, Lynam, & Widiger, 2011).

Nevertheless, one of the main issues underlying the evaluation of psychopathy is the identification and analysis of the risk of violence (Vitacco et al., 2016), not only in populations associated with crime and delinquency, but also in inmates (Vitacco, Rogers, & Neumann, 2003).

In turn, in recent decades there has been a growing recognition of the need to invest in early screening and consequent intervention during adolescence (Salekin & Lynam, 2010) to implement preventive measures.

This need is the result of scientific evidence that criminal recidivism alone, high in adolescence (Yang et al., 2019), tends to increase with advancing age and, in contrast, the response to treatment decreases (Liang et al., 2020; Salekin, 2017). Also, the association between psychopathic traits and antisocial behavior, substance abuse, and early involvement in the world of crime stands out (Hare & Neumann, 2005).

For the reasons mentioned above, there must be a rigorous evaluation in the context of justice (Neal & Sellbom, 2012), not only because of ethical issues and psychological implications (Evans & Tully, 2016), but also because an understanding of the nature, specificities, and degree of psychopathy can help in the consideration of the

Psychopathy and Criminal Behavior. https://doi.org/10.1016/B978-0-12-811419-3.00022-4

criminal penalty and the recommended intervention (Tew, Harkins, & Dixon, 2013). For example, in the case of adolescents, when evaluating traits of psychopathy, it becomes possible to distinguish whether the dysfunctional behavior has a transitory and less severe nature, or whether it corresponds to a stable pattern of behavior (Kruh, Frick, & Clements, 2005).

Also, the imperative need for rigor and excellence associated with the instruments of evaluation of children, adolescents, and adults has fostered numerous debates in scientific research on the nature of the construct of psychopathy (Cooke, Michie, & Skeem, 2007; Hare & Neumann, 2008; Kavish et al., 2020; Miller & Lynam, 2012; Wall, Wygant, & Sellbom, 2015).

In recent years, evidence has shown that the structure of psychopathy presents a dimensional rather than a categorical nature, in that the traces of this pathology are distributed throughout the population (Neumann & Hare, 2008), and people diagnosed with psychopathy meet and represent the limit of this distribution (Hare & Neumann, 2008).

Even so, there is a variety of perspectives on what precisely constitutes the concept of psychopathy (Kavish et al., 2020) and, therefore, some debates about the most appropriate factorial model that prevails (e.g., the factorial model of psychopathy, Cooke et al., 2007; Hare & Neumann, 2006), and the centrality of certain characteristics for the construct of psychopathies, such as antisocial or criminal behavior and boldness (Hare & Neumann, 2010; Lilienfeld et al., 2012; Miller & Lynam, 2012; Skeem & Cooke, 2010). Discussion also occurs around the elements necessary to constitute a psychopathic personality disorder, including whether interpersonal-affective traits (e.g., insensitivity, absence of remorse, dishonesty, and grandiosity) are sufficient for diagnosis (Lilienfeld, 1994; Poythress & Hall, 2011) and, in contrast, whether behavioral traits (e.g., impulsiveness) are necessary (Poythress & Hall, 2011). As it can be easily understood, these scientific concerns are relevant to the field of evaluation.

According to the traditional perspective of psychopathy (e.g., Harpur, Hare, & Hakstian, 1989), this construct integrates two domains, namely primary psychopathy, characterized by personality traits, such as the absence of empathy or feelings of guilt, and secondary psychopathy, defined by behavioral tendencies, such as the sexual promiscuity and the antisocial lifestyle (Blackburn & Maybury, 1985; Visser & Campbell, 2018).

The three-factor model was initially proposed by Cooke and Michie (2001) and Cooke et al. (2007), who suggested that the items of the Hare Psychopathy Checklist-Revisited (PCL-R; Hare, 2003) designed to evaluate antisocial trends should be excluded, as they are not a central feature of the construct of psychopathy. Sellbom (2011) states that this integrated the following three factors: affective (e.g., insensitivity and lack of remorse), interpersonal (e.g., grandiosity, manipulation, and dominance), and behavioral (e.g., impulsiveness, irresponsibility, and search for sensations). Nevertheless, some investigations (e.g., Hare, 2003; Neumann, Hare, & Newman, 2007) criticized the three-factor model, in particular the exclusion of items. According to the previous investigations, antisocial behavior is a fundamental aspect of defining the construct of psychopathy (Visser & Campbell, 2018).

Later, the triadic model is developed (Patrick, Fowles, & Krueger, 2009), which integrates three factors that, according to Hyatt et al. (2020), were based on the Five

Factors Model (FFM) of personality, namely boldness (low neuroticism + high extroversion), meanness (low pleasantness), and disinhibition (low conscientiousness). As opposed to other models, this one integrates a concept that concerns adaptive traits, namely boldness. The concept of boldness integrates other characteristics such as courage, low sensitivity to stress, bravery, and social charm (Hyatt et al., 2020). Based on this model, the self-reported Triadic Psychopathy Measure (Triarchic Psychopathy Measure—TriPM; Patrick, 2010), which we will discuss below, stands out.

Regarding the four-factor models (e.g., Hare & Neumann, 2008; Vitacco, Neumann, & Jackson, 2005), stands out the factorial model that can be applied to PCL-R (Hare, 2003; Hare & Neumann, 2006), whose factorial flexibility allows the organization of traits, for example, in two-factor models (Hare, 1991) and three-factor models (Cooke & Michie, 2001). The four-factor model of PCL-R distinguishes between interpersonal domain (e.g., lack of honesty and trust in interpersonal relationships), affective domain (e.g., lack of empathy and feelings of guilt), lifestyle domain (e.g., lack of financial responsibility and disregard for security), and antisocial domain (e.g., crime).

Within the four-factor models, there are differences. As opposed to PCL-R, the Hare Self-Report Psychopathy Scale (SRP-III) stands out, which includes several items relating to antisocial behavior higher than the previous instrument. In this SRP-III instrument, the model integrates the four factors (e.g., Visser & Campbell, 2018), namely interpersonal manipulation (e.g., pathological lying), affective insensitivity (e.g., absence of remorse and empathy), deviant lifestyle (e.g., recklessness and unpredictability), and antisocial behavior (e.g., the versatility of criminal activity). The following version, SRP-IV, has again undergone changes in the factorial structure, namely concerning the designation of factors, which appear with nomenclature: 1. Interpersonal Manipulation, 2. Callous Affect, 3. Erratic Lifestyle, and 4. Criminal Tendencies (Visser & Campbell, 2018).

In short, since the construction of the Hare Psychopathic Scale and consequently revised versions (PCL-R; Hare, 2003), there has been an exponential growth in the study of psychopathy (Garofalo, Noteborn, Sellbom, & Bogaerts, 2019) and its evaluation instruments.

Shou, Sellbom, and Han (2017) point out the following as the main measures of self-reporting: Hare Self-Report Scale (SRP; Paulhus, Neumann, Hare, Williams, & Hemphill, 2016); Psychopathic Personality Inventory-Revised (PPI-R; Lilienfeld & Widows, 2005); Triadic Psychopathy Measure (Triarchic Psychopathy Measure—TriPM; Patrick, 2010); and Levenson Psychopathy Self-Report Scale (Levenson Self-Report Psychopathy Scale—LSRP; Levenson, Kiehl, & Fitzpatrick, 1995). The investigation shows the relevance of other inventories in forensic evaluations of criminal adults, namely Minnesota Multiphasic Personality Inventory (MMPI-2) (Butcher et al., 2001) and Personality Assessment Inventory (PAI) (Morey, 1991).

These and other instruments, accompanied by other measures that evaluate psychopathy, will be explored in this chapter, with particular analysis of their specificities, from psychometric qualities to the underlying factorial model and its potentialities and limitations. It should be noted, however, that this chapter does not intend to exhaust the universe of evaluation instruments, and there are others that, due to the chapter's dimension, have not been addressed here (e.g., The Youth Psychopathic Traits

Inventory—YPI, Andershed, Kerr, Stattin, & Levander, 2002; The Youth Psychopathic Traits Inventory-Short Version—YPI-S, van Baardewijk et al., 2010).

Hare Psychopathy Checklist-Revisited (PCL-R; Hare, 2003)

Hare's Psychopathy Scale-Revised version (Hare Psychopathy Checklist-Revisited, PCL-R), authored by Hare (2003), is the instrument considered golden standard in research and clinical and forensic contexts (Hare & Neumann, 2006; Vitacco et al., 2005). Although not directly designed to assess the risk of antisocial or criminal behavior, such as the risk of violence, PCL-R scales work as well in risk assessment as instruments specifically designed for this purpose (e.g., Mokros, Vohs, & Habermeyer, 2014). This is one of the most frequently used tools for risk assessment, management, and monitoring (Hurducas, Singh, de Ruiter, & Petrila, 2014; Singh et al., 2014), as the identification of psychopathy through PCL-R has proven to be a consistent predictor of criminal, antisocial, and violent behavior (e.g., Hare, 2003; Walters, 2003).

Tendentiously used with forensic populations, PCL-R is intended for the entire adult population (i.e., 18 years of age or older), female (Carabellese et al., 2020; Eisenbarth, Krammer, Edwards, Kiehl, & Neumann, 2018; Smith, Gacono, & Cunliffe, 2020), and male (Cunha, Braga, Gomes, & Abrunhosa Gonçalves, 2020; Lehmann et al., 2019; Reynolds, Maurer, Cook, Harenski, & Kiehl, 2020).

The instrument consists of 20 items (glibness/superficial charm; grandiose sense of self-worth; the need for stimulation/proneness to boredom; pathological lying; conning and manipulative; lack of remorse or guilt; shallow affect; callous and lack of empathy; parasitic lifestyle; poor behavior controls; promiscuous sexual behavior; early behavior problems; lack of realistic, long-term goals; impulsivity; irresponsibility; failure to accept responsibility for own actions; many short-term marital relationships; juvenile delinquency; revocation of conditional release; and criminal versatility) that are evaluated on a scale of three ordinal points (0, 1, or 2), taking into account their absence or presence (Hare, Neumann, & Mokros, 2018). The items correspond to explicit behaviors (e.g., reduced self-control and impulsiveness) and disguised behaviors (e.g., manipulation and absence of feelings of guilt) that characterize psychopathy (e.g., Forsman, Lichtenstein, Andershed, & Larsson, 2010; Neumann, Hare, & Pardini, 2015).

Initially, PCL-R was organized in a two-factor model, namely factor 1, referring to personality traits, and factor 2, referring to the antisocial lifestyle (Gonçalves & Cunha, 2017; Hare, 1991), a model that continues to be used and validated empirically until today (e.g., Douglas, Bore, & Munro, 2012; Kavish et al., 2019).

Over the past decade, numerous analyses of latent variables at the item level have provided strong support to the four-factor model, reinforcing its construction validity (Mokros et al., 2015). It is a suitable model regardless of sample and evaluation method (Neumann et al., 2015), highlighting the clear and coherent internal structure as one of the strong PCL-R evidenced by the literature (Hare, Neumann, & Mokros, 2018).

The four-factor model is organized into the following four domains of correlated latent traits: 1. Interpersonal Factor (e.g., pathological lying and manipulation); 2.

Affective Factor (e.g., absence of remorse and affective superficiality); 3. Lifestyle Factor (e.g., impulsiveness and irresponsibility); and 4. Antisocial Factor (e.g., reduced behavioral control and criminal versatility).

Regarding psychometric qualities, strong evidence is provided regarding the reliability of PCL-R items, as well as regarding the scores of each factor and total scores. For example, in the instrument manual, PCL-R presented an alpha of 0.87, an inter-item correlation of 0.25, and a score of 0.87 and 0.93, respectively, for the ICC1 and ICC2 values (Hare, Neumann, & Mokros, 2018).

In a sample from the United Kingdom (Tew, Harkins, & Dixon, 2015), the alpha coefficient was 0.79, while the ICC1 and ICC2 reached values of 0.89 and 0.94, respectively. The four facets represented in the items also showed high levels of internal consistency (Facet 1: $\alpha=0.81$; Facet 2: $\alpha=0.73$; Facet 3: $\alpha=0.77$). Only facet 4, referring to the antisocial facet, showed a questionable internal consistency level ($\alpha=0.67$). This study also showed a positive correlation with other measures of psychopathy, namely with the Hare Self-Report Psychopathy Scale—SRP ($r=0.41$, $P<0.01$) and the Hare Self-Report Psychopathy Scale: Short Form—SRP-SF ($r=0.40$, $P<0.01$).

According to Hare, Neumann, & Mokros, 2018, the literature shows some ease in obtaining a high reliability among the ratings given by different evaluators, often recorded in the range 0.85–0.90. Even similar values are pointed out between ratings given in research and clinical practice (e.g., Willemsen, Vanheule, & Verhaeghe, 2011; Woodworth & Porter, 2002).

The standard management procedure integrates the implementation of a semistructured interview and the integration of information about the person being evaluated. The interview can take between 90 and 120 min and require several sessions. It integrates the main areas of the subject's life history (Hare, 1991, 2003), explored in a detailed, careful, and rigorous way. Take family life, interpersonal and sexual behavior, drug use, and antisocial behavior in childhood, among others.

As far as the interview is concerned, it can be omitted on the condition that the evaluator has access to rich and updated complementary files (Hare & Neumann, 2005). The evaluator must know that people with psychopathy tend to strive to convey a positive image, particularly in the interview. In a literature review, Harris, Rice, and Cormier (2013) concluded that in risk assessments, the predictive validity of PCL-R scoring, when the assessor only had access to information files, tended to exceed the scoring obtained from the interview.

In the interpretation and quotation of the items, the typical functioning of the subject must be taken into account, to the detriment of its state during the interview. PCL-R evaluates traits and not states. The final result corresponds to the sum of the quotations of the items in the scale and can be interpreted in dimensional terms, allowing to evaluate how much the individual corresponds to the psychopathic prototype or categorically, to help identify or diagnose psychopathy. Fundamentally, there is a focus not only on the total score but also on the subscales where the score is higher or on the potential differentiation of values between the different subscales. This information is important to understand the specifics of the operation and, particularly, the risk of recurrence (Gonçalves & Cunha, 2017).

The total score can range from 0 to 40 and reflects the extent to which the subject fits the psychopath profile (Hare, 2002). In general, a score of 30 or more points to the existence of psychopathy (Gonçalves & Cunha, 2017).

The cutoff point is one of the criticisms that have been leveled at this instrument, given the influence of cultural differences on the expression of psychopathy (Douglas, Strand, Belfrage, Fransson, & Levander, 2005), and, not infrequently, the use of a cutoff point to make clinical or forensic decisions is discouraged (Hare, Black, & Walsh, 2013). In order to overcome this limitation, it may be important to point out how far one distances oneself from the psychopathic prototype and analyze what traits characterize its functioning, rather than using cutoff points rigidly (Gonçalves & Cunha, 2017).

It is important to note that even in community samples, such as the Neumann and Hare (2008) research, a total score is recorded in PCL-R with an average of 3.53 for men and 2.61 for women. With higher scores, DeMatteo, Heilbrun, and Marczyk (2005), with a sample of people with no criminal record or history of institutionalization, obtained total PCL-R scores of 9.7. Even in 1989, Trevethan and Walker's study showed PCL-R total scores of 8.5 for a sample of university students, as well as Forth and colleagues' research Forth, Brown, Hart, and Hare (1996), in which the total scores of men in PCL-R corresponded to an average of 6.4 and, for women, an average of 2.7.

Its main advantages and potentialities are crucial for making this the most used instrument in the forensic context. Take, for example, the more objective and more rigorous psychometric criteria in the evaluation of psychopathy; the high psychometric characteristics; the usefulness in the evaluation of the risk of violence and criminal and violent recidivism; the evaluation of traits to the detriment of states that make it possible to see how the examinee works; the possibility of filling in the scale only based on individual information files, as long as this is reliable and abundant; and the need for training of the evaluator and the requirements of administration and quotation, as criteria for the quality of the evaluations. Also, this scale has the advantage of overcoming the limitations of self-reporting tools such as simulation, social desirability, denial, or behavior minimization (Edens, Petrila, & Buffington-Vollum, 2001; Gonçalves & Cunha, 2017; Hare, Neumann, & Mokros, 2018).

On the other hand, the main limitations are, according to Martens (2008), the speculative and subjective nature of some items, which makes the process of evaluation and response of the evaluator difficult (e.g., volubility/surface charm; affective superficiality), as well as the difficulties in the quotation of PCL-R when it is exclusively developed from individual files, which tend to be unavailable or incomplete, thus omitting important information that can considerably affect the validity of the construction of the instrument (Edens, Petrila, & Buffington-Vollum, 2001; Edens, Poythress, & Watkins, 2001).

Hare Psychopathy Checklist: Screening Version (PCL:SV; Hart, Cox, & Hare, 1995b)

This instrument, as a screening version of the previous instrument (PCL:SV; Hart et al., 1995b), is brief in its administration, scoring, and interpretation and can be used in clinical and forensic contexts for the evaluation of male and female psychopathy (Bo, Pedersen, Christensen, & Rasmussen, 2019).

This version includes 12 items (superficial; grandiose; deceitful; lacks remorse; lacks empathy; doesn't accept responsibility; impulsive; lacks goals; irresponsible; poor behavior controls; adolescent antisocial behavior; and adult antisocial behavior), organized in a three-point Likert scale (0, 1, or 2) in which the total scores can vary from 0 to 24 points (Bo et al., 2019). High scores alert the clinician to the need for an in-depth evaluation of psychopathy (Loving, 2002), and values equal to or higher than 18 tend to be indicative of the presence of psychopathy (Bo et al., 2019).

The interview tends to take about 45 min and the review of collateral information about 35 min.

PCL:SV relates to PCL-R conceptually, psychometrically, and empirically (e.g., Cooke, Michie, Hart, & Hare, 1999; Guy & Douglas, 2006; Hart, Cox, & Hare, 1995a). There is growing evidence about the constructive validity of PCL:SV, including the ability to predict aggression and violence, in clinical and forensic populations (Hare, Neumann, & Mokros, 2018).

In the systematic review by Higgs, Tully, and Browne (2017), regarding the psychometric properties of PCL-SV in forensic settings, a diagnostic agreement with PLC-R was revealed, as well as a good performance of this screening version regarding the predictive validity of violence.

Regarding reliability, the various studies with forensic population integrated into the previous systematic review (Higgs et al., 2017) point to an internal consistency with an alpha of 0.85, on average, and a correlation between items ranging from 0.21 to 0.50.

As for concurrent validity, there are correlations with the PPI-R ($r=0.55$; Hughes, Stout, & Dolan, 2013) and its prereview version, the PPI ($r=0.62$; Kruh et al., 2005); with the Comprehensive Assessment of Psychopathic Personality ($r=0.90$; Pedersen, Kunz, Elsass, & Rasmussen, 2010); and with the Hare Self-Report Psychopathy Scale ($r=0.53$; Hart et al., 1995a).

As for predictive validity, once again, this screening instrument acts in accordance with PCL-R. For example, in the study by Mokros et al. (2014), PCL:SV showed a sensitivity of 28% and a specificity of 90% in predicting behaviors and violent offenses, such as sexual assault.

Psychopathy Checklist: Youth Version (PCL:YV; Forth, Kosson, & Hare, 2003)

Hare's Psychopathy Scale: Youth Version (PCL:YV; Forth, Kosson, & Hare, 2003) is a scale for adolescents, male and female, aged between 12 and 18 years, consisting of 20 items (impression management; grandiose sense of self-worth; pathological lying; manipulation for personal gain; lack of remorse; shallow effect; callous/lack of empathy; failure to accept responsibility; stimulation-seeking; parasitic orientation; lacks goals; impulsivity; irresponsibility; poor anger control; early behavior problems; serious criminal behavior; serious violations of release conditions; criminal versatility; interpersonal sexual behavior; and unstable interpersonal relationships).

Such as the PCL-R and PCL:SV, each item is scored on a three-point scale (0, 1, or 2), with total scores ranging from 0 to 40 values. According to Forth and Brazil (2019), the research points to cut scores between 25 and 30, where young people with total values higher than those mentioned tend to present psychopathic traits. The scores on each item are based on (a) a semistructured interview with the youth, (b) a review of official court documents, if any, and (c) an interview with a parent or legal guardian.

This tool requires the interviewer to evaluate the young person's style and interpersonal attitudes; their functioning in the psychological, educational, occupational, family, and social/people domains; and their credibility when comparing their statements with official records, or collateral reports, such as the parent's allegations (Cauffman, Kimonis, Dmitrieva, & Monahan, 2009). The interview lasts about 90 min and the collection of collateral information between 69 and 90 min.

According to Maurer, Paul, Anderson, Nyalakanti, and Kiehl (2020), although some investigations continue to use the two-factor model (i.e., factor 1—interpersonal and affective traits and factor 2—antisocial and lifestyle traits) and the four-factor model, factor analysis studies at PCL:YV found support for the three-factor model in samples of juvenile offenders (Forth, Kosson, & Hare, 2003; Jones, Cauffman, Miller, & Mulvey, 2006; Salekin, 2006; Salekin, Brannen, Zalot, Leistico, & Neumann, 2006).

The three-factor personality-centered model comprises (i) the arrogant and dishonest interpersonal style (ADI; Factor 1); (ii) the deficient affective experience (DAE; Factor 2); and (iii) the impulsive and irresponsible behavioral style (IIB; Factor 3). Some investigations consider this model to be the most appropriate for adolescents when compared to the four-factor model, which includes the Antisocial Factor (Neumann, Kosson, Forth, & Hare, 2006), or Criminal Behavior (Jones et al., 2006).

This instrument presents the same psychometric and predictive properties as its counterpart for the adult population (e.g., Anderson & Kiehl, 2014; Walters & Kiehl, 2015), as well as adequate adaptation between ethnic groups and different countries (e.g., Book, Forth, & Clark, 2013; Dolan & Rennie, 2006; Hillege, de Ruiter, Smits, van der Baan, & Das, 2011; McCoy & Edens, 2006; Schrum & Salekin, 2006; Tsang et al., 2015; Walters & Kiehl, 2015).

According to Forth and Brazil (2019), the psychometric characteristics of this instrument tend to be high, namely an internal consistency, for the total scale, which tends to present an alpha of Cronbach with values between 0.85 and 0.94; interassessor reliability reaching values from acceptable to excellent (0.70–0.90); and, finally, a correlation between factors with an internal consistency pointing to alpha values between 0.22 (questionable) and 0.86 (excellent).

In a recent research by Maurer et al. (2020), with young people with psychopathic traits, this instrument presented an alpha of Cronbach for the total scale of 0.80, revealing a good internal consistency and alphas for the four facets of 0.72 (interpersonal facet), 0.77 (emotional facet), 0.73 (lifestyle facet), and 0.67 (antisocial facet), respectively.

In particular, regarding the validity of a construction, in Pechorro's investigation Pechorro, Barroso, Maroco, Vieira, and Gonçalves (2014), significant associations were revealed in instruments such as the Child and Adolescent Taxon Scale—CATS (Quinsey, Harris, Rice, & Cormier, 2006, $r=0.44$; $P=0.001$) and the Youth Level of

Service/Case Management Inventory—YLS/CMI (Hoge & Andrews, 2002; 0.53, $P=0.001$). In this study, the internal consistency of the total scale converged to an alpha of 0.71, and the three factors presented equally adequate alpha values, interpersonal facet ($\alpha=0.65$), affective facet ($\alpha=0.69$), and behavioral facet ($\alpha=0.64$), respectively.

It is important to note that, as a potential limitation, concerns about the use of this instrument in the criminal justice system stand out. These relate to three factors, namely: (a) the danger of labeling an adolescent as a psychopath; (b) the possibility of some characteristics measured by the PCL:YV corresponded to behaviors considered normative in adolescence; and (c) the degree of stability of traits related to psychopathy, from late childhood to early adulthood (Hare, Neumann, & Mokros, 2018).

Although psychopathy and respective traits do not appear suddenly in early adulthood, it would be inappropriate to label an adolescent as a psychopath, or to use a high score in PCL:YV as the basis for a more severe sentence (Hare, Neumann, & Mokros, 2018). Thus, this tool is not used to diagnose psychopathy, but to evaluate its precursors and characteristics of adolescent functioning, developing appropriate intervention strategies.

The potential disadvantages of this scale are the reduction in the ability to predict long-term offenses. In the research of Cauffman et al. (2009), when other psychopathic measures were included (i.e., Youth Psychopathic Traits Inventory; NEO Personality Inventory Revised), PCL:YV was unable to predict the offense 3 years later.

Self-Report Psychopathy Scale-4 (SRP-4; Paulhus, Neumann, Hare, Williams, & Hemphill, 2016)

The Self-Report Psychopathy Scale (SRP-4), by Paulhus, Neumann, Hare, Williams, & Hemphill, 2016, is a self-reported scale that evaluates the presence of psychopathic traits in adults, female and male, using 64 items classified on a five-point scale, from "strongly agree" to "strongly disagree" (Visser & Campbell, 2018).

Initially, this scale was designed to be the self-reported version of the PCL-R instrument (Hare, 2003), whose admiration time is considerably shorter, namely about 10 to 15 min. Currently, SRP-4 is predominantly used to evaluate subclinical psychopathology (Demetrioff, Porter, & Baker, 2016). Previous versions of SRP-4 have demonstrated excellent reliability and validity, associated with a structure of factors congruent with the underlying PCL-R scale model (Visser & Campbell, 2018) and which are significantly correlated (Neumann et al., 2015).

According to Demetrioff et al. (2016), this is the only scale that maps the four facets of psychopathy (Neumann et al., 2015) covered by the PCL-R, namely the interpersonal, affective, lifestyle, and antisocial facets. These appear in this model with the following nomenclature: 1. Interpersonal Manipulation; 2. Callous Affect; 3. Erratic Lifestyle; and 4. Criminal Tendencies (Visser & Campbell, 2018).

However, the items of the SRP-4 instrument can also be organized in the two-factor model of the dimensions of psychopathy (Seara-Cardoso, Dolberg, Neumann, Roiser,

& Viding, 2013), which comprises, on the one hand, the affective-interpersonal dimensions (Factor 1) and, on the other, the antisocial lifestyle (Factor 2).

The SRP-4 has been shown to integrate good reliability and validity, evaluated in university and community samples, described in the instrument manual (Visser & Campbell, 2018).

According to Sellbom, Lilienfeld, Fowler, & McCray, 2018, this instrument has adequate psychometric qualities. Regarding internal consistency, an alpha of 0.92 for the total inventory and alphas between 0.75 and 0.82 for each of the scale factors, namely interpersonal manipulation ($\alpha = 0.82$), callous affect ($\alpha = 0.78$), erratic lifestyle ($\alpha = 0.79$), and criminal tendencies ($\alpha = 0.75$), are evidenced.

Concerning the limitations of this instrument, the results tend to be lower in the items of antisocial behavior in community samples that can influence the final score (e.g., "I was convicted of a serious crime"). Nevertheless, the manual provides standards for the community, student, and offender samples, allowing researchers to better contextualize and interpret scores. Another limitation is that SRP-4 has recently become the property of Multi-Health Systems, which requires financial costs for its use (Visser & Campbell, 2018).

The need for further investigation and validation of this instrument is also highlighted, given the reduced associations that have been identified between the SRP-4 scores and the traits of psychopathy considered fundamental. This weakness seems to have been originated by the removal of items related to anxiety and fear, which were replaced by items associated with antisocial behavior, to achieve greater proximity to PCL-R. Nevertheless, this alteration has potentiated a smaller coverage of the boldness domain concerning previous versions of the instrument, such as the SRP-II, and, therefore, items related to antisocial behavior prevail in the scale, which are less specific in their relations with other measures of psychopathy (Sellbom, Lilienfeld, Fowler, & McCray, 2018).

One of the potentialities of SRP-4 is the possibility of analyzing the items according to a two-factor model. According to Hare (2003), research has shown that primary psychopathy (tending to be called "factor 1" which comprises the facets of interpersonal manipulation and insensitivity) presents correlations and specificities different from secondary psychopathy (often called "factor 2" which refers to facets of erratic lifestyle and antisocial behavior). In general, secondary psychopathy is associated with risk-taking and social deviation, while primary psychopathy integrates the manipulation and insensitivity of the psychopathic personality. In this way, the flexibility of the structure of the scale is important for a greater understanding of the specificities of the pathology and functioning of the person being evaluated.

Still, in the sense of potentialities, it is possible to allude to the reduced version of this instrument, the Self-Report Psychopathy Scale: Short Form (Paulhus, Neumann, Hare, Williams, & Hemphill, 2016), which includes 29 items (Visser & Campbell, 2018), organized based on a model of four factors (Neumann et al., 2015) and evaluated in community and forensic population samples from different geographic areas (Gordts, Uzieblo, Neumann, Van den Bussche, & Rossi, 2017; León-Mayer, Folino, Neumann, & Hare, 2015; Neumann et al., 2015).

The SRP-SF demonstrates good psychometric properties and evaluates the same constructs as the complete and previous versions of the SRP and the reference instrument of psychopathy evaluation itself, the PCL-R (Carré, Hyde, Neumann, Viding, & Hariri, 2013; Gordts et al., 2017; Neumann & Pardini, 2014; Neumann et al., 2015). The research of Gordts et al. (2017) shows that the internal consistency of the total scale corresponded to an alpha of 0.84 and the subscales reached values between 0.44 and 0.73. As for the validity of the retest, an alpha of 0.89 was reached.

Hare P-SCAN (Hare & Herve, 1999)

The Hare P-SCAN instrument (Hare & Herve, 1999) is a screening measure designed for rapid identification of teenagers and adults (from the age of 13), male and female, with psychopathic characteristics, which are referenced for a more rigorous and accurate evaluation (McKee, Waples, & Tullis, 2017). The administration time for this instrument is about 10 to 15 min.

This checklist integrates 90 items organized in a model of three factors, namely the interpersonal, affective, and lifestyle factors (Brackett, Jackson, & Richards, 2008; McKee et al., 2017).

Items 1–30 represent the interpersonal facet and evaluate relationships and interactions with others; items 31–60 concern the affective facet that analyzes the examinee's emotions and feelings; and, finally, items 61–90 concern the lifestyle facet and refer to impulsiveness, lack of goals, and parasitic lifestyle typical of psychopathic functioning (Brackett et al., 2008; Mathieu, Neumann, Hare, & Babiak, 2014; Neumann et al., 2007).

Each item is scored on a three-point Likert scale (0, 1, or 2), where the total score is the sum of the total of each of the three facets (Elwood, Poythress, & Douglas, 2004). As far as the evaluator is concerned, he or she does not need to have any training in psychology. He may be, for example, the probation officer. He is not required to conduct an interview, but only to fill out the instrument according to the information obtained through contact with the individual and relevant data present in files relating to his or her history (Brackett et al., 2008).

The total score can reach values from 0 to 60, with values between 32 and 44 being considered high and a target of concern, and values from 45 onwards are already considered quite high (Elwood et al., 2004). Thus, the authors recommend that from the value 30 on, the person should be referenced for a more rigorous assessment, performed by a trained professional using an assessment (i.e., PCL-R, PCL:SV, PCL:YV), rather than a screening tool (Brackett et al., 2008).

In McKee et al. (2017) research, the scale for interpersonal behaviors reached an alpha of 0.93 concerning reliability, the scale for emotional behaviors reached an alpha of 0.96, and the scale for lifestyle behaviors reached a value of 0.95.

In an investigation by Warren, Chauhan, and Murrie (2005), with women in correctional facilities, P-SCAN presented high psychometric characteristics, namely an internal consistency for the total scale and for the three facets exceptionally high, with alpha values exceeding 0.96; strong interitems correlations, which ranged from

0.31 to 0.84; as well as correlations between the three facets of psychopathy, which ranged from 0.97 (i.e., a high level of psychopathy), (i.e., the relationship between the affective facet and the lifestyle facet), and 0.93 (i.e., the relationship between the interpersonal facet and the lifestyle facet).

In the study by Brackett et al. (2008), in addition to a high internal consistency, where the total scale reached an alpha of 0.98, and the subscale values between 0.93 and 0.95, significant convergent correlations were revealed between this instrument and the PCL-R facets (i.e., Interpersonal: $r=0.43$, $P<0.01$; Affective: $r=0.40$, $P<0.01$; and Lifestyle: $r=0.40$, $P<0.01$).

Levenson Self-Report Psychopathy (LSRP; Levenson et al., 1995)

The first self-report instrument published to assess psychopathic traits in community samples of the adult population was the Levenson Self-Report Psychopathy scale (LSRP; Levenson et al., 1995), composed of 26 items, 7 of which are inverted to reduce the risk of response bias (Brinkley, Schmitt, Smith, & Newman, 2001).

The response is attributed on a four-point scale, between which *I strongly disagree* (1) and *I agree* (4) (Alzeer, Michailidou, Munot, & Kyranides, 2019), where scores greater than 58 point to psychopathy (Brinkley et al., 2001).

Despite its small size as a result of the need to develop self-reported measures to apply in situations where the use of PCL-R was not feasible (Sellbom, Lilienfeld, Fowler, & McCray, 2018), this instrument is an efficient measure for evaluating psychopathy in various contexts (Shou et al., 2017), from university, forensic, correctional to community samples (e.g., Brinkley, Diamond, Magaletta, & Heigel, 2008; Jones & Miller, 2012; Poythress et al., 2010; Salekin, Chen, Sellbom, Lester, & MacDougall, 2014). The test administration time is about 5–10 min.

According to Kavish et al. (2019), LSRP has been showing good psychometric properties. The total scores often refer to high levels of reliability (Cronbach's alpha values higher than 0.80), and the subscales tend to have strong correlations with other self-reported measures such as SRP-III and PPI-R (Ross et al., 2007; Seibert et al., 2011; Sellbom, 2011), as well as with PCL-R (Brinkley et al., 2001; Poythress et al., 2010).

In an investigation with people inserted in the community and in a prison context (Sellbom, 2011), the instrument revealed a total alpha of 0.84 for the total scale, as well as adequate alpha values for the subscales, 0.83 (egocentrism); 0.61 (callous); and 0.62 (antisocial), respectively. Regarding the interitems correlation, the results were equally good, 0.36 (egocentrism), 0.29 (callous), and 0.24 (antisocial), respectively.

Despite the psychometric qualities, inconsistencies prevail over the most appropriate factorial model for this instrument. Originally, the LSRP was based on a model of two factors, namely primary psychopathy (16 items, $\alpha=0.79$), characterized by traits such as manipulation, egocentrism, and cruelty; and secondary psychopathy (10 items, $\alpha=0.68$), defined by the psychopathic traits referring to anxiety and impulsiveness, associated with antisocial behavior and aggressiveness (Salekin et al., 2014; Seibert et al., 2011). This model began to be questioned by the inadequate adjustment that was revealed in numerous studies (e.g., Brinkley et al., 2008; Chabrol & Leichsenring, 2006; Salekin et al., 2014; Sellbom, 2011; Somma, Fossati, Patrick, Maffei, & Borroni, 2014), not infrequently due to the low reliability of the secondary psychopathy factor (Brinkley et al., 2001; Yokota, 2012), as opposed to the primary psychopathy construct, with relatively high levels of internal consistency (Hall et al., 2014; Poythress et al., 2010; Ross et al., 2007; Seibert et al., 2011; Walters, 2008).

In 2008, a three-factor model was proposed by Brinkley and colleagues, consisting of 19 of the 26 original items and which has been explored and elaborated by other authors over the last few years (e.g., Christian & Sellbom, 2016; Salekin et al., 2014), namely: 1. Egocentrism (i.e., captures the interpersonal domain of psychopathy and describes a Machiavellian, evil, and self-centered interpersonal style), 2. Callousness (i.e., integrates the affective domain, which reflects the absence of empathy and emotional involvement with others), and 3. Antisocial Posture (i.e., assesses antisocial behaviors).

This model has shown to be adequate in community and forensic samples (e.g., Christian & Sellbom, 2016; Salekin et al., 2014; Seibert et al., 2011; Sellbom, 2011), and when compared, it tends to be superior to the two-factor model (e.g., Anestis, Green, Arnau, & Anestis, 2019; Brinkley et al., 2008; Salekin et al., 2014).

The convergent validity of these three factors has been studied. Take, for example, the high correlation of the egocentric factor with scales that evaluate narcissism and the association between the insensitivity factor and the meanness factor of the triadic model of psychopathology (Sellbom & Phillips, 2013), as well as the association of the antisocial factor with scales that evaluate impulsiveness, violation of norms, and disobedience of rules (Anderson, Sellbom, Wygant, & Edens, 2013; Few et al., 2013; Seibert et al., 2011).

The investigation of Garofalo et al. (2019), using the three-factor model, showed an internal consistency with a total alpha of 0.79, in which the subscales revealed alpha values of 0.79 (egocentrism), 0.56 (callousness), and 0.52 (antisocial), respectively. Regarding the validity of the construct, a high correlation with the Self-Report Psychopathy Scale-III (SRP-III; $r=0.69$, $P<0.001$) was pointed out, as well as positive associations between the total LSRP score and borderline and narcissistic personality traits, reduced self-control, identity problems, and difficulties in relational functioning. Previous investigations had already pointed to associations between this instrument and other variables, such as the search for sensations, low school performance, and substance abuse (e.g., Brinkley et al., 2001; Levenson et al., 1995).

Nevertheless, in a recent study by Kavish et al. (2019), the two-factor model and the total scale of the LSRP showed an internal consistency between adequate and good (Cronbach alphas ranged from 0.73 to 0.84), which suggests the potential need for studies to explore the origins of these inconsistencies.

As a potential of this instrument, the main distinguishing factor of the LSRP is the fact that the items do not have any explicit reference to observable antisocial behavior, which facilitates the evaluation of potential associations with other measures of antisocial behavior without contamination by criteria (Garofalo et al., 2019). In contrast, as a limitation, the inconsistencies regarding the most appropriate factorial model for the instrument prevail.

Psychopathic Personality Inventory (PPI; Lilienfeld & Andrews, 1996)

The Psychopathic Personality Inventory (PPI), by Lilienfeld and Andrews (1996), is a self-reporting instrument made up of 187 items, for both male and female adults, whose response integrates a Likert scale of four points (1, 2, 3, or 4) that evaluates the potential presence of traces of psychopathy. The administration time varies from 15 to 25 min.

The original instrument, built in 1996, had eight scales associated with the dimensions of psychopathy, accompanied by three validity scales regarding the management of socially desirable impressions (e.g., "I've always been completely fair to others"), deviant responses (e.g., "I look down on the ground whenever I hear a plane flying above my head"), and inconsistent responses (i.e., several random responses greater than 40 invalidate the validity of the responses).

Regarding the psychometric qualities of this instrument, satisfactory psychometric properties were evidenced in samples of adult prisoners and young offenders (Poythress, Edens, & Lilienfeld, 1998; Sandoval, Hancock, Poythress, Edens, & Lilienfeld, 2000). Regardless of the sample, from young graduates (Lilienfeld & Andrews, 1996) to young offenders (Poythress et al., 1998), the internal consistency for the total set of PPI items tends to be high (alphas between 0.90 and 0.93). A greater variability tends to be observed in the internal consistency of the PPI subscales (alphas between 0.72 and 0.91). Regarding the validity of the reliability test-retest, it also tends to be high. Take, for example, the samples of recently graduated students (Lilienfeld & Andrews, 1996), where the retest-test reached an alpha value of 0.95 for the total score and alpha values between 0.82 and 0.94 for the subscale scores.

In 2005, the revised version of this instrument was developed (Psychopathic Personality Inventory-Revised; Lilienfeld & Widows, 2005). It consists of 154 items, in a Likert scale of four points (1, 2, 3, or 4). In light of the original, the PPI-R also includes four scales of validity, and in both versions, the punctuation corresponds to the sum of the items of the eight subscales.

Regarding psychometric characteristics, the PPI-R presents an alpha of 0.89, in which the eight subscales that evaluate the main characteristics of psychopathy also show an adequate alphas, namely: Machiavellian egocentricity ($\alpha=0.82$), rebellious nonconformity ($\alpha=0.88$), blame externalization ($\alpha=0.76$), carefree nonplanfulness ($\alpha=0.53$), social influence ($\alpha=0.07$), fearlessness ($\alpha=0.63$), stress immunity ($\alpha=0.61$), and cold-heartedness ($\alpha=0.75$).

In the study by Culhane, Walker, and Hildebrand (2019), where the population sample corresponded to male serial killers, this version presented positive correlations with instruments such as the Levenson Self-Report Psychopathy (0.83, $P<0.001$) and the Self Report Psychopathy Scale-III (0.87, $P<0.001$).

In an investigation by Chapman, Gremore, and Farmer (2003), with women in a prison setting, the internal consistency of the PPI corresponded to an alpha of 0.85 for the total scale score and alpha values between 0.79 and 0.89 for the eight subscales. Regarding the retest, the instrument showed high values for the total scale ($r=0.92$) and for the respective subscales ($r=0.77$ to 0.90).

The Triarchic Psychopathy Measure (TriPM; Patrick, 2010)

This instrument is a self-reported measure for adults, male and female, composed of 58 items organized on a four-point Likert scale—predominantly false, false, predominantly true, or true (Evans & Tully, 2016). The administration time of TriPM integrates about 15 min.

This measure is organized according to the three constructs that define psychopathy according to the triadic model proposed by Patrick et al. (2009), namely meanness, boldness, and disinhibition (Evans & Tully, 2016).

The meanness scale integrates 19 items and refers to characteristics of psychopathy such as coldness, cruelty, insensitivity, hostility, violence, and aggressiveness (Pechorro, DeLisi, Alberto, Ray, & Simões, 2018). According to Patrick (2010), this scale integrates behavioral manifestations that tend to be present in the life history of a person with a psychopathic functioning. Examples include cruelty to animals and people, various forms of aggression, the exploitation of others for personal gain, or the challenge to authority (Pechorro et al., 2018).

The scale boldness consisting of 19 items concerns an assertive, dominant, and adventurous interpersonal style; a high degree of self-confidence, tolerance of the unknown and of danger; and the ability to quickly recover from stressful situations (Pechorro et al., 2018).

The 20 items that define the scale of disinhibition relate to impulsiveness, irresponsibility, and a tendency to be impatient and to fail in the management and inhibition of one's own behavior. In other words, it refers to the deficit in the capacity of emotional self-regulation and the consequent control of one's own conduct, for example, through the use of sanctioning emotions such as shame or guilt, which tend to inhibit negative behavior (Pechorro et al., 2018).

As far as the psychometric qualities of this instrument are concerned, they tend to be adequate. As for the internal consistency, in the Sellbom and Phillips (2013) investigation with a forensic sample, the alpha of the subscales corresponded to 0.89 (boldness), 0.90 (malice), and 0.89 (disinhibition). Similarly, in the study by Stanley, Wygant, and Sellbom (2013) the alphas ranged from 0.77 (boldness), 0.84 (disinhibition), and 0.88 (meanness).

In the study by Sellbom and Phillips (2013), which integrated a forensic sample (i.e., women in a prison setting) and a community sample (i.e., young university students), revealed that, in the first sample, meanness proved to be positively associated with Machiavellian traits and negatively associated with empathy; boldness found itself positively correlated with narcissism and the search for sensations, emotions, and adventure and negatively correlated with the system of inhibition of behavior and, finally, disinhibition proved to be positively associated with the search for sensations and fun, as well as high susceptibility to boredom.

Regarding the second sample, the meanness dimension was positively related to other measures, such as insensitivity, cruelty, egocentrism, and narcissism; boldness was positively correlated with courage and low susceptibility to stress; and, finally, disinhibition was positively associated with measures such as impulsiveness, antisocial behavior, nonconformity, and responsibility of the other for actions, among others.

Specifically regarding the scales and subscale, it was revealed convergent validity with the PPI instrument in the forensic sample. The TriPM scales presented positive associations with the total scale of the PPI ($r=0.64$) and with its respective subscales, as for example between the meanness subscale and Machiavellian self-centeredness ($r=0.67$) and insensitivity ($r=0.38$), as well as between the self-centered impulsivity subscale and disinhibition ($r=0.60$) and with the Machiavellian self-centered subscale ($r=0.52$).

As for the potential of TriPM, this instrument overcomes some of the limitations of other measures that evaluate psychopathy, such as PCL-R. According to Wall et al. (2015), it is the boldness dimension that explains the differences between antisocial personality disorder and psychopathic personality disorder. In this sense, instruments such as PCL-R do not evaluate or differentiate these distinct constructs (Patrick, Drislane, & Strickland, 2012; Patrick, Durbin, & Moser, 2012), nor do they capture important elements of psychopathy (Evans & Tully, 2016).

On the other hand, as far as limitations are concerned, the need for greater investment in studies that evaluate the psychometric qualities of this measure, particularly to evaluate the validity of external constructs, is highlighted. These studies are fundamental for this measure to be considered a reliable tool to be implemented in the criminal justice system (Evans & Tully, 2016).

Reference should also be made to the existence of a version for young people called youth psychopathic traits inventory—Triarchic (YPI-Tri; Drislane et al., 2015). It is a self-reported measure consisting of 33 items, selected from the original version of the instrument inventory of psychopathic traits in youth (YPI; Andershed, Kerr, Stattin, & Levander, 2002), but with particular and distinct relevance to the triadic model of psychopathy

Thus, YPI-Tri integrates three scales, namely boldness (10 items), meanness (10 items), and disinhibition (13 items), in light of the adult version.

As for psychometric properties, the research of Drislane et al. (2015) revealed that the YPI-Tri scales have an acceptable internal consistency, namely with alpha values of 0.82 (disinhibition), 0.81 (meanness), and 0.75 (boldness), respectively. In this study concerning convergent validity, associations with other measures of psychopathy are highlighted, such as the Inventory of Callous-Unemotional Traits (Frick, 2004), Antisocial Process Screening Device (Frick & Hare, 2001), and Child Psychopathy Scale (Lynam, 1997).

Antisocial Process Screening Device (APSD; Frick & Hare, 2001)

The Antisocial Process Screening Device (APSD) instrument is a self-reporting scale made up of 20 items, quoted on a Likert scale of 3 points (0, 1, or 2), in which scores greater than 15 point to the presence of psychopathic traits (Vitacco et al., 2003).

The APSD includes the self-reported version for young people (APSD-SR, Caputo et al., 1999) and the version for adults, specifically for parents (APSD-PR, Frick, Ray, Thornton, & Kahn, 2014) and teachers (APSD-TR; Frick et al., 2014), whose administration time for each of these three forms takes about 10 min. All versions of this instrument are widely administered in samples of different cultural backgrounds and different evaluation scenarios (e.g., Dong, Wu, & Waldman, 2014; Goulter, Kimonis, & Heller, 2018; Laajasalo et al., 2014).

The scale of self-reporting tends to be particularly useful in circumstances where parents or teachers are absent, or in situations where, as a result of reduced contact, parents are unable to provide information or clarify the antisocial characteristics of young people (Loney, Frick, Clements, Ellis, & Kerlin, 2003). Examples include dysfunctional families with reduced contact or young people who are in a judicial environment at the time of evaluation.

Regarding the factorial structure, this instrument aggregates a model of three factors (Frick, Bodin, & Barry, 2000a, 2000b), namely: (a) Impulsivity (IMP); (b) Callous/Unemotional (C/U); and (c) Narcissism (NAR).

In an investigation by Liang et al. (2020), the psychometric characteristics of this instrument were evaluated using multiple forms of information (i.e., self-reporting of children versus report of caregivers) and through diversified demographic samples, namely adolescents inserted in the community (sample 1), adolescents incarcerated (sample 2), and children and their caregivers (sample 3).

About the psychometric qualities, the internal consistency integrated alpha values considered valid in all samples, 0.81 (sample 1), 0.72 (sample 2), and 0.76 (sample 3), respectively. Nevertheless, when analyzing the alpha coefficients of each of the three factors mentioned, some fragilities were identified, particularly in samples 2 and 3. These fragilities had already been identified in previous investigations (e.g., Goodwin, Sellbom, & Salekin, 2015; Goulter et al., 2018).

In the first sample, with young people inserted in the community, the alpha coefficient did not show any weaknesses, because, in light of what is referred to by the investigations, the stability of psychopathy increases as the human being grows (Salekin & Lynam, 2010). Also, adolescents inserted in the community and with higher levels of education tend to be more competent in the emotional domain, in the sense of experiencing and understanding their emotions and, in turn, in the recognition of the symptoms in the instrument, given the greater semantic understanding of the items (Liang et al., 2020).

Regarding the second sample, with adolescents inserted in justice systems, it was found that the coefficient of each factor presented low reliability. This result is in line with studies that show that psychopathy differs between young people involved in justice and young people inserted in the community (e.g., Lee, Vincent, Hart, & Corrado, 2003). One possible explanation refers to the often fraudulent and defensive response style of young offenders (Colins, Bijttebier, Broekaert, & Andershed, 2014), who tend to respond to items in order to hide their true emotions.

Finally, in sample 3, referring to the reporting of children and their caregivers, the alpha coefficients were marginal, especially regarding the Callous/Unemotional. A potential explanation is that children tend not to reveal their feelings and often their emotions may not correspond to what is observed by the caregivers. Thus, this research highlights and supports the findings of previous studies in referring to the usefulness of the self-report questionnaire for young people, given the limitations of the accuracy of the information given by the measures attributed to the caregivers (e.g., Frick et al., 2000a, 2000b). According to Kamphaus and Frick (2005), self-reporting becomes, consecutively, the most reliable and valid strategy as the child enters adolescence.

The validity of the instrument construction was supported in the three samples, showing robust correlations with other psychopathic measures, such as Youth Psychopathic Traits Inventory (YPI) and Child Problematic Traits Inventory (CPTI).

Concerning convergent validity, consistent results were identified regarding the behavioral factor (Impulsivity) and the interpersonal factor (Narcissism), which correlated significantly with similar dimensions present in other psychopathy measures (e.g., CPTI). Nevertheless, in light of what was reported by other investigations (e.g., Gillen, MacDougall, Forth, Barry, & Salekin, 2019; Wang et al., 2017), the correlation of the Callous/Unemotional in sample 1 and sample 2, with other similar measures, was weak and insignificant, which did not happen with sample 3. A potential justification is that in sample 3 the response of adults may integrate high levels of social desirability (Muñoz & Frick, 2007). In other words, parents tend to respond negatively to items of this Callous/Unemotional and, in turn, scores are lower, preventing a positive correlation with other instruments (Liang et al., 2020).

In a previous investigation, by Vitacco et al. (2003), the cutoff point of this instrument was evaluated, namely sensitivity, specificity, positive predictive power (PPP), negative predictive power (NPP), and success rate. It was revealed that a result greater than or equal to 15 was associated with high sensitivity (≥ 0.96). Still, despite the modest positive predictive power (PPP), i.e., the probability of an adolescent obtaining a score above the cutoff point of the instrument presenting psychopathy, the APSD failed to identify several adolescents with the pathology. These results point to this instrument as a screening tool, but not as a diagnostic measure—one of the limitations of the APSD.

Other limitations of this instrument refer to the reduced accuracy of the information given by the measures attributed to parents or caregivers (e.g., Frick et al., 2000a, 2000b) and the fact that there is no consensus on the most appropriate factorial model for the instrument (Liang et al., 2020). One of the reasons identified for the inconsistency of the APSD factor structure among studies is the variety of informants associated with them (teachers, parents, and adolescents).

In contrast, regarding the potentialities of this instrument, the diversity of information sources stands out, as well as the positive correlation with other instruments that evaluate psychopathy and self-reporting, while the most reliable and valid strategy in adolescence (Kamphaus & Frick, 2005).

Comprehensive Assessment of Psychopathic Personality

The Comprehensive Assessment of the Psychopathic Personality model (CAPP; Cooke, Hart, Logan, & Michie, 2004), developed from a systematic review of the literature on psychopathy, accompanied by evidence from clinical and forensic practice (Kavish et al., 2020), has fostered the development of a series of assessment tools for adults, male and female (e.g., semistructured interview, self-reported scales).

As a comprehensive model of psychopathic personality disorder, it covers all signs of psychopathy and therefore focuses on personality traits rather than the potential behavioral consequences of the pathology (Kreis, Cooke, Michie, Hoff, & Logan, 2012). In this way, it avoids potential confusion between personality traits and specific behaviors (e.g., antisocial behavior and criminal behavior), a phenomenon that negatively affects measures of psychopathy (e.g., Skeem & Cooke, 2010).

The CAPP conceptual map is based on six principles (Cooke, Hart, Logan, & Michie, 2012), namely:

1. Traits of psychopathic personality disorder are associated with a pathological personality; i.e., they are an individual deviation and not a deviation of a cultural or social nature (Skeem & Cooke, 2010).
2. Traits are clearly defined, in atomic terms, without the use of names that integrate complex mixtures of symptoms that could be analyzed in multiple symptoms (Cooke & Logan, 2018).
3. Personality traits are "described using common language adjectives to define psychological functioning" (Mollaret, 2009, p. 316)—lexical approach to personality (Kavish et al., 2020).
4. Psychopathy is conceptualized as a pathology of a dynamic nature and based on personality, and, therefore, this model allows one to evaluate the change in the severity of symptoms over time, as opposed to other measures such as PCL-R (Hare, 2003), which are static and were not designed to evaluate change (Kreis et al., 2012).
5. The CAPP is presented as a hierarchical conceptual map, in which the symptoms are organized into several domains, which provides an additional framework for the interpretation of symptoms. The 33 symptoms are then organized into six domains that define the functioning of the psychopathic personality, namely: (1) Bonding, (2) Behavior, (3) Cognition, (4) Domain, (5) Self, and (6) Emotions (Kavish et al., 2020). Each of the symptoms inserted in these domains is defined using three adjectives, or through a small sentence that describes the trace. For example, the trait "Dominant" can be defined using three objectives, namely Arrogant, Authoritarian, and Controlling, decreasing the risk of ambiguities associated with the meaning of the psychopathy traits evaluated.
6. The conceptual map was designed to be comprehensive in including symptoms associated with psychopathic functioning.

Under the Comprehensive Assessment of the Psychopathic Personality model (CAPP; Cooke, Hart, et al., 2004), should be mentioned the existence of the Institutional Rating Scale (CAPP-IRS, Cooke et al., 2012) and the CAPP Lexical Rating Scale (CAPP Lexical Rating Scale; CAPP-LRS; Sellbom, Cooke, & Hart, 2015).

Minnesota Multiphasic Personality Inventory (Ben-Porath & Tellegen, 2008; Butcher et al., 2001)

The Minnesota Multiphasic Personality Inventory-2 (MMPI-2; Butcher, Dahlstrom, Graham, Tellegen, & Kaemmer, 1989; Butcher et al., 2001) and the Minnesota Multiphasic Personality Inventory-Restructured Form (MMPI-2-RF; Ben-Porath & Tellegen, 2008) are the updated versions of the original Minnesota Multiphasic Personality Inventory (MMPI; Hathaway & McKinley, 1943). The new MMPI-3 (Ben-Porath & Tellegen, 2020a, 2020b) is an updated version of the MMPI-2-RF. Since its original development, the MMPI has become the most widely used clinical personality inventory. Although they do not exhaust the objective of evaluating psychopathy, for this general purpose, MMPI-2 has a clinical Scale 4 (Psychopathic Deviate—Pd), and MMPI-2-RF includes the Restructured Clinical scale (Antisocial Behavior—RC4).

The **MMPI-2**, a broadband self-report measure of psychopathology, is appropriate for individuals aged 18 years or older and requires examinees to respond "true" or "false" to 567 statements describing personal characteristics, behaviors, experiences, and beliefs. The MMPI-2 have 10 clinical/personality scales (e.g., *Depression, Paranoia, Psychasthenia, Schizophrenia*, and includes also a *Psychopathic deviate* scale), 9 validity scales (e.g., *Variable Response Inconsistency, Infrequency psychopathology, Lie*), and 15 additional content scales measuring specific personality factors (e.g., *Anxiety, Health concerns, Fears, Anger, Antisocial practices, Family problems, Work interference*).

With 50 items, the purpose of MMPI-2 Scale 4 **Psychopathic Deviate (*Pd*)** is to assess aspects of the person's general level of social adjustment. More specifically, the Scale 4 (*Pd*) evaluates inability to profit from experience, break rules, disregard for laws or social conventions, engage in illegal behavior, problems, and conflicts with authorities, frequent relationships, hedonism, and work difficulties. For example, an elevated score on Scale 4 (*Pd*) suggests that the person taking the test might manifest feelings, attitudes, and behavior similar to the group of juvenile delinquents used to derive the scale. The most commonly elevated scale are among offenders. One T-score greater than 65 indicates clinical significance on a specific scale (Graham, 2011).

While it was originally designed to measure the psychopathic personality (Hathaway & McKinley, 1943), research has suggested that the **overall *Pd* scale score is a poor measure of psychopathy** (Graham, 2011). For example, Hare and Cox (1978) and Hare (1985) found only modest associations between *Pd* scale of the MMPI-2 and clinician ratings [e.g., Psychopathy Checklist (PCL)] of psychopathy. Hockey (2016) research results showed that individuals who scored highly on the *Pd* scale did not score any higher on the PCL-R than individuals who scored lower on the Psychopathic Deviate scale. The study by Walters (1985) with 225 male military criminal offenders supports the utility of MMPI-2 Scale 4 as a general measure of Antisocial Personality (evaluated with the Psychiatric Diagnosis Interview).

Still from an interpretive point of view, but in a more complex record, **Scale 4 Psychopathic Deviate** can be broken down into **different specific subscales**: *Pd1/ Familial Discord* (family that was unsupportive, critical, and interfered with independence); *Pd2/Authority Conflict* (beliefs of right/wrong that disregard societal rules, rebellion against societal norms, legal/academic difficulties); *Pd3/Social Imperturbability* (stubborn, socially confident, honest); *Pd4/Social Alienation* (feels poorly understood, isolated from others); and *Pd5/Self-Alienation* (unhappy with self, guilt and regret regarding past behavior) (e.g., Graham, 2011; Harris & Lingoes, 1968; Hockey, 2016). The *Authority Conflict* **subscale (*Pd2*)** was consistently the strongest correlate of different measures of psychopathy, namely Psychopathic Personality Inventory (PPI) (Lilienfeld, 1999) and also correlated with the interpersonal, impulsive, and antisocial facets of psychopathy (Hockey, 2016). In other study, although the *Pd2* was the only one that significantly correlated with the total PCL-R scores, the relationship ($r=0.31$) was modest (Meloy & Gacono, 1995). Further, the *Familial Discord* (*Pd1*), *Social Alienation* (*Pd4*), and *Self-Alienation* (*Pd5*) subscales are likely capturing the behavioral and impulsive aspect of psychopathy, and *Social Imperturbability* (*Pd3*) is able to somewhat capture the interpersonal aspect of psychopathy. Finally, individuals who score highly on *Pd1*, *Pd4,* and *Pd5* are likely to act impulsively and irresponsibly (Hockey, 2016). From this complex data diversity within the *Pd* scale, Caldwell (2006) concludes that *Pd scale* acts as a strength when measuring psychopathy, as a heterogeneous construct.

The MMPI-2 scales also organize clusters of **content-related items**. For this reason, the different dimensions of each scale can be more clearly differentiated. For example, *Family Problems* (FAM), *Anger* (ANG), and *Antisocial Practices* (ASP) content scales could be useful for problems like the degree of alienation from family, social imperviousness, difficulties with school and authority figures, and alienation from self and society, impulsivity. On the other hand, when FAM is elevated but not ASP, the elevated Scale 4 seems to have more to do with family alienation and conflict than criminal and other forms of antisocial behavior. The content scale ***Antisocial Practices*** **(ASP)** was developed primarily through a rational and statistical strategy to assess a face valid content domain associated with antisocial personality. It has been found to be superior to *Pd* Scale 4 in the prediction of psychopathic personality traits in several different college student samples (Sellbom, Ben-Porath, Lilienfeld, Patrick, & Graham, 2005). For example, and with implications for interpretation and case management, it might be found that an elevation on *Pd* scale can resulted in the context of criminal acting out that might be suggested by subscale elevations on authority conflict and social imperturbability or resulted primarily from family discord. Additionally, information from content scales can be instructive and useful to incrementally increase the validity of the clinical scales and refine their meanings (e.g., of high scores on *Pd* scale). So, the MMPI-2 content scales can be useful to extend, supplement, confirm, and refine interpretations derived from the validity and basic standard clinical scales, like *Pd* scale.

With 338 items, the **MMPI-2-RF** is a measure related conceptually and empirically to modern theories and models of personality dysfunction and maladaptation. The MMPI-2-RF is comprised of six sets of scales: Validity (e.g., Symptom Validity—FBS-r, Response Bias Scale—RBS); Higher Order (e.g., Emotional/Internalizing Dysfunction—EID, Behavioral/Externalizing Dysfunction—BXD); Restructured Clinical (e.g., Demoralization—RCd, Low Positive Emotions—RC2, Cynicism—RC3, Antisocial Behavior—RC4); Specific Problem (e.g., Juvenile Conduct Problems—JCP, Substance Abuse—SUB, Aggression—AGG); Interest (e.g., Aesthetic-Literary Interests—AES); and Personality Psychopathology Five (e.g., Aggressiveness—AGGR-r, Disconstraint—DISC-r).

The nine MMPI-2-RF Restructured Clinical (RC) Scales were developed to address problems in the original clinical scales, including the lack of theoretical grounding, higher than expected intercorrelations, and the inclusion of questionable subtle items. The **Antisocial Behavior (RC4)** consists of 22 items that evaluate various undercontrolled behavioral proclivities including antisocial behaviors and family conflict, and analyzes various past characteristics and tendencies such as risk-taking behaviors, juvenile delinquency, aggression, criminal and disinhibitory behaviors, family problems, substance abuse, lying, cheating, stealing, and failure to conform to social norms. Higher scores on RC4 scale are associated with acting out behavior, substance abuse, and family problems and are also representative of past (and current) criminal conduct history of breaking rules and impulsivity legal difficulties, poor achievement in general, and possibly a history of sexual acting out (Phillips, Sellbom, Ben-Porath, & Patrick, 2014; Sellbom et al., 2012). The Antisocial Behavior Restructured Clinical (RC4) had significantly greater convergent validity in predicting psychopathy as measured by the Psychopathy Checklist: Screening Version (Hart et al., 1995a) and behavioral criteria associated with this construct (Sellbom, Ben-Porath, & Stafford, 2007). With a criminal court clinic samples, Sellbom et al. (2007) concluded that the Antisocial Behavior (RC4), the content scale Antisocial Practices (ASP), and Personality Psychopathology Five Scale Disconstraint (DISC) consistently outperform Scale 4 (*Pd*) in predicting psychopathy and related criteria when assessed from a dimensional perspective. It is important to remember that the DISC scale was constructed to assess a stable personality trait associated with antisocial personality disorder and psychopathy and includes admission of delinquent conduct, reflects a broad dimension of behavioral undercontrol, impulsivity and disinhibition sensation seeking (Harkness, McNulty, & Ben-Porath, 1995). These researchers assert that RC4 was the best measure of the social deviance traits of psychopathy but it is not associated to affective-interpersonal traits of psychopathy (see also Sellbom et al., 2005).

Conclusions about the validity and usefulness of the investigation with MMPI-2 and MMPI-2-RF concerning psychopathy are not convergent. For example, it is often stressed that the various general used self-report measures of psychopathy, like the MMPI-2 *Pd* scale, are widely unrelated to the fundamental personality features of this condition (Harpur et al., 1989; Hawk & Peterson, 1973) or that the MMPI was unable to capture all the construct dimensions of psychopathy (Hundleby & Ross, 1977). In the same sense, Krueger, Markon, Patrick, Benning, and Kramer (2007) conclude these MMPI scales appear to be indicators of broad-based externalizing tendencies, which do not distinguish psychopathy from a variety of other conditions often associated with antisocial and criminal behavior.

But, in a comparative analysis between different versions of MMPI, Caldwell (2006) suggests the validity of the MMPI-2 Scale 4 (Psychopathic Deviate), defends that *Pd* measures the same "psychopathic constellation" as the PCL-R, and concludes the heterogeneous syndrome of psychopathy is better evaluated by the heterogeneity of this scale than the corresponding RC4 (Antisocial Behavior) scale of the MMPI-2-RF. But it is important to mention that the Caldwell's suggestion that MMPI-2 *Pd* Scale 4 is a better measure of the psychopathy construct than MMPI-2-RF RC4 is predicated on the questionable assumption that psychopathy is a syndromal, and categorical, construct, and not a dimensional variable.

Several researchers defend that a combination of MMPI-2-RF trait scales (including estimated psychopathy index scores of impulsive-antisociality, disaffiliativeness, fearfulness, and anxiety) is required to give account of the full scope of the psychopathy construct (e.g., Grossi et al., 2015; Phillips et al., 2014; Sellbom et al., 2016) and that such estimated psychopathy indices on the MMPI-2-RF were useful in predicting treatment completion and recidivism for convicted male batterers (Rock, Sellbom, Ben-Porath, & Salekin, 2013).

The psychometric research regarding the reliability (internal consistency) of these MMPI-2 and MMPI-2-RF scales identifies Cronbach's alpha values that are generally good or acceptable. Specifically, for the Antisocial Behavior (RC4) of the MMPI-2-RF: 0.72, intermediate value between the values 0.91 (Demoralization) and 0.63 (Disaffiliativeness), in a sample of 230 women incarcerated at a state correctional facility (Phillips et al., 2014); 0.80, on the college sample of 724 undergraduate students and 0.82 on a 703 male prison inmates correctional sample, compared to values of 0.91/0.91 (Demoralization) and 0.58/0.54 (Disaffiliativeness), identified respectively in those two samples (Sellbom et al., 2012). Finally, the internal consistencies for the scales used in Sellbom et al. (2007) research are as follows: 0.74 and 0.82 (RC4), 0.63 and 0.76 (Scale 4, *Pd*, MMPI-2), 0.82 and 0.82 (ASP, content MMPI-2 scale), respectively, for a sample of 85 individuals who were undergoing pretrial forensic psychological evaluations at one court clinic and for a sample of 1592 individuals who had been evaluated at a forensic center.

Finally, the new MMPI-3 provides enhanced coverage of constructs related to personality and psychopathology has not yet published research concerning psychopathy.

Personality Assessment Inventory (Morey, 1991)

The Personality Assessment Inventory (PAI; Morey, 1991) is a self-administered, multiscale personality inventory providing psychological assessment information about psychopathology, personality, and psychosocial environment, measuring constructs relevant to clinical diagnosis and decision-making, suitable for use with individuals aged 18+. It applies to diverse types of settings, with surveys of practicing clinicians indicating the PAI as one of the most popular, widely used, clinical measures in mental health, forensic/correctional, screening, and training contexts (e.g., Archer, Buffington-Vollum, Stredny, & Handel, 2006).

The PAI is organized into four sets of scales—four validity scales, 11 clinical scales, five treatment scales, and two interpersonal scales, with many of the full scales also including subscales. The questionnaire includes 344 items, and completion typically takes 45–60 min using either paper and pencil or computer; it requires a fourth-grade reading level to complete. Response options are on a four-point scale, ranging from "totally false, not at all true" to "very true." Items are summed into raw scores which are then transformed to *T*-scores (mean of 50, standard deviation of 10), and interpretation is provided relative to a standardization sample of 1000 community-dwelling adults from the United States, selected to match US census characteristics based on gender, race, and age. Internal consistency alphas for the full scales are generally found to be in the .80 in a variety of different settings, and test-retest reliability in nonclinical samples yields similar estimates. Such reliability values provide an estimate of the standard error of measurement of roughly three to four T-score points, with 95% confidence intervals of ± six to eight T-score points. For a comprehensive presentation of available validity evidence, see the PAI manual (Morey, 2007).

The four validity scales of the PAI—Negative Impression Management (NIM), Positive Impression Management (PIM), Inconsistency (ICN), and Infrequency (INF)—were developed to assess profile distortion, which can result from either random (assessed with ICN and INF) or systematic (assessed with NIM and PIM) sources of response distortion. Systematic profile distortion can be further broken down into effortful (i.e., intentional) or noneffortful forms. Effortful distortion occurs when respondents intentionally present themselves in a manner that is at odds with their experience or historical fact (i.e., they might malinger, or fake good). In noneffortful distortion, respondents may present themselves in a manner which is consistent with their subjective experience, but which an experienced clinician might see as lacking insight (most commonly, when overly positive), or as an exaggeration (if overly negative) of symptoms. The PAI provides supplemental indices that assist in distinguishing between these different forms of systematic distortion. Because of the potential reporting biases that might be present in the assessment of psychopathy, the availability of validated response validity scales on the PAI represents an important advantage for test interpretation.

While several of the substantive scales from the PAI are relevant to the assessment of psychopathy, the most commonly researched scale for this application is the Antisocial Features (ANT) scale. This scale includes three conceptually distinct subscales intended to measure facets of antisociality: ANT-A (Antisocial Behaviors), which assesses a history of conduct problems and criminality; ANT-E (Egocentricity), which measures a self-centered, callous, and remorseless interpersonal style; and ANT-S (Stimulus Seeking), which reflects a tendency to take risks and a strong desire for novelty. The ANT scale has shown to be a robust predictor of theoretically relevant forms of social deviance, such as institutional misconduct and criminal recidivism (e.g., Reidy, Sorensen, & Davidson, 2016). A recent meta-analytic review (Gardner, Boccaccini, Bitting, & Edens, 2015) indicated that ANT scores consistently emerged as a small to moderate predictor of institutional misconduct in both correctional and treatment settings.

Research has generally shown that ANT scores are moderate to strongly associated with both self-report and interview-based assessment of both an antisocial personality disorder and psychopathy (Douglas, Guy, Edens, Boer, & Hamilton, 2007; Edens, Poythress, & Watkins, 2001; Guy, Poythress, Douglas, Skeem, & Edens, 2008). However, there is some evidence to suggest that the ANT scale may be more strongly related to behavioral deviance than to interpersonal or affective features of psychopathy (Douglas et al., 2007; Lilienfeld, Fowler, & Patrick, 2006). This is supported by findings of higher associations with Factor 2 (the social deviance factor) of the Psychopathy Checklist-Revised (PCL-R; Hare, 2003), with smaller associations between the ANT Scale and affective and interpersonal deficits as assessed by the PCL-R (Douglas et al., 2007; Edens, Hart, Johnson, Johnson, & Olver, 2000; Kucharski, Petitt, Toomey, & Duncan, 2008; Walters, Duncan, & Geyer, 2003). While research suggests the pragmatic utility of the PAI in criminal justice settings, with predictive validity, estimates often comparable to those provided by the PCL-R (Walters & Duncan, 2005), the two instruments should be viewed as complementary rather than as a proxy for one another, as both seem to contribute somewhat independently to prediction of important outcomes (e.g., Buffington-Vollum, Edens, Johnson, & Johnson, 2002).

Another PAI scale that is theoretically relevant to the assessment of psychopathy is Aggression (AGG). The AGG scale assesses anger, hostility, and aggression and is comprised of three subscales: Aggressive Attitude (AGG-A), Verbal Aggression (AGG-V), and Physical Aggression (AGG-P). Similar to the ANT scale, the AGG scale has proven to be a robust predictor of institutional misconduct in both correctional and treatment settings, as well as of postrelease recidivism (Gardner et al., 2015; Reidy et al., 2016). Additionally, the AGG scale has demonstrated incremental utility above PCL-R Factor 2 in the prediction of institutional misconduct (Walters et al., 2003). Given that psychopathic individuals tend to be described as prone to violence and aggression, research has reported the AGG scale to demonstrate moderate correlations with self-report and interview-based indices of psychopathy (Edens, Poythress, & Watkins, 2001; Walters, Duncan, & Geyer, 2003). For example, Edens, Poythress, and Watkins (2001) reported AGG, in addition to the ANT scale, as being a significant behavioral correlate of the Psychopathic Personality Inventory (PPI; Lilienfeld & Andrews, 1996).

In addition to the basic scales of the PAI, supplemental indicators for the PAI have been developed that may provide useful information regarding the assessment of psychopathy and violence risk. The Violence Potential Index (VPI; Morey, 1996) incorporates 20 different features of the PAI profile that serve as putative risk factors for violent behavior. Such features include anger, hostile control in relationships, sensation seeking, impulsivity, agitation, antisocial behavior, grandiosity, and alcohol and drug abuse, among others. Research has shown moderate-sized effects for VPI in predicting both violent and nonviolent recidivism (Boccaccini, Murrie, Hawes, Simpler, & Johnson, 2010; Reidy et al., 2016). The VPI has been shown to correlate with a self-report measure of psychopathic features such as Hare's 1985 self-report measure of psychopathy (SRP-R) and a diagnostic interview for ASPD (Edens et al., 2000; Morey, 1996).

Aside from the scales most commonly used to assess psychopathy with the PAI (i.e., ANT and AGG), there are a variety of other PAI scales that are theoretically related to the construct. Relevant PAI scales such as Alcohol Problems (ALC) and Drug Problems (DRG), Borderline Features (BOR), Mania (MAN), Paranoia (PAR), Stress (STR), and Treatment Rejection (RXR) have been investigated as correlates of PCL-R defined psychopathy (e.g., Douglas et al., 2007) and of the Psychopathic Personality Inventory (e.g., Patrick, Edens, Poythress, Lilienfeld, & Benning, 2006). Moreover, as interpersonal style theoretically overlaps with core personality traits of psychopathy, several researchers have examined the relationship between the interpersonal scales of the PAI (e.g., Dominance and Warmth) and psychopathic personality. The Dominance (DOM) scale assesses the extent to which one is controlling and independent in personal relationships, while the Warmth (WRM) scale assesses the extent to which a person is interested in supportive and empathic personal relationships. Previous research has shown particular support for the use of the DOM scale as a relevant indicator of interpersonal features of psychopathy (Douglas et al., 2007; Edens, 2009; Patrick et al., 2006). For example, in a sample of 281 Canadian federal offenders, Douglas et al. (2007) found that only the DOM scale predicted Factor 1 (the interpersonal and affective deficit factor) of the PCL-R.

In tandem with the use of specific scales of the PAI to assess psychopathy, recent research has investigated the ability of higher-order factors of the PAI to capture the construct. Such higher-order factors include the broad psychopathological domains of internalizing (INT) and externalizing (EXT) features. In a large correctional sample, Blonigen et al. (2010) explored convergent and discriminant relations between factors of psychopathy measures and latent criteria of INT and EXT derived from the PAI (Blonigen et al., 2010). Using a multimethod approach of both self-report and interview/file review, results indicated scores reflective of affective and interpersonal traits of psychopathy were negatively associated with INT, whereas scores reflective of social deviance exhibited positive associations with both INT and EXT of the PAI.

Conclusions

Psychopathy has long been recognized as a forensic construct with implications and influence in decision-making in the legal context, and, therefore, the ethics associated with forensic practice require professionals to be aware of the limitations of the instruments (Cooke, 2010), without neglecting their potential.

Throughout the chapter, instruments were explored, with the following potentialities: (a) temporal and financial costs tend to be lower (Hare, Neumann, & Mokros, 2018); (b) a facility associated with filling out and administering the instrument, which does not require appraisers to make subjective judgments about the person's functioning that are not observable, as the lack of empathy (Lilienfeld & Fowler, 2006); and (c) the opportunity to develop large population reference samples (Muñoz & Frick, 2007) and to identify specific subjective dispositions, such as guilt or intentions in people's actions, such as manipulation (Colins et al., 2014). Examples are the Self-Assessment of Psychopathy Scale (SRP-4), the Hare P-Scan, the Levenson Psychopathy Self-Relate Scale (LSRP), and the Triadic Psychopathy Measure (TriPM).

Another potentiality, present in instruments such as the PCL-R and its screening version (PLC:SV) and for adolescents (PCL:YV), as well as in the APSD version intended for parents (APSD-PR) and teachers (APSD-TR), and the CAPP Institutional Assessment Scale (CAPP-IRS), results from the fact that consultation with other elements and sources of information mitigates the risk of the results being contaminated merely by criminal history (Muñoz & Frick, 2007).

Concerning limitations, the cooperation of the person is highlighted as an essential factor for self-reported measures (Tew et al., 2015) and, in turn, the risk of the person in resorting to manipulation in response to items, distorting responses to make characteristics more or less socially desirable (Colins et al., 2017; Pechorro, Da Silva, Rijo, Gonçalves, & Andershed, 2017; Pechorro, Goncalves, Andershed, & Delisi, 2017). With the exception of the Psychopathic Personality Inventory (PPI), the other instruments presented do not include validity scales. In this sense, instruments such as the PCL-R and its screening version (PLC:SV) and for adolescents (PCL:YV), the APSD version for parents (APSD-PR) and teachers (APSD-TR), and the CAPP Institutional Assessment Scale (CAPP-IRS) stand out once again for overcoming the limitations of self-reported instruments such as simulation, social desirability, denial, or behavior minimization (Edens, Petrila, & Buffington-Vollum, 2001).

Therefore, it is essential to reflect on the limitations of the instruments according to the specificities of the target population of the evaluation before resorting to them. Take, for example, young people in prison settings where financial resources for comprehensive evaluations are often lacking (Colins, Noom, & Vanderplasschen, 2012), and access to important diagnostic information provided by parents and teachers is scarce (Colins, Vermeiren, Schuyten, Broekaert, & Soyez, 2008).

Also noteworthy is the adaptation of the instrument in different cultures (Shou et al., 2017), where the cutoff point may have to change depending on the specificities and influence of the evaluated person's culture. The same is true for the female population, where the expression of risk factors for violence tends to be different in women (Van Voorhis, Wright, Salisbury, & Bauman, 2010) and, therefore, the different and gender-appropriate methods of evaluation for each population sample (Geraghty, 2015).

The specificities of the sample are also important. For example, in an investigation by Mossière, Olver, and Marche (2020), the SRP-SF proved to be a particularly useful tool in predicting violence and identifying antisocial behavior. The same applies to PCL-R as a golden standard instrument in the clinical and forensic context (Hare & Neumann, 2006; Vitacco et al., 2005), which works both at the level of psychopathy diagnosis and risk assessment (e.g., Mokros et al., 2014).

References

Alzeer, S. M., Michailidou, M. I., Munot, M., & Kyranides, M. N. (2019). Attachment and parental relationships and the association with psychopathic traits in young adults. *Personality and Individual Differences*, *151*(1), 1–6. https://doi.org/10.1016/j.paid.2019.07.009.

Anderson, N. E., & Kiehl, K. A. (2014). Psychopathy and aggression: When paralimbic dysfunction leads to violence. *Current Topics in Behavioral Neurosciences*, *17*, 369–393. https://doi.org/10.1007/7854_2013_257.

Andershed, H., Kerr, M., Stattin, H., & Levander, S. (2002). Psychopathic traits in non-referred youths: A new assessment tool. In E. Blaauw, & L. Sheridan (Eds.), *Psychopaths: Current international perspectives* (pp. 131–158). The Hague: Elsevier.

Anderson, J. L., Sellbom, M., Wygant, D. B., & Edens, J. F. (2013). Examining the necessity for and utility of the psychopathic personality inventory–revised (PPI–R) validity scales. *Law and Human Behavior*, *37*(5), 312–320. https://doi.org/10.1037/lhb0000018.

Anestis, J. C., Green, B. A., Arnau, R. C., & Anestis, M. D. (2019). Psychopathic personality traits in the military: An examination of the Levenson self-report psychopathy scales in a novel sample. *Assessment*, *26*(4), 670–683. https://doi.org/10.1177/1073191117719511.

Archer, R. P., Buffington-Vollum, J. K., Stredny, R. V., & Handel, R. W. (2006). A survey of psychological test use patterns among forensic psychologists. *Journal of Personality Assessment*, *87*(1), 84–94. https://doi.org/10.1207/s15327752jpa8701_07.

Ben-Porath, Y. S., & Tellegen, A. (2008). *MMPI-2-RF (MMPI-2-restructured form) manual for administration*. Minnesota, MN: University of Minnesota Press.

Ben-Porath, Y. S., & Tellegen, A. (2020a). *MMPI-3 manual for administration, scoring, and interpretation*. Minnesota, MN: University of Minnesota Press.

Ben-Porath, Y. S., & Tellegen, A. (2020b). *MMPI-3 technical manual*. Minnesota, MN: University of Minnesota Press.

Blackburn, R., & Maybury, C. (1985). Identifying the psychopath: The relation of Cleckley's criteria to the interpersonal domain. *Personality and Individual Differences*, *6*(3), 375–386. https://doi.org/10.1016/0191-8869(85)90062-5.

Blonigen, D. M., Patrick, C. J., Douglas, K. S., Poythress, N. G., Skeem, J. L., Lilienfeld, S. O., … Krueger, R. F. (2010). Multimethod assessment of psychopathy in relation to factors of internalizing and externalizing from the personality assessment inventory: The impact of method variance and suppressor effects. *Psychological Assessment*, *22*, 96–107. https://doi.org/10.1037/a0017240.

Bo, S., Pedersen, L., Christensen, K. B., & Rasmussen, K. (2019). Psychopathy in a forensic sample – The factor structure of the PCL:SV in a Danish forensic sample. *Scandinavian Journal of Psychology*. https://doi.org/10.1111/sjop.12566.

Boccaccini, M. T., Murrie, D. C., Hawes, S. W., Simpler, A., & Johnson, J. (2010). Predicting recidivism with the personality assessment inventory in a sample of sex offenders screened for civil commitment as sexually violent predators. *Psychological Assessment*, *22*(1), 142–148. https://doi.org/10.1037/a0017818.

Book, A. S., Forth, A. E., & Clark, H. J. (2013). The Hare psychopathy checklist—Youth version. In R. P. Archer, & E. M. A. Wheeler (Eds.), *Forensic uses of clinical assessment instruments* (pp. 266–290). New York, NY: Routledge/Taylor & Francis Group.

Brackett, R. E., Jackson, R. L., & Richards, H. J. (2008). The Hare PSCAN and its relationship to psychopathy in a sample of civilly committed sexual offenders. *International Journal of Forensic Mental Health*, *7*(1), 29–37. https://doi.org/10.1080/14999013.2008.9914401.

Brinkley, C. A., Diamond, P. M., Magaletta, P. R., & Heigel, C. P. (2008). Cross-validation of Levenson's psychopathy scale in a sample of federal female inmates. *Assessment*, *15*(4), 464–482. https://doi.org/10.1177/1073191108319043.

Brinkley, C. A., Schmitt, W. A., Smith, S. S., & Newman, J. P. (2001). Construct validation of a self-report psychopathy scale: Does Levenson's self-report psychopathy scale measure the same constructs as Hare's psychopathy checklist revised? *Personality and Individual Differences*, *31*(7), 1021–1038. https://doi.org/10.1016/S0191-8869(00)00178-1.

Buffington-Vollum, J., Edens, J. F., Johnson, D. W., & Johnson, J. K. (2002). Psychopathy as a predictor of institutional misbehavior among sex offenders: A prospective replication. *Criminal Justice and Behavior*, *29*(5), 497–511. https://doi.org/10.1177/009385402236730.

Butcher, J. N., Dahlstrom, W. G., Graham, J. R., Tellegen, A., & Kaemmer, B. (1989). *Manual for administration and scoring: MMPI-2*. Minneapolis, MN: University of Minnesota Press.

Butcher, J. N., Graham, J. R., Ben-Porath, Y. S., Tellegen, A., Dahlstrom, W. G., & Kaemmer, B. (2001). *Minnesota multiphasic personality inventory-2: Manual for administration and scoring* (2nd ed.). Minneapolis: University of Minnesota Press.

Caldwell, A. B. (2006). Maximal measurement or meaningful measurement: The interpretive challenges of the MMPI-2 Restructured Clinical (RC) Scales. *Journal of Personality Assessment*, *87*, 193–201.

Carabellese, F., Felthous, A. R., La Tegola, D., Rossetto, I., Franconi, F., Lucchini, G., & Catanesi, R. (2020). Female psychopathy: A descriptive national study of socially dangerous female NGRI offenders. *International Journal of Law and Psychiatry*, *68*, e101455. https://doi.org/10.1016/j.ijlp.2019.101455.

Carré, J. M., Hyde, L. W., Neumann, C. S., Viding, E., & Hariri, A. R. (2013). The neural signatures of distinct psychopathic traits. *Social Neuroscience*, *8*(2), 122–135. https://doi.org/10.1080/17470919.2012.703623.

Cauffman, E., Kimonis, E. R., Dmitrieva, J., & Monahan, K. C. (2009). A multimethod assessment of juvenile psychopathy: Comparing the predictive utility of the PCL: YV, YPI, and NEO-PRI. *Psychological Assessment, 21*(4), 528–542. https://doi.org/10.1037/a0017367.

Chabrol, H., & Leichsenring, F. (2006). Borderline personality organization and psychopathic traits in nonclinical adolescents: Relationships of identity diffusion, primitive defense mechanisms and reality testing with callousness and impulsivity traits. *Bulletin of the Menninger Clinic, 70*(2), 160–170. https://doi.org/10.1521/bumc.2006.70.2.160.

Chapman, A. L., Gremore, T. M., & Farmer, R. F. (2003). Psychometric analysis of the psychopathic personality inventory (PPI) with female inmates. *Journal of Personality Assessment, 80*(2), 164–172. https://doi.org/10.1207/S15327752JPA8002_05.

Christian, E., & Sellbom, M. (2016). Development and validation of an expanded version of the three-factor Levenson self report psychopathy scale. *Journal of Personality Assessment, 98*(2), 155–168. https://doi.org/10.1080/00223891.2015.1068176.

Colins, O. F., Bijttebier, P., Broekaert, E., & Andershed, H. (2014). Psychopathic-like traits among detained female adolescents: Reliability and validity of the antisocial process screening device and the youth psychopathic traits inventory. *Assessment, 21*(2), 195–209. https://doi.org/10.1177/1073191113481997.

Colins, O. F., Fanti, K. A., Andershed, H., Mulder, E., Salekin, R. T., Blokland, A., & Vermeiren, R. R. (2017). Psychometric properties and prognostic usefulness of the youth psychopathic traits inventory (YPI) as a component of a clinical protocol for detained youth: A multiethnic examination. *Psychological Assessment, 29*(6), 740–753. https://doi.org/10.1037/pas0000437.

Colins, O. F., Noom, M., & Vanderplasschen, W. (2012). Youth psychopathic traits inventory-short version: A further test of the internal consistency and criterion validity. *Journal of Psychopathology and Behavioral Assessment, 34*, 476–486. https://doi.org/10.1007/s10862-012-9299-0.

Colins, O., Vermeiren, R., Schuyten, G., Broekaert, E., & Soyez, V. (2008). Informant agreement in the assessment of disruptive behavior disorders in detained minors in Belgium: A diagnosis-level and symptom-level examination. *Journal of Clinical Psychiatry, 69*, 141–148. https://doi.org/10.4088/JCP.v69n0119.

Cooke, D. (2010). Psychopathy. In J. M. Brown, & E. A. Campbell (Eds.), *The Cambridge handbook of forensic psychology* (pp. 292–298). Cambridge: Cambridge University Press. https://doi.org/10.1017/CBO9780511730290.037.

Cooke, D. J., Hart, S. D., Logan, C., & Michie, C. (2004). *Comprehensive assessment of psychopathic personality-institutional rating scale (CAPP-IRS)*. Unpublished manuscript.

Cooke, D. J., Hart, S. D., Logan, C., & Michie, C. (2012). Explicating the construct of psychopathy: Development and validation of a conceptual model, the comprehensive assessment of psychopathic personality (CAPP). *International Journal of Forensic Mental Health, 11*(4), 242–252. https://doi.org/10.1080/14999013.2012.746759.

Cooke, D. J., & Logan, C. (2018). Capturing psychopathic personality: Penetrating the mask of sanity through clinical interview. In C. J. Patrick (Ed.), *Handbook of psychopathy* (pp. 189–210). New York, NY: The Guilford Press.

Cooke, D. J., & Michie, C. (2001). Refining the construct of psychopathy: Towards a hierarchical model. *Psychological Assessment, 13*(2), 171–188. https://doi.org/10.1037//1040-3590.13.2.171.

Cooke, D. J., Michie, C., Hart, S. D., & Hare, R. D. (1999). Evaluating the screening version of the Hare psychopathy checklist—Revised (PCL: SV): An item response theory analysis. *Psychological Assessment, 11*(1), 3–13. https://doi.org/10.1037/1040-3590.11.1.3.

Cooke, D. J., Michie, C., & Skeem, J. (2007). Understanding the structure of the psychopathy checklist–revised: An exploration of methodological confusion. *The British Journal of Psychiatry*, *190*(49), 39–50. https://doi.org/10.1192/bjp.190.5.s39.

Culhane, S. E., Walker, S., & Hildebrand, M. M. (2019). Serial homicide perpetrators' self-reported psychopathy and criminal thinking. *Journal of Police and Criminal Psychology*, *34*(1), 1–13. https://doi.org/10.1007/s11896-017-9245-x.

Cunha, O., Braga, T., Gomes, H. S., & Abrunhosa Gonçalves, R. (2020). Psychopathy checklist-revised (PCL-R) factor structure in male perpetrators of intimate partner violence. *Journal of Forensic Psychology Research and Practice*, *20*(3), 241–263. https://doi.org/10.1080/24732850.2020.1717279.

DeMatteo, D., Heilbrun, K., & Marczyk, G. (2005). Psychopathy, risk of violence, and protective factors in a noninstitutionalized and noncriminal sample. *International Journal of Forensic Mental Health*, *4*(2), 147–157. https://doi.org/10.1080/14999013.2005.10471220.

Demetrioff, S., Porter, S., & Baker, A. (2016). I know how you feel: The influence of psychopathic traits on the ability to identify micro-expressions. *Psychology, Crime & Law*, *23*(3), 274–290. https://doi.org/10.1080/1068316X.2016.1247159.

Dolan, M., & Rennie, C. (2006). Psychopathy checklist: Youth version and youth psychopathic trait inventory: A comparison study. *Personality and Individual Differences*, *41*(4), 779–789. https://doi.org/10.1016/j.paid.2006.03.021.

Dong, L., Wu, H., & Waldman, I. D. (2014). Measurement and structural invariance of the antisocial process screening device. *Psychological Assessment*, *26*(2), 598–608. https://doi.org/10.1037/a0035139.

Douglas, H., Bore, M., & Munro, D. (2012). Construct validity of a two-factor model of psychopathy. *Psychology*, *3*(3), 243–248. https://doi.org/10.4236/psych.2012.33034.

Douglas, K. S., Guy, L. S., Edens, J. F., Boer, D. P., & Hamilton, J. (2007). The personality assessment inventory as a proxy for the psychopathy checklist–revised: Testing the incremental validity and cross-sample robustness of the antisocial features scale. *Assessment*, *14*(3), 255–269. https://doi.org/10.1177/1073191107302138.

Douglas, K. S., Strand, S., Belfrage, H., Fransson, G., & Levander, S. (2005). Reliability and validity evaluation of the psychopathy checklist: Screening version (PCL: SV) in Swedish correctional and forensic psychiatric samples. *Assessment*, *12*(2), 145–161. https://doi.org/10.1177/1073191105275455.

Drislane, L. E., Brislin, S. J., Kendler, K. S., Andershed, H., Larsson, H., & Patrick, C. J. (2015). A Triarchic model analysis of the youth psychopathic traits inventory. *Journal of Personality Disorders*, *29*(1), 15–41. https://doi.org/10.1521/pedi_2014_28_144.

Edens, J. F. (2009). Interpersonal characteristics of male criminal offenders: Personality, psychopathological, and behavioral correlates. *Psychological Assessment*, *21*(1), 89–98. https://doi.org/10.1037/a0014856.

Edens, J. F., Hart, S. D., Johnson, D. W., Johnson, J. K., & Olver, M. E. (2000). Use of the personality assessment inventory to assess psychopathy in offender populations. *Psychological Assessment*, *12*(2), 132–139. https://doi.org/10.1037/1040-3590.12.2.132.

Edens, J. F., Petrila, J., & Buffington-Vollum, J. K. (2001). Psychopathy and the death penalty: Can the psychopathy checklist-revised identify offenders who represent "a continuing threat to society"? *The Journal of Psychiatry & Law*, *29*(4), 433–481. https://doi.org/10.1177/009318530102900403.

Edens, J. F., Poythress, N. G., & Watkins, M. M. (2001). Further validation of the Psychopathic Personality Inventory among offenders: Personality and behavioral correlates. *Journal of Personality Disorders*, *15*(5), 403–415. https://doi.org/10.1521/pedi.15.5.403.19202.

Eisenbarth, H., Krammer, S., Edwards, B. G., Kiehl, K. A., & Neumann, C. S. (2018). Structural analysis of the PCL-R and relationship to BIG FIVE personality traits and parenting characteristics in an Hispanic female offender sample. *Personality and Individual Differences, 129*, 59–65. https://doi.org/10.1016/j.paid.2018.03.015.

Elwood, C. E., Poythress, N. G., & Douglas, K. S. (2004). Evaluation of the Hare P-SCAN in a non-clinical population. *Personality and Individual Differences*, *36*(4), 833–843. https://doi.org/10.1016/S0191-8869(03)00156-9.

Evans, L., & Tully, R. J. (2016). The triarchic psychopathy measure (TriPM): Alternative to the PCL-R? *Aggression and Violent Behavior*, *27*, 79–86. https://doi.org/10.1016/j.avb.2016.03.004.

Few, L. R., Miller, J. D., & Lynam, D. R. (2013). An examination of the factor structure of the elemental psychopathy assessment. *Personality Disorders: Theory, Research, and Treatment*, *4*(3), 247. https://doi.org/10.1037/per0000016.

Forsman, M., Lichtenstein, P., Andershed, H., & Larsson, H. (2010). A longitudinal twin study of the direction of effects between psychopathic personality and antisocial behaviour. *Journal of Child Psychology and Psychiatry*, *51*(1), 39–47. https://doi.org/10.1111/j.1469-7610.2009.02141.x.

Forth, A., & Brazil, K. (2019). Psychopathy Checklist: Youth Version (PCL:YV). In R. Morgan (Ed.), *The SAGE encyclopedia of criminal psychology* (pp. 1193–1196). Thousand Oaks, CA: Sage Publications, Inc.

Forth, A. E., Brown, S. L., Hart, S. D., & Hare, R. D. (1996). The assessment of psychopathy in male and female noncriminals: Reliability and validity. *Personality and Individual Differences*, *20*(5), 531–543. https://doi.org/10.1016/0191-8869(95)00221-9.

Forth, A. E., Kosson, D. S., & Hare, R. D. (2003). *Hare psychopathy checklist: Youth version*. Toronto: Multi-Health Systems.

Frick, P. J. (2004). *The inventory of callous-unemotional traits*. New Orleans, LA: UNO.

Frick, P. J., Bodin, S. D., & Barry, C. T. (2000a). Psychopathic traits and conduct problems in community and clinic-referred samples of children: Further development of the psychopathy screening device. *Psychological Assessment*, *12*(4), 382–393. https://doi.org/10.1037/1040-3590.12.4.382.

Frick, P. J., Bodin, S. D., & Barry, C. T. (2000b). Applying the concept of psychopathy to children: Implications for the assessment of antisocial youth. In C. Gacono (Ed.), *The clinical and forensic assessment: A practitioner's guide* (pp. 1–24). New York, NY: Lawrence Erlbaum.

Frick, P. J., & Hare, R. D. (2001). *The antisocial process screening device*. Toronto, ON: Multi-Health Systems.

Frick, P. J., Ray, J. V., Thornton, L. C., & Kahn, R. E. (2014). Can callous-unemotional traits enhance the understanding, diagnosis, and treatment of serious conduct problems in children and adolescents? A comprehensive review. *Psychological Bulletin*, *140*(1), 1–57. https://doi.org/10.1037/a0033076.

Gao, Y., & Raine, A. (2010). Successful and unsuccessful psychopaths: A neurobiological model. *Behavioral Sciences & the Law*, *28*(2), 194–210. https://doi.org/10.1002/bsl.924.

Gardner, B. O., Boccaccini, M. T., Bitting, B. S., & Edens, J. F. (2015). Personality assessment inventory scores as predictors of misconduct, recidivism, and violence: A meta-analytic review. *Psychological Assessment*, *27*(2), 534–544. https://doi.org/10.1037/pas0000065.

Garofalo, C., Noteborn, M. G., Sellbom, M., & Bogaerts, S. (2019). Factor structure and construct validity of the Levenson self-report psychopathy scale (LSRP): A replication and extension in Dutch nonclinical participants. *Journal of Personality Assessment*, *101*(5), 481–492. https://doi.org/10.1080/00223891.2018.1519830.

Geraghty, K. A. (2015). *Assessing risk in female offenders* (Doctoral dissertation). Birmingham: University of Birmingham.

Gillen, C. T. A., MacDougall, E. A. M., Forth, A. E., Barry, C. T., & Salekin, R. T. (2019). Validity of the youth psychopathic traits inventory–short version in justice-involved and at-risk adolescents. *Assessment*, *26*(3), 479–491. https://doi.org/10.1177/1073191117700723.

Gonçalves, R. A., & Cunha, O. (2017). Escala de Psicopatia de Hare. In M. Simões, L. Almeida, & M. Gonçalves (Eds.), *Psicologia Forense: Instrumentos de Avaliação* (pp. 2–41). (Pactor).

Goodwin, B. E., Sellbom, M., & Salekin, R. T. (2015). Elucidating the construct validity of the antisocial process screening device (APSD) in a sample of young adults. *Journal of Psychopathology and Behavioral Assessment*, *37*(1), 1–11. https://doi.org/10.1007/s10862-014-9444-z.

Gordts, S., Uzieblo, K., Neumann, C., Van den Bussche, E., & Rossi, G. (2017). Validity of the self-report psychopathy scales (SRP-III full and short versions) in a community sample. *Assessment*, *24*(3), 308–325. https://doi.org/10.1177/1073191115606205.

Goulter, N., Kimonis, E. R., & Heller, E. (2018). Antisocial process screening device subscales predict recidivism in an Australian juvenile offender sample. *Journal of Psychopathology and Behavioral Assessment*, *40*(2), 159–168. https://doi.org/10.1007/s10862-018-9669-3.

Graham, J. R. (2011). *MMPI-2: Assessing personality and psychopathology* (5th ed.). Oxford: Oxford University Press.

Grossi, L. M., Green, D., Belfi, B., McGrath, R. E., Griswold, H., & Schreiber, J. (2015). Identifying aggression in forensic inpatients using the MMPI-2-RF: An examination of MMPI-2-RF scale scores and estimated psychopathy indices. *International Journal of Forensic Mental Health*, *14*(4), 231–244. https://doi.org/10.1080/14999013.2015.1108943.

Guy, L. S., & Douglas, K. S. (2006). Examining the utility of the PCL: SV as a screening measure using competing factor models of psychopathy. *Psychological Assessment*, *18*(2), 225–230. https://doi.org/10.1037/1040-3590.18.2.225.

Guy, L. S., Poythress, N. G., Douglas, K. S., Skeem, J. L., & Edens, J. F. (2008). Correspondence between self-report and interview-based assessments of antisocial personality disorder. *Psychological Assessment*, *20*(1), 47–54. https://doi.org/10.1037/1040-3590.20.1.47.

Hall, J. R., Drislane, L. E., Patrick, C. J., Morano, M., Lilienfeld, S. O., & Poythress, N. G. (2014). Development and validation of triarchic construct scales from the psychopathic personality inventory. *Psychological Assessment*, *26*(2), 447–461. https://doi.org/10.1037/a0035665.

Hare, R. (2002). La naturaleza del psicópata: algunas observaciones para entender la violencia depredadora humana. In A. Raine, & J. Sanmartín (Eds.), *Violencia y psicopatía* (pp. 15–58). Editorial Ariel.

Hare, R. D. (1985). Checklist for the assessment of psychopathy in criminal populations. In M. H. Ben-Aron, S. J. Hucker, & C. D. Webster (Eds.), *Clinical criminology* (pp. 157–167). Toronto, ON: University ofClarke Institute of Psychiatry.

Hare, R. D. (1991). *The Hare Psychopathy Checklist – Revised*. Toronto, ON: Multi-Health Systems.

Hare, R. D. (2003). *Manual for the revised psychopathy checklist* (2nd). Toronto, ON: Multi-Health Systems.

Hare, R. D., Black, P., & Walsh, Z. (2013). The PCL-R: Forensic applications and limitations. In R. P. Archer, & E. M. A. Wheeler (Eds.), *Forensic uses of clinical assessment instruments* (2nd, pp. 230–265). New York, NY: Routledge.

Hare, R. D., & Cox, D. N. (1978). Clinical and empirical conceptions of psychopathy, and the selection of subjects for research. In R. D. Hare, & D. Schalling (Eds.), *Psychopathic behaviour: Approaches to research* (pp. 1–21). Chichester, England: John Wiley & Sons, Inc.

Hare, R. D., & Herve, H. F. (1999). *Hare P-SCAN*. Toronto: Multi-Health Systems.

Hare, R. D., & Neumann, C. S. (2005). Structural models of psychopathy. *Current Psychiatry Reports*, *7*(1), 57–64. https://doi.org/10.1007/s11920-005-0026-3.

Hare, R. D., & Neumann, C. S. (2006). The PCL-R assessment of psychopathy: Development, structural properties, and new directions. In C. J. Patrick (Ed.), *Handbook of psychopathy* (pp. 58–88). New York, NY: The Guilford Press.

Hare, R. D., & Neumann, C. S. (2008). Psychopathy as a clinical and empirical construct. *Annual Review of Clinical Psychology*, *4*, 217–246. https://doi.org/10.1146/annurev.clinpsy.3.022806.091452.

Hare, R. D., & Neumann, C. S. (2010). The role of antisociality in the psychopathy construct. *Psychological Assessment*, *22*, 446–454. https://doi.org/10.1037/a0013635.

Hare, R. D., Neumann, C. S., & Mokros, A. (2018). The PCL-R assessment of psychopathy: Development, properties, debates, and new directions. In C. J. Patrick (Ed.), *Handbook of psychopathy* (pp. 39–79). New York, NY: The Guilford Press.

Harkness, A. R., McNulty, J. L., & Ben-Porath, Y. S. (1995). The personality psychopathology five (PSY-5): Constructs and MMPI-2 scales. *Psychological Assessment*, *7*, 104–114. https://doi.org/10.1037/a0025830.

Harpur, T. J., Hare, R. D., & Hakstian, A. R. (1989). Two-factor conceptualization of psychopathy: Construct validity and assessment implications. *Psychological Assessment*, *1*(1), 6–17. https://doi.org/10.1037/1040-3590.1.1.6.

Harris, R. E., & Lingoes, J. C. (1968). *Subscales for the MMPI: An aid to profile interpretation*. Los Angeles, CA: University of California, Department of Psychiatry.

Harris, G. T., Rice, M. E., & Cormier, C. A. (2013). Research and clinical scoring of the psychopathy checklist can show good agreement. *Criminal Justice and Behavior*, *40*(11), 1349–1362. https://doi.org/10.1177/0093854813492959.

Hart, S. D., Cox, D. N., & Hare, R. D. (1995a). *Hare psychopathy checklist: Screening version (PCL: SV)*. Toronto: Multi-Heath Systems.

Hart, S. D., Cox, D. N., & Hare, R. D. (1995b). *Manual for the Psychopathy Checklist: Screening Version (PCL:SV)*. Toronto: Multi-Health Systems.

Hathaway, S. R., & McKinley, J. C. (1943). *Manual for administering and scoring the MMPI*. Minneapolis, MN: University of Minnesota Press.

Hawk, S. S., & Peterson, R. A. (1973). Do MMPI psychopathic deviancy scores reflect psychopathic deviancy or just deviancy? *Journal of Personality Assessment*, *38*(4), 362–368. https://doi.org/10.1080/00223891.1974.10119986.

Higgs, T., Tully, R. J., & Browne, K. D. (2017). Psychometric properties in forensic application of the screening version of the psychopathy checklist. *International Journal of Offender Therapy and Comparative Criminology*, *62*(7), 1869–1887. https://doi.org/10.1177/0306624x17719289.

Hillege, S., de Ruiter, C., Smits, N., van der Baan, H., & Das, J. (2011). Structural and metric validity of the Dutch translation of psychopathy checklist: Youth version (PCL: YV). *International Journal of Forensic Mental Health*, *10*(4), 346–357. https://doi.org/10.1080/14999013.2011.631207.

Hockey, L. (2016). *An exploration of the relationship between psychopathy and the MMPI-2* (Doctoral dissertation). Victoria: Deakin University.

Hoge, R. D., & Andrews, D. A. (2002). *The Youth Level of Service/Case Management Inventory manual and scoring key*. North Tonawanda, NY: Multi-Health Systems.

Hughes, M. A., Stout, J. C., & Dolan, M. C. (2013). Concurrent validity of the psychopathic personality inventory-revised and the psychopathy checklist. *Criminal Justice and Behavior, 40*(7), 802–813. https://doi.org/10.1177/0093854812475135.

Hundleby, J. D., & Ross, B. E. (1977). Comparison of measures of psychopathy. *Journal of Consulting and Clinical Psychology, 45*(4), 702–703. https://doi.org/10.1037//0022-006x.45.4.702.

Hurducas, C. C., Singh, J. P., de Ruiter, C., & Petrila, J. (2014). Violence risk assessment tools: A systematic review of surveys. *International Journal of Forensic Mental Health, 13*(3), 181–192. https://doi.org/10.1080/14999013.2014.942923.

Hyatt, C. S., Crowe, M. L., Lynam, D. R., & Miller, J. D. (2020). Components of the triarchic model of psychopathy and the five-factor model domains share largely overlapping nomological networks. *Assessment, 27*(1), 72–88. https://doi.org/10.1177/1073191119860903.

Jones, S., Cauffman, E., Miller, J. D., & Mulvey, E. (2006). Investigating different factor structures of the psychopathy checklist: Youth version: Confirmatory factor analytic findings. *Psychological Assessment, 18*(1), 33–48. https://doi.org/10.1037/1040-3590.18.1.33.

Jones, S., & Miller, J. D. (2012). Psychopathic traits and externalizing behaviors: A comparison of self- and informant reports in the statistical prediction of externalizing behaviors. *Psychological Assessment, 24*(1), 255–260. https://doi.org/10.1037/a0025264.

Kamphaus, R. W., & Frick, P. J. (2005). *Clinical assessment of child and adolescent personality and behavior* (2nd ed.). Springer Science.

Kavish, N., Boisvert, D., Wells, J., Lewis, R., Cooke, E., Woeckener, M., & Armstrong, T. (2019). On the associations between indicators of resting arousal levels, physiological reactivity, sensation seeking, and psychopathic traits. *Personality and Individual Differences, 141*, 218–225. https://doi.org/10.1016/j.paid.2019.01.013.

Kavish, N., Schiafo, M., Sellbom, M., & Anderson, J. L. (2020). Construct validity of the comprehensive assessment of psychopathic personality (CAPP) lexical rating scale. *Personality Disorders, Theory, Research, and Treatment, 11*(6), 418–430. https://doi.org/10.1037/per0000390.

Kreis, M. K., Cooke, D. J., Michie, C., Hoff, H. A., & Logan, C. (2012). The comprehensive assessment of psychopathic personality (CAPP): Content validation using prototypical analysis. *Journal of Personality Disorders, 26*(3), 402–413. https://doi.org/10.1521/pedi.2012.26.3.402.

Krueger, R. F., Markon, K. E., Patrick, C. J., Benning, S. D., & Kramer, M. D. (2007). Linking antisocial behavior, substance use, and personality: An integrative quantitative model of the adult externalizing spectrum. *Journal of Abnormal Psychology, 116*(4), 645–666. https://doi.org/10.1037/0021-843X.116.4.645.

Kruh, I. P., Frick, P. J., & Clements, C. B. (2005). Historical and personality correlates to the violence patterns of juveniles tried as adults. *Criminal Justice and Behavior, 32*(1), 69–96. https://doi.org/10.1177/0093854804270629.

Kucharski, L. T., Petitt, A. N., Toomey, J., & Duncan, S. (2008). The utility of the personality assessment inventory in the assessment of psychopathy. *Journal of Forensic Psychology Practice, 8*(4), 344–357. https://doi.org/10.1080/15228930802199267.

Laajasalo, T., Saukkonen, S., Kivivuori, J., Salmi, V., Lipsanen, J., & Aronen, E. T. (2014). Brief report: Self-reported psychopathic-like features among Finnish community youth: Investigation of the factor structure of the antisocial personality screening device. *Journal of Adolescence, 37*(7), 1185–1188. https://doi.org/10.1016/j.adolescence.2014.08.010.

Lee, Z., Vincent, G. M., Hart, S. D., & Corrado, R. R. (2003). The validity of the antisocial process screening device as a self-report measure of psychopathy in adolescent offenders. *Behavioral Sciences & the Law, 21*(6), 771–786. https://doi.org/10.1002/bsl.561.

Lehmann, R. J. B., Neumann, C. S., Hare, R. D., Biedermann, J., Dahle, K. P., & Mokros, A. (2019). A latent profile analysis of violent offenders based on PCL-R factor scores: Criminogenic needs and recidivism risk. *Frontiers in Psychiatry*, *10*(627), 1–10. https://doi.org/10.3389/fpsyt.2019.00627.

León-Mayer, E., Folino, J. O., Neumann, C., & Hare, R. D. (2015). The construct of psychopathy in a Chilean prison population. *Brazilian Journal of Psychiatry*, *37*(3), 191–196. https://doi.org/10.1590/1516-4446-2014-1540.

Levenson, M. R., Kiehl, K. A., & Fitzpatrick, C. M. (1995). Assessing psychopathic attributes in a noninstitutionalized population. *Journal of Personality and Social Psychology*, *68*(1), 151. https://doi.org/10.1037/0022-3514.68.1.151.

Liang, J., Wang, M. C., Luo, J., Liang, J., Zhang, X., & Gao, Y. (2020). Elaborating on the construct validity of the antisocial process screening device in Chinese children and adolescents: Across-informants and across-samples. *Current Psychology*, 1–13. https://doi.org/10.1007/s12144-020-00777-2.

Lilienfeld, S. O. (1994). Conceptual problems in the assessment of psychopathy. *Clinical Psychology Review*, *14*, 17–38.

Lilienfeld, S. O. (1999). The relation of the MMPI-2 Pd Harris–Lingoes subscales to psychopathy, psychopathy facets, and antisocial behavior: Implications for clinical practice. *Journal of Clinical Psychology*, *55*(2), 241–255. https://doi.org/10.1002/(sici)1097-4679(199902)55:2<241::aid-jclp12>3.0.co;2-i.

Lilienfeld, S. O., & Andrews, B. P. (1996). Development and preliminary validation of a self-report measure of psychopathic personality traits in noncriminal population. *Journal of Personality Assessment*, *66*(3), 488–524. https://doi.org/10.1207/s15327752jpa6603_3.

Lilienfeld, S. O., & Fowler, K. A. (2006). The self-report assessment of psychopathy: Problems, pitfalls, and promises. In C. J. Patrick (Ed.), *Handbook of psychopathy* (pp. 107–132). New York, NY: The Guilford Press.

Lilienfeld, S. O., Fowler, K. A., & Patrick, C. (2006). The self-report assessment of psychopathy. In C. J. Patrick (Ed.), *Handbook of psychopathy* (pp. 107–132). New York, NY: Guilford Press.

Lilienfeld, S. O., Patrick, C. J., Benning, S. D., Berg, J., Sellbom, M., & Edens, J. F. (2012). The role of fearless dominance in psychopathy: Confusions, controversies, and clarifications. *Personality Disorders*, *3*(3), 327–340. https://doi.org/10.1037/a0026987.

Lilienfeld, S. O., & Widows, M. (2005). *Professional manual for the psychopathic personality inventory-revised (PPI-R)*. North Florida, FL: Psychological Assessment Resources.

Loney, B. R., Frick, P. J., Clements, C. B., Ellis, M. L., & Kerlin, K. (2003). Callous-unemotional traits, impulsivity, and emotional processing in antisocial adolescents. *Journal of Clinical Child and Adolescent Psychology*, *32*(1), 139–152. https://doi.org/10.1207/S15374424JCCP3201_07.

Loving, J. L. (2002). Treatment planning with the psychopathy checklist–revised (PCL-R). *International Journal of Offender Therapy and Comparative Criminology*, *46*(3), 281–293. https://doi.org/10.1177/0306624X02463003.

Martens, W. H. (2008). The problem with Robert Hare's psychopathy checklist: Incorrect conclusions, high risk of misuse, and lack of reliability. *Medicine and Law*, *27*, 449–462.

Mathieu, C., Neumann, C. S., Hare, R. D., & Babiak, P. (2014). A dark side of leadership: Corporate psychopathy and its influence on employee well-being and job satisfaction. *Personality and Individual Differences*, *57*, 83–88. https://doi.org/10.1016/j.paid.2013.11.010.

Maurer, J. M., Paul, S., Anderson, N. E., Nyalakanti, P. K., & Kiehl, K. A. (2020). Youth with elevated psychopathic traits exhibit structural integrity deficits in the uncinate fasciculus. *NeuroImage: Clinical*, *26*, 102236. https://doi.org/10.1016/j.nicl.2020.102236.

McCoy, W. K., & Edens, J. F. (2006). Do black and white youths differ in levels of psychopathic traits? A meta-analysis of the psychopathy checklist measures. *Journal of Consulting and Clinical Psychology*, *74*(2), 386–392. https://doi.org/10.1037/0022-006X.74.2.386.

McKee, V., Waples, E. P., & Tullis, K. J. (2017). A desire for the dark side: An examination of individual personality characteristics and their desire for adverse characteristics in leaders. *Organization Management Journal*, *14*(2), 104–115. https://doi.org/10.1080/15416518.2017.1325348.

Meloy, J. R., & Gacono, C. (1995). Assessing the psychopathic personality. In J. Butcher (Ed.), *Clinical personality assessment: Practical approaches* (pp. 567–581). Oxford: Oxford University Press.

Miller, J. D., & Lynam, D. R. (2012). An examination of the psychopathic personality Inventory's nomological network: A meta-analytic review. *Personality Disorders, Theory, Research, and Treatment*, *3*(3), 305–326. https://doi.org/10.1037/a0024567.

Mokros, A., Hare, R. D., Neumann, C. S., Santtila, P., Habermeyer, E., & Nitschke, J. (2015). Variants of psychopathy in adult male offenders: A latent profile analysis. *Journal of Abnormal Psychology*, *124*(2), 372–386. https://doi.org/10.1037/abn0000042.

Mokros, A., Vohs, K., & Habermeyer, E. (2014). Psychopathy and violent reoffending in German-speaking countries. *European Journal of Psychological Assessment*, *30*(2), 117–129. https://doi.org/10.1027/1015-5759/a000178.

Mollaret, P. (2009). Using common psychological terms to describe other people: From lexical hypothesis to polysemous conception. *Theory & Psychology*, *19*(3), 315–334. https://doi.org/10.1177/0959354309104157.

Morey, L. C. (1991). *The personality assessment inventory: Professional manual*. Psychological Assessment Resources.

Morey, L. C. (1996). *An interpretive guide to the personality assessment inventory*. Psychological Assessment Resources.

Morey, L. C. (2007). *Professional manual for the personality assessment inventory* (2nd ed.). Psychological Assessment Resources.

Mossière, A. M., Olver, M., & Marche, T. (2020). Psychopathy, emotionality, and offending. *The Journal of Forensic Psychiatry & Psychology*, *31*(4), 1–21. https://doi.org/10.1080/14789949.2020.1772341.

Muñoz, L. C., & Frick, P. J. (2007). The reliability, stability, and predictive utility of the self-report version of the antisocial process screening device. *Scandinavian Journal of Psychology*, *48*(4), 299–312. https://doi.org/10.1111/j.1467-9450.2007.00560.x.

Neal, T. M., & Sellbom, M. (2012). Examining the factor structure of the hare self-report psychopathy scale. *Journal of Personality Assessment*, *94*(3), 244–253. https://doi.org/10.1080/00223891.2011.648294.

Neumann, C. S., & Hare, R. D. (2008). Psychopathic traits in a large community sample: Links to violence, alcohol use, and intelligence. *Journal of Consulting and Clinical Psychology*, *76*(5), 893–899. https://doi.org/10.1037/0022-006X.76.5.893.

Neumann, C. S., Hare, R. D., & Newman, J. P. (2007). The super-ordinate nature of the psychopathy checklist-revised. *Journal of Personality Disorders*, *21*(2), 102–117. https://doi.org/10.1521/pedi.2007.21.2.102.

Neumann, C. S., Hare, R. D., & Pardini, D. A. (2015). Antisociality and the construct of psychopathy: Data from across the globe. *Journal of Personality*, *83*(6), 678–692. https://doi.org/10.1111/jopy.12127.

Neumann, C. S., Kosson, D. S., Forth, A. E., & Hare, R. D. (2006). Factor structure of the Hare Psychopathy Checklist: Youth version in incarcerated adolescents. *Psychological Assessment*, *18*(2), 142–154.

Neumann, C. S., & Pardini, D. (2014). Factor structure and construct validity of the self-report psychopathy (SRP) scale and the youth psychopathic traits inventory (YPI) in young men. *Journal of Personality Disorders*, *28*(3), 419–433. https://doi.org/10.1521/pedi_2012_26_063.

Patrick, C. J. (2010). Triarchic psychopathy measure (TriPM). In *PhenX Toolkit Online Assessment Catalog*. Retrieved from https://www.phenxtoolkit.org/protocols/view/121601.

Patrick, C. J., Drislane, L. E., & Strickland, C. (2012). Conceptualising psychopathy in triarchic terms: Implications for treatment. *International Journal for Forensic Mental Health*, *11*(4), 253–266. https://doi.org/10.1080/14999013.2012.746761.

Patrick, C. J., Durbin, C. E., & Moser, J. S. (2012). Reconceptualizing antisocial deviance in neurobehavioral terms. *Development and Psychopathology*, *24*(3), 1047–1071. https://doi.org/10.1017/S0954579412000533.

Patrick, C. J., Edens, J. F., Poythress, N. G., Lilienfeld, S. O., & Benning, S. D. (2006). Construct validity of the psychopathic personality inventory two-factor model with offenders. *Psychological Assessment*, *18*(2), 204–208. https://doi.org/10.1037/1040-3590.18.2.204.

Patrick, C. J., Fowles, D. C., & Krueger, R. F. (2009). Triarchic conceptualization of psychopathy: Developmental origins of disinhibition, boldness, and meanness. *Development and Psychopathology*, *21*(3), 913–938. https://doi.org/10.1017/S0954579409000492.

Paulhus, D. L., Neumann, C. S., Hare, R. D., Williams, K. M., & Hemphill, J. F. (2016). *Self-report psychopathy scale 4th edition-technical manual*. Toronto: Multi-Health Systems.

Pechorro, P., Barroso, R., Maroco, J., Vieira, R. X., & Gonçalves, R. A. (2014). Psychometric properties of the psychopathy checklist: Youth version among Portuguese juvenile delinquents. *International Journal of Offender Therapy and Comparative Criminology*, *59*(12), 1322–1337. https://doi.org/10.1177/0306624X14535558.

Pechorro, P., Da Silva, D. R., Rijo, D., Gonçalves, R. A., & Andershed, H. (2017). Psychometric properties and measurement invariance of the youth psychopathic traits inventory-short version among Portuguese youth. *Journal of Psychopathology and Behavioral Assessment*, *39*(3), 486–497. https://doi.org/10.1007/s10862-017-9597-7.

Pechorro, P., DeLisi, M., Alberto, I., Ray, J. V., & Simões, M. R. (2018). The triarchic model of psychopathy among incarcerated male youths: A psychometric study. In M. DeLisi (Ed.), *Routledge international handbook of psychopathy and crime* (pp. 265–275). Routledge.

Pechorro, P., Goncalves, R. A., Andershed, H., & Delisi, M. (2017). Female psychopathic traits in forensic and school context: Comparing the antisocial process screening device self-report and the youth psychopathic traits inventory-short. *Journal of Psychopathology & Behavioral Assessessment*, *39*, 642–656. https://doi.org/10.1007/s10862-017-9605-y.

Pedersen, L., Kunz, C., Elsass, P., & Rasmussen, K. (2010). Psychopathy as a risk factor for violent recidivism: Investigating the psychopathy check-list screening version (PCL:SV) and the comprehensive Assessment of psychopathic personality (CAPP) in a forensic psychiatric setting. *International Journal of Forensic Mental Health*, *9*(4), 308–315. https://doi.org/10.1080/14999013.2010.526681.

Phillips, T. R., Sellbom, M., Ben-Porath, Y. S., & Patrick, C. J. (2014). Further development and construct validation of MMPI-2-RF indices of global psychopathy, fearless-dominance, and impulsive-antisociality in a sample of incarcerated women. *Law and Human Behavior*, *38*(1), 34–46. https://doi.org/10.1037/lhb0000040.

Poythress, N. G., Edens, J. F., & Lilienfeld, S. O. (1998). Criterion-related validity of the psychopathic personality inventory in a prison sample. *Psychological Assessment*, *10*(4), 426–430. https://doi.org/10.1037/1040-3590.10.4.426.

Poythress, N. G., & Hall, J. (2011). Psychopathy and impulsivity reconsidered. *Aggression and Violent Behavior*, *16*(2), 120–134.

Poythress, N. G., Lilienfeld, S. O., Skeem, J. L., Douglas, K. S., Edens, J. F., Epstein, M., & Patrick, C. J. (2010). Using the PCL-R to help estimate the validity of two self-report measures of psychopathy with offenders. *Assessment, 17*(2), 206–219. https://doi.org/10.1177/1073191109351715.

Quinsey, V. L., Harris, G. T., Rice, M. E., & Cormier, C. A. (2006). *Violent offenders: Appraising and managing risk* (2nd). American Psychological Association.

Reidy, T. J., Sorensen, J. R., & Davidson, M. (2016). Testing the predictive validity of the personality assessment inventory (PAI) in relation to inmate misconduct and violence. *Psychological Assessment, 28*(8), 871–884. https://doi.org/10.1037/pas0000224.

Reynolds, B. L., Maurer, J. M., Cook, A. M., Harenski, C., & Kiehl, K. A. (2020). The relationship between psychopathic traits and risky sexual behavior in incarcerated adult male offenders. *Personality and Individual Differences, 156*, 1–6. https://doi.org/10.1016/j.paid.2019.109798.

Rice, M. E., & Harris, G. T. (2013). Psychopathy and violent recidivism. In K. A. Kiehl, & W. P. Sinnott-Armstrong (Eds.), *Oxford series in neuroscience, law, and philosophy. Handbook on psychopathy and law* (pp. 231–249). Oxford: Oxford University Press.

Rock, R. C., Sellbom, M., Ben-Porath, Y. S., & Salekin, R. T. (2013). Concurrent and predictive validity of psychopathy in a batterer's intervention sample. *Law and Human Behavior, 37*(3), 145–154. https://doi.org/10.1037/lhb0000006.

Ross, S. R., Molte, J., Poy, R., Segarra, P., Pastor, M. C., & Montañés, S. (2007). Gray's model and psychopathy: BIS but not BAS differentiates primary from secondary psychopathy in noninstitutionalized young adults. *Personality and Individual Differences, 43*(7), 1644–1655. https://doi.org/10.1016/j.paid. 2007.04.020.

Salekin, R., & Lynam, D. (2010). Child and adolescent psychopathy: An introduction. In R. Salekin, & D. Lynam (Eds.), *Handbook of child and adolescent psychopathy* (pp. 1–12). New York, NY: The Guilford Press.

Salekin, R. T. (2006). Psychopathy in children and adolescents: Key issues in conceptualization and assessment. In C. J. Patrick (Ed.), *Handbook of psychopathy* (pp. 389–414). New York, NY: The Guilford Press.

Salekin, R. T. (2017). Research review: What do we know about psychopathic traits in children? *Journal of Child Psychology and Psychiatry, 58*(11), 1180–1200. https://doi.org/10.1111/jcpp.12738.

Salekin, R. T., Brannen, D. N., Zalot, A. A., Leistico, A. M., & Neumann, C. S. (2006). Factor structure of psychopathy in youth: Testing the applicability of the new four-factor model. *Criminal Justice and Behavior, 33*(2), 135–157. https://doi.org/10.1177/0093854805284416.

Salekin, R. T., Chen, D. R., Sellbom, M., Lester, W. S., & MacDougall, E. (2014). Examining the factor structure and convergent and discriminant validity of the Levenson self-report psychopathy scale: Is the two-factor model the best fitting model? *Personality Disorders, Theory, Research, and Treatment, 5*(3), 289–304. https://doi.org/10.1037/per 0000073.

Sandoval, A.-M., Hancock, D., Poythress, N., Edens, J. F., & Lilienfeld, S. (2000). Construct validity of the psychopathic personality inventory in a correctional sample. *Journal of Personality Assessment, 74*(2), 262–281. https://doi.org/10.1207/S15327752JPA7402_7.

Schrum, C. L., & Salekin, R. T. (2006). Psychopathy in adolescent female offenders: An item response theory analysis of the psychopathy checklist: Youth version. *Behavioral Sciences & the Law, 24*(1), 39–63. https://doi.org/10.1002/bsl.679.

Seara-Cardoso, A., Dolberg, H., Neumann, C., Roiser, J. P., & Viding, E. (2013). Empathy, morality and psychopathic traits in women. *Personality and Individual Differences, 55*(3), 328–333. https://doi.org/10.1016/j.paid.2013.03.011.

Seibert, L. A., Miller, J. D., Few, L. R., Zeichner, A., & Lynam, D. R. (2011). An examination of the structure of self-report psychopathy measures and their relations with general traits and externalizing behaviors. *Personality Disorders, Theory, Research, and Treatment*, *2*(3), 193–208. https://doi.org/10.1037/a0019232.

Sellbom, M. (2011). Elaborating on the construct validity of the Levenson self-report psychopathy scale in incarcerated and non-incarcerated samples. *Law and Human Behavior*, *35*, 440–451. https://doi.org/10.1007/s10979-010-9249-x.

Sellbom, M., Ben-Porath, Y. S., Lilienfeld, S. O., Patrick, C. J., & Graham, J. R. (2005). Assessing psychopathic personality traits with the MMPI–2. *Journal of Personality Assessment*, *85*(3), 334–343. https://doi.org/10.1207/s15327752jpa8503_10.

Sellbom, M., Ben-Porath, Y. S., Patrick, C. J., Wygant, D. B., Gartland, D. M., & Stafford, K. P. (2012). Development and construct validation of MMPI-2-RF indices of global psychopathy, fearless-dominance, and impulsive-antisociality. *Personality Disorders, Theory, Research, and Treatment*, *3*(1), 17–38. https://doi.org/10.1037/a0023888.

Sellbom, M., Ben-Porath, Y. S., & Stafford, K. P. (2007). A comparison of MMPI-2 measures of psychopathic deviance in a forensic setting. *Psychological Assessment*, *19*(4), 430–436. https://doi.org/10.1037/1040-3590.19.4.430.

Sellbom, M., Cooke, D. J., & Hart, S. D. (2015). Construct validity of the Comprehensive Assessment of Psychopathic Personality (CAPP) concept map: Getting closer to the core of psychopathy. *International Journal of Forensic Mental Health*, *14*, 172–180.

Sellbom, M., Drislane, L. E., Johnson, A. K., Goodwin, B. E., Philips, T. R., & Patrick, C. J. (2016). Development and validation of MMPI-2-RF scales for indexing triarchic psychopathy constructs. *Assessment*, *23*(5), 527–543. https://doi.org/10.1177/1073191115590853.

Sellbom, M., Lilienfeld, S., Fowler, K. A., & McCray, K. L. (2018). The self-report assessment of psychopathy: Challenges, pitfalls, and promises. In C. Patrick (Ed.), *Handbook of psychopathy* (pp. 211–258). New York, NY: The Guilford Press.

Sellbom, M., & Phillips, T. R. (2013). An examination of the triarchic conceptualization of psychopathy in incarcerated and nonincarcerated samples. *Journal of Abnormal Psychology*, *122*(1), 208–214. https://doi.org/10.1037/a0029306.

Shou, Y., Sellbom, M., & Han, J. (2017). Evaluating the construct validity of the Levenson self-report psychopathy scale in China. *Assessment*, *24*(8), 1008–1023. https://doi.org/10.1177/1073191116637421.

Singh, J. P., Desmarais, S. L., Hurducas, C., Arbach-Lucioni, K., Condemarin, C., Dean, K., … Ho, R. M. Y. (2014). International perspectives on the practical application of violence risk assessment: A global survey of 44 countries. *International Journal of Forensic Mental Health*, *13*(3), 193–206. https://doi.org/10.1080/14999013.2014.922141.

Skeem, J. L., & Cooke, D. J. (2010). Is criminal behavior a central component of psychopathy? Conceptual directions for resolving the debate. *Psychological Assessment*, *22*(2), 433–445. https://doi.org/10.1037/a0008512.

Smith, J. M., Gacono, C. B., & Cunliffe, T. B. (2020). Female psychopathy and aggression: A study with incarcerated women and Rorschach aggression scores. *Journal of Aggression, Maltreatment & Trauma*, *29*(8), 936–952. https://doi.org/10.1080/10926771.2020.1738614.

Somma, A., Fossati, A., Patrick, C., Maffei, C., & Borroni, S. (2014). The three-factor structure of the Levenson self-report psychopathy scale: Fool's gold or true gold? A study in a sample of Italian adult non-clinical participants. *Personality and Mental Health*, *8*(4), 337–347. https://doi.org/10.1002/pmh.1267.

Stanley, J. H., Wygant, D. B., & Sellbom, M. (2013). Elaborating on the construct validity of the triarchic psychopathy measure in a criminal offender sample. *Journal of Personality Assessment*, *95*(4), 343–350. https://doi.org/10.1080/00223891.2012.735302.

Tew, J., Harkins, L., & Dixon, L. (2013). What works in reducing violent reoffending in psychopathic offenders. In L. A. Craig, L. Dixon, & T. A. Gannon (Eds.), *What works in offender rehabilitation* (pp. 129–141). New Jersey: Wiley Blackwell.

Tew, J., Harkins, L., & Dixon, L. (2015). Assessing the reliability and validity of the self-report psychopathy scales in a UK offender population. *The Journal of Forensic Psychiatry & Psychology*, *26*(2), 166–184. https://doi.org/10.1080/14789949.2014.981565.

Tsang, S., Schmidt, K. M., Vincent, G. M., Salekin, R. T., Moretti, M. M., & Odgers, C. L. (2015). Assessing psychopathy among justice involved adolescents with the PCL: YV: An item response theory examination across gender. *Personality Disorders, Theory, Research, and Treatment*, *6*(1), 22–31. https://doi.org/10.1037/per0000094.

van Baardewijk, Y., Andershed, H., Stegge, H., Nilsson, K. W., Scholte, E., & Vermeiren, R. (2010). Development and tests of short versions of the Youth Psychopathic Traits Inventory and the Youth Psychopathic Traits Inventory-Child Version. *European Journal of Psychological Assessment*, *26*(2), 122–128.

Van Voorhis, P., Wright, E. M., Salisbury, E., & Bauman, A. (2010). Women's risk factors and their contributions to existing risk/needs assessment: The current status of a gender-responsive supplement. *Criminal Justice and Behavior*, *37*(3), 261–288. https://doi.org/10.1177/0093854809357442.

Visser, B. A., & Campbell, S. (2018). Measuring the dark side of personality. In V. Zeigler-Hill, & T. K. Shackelford (Eds.), *The SAGE handbook of personality and individual differences: Origins of personality and individual differences* (pp. 573–591). London: Sage.

Vitacco, M. J., Neumann, C. S., & Jackson, R. L. (2005). Testing a four-factor model of psychopathy and its association with ethnicity, gender, intelligence, and violence. *Journal of Consulting and Clinical Psychology*, *73*(3), 466–476. https://doi.org/10.1037/0022-006X.73.3.466.

Vitacco, M. J., Neumann, C. S., Welch, L. T., & Buckley, P. (2016). The clinical assessment of psychopathy. In R. Jackson, & R. Roesch (Eds.), *Learning forensic assessment: Research and practice* (pp. 116–130). Routledge/Taylor & Francis Group.

Vitacco, M. J., Rogers, R., & Neumann, C. S. (2003). The antisocial process screening device: An examination of its construct and criterion-related validity. *Assessment*, *10*(2), 143–150. https://doi.org/10.1177/1073191103010002005.

Wall, T. D., Wygant, D. B., & Sellbom, M. (2015). Boldness explains a key difference between psychopathy and antisocial personality disorder. *Psychiatry, Psychology and Law*, *22*(1), 94–105. https://doi.org/10.1080/13218719.2014.919627.

Walters, G. D. (1985). Scale 4 (Pd) of the MMPI and the diagnosis antisocial personality. *Journal of Personality Assessment*, *49*(5), 474–476. https://doi.org/10.1207/s15327752jpa4905_3.

Walters, G. D. (2003). Predicting institutional adjustment and recidivism with the psychopathy checklist factor scores: A meta-analysis. *Law and Human Behavior*, *27*, 541–558. https://doi.org/10.1023/A:1025490207678.

Walters, G. D. (2008). Self-report measures of psychopathy, antisocial personality, and criminal lifestyle: Testing and validating a two-dimensional model. *Criminal Justice and Behavior*, *35*(12), 1459–1483. https://doi.org/10.1177/0093854808320922.

Walters, G. D., & Duncan, S. A. (2005). Use of the PCL-R and PAI to predict release outcome in inmates undergoing forensic evaluation. *Journal of Forensic Psychiatry & Psychology*, *16*(3), 459–476. https://doi.org/10.1080/14789940500034405.

Walters, G. D., Duncan, S., & Geyer, M. (2003). Predicting disciplinary adjustment in inmates undergoing forensic evaluation: A direct comparison of the PCL-R and the PAI. *Journal of Forensic Psychiatry & Psychology*, *14*(2), 382–393. https://doi.org/10.1080/1478994031000136527.

Walters, G. D., & Kiehl, K. A. (2015). Limbic correlates of fearlessness and disinhibition in incarcerated youth: Exploring the brain–behavior relationship with the Hare psychopathy checklist: Youth version. *Psychiatry Research*, *230*(2), 205–210. https://doi.org/10.1016/j.psychres.2015.08.041.

Wang, M. C., Gao, Y., Deng, J., Lai, H., Deng, Q., & Armour, C. (2017). The factor structure and construct validity of the inventory of callous-unemotional traits in Chinese undergraduate students. *PLoS One*, *12*(12), 0189003. https://doi.org/10.1371/journal.pone.0189003.

Warren, J. I., Chauhan, P., & Murrie, D. C. (2005). Screening for psychopathy among incarcerated women: Psychometric properties and construct validity of the Hare P-Scan. *International Journal of Forensic Mental Health*, *4*(2), 175–189. https://doi.org/10.1080/14999013.2005.10471222.

Willemsen, J., Vanheule, S., & Verhaeghe, P. (2011). Psychopathy and lifetime experiences of depression. *Criminal Behaviour and Mental Health*, *21*(4), 279–294. https://doi.org/10.1002/cbm.812.

Wilson, L., Miller, J. D., Zeichner, A., Lynam, D. R., & Widiger, T. A. (2011). An examination of the validity of the elemental psychopathy assessment: Relations with other psychopathy measures, aggression, and externalizing behaviors. *Journal of Psychopathology and Behavioral Assessment*, *33*(3), 315–322. https://doi.org/10.1007/s10862-010-9213-6.

Woodworth, M., & Porter, S. (2002). In cold blood: Characteristics of criminal homicides as a function of psychopathy. *Journal of Abnormal Psychology*, *111*(3), 436–445. https://doi.org/10.1037/0021-843X.111.3.436.

Yang, W., Zhang, X., Wang, M., Zhong, C., Luo, J., & Gao, Y. (2019). Factor structure and construct validity of the youth psychopathic traits inventory and its shorten version in Chinese detained boys. *Frontiers in Psychology*, *10*, 18–31. https://doi.org/10.3389/fpsyg.2019.01831.

Yokota, K. (2012). The validity of a three-factor model in PPI-R and social dominance orientation in Japanese sample. *Personality and Individual Differences*, *53*(7), 907–911. https://doi.org/10.1016/j.paid.2012.07.006.

The concept of psychopathy and risk assessment: Historical developments, contemporary considerations, and future directions

7

Ryan Veal and James R.P. Ogloff

Introduction

Few constructs have been as closely associated with offending and violence as psychopathy. The very term psychopathy has become practically synonymous with offending, particularly in the popular media. Such connotations have led to confusion and obfuscation regarding the actual relationship between psychopathy and offending. Attempts have been made over the past century to adopt terms for psychopathy that are less stigmatizing and emotionally laden (e.g., sociopathy, antisocial personality disorder, dissocial personality disorder). On its own, however, psychopathy is neither a necessary or sufficient explanation for offending and violence. The vast majority of offenders are not psychopathic and, increasingly, it is clear that many psychopaths do not necessarily offend. It is the case, however, that decades of research have confirmed that psychopathy is an important consideration in the assessment of risk for offending and violence. This chapter will provide an overview of the relationship between psychopathy and forensic risk assessment. Taking an historical perspective, we clarify the essential considerations of psychopathy in the assessment of recidivism risk against the background of the evolving nature of psychopathy conceptualized within risk assessment practice.

The traits considered essential in any conceptualization of the psychopathy construct (Cleckley, 1941; Cooke, Hart, Logan, & Michie, 2012; Hare, 2003; McCord & McCord, 1964) are largely consistent with personality features and behavioral patterns that correlate with rule violation, criminal behavior, and reoffending (e.g., Eysenck's in 1977 about the *three-factor model of criminal personality;* Miller & Lynam's in 2001 about the *five-factor model of antisocial behavior;* and Bonta & Andrews' in 2017 about the *Antisocial Personality Pattern*). Accordingly, the development of psychopathy assessment measures—particularly the *Psychopathy Checklist-Revised* (PCL-R; Hare, 2003)—has coincided with the research, development, and application of standardized forensic risk assessment measures and approaches. The implications associated with the diagnostic label of "psychopath" in the criminal justice system mean the use of the psychopathy construct in forensic risk assessment—particularly in adversarial legal

Psychopathy and Criminal Behavior. https://doi.org/10.1016/B978-0-12-811419-3.00011-X

settings—can be fraught with ethical as well as legal concerns (Kelley, Edens, Mowle, Penson, & Rulseh, 2019; Lyon, Ogloff, & Shepherd, 2016). In part because of these implications, the relationship between psychopathy and risk for recidivism has been extensively researched and the extent of the literature is overwhelming.

A number of authors have identified contemporary issues for clinicians and researchers utilizing the psychopathy construct in violence risk assessment. For example, recent articles have considered psychopathy and the use of the PCL-R in assessing risk of violence recidivism (Bergstrøm, Larmour, & Farrington, 2018; Serin, Brown, & De Wolf, 2016) and correct interpretations of the broad recidivism and psychopathy research (Douglas, Vincent, & Edens, 2018; Hemphill, 2007). Concerns raised include, but are not limited to, the importance of considering: base rates for the type of offending population (Hemphill, 2007; Serin et al., 2016); the utility of PCL measures cut-scores relative to decision error (false positive and false negative rates) (Hemphill, 2007; Serin et al., 2016); potential moderator and mediator effects that influence predictive accuracy of the psychopathy construct (Bergstrøm et al., 2018; Douglas et al., 2018); limitations in the reported effect sizes for associations between PCL scores and indices of recidivism (Douglas et al., 2018; Hemphill, 2007); and the utility of the psychopathy construct in explaining—rather than predicting—recidivism (Bergstrøm et al., 2018).

The chapter begins with a brief history of psychopathy relative to antisocial behavior, including the early to current influential research on the association between PCL measures psychopathy and criminal offending behaviors. We then consider the mutual influence of the psychopathy concept and violence risk assessment. This will include discussion of the use of the PCL-R and related measures—both as stand-alone measures and in a combined approach with forensic risk assessment measures—in violence risk assessment practice, and the evolving nature of psychopathy within the violence risk assessment approach of structured professional judgment. Contemporary considerations with regard to the most commonly used structured professional judgment guidelines are then discussed, including general offending behavior risk assessment practice more broadly, and alternative assessment approaches to the PCL-R. The chapter will conclude with a summary of the considerations based on the intertwined history of violence risk assessment and the psychopathy construct, and posit future directions for research.

Historical developments: The psychopathy construct relative to offending

A brief history of the psychopathy construct relative to risk of recidivism

Long before the development of the first edition of the Psychopathy Checklist (PCL; Hare, 1980), the personality traits consistently identified in the literature—including emotional shallowness, empathy deficits, lack of remorse, manipulation and exploitation, and behavioral disinhibition—had been implicated in violent, sexually aggressive, and general antisocial behavior (Cleckley, 1941; Hare, 1970; Karpman, 1951; Pinel, 1806). As summarized in a review of psychopathic behavior by Pichot (1978), the construct of psychopathy has been traced to the clinical writings of Pinel (1806) on *manie sans delire*—a form of mental disorder based on the existence of perverse behavior and an undisciplinable disposition, but without the presence of delusion. Nineteenth-century notions of antisocial behavior differ from modern conceptualizations with respect to criminality and social norms (Berrios, 1993), yet it is behavior—specifically repetitive criminal behavior, for which punishment has little deterrent effect (Crego & Widiger, 2015)—that became the focus for the latter 19th and early 20th century conceptualization of psychopathy.

By the early 20th century, psychopathy remained ill-defined, with a common problem being the tendency of many psychiatrists to use the label "psychopathic personality" as a last resort for otherwise unclassifiable personality disorders (McCord & McCord, 1964). In the mid-20th century, writers such as Cleckley (1941) and Karpman (1941, 1951) documented psychopathic personality case studies of individuals exhibiting varied antisocial and criminal behaviors—often of an instrumental and predatory nature—which assisted in streamlining the concept of psychopathy. Cleckley's (1941) identification of 16 characteristics associated with psychopathy, in particular, helped form the basis from which modern conceptions of psychopathy as a form of personality disorder have advanced (Hare, 2003; Patrick, 2006). Cleckley's reliance on case studies and the vague way in which the psychopathy characteristics were described meant his list of characteristics were insufficient to measure psychopathy in a valid and reliable manner (Cooke et al., 2012; Hare & Neumann, 2008). Further, in the absence of a reliable and valid assessment measure for the psychopathy construct for recidivism research, the relevance of personality traits in explaining criminal behavior was also disputed (Tennenbaum, 1977).

Development of the Psychopathy Checklist

For almost 40 years, psychopathy has become almost inseparable from the Hare Psychopathy Checklist (Hare, 1980, 1991, 2003). While the construct and its measurement must not be confused, the contributions of the Psychopathy Checklist, Revised (PCL-R; Hare, 1991, 2003) have been immeasurable. The first edition of the PCL (Hare, 1980) arose primarily from the need for a valid assessment tool to reliably measure the clinical construct of psychopathy (Hare, 1980, 2003), and the necessity for such a tool being explicit in research and the criminal justice system (Hare, 2007; Hare & Cox, 1978). Self-report personality measures, such as the Minnesota Multiphasic Personality Inventory (MMPI; Hathaway & McKinley, 1940), did not validly assess psychopathy (Hare, 1985). Diagnostic criteria for antisocial personality disorder (and personality disorder, antisocial type, American Psychiatric Association, 1968) focused on personality, interpersonal, and behavioral characteristics, many of which overlapped with Cleckley's description, and were largely indicative of the psychopathic construct (Arrigo & Shipley, 2001; Ogloff, 2006). Subsequent editions of the DSM, however, have essentially devolved to behavioral trait lists (DSM-III, American Psychiatric Association, 1980; DSM-V, American Psychiatric Association, 2013) and have been found to be poor proxies for psychopathy (for a review on the differences between psychopathy and APD, see Ogloff, 2006). The PCL, revised editions (Hare, 1991, 2003), and derivative measures—the screening version (PCL:SV; Hart, Cox, & Hare, 1995) and youth version (PCL:YV; Forth, Kosson, & Hare, 2003)—hereafter described as the PCL measures, went on to revolutionize the clinical and forensic assessment of psychopathy in part because of the ability to reliably measure the core personality traits of psychopathy in addition to the behavioral traits. A three-factor PCL model proposed by Cooke and Michie (2001) has support for construct validity (Cooke & Sellbom, 2019; Skeem, Mulvey, & Grisso, 2003); however, the two-factor (*Interpersonal/Affective* and *Lifestyle/Antisocial*) and four-factor (*Interpersonal, Affective, Lifestyle* and *Antisocial*) structure of the PCL measures have remained the most dominant in risk assessment practice and research (Hare, 2016; Richards et al., 2016).

The PCL measures and offending

In addition to capacity of the PCL measures to capture the psychopathy construct in a valid and reliable way, the success of these tools in forensic risk assessment can be partly attributed to PCL total and factor score associations with recidivism, particularly violent and general reoffending. Meta-analyses following the release of the PCL-R (Hare, 1991) reported average correlations (r values between 0.27 and 0.28) between PCL-R scores and violent recidivism that indicated moderate predictive validity (Campbell, French, & Gendreau, 2009; Hemphill, Hare, & Wong, 1998), and these findings were consistent with meta-analyses on the relationship between general recidivism and PCL-R psychopathy (average r values between 0.27 and 0.28) (Gendreau, Little, & Goggin, 1996; Salekin, Rogers, & Sewell, 1996). Somewhat smaller weighted effect sizes for violent ($r=0.21$) and general ($r=0.23$) recidivism were subsequently reported in a meta-analysis by Gendreau, Goggin, and Smith (2002). Hemphill (2007) reported on the methodological differences underlying the effect size heterogeneity in PCL measures predictive accuracy findings in meta-analyses, including: sample inconsistencies across studies, misuse of the PCL measures as predictor variables, criterion variable differences (e.g., offending types and predictive versus postdictive study design), variation in measurement of recidivism (e.g., length of follow-up), and different types of statistical indices used as effect sizes.

The utility of PCL measures cut-scores dichotomizing offenders as psychopathic or nonpsychopathic in 2×2 study designs (true positive, true negative, false positive, and false negative) for recidivism prediction was also questioned by Hemphill as oversimplifying the complex nature of risk assessment—disregarding false positive and false negative rates (decision errors) in risk assessments when using the PCL measures cut-scores has subsequently been suggested as a practical concern (Serin et al., 2016). Research exploring the relationship between the PCL measures and recidivism, however, has continued unabated. In one of the largest ($k=95$ studies) and most cited of these meta-analyses, Leistico, Salekin, DeCoster, and Rogers (2008) used broader criteria for general recidivism and reported a moderate effect size for the PCL measures and recidivism ($r=0.27$), as well as the finding that, although both significant, Factor 2 (*Lifestyle/Antisocial*) was a better predictor than Factor 1 (*Interpersonal/Affective*). Edens, Campbell, and Weir (2007) reported largely consistent meta-analytic findings for PCL measures and risk for both violent and general recidivism in young offenders. Walters (2007) previously reported that Factor 2 and its facets (*Lifestyle* and *Antisocial*) were better predictors of recidivism than

Factor 1. This finding has been consistently reported in influential meta-analyses for both general and violent recidivism (Hemphill, Hare, et al., 1998; Kennealy, Skeem, Walters, & Camp, 2010; Yang, Wong, & Coid, 2010). This finding should be hardly surprising, however, since the items on those two facets are largely measures of behavior, including adolescent offending and criminal versatility, that should naturally correlate with subsequent offending (Evans, Ogloff, & Wood, 2013).

An association of similar magnitude between other criminal behaviors and the psychopathy concept has been less clearly evinced in the meta-analytic research, particularly for sexual recidivism (for an overview, refer to McCuish, Chapter 15, this edition). Early research by Hemphill, Hare, et al. (1998) found weaker relationships between PCL psychopathy and sexual recidivism ($r=0.23$) compared to general and violent recidivism ($r=0.27$). Similar findings have been reported in other reviews and meta-analyses (Hanson & Bussière, 1998; Hanson & Morton-Bourgon, 2005, 2009; Hemphill, Templeman, Wong, & Hare, 1998). The research confirms that most sexual offenders, particularly child sexual offenders, are not psychopathic (Porter et al., 2000). However, the PCL measures remained popular for assessing risk of sexual violence (Lally, 2003), in part because of standout caveats on the psychopathy construct and sexual recidivism research at the turn of the century that would go on to inform current future sexual offending risk assessment practice and research.

Studies have shown that PCL measures—including for Factor 1 (*Interpersonal/Affective*)—retained predictive accuracy for (nonsexual) violent and general recidivism among sexual offenders (Olver & Wong, 2006; Porter et al., 2000). Further, as reported in a more recent meta-analysis (Hawes, Boccaccini, & Murrie, 2013), when moderated by sexual deviance, an increase in the predictive accuracy of psychopathy for sexual recidivism is produced. This finding was recently supported in a study of sexual homicides (Darjee, 2019), which reported a significant moderate association for PCL-R Total, and both Factor 1 (*Interpersonal/Affective*) and 2 (*Lifestyle/Antisocial*) scores with sexual sadism in a sample ($n=51$) of sexual homicide offenders. In contrast to the research on other types of offending, a recent review by Ogloff, Veal, Shea, and McEwan (in press) summarized the limited research on the psychopathy construct in risk assessment for stalking recidivism. Underscoring the importance of knowledge of base rates for predictive accuracy in risk assessment, the review of Ogloff et al. indicates restricted predictive utility considering the prevalence of psychopathy among stalkers compared to other offenders—potentially due to the lack of desire or capacity to form close attachments typical in psychopathy, unless the stalker is of the *resentful* or *predatory* subtype.

Mutual influence of the psychopathy concept and violence risk assessment

Use of the PCL measures in violence risk assessment

Considering the literature on PCL-R psychopathy and associations with general and violent recidivism, it is unsurprising that the PCL measures have been at the forefront of forensic risk assessment measures and methods. This influence can be charted through an examination and overview of the commonly used risk assessment measures—both actuarial and structured professional judgment (SPJ) approaches—since the time of the first edition of the PCL (Hare, 1980). Hare initially designed the PCL to assess the presence of psychopathy for clinical and research purposes, and has maintained that the PCL measures were not intended to be used as risk assessment measures (Hare, 1991, 2003). Specifically, Hare (2006) reported that the tools are used most appropriately when assessing risk for recidivism "...as part of a battery of variables and factors relevant to forensic psychology and psychiatry" (p. 710). Notwithstanding, the PCL filled a necessary void in risk assessment for recidivism, and repeated findings (Harris, Rice, & Cormier, 1991; Hemphill, Hare, et al., 1998; Hemphill, Templeman, et al., 1998; Salekin et al., 1996) associating the PCL-R (Hare, 1991) with recidivism invariably led to its utility as a risk assessment measure—sometimes on its own and sometimes embedded within other risk assessment measures. Support for the use of the PCL-R (Hare, 1991) to predict violent recidivism when scored exclusively from file review also contributed to its use in risk assessment (Harris, Rice, & Quinsey, 1993).

The psychopathy construct began to shift from a clinical concept to an actuarial tool in the PCL-R. A key moment in the use of a psychopathy assessment measure in violence risk assessment arose in the comprehensive MacArthur Study of Mental Disorder and Violence (Monahan & Steadman, 1994), during which time the PCL:SV was developed (Hart et al., 1995). Of 134 potential predictors of violence, the PCL:SV was determined to be the strongest predictor in the extensive follow-up of (n=939) civil psychiatric patients. Follow-up research using the MacArthur Study sample demonstrated the strongest correlation with violence to be for Factor 3 (*Affective*) and 4 (*Antisocial*) in the four-factor model of the PCL:SV (Vitacco, Neumann, & Jackson, 2005). While Factor 1 (*Interpersonal/Affective*) scores had also been associated with predicting violent recidivism (Serin, 1996), the predictive power of the PCL measures was also criticized as being primarily from the inclusion of Factor 4 (*Antisocial*) traits not considered in keeping with a personality assessment measure (Cooke & Michie, 2001; Skeem & Mulvey, 2001). Regardless, the predictive validity of the PCL measures for recidivism and violence has undoubtedly contributed to the dominance of these measures for psychopathy assessment in the area of forensic risk assessment for several decades (Hurducas, Singh, De Ruiter, & Petrila, 2014; Neal & Grisso, 2014), and, as will be discussed, also influenced the development of contemporary risk assessment measures. Despite this link to violence and antisocial behavior, a diagnosis of psychopathy—albeit with a lack of empathy and lack of remorse—has never been proposed as being sufficient for use as a single measure in violence risk assessment (Hare, 2003, 2016; Hart, 1998; Widiger & Trull, 1994). The actuarial use of psychological assessment tools—including the PCL measures—in unstructured approaches to risk assessment has been rightly criticized as lacking evidence base (Douglas, Ogloff, Nicholls, & Grant, 1999; Hart & Logan, 2011).

The PCL measures within actuarial and structured professional judgment approaches

Both the PCL:SV and the PCL-R have regularly been used in concurrent validity analyses in the development of violence risk assessment measures, for example, the Spousal

Assault Risk Assessment guide (SARA; Kropp, Hart, Webster, & Eaves, 1994, 1995, 1998) and the Historical Clinical Risk Management-20 (HCR-20^{V2}; Webster, Douglas, Eaves, & Hart, 1997). Further, the item-structure and use of brief, ordinal item-rating scales in the PCL measures have also been the prototype in developing risk assessment measures for both nondiscretionary (actuarial) and discretionary (clinical judgment) approaches. The psychopathy construct—predominantly through PCL measures of psychopathy—has also informed or fully formed the items within these tools.

From the point of actuarial use of the PCL-R in violence risk assessment, the PCL measures went on to influence actuarial violence risk assessment measures, most notably, the Violence Risk Appraisal Guide (VRAG; Harris et al., 1993; Rice & Harris, 1995)—the VRAG and revised version (Rice, Harris, & Lang, 2013) are among the most empirically supported methods for violence risk assessment. In the development of the VRAG, Harris et al. (1993) reported analyzing approximately 50 candidate variables from the violent recidivism research in violent offenders ($n=618$) assessed pretrial in a secure psychiatric hospital for the outcome variable: criminal charge for violent reoffending in an average seven year follow-up. Multiple-regression analyses were used to select the strongest combination of predictor variables, and the decided upon 12 items for inclusion were shown to predict violent recidivism with a high degree of accuracy (AUC=0.76)—subsequent meta-analyses reported similar findings (Fazel, Singh, Doll, & Grann, 2012; Singh, Grann, & Fazel, 2011). Item weights—based on the bivariate relationship between each item and recidivism—were assigned to each of these 12 predictor variables, and the PCL-R (Hare, 1991) was reported to be the strongest predictor. The inclusion of the PCL-R total score as one of the 12 items in the VRAG was criticized because the PCL-R was the predominant predictive validity item in the measure, accounting for approximately 75% of overall predictive accuracy (Douglas, Hart, Webster, & Belfrage, 2013).

In contrast to the actuarial approach to risk assessment, the HCR-20^{V1} (Webster, Eaves, Douglas, & Wintrup, 1995) was developed to provide a set of structured professional judgment (SPJ) guidelines for the assessment of risk of future violence. The HCR-20 includes 20 violence recidivism items from epidemiological and clinical research organized into three domains of risk associated with reoffending: *Historical* (static), *Clinical* (dynamic), and *Risk Management* (future adjustment). The three subscales combine to provide a guide to assist the clinician in making an overall risk judgment—unlike in research, in clinical practice assessors are discouraged from calculating a total score. The initial version of the HCR-20 included the historical item, *Psychopathy*, requiring full PCL-R assessment (PCL:SV assessment also being permissible in Version 2) and use of the suggested PCL measures cut-scores when scoring this HCR-20 item. In the second version, Webster et al. (1997) cited the available research on predicting violent recidivism (e.g., the meta-analysis of Salekin et al., 1996) as guiding the inclusion of this item, and emphasized the *Psychopathy* item should be removed from an overall HCR-20^{V2} assessment if the PCL measures were not used in assessment of the item. Early research on the HCR-20^{V2} led to comparable predictive accuracy to the PCL:SV (Douglas et al., 1999), and meta-analyses have reported modest to moderately good predictive accuracy for the HCR-20^{V2} in violence risk assessment (AUC values between.64 and.76) (Singh et al., 2011). Akin to the use of the psychopathy construct within the VRAG (Harris et al., 1993) actuarial violence risk assessment, the PCL measures were considered to be essential in the HCR-20^{V2} risk assessment.

The PCL measures against other risk assessment approaches

Meta-analyses and related reviews have generally demonstrated that the SPJ approach to risk assessment was equal to, or marginally superior than, actuarial risk assessment measures for prediction of violent recidivism (Campbell et al., 2009; Fazel et al., 2012; Guy, 2008; Guy, Douglas, & Hendry, 2010; Monahan & Skeem, 2014; Singh et al., 2011; Yang et al., 2010). Within these analyses, less support is typically reported for the predictive validity of PCL compared to both actuarial and SPJ guidelines measures for violent recidivism—including for young offenders (Olver, Stockdale, & Wormith, 2009). Comparable predictive validity findings between the PCL-R and other violence risk assessments—including the HCR-20^{V2} and VRAG—were also demonstrated for violent recidivism by Campbell et al. (2009); however, an often cited meta-analytic comparison of the PCL measures predictive accuracy compared to the HCR-20^{V2} by Guy et al. (2010) reported that the HCR-20^{V2} (with the *Psychopathy* item removed) added incrementally to the PCL measures, yet the converse was not true for the PCL measures.

Similar support for the HCR-20^{V2} over the PCL-R was reported in other meta-analyses with regard to effect size comparisons (Fazel et al., 2012; Singh et al., 2011), yet only Yang et al. (2010) also tested the incremental validity of the PCL-R, finding the HCR-20^{V2} and the actuarial Offender Group Reconviction Scale (OGRS; Copas & Marshall, 1998) to be significantly more strongly related to violent recidivism. Douglas et al. (2018) recently highlighted the importance of incremental validity research—including which composite parts of the psychopathy concept add predictive utility over others—in risk assessment research. As will be discussed, it is this line of inquiry that has influenced the utility of both the SPJ approach and the psychopathy concept in contemporary violence risk assessment. The heterogeneity of incremental validity in risk assessment findings using the PCL measures led to the recommendation by Camp, Skeem, Barchard, Lilienfeld, and Poythress (2013) "…against making broad generalizations about the relation between psychopathy and violence" (p. 467).

Different perspectives on the utility of the PCL measures in risk assessment practice resulted from the increase in comparative measures research, often with regard to the necessity of the psychopathy concept when properly utilized (Hare, 1998) or the utility of actuarial and SPJ approaches to risk assessment (Monahan & Skeem, 2014). The debate on the benefits and disadvantages between actuarial and evidence-based SPJ risk assessment guidelines is beyond the scope of this discussion—refer to Hart and Logan (2011) for a review. In brief, typical criticisms of the actuarial approach include: the inability to address factors that may be important for the risk assessment that are not listed on the actuarial instrument; the failure to include opportunity to address intervention in addition to prediction, given focus is on static, historical factors without emphasis on dynamic treatment targets; and the inclusion of "high-fidelity" predictors, meaning the ability of the measure is to assess only specific outcomes over specific timeframes, in specific populations. In addition, one of the key criticisms of the actuarial approach can be elicited in considering the use of the psychopathy construct within what is one of the most widely used SPJ procedure measures for sexual recidivism assessment—the Sexual Violence Risk-20 (Boer, Hart, Kropp, & Webster, 1997). Unlike the commonly used actuarial Static-99R (Harris, Phenix, Hanson, & Thornton, 2003), which includes empirically sourced predictors for sexual-recidivism only (and therefore has no psychopathy construct-related item), consideration of the psychopathy construct in the SVR-20 is guided by the empirically established relationship to *nonsexual violent* recidivism for sexual offenders who score high on the PCL measures, as previously discussed (Olver & Wong, 2006; Porter et al., 2000). Consistent with the HCR-20^{V2}, the SVR-20 item, *Psychopathic Personality Disorder,* refers the assessor to adhere to the psychopathy construct exclusively according to the PCL measures. The need to manage risk in addition to predict risk, as reported by Hart (1998), is an essential component and strength of the SPJ approach. While the actuarial approach has merit if the purpose of the risk assessment is purely prediction (Monahan & Skeem, 2014), as will be discussed, risk management and intervention is a pertinent addition to prediction when considering the psychopathy construct in contemporary risk assessment practice.

The move away from PCL inclusion

In contrast to the initial version of the actuarial VRAG and early versions of the HCR-20, several SPJ procedure measures developed around the turn of this century contain items related to the psychopathy construct without requiring assessment within the tool using the PCL measures; instead, utilizing a broader consideration of the psychopathy construct. The Violence Risk Scale (VRS; Wong & Gordon, 1998, 2000, 2003) includes a *Criminal Personality* item, which is integrated as a dynamic item in consideration that "behavioral manifestations of the personality may change" (Wong & Gordon, 2000; p. 34). Wong et al. presented key stages of change—according to Prochaska and DiClemente (1992)—for this dynamic item, thereby encouraging intervention options. Further, although explicitly acknowledging the item was largely influenced by the PCL-R (Hare, 1991), the VRS does not consider a PCL-R assessment an essential aspect of the assessment of this item, instead making reference to consideration of the personality characteristics. Specifically, the purpose of the *Criminal Personality* item is to capture the Factor 1 (*Interpersonal/Affective*) aspects of psychopathy most relevant to violence; the relevant behavioral aspects of Factor 2 (*Lifestyle/Antisocial*) are captured elsewhere (e.g., the *Violence throughout Lifespan* and *Impulsivity* items in the VRS).

Other SPJ guidelines developed at this time also include broader descriptions for items concerning the psychopathy construct, and do not include explicit recommendations that only PCL measures may be used for scoring these items. The SARA (Kropp et al., 1998) includes the item *Personality Disorder with Anger, Impulsivity, or Behavioral Instability,* and refers to personality disorder assessment with DSM-IV when scoring. Further, the RSVP (Hart, Kropp, & Laws, 2003), while continuing the acknowledgment of the limited utility of psychopathy for risk accuracy of sexual recidivism detailed in its precursor tool—the SVR-20—expands the *Psychopathic Personality Disorder* item description to allow for dissocial personality disorder criteria according to the *International classification of diseases and related health problems* (World Health Organization, 1990) should PCL measures assessment be unavailable. It is noteworthy, however, that the RSVP has not been validated since publication.

Relevant violence research within the previous two decades (Guy et al., 2010; Yang et al., 2010) has resulted in a shift of the influence of the psychopathy construct—particularly as measured by the PCL-R—within each of the most commonly used actuarial and SPJ procedures to violence risk assessment. A subsequent revision in the VRAG-R (Rice et al., 2013) included a refinement of certain measure items and replacement of others. Based on yielding the largest incremental effect when compared to both the PCL-R Total score and the PCL-R Factor 2 (*Lifestyle/Antisocial*) score in the revision validation study, the *PCL-R Total* item in the VRAG was replaced in the VRAG-R with the score of PCL-R Factor 4 (*Antisocial*)—the new item being labeled *Antisociality*. The inclusion of items exclusively from PCL-R Factor 4 in the VRAG-R negate previous criticisms that the predictive power of the VRAG was drawn exclusively from the original *PCL-R Total* item; when scoring the VRAG-R in the validation study with the *Antisociality* item as missing (using prorating), the predictive accuracy was reported as minimally affected (AUC = 0.75) compared to scoring the VRAG-R with the item (AUC = 0.75).

The third version of the HCR-20 (Douglas et al., 2013) continues on from previous versions as one of the most widely used assessment measure for violence risk (Douglas et al., 2014). A major change from the earlier versions to the HCR-20^{V3} relevant to this discussion was the replacement of the Historical item, *Psychopathy*, with the item, *History of Problems with Personality Disorder.* The replaced item definition encourages the clinician to consider both "personality disorders of the antisocial type (variously referred to as antisocial, psychopathic, and dissocial personality disorders)" (p. 79) as well as all other personality disorders. In addition to expanding this definition of the psychopathy construct to broadly include item description indicators of any antisocial-type personality disorder—and relevant indicators from other personality disorders—a considerable change from the previous *Psychopathy* item is the removal of the requirement that the PCL-R or PCL:SV must be used in Version 3 when scoring the item. Nonetheless, the value of the use of a PCL assessment is acknowledged in the HCR-20^{V3} manual, as follows:

> *For those evaluators who are interested specifically in the assessment and diagnosis of psychopathic personality disorder, we recommend but do not require they use the PCL-R or PCL:SV. Evaluators may use country-adjusted cut-scores on the PCL-R and PCL:SV. Evaluators may use other assessment procedures to the extent that justification exists for doing so (p. 79).*

The expansion of new HCR-20^{V3} personality item to broadly include relevant personality indicators paralleled expansion of the *Violence* historical item in the HCR-20^{V3}, and the inclusion of a new *Other Antisocial Behavior* historical item. The removal of the requirement to use the PCL measures does not suggest diminished value in these psychopathy assessment measures—indeed, consistent with the development of earlier SPJ procedures, both the PCL-R (Smith & Edens, 2013) and PCL:SV (Douglas et al., 1999) were reported as used in concurrent validity on the HCR-20^{V3}. Rather, the item update reflects the necessity of item inclusion in SPJ guideline risk assessment practice to match the empirical base (Coid et al., 2011), and endorses the assertion of Hare (2007) that the PCL measures be used where indicated as part of a sophisticated assessment battery, rather than the psychopathy construct being the risk assessment itself.

Contemporary considerations of the psychopathy construct in forensic risk assessment

On general recidivism

In broadening the scope of the psychopathy construct beyond the PCL measures relative to the assessment of violence risk, the empirical research and SPJ procedures have largely aligned with general recidivism risk assessment according to the *Risk, Need, Responsivity* (RNR) principles (Bonta & Andrews, 2017). Extensive research on recidivism risk factors led to the development of one of the first empirically driven risk assessment measures in the Level of Service Inventory (LSI, Andrews, 1982), and the subsequent revised version (LSI-R, Andrews & Bonta, 1995) is the most commonly used risk assessment measure for general recidivism in the United States (Olver, Stockdale, & Wormith, 2014). In contrast to the HCR-20^{V2} and the VRAG, these earlier Level of Service (LS) measures did not include psychopathy-construct related items for the assessment of general recidivism risk. Perhaps the main reason for this is that the LS measures do not have to be completed by clinicians, and are typically employed by community corrections and corrections officers.

Meta-analytic updates to the risk research by Gendreau et al. (1996) informed the inclusion of the *Antisocial Personality Pattern* (APP) risk/need factor, one of the *Central Eight* risk/need factors in the more recent LS/CMI (Andrews, Bonta, & Wormith, 2004) and LS/RNR (Andrews, Bonta, & Wormith, 2008) measures. Meta-analyses on the predictive accuracy of the LS measures show moderate support for the *Central Eight* risk/need factors correlating with general recidivism (r values between 0.29 and 0.30, Olver et al., 2014), and have also reported comparable—in some cases superior—predictive accuracy for violent recidivism compared to the PCL-R and VRAG (Campbell et al., 2009; Gendreau et al., 2002; Yang et al., 2010).

Despite item overlap with the psychopathy construct in both the PCL measures and DSM-5 APD (e.g., impulsivity, callousness), the APP risk/need factor is proposed by Bonta and Andrews (2017) as a general collection of behaviors and personality traits in their *General Personality and Cognitive Social Learning* theory of criminal behavior. APP is explicitly not considered as a form of personality psychopathology. This risk/need factor is also considered in terms of the trademark RNR *dynamic need*, allowing targets for intervention. Notwithstanding, these LS measures include the psychopathy construct—according to either high scores on the PCL-R or an APD diagnosis—as a responsivity factor that does not contribute to the overall risk-rating score, yet may provide grounds for a clinician to make clinical override to the risk rating, and may be relevant to case planning based on the LS assessment. Within the RNR framework, depending on the overall LS scores, psychopathic offenders may simply be considered as high-risk, high-need offenders, and any formal diagnosis of the psychopathy construct contributes to risk management rather than risk assessment (Bonta & Andrews, 2017). Inclusion of the psychopathy construct in the LS measures in this format is consistent with its inclusion as a specific *Red flag risk factor* in the Stalking Risk Profile (SRP; MacKenzie et al., 2009), which recommends a high-risk judgment or additional assessment because of the low base rates of this disorder in stalking and potential relationship to violence. Akin to other SPJs developed in the previous decade, Mackenzie et al. advise use of a formal psychopathy assessment, yet do not mandate that the PCL measures only be used. The SRP also emphasizes the psychopathy construct as a risk management consideration in addition to a risk assessment consideration.

Utility of the psychopathy concept alongside contemporary violence and general risk assessment: Formulation, risk management, and intervention

While these SPJ procedures have moved away from including psychopathy as essential in the risk assessment for violent recidivism, the changes do not preclude the invaluable contribution of assessment of the psychopathy construct—as has been shown in the development of contemporary SPJ procedures—as part of general or violent risk assessment and risk management considerations. For example, Coid, Ullrich, and Kallis (2013) reported the earlier version violence risk assessment measures (including the VRAG and HCR-20^{V2}) are extremely limited in predicting future violence in offenders scoring high (≥ 30) on the PCL-R, underscoring the importance of a comprehensive diagnostic assessment *prior to* any risk assessment—which may result in a clinical override—until the latest versions of these risk assessment measures have been subjected to comprehensive meta-analyses on predictive validity relative to psychopathy concept.

Undoubtedly, the psychopathy construct is not a protective factor for violence risk assessment; however, consideration of protective factors in combination with the psychopathy construct for the purpose of risk assessment and risk management is made clear in the SAPROF (2nd ed.; de Vogel, de Ruiter, Bouman, & de Vries Robbé, 2012), which offers warning that "…under certain circumstances, almost every protective factor can be a risk factor" (p. 23). de Vogel et al. provide the useful example that the protective factor of intelligence can be transformed to a risk factor for an offender with psychopathic traits, who can use intelligence to avoid criminal justice detection or is skilled at manipulating other people. As with the aforementioned discussion on sexual deviance potentially moderating the of risk of sexual recidivism with the psychopathy concept (Hawes et al., 2013), this consideration highlights the importance of psychopathy assessment alongside risk assessment in the SPJ approach to identify interactive effects with other risk factors in formulation of violence and general risk assessment.

Integrating risk management and intervention targets in the SPJ approach—often referred to as fourth-generation risk assessment practice (Bonta & Andrews, 2017)—is an additional psychopathy construct consideration in any risk assessment. A unique meta-analysis by Blais, Solodukhin, and Forth (2014) that differentiated between instrumental and reactive violence—albeit with high number of postdictive studies included in the analysis—reported evidence for stronger relations between instrumental violence and Factor 1 (*Interpersonal/Affective*) compared to Factor 2 (*Lifestyle/Antisocial*). Although both factors were significantly associated with both instrumental and reactive violence, these findings offer further understanding on utility of the PCL measures in violence risk formulation. It is in formulation that intervention can take place, and the utility of the PCL measures is maintained by recent research by Polascheck and colleagues (2013, 2014) as well as Olver, Wong and colleagues (2013, 2016) proposing offenders who score high on the PCL measures can benefit from intervention with regard to risk reduction if the correct dynamic risk needs within the measures are targeted. The psychopathy construct is decreasingly a cause for pessimism with regard to treatment (refer to Olver, Chapter 22, this edition for a review). In light of these considerations, the chapter now turns to what alternatives to the PCL measures can offer to contemporary violent and general risk assessment approaches.

On alternative assessment measures

The *Comprehensive Assessment of Psychopathic Personality* (CAPP; Cooke, Hart, Logan, & Michie, 2004; Cooke et al., 2012) was developed to provide a conceptualization of psychopathy distinctly separate from the operationalized criteria used for diagnosis in the PCL measures. The *Comprehensive Assessment of Psychopathic Personality—Institutional Rating Scale* (CAPP-IRS, Cooke et al., 2004, 2012) is the emerging primary assessment alternative to the PCL measures for use in forensic settings, although the research literature is still scant compared to the PCL measures. Opposition to adoption of the operationalized PCL factor structure as the universally accepted conceptualization of psychopathy assessment (Cooke & Michie, 2001; Skeem & Cooke, 2010; Skeem, Polaschek, Patrick, & Lilienfeld, 2011)—primarily because of the role of antisocial and criminal behavior within these measures—contributed to the development of the CAPP, which includes a conceptual model of the psychopathic personality disorder comprising 33 symptoms in six domains (self, emotional, dominance, attachment, behavioral, and cognitive) of personality functions. The validity and utility of the CAPP conceptualization (Cooke et al., 2012; Sellbom, Cooke, & Hart, 2015) and the associated semistructured clinical interview and informant rating form, the CAPP-IRS (Cooke & Logan, 2015), to assess psychopathy has complemented support for prototypical ratings (see Cooke, 2018 for a review); however, very limited recidivism research exists to evaluate the utility of the CAPP in risk assessment.

In the only study to compare the PCL measures with the CAPP for predictive validity, Pedersen, Kunz, Rasmussen, and Elsass (2010) reported no significant difference in the moderate predictive accuracy for recidivism of the PCL:SV and CAPP-IRS (Danish research-version) in a sample of Danish forensic psychiatric patients ($n=96$;

follow-up period of 5.7 years), providing preliminary yet tentative predictive validity for the personality-based CAPP with fewer items reflecting antisocial behavior. Notwithstanding the research disparity in predictive validity between the two conceptualizations, a review of the differences between the CAPP and PCL measures relative to utility in violence risk assessment hypothesized a key advantage of the CAPP over the PCL measures (Bergstrøm et al., 2018). That being the larger concentration of dynamic factors to aid in explaining—and therefore intervening to reduce—violence risk, rather than predicting risk. This proposal for the increased utility of the CAPP aligns with the principles of RNR within fourth-generation violence risk assessment approaches (Bonta & Andrews, 2017) to allow for high violence risk offenders to receive high dynamic need management and intervention. A major drawback of the CAPP is the length of time required for administration due to its comprehensiveness, yet its potential utility, as outlined by Bergstrøm et al. (2018), alongside fourth-generation risk assessment measures for the purposes of identifying treatment targets is compelling. Research on the CAPP continues to increase, and with the CAPP–Self-Report (CAPP-SR; Sellbom, Cooke, & Shou, 2019) recently developed, a screening version suitable for use in forensic population may contribute to increased use in forensic risk assessment and research.

No self-report measure for psychopathy has been adequately validated for clinical use in violence risk assessment. Despite some findings on the utility of the Psychopathic Personality Inventory (PPI; Lilienfeld & Andrews, 1996) providing incremental validity over the PCL-R in predicting violent recidivism (Camp et al., 2013), self-report psychopathy measures have understandably not been adopted for forensic practice when considering the propensity for deception and manipulation considered core to the psychopathy concept. Regardless, research using self-report measures such as the NEO-Personality Inventory-Revised (NEO-PI-R; Costa & McCrae, 2008) and the Elemental Psychopathy Assessment (EPA; Lynam et al., 2011) investigating the link between the dimensional *Five Factor Model* (FFM; Costa & McCrae, 1992) personality conceptualization and antisocial behavior provides tentative support to the suggestion of both Widiger and Lilienfeld, and their respective colleagues (Bagby & Widiger, 2018; Lilienfeld, Watts, Francis Smith, Berg, & Latzman, 2015; Widiger & Lynam, 1998) to merge the psychopathy construct within the general personality literature, rather than consider it as a stand-alone pathology. The evidence indicates the higher order factor and lower order facet traits of the FFM—typically those related to low agreeableness and low conscientiousness—reliably demonstrate associations with both psychopathy (Lynam & Miller, 2015) and antisocial behavior (Vize, Miller, & Lynam, 2018). However, consistent with the CAPP, research on the predictive utility of the FFM is in an infancy stage compared to the PCL measures.

Conclusions

Although simple in approach, this historical overview encourages the reader to consider the evolving nature of both the utility of psychopathy in forensic risk assessment, and also, of the psychopathy construct itself. Psychopathy—overwhelmingly assessed using the PCL measures—is a core component of risk assessment in many forensic settings, and the PCL measures have directly influenced modern risk assessment methods and measures, particularly for violence risk assessment, in part because of impressive predictive accuracy. Psychopathy as a construct, however, is distinct from risk for recidivism; a high score on a PCL measure does not necessarily equate with high risk, and the converse is also true. Research on incremental validity for the PCL-R with established risk assessment measures has demonstrated the psychopathy construct may be less applicable in predicting risk than previously reported in recent decades. Risk assessment practice continues to develop an increasingly sophisticated understanding of the essential risk factors—assisted by nuanced research on the PCL measures predictive accuracy—and the PCL-R is no longer included as a necessary component in the most widely used contemporary violence risk assessment measures, the VRAG-R (Rice et al., 2013) and HCR-20^{V3} (Douglas et al., 2013)—although these revisions are yet to be adequately validated.

The psychopathy concept assessed with the PCL measures or the CAPP-IRS, however, still retains critical importance in SPJ risk assessment approaches, which remain the premier violence risk assessment choice over actuarial measures because of the advantage of risk management and intervention in addition to risk assessment. Within these approaches, mediating and moderating factors alongside high scores on a psychopathy assessment can result in an increase in risk, which may merit a risk assessment clinical override.

Further, use of the psychopathy concept in general recidivism risk assessment according to the RNR principles—utilizing relevant personality traits and behaviors as risk/need factors, and any formal psychopathic personality diagnosis as a responsivity factor that may also override a clinical risk rating depending on severity—is now largely consistent with the SPJ procedural approach to formulation of violence risk in the HCR-20^{V3}, as well as the SPJ guidelines to assess risk of other criminal behaviors. Established considerations in risk assessment using the psychopathy construct, such as knowledge of base rates in an offending population and the utility of psychopathy assessment measure cut-scores, remain pertinent when utilizing a psychopathy assessment within these contemporary risk assessment approaches. In the assessment of violence risk, prior assessment for psychopathy where indicated is still strongly advised. The importance of psychopathy as it relates to both risk and interventions suggests that psychopathy assessments are still indicated as part of a comprehensive risk and management plan.

In considering the increased optimism in the previous decade—although still largely unproven—for the treatment of psychopathic offenders to reduce recidivism risk, the utmost utility of the psychopathy construct in risk assessment may prove to be in intervention as opposed to risk assessment, thereby increasing the need for the use of psychopathy assessment measures that consider dynamic factors rather than those that have predominantly static factors. An understanding of the causes of violence to prevent recurrence is more imperative than the prediction and management of violent behavior (Monahan & Skeem, 2014).

Finally, in terms of future directions, the following four research recommendations are provided to assist in strengthening the utility of the psychopathy concept alongside SPJ procedures to inform the formulation of recidivism risk assessments:

- The PCL measures demonstrate moderate support for predicting violent and general offending recidivism. Further research on the predictive validity—with regard to methodological limitations of the psychopathy construct in recidivism research (Douglas et al., 2018; Hemphill, 2007)—of the CAPP measures is also warranted, both as stand-alone assessment measures, and in comparison to the PCL measures. While the CAPP-IRS may prove to have beneficial utility for SPJ approaches because of the ability to target a wider variety of dynamic factors and items for intervention, predictive accuracy to at least match the PCL measures will be essential if the psychopathy construct is to also be used for a clinical override of risk assessment. A screening version of the CAPP-IRS will likely increase the research base.
- Following on from the need for research using alternative psychopathy assessment measures, consideration of unifying psychopathy into the generalist perspective in personality psychology (Lilienfeld et al., 2015; Widiger & Lynam, 1998) is in keeping with the RNR *General Personality and Cognitive Social Learning* of criminal behavior, which disregards personality psychopathology in favor of identifying dynamic risk/needs to reduce risk, and has empirical support for doing so (Bonta, Blais, & Wilson, 2014). The development of SPJ procedures that include the psychopathy-relevant FFM traits could inform nuanced interventions without the stigmatized label of "psychopathy" that may influence an offender's future in the institutional and legal systems (Berryessa & Wohlstetter, 2019).
- Future utility of the psychopathy construct in violence risk assessment includes emphasis on risk management and intervention. Longitudinal research combining fourth-generation risk assessment approaches and a focus on targeted intervention to the risk factors and individual items identified within the PCL measures that have demonstrated utility (Olver et al., 2013)—and those dynamic factors and items proposed to have intervention utility in alternative assessment measures—in reducing violence risk will be desirable considering the prevalence of psychopathy in high-risk violent offenders (Hart & Cook, 2012).
- A final consideration is for an increase in violent recidivism research using the VRAG-R as well as the HCR-20^{V3} compared to the PCL measures to allow for predictive accuracy to be subsequently assessed in meta-analyses. Considering Coid et al. (2013) reported the utility of previous versions of the most commonly used violence risk assessment measures was poor for individuals with PCL-R psychopathy, further research is therefore required using these updated violence risk assessment measures to determine predictive validity for offenders who score highly on a psychopathy assessment prior to a formal risk assessment.

References

American Psychiatric Association. (1968). *Diagnostic and statistical manual of mental disorders* (2nd ed.). Washington DC: Author.

American Psychiatric Association. (1980). *Diagnostic and statistical manual of mental disorders* (3rd ed.). Washington, DC: Author.

American Psychiatric Association. (2013). *Diagnostic and statistical manual of mental disorders* (5th ed.). Washington, DC: Author.

Andrews, D. A. (1982). *The level of supervision inventory: The first follow-up*. Toronto, Canada: Ontario Ministry of Correctional Services.

Andrews, D. A., & Bonta, J. (1995). *Level of service inventory–revised (LSI–R): An offender assessment system: User's guide*. Toronto, Canada: Multi-Health Systems.

Andrews, D. A., Bonta, J., & Wormith, J. S. (2004). *Level of service/case management inventory (LS/CMI): An offender assessment system: User's guide*. Toronto, Canada: Multi-Health Systems.

Andrews, D. A., Bonta, J., & Wormith, J. S. (2008). *Level of service/risk, need, responsivity (LS/RNR): An offender assessment system: User's guide*. Toronto, Canada: Multi-Health Systems.
Arrigo, B. A., & Shipley, S. (2001). The confusion over psychopathy (I): Historical considerations. *International Journal of Offender Therapy and Comparative Criminology, 45*, 325–344.
Bagby, R. M., & Widiger, T. A. (2018). Five factor model personality disorder scales: An introduction to a special section on assessment of maladaptive variants of the five factor model. *Psychological Assessment, 30*, 1–9. https://doi.org/10.1037/pas0000523.
Bergstrøm, H., Larmour, S. R., & Farrington, D. P. (2018). The usefulness of psychopathy in explaining and predicting violence: Discussing the utility of competing perspectives. *Aggression and Violent Behavior, 42*, 84–95. https://doi.org/10.1016/j.avb.2018.07.006.
Berrios, G. E. (1993). Personality disorders: A conceptual history. In G. Stein, & P. Tyrer (Eds.), *Personality disorder reviewed* (pp. 17–41). London, UK: Gaskell/Royal College of Psychiatrists.
Berryessa, C. M., & Wohlstetter, B. (2019). The psychopathic "label" and effects on punishment outcomes: A meta-analysis. *Law and Human Behavior, 43*, 9–25. https://doi.org/10.1037/lhb0000317.
Blais, J., Solodukhin, E., & Forth, A. E. (2014). A meta-analysis exploring the relationship between psychopathy and instrumental versus reactive violence. *Criminal Justice and Behavior, 41*, 797–821. https://doi.org/10.1177/0093854813519629.
Boer, D. P., Hart, S. D., Kropp, P. R., & Webster, C. D. (1997). *Manual for the sexual violence risk-20: Professional guidelines for assessing risk of sexual violence*. Vancouver, Canada: Mental Health, Law, and Policy Institute.
Bonta, J., & Andrews, D. A. (2017). *The psychology of criminal conduct* (6th ed.). New York, NY: Routledge.
Bonta, J., Blais, J., & Wilson, H. A. (2014). A theoretically informed meta-analysis of the risk for general and violent recidivism for mentally disordered offenders. *Aggression and Violent Behavior, 19*, 278–287. https://doi.org/10.1016/j.avb.2014.04.014.
Camp, J. P., Skeem, J. L., Barchard, K., Lilienfeld, S. O., & Poythress, N. G. (2013). Psychopathic predators? Getting specific about the relation between psychopathy and violence. *Journal of Consulting and Clinical Psychology, 81*, 467–480. https://doi.org/10.1037/a0031349.
Campbell, M. A., French, S., & Gendreau, P. (2009). The prediction of violence in adult offenders: A meta-analytic comparison of instruments and methods of assessment. *Criminal Justice and Behavior, 36*, 567–590. https://doi.org/10.1177/0093854809333610.
Cleckley, H. (1941). *The mask of sanity*. St Louis, MO: Mosby.
Coid, J. W., Ullrich, S., & Kallis, C. (2013). Predicting future violence among individuals with psychopathy. *The British Journal of Psychiatry, 203*, 387–388. https://doi.org/10.1192/bjp.bp.112.118471.
Coid, J. W., Yang, M., Ullrich, S., Zhang, T., Sizmur, S., Farrington, D., et al. (2011). Most items in structured risk assessment instruments do not predict violence. *The Journal of Forensic Psychiatry & Psychology, 22*, 3–21. https://doi.org/10.1080/14789949.2010.495990.
Cooke, D. J. (2018). Psychopathic personality disorder: Capturing an elusive concept. *European Journal of Analytic Philosophy, 14*, 15–32. https://doi.org/10.31820/ejap.14.1.1.
Cooke, D., Hart, S. D., Logan, C., & Michie, C. (2004). *Comprehensive assessment of psychopathic personality—Institutional rating scale (CAPP-IRS)*. Unpublished manuscript.
Cooke, D. J., Hart, S. D., Logan, C., & Michie, C. (2012). Explicating the construct of psychopathy: Development and validation of a conceptual model, the comprehensive assessment of psychopathic personality (CAPP). *International Journal of Forensic Mental Health, 11*, 242–252. https://doi.org/10.1080/14999013.2012.746759.

Cooke, D. J., & Logan, C. (2015). Capturing clinical complexity: Towards a personality-oriented measure of psychopathy. *Journal of Criminal Justice*, *43*, 262–273. https://doi.org/10.1016/j.jcrimjus.2015.04.004.

Cooke, D. J., & Michie, C. (2001). Refining the construct of psychopathy: Towards a hierarchical model. *Psychological Assessment*, *13*, 171–188. https://doi.org/10.1037//1040-3590.13.2.171.

Cooke, D. J., & Sellbom, M. (2019). An examination of psychopathy checklist-revised latent factor structure via exploratory structural equation modeling. *Psychological Assessment*, *31*, 581–591. https://doi.org/10.1037/pas0000676.

Copas, J., & Marshall, P. (1998). The offender group reconviction scale: The statistical reconviction score for use by probation officers. *Journal of the Royal Statistical Society*, *47*, 159–171. https://doi.org/10.1111/1467-9876.00104.

Costa, P. T., & McCrae, R. R. (1992). The five-factor model of personality and its relevance to personality disorders. *Journal of Personality Disorders*, *6*, 343–359. https://doi.org/10.1521/pedi.1992.6.4.343.

Costa, P. T., & McCrae, R. R. (2008). The revised NEO personality inventory (NEO-PI-R). In *The SAGE handbook of personality theory and assessment: Volume 2—Personality measurement and testing* (pp. 179–198). Los Angeles, CA: Sage. https://doi.org/10.4135/9781849200479.n9.

Crego, C., & Widiger, T. A. (2015). Psychopathy and the DSM. *Journal of Personality*, *83*, 665–677. https://doi.org/10.1111/jopy.12115.

Darjee, R. (2019). Sexual sadism and psychopathy in sexual homicide offenders: An exploration of their associates in a clinical sample. *International Journal of Offender Therapy and Comparative Criminology*, 1–29. https://doi.org/10.1177/0306624x19836872.

de Vogel, V., de Ruiter, C., Bouman, Y., & de Vries Robbé, M. (2012). *SAPROF. Guidelines for the assessment of protective factors for violence risk* (2nd ed.). Utrecht, The Netherlands: Forum Educatief.

Douglas, K., Hart, S., Webster, C., & Belfrage, H. (2013). *HCR-20 (version 3): Assessing risk for violence—User guide*. Burnaby, Canada: Mental Health, Law, and Policy Institute, Simon Fraser University.

Douglas, K. S., Ogloff, J. R. P., Nicholls, T. L., & Grant, I. (1999). Assessing risk for violence among psychiatric patients: The HCR-20 violence risk assessment scheme and the psychopathy checklist: Screening version. *Journal of Consulting and Clinical Psychology*, *67*, 917–930. https://doi.org/10.1037/0022-006X.67.6.917.

Douglas, K. S., Shaffer, C., Blanchard, A. J. E., Guy, L. S., Reeves, K., & Weir, J. (2014). *HCR-20 violence risk assessment scheme: Overview and annotated bibliography (HCR-20 violence risk assessment white paper series, no. 1)*. Burnaby, British Columbia, Canada: Mental Health, Law, and Policy Institute, Simon Fraser University.

Douglas, K. S., Vincent, G. M., & Edens, J. F. (2018). Risk for criminal recidivism: The role of psychopathy. In C. J. Patrick (Ed.), *Handbook of psychopathy* (2nd ed., pp. 682–709). New York, NY, US: The Guilford Press.

Edens, J., Campbell, J., & Weir, J. (2007). Youth psychopathy and criminal recidivism: A meta-analysis of the psychopathy checklist measures. *Law and Human Behavior*, *31*, 53–75. https://doi.org/10.1007/s10979-006-9019-y.

Evans, J., Ogloff, J. R. P., & Wood, M. (2013). Understanding psychopathy. In O. J. Thienhaus, & M. Piasecki (Eds.), *Correctional psychiatry: Practice guidelines and strategies*. Civic Research Institute: Kingston, NJ.

Eysenck, H. J. (1977). *Crime and personality* (2nd ed.). London, UK: Routledge.

Fazel, S., Singh, J. P., Doll, H., & Grann, M. (2012). Use of risk assessment instruments to predict violence and antisocial behaviour in 73 samples involving 24,827 people: Systematic review and meta-analysis. *British Medical Journal, 345*. https://doi.org/10.1136/bmj.e4692.

Forth, A. E., Kosson, D. S., & Hare, R. D. (2003). *The Hare psychopathy checklist: Youth version*. Toronto, ON: Multi-Health Systems.

Gendreau, P., Goggin, C., & Smith, P. (2002). Is the PCL-R really the "unparalleled" measure of offender risk? A lesson in knowledge cumulation. *Criminal Justice and Behavior, 29*, 397–426. https://doi.org/10.1177/0093854802029004004.

Gendreau, P., Little, T., & Goggin, C. (1996). A meta-analysis of the predictors of adult offender recidivism: What works! *Criminology, 34*, 575–608. https://doi.org/10.1111/j.1745-9125.1996.tb01220.x.

Guy, L. S. (2008). *Performance indicators of the structured professional judgment approach for assessing risk for violence to others: A meta-analytic survey*. Unpublished doctoral dissertation Burnaby, Canada: Simon Fraser University.

Guy, L. S., Douglas, K. S., & Hendry, M. C. (2010). The role of psychopathic personality disorder in violence risk assessments using the HCR-20. *Journal of Personality Disorders, 24*, 551–580. https://doi.org/10.1521/pedi.2010.24.5.551.

Hanson, R. K., & Bussière, M. T. (1998). Predicting relapse: A meta-analysis of sexual offender recidivism studies. *Journal of Consulting and Clinical Psychology, 66*, 348–362. https://doi.org/10.1037/0022-006X.66.2.348.

Hanson, R. K., & Morton-Bourgon, K. E. (2005). The characteristics of persistent sexual offenders: A meta-analysis of recidivism studies. *Journal of Consulting and Clinical Psychology, 73*, 1154–1163. https://doi.org/10.1037/0022-006x.73.6.1154.

Hanson, R. K., & Morton-Bourgon, K. E. (2009). The accuracy of recidivism risk assessments for sexual offenders: A meta-analysis of 118 prediction studies. *Psychological Assessment, 21*, 1–21. https://doi.org/10.1037/a0014421.

Hare, R. D. (1970). *Psychopathy: Theory and research*. Chichester, NY: Wiley.

Hare, R. D. (1980). A research scale for the assessment of psychopathy in criminal populations. *Personality and Individual Differences, 1*, 111–119. https://doi.org/10.1016/0191-8869(80)90028-8.

Hare, R. D. (1985). Comparison of procedures for the assessment of psychopathy. *Journal of Consulting and Clinical Psychology, 53*, 7–16. https://doi.org/10.1037/0022-006X.53.1.7.

Hare, R. D. (1991). *The Hare psychopathy checklist—revised*. Toronto, ON: Multi-Health Systems.

Hare, R. D. (1998). The Hare PCL-R: Some issues concerning its use and misuse. *Legal and Criminological Psychology, 3*, 99–119. https://doi.org/10.1111/j.2044-8333.1998.tb00353.x.

Hare, R. D. (2003). *The Hare psychopathy checklist-revised* (2nd ed.). Toronto, ON: Multi-Health Systems.

Hare, R. D. (2006). Psychopathy: A clinical and forensic overview. *Psychiatria Clinica, 29*, 709–724.

Hare, R. D. (2007). Forty years aren't enough: Recollections, prognostications, and random musings. In H. Hervé, & J. C. Yuille (Eds.), *The psychopath: Theory, research, and practice* (pp. 3–28). Mahwah, NJ: Lawrence Erlbaum Associates Publishers.

Hare, R. D. (2016). Psychopathy, the PCL-R, and criminal justice: Some new findings and current issues. *Canadian Psychology/Psychologie Canadienne, 57*, 21–34. https://doi.org/10.1037/cap0000041.

Hare, R. D., & Cox, D. N. (1978). Clinical and empirical conceptions of psychopathy, and the selection of subjects for research. In R. D. Hare, & D. Schalling (Eds.), *Psychopathic behaviour: Approaches to research* (pp. 1–21). Chichester, NY: Wiley.

Hare, R. D., & Neumann, C. S. (2008). Psychopathy as a clinical and empirical construct. *Annual Review of Clinical Psychology, 4*, 217–246. https://doi.org/10.1146/annurev.clinpsy.3.022806.091452.

Harris, A. J. R., Phenix, A., Hanson, R. K., & Thornton, D. (2003). *Static-99 coding rules: Revised 2003*. Ottawa, ON: Solicitor General Canada.

Harris, G. T., Rice, M. E., & Cormier, C. A. (1991). Psychopathy and violent recidivism. *Law and Human Behavior, 15*, 625–637. https://doi.org/10.1007/BF01065856.

Harris, G. T., Rice, M. E., & Quinsey, V. L. (1993). Violent recidivism of mentally disordered offenders: The development of a statistical prediction instrument. *Criminal Justice and Behavior, 20*, 315–335. https://doi.org/10.1177/0093854893020004001.

Hart, S. D. (1998). The role of psychopathy in assessing risk for violence: Conceptual and methodological issues. *Legal and Criminological Psychology, 3*(Pt 1), 121–137. https://doi.org/10.1111/j.2044-8333.1998.tb00354.x.

Hart, S. D., & Cook, A. N. (2012). Current issues in the assessment and diagnosis of psychopathy (psychopathic personality disorder). *Neuropsychiatry, 2*, 497–508. https://doi.org/10.2217/npy.12.61.

Hart, S. D., Cox, D., & Hare, R. D. (1995). *Manual for the psychopathy checklist: Screening version*. Toronto, ON: Multi-Health Systems.

Hart, S. D., Kropp, P. R., & Laws, D. R. (2003). *The risk for sexual violence protocol (RSVP)*. Burnaby, BC: Simon Fraser University, Mental Health, Law, and Policy Institute.

Hart, S. D., & Logan, C. (2011). Formulation of violence risk using evidence-based assessments: The structured professional judgment approach. In P. Sturmey, & M. McMurran (Eds.), *Forensic case formulation* (pp. 81–106). Chichester, UK: John Wiley & Sons, Ltd.

Hathaway, S. R., & McKinley, J. C. (1940). A multiphasic personality schedule (Minnesota): I. Construction of the schedule. *The Journal of Psychology: Interdisciplinary and Applied, 10*, 249–254. https://doi.org/10.1080/00223980.1940.9917000.

Hawes, S. W., Boccaccini, M. T., & Murrie, D. C. (2013). Psychopathy and the combination of psychopathy and sexual deviance as predictors of sexual recidivism: Meta-analytic findings using the psychopathy checklist—Revised. *Psychological Assessment, 25*, 233–243. https://doi.org/10.1037/a0030391.

Hemphill, J. F. (2007). The Hare psychopathy checklist and recidivism: Methodological issues and critically evaluating empirical evidence. In H. Hervé, & J. C. Yuille (Eds.), *The psychopath: Theory, research, and practice* (pp. 141–170). Mahwah, NJ: Lawrence Erlbaum Associates Publishers.

Hemphill, J. F., Hare, R. D., & Wong, S. (1998). Psychopathy and recidivism: A review. *Legal and Criminological Psychology, 3*, 139–170. https://doi.org/10.1111/j.2044-8333.1998.tb00355.x.

Hemphill, J. F., Templeman, R., Wong, S., & Hare, R. D. (1998). Psychopathy and crime: Recidivism and criminal careers. In D. J. Cooke, A. E. Forth, & R. D. Hare (Eds.), *NATO ASI series (series D: Behavioural and social sciences): Vol. 88. Psychopathy: Theory, research and implications for society*. Dordrecht: Springer.

Hurducas, C. C., Singh, J. P., De Ruiter, C., & Petrila, J. (2014). Violence risk assessment tools: A systematic review of surveys. *International Journal of Forensic Mental Health, 13*, 181–192. https://doi.org/10.1080/14999013.2014.942923.

Karpman, B. (1941). On the need of separating psychopathy into two distinct clinical types: The symptomatic and the idiopathic. *Journal of Criminal Psychopathology, 3*, 112–137.

Karpman, B. (1951). The sexual psychopath. *Journal of Criminal Law, Criminology, and Police Science*, *42*, 184–198. https://doi.org/10.2307/1139876.

Kelley, S. E., Edens, J. F., Mowle, E. N., Penson, B. N., & Rulseh, A. (2019). Dangerous, depraved, and death-worthy: A meta-analysis of the correlates of perceived psychopathy in jury simulation studies. *Journal of Clinical Psychology*, *75*, 627–643. https://doi.org/10.1002/jclp.22726.

Kennealy, P. J., Skeem, J. L., Walters, G. D., & Camp, J. (2010). Do core interpersonal and affective traits of PCL-R psychopathy interact with antisocial behavior and disinhibition to predict violence? *Psychological Assessment*, *22*, 569–580. https://doi.org/10.1037/a0019618.

Kropp, P. R., Hart, S. D., Webster, C. W., & Eaves, D. (1994). *Manual for the spousal assault risk assessment guide*. Vancouver, BC: British Columbia Institute on Family Violence.

Kropp, P. R., Hart, S. D., Webster, C. W., & Eaves, D. (1995). *Manual for the spousal assault risk assessment guide* (2nd ed.). Vancouver, BC: British Columbia Institute on Family Violence.

Kropp, P. R., Hart, S. D., Webster, C. W., & Eaves, D. (1998). *Spousal assault risk assessment: User's guide*. Toronto, ON: Multi-Health Systems, Inc.

Lally, S. J. (2003). What tests are acceptable for use in forensic evaluations? A survey of experts. *Professional Psychology: Research and Practice*, *34*, 491–498. https://doi.org/10.1037/0735-7028.34.5.491.

Leistico, A.-M. R., Salekin, R. T., DeCoster, J., & Rogers, R. (2008). A large-scale meta-analysis relating the Hare measures of psychopathy to antisocial conduct. *Law and Human Behavior*, *32*, 28–45. https://doi.org/10.1007/s10979-007-9096-6.

Lilienfeld, S. O., & Andrews, B. P. (1996). Development and preliminary validation of a self-report measure of psychopathic personality traits in noncriminal population. *Journal of Personality Assessment*, *66*, 488–524. https://doi.org/10.1207/s15327752jpa6603_3.

Lilienfeld, S. O., Watts, A. L., Francis Smith, S., Berg, J. M., & Latzman, R. D. (2015). Psychopathy deconstructed and reconstructed: Identifying and assembling the personality building blocks of Cleckley's chimera. *Journal of Personality*, *83*, 593–610. https://doi.org/10.1111/jopy.12118.

Lynam, D. R., Gaughan, E. T., Miller, J. D., Miller, J. D., Mullins-Sweatt, S., & Widiger, T. A. (2011). Assessing the basic traits associated with psychopathy: Development and validation of the elemental psychopathy assessment. *Psychological Assessment*, *23*, 108–124. https://doi.org/10.1037/a0021146.

Lynam, D. R., & Miller, J. D. (2015). Psychopathy from a basic trait perspective: The utility of a five-factor model approach. *Journal of Personality*, *83*, 611–626. https://doi.org/10.1111/jopy.12132.

Lyon, D. R., Ogloff, J. R. P., & Shepherd, S. M. (2016). Legal and ethical issues in the assessment of psychopathy. In C. B. Gacono (Ed.), *Personality and clinical psychology series. The clinical and forensic assessment of psychopathy: A practitioner's guide* (2nd Ed., pp. 193–216). Routledge/Taylor & Francis Group: New York, NY.

MacKenzie, R., McEwan, T., Pathé, M., James, D., Ogloff, J. R. P., & Mullen, P. (2009). *Stalking risk profile: Guidelines for the assessment and management of stalkers*. Melbourne, Australia: StalkInc. and Centre for Forensic Behavioural Science.

McCord, W., & McCord, J. (1964). The psychopath: An essay on the criminal mind. In *Princeton*. NJ: Van Nostrand.

Miller, J. D., & Lynam, D. (2001). Structural models of personality and their relation to antisocial behavior: A meta-analytic review. *Criminology*, *39*, 765–798. https://doi.org/10.1111/j.1745-9125.2001.tb00940.x.

Monahan, J., & Skeem, J. L. (2014). The evolution of violence risk assessment. *CNS Spectrums*, *19*, 419–424. https://doi.org/10.1017/s1092852914000145.

Monahan, J., & Steadman, H. J. (1994). *Violence and mental disorder: Developments in risk assessment*. Chicago: University of Chicago Press.

Neal, T. M. S., & Grisso, T. (2014). Assessment practices and expert judgment methods in forensic psychology and psychiatry: An international snapshot. *Criminal Justice and Behavior*, *41*(12), 1406–1421. https://doi.org/10.1177/0093854814548449.

Ogloff, J. R. P. (2006). Psychopathy/antisocial personality disorder conundrum. *Australian and New Zealand Journal of Psychiatry*, *40*, 519–528. https://doi.org/10.1080/j.1440-1614.2006.01834.x.

Ogloff, J. R. P., Veal, R. G., Shea, D. E., & McEwan, T. (in press). The role of psychopathy in stalking. In: A. R. Felthous, & H. Saß (Eds.), The Wiley international handbook of psychopathic disorders and the law (Vol. II, 2nd ed.). Chichester, England: John Wiley & Sons, Ltd.

Olver, M. E. (2016). Treatment of psychopathic offenders: Evidence, issues, and controversies. *Journal of Community Safety and Well-Being*, *1*, 75–82.

Olver, M. E., Lewis, K., & Wong, S. (2013). Risk reduction treatment of high-risk psychopathic offenders: The relationship of psychopathy and treatment change to violent recidivism. *Personality Disorders*, *4*, 160–167. https://doi.org/10.1037/a0029769.

Olver, M. E., Stockdale, K. S., & Wormith, J. S. (2009). Risk assessment with young offenders: A meta-analysis of three assessment measures. *Criminal Justice and Behavior*, *36*, 329–353. https://doi.org/10.1177/0093854809331457.

Olver, M. E., Stockdale, K. C., & Wormith, J. S. (2014). Thirty years of research on the level of service scales: A meta-analytic examination of predictive accuracy and sources of variability. *Psychological Assessment*, *26*, 156–176. https://doi.org/10.1037/a0035080.

Olver, M. E., & Wong, S. (2006). Psychopathy, sexual deviance, and recidivism among sex offenders. *Sexual Abuse: A Journal of Research and Treatment*, *18*, 65–82. https://doi.org/10.1177/107906320601800105.

Patrick, C. J. (2006). Back to the future: Cleckley as a guide to the next generation of psychopathy research. In C. J. Patrick (Ed.), *Handbook of psychopathy* (pp. 605–617). New York, NY, US: The Guilford Press.

Pedersen, L., Kunz, C., Rasmussen, K., & Elsass, P. (2010). Psychopathy as a risk factor for violent recidivism: Investigating the psychopathy checklist screening version (PCL:SV) and the comprehensive assessment of psychopathic personality (CAPP) in a forensic psychiatric setting. *International Journal of Forensic Mental Health*, *9*, 308–315. https://doi.org/10.1080/14999013.2010.526681.

Pichot, P. (1978). Psychopathic behavior: A historical overview. In R. D. Hare, & D. Schalling (Eds.), *Psychopathic behavior: Approaches to research* (pp. 55–70). Chichester, NY: Wiley.

Pinel, P. (1806). Section IV: Mental derangement distributed into different species: Second species of mental derangement. In *A treatise on insanity* (pp. 150–156). London, UK: Messers Cadell & Davies, Strand.

Polaschek, D. L. L. (2014). Adult criminals with psychopathy: Common beliefs about treatability and change have little empirical support. *Current Directions in Psychological Science*, *23*, 296–301. https://doi.org/10.1177/0963721414535211.

Polaschek, D. L. L., & Daly, T. E. (2013). Treatment and psychopathy in forensic settings. *Aggression and Violent Behavior*, *18*, 592–603. https://doi.org/10.1016/j.avb.2013.06.003.

Porter, S., Fairweather, D., Drugge, J., Hervé, H., Birt, A., & Boer, D. P. (2000). Profiles of psychopathy in incarcerated sexual offenders. *Criminal Justice and Behavior*, *27*, 216–233. https://doi.org/10.1177/0093854800027002005.

Prochaska, J. O., & DiClemente, C. C. (1992). The transtheoretical approach. In J. C. Norcross, & M. R. Goldfried (Eds.), *Handbook of psychotherapy integration* (pp. 300–334). New York, NY: Basic Books.

Rice, M., & Harris, G. (1995). Violent recidivism: Assessing predictive validity. *Journal of Consulting and Clinical Psychology*, *63*, 737–748. https://doi.org/10.1037/0022-006X.63.5.737.

Rice, M. E., Harris, G. T., & Lang, C. (2013). Validation of and revision to the VRAG and SORAG: The violence risk appraisal guide—Revised (VRAG-R). *Psychological Assessment*, *25*, 951–965. https://doi.org/10.1037/a0032878.

Richards, H. J., Gacono, C. B., Cunliffe, T. B., Kivisto, A. J., Smith, J. M., & Bodholdt, R. (2016). Assessing psychopathy in adults: The Hare psychopathy checklist—Revised and psychopathy checklist screening version. In C. B. Gacono (Ed.), *The clinical and forensic assessment of psychopathy: A practitioner's guide* (2nd ed., pp. 137–166). New York, NY: Routledge/Taylor & Francis Group.

Salekin, R. T., Rogers, R., & Sewell, K. W. (1996). A review and meta-analysis of the psychopathy checklist and psychopathy checklist—Revised: Predictive validity of dangerousness. *Clinical Psychology: Science and Practice*, *3*, 203–215. https://doi.org/10.1111/j.1468-2850.1996.tb00071.x.

Sellbom, M., Cooke, D. J., & Hart, S. D. (2015). Construct validity of the comprehensive assessment of psychopathic personality (CAPP) concept map: Getting closer to the core of psychopathy. *International Journal of Forensic Mental Health*, *14*, 172–180. https://doi.org/10.1080/14999013.2015.1085112.

Sellbom, M., Cooke, D. J., & Shou, Y. (2019). Development and initial validation of the comprehensive assessment of psychopathic personality–self-report (CAPP-SR). *Psychological Assessment*, *31*, 878–894. https://doi.org/10.1037/pas0000714.

Serin, R. C. (1996). Violent recidivism in criminal psychopaths. *Law and Human Behavior*, *20*, 207–217. https://doi.org/10.1007/BF01499355.

Serin, R. C., Brown, S. L., & De Wolf, A. H. (2016). The clinical use of the Hare psychopathy checklist—Revised (PCL-R) in contemporary risk assessment. In C. B. Gacono (Ed.), *Personality and clinical psychology series. The clinical and forensic assessment of psychopathy: A practitioner's guide* (2nd ed., pp. 293–310). Routledge/Taylor & Francis Group: New York, NY, US.

Singh, J. P., Grann, M., & Fazel, S. (2011). A comparative study of violence risk assessment tools: A systematic review and metaregression analysis of 68 studies involving 25,980 participants. *Clinical Psychology Review*, *31*, 499–513. https://doi.org/10.1016/j.cpr.2010.11.009.

Skeem, J. L., & Cooke, D. J. (2010). Is criminal behavior a central component of psychopathy? Conceptual directions for resolving the debate. *Psychological Assessment*, *22*, 433–445. https://doi.org/10.1037/a0008512.

Skeem, J. L., & Mulvey, E. P. (2001). Psychopathy and community violence among civil psychiatric patients: Results from the MacArthur violence risk assessment study. *Journal of Consulting and Clinical Psychology*, *69*, 358–374. https://doi.org/10.1037/0022-006X.69.3.358.

Skeem, J. L., Mulvey, E. P., & Grisso, T. (2003). Applicability of traditional and revised models of psychopathy to the psychopathy checklist: Screening version. *Psychological Assessment*, *15*, 41–55. https://doi.org/10.1037/1040-3590.15.1.41.

Skeem, J. L., Polaschek, D. L. L., Patrick, C. J., & Lilienfeld, S. O. (2011). Psychopathic personality: Bridging the gap between scientific evidence and public policy. *Psychological Science in the Public Interest*, *12*, 95–162. https://doi.org/10.1177/1529100611426706.

Smith, S., & Edens, J. F. (2013). *Concurrent validity between the HCR-20 (version 3) and the PCL-R among male pre-trial offenders in Texas*. Unpublished data analyses College Station, TX: Texas A&M University.

Tennenbaum, D. J. (1977). Personality and criminality: A summary and implications of the literature. *Journal of Criminal Justice*, *5*, 225–235. https://doi.org/10.1016/0047-2352(77)90041-1.

Vitacco, M. J., Neumann, C. S., & Jackson, R. L. (2005). Testing a four-factor model of psychopathy and its association with ethnicity, gender, intelligence, and violence. *Journal of Consulting and Clinical Psychology*, *73*, 466–476. https://doi.org/10.1037/0022-006X.73.3.466.

Vize, C. E., Miller, J. D., & Lynam, D. R. (2018). FFM facets and their relations with different forms of antisocial behavior: An expanded meta-analysis. *Journal of Criminal Justice*, *57*, 67–75. https://doi.org/10.1016/j.jcrimjus.2018.04.004.

Walters, G. D. (2007). Predicting institutional adjustment with the lifestyle criminality screening form and the antisocial features and aggression scales of the PAI. *Journal of Personality Assessment*, *88*, 99–105. https://doi.org/10.1207/s15327752jpa8801_13.

Webster, C. D., Douglas, K. S., Eaves, D., & Hart, S. D. (1997). *HCR-20: Assessing risk for violence (version 2)*. Burnaby, Canada: Simon Fraser University, Mental Health, Law, and Policy Institute.

Webster, C. D., Eaves, D., Douglas, K. S., & Wintrup, A. (1995). *The HCR-20 scheme: The assessment of dangerousness and risk*. Vancouver, Canada: Forensic Psychiatric Services Commission of British Columbia.

Widiger, T. A., & Lynam, D. R. (1998). Psychopathy and the five-factor model of personality. In T. Millon, E. Simonsen, M. Birket-Smith, & R. D. Davis (Eds.), *Psychopathy: Antisocial, criminal, and violent behavior* (pp. 171–187). New York, NY, US: The Guilford Press.

Widiger, T. A., & Trull, T. J. (1994). Personality disorders and violence. In J. Monahan, & H. J. Steadman (Eds.), *Violence and mental disorder* (pp. 203–226). Chicago, IL: University of Chicago Press.

Wong, S., & Gordon, A. (1998). *Violence risk scale*. Canada: Department of Psychology, University of Saskatchewan.

Wong, S., & Gordon, A. (2000). *Violence risk scale*. Canada: Department of Psychology, University of Saskatchewan.

Wong, S., & Gordon, A. (2003). *Violence risk scale*. Canada: Department of Psychology, University of Saskatchewan.

World Health Organization. (1990). *International classification of diseases and related health problems* (10th ed.). Geneva: World Health Organization.

Yang, M., Wong, S., & Coid, J. (2010). The efficacy of violence prediction: A meta-analytic comparison of nine risk assessment tools. *Psychological Bulletin*, *136*, 740–767. https://doi.org/10.1037/a0020473.

Communicating with psychopaths in law enforcement settings

8

Jeff Thompson, Paulo Barbosa Marques, Laura Alho, and Mauro Paulino

The person you are talking to consistently shows a lack of regard for others' feelings or violates people's rights. Each time you mention his victims, you realize he seemingly refers to them as inanimate objects that are suitable for disposal once they no longer serve his purpose. In a hostage negotiation setting, as time progresses, you begin to realize he seems just as calm as you if not more, despite the chaos reigning outside the building and the audible sounds of hostages crying inside. As your conversation continues, even in such tense and serious events, he displays a demeanor that could easily be described as a charming and convincing.

He tells you stories to try and convince you he is the brightest man you have ever known and the cause of the current predicament and other failings in his life are clearly due to the faults of lesser-minded people. He often tries to gain control of the interaction when he is being questioned by the police, including questioning multiple times if you really are the most experienced person and worthy to be his counterpart. In hostage negotiations, he goes as far as asking you to take a deep introspective reflection to ask yourself, "Are you doing enough to ensure his safety and that of the hostages?"

You are a police officer and your counterpart is demonstrating indicators that correspond with those of a psychopath. In a critical incident, your job might be to get him to voluntarily surrender because he has multiple hostages being held at gunpoint and it is their safety that is your utmost concern. In an investigative interview, your job is to get him to cooperate by talking and gather information that will help guide your investigation. These interactions demonstrate that mastering communication skills is key in the criminal justice and policing landscape.

Introduction

Human communication is one of the most important skills for the harmonious development of an individual.

The selection and even the improvement of emotional expression behaviors throughout the evolution of the species highlights their central role in survival: they ensure the essential of intra- and even interspecific communication, providing group, child-parental, and peer interactions, allowing the definition of hierarchies and leaderships, preserving group cohesion, developing cooperation strategies toward a common objective, effectively defending the territory, ensuring family cohesion and the efficiency of many of the protection measures for the offspring, etc. (Darwin, 1872).

Psychopathy and Criminal Behavior. https://doi.org/10.1016/B978-0-12-811419-3.09989-1

Several studies in the field of developmental psychology demonstrate the importance of communication in the mother–child dyad, considering this early child-parental interaction as a determinant of the child's mental health. The psychiatrist John Bowlby had a significant role in integrating this view of the mother–infant relationship into our understanding of human attachment, eventually leading to the formulation of his important Attachment Theory. According to Bowlby (1988), the newborn shows, from the beginning, that he gives preference to the mother's voice over that of other women, and the bond between mother and child critically depends on the quantity and quality of the interactions they establish with each other. Bowlby's Attachment Theory suggests that due to the critical importance of attachment for the long-term emotional well-being of the infant, evolution has led children to become biologically preprogrammed to form attachments to their caregiver.

This means that from an early age, human beings establish different forms of communication and the quality of their interactions (e.g., infant–caregiver relationship) is crucial in the development of different psychopathological disorders, namely personality disorders, including psychopathy (Alzeer, Michailidou, Munot, & Kyranides, 2019; Kohlhoff et al., 2020; Van Der Zouwen, Hoeve, Hendriks, Asscher, & Stams, 2018).

Psychopathy is characterized by both affective–interpersonal as well as behavioral–lifestyle features. Recent theories point out that the affective–interpersonal facet might result from an inborn deficit, whereas the behavioral–lifestyle facet might be more under the influence of environmental risk factors like neglecting or abusive parenting (Lykken, 1995; Poythress & Skeem, 2006; Skeem, Poythress, Edens, Lilienfeld, & Cale, 2003).

In the domain of parenting, human communication is also central, and if scientific evidence demonstrates that poor parental bonding and childhood physical abuse are both associated with a psychopathic personality (e.g., Gao, Raine, Chan, Venables, & Mednick, 2010), an inconsistent verbal and nonverbal communication may also lead the adult to positively or negatively reinforce certain patterns of behavior in the child. According to the theory of transactional analysis (TA) developed by Eric Berne in the 1950s as a theory of human personality and social behavior and as a comprehensive form of psychotherapy, individuals can develop long-term problems in their ego states, social functioning, and self-efficacy as the result of unfavorable messages from their social context (negative parental messages in early life, lack of developing mature coping mechanisms, intergenerational messages, negative stroke balance), script decisions (accepting or rejecting unfavorable messages via behavior, emotional disconnection, or cognitive styles), life events, and genetics/temperament (Vos & van Rijn, 2021). Thus certain mimic and gestural signs, a certain tone of voice, the adoption of a certain distance (greater or lesser), the option for certain communicational interactions (the "poor thing," or on the other hand, the "rogue") may affect a role in the future of victim or offender, a losing or winning life narrative, a positive or negative existential attitude (Berne, 1972).

The psychopathic "label" and effects on communication

Psychopathy is a complex, multifaceted construct expressing itself in affectively cold, interpersonally deceptive, behaviorally reckless, and often overtly antisocial behavior.

Those with psychopathy often possess an impaired moral conscience, a lack of emotional sensitivity, and social relatedness. According to Hare (1996), psychopaths can be described as intra-specific predators who resort to charm, manipulation, intimidation, and violence to control others and achieve immediate satisfaction of their desires (impulsiveness) and their own selfish needs (narcissism). Lacking feelings for other people, psychopathic individuals act coldly, violating social norms and expectations without any sense of guilt or regret. Their personality attributes typically include a grandiose sense of self-worth and superficial charm, and they often display a seductive behavior in order to manipulate others. Psychopathic personalities are characterized by their intolerance to frustration and inability to accept their mistakes and learn from them. The concept of psychopathy is also associated with lying, deceit, and manipulation (Hare, Forth, & Hart, 1989).

However, labeling the psychopath as a pathological liar can prove problematic in criminal justice settings, namely in the intervention of law enforcement agencies (LEAs) when confronted with a psychopath. There is a wide range of possibilities in which a police officer can interact with a psychopath, whether performing frontline police duties as a patrol officer or at the level of criminal investigation. Probably the markedly communicational contexts in which this social interaction is most likely to occur are police negotiations and investigative interviews.

There is undeniable evidence to suggest that characterizing defendants as "psychopaths" has a considerable detrimental impact that may make jurors more prone to support the death penalty for them (Kelley, Edens, Mowle, Penson, & Rulseh, 2019).

The potential influence of labeling someone as psychopathic (e.g., Berryessa & Wohlstetter, 2019; Kelley et al., 2019; Truong, Kelley, & Edens, 2021) may go beyond the courtroom door and have a far-reaching impact in other interactions with the criminal justice system. For instance, the introduction of the label "psychopath" may well affect the communication process that occurs during a police negotiation or an investigative interview. Labeling a suspect as psychopath, deceptive, or pathological liar can contribute to confirmation bias, a psychological tendency to pursue information that confirms investigators' expectations (Lidén, Gräns, & Juslin, 2018). The label can color law enforcement officers' (LEOs) expectations, which may lead to guilt-presumptive investigative activities, reluctance to gathering and analyzing exonerating evidence, or adopting an accusatorial approach to interviewing (e.g., Hill, Memon, & McGeorge, 2008; Kassin, Goldstein, & Savitsky, 2003; Lidén et al., 2018). For this reason, adopting an information-gathering approach, such as in the cognitive interview model (Geiselman & Fisher, 1988), is regarded as preferable, as opposed to accusatory or confession-driven interviews. However, even in information-gathering interviews, the tactics used by law enforcement officers to accomplish these objectives are subjective and prone to the interviewer's beliefs. This can result in a situation where the interviewer is more likely to formulate accusatory questions and use a higher verb abstraction with negative valence, resulting in a communication process more about proving the interviewer's beliefs to be true and less about fact or truth finding (Adams-Quackenbush, Vrij, Horselenberg, et al., 2020).

If, on the one hand, an individual with characteristics of this nature justifies very careful planning of the operation or interview, what must be avoided is that this label contributes to an eventual presumption of guilt or the adoption of an investigative process conditioned by a confirmatory bias (e.g., Lidén et al., 2018), with serious consequences in the development of rapport or in the establishment of a communication that may prove to be productive in resolving the situation.

Police personnel should establish clearly defined goals prior to interviewing potential suspects. For a person under investigation, the impression of the person having committed a crime is argued to be very significant because it establishes whether police interviewers proceed to interview suspects with a presumption of guilt which, in turn, can predispose an inclination to ask guilt-presumptive and confirmatory questions, as well as using persuasive tactics, and attempt to obtain confessions (Hill et al., 2008; Kassin et al., 2003). If police interviewers presume suspects to be guilty prior to the interview, they would conduct their interviews by seeking or interpreting evidence in ways that are partial to existing beliefs or hypotheses (Minhas & Walsh, 2018).

In the context of police negotiation, the capacity of law enforcement personnel to prove immune to the idea that they may be being deceived or manipulated by the psychopathic subject may prove to be more productive. As will be explored in this chapter, it is essential to adopt a tactical communication, more focused on the individual's behaviors than on the arguments that occasionally prove to be contradictory during the communication. When a negotiator demonstrates interest or curiosity, utilizing active listening skills combined with positive strength statements in contrast to judging or criticizing what the subject is saying, and shows a level of respect by genuinely wanting to hear about his or her (the male pronoun will be used in the remainder of the chapter for brevity purposes) perspective, it can contribute to the success of the operation.

Communication skills when negotiating with psychopaths

Regardless of the style or model used by a crisis and hostage negotiation team (CHNT), the universal strategies include the following: the use of active listening skills, a team concept where CHNT members all play various specific and vital roles, building rapport and demonstrating empathy genuinely in order to influence the subject, joint problem-solving with him or her, continually assessing the situation and adapting when necessary, and working collaboratively with other police units including the tactical team (Greenstone, 1995; Grubb, 2010; Johnson, Thompson, Hall, & Meyer, 2017; McMains, Mullins, & Young, 2020; Miller, 2005; Oostinga, Giebels, & Taylor, 2018; Thompson, 2014a; Vecchi, 2009).

As mentioned previously, the goal of the crisis hostage negotiator is to influence a positive behavioral change in the subject to gain his or her voluntary compliance (Fuselier, 1981; Giebels & Noelanders, 2004; Vecchi, Van Hasselt, & Romano, 2005). The CHNT's purpose is seeking a resolution of the immediate crisis; it is not an attempt to remedy the long-term causes of the crisis or instill new habits in the subject. The core skills to achieving this goal are the effective use of communication skills by the negotiator throughout the incident.

Part of being able to influence the subject (the person the CHNT is engaging) is understanding their thinking, emotions, and behaviors. From a strategic perspective, it makes practical sense to understand the subject's current thinking, emotions, and behavior if the negotiator is seeking to change each of those in the subject in order to influence a behavioral change and ultimately get their surrender. For subjects who might have a mental illness, it is important for the negotiator to be familiar with various mental health conditions, specifically the indicators and symptoms. This gives the negotiator better insight into the tactics, insight, and mindset that is dictating the subject's actions. This is described as empathy and it demonstrates the need for the negotiator to be empathetic (Grubb, Brown, & Hall, 2015; Slatkin, 2005; Strentz, 2006; Thompson, 2015; Thompson, Ebner, & Giddings, 2017).

The incidents law enforcement crisis hostage negotiators are involved in have been described as tense, unpredictable, (potentially) volatile, stressful, and emotionally driven (McMains et al., 2020; Thompson, 2014b; Vecchi et al., 2005). When the subject displays the traits of a psychopath, it further complicates matters due to their corresponding actions, current disposition, and behaviors. This complication is compounded when the psychopathic subject is holding hostages.

Despite these numerous complications, experience and research in psychology, psychopathology, crisis communication, and crisis hostage negotiation have demonstrated that it is possible to not only communicate with a psychopathic subject but it is also possible to negotiate with him and convince him to capitulate.

Among the numerous tasks and functions a CHNT must perform during a crisis incident, diagnosing a person with a mental illness is fortunately not one of them. This is not to dismiss the importance of the team needing to possess an understanding of psychopathology. It is imperative that hostage negotiators have a comprehensive understanding of various mental illnesses, including psychopaths (Ireland, Fisher, & Vecchi, 2011). Although the negotiator is not diagnosing the subject with a mental illness, first and foremost having a thorough and detailed comprehension of mental illnesses (and psychopaths for the purpose of this chapter) is a necessary element of their overall negotiating strategy.

The proficient hostage negotiator has been described as someone who is an effective listener; patient, calm, and stable; flexible, adaptable, and a quick thinker; determined and focused; and emotionally stable (for example, see McMains et al., 2020). The effective negotiator utilizes these skills appropriately based on the individual subject. Thus if the subject is displaying traits and behaviors of a psychopath, it is necessary for the negotiator and entire CHNT to have a substantial understanding of what a psychopath is.

When communicating with a psychopath, it could be foolish for the negotiator to ask the subject to consider the plight of the hostages, although ostensibly one might think this could be a worthwhile tactic. In reality, at best this approach will most likely be fruitless and at worse, it could put the hostages at further risk (Ireland et al., 2011; Strentz, 2006). The psychopathic subject, as already stated, does not care about the consequences of his actions which could have involved innocent people getting hurt (or killed). Even worse, he can view the hostages as "pawns" in his game to achieve something that might not even be instrumental (such as money or speaking to a governmental official) but instead be expressive—he is finding joy in the fear, pain, and suffering the hostages are experiencing (Ireland et al., 2011). Thus by the negotiator pleading for the hostages' well-being could in fact only further increase the subject's perception that he is winning (i.e., *Machiavellian egocentricity* and *coldheartedness*). The psychopathic subject could also absolve himself of blame for their emotional and physical injuries and instead blame the negotiator (i.e., *blame externalization*). Not only can this instill doubt in the negotiator and have him doubt his tactics, the subject can further complicate the incident by using his manipulative abilities to influence the hostages to advocate on his behalf (i.e., *social potency*). What is critical for the negotiator to understand is if he does choose to discuss the hostages with the subject and their release, it should be framed in a manner that promotes the action as being beneficial to the subject, it being directly connected to his own well-being, and that it will be viewed as an advantageous action by the subject.

A major concern with engaging the psychopath is how they embrace the constructs of rapport building and demonstrating empathy. Babiak and Hare's (2019) work regarding psychopaths working in a business environment shows that they use charm and language to display like-mindedness to get the coworker to have trust in the psychopathic coworker where they believe they understand them and they share similar perspectives and values. Of course, the psychopath is not being genuine but rather he is strategically using this to get whatever he wants.

For the negotiator, this calls for much concern. First, he must be sure not to be tricked by the tactics used by the subject into falsely believing he see's things similarly and a bond (or rapport) has been created. Next, the negotiator uses these same skills in a much similar fashion. However, negotiators are trained to use these skills in order to genuinely establish rapport and demonstrate empathy—not to manipulate subjects. By being genuine and having this knowledge, the negotiator can try to ensure the negotiating advantage remains with the CHNT by not being fooled by the subject's attempts at false rapport building.

Further, the CHNT should be mindful of this with how the tactics might be used by the psychopathic subject on a much more untrained and vulnerable audience—the hostages. Without being aware of this, the CHNT can falsely think the hostages are advocating on behalf of the subject due to suffering from "Stockholm Syndrome". In reality, it can be more accurate that the hostages, influenced by the subject, are also trying whatever tactics they can to keep themselves alive which includes being cooperative and trying to develop rapport with the subject (Fuselier, 1999; de Fabrique et al., 2007). Some research has suggested that psychopaths have a keen ability to recognize among a group the most vulnerable persons. In a hostage-taking setting, the subject can use this type of hostage as a pawn to manipulate them into pleading for their lives driving the emotions of everyone, including the CHNT, toward an uncontrollable level while he remains calm. Regardless of the motivating factor, the use of hostages as the communicators instead of the subject negotiating directly with the CHNT has been described as concerning (McMains et al., 2020; Strentz, 2006; Thompson, 2018) for a variety of reasons, including the possibility that the hostages' behavior is understandably being emotionally driven and also potentially irrational.

The negotiator should seek to remain calm, especially in these circumstances while not falling into the same approach of the subject (i.e., treating the hostage as a pawn).

By focusing on wanting to solely negotiate with the hostage taker (instead of communicating with the hostages as well), the negotiator can unfortunately become dismissive of the plight of the hostage and treat him or her like a pawn, similarly to how the subject is. An issue with giving the perception that the CHNT is dismissing the hostage(s) is the hostage might be fooled into thinking the hostage taker cares about their well-being due to the false rapport that has been developed between the two. This can create an inaccurate perception that the negotiator and entire CHNT as being inept, not wanting to genuinely negotiate, and not looking out for the best interests and safety of the hostages.

Worse, this could lead to the hostage feeling abandoned by the CHNT and thus seek to try and take matters into their own hands. This could initiate a downward spiral of events as it can increase the chances of a violent interaction between the hostage and subject. Additionally, this can then lead to the initiation of an unplanned tactical entry by the special operations team because of these actions. All of this can increase the chances of injuries or worse, fatalities.

Another recommendation is acceptance. The negotiator should accept the fact that some people have no conscience and a negotiation with them will not somehow magically give them a conscience that they have lacked their entire life. The CHNT has to be realistic in what they can do and to best prepare to engage the subject with the realistic expectations. The best way for a CHNT is to continually train and include opportunities for constructive criticism. It is better for the negotiator to have their flaws and areas needing improvement to happen during a practice session instead of it occurring during a real-life incident where the psychopathic subject is now using these negotiator flaws to his advantage.

Considering the psychopathic subject can have a penchant for lying, it could be confusing for the negotiator to understand what is truthful while also becoming frustrated with repeated promises being broken. Stout (2006) explains how repeated lies are representative of psychopaths. It is important to focus on the actions of the subject in comparison to what he says. Being aware of both his actions and words allows the CHNT to discern the discrepancies between the two (this is further discussed below).

An important strategy the negotiator may also consider is to provide multiple options where the subject can maintain a sense of control over their outcome and have the sense and perspective as if they are making choice what to do. This can then potentially lead to the subject selecting which surrender option works best for them. This is a demonstration of a basic foundational hostage negotiation skill of joint problem-solving. For the psychopath, having him be part of the process is important as it gives the subject a sense of personal empowerment as it embraces their aggression and uses it constructively (Simon, 2010).

Additional considerations specific to hostage negotiation are maintaining focus, self-control, active listening skills, possessing curiosity and being nonjudgmental, utilizing situational boards and communication logs, and finally, and as previously stated, embracing the traits and behaviors of the psychopath to the CHNT's advantage. Each is further described as follows.

Considering how negotiating with a psychopathic subject has previously been stated as one of the tensest negotiating incidents a negotiator can be involved in (Strentz,

2006), maintaining focus and possessing self-control are necessary for any chances of success to occur. Part of maintaining focus includes not getting baited by the subject, being lured into providing personal information, or beginning to second guess yourself based on the subject's prodding. All of these can be tactics the subject might seek to use. One example of how focus can be maintained is by taking a "timeout," as suggested by Goergen (2006). This can be advantageous for the negotiator when engaging the psychopath, as it allows the negotiator to assess the situation to review both his communicative tactical approach as well as that of the subject. By taking this "timeout," it can "stall for time" (Noesner, 2010), and let the negotiator rationally analyze with the rest of the CHNT what has already taken place. This then can further allow the negotiator to determine what path to take next to seek the release of hostages and the subject's surrender.

Self-control is closely linked to maintaining focus. Effective negotiators have been stated as having to be able to remain calm and emotionally stable (Johnson et al., 2017). In order to handle such tense situations, it is necessary that they continually train and prepare for such incidents. Training is particularly necessary given the how rare actual hostage-taking incidents actually occur (Call, 2003; Thompson, 2014a). Thus, regardless of experience, continually training is not just a suggestion, it needs to be mandatory. Specifically, training should move beyond typical and expected training that includes scenarios and role-play exercises as well as reviewing and understanding mental illnesses. It should be noted that when conducting scenario training and role-play exercises, CHNT's should consider employing improve actors and consult mental health subject matter experts to increase the accuracy and realism of the training.

Enhanced trainings should involve stress control techniques such as breath control, mindfulness practices to ease anxiety, mental rehearsal strategies, understanding how cognitive behavioral therapy practices can be utilized, and how acknowledgment of emotions can help ensure they do not dictate a negotiator's actions. For situations involving a psychopathic subject, self-control is one of the most important traits for a negotiator to possess. Therefore, practices in this area must be well established long before the incident occurs.

Active listening skills are considered to be one of the most important skills that a negotiator must be proficient at in order to be effective and have any hope of gaining the subject's voluntary compliance. Active listening allows slowing a situation down, encourages continued dialogue, deescalates tense and negative emotions, demonstrates empathy, builds rapport between the negotiator and subject, and importantly, it provides valuable information to the negotiator and entire CHNT (McMains et al., 2020).

When used effectively with the psychopathic subject, active listening can contribute toward making valuable gains toward seeking voluntary compliance. Curiosity and being nonjudgmental is connected to the skillful use of active listening skills on the part of the negotiator.

Admittedly the existing research on the psychopath has stated rapport is nearly impossible to establish with the psychopath. However, by utilizing active listening skills, a level of mutual respect can potentially be gained. Showing interest (or curiosity), in contrast to judging what is said, can demonstrate how the negotiator is remaining calm and instead of criticizing what the subject is saying, the negotiator is displaying a level of respect by genuinely wanting to hear about the subject's perspective. When done effectively, this can display the negotiator's level of expertise and credibility, while also demonstrating he is seeking the subject to be an equal counterpart in attaining a mutually suitable solution.

Further, the negotiator can delicately use positive strength statements such as stating how he (the negotiator) is impressed with how intelligent he is (if the subject shares past information) as well as being impressed with how the subject is remaining calm—just like how the negotiator is. This active listening tactic (Thompson, 2020) of "positive strength statements" not only embraces the "stress immunity" trait of a psychopath but it also connects that trait as also being the same as a negotiator. Avoiding the semantic argument of this, when used successful, regardless if you describe this as "rapport" or "mutual respect," the purpose is the same—gaining a perspective change in the subject to see the negotiator as being someone who genuinely wants to hear from him, is not judging his actions (yet noticeably not necessarily agreeing either), and is pointing out his attributes.

Of course, as the negotiator is doing this genuinely, it is not absent of purpose. Instead, the use of active listening skills is strategic and allows the CHNT to gain a deeper insight into the psychopathic subject's perspective and what is motivating him, without ever losing focus of the process (influencing a positive behavioral change) to achieve the goal (surrendering through voluntary compliance).

Crisis incidents for CHNTs include numerous tasks being conducted by a variety of team members while often, due to an assortment of reasons, team members frequently perform more than one of those tasks. Sometimes because of this, the situational boards and communication logs are dismissed unintentionally or on purpose. When negotiating with a psychopathic subject, ensuring the situational boards and communication logs are accurately and consistently updated is paramount and should be considered mandatory. Situational boards help identify important information that the subject has shared (McMains et al., 2020; Thompson, 2017), while the communication logs assist the CHNT team with keeping an accurate timeline of when communication takes place and the important information revealed during each interaction.

Considering a psychopathic trait can include frequently state one thing and do another, these notes will help keep track of both the actions and words of the psychopathic subject. Importantly, it can reveal either the congruence or incongruence between the two. This also includes promises made (such as the release of hostages), specific people they are blaming (blame externalization), and positive aspects of their life (referred to as "hooks" in hostage negotiation terminology). These hooks could then be used to try to lure them toward surrendering. Since the psychopathic subject cares about his own well-being and not others, a specific hook could be their own survival (in congruence with their Machiavellian Egocentricity trait).

Knowledge of these traits and behaviors associated with a psychopathic person allows the CHNT members to understand their subject more deeply. The expert negotiator is then able to use that information to their benefit and try to incorporate it as part of their communication and negotiation strategies. Thus utilizing the traits and behaviors of the psychopath in this manner strategically can benefit the CHNT and should be explored as "Stress Immunity" and "Machiavellian Egocentricity" in the examples already shared. Also shared earlier was having the psychopathic subject feel like an equal partner in the exploration of mutually suitable resolutions due to their inflated sense of their ego. This can be effective as it importantly can counter their impulsive behavior. Specifically, keeping the subject busy and engaged with the negotiator can reduce their impulsive tendencies. This also can take their attention off the hostages, especially if they have made negative statements about them, which would not be surprising as the psychopath is known to be coldhearted. This once again demonstrates how delicate, meticulous, and purposeful the negotiator needs to be with each and every tactic used when communicating with the subject.

A negotiator should consider an attempt at rationalizing how events in the past were not necessarily his fault and (externalizing blame) due to his competence and abilities, the negotiator believes the two of them can work toward a solution that allows him to get out safely. Additionally, by the subject choosing this option, he can continue to make sure people get to hear from him directly about what has happened. Again, playing to his ego, the negotiator can take advantage of this by following that up by asking him, "Besides, who else is better than you to tell your story?"

The above are a few examples of what can often be seen as negative traits and behaviors of the psychopath (understandably), can now be used by the negotiator as part of their positive approach to work toward resolving the incident safely. Considering how intelligent the psychopathic subject could be, the negotiator should be reminded that they are part of a team and the team concept can further help explore the best possible approaches and when to importantly adapt if necessary (McMains et al., 2020).

It is important to note how each of the skills shared are interconnected and when used successfully, one contributes to the effective use of others. Unfortunately, the same is true for the opposite—when used inefficiently, the "contagion" impact is also felt in a negative way. Therefore, the negotiator must remember how all of the skills, techniques, and strategies work in a gestalt manner where each must be used purposefully in a manner that understands the implications it has in the immediate moment and for subsequent moments later during the incident.

Conclusions

Police officers are regularly tasked with the resolution of incidents involving antisocial behavior. However, conflict resolution and achieving compliance is not limited to the use of force (Vecchi et al., 2005). Therefore proficiency in communication and negotiation skills aiming at establishing a productive human interaction with antisocial or psychopathic individuals is needed.

Communication skills can influence human behavior and decision making in several ways that may impact the effectiveness of key policing tasks, such as the investigative interviewing of suspects or crisis and hostage negotiations.

Police training manuals and research literature emphasize that establishing and maintaining rapport is crucial to the outcome of police communication-based interventions. Accordingly, Fisher and Geiselman (1992) suggest that empathy, in addition to personalizing the interview, should be one of the guiding principles for developing rapport. Moreover, based on the findings of prior studies, violent offenders and sex crime perpetrators are more likely to disclose information and confess during a police interview if the investigators develop a positive, empathic, nonjudgmental, respectful, and humanitarian interview style.

While information disclosure is an important investigative interview outcome per se, the unique nature of the crimes committed by psychopaths is such that the importance of this outcome is heightened. It is possible that the psychopathic personality features of the suspect and the type of offense perpetrated influence the way the investigator conducts the investigative interview, which in turn might affect the likelihood of eliciting information. An example of this dynamics can be observed in Vrij, Mann, Kristen, and Fisher (2007) study showing that an accusatory interview style (indicating a higher degree of suspicion) had a negative effect on the length of suspects' statements and on the amount of verbal cues to deception contained in the statements. Other authors found that the use of active listening skills (indicating a lower degree of suspicion) was positively related with suspects' willingness to cooperate (e.g., Beune, Giebels, & Sanders, 2009).

It is also clear that rapport building is paramount to a successful hostage negotiation. Additionally, the ability to display empathy toward the subject's situation forms a key component of active listening that is used to help establishing rapport and building trust between the negotiator and the person in crisis or hostage taker. Both active listening and empathy are considered core skills that should equip law enforcement crisis hostage negotiators when dealing with a psychopathic subject. This still holds true while acknowledging how hard it could be to develop rapport with a person demonstrating psychopathic traits as this approach can still contribute to mutual respect, influencing the subject, and advancing towards achieving the goal (cooperation or voluntary compliance).

Examining both contexts (i.e., the investigative interview and the crisis and hostage negotiations setting), by analyzing the interplay between police officers and psychopathic suspects, we can conclude that ethically based approaches to interpersonal interactions are associated with a greater likelihood of obtaining the desired outcomes. Even with psychopaths, only a human rights-compliant interpersonal interaction is acceptable and tends to lead to positive results.

References

Adams-Quackenbush, N. M., Vrij, A., Horselenberg, R., et al. (2020). Articulating guilt? The influence of guilt presumption on interviewer and interviewee behaviour. *Current Psychology*. https://doi.org/10.1007/s12144-020-00726-z.

Alzeer, S. M., Michailidou, M. I., Munot, M., & Kyranides, M. N. (2019). Attachment and parental relationships and the association with psychopathic traits in young adults. *Personality and Individual Differences*, *151*, 109499. https://doi.org/10.1016/j.paid.2019.07.009.

Babiak, P., & Hare, R. D. (2019). *Snakes in suits*. New York: Harper.

Berne, E. (1972). *What do you say after you say hello?: The psychology of human destiny*. New York: Grove Press.

Berryessa, C. M., & Wohlstetter, B. (2019). The psychopathic "label" and effects on punishment outcomes: A meta-analysis. *Law and Human Behavior*, *43*(1), 9–25. https://doi.org/10.1037/lhb0000317.

Beune, K., Giebels, E., & Sanders, K. (2009). Are you talking to me? Influencing behaviour and culture in police interviews. *Psychology, Crime & Law*, *15*(7), 597–617. https://doi.org/10.1080/10683160802442835.

Bowlby, J. (1988). *A Secure Base: Parent-child attachment and healthy human development*. New York: Basic Books.

Call, J. A. (2003). Negotiating crises: The evolution of hostage/barricade crisis negotiation. *Journal of Threat Assessment*, *2*, 69–94.

Darwin, C. (1872). *The expression of the emotions in man and animals*. John Murray.

De Frabrique, N., Romano, S. J., Vecchi, G. M., & Van Hasselt, V. B. (2007). Understanding Stockholm syndrome. *FBI Law Enforcement Bulletin*, *7*(76), 10–15.

Fisher, R. P., & Geiselman, R. E. (1992). *Memory-enhancing techniques for investigative interviewing: The cognitive interview*. Charles C Thomas.

Fuselier, G. D. (1981). A practical overview of hostage negotiation (Part I). *FBI Law Enforcement Bulletin*, *50*(6), 2–6.

Fuselier, G. D. (1999). Placing the Stockholm syndrome in perspective. *FBI Law Enforcement Bulletin*, *7*(68), 22–25.

Gao, Y., Raine, A., Chan, F., Venables, P. H., & Mednick, S. A. (2010). Early maternal and paternal bonding, childhood physical abuse and adult psychopathic personality. *Psychological Medicine*, *40*(6), 1007–1016. https://doi.org/10.1017/S0033291709991279.

Geiselman, R. E., & Fisher, R. P. (1988). The cognitive interview: An innovative technique for questioning witnesses of crime. *Journal of Police and Criminal Psychology*, *4*, 2–5. https://doi.org/10.1007/BF02806548.

Giebels, E., & Noelanders, S. (2004). *Crisis negotiations: A multiparty perspective*. Veenendaal, The Netherlands: Universal Press.

Goergen, M. G. (2006). *Crisis negotiators field guide*. Minneapolis, MN: Eagle Training.

Greenstone, J. L. (1995). Tactics and negotiating techniques (TNT): The way of the past and the way of the future. In M. I. Kurke, & E. M. Scrivner (Eds.), *Police psychology into the 21st century* (pp. 357–371). Lawrence Erlbaum Associates, Inc.

Grubb, A. (2010). Modern day hostage (crisis) negotiation: The evolution of an art form within the policing arena. *Aggression and Violent Behavior*, *15*, 341–348.

Grubb, A., Brown, S., & Hall, P. (2015). Personality traits and coping styles in UK police officers: Do negotiators differ from their non-negotiator colleagues? *Psychology, Crime & Law*, *21*, 347–374.

Hare, R. D. (1996). Psychopathy: A clinical construct whose time has come. *Criminal Justice and Behavior*, *23*, 25–54.

Hare, R. D., Forth, A. E., & Hart, S. D. (1989). The psychopath as prototype for pathological lying and deception. In J. C. Yuille (Ed.), *Series D: Behavioural and social sciences: vol. 47. Credibility assessment. Nato science*. Dordrecht: Springer. https://doi.org/10.1007/978-94-015-7856-1_2.

Hill, C., Memon, A., & McGeorge, P. (2008). The role of confirmation bias in suspect interviews: A systematic evaluation. *Legal and Criminological Psychology*, *13*, 357–371. https://doi.org/10.1348/135532507X238682.

Ireland, C., Fisher, M., & Vecchi, G. (Eds.). (2011). *Conflict and crisis communication*. London: Routledge.

Johnson, K. E., Thompson, J., Hall, J. A., & Meyer, C. (2017). Crisis (hostage) negotiators weigh in: The skills, behaviors, and qualities that characterize an expert crisis negotiator. *Police Practice and Research*, *19*(5), 472–489. https://doi.org/10.1080/15614263.2017.1419131.
Kassin, S. M., Goldstein, C. C., & Savitsky, K. (2003). Behavioral confirmation in the interrogation room: On the dangers of presuming guilt. *Law and Human Behavior*, *27*, 187–203. https://doi.org/10.1023/A:1022599230598.
Kelley, S. E., Edens, J. F., Mowle, E. N., Penson, B. N., & Rulseh, A. (2019). Dangerous, depraved, and death-worthy: A meta-analysis of the correlates of perceived psychopathy in jury simulation studies. *Journal of Clinical Psychology*, *75*(4), 627–643. https://doi.org/10.1002/jclp.22726.
Kohlhoff, J., Mahmood, D., Kimonis, E., Hawes, D. J., Morgan, S., Egan, R., et al. (2020). Callous–unemotional traits and disorganized attachment: Links with disruptive behaviors in toddlers. *Child Psychiatry & Human Development*, *51*(3), 399–406. https://doi.org/10.1007/s10578-019-00951-z.
Lidén, M., Gräns, M., & Juslin, P. (2018). The presumption of guilt in suspect interrogations: Apprehension as a trigger of confirmation bias and debiasing techniques. *Law and Human Behavior*, *42*(4), 336–354. https://doi.org/10.1037/lhb0000287.
Lykken, D. T. (1995). *The antisocial personalities*. Lawrence Erlbaum Associates, Inc.
McMains, M. J., Mullins, W. C., & Young, A. T. (2020). *Crisis negotiations: Managing critical incidents and hostage situations in law enforcement and corrections*. New York: Routledge.
Miller, L. (2005). Hostage negotiation: Psychological principles and practices. *International Journal of Emergency Mental Health*, *7*, 277–298.
Minhas, R., & Walsh, D. (2018). Influence of racial stereotypes on investigative decision-making in criminal investigations: A qualitative comparative analysis. *Cogent Social Sciences*, *4*, 1. https://doi.org/10.1080/23311886.2018.1538588.
Noesner, G. (2010). *Stalling for time: My life as an FBI negotiator*. New York: Random House.
Oostinga, M. S. D., Giebels, E., & Taylor, P. (2018). "An error is feedback": The experience of communication error management in crisis negotiations. *Police Practice and Research*, *19*(1), 17–30. https://doi.org/10.1080/15614263.2017.1326007.
Poythress, N. G., & Skeem, J. L. (2006). Disaggregating psychopathy: Where and how to look for subtypes. In C. J. Patrick (Ed.), *Handbook of psychopathy* (pp. 172–192). New York, NY: The Guilford Press.
Simon, G. K. (2010). *In Sheep's clothing: Understanding and dealing with manipulative people*. Marion, MI: Parkhurst Brothers.
Skeem, J. L., Poythress, N., Edens, J. F., Lilienfeld, S. O., & Cale, E. M. (2003). Psychopathic personality or personalities? Exploring potential variants of psychopathy and their implications for risk assessment. *Aggression and Violent Behavior*, *8*(5), 513–546. https://doi.org/10.1016/S1359-1789(02)00098-8.
Slatkin, A. A. (2005). *Communication in crisis and hostage negotiations: Practical communication techniques, stratagems, and strategies for law enforcement, corrections and emergency service personnel in managing critical incidents*. Springfield, IL: Charles C. Thomas.
Stout, M. (2006). *The sociopath next door*. New York: Harmony.
Strentz, T. (2006). *Psychological aspects of crisis negotiation*. Boca Raton, FL: Taylor & Francis.
Thompson, J. (2014a). *Crisis or hostage negotiation? The distinction between two important terms*. March: FBI Law Enforcement Bulletin. Retrieved from https://leb.fbi.gov/2014/march/crisis-or-hostage-negotiation-the-distinction-between-two-important-terms.
Thompson, J. (2014b). Applying hostage and crisis negotiation intervention strategies in commercial dispute resolution. *Alternatives to the High Cost of Litigation*, *32*(4), 52/63–65.

Thompson, J. (2015). *Nonverbal communication and the skills of effective mediators: Developing rapport, building trust, and displaying professionalism*. Doctoral thesis, Griffith University]. Retrieved from https://doi.org/10.25904/1912/3625.

Thompson, J. (2017). Terrorism and hostage negotiation: Law enforcement strategies, preparation, and training (part I). In *The command post, 39/spring edition* (pp. 5–7). https://canadiancriticalincident.com/newsletters.

Thompson, J. (2018). Terrorism and hostage negotiation: Law enforcement strategies, preparation, and training (part II). In *The command post, 40/spring edition* (pp. 5–8). https://canadiancriticalincident.com/newsletters.

Thompson, J. (2020). *Active listening: Using "PRIME SOS+" to recall the critical skills of crisis intervention specialists*. (Training materials).

Thompson, J., Ebner, N., & Giddings, J. (2017). Nonverbal communication in negotiation. In C. Honeyman, & A. K. Schneider (Eds.), *The Negotiator's desk reference*. St Paul: DRI Press. Retrieved from: https://ssrn.com/abstract=3136798.

Truong, T. N., Kelley, S. E., & Edens, J. F. (2021). Does psychopathy influence juror decision-making in capital murder trials? "The devil is in the (methodological) details". *Criminal Justice and Behavior*, *48*(5), 690–707. https://doi.org/10.1177/0093854820966369.

Van Der Zouwen, M., Hoeve, M., Hendriks, A. M., Asscher, J. J., & Stams, G. J. J. (2018). The association between attachment and psychopathic traits. *Aggression and Violent Behavior*, *43*, 45–55. https://doi.org/10.1016/j.avb.2018.09.002.

Vecchi, G. M. (2009). Conflict and crisis communication: The behavioral influence stairway model and suicide intervention. *Annals of the American Psychotherapy Association*, *12*, 32–39.

Vecchi, G. M., Van Hasselt, V. B., & Romano, S. J. (2005). Crisis (hostage) negotiation: Current strategies an issues in high-risk conflict resolution. *Aggression and Violent Behavior*, *10*, 533–551.

Vos, J., & van Rijn, B. (2021). The evidence-based conceptual model of transactional analysis: A focused review of the research literature. *Transactional Analysis Journal*, *51*(2), 160–201. https://doi.org/10.1080/03621537.2021.1904364.

Vrij, A., Mann, S., Kristen, S., & Fisher, R. (2007). Cues to deception and ability to detect lies as a function of police interview styles. *Law and Human Behavior*, *31*, 499–518.

Negotiating with the psychopathic hostage taker

9

James L. Greenstone

Introduction

The psychopath is an amoral, asocial, short-run hedonist. As such, police hostage negotiations with such an actor present special concerns. Detailed research and definitions have been provided by the experts in this field (Babiak & Hare, 2006; Gacono, 2000; Hare, 1993). Here will be identified specific related research, the purpose of negotiations, and the strategies for intervention. Fundamentals of negotiations with the psychopath will be examined and presented.

The psychopath

To successfully negotiate with a psychopath who is holding hostages, it is vital to understand the inner workings of such a person. To begin with, they sound like we sound, they tend to look like we look, and they will use the same words and intellect that we use and that of others we know. They are just like us in so many ways and unlike us in so many other and critical ways. This makes it hard to differentiate the psychopath from the nonpsychopaths with whom we deal on a daily basis. Their behavior, either verbal or nonverbal, is not motivated by or dependent on the moral, social, religious, or ethical guidelines that function within most people. The motivation of the psychopath is governed by those behaviors that satisfy their needs and pleasures regardless of the effects of those behaviors on other people. Moreover, the psychopathic individual will do whatever is necessary to do what they want to do regardless of what they must do to achieve their goal and regardless of the effect of their behavior on others (Greenstone, 1992a, 1992b, 1993, 1994, 1995a, 1995b, 1995c, 2005; Greenstone & Leviton, 1987). The negotiator must recognize the psychopath early and differentiate them from others with whom the negotiator might engage. The psychopath cannot be evaluated on the same basis as we would evaluate other beings who might be holding hostages, or expressing suicidal ideas or who may be involved in domestic disputes. This must be understood, not because it is easy but because it is hard and the endgame will be either positively or negatively affected as a result. Behavior will not lie to the negotiator if the negotiator will follow clues that might be present or the inklings or partial awareness that will inevitably present. The negotiator with the normally derived social and ethical awareness may tend to interpret the behavior of the psychopath according to these ingrained values. In many negotiation or crisis situations, these ingrained values and morals inculcated within will serve

Psychopathy and Criminal Behavior. https://doi.org/10.1016/B978-0-12-811419-3.00005-4

the negotiator well. In negotiating with the psychopath, they may not serve so well or even impede the negotiation process with this type of actor. The psychopath does not care what he must do to achieve what he wants or who he has to hurt to get what he wants. And, while he does not care about the needs of others, except if it serves his plan, he will avoid personal pain and discomfort whenever possible. He will do whatever serves his purposes. Some psychopathic killers have gone on to be model prisoners in prison because it gets them what they want, not because of personal rehabilitation. When they get out of prison, they may engage in the same behavior that resulted in the prison time to begin with. Maybe, if they live long enough, their psychopathic behaviors may burn themselves out in their mid 30s or 40s (e.g. Harpur & Hare, 1994). Marginal existence seems to follow that burnout.

Greenstone, Kosson and Gacono (2000) present some preliminary thoughts and findings that may add clarity to overall understanding in this particular area. Hostage and crisis negotiations team members are not often instructed as to the differentiation between the psychopath and the antisocial personality. There may be considerable value in the differentiation in some cases. Psychopathy has been associated with specific forms of violence, both planned and purposeful. Differently the definitions of the antisocial personality reflect mainly overt behaviors. This could include prison inmates as well as those with mental disorders. The presence of such traits as egocentricity, shallow affect, manipulativeness, and lack of empathy and remorse differentiates the psychopath. To the extent that these differences may be predictive, they may well be helpful to the hostage negotiator (Hare, 1993; McMains & Mullins, 2001).

Specific related research

Direct research relating to the field assessments of psychopathy during police hostage situations is somewhat limited. In the affirmative, the ability to accurately assess psychopathy versus antisocial personality and/or other psychological types in these situations would be extremely valuable. Reasons for the need for such accurate assessments are based, in part, on the predilection for the psychopath to exhibit purposeful and planned violence (Hare, 1991, 1993; Hare & McPherson, 1984; Meloy, 1988; Quinsey, Harris, Rice, & Cormier, 1988).

In an attempt to provide instrumentation for the law enforcement hostage negotiator, a research study was undertaken (Greenstone et al., 2000). To accomplish this very specific goal, items from the Hare Psychopathy Checklist: Screening Version (PCL: SV; Hart, Cox, & Hare, 1995) were modified along with modifications to the Interpersonal Measure of Psychopathy (IMP, Kosson, Steuerwald, Forth, & Kirkhart, 1987). It must be noted that all 12 items of the PCL: SV were retained. The main question concerned whether or not police negotiators could use these instruments to effectively discriminate various hostage-taker types.

In trying to accomplish the research in the most useful manner, it is important to understand that functioning during a hostage situation will often impose multiple limitations on the use of screening instruments.

These include:

1. Negotiators and negotiation team members have many related tasks to be completed and that are ongoing during an active situation (Greenstone, 1998; Hillmann, 1988). It is a very busy time and one with many separate and supportive responsibilities.
2. Complete information about the hostage taker and about the entire situation are often not immediately available. Such information will continue to be received and evaluated throughout the event. This makes the utilization of any instruments difficult and often without a complete accounting of needed information.
3. Hostage situations change rapidly. Any screening instrument must take this into account and yet be useful with partial information, changing information, or with the receipt of updated information. Incomplete information may lead to incomplete or inaccurate assessments under circumstances where accuracy is vital and may be related to life and death issues.
4. Police negotiations are often conducted by telephone or other telecommunications apparatus. Some negotiations may be conducted face-to-face. Any instrument developed must be able to be utilized under either and both situations as well as under austere circumstances. Changing the revised instrument responses to "present" or "absent" is thought to help under these circumstances.

The scoring of the Psychopathy Checklist-Screening Version-Hostage Negotiations (PCL-SV-HN) differed from the usual scoring of the PCL: SV to take into account the specific nature of the active police hostage negotiation situation and the variables that are always present to a more or less degree depending on the specifics encountered. It also takes into account the ongoing nature of intelligence gathering and utilization of other sources to gather needed information. Officers may only receive rudimentary training on the use of the various instruments involved. Basically, the IMP was treated in the same way.

> *In this preliminary project, investigators sought to determine whether (a) the instruments could be integrated into actual hostage situations, (b) the modified instruments could be completed by paraprofessionals in a reliable manner, and (c) psychopathy scores could differentiate among hostage takers regarding real-world behavior.*
>
> *Greenstone et al. (2000, p. 394)*

The results of this study utilizing the PCL-SV-HN were promising in that they tended to support the necessary differentiations that needed to be made in the field under challenging conditions. This will prove helpful in deciding on the need for more cautious strategies and approaches. The results were suggestive that the PCL-SV-HN could be helpful in distinguishing the psychopath in these critical situations. Differentiation between violence prone psychopaths and those seeking "suicide by cop" may be now possible (McMains & Mullins, 2001).

Substantial work is needed on the PCL-SV-HN and its effective in-the-field utilization. Further evaluation of the reliability and validity of the instrument is needed. It is hoped that input from those who utilize this instrument, both effectively and ineffectively will be communicated to the author for use in gaining a better understanding of how negotiators can use it to their collective advantage.

The basics of negotiations

The "shotgun" approach to negotiations on any level is probably misguided to say the least. Talking for the sake of talking or attempting to resolve a hostage or barricade situation by exerting police powers or attitudes is foolhardy. Accurate field diagnosis of the actor with whom you have encountered informs negotiation strategies. The approach that might be effective with a suicidal or psychotic hostage taker may fall flat when attempted with the psychopath and lead to further and more nearly difficult and even deadly consequences. Exceptions can always exist in the field to the standard diagnostics utilized. Not all people who commit crimes are psychopaths. Not all people who are depressed will attempt suicide. Not all who are suicidal are necessarily mentally ill. It is critical that the police negotiator is able to get "inside the head" of the person with whom they are negotiating. Never more important is this than with the psychopath.

The psychopath, often referred to and/or confused with the Antisocial Personality, lacks the moral and social development that most received during their early years and which are reinforced throughout life. It may be of importance to acquaint one's self with the distinctions that are made between the psychopathic personality and the antisocial personality. The main focus and language used here will be focused on the psychopath.

The development of effective negotiation techniques may be based on the understanding by the negotiator that they are encountering someone who is motivated by their own needs and pleasures regardless of what they must do to achieve those needs. The psychopath knows the rules of the "game" and the rules of society but to his way of thinking, these rules do not apply to him. They are there to be used to manipulate others and his satisfaction is the only outcome sought. This actor may well have a history of being unable to sustain meaningful work relationships and is often lacking in the ability to be a responsible parent.

The psychopath may well know the surrounding social norms but fails to accept them.

Practical to the diagnostics done by the negotiator, is the observations that this actor is self-centered to the point that he will satisfy himself even if it means hurting others. Lasting personal relationships are not possible for this individual but are often feigned. Behavior seldom, if ever, lies and should be scrutinized by the negotiator in preparing to engage any hostage taker but especially this one.

In conversation, the psychopath may come across as very cool and even calculating. They may have high verbal skills and can be very manipulative. During the negotiation process, they may even end up interviewing the negotiator. Look for the clues, evaluate them, and use them to the negotiator's advantage. Additionally, this actor may have some difficulty accepting responsibility for his own actions. The result will be to continually blame others for his missteps in life or in the immediate situation.

Of note, as mentioned earlier, is the high possibility that even if incarcerated, this individual may end up being seen as a model prisoner. If it gets him what he wants and needs, the necessary behavior will be utilized and exploited. Also, it should not be surprising that once released from custody that he will return to previous behaviors that satisfy his needs at that time.

Negotiation strategies should always be developed for the particular situation faced by the police negotiator. This involves understanding all that is mentioned here and an in-depth understanding of the various types of persons and problems that may lead someone to take hostages, barricade themselves, or threaten suicide, to mention a few.

If, based on observed behavior and/or historical data, you are possibly encountering a subject who may be psychopathic, avoid getting into a contest of wills; yours against his. To the other extreme, also do not expect interpersonal or human bonding with this person. Such bonding is not uncommon with other types of hostage takers or with those experiencing other types of human crises.

In these particular situations, the use of nonpolice negotiators is not a good idea. There are those who advocate the use of nonpolice negotiators in other type of hostage takings or crisis interventions. Utilization of such other here, may only cause the situation to worsen or become more difficult, or both.

Additionally, with the psychopath, the main motivators by the negotiator for the actor will be a threat to their own ego or the positive stimulation of that ego. This individual will avoid causing harm, or having harm caused, to himself. He may also respond to those comments or actions that he perceives makes him the good guy or the hero in these situations. To some degree, the release of hostages may be gained in this way. If presented well by the negotiator, the taker may be able to believe that he is the "good guy" or the "hero" for the release of captured individuals, children, the sick and injured, etc.

The negotiator should attempt to keep the subject in a problem-solving mode. Also, always remember the taker's egocentricities. Stay reality oriented. The demands of the psychopath in these situations will usually be realistic and precise.

In almost all hostage taking, barricaded, and crisis situations when negotiators are properly trained and given the time necessary to negotiate, the result is peaceful resolution with minimal injuries, if any, to either side. A major exception to that outcome rule is when someone has decided to end their own life and does so. Otherwise the rule seems to apply. Not only does it apply, but surrender usually follows without tactical intervention. The actor is "talked" out.

Another exception to high success rates without tactical intervention is the endgame with the psychopath. Although every attempt must still be made through negotiations to end such a situation, negotiators must be aware that the solution here may need to be a tactical one.

Suggested negotiation strategies

Entering into negotiations should never be taken lightly or without due consideration. The fate of the negotiations itself, and perhaps the fate of those involved, will be determined by what the negotiator does at the outset of negotiations and even before. The serious business of negotiating with a hostage taker or with persons in crisis requires special care. This care includes doing the following (Greenstone, 1992a, 1992b, 1993, 1994, 1995a, 1995b, 1995c, 1997, 2005, 2015; Greenstone & Leviton, 1987):

1. Prepare and know your opening statement to the subject prior to making contact. Without this, you may lose the chance to set up meaningful communications.
2. Early in the negotiations, ask the subject to surrender and to come out. Attempting this can lead to early, often unexpected success.
3. If the subject will not respond favorably to your early attempt to come out, move on from there and come back to this request later as appropriate. Do not press the point. Just move on.
4. Try to ignore the hostages. Focus on the hostage taker. Make the taker the focus of your attention. The rest will follow.
5. Use cover to provide for your own security, as needed and as appropriate.
6. Do not tell the hostage taker "No." The term is too final and may lead to undesirable results. Work around things that you cannot do or situations that you cannot affect.
7. Avoid volunteering information to the subject. Too much, too fast can be dangerous.
8. Let the hostage taker talk about whatever they might want to talk about. This is especially important early in the negotiations.
9. If at a loss for words in a particular instance during negotiations, repeat the last statement uttered by the taker or use "pat" phrases or "minimal encouragers." Sometimes, something as simple as a well-placed grunt will work very well.
10. Try to make the hostage taker feel as though they are important to you. You are there to listen to them and to help them to get out of their present circumstances.
11. Pay attention to the demands made by the taker. Write them down rather than trusting them to memory. Avoid trivializing demands that are made. Acknowledge them.
12. Use the hostage taker's first name during negotiations, as appropriate. If in doubt, ask permission.
13. Let the subject talk as they need to. Try not to cut them off when they are speaking. Pay attention to what is said. Take notes as possible rather than trusting your memory. This will help avoid negotiator errors.
14. Always listen and observe carefully to what is going on in the forefront and in the background of the conversation.
15. Do not make promises to the hostage taker that you cannot keep or do not intend to keep. If lying is absolutely necessary, lie only about big things and never about small things.
16. Do not offer your evaluation of the beliefs stated by the subject. Remember, that is the way that they see things at the moment.
17. Let the subject know that you are really trying to understand their points of view as expressed. Agreement or disagreement is not necessary.
18. Remember that accepting the taker's point of view is not the same as agreeing with that point of view.
19. Make the subject work for everything they may get or receive.
20. Be sure to review the earlier steps prior to beginning any negotiations and regardless of how much experience the negotiator may have.

In addition, the understanding of certain risk factors when negotiating with the psychopath and others may be helpful at this point. First developed by the Federal Bureau of Investigation, a list of high-risk factors in a hostage or barricade situation has been identified to assist negotiators. These factors provide indicators suggesting a substantial risk of violence in the particular situation at hand. Note that the cumulative value of the factors may indicate even greater risk. If any of the factors are identified, SWAT and command should be notified of the risk and of the potential need for tactical intervention in order to resolve the situation. Negotiations should continue, if possible. At the point at which negotiations are no longer possible, SWAT and command should again be notified. A tactical resolution should be considered and planned. Although not an exhaustive list, some of the factors include the following:

1. The actions of the subject in this particular hostage or barricaded scene would lead one to conclude that he or she wanted to get the police involved with him or her at this time. The actions of the subject were purposeful in this regard.
2. The person being detained by the subject was specifically selected rather than being held as a matter of random circumstance. The subject may have had, or could be currently having, some sort of involvement with the selectee.
3. The police have been called to deal with this subject before. The situation may have been similar to the current one, but also may have involved personal violence, restraining orders, the court system, or other similar problems.
4. Detention of another person without substantive demands, as would be found in a true hostage situation.
5. Threats against the person being detained that seem to be personal rather than general in nature. A hostage taker, for instance, may make threats to hurt or kill someone for not doing as he or she asks during the siege. This individual seems to personalize the threats, and it may seem that they stem from something ongoing between the two individuals.
6. This actor has done this type of thing before.
7. When you evaluate the stress level present in the subject's life, either currently or in the recent past, it is high and extremely significant to the person. The actor may be in crisis or have experienced singular or multiple crisis situations in his or her life that are not resolved or that they believe cannot be resolved.
8. Remember, crisis is in the eye of the beholder. If the subject thinks that he or she is experiencing a crisis, for the subject, he or she is in crisis. It is important to understand the subject within this framework in order to be successful.
9. The background and rearing of the subject in this situation is such that he or she believes that he or she cannot back down without being personally degraded as a person. For instance, the subject's reluctance to surrender seems to be tied more to what others will think than to the practicality of peacefully resolving the situation and getting on with life. There is no "honorable" way out, would be another example. Negotiations may seem to be productive with this person, and then turn sour for seemingly no other explainable reason.
10. As part of the crisis, or impending crisis, in the subject's life, he or she feels that there is no one to whom they can turn for nurture and/or support. The subject feels alone and isolated without the social support systems that most of us have and can turn to in times of severe stress and crisis. This should not be interpreted to mean that no such systems exist; only that the subject believes that they are nonexistent or nonavailable.
11. The subject tells you that he is going to commit suicide. Take this seriously regardless of the context. People who talk about suicide do take their own lives. As you may see, this statement of intent may be tied to some of the other factors mentioned. Even if the subject recants the threat, continue to monitor for the possibility of suicide, and actively make plans to counter such an attempt and/or to suggest a rescue of the subject.

12. The subject's verbalizations seem to change direction and sound more and more like a final spiritual confession. This may happen in combination with a suicidal statement or seem to stand alone. Remember that the direction in which they are headed is the same. The subject may ask you to tell his or her family certain things, or to have someone retrieve certain documents for him or her, etc. The subject may ask for extended time off of the phone in order to "take care of some things" or to "make some decisions." Listen carefully for this change of emphasis. From a negotiating standpoint, you may want to interrupt this line of verbalization rather than allow it to continue. If the subject cannot complete the confession, he or she may not feel that he can kill himself. If you suspect suicide, regardless of the verbalizations to the contrary, you may want to try to keep the subject on the phone rather than allowing him or her to disconnect and remain alone.

Conclusions

Police negotiation is a difficult and intense process. Negotiating with a psychopath is no less difficult and also presents special problems and understandings that the negotiator must embrace and solve. It is probably true that the perfect negotiator does not exist. All will make mistakes from time to time. The real effort of the negotiator should be expanded to understand the psychopath and to avoid the potentially negotiation-ending or even career-ending errors (see Greenstone, 2007).

Some of these errors follow with suggested fixes in order to avoid these mistakes:

Error Number 1: Choosing the wrong negotiator for the specific negotiations.

The Fix: Negotiators should be prepared to negotiate each dispute, and recognize that they may not be successful with every dispute. The skills of one negotiator may be better suited for a particular situation and not for another. Prepare your team with multiple skills and with multiple negotiators. Use them where they are most effective.

Error Number 2: Not understanding the type of situation to be negotiated.

The Fix: Prior to entering negotiations, take time to understand the specifics presented to you. The more you know the better.

Error Number 3: Timing the negotiations incorrectly.

The Fix: Evaluating when to negotiate and when not to negotiate takes some skill. Certain issues may become relevant at a particular time and not at others. What you say at a particular time or in a particular way may have a greater impact if timed properly based on what you observe happening in the negotiations. Bargaining may not be possible without establishing rapport first. Negotiation is not a single process. It is a multistage involvement.

Error Number 4: Not making meaningful contact with the other party.

The Fix: Negotiators must convey a sense of seriousness and of interest in the process and in the other side. It must appear as though you care about what is going on. This must be demonstrated throughout the process for it to be effective.

Error Number 5: Failing to use appropriate intelligence intelligently.

The Fix: Do your homework. Gather as much information as you can about the other parties to the negotiations. Intelligence information must be used intelligently if it is to have the desired effect on preparations, planning, and delivery. Generally, information is power if gathered and utilized effectively.

Error Number 6: Failure to keep all parties focused on problem-solving.

The Fix: Focus, focus, focus. It is easy to get off-track. And, sometimes you will. Move the negotiations back to the mode of problem-solving. Negotiations revolve around some sort of dispute or perceived problem. The goal is to solve the problem and resolve the dispute. Enlist the other side's help in solving problems. Listen to what they say.

Error Number 7: Not recognizing the strengths and weaknesses of the other side.

The Fix: Negotiations and bargaining do not happen in a vacuum. Each party brings to the table both strengths and weaknesses. Understand theirs. Understand yours. This should be a continuous evaluative process. Don't underestimate either side.

Error Number 8: Not understanding the mind-set of the other party.

The Fix: What is the other side experiencing? How do they see negotiations? What problems and issues do they bring to the table? What is their intention? Are there impending latent problems? Are there hidden agenda that must be uncovered? Pay attention to mind-set and try to understand it.

Error Number 9: Avoiding safety issues.

The Fix: This is a big one. Most nonpolice or nonmilitary negotiators see safety as a secondary issue. It is not. Safety issues can arise in all venues. And, a breach in safety only has to happen one time to ruin the bargaining and perhaps your own security. Always remain aware of what is going on around you or around the actor.

Error Number 10: Negotiating without sufficient time.

The Fix: It takes time to bargain effectively. Arrange for the time you need. Otherwise consider not entering the process until the needed time is available. Try to resolve pressures that you know will affect your time allotment prior to starting the negotiations. Do not succumb to time pressures from anyone, not even your boss. Negotiators can only be successful if they have the time to produce that success.

Error Number 11: Not knowing when to walk away from the negotiations.

The Fix: Before entering negotiations, and based on the best information you have about your side and the other side, what is the best you can do short of a successful negotiated resolution? How will this ultimately serve your needs? What is available to you and what are you willing to do if you cannot reach the desired negotiated outcome? Resolving a dispute by other than negotiations is not a failure. It is a resolution.

Error Number 12: Negotiating without understanding your prime objective.

The Fix: The objectives may change. Understand what the objective is for you and for the other side. Is the objective life, money, power, other. Your objective will not be the same as the other parties to the process. Knowing both yours and theirs can be crucial to outcome.

Error Number 13: Failure to understand the interests of the other side.

The Fix: Generally, we will be aware of our interests in negotiating a subject. Not taking time to attempt to evaluate the interests of the other side could sabotage your efforts. Most of the time, the other party will be more interested in achieving their interests than yours. If you can convey to them that you are also interested in helping them achieve their interests, you may be much more effective in getting both accomplished. Consider that all parties to the negotiations may be able to satisfy their interests. Find a way to make that happen. It will require some work and some imagination.

Error Number 14: Not appreciating the validity of an argument.

The Fix: Just because the other side poses an argument, that does not make it invalid. And, just because you pose an argument, does not automatically make it valid. A legitimate argument must be recognized when it occurs regardless of the origin. Being able to do this affects your credibility and the recognized credibility of the other side.

Error Number 15: Having no sense of alternatives to negotiations.

The Fix: Plan your alternative to negotiations before entering the process. Reevaluate these alternatives continually. Do not be caught in a nonnegotiable situation without a viable alternative to what you are attempting. Alternatives are what you do instead of negotiations. They represent your plan when you may need to terminate negotiations for lack of progress or solution.

Error Number 16: Failure to understand the nature of the relationships between you and the subject with whom you are negotiating.

The Fix: Some relationships may have to survive the negotiations; others will not have this need. Also, the relationship between other parties to the negotiations may be important to understand when doing strategic planning. Additionally, how important is the relationship likely to be between you and the other side when negotiations are concluded, and they are ready to surrender. Plan accordingly.

Error Number 17: Utilizing ineffective communication skills.

The Fix: This is an important one but not an easy one. Most police negotiators think that they are good communicators. Most do not practice these skills. Probably more mistakes are made in this area than in any other. Review the skills and practice them over and over again. The key to successful negotiations will always be effective communications regardless of the forum. Role-play what is to be said, either before or during actual bargaining. Talking, listening, hearing, responding, and all the rest are acquired skills that cannot be underestimated. Above all else, heed this.

Error Number 18: Proceeding without knowing the willingness and ability of the subject to make and abide by their commitments.

The Fix: If more than one actor is involved in the negotiations, always know who the decision-makers are before getting too involved in the process. Evaluate responses to small agreements before entering into big ones. Always know with whom you are doing business. Try to do business only with those who can enter into an agreement should one be reached.

Error Number 19: Entering negotiations without considering options.

The Fix: Options are what you do during negotiations. They are similar to arrows in a quiver. If you are hunting with only one arrow, you better be 100% all of the time. Few of us are. Always know where you will find your next arrow if the current one fails. Opt for options and keep your quiver full.

Error Number 20: Approaching negotiations without first analyzing the perspectives of all parties to the situation at hand.

The Fix: Negotiations do not happen by accident. Hostage, barricaded, and crisis situations arise for a reason. People submit to negotiations for many and varied reasons. Not all of the reasons are consistent with a positive outcome. Some are designed to achieve hidden agenda. In our attempts to be of help, we may lose valuable time and ground by being blindsided because we have not done our homework or have not been good observers.

Error Number 21: Taking the attitude of "winner-take-all" and "loser-takes-nothing."

The Fix: Traditionally, many have been taught this approach. We are told that the purpose of negotiations is to take all we can and that the other side's needs and interests are unimportant. Success may be achieved better and quicker if the conveyed goal is for both parties to the issues at hand to come away with what they need to the greatest extent possible. Note that the issue is "need" and is not "want." Careful analysis of the real issues and needs may reveal how this can be accomplished. If you do not look for it, you probably will not find it.

Error Number 22: Adding information to the negotiations, or doing something during negotiations, "for what it's worth."

The Fix: "For what it's worth" is worthless. Just do not do it. Have a reason for everything that you make part of the negotiation process. Adding material "for what it's worth" injects unconsidered variables that may adversely affect the process. Always have a reason to make an insertion. You may not always be correct; however, at least you have attempted to think through the information and to decide on its relevance and helpfulness.

Error Number 23: Failure to practice negotiation skills.

The Fix: Practice, practice, practice. Practice individual skills. Practice team skills as a team.

Error Number 24: Treating the negotiations as an individual endeavor rather than a team process.

The Fix: Everyone understands that two heads are better than one. Imagine the power of a team when properly deployed and utilized to resolve a hostage, barricaded, or crisis situation. Teamwork is the key to success in negotiations. All members of the team support the efforts of the primary negotiator. All have input to the process. A team wins together and loses together.

Error Number 25: Failure to remember and to avoid the other 24 errors.

The Fix: Pay close attention to the possible errors. The success of your next encounter may well depend on it. Postevent critiques should be open and honest attempts to understand and to correct any of the errors made. Even successful events should be critiqued for errors and for recommended improvements.

This is a reminder that successful hostage negotiations may well depend on our understanding of the possible errors that a negotiator might make and the need to avoid them. The errors occur because of the assumptions we make, our failure to acquire and practice the needed skills, or because we have never taken the time to think about them. The previous mentioned errors have all happened to some hostage negotiator somewhere and at some time in the performance of their duties. They are real and really do require the needed attention by all working in this field. Avoiding errors will increase effectiveness. Negotiating with the psychopath makes attention to these details essential (Greenstone, 2017).

References

Babiak, P., & Hare, R. (2006). *Snakes in suits: When psychopaths go to work*. New York: HarperCollins Publishers.

Gacono, C. (2000). *The clinical and forensic assessment of psychopathy: A practitioner's guide*. New Jersey: Lawrence Erlbaum Associates, Publishers.

Greenstone, J. L. (1992). The art of negotiating: Tactics and negotiating techniques—The way of the past and the way of the future. *Command: Journal of The Texas Tactical Police Officers Association*, *1*, 11–18.

Greenstone, J. L. (1992). The negotiator's equipment: Tools of the trade; mark of the professional. *Law Enforcement Product News*, *10*, 1–3.

Greenstone, J. L. (1993). Dr. Greenstone's 150 laws of hostage and crisis negotiations. *Police and Security News*, *15*, 36–38.

Greenstone, J. L. (1994). Crisis intervention skills training for police negotiators in the 21st century. *Journal of Police and Criminal Psychology*, *10*, 57–61.

Greenstone, J. L. (1995a). Tactics and negotiating techniques (TNT): The way of the past and the way of the future. In M. I. Kurke, & E. M. Scrivner (Eds.), *Police psychology into the 21st century* (pp. 357–371). Hillsdale, New Jersey: Lawrence Erlbaum Associates.

Greenstone, J. L. (1995b). Hostage negotiations team training for small police departments. In M. I. Kurke, & E. M. Scrivner (Eds.), *Police psychology into the 21st century* (pp. 23–48). Hillsdale, NJ: Lawrence Erlbaum Associates.

Greenstone, J. L. (1995c). Crisis intervention skills: Training for police negotiators. *Police Chief*, *62*(8), 30–34.

Greenstone, J. L. (1997). Krisenintervention: Mitteilungen/crisis intervention communications in hostage and crisis negotiations. In *Paper and presentation to the Internationale Seminar-Fuhrung, Einsatz, Ausbildung und Ausstaattung von Specialeinheiten, Polizei-Fuhrungsakademie, Munster, Germany, August*.

Greenstone, J. L. (1998). *Basic course for hostage and crisis negotiators*. Arlington, TX: Regional Police Academy, North Central Texas Council of Governments.

Greenstone, J. L. (2005). *The elements of police hostage and crisis negotiations: Critical incidents and how to respond to them*. Binghamton, NY: The Haworth Press, Inc.

Greenstone, J. L. (2007). The twenty-five most serious errors made by police hostage and crisis negotiators. *Journal of Police Crisis Negotiations*, *7*(2), 107–116.

Greenstone, J. L. (2015). *Emotional first aid: Field guide to crisis intervention and psychological survival*. Duluth, MN: Whole Person Associates.

Greenstone, J. L. (2017). *On Policing: From swords into plowshares*. CreateSpace Independent Publishing Platform.

Greenstone, J. L., Kosson, D. S., & Gacono, C. B. (2000). Psychopathy and hostage negotiations: Some preliminary thoughts and findings. In C. B. Gacono (Ed.), *The clinical and forensic assessment of psychopathy: A practitioner's guide* (pp. 385–404). Hillsdale, NJ: Lawrence Erlbaum Associates.

Greenstone, J. L., & Leviton, S. (1987). Crisis intervention. In R. Corsini (Ed.), *Concise encyclopedia of psychology*. New York: John Wiley Interscience.

Hare, R. D. (1991). *Manual for the revised psychopathy checklist*. Toronto, Canada: Multi-Health Systems.

Hare, R. (1993). *Without conscience: The disturbing world of the psychopaths among us*. New York: Pocket Books.

Hare, R. D., & McPherson, L. M. (1984). Violent and aggressive behavior by criminal psychopaths. *International Journal of Law and Psychiatry*, *7*, 35–50.

Harpur, T. J., & Hare, R. D. (1994). Assessment of psychopathy as a function of age. *Journal of abnormal psychology*, *103*(4), 604–609. https://doi.org/10.1037//0021-843x.103.4.604.

Hart, S. D., Cox, D. N., & Hare, R. D. (1995). *Manual for the psychopathy checklist: Screening version (PCL:SV)*. Toronto: Multi-Health Systems.

Hillmann, M. (1988). Tactical intelligence operations and support during a major barricade/hostage event. *Police Chief*, *55*(2), 18–30.

Kosson, D. S., Steuerwald, B. L., Forth, A. E., & Kirkhart, K. J. (1987). A new method for assessing the interpersonal behavior of psychopaths: Preliminary validation studies. *Psychological Assessment*, *9*, 89–101.

McMains, M. J., & Mullins, W. C. (2001). *Crisis negotiations: Managing critical incidents and hostage situations in law enforcement and corrections*. Cincinnati, OH: Anderson Publishing Company.

Meloy, R. (1988). *The psychopathic mind: Origins, dynamics and treatments*. Northvale, NJ: Jason Aronson, Inc.

Quinsey, A., Harris, B., Rice, D., & Cormier, C. (1988). *Violent offenders: Appraising and managing risk*. Washington, DC: American Psychological Association. Related Readings and Resources.

Interviewing psychopaths: Toward a science of investigative interviewing of psychopathic suspects

10

Paulo Barbosa Marques and Michel St-Yves

Introduction

The word "psychopath" is often associated with serial killers and sadistic rapists. And for good reason since most of these are psychopaths (Porter, Woodworth, Earle, Drugge, & Boer, 2003). However, the vast majority of psychopaths are not serial killers or sadists. This personality disorder affects approximately 1% of the general population and up to 25% of the prison population (Hare, 1998; Neumann & Hare, 2008). There are mainly violent repeat offenders and sex offenders (Serin, Peters, & Barbaree, 1990), whose crimes are often premeditated (Herve & Yuille, 2007), but also perpetrators of financial crimes such as Babiak and Hare (2006) called "Snakes in Suits."

Despite the relatively large number of psychopaths arrested and questioned by the police, there is very little written on this subject. The science of interrogation has taught us that the perception of the evidence and the attitude of the investigator are two of the most determining factors during police interrogation[a] (Alison, Alison, Noone, Elntib, & Christiansen, 2013; Holmberg & Christianson, 2002; St-Yves & Meissner, 2014; Walsh & Bull, 2015; Williamson, 1990). The nature and gravity of the crime can also influence the collaboration of a suspect (Deslauriers-Varin, Lussier, & St-Yves, 2011; Moston, Stephenson, & Williamson, 1992). As well as certain individual factors, such as age, gender, and family status (St-Yves, 2002). But the personality of the suspect is probably one of the most important factors to consider during a police interview. When interviewing a suspect, it is not a crime to be questioned, but first a person who might have committed a criminal offense.

In this chapter, we will see that knowing the profile of a suspect's personality can help to personalize the investigative interview and more easily achieve the objectives. In addition, we will analyze and integrate the contributions of scientific evidence and what constitute best practices in the field of investigative interviewing (namely suspect interviewing in connection with high-risk crimes, such as murder, sexual offenses, and terrorism).

[a] In this text, the word interrogation is used to designate an investigative interview with a suspect.

Psychopathy and Criminal Behavior. https://doi.org/10.1016/B978-0-12-811419-3.00045-5

The evolution of practices in police interrogation

Despite the persistence, to this day, of certain controversial practices (see Kelly & Meissner, 2016; Miller, Redlich, & Kelly, 2018; Snook, Eastwood, Stinson, & Tedeschini, 2010; St-Yves, 2014), police interrogation has greatly evolved since the 1990s. This evolution is linked in large part to the reporting of certain practices deemed unethical and prejudicial to the suspect, to the increasingly frequent presence of a witness in the interview room (lawyer and/or videotape), as well as advances in research in this area. If, in the past, conducting an investigative interview was considered an art, today it can be said that it is a science (St-Yves, 2014). The methods taught are now largely based on science and respect of human rights (Vrij et al., 2017). Such more evidence based, ethical, and human rights-compliant interviewing practices are not only more effective, but also they greatly reduce the risk of false confessions (Gudjonsson, 2021; Gudjonsson & Pearse, 2011) and miscarriages of justice (Poyser & Milne, 2021).

While the accusatorial and confession-based approach known as the Reid technique (Inbau, Reid, Buckley, & Jayne, 2013) and the information-gathering approach, namely the PEACE[b] model (see Clarke & Milne, 2001), have been competing for almost three decades, new science-based interviewing models are emerging and constitute promising practices for the gathering of information from various sources (e.g., Luke, 2021; Surmon-Böhr, Alison, Christiansen, & Alison, 2020). These methods also take a strategic approach to introducing the available evidence against the defendant and identifying contradictions in a narrative (see Bull, 2014; Hartwig, Granhag, & Luke, 2014; May, Granhag, & Tekin, 2017; Oleszkiewicz & Watson, 2021; Walsh & Bull, 2015).

Developed by Fred Inbau and John Reid, the Reid technique (Inbau et al., 2013) has been the predominant interrogation method used by the police in the United States and Canada, with hundreds of thousands of law enforcement agents trained to use the method since the 1960s. It consists of three distinct stages with specific objectives. The process begins with a careful factual analysis of the case, followed by the behavior analysis interview (a nonaccusatory interview designed to gather investigative and behavioral information), followed when appropriate by the Reid nine steps of interrogation aimed at breaking the suspect's resistance (using an accusatory approach based on an assumption of guilt). According to Inbau and colleagues, individuals should be interrogated only when the information obtained from the interview and investigation indicates that the subject is involved in the commission of the crime, which, very often, is based only on a subjective analysis of the suspect's answers and behaviors (Kassin, 2014; Kelly & Meissner, 2016; King & Snook, 2009).

As for the PEACE model, it was developed in the early 1990s as a collaborative effort between law enforcement and psychologists in England and Wales. It was conceived as a way to stem the proliferation of miscarriages of justice that were resulting

[b] PEACE is the acronym of each phase of the interview: preparation and planning; engage and explain; account and clarification; closure; evaluation.

from police interrogations. PEACE is a nonaccusatory, information-gathering approach to investigative interviewing, considered to be effective at generating information while avoiding potential pitfalls associated with accusatory approaches such as false confessions. The PEACE framework is often considered the current best practice and has the advantage of being suitable for interviews with victims, witnesses, or suspects (Bull, 2014; Meissner, Kelly, & Woestehoff, 2015; Milne & Bull, 1999; Russano, Kelly, & Meissner, 2019; Vrij et al., 2017).

Good investigative interviewing practices are based on a better understanding of the psychological processes involved in the interrogation process, as well as factors likely to encourage the collaboration of a suspect. Upon his arrest, the suspect will be informed of his rights (e.g., right to remain silent; right to receive legal advice), then, through respect and listening, the investigator will try to establish an empathetic relationship with him in order to promote his collaboration. Then, the investigator will ask questions to validate certain elements of the investigation and will offer the suspect the opportunity to give his version of the facts. It is only after obtaining this version (if the suspect wishes to explain himself) that the investigator will progressively present him with the evidence (when it is available), thus allowing the suspect to give an explanation or to change his version of the facts. If the suspect continues to deny or decides to exercise his right to remain silent, the investigator will explore his resistance and fears, which are generally associated with legal and personal consequences. When information contributing to the investigation or a confession is obtained, the investigator will try to corroborate as much information as possible in order to ensure its authenticity (see St-Yves & Meissner, 2014, for a detailed description stages of a police interrogation).

Do these procedures apply to all suspects? Are there more effective ways for interviewing a psychopath? We will see in the next section how psychopaths might differ from other suspects, and how important it is to take these differences into account in order to achieve goals.

Preparing to interview a psychopath

Many researchers have argued for the importance of preparing for a suspect's interview, as well as the importance of building rapport with them (see Abbe & Brandon, 2013; Bull & Soukara, 2010; Holmberg & Christianson, 2002; Kelly, Miller, & Redlich, 2016; St-Yves & Meissner, 2014; Vallano & Schreiber Compo, 2015; Vanderhallen, Vervaeke, & Holmberg, 2011; Wachi et al., 2018). Being empathetic and attentive makes it possible to obtain better cooperation from the suspect and to gather more information (Alison et al., 2013; Brimbal et al., 2021; Cleary & Bull, 2019; Kieckhaefer, Vallano, & Compo, 2013; Redlich, Kelly, & Miller, 2014; St-Yves, 2014; Vanderhallen et al., 2011; Walsh & Bull, 2010a, 2010b, 2012a, 2012b).

The investigative interviewing of a psychopathic suspect is an act that does not leave any police investigator indifferent. As such, it is essential that the planning phase of the interview is taken with the utmost seriousness, constituting the ideal time for the researcher to reflect on preexisting attitudes, expectations, biases, preconceived notions, which can enhance a guilty presumptive mindset. This prior reflection on the characteristics of the investigator and other intervening parties that may exist (e.g., interpreter) allows anticipating and resolving any constraints in establishing an empathetic relationship with the suspect. The establishment of rapport is likely not the only means by which interviewers could overcome resistance and increase information disclosure. For example, contextual factors that are independent of an interviewer's tactics can influence the reporting of information by interview subjects (Dawson et al., 2017; Dianiska et al., 2019; Hoogesteyn et al., 2019; Hoogesteyn et al., 2020a, 2020b).

Goodman-Delahunty et al. (2014) examined an international sample of practitioners and high-value detainees ($N=64$) and concluded that noncoercive physical interview settings were associated with an increase in disclosures of incriminating information by the detainees. The authors noted that the comfortable setting may have fostered rapport, which in turn facilitated disclosure.

Emerging research suggests a positive outcome of context manipulations in investigative interviews quality. Dawson et al. (2017) manipulated both architectural and interior features of the interview room and concluded that the larger physical spaciousness of the room resulted in higher information disclosure. Similarly, Hoogesteyn et al. (2019) offered compelling evidence that spaciousness of the room is related with interviewees' report of more positive perceptions of rapport building. Hoogesteyn et al. (2020a) examined the beliefs of detainees and general population individuals on two different police interview environments, one "typical" room and one designed to be more comfortable and inviting. Both detainees and lay people rated the decorated room as eliciting higher feelings of cooperation, supporting that the interview room atmosphere could affect suspects' cooperation efforts, echoing Goodman-Delahunty et al.'s (2014) findings.

In addition to the physical spaciousness of the interview room, other contextual aspects are relevant to investigative interviewing practice. Based on the *context manipulation* domain from the Kelly et al.'s (2013) taxonomy of interviewing techniques, Hoogesteyn et al. (2020b) examined a sample of 81 police investigators to determine what other context manipulation techniques investigators use and believe to be useful in their interviewing practice. Considering their physical appearance (i.e., wearing formal or casual clothing), the seating distance, and making the room appear warm and comfortable were (respectively) reported to be the three most useful techniques. Investigators reported that leaving suspects alone in the interview room was helpful for allowing them time to think and take a mental break from the interview. Conducting the interview in a small room was reported as the least useful technique.

Concluding, context manipulation techniques can be used to foster a productive investigator–suspect relationship, rather than control. The same assumptions apply to the preparation of the context where the investigative interview of a psychopathic suspect will take place. Rather than opting for an uncomfortable and hostile space, investigators should opt for a room that conveys respect, dignity, and neutrality and that allows and encourages suspects to speak freely.

Preparation was considered by investigators to be a key element of successful investigative interviews with suspects (Soukara et al., 2002), and the skillful investigator reflects on the best way to structure the interview (Baldwin, 1993). In fact, there has been found an association between its undertaking and the interview aim of gaining comprehensive information/evidence (Walsh & Bull, 2010a, 2010b).

Despite the importance of planning the interview ahead, preparation has been often found to be misunderstood and underutilized (Clarke & Milne, 2001; Walsh & Milne, 2007). The main reason given for negligence in relation to this important phase of any investigative interview was the lack of time to undertake the task. Moreover, in a study with South Korean investigators, Kim et al. (2018) found that investigators' propensity to plan was less associated with perceived time pressures, but more so with (i) organizational cultures (e.g., overt or more subtle messages that signal to interviewers that interview planning is not always necessary), (ii) officers' beliefs in their own ability to interview effectively without planning, and (iii) officers suggesting that they often conduct interviews having already made enough investigative enquiries and evidence gathering to know what had happened (without entertaining other possibilities or testing their hypothesis robustly).

Contrary to an important principle of modern investigative interviewing—retaining an open mind—some investigators assume the suspect's alleged culpability even before starting the interview (Walsh & Bull, 2011; Walsh & Milne 2007). Such presumptions of guilt are even more likely to occur with suspects with a psychopathic personality and are also thought to lead to insufficient preparation (and most likely insufficient investigative inquiries, information and evidence gathering). The potential effects of investigators generating a single hypothesis prematurely, as to what happened to whom and by whom, and its impact on an investigative interview with a psychopath may well result in investigative failure. Thus proper interview preparation includes obtaining information about the interviewee under a neutral stance.

Several sources of information can help in drawing the psychological profile of a suspect: social environment, institutional files, criminal history and, of course, an interview with the suspect. Determining the suspect's profile allows the interviewer to know who he is dealing with, to position himself, and then to adopt specific strategies. In other words, this allows for a "tailor-made" interrogation (see St-Yves, 2004b).

The identification of a psychopathic profile is usually done by the identification of specific criteria identified by Hare (1991). These are 20 traits that characterize psychopathy. The subject does not need to have all of the features. Although the Hare Psychopathy Scale cannot be used during an interview to make a diagnosis, the psychopath rarely goes unnoticed. The investigator must be prepared to manage the relationship based on certain behaviors typical of psychopaths, including superficial charm, lack of remorse and empathy, grandiosity, lying and manipulation. He can even sometimes be charismatic. In order to appear credible in the eyes of the suspect, the investigator must project the image of a confident and in control investigator, who controls his file. The psychopath will often try to destabilize the investigator, identify his weaknesses (and that of the investigation), and then exploit them (O'Toole et al., 2012; Quayle, 2008; St-Yves, 2004b). In the eyes of the suspect, the way the interviewer behaves and conducts the interview demonstrates the strength of the criminal evidence held against him.

Because psychopaths are narcissists and like to feel important, Quayle (2008) recommends dressing in a professional manner and using titles of civility such as "Mr," or any other official and appropriate title. Also, because one of the traits of psychopathy is the need for stimulation—the psychopath gets bored easily—O'Toole et al. (2012) suggest using two investigators, or finding a dynamic and interactive way to questioning. This can be done by using visual outputs, such as sketching while narrating (Deeb et al., 2021; Eastwood et al., 2018).

According to Perri (2010), postoffense behavior is an important indicator of the presence of traits of psychopathy and that investigators cannot ignore when developing an interview strategy. Psychopaths are more likely not to display traumatic behaviors after the offense because murder is more often instrumental and committed without emotion (Hakkanen-Nyholm & Hare, 2009).

Some authors tried to summarize the set of tasks to be considered when planning the interview (e.g., Kim et al., 2018; Schollum, 2005), the following being essential in the specific case of the interview with a psychopath:

- Understanding the purpose of the interview;
- Obtaining background information on the incident under investigation;
- Obtaining background information on the interviewee;
- Anticipate and have a strategy to face the suspect's potential defenses;
- Defining the aims and objectives of the interview;
- Organizing the sequence of themes to explore and questions each need;
- Understanding and recognizing the points to prove;
- Assessing what evidence is available and from where it was obtained;
- Assessing what evidence is needed and how it can be obtained;
- Considering the method/order of disclosing items of evidence/information;
- Understanding the legislation, guidelines, and special considerations;
- Preparing the interview setting and other logistics (e.g., interpreter, lawyer).

The establishment of rapport with a psychopath

The relational dimension is very important in an investigative interview. We now know that establishing rapport with the interviewee has a positive impact not only on the course of the interview but also on its outcome (see Alison et al., 2013; Holmberg & Christianson, 2002; St-Yves, 2006, 2014; Vanderhallen et al., 2011; Walsh & Bull, 2012a, 2012b).

Despite the construction of rapport to which the important phase of "engage and explain" refers being a central element of an effective information-gathering interview based on the PEACE framework, its definition in the scientific literature is not consensual. However, the various definitions seem to highlight common attributes, such as communication, mutuality, positivity, respect, successful outcomes, and trust (Neequaye & Mac Giolla, 2021). Vanderhallen et al. (2011) based their definition on a "working alliance." On the other hand, this alliance is built on the basis of trust and respect between the investigator and the interviewee (Russano et al., 2014) and coordinated in a positive way toward mutual understanding of goals and needs (Tickle-Degnen & Rosenthal, 1990).

While nuanced differences in rapport definitions persist, there is a general agreement, which has been forged through the literature, as to the benefits of both building and maintaining rapport in interviews. Such benefits have been those pertaining to the gathering of more complete (and more reliable) information (Redlich et al., 2014).

Unlike people who feel emotion and feel remorse for their crime, interrogation with a psychopath is like a chess game (St-Yves, 2004b). The interview should be based on a nonemotional format and the dialogue should be structured around specific facts and evidence (Perri & Lichtenwald, 2008). The investigator should also avoid projecting his own emotions (for example, regarding the disturbing nature of an offense) when considering an interview strategy (Quayle, 2008). Psychopaths often perceive emotionality as a sign of weakness. Quayle (2008) also recommends that the interviewer shows genuine interest in the interviewee and his narrative.

This notion of nonemotionality and genuine interest calls for a stance of neutrality based on listening actively to what the interviewee is narrating. In fact, studies conducted with prisoners, including violent and sex offenders, conclude that suspects strongly endorse rapport-building strategies and techniques that promote respect, humanity, and neutrality (see Cleary & Bull, 2019; Kebbell et al., 2010; May et al., 2021). Further, using measures drawn from Miller and Rollnick's (2002) motivational interviewing paradigm, rapport in interviews with actual terrorist suspects has been found to overcome initial resistance (Alison et al., 2013).

According to Quayle (2008), the psychopathic suspect may view the police interview as a "game." He can anticipate questions or try to take control of the interview by talking about it at length, refusing to answer simple questions, asking questions of the interviewers, or trying to provoke reactions from the interviewers. He can try to intimidate the investigator by maintaining direct eye contact, using extended hand gestures and, if possible, invading the investigators' personal space. The more the psychopathic individual feels in control of the interview, the more he will be resistant to attempts to obtain a confession or useful information (Quayle, 2008). It may therefore be necessary to tactfully interrupt the interviewee in order to reframe the interview and subtly elude the questions he is asking.

It is important to note here that not all psychopaths are uncooperative and, most importantly, not all resistance should be viewed as signs of suspects concealing their guilt.

Rapport has been found believed to help facilitate a pathway to the obtaining of reliable confessions (provided by those suspected of serious offenses, such as either sex offenders or murderers) to their wrongdoing (Holmberg & Christianson, 2002; Kebbell et al., 2010; Leahy-Harland & Bull, 2017). In another study with convicted sex offenders, Kebbell, Hurren, and Mazerolle (2006) found that only 20% of these offenders said that they entered interviews with a firm denial strategy, while half of their sample said they were undecided at that initial stage (with the remaining 30% advising that they had decided that they would admit their guilt). According to the authors, the decisions among the 'undecided' half rested on the manner as to how they were treated in the interview. Those offenders, who said they felt that their interviewers were nonjudgmental and respectful, stated that they acknowledged their culpability in the interviews. This finding is consistent with the study conducted by Holmberg and Christianson (2002) also involving convicted offenders. In that research, the authors found an association between interviewing styles and the predisposition to recognize guilt in the interview. That is, those who said that their interviewers adopted a humanitarian style of investigative interviewing were more likely to be found as those who confessed when being questioned.

Obtaining an account and presenting the evidence

The objective of knowing the suspect's version of events is to discover new elements of the investigation and to give him the opportunity to explain himself or even to exonerate himself, because the suspect may be innocent.

The attitudes of interviewers are unlikely to be by themselves the sole pivot on which suspects cooperate. What tactics investigators actually undertake when interviewing a psychopathic individual are also important.

The psychopath tends to be careful, even to remain silent, as long as he does not know what the investigation shows about him. They are calculators and they are interested in the evidence being held by the investigators only for the purpose of knowing whether it is better to collaborate or not. This is why it is recommended to obtain the version of the facts before presenting the evidence (see St-Yves & Meissner, 2014).

Associations between disclosing strong evidence and confessions from suspects have been found in several studies (Cassell & Hayman, 1996; Gudjonsson & Petursson, 1991; Kebbell, Hurren, & Mazerolle, 2006; Kebbell, Hurren, & Roberts, 2006Moston et al., 1992; Sellers & Kebbell, 2009; Soukara et al., 2009; Walsh & Bull, 2012b).

In a study conducted by Leo (1996) in the USA, the author examined 182 interrogations and concluded that certain tactics have a significant effect on a suspects' likelihood of providing information that incriminated them in criminal activity. One of these tactics found in over 90% of the interviews was the police *emphasizing contradictions*, either between the various statements the suspects provided or with the evidence they had in their possession.

In another study, Bull and Soukara (2010) examined the techniques undertaken by investigators in 40 interviews where the suspect in those interviews had first denied any offense (only to admit to the same later in the interview). Bull and Soukara noted that, either at the point of confession or in the 10 min prior to confessions, the investigators always used certain tactics. While, as in Leo's (1996) study, *emphasizing contradictions* was often employed as a tactic by interviewers in these important time segments, the use of *open questions* and the undertaking of *evidence disclosure* were also found to be always present.

Walsh and Bull (2012b) also analyzed how interviewers attempted to overcome suspects' denials as to suspected wrongdoing. They found that the skillful use of a range of tactics that were consistent with those prescribed by the PEACE promoted either partial or full confessions, from suspects who began interviews in denial. Harsh and deceptive interrogation tactics such as *maximization*, *minimization*, or *intimidation* were very rarely found in Walsh and Bull's (2012b) study because of their oppressive nature that could prompt false confessions. Indeed, these tactics were found to increase suspects' resistance. Moreover, of those techniques that were found in their study to have a positive relationship with movements toward confessions, it was the *disclosure of evidence* that was found most associated with admissions of guilt by suspects of their offenses.

Even if the phenomenon of confession is linked to a combination of factors (Gudjonsson, 2003; St-Yves, 2004a), the suspect's perception of the evidence is the determining factor for obtaining a confession (Cassell & Hayman, 1996; Deslauriers-Varin et al., 2011; Gudjonsson, 2007; Gudjonsson & Petursson, 1991; Kebbell, Hurren, & Roberts, 2006; Leo, 2008; Moston et al., 1992; Sellers & Kebbell, 2009). Two in three suspects (66.7%) admitted their crime when the evidence seemed strong, compared to one in three (36.4%) when the quality of the evidence seemed weak, then 1 in 10 (9.9%) when there was little or no evidence (Williamson, 1990). Gudjonsson and colleagues observed that almost 70% of people admitted that they would never have made a confession if they had not been suspected by the police, then between 55% and 60% confessed because they believed that the police had enough evidence to charge them and have them convicted (Gudjonsson & Bownes, 1992; Gudjonsson & Petursson, 1991; Sigurdsson & Gudjonsson, 1994). Deslauriers-Varin and St-Yves (2006) observed that the rate of confessions almost doubled (from 31.4% to 55.6%) when the evidence was perceived by the suspect as being relatively strong. The principle is simple: in the face of overwhelming evidence, denial becomes futile. For the suspect, there are only two choices left: keep silent or give a version that allows him to explain himself and, suddenly, to try to get out of it with minor consequences.

According to Hakkanen-Nyholm and Hare (2009) the psychopathic suspect shows an ability to lie, without being destabilized, even when inconsistencies or evidence is presented to him. Even though Klaver et al. (2007), who have studied deception in psychopaths, have been able to demonstrate that even having great reputation for being good liars, certain indicators of deception can be detected.

Several studies have found that certain evidence disclosure strategies appear to be more productive than other strategies in establishing the credibility of suspects narrative (Dando et al., 2015; Granhag et al., 2012; Hartwig et al., 2006; Hartwig et al., 2005; Sorochinski et al., 2014). However, while these range of studies all reflect the importance of evidence disclosure, it is less understood as to what particular methods of evidence disclosure are more effective than others.

In brief, the literature indicates there are essentially three methods of disclosure of evidence, being "early," "late," or "gradual."

Early disclosure refers to that evidence being completely revealed shortly after the beginning of the interview (Leo, 1996; Moston et al., 1992; Sellers & Kebbell, 2009). Sellers and Kebbell (2009) conducted a laboratory-based study and found that suspects were prone to confess their crimes when investigators presented strong evidence right at the outset of the interview. In an earlier study that was conducted by the police in England and Wales prior to the implementation of the PEACE framework, Moston et al. (1992) reached the same conclusions (i.e., only when the evidence was viewed as strong were such admissions forthcoming).

When interviewing a psychopath, as with other suspects, the strategy of presenting evidence at the beginning of the interview can prove problematic. When the evidence had been fully disclosed early, there is little room for interviewers to overcome possible denials from the suspect by adding more. Having seen the evidence or in sight of the evidence psychopaths can deny and adjust their narrative to fit the disclosed evidence (see Walsh & Bull, 2015).

In addition to the scarcity of remaining strategies to deal with such denials, if there was a confession, then the interview would come quickly thereafter to a close (since the interviewer's goal had apparently been obtained). As discussed in this chapter, even with a psychopathic suspect, this temptation not to pursue a fact-finding attitude and opt for a confession strategy can lead to miscarriages of justice (see Walsh & Marques, 2021). Early disclosure of evidence might prompt highly vulnerable suspects to adjust their narrative and provide a false confession to fit with that evidence disclosed, no matter how inaccurate or incomplete that evidence was in revealing the full story.

Further, it was found that, despite the apparent aim of investigators in obtaining quick admissions of the offenses charged against the suspect, confronting him with evidence at such an early stage of the interview is largely unsuccessful in actually prompting confessions from suspects (Walsh & Bull, 2015).

Regarding the 'late' disclosure of evidence in interviews, this approach involves allowing the psychopathic suspect (who is unaware of what, if any, evidence is possessed by the investigators that shows their possible involvement in the crime) to present his version of the facts and reveal the evidence at a later stage of the interview. In this way, police investigators adopt a strategy that is said to ensure exhaustive coverage of all possible alibis and excuses before disclosing what evidence they held (Hartwig et al., 2005; Hartwig et al., 2006; Sorochinski et al., 2014).

Several studies have shown that it is best to present the evidence later in the interview (Baldwin, 1992; Bull & Milne, 2004; Hartwig et al., 2005). Defined as the Strategic Use of Evidence approach (or SUE), Hartwig et al. (2006) found that revealing the evidence later enabled investigators to be more accurate in detecting whether suspects were either lying or telling the truth (than was the case in their study where interviewers revealed evidence early). According to Jordan et al. (2012), such late disclosure of evidence only traps the culprits and has no cost to the innocent. Liars become less consistent than those who tell the truth when the evidence is presented later in the interview.

Hartwig et al. (2005) suggest to present more and more precise evidence as the interrogation progresses, starting with the presentation of vague evidence and adding more and more details by the following. This method allows for a more precise determination of innocence or guilt when examining the consistency of the statements in relation to the evidence.

As mentioned earlier in this chapter, when interviewing a psychopathic suspect, the investigator should seek to adopt a neutral stance in the interview to be conducted in an equally neutral environment and not revealing a possible label of "guilty" or "psychopath." The objective is, by not revealing the potential evidence one might have, allow the psychopathic suspect to be motivated and engaged (see Surmon-Böhr et al., 2020 about the use of motivational interviewing with suspects) and make statements, which may prove to be consistent or in contradiction with the undisclosed evidence to hand. As such, the psychopath would have little room to satisfactorily explain any contradictions between what they have said, and what then they came to learn that the interviewer actually knows, once the evidence held was revealed.

Walsh and Marques (2021) state that the impact of a late evidence disclosure strategy in uncovering the truth might well be reduced in many jurisdictions with a legal representation strategy characterized by the advice to suspects to remain in silence when questioned by the police. It therefore is of no surprise to see those SUE researchers now beginning to examine "drip feed" strategies of evidence disclosure in their research directions.

Faced with a situation in which the psychopathic suspect is advised to remain silent, it is important that the investigator maintain a serene and professional posture and inform the suspect that this is one of his rights, but on the other hand it is up to him the final decision to present his version of the facts and to participate in a procedural act where he will be confronted with available evidence (if any) and, thus, will have the possibility to present its defense. This approach, where the investigator conveys serenity in the face of the barrier, respect for the interviewee's rights, availability and genuine interest to listen to him, and transfers control to the suspect, constitutes a very productive approach that suits the idiosyncrasies of the psychopath.

The "gradual" disclosure of evidence involves an incremental approach of "drip-feeding" evidence throughout the interview (Granhag et al., 2012). Walsh et al. (2016) asked 224 British investigators which of "early," "late," and "gradual" evidence disclosure approaches they preferred, finding that the vast majority opted for a gradual approach. This is in line with their training in the PEACE model, which advocates that, after gaining a first account from suspects, evidence should be disclosed in a phased manner.

A correct adoption of the "gradual" disclosure of evidence approach requires that the investigator master and resort to an adequate questioning method. Griffiths and Milne (2006) advocated an approach where questioning (on each topic in the interview) would start with an open enquiry, followed by probing questions designed to seek out the required micro-detail (while avoiding use of the nonproductive questions). Walsh and Bull (2015) found this approach to be strongly associated with interviews that were more successful in gathering comprehensive information, as well as (as was noted earlier) overcoming denials.

In conclusion, the tactics recommended in the PEACE framework are more successful in moving resistant suspects to confess to crimes (without the use of unethical tactics), by first giving suspects opportunity to provide their versions of stories before gradually disclosing evidence and emphasizing the inconsistencies between that evidence and their given accounts.

Thus considering the various contributions in modern investigative interviewing science and practices, many of them resulting from methodologically robust studies with samples from prison/correction settings (where the prevalence of psychopaths is more significant), the PEACE model is likely to prove effective in the interview with psychopaths. The tactics recommended in the PEACE framework are more successful in moving resistant suspects to confess to crimes (without the use of unethical tactics), providing important guarantees in safeguarding the authenticity of a confession (St-Yves & Meissner, 2014).

Confession in psychopaths

The investigative interview of a psychopath is a specialist task that can be very demanding. Investigators need to perform several methodological and systematic procedures, where keen attention to detail, good communication skills, and the ability to gather accurate and fulsome information are key. This not only means ensuring vast awareness about the case under investigation (e.g., existing evidence, antecedent history, and current condition of the suspect) and the strategy to be employed but also anticipate how the suspect is expected to perform in response to the strategy or questioning tactics (Quayle, 2008).

The literature shows that between 40% and 60% of suspects confess to their crimes during police interrogation (see Deslauriers-Varin et al., 2011; St-Yves & Meissner, 2014). Statistically, there is therefore a 50% chance of not obtaining a confession. Many criminal investigators believe that in order to consider the interview a success, it is imperative to get a confession (Perri, 2010). However this "confession culture," characterized by the use of accusatorial and often "persuasive" interrogation techniques in the quest of a confession, must be questioned. Such tactics may violate suspects' rights and are more likely to elicit false confessions (Gudjonsson, 2018; Kassin et al., 2010; Kassin & Gudjonsson, 2004; Walsh & Marques, 2021).

A number of large-scale studies of false confessions, carried out in Iceland, show the importance of antisocial personality traits and history of offending both among prison inmates and community samples, when considering the reliability of suspects' confessions. The findings indicate that false confessions and false denials were significantly associated with antisocial personality traits (Gudjonsson, Sigurdsson, Bragason, et al., 2004; Gudjonsson, Sigurdsson, &Einarsson, 2004; Sigurdsson & Gudjonsson, 1996).

One interpretation of the abovementioned findings is that psychopaths are more likely to be involved in offending, consequently more prone to be interviewed by police, particularly susceptible to lie for short-term instrumental gain, and less concerned about the consequences of their behavior. This increases their propensity to make false denials as well as false confessions depending on their need at any given time (Kassin et al., 2010). Moreover, psychopaths' lifestyle factors such as impulsivity and/or poor behavior control may be related to interrogative compliance. This relationship may be related to the instant gratification of leaving the interrogation room after falsely confessing. Interpersonal manipulation was also found to be related to false confessions. One possible explanation for this association may have been to cover up a more serious offense (Larmour et al., 2015). Quayle (2008) states that in certain cases, the need to fill the psychopath's ego outweighs his desire to avoid legal consequence and he seeks to impress with his audacity in confessing a crime that makes him proud. However, these assumptions are not supported empirically.

The purpose of interviewing a psychopathic suspect is therefore not necessarily to obtain a confession, because the psychopath does not crack, but rather to adopt a fact-finding stance in order to gather information about his participation (if any) in the offense, discover the degree of premeditation of the crime, and the motivation behind it (see St-Yves & Kebbell, 2018).

Closing the interview and authenticating a confession

The Closure stage of the interview involves the interviewer summarizing the account for the suspect, with the aim of encouraging further recall or to clarify any areas of uncertainty, and providing information pertaining to follow-up procedures. Closing the interview facilitates a shared understanding of the interview and should include the following tasks:

- **Summarize account:** the investigator provides a detailed summary of the suspect's entire account. In cases where a written document (e.g., a statement) is produced, the investigator should read it.
- **Confirm account summary:** The investigator asks the suspect if the summary of the account is correct and provides the opportunity and time for the suspect to correct, alter, or add to their account.
- **Follow-up procedure:** The investigator acknowledges the collaboration of all participants (e.g., suspect, lawyer, interpreter); demonstrates availability to be contacted in case further clarification is needed or if the suspect wishes to speak/add some information; informs and explains any procedural acts that may occur in the future (e.g., police and judicial proceedings).
- **Contact details:** The investigator provides the suspect (or his lawyer) with his name and contact details, explains the terms on which the contact should be used, and asks the suspect to contact him if he thinks of anything.

Even though the closure phase is the part of an interview that the interviewee is likely to remember most, research suggests that this phase is the least skillfully covered by investigators, with summarizing the account and providing information pertaining to follow-up procedures often being covered at less than adequate levels (Walsh & Bull, 2010a, 2010b, 2012a; Walsh & Milne, 2007).

When the interview of a suspect results in a confession, the fact that the suspect has a psychopathic personality should not be a reason for this confession not to be adequately substantiated by the investigator. The confession is in fact intended to compensate for the lack of material evidence (Baldwin, 1993). The pressure on the suspect is generally inversely proportional to the quality of the evidence. The less evidence there is, the more the investigator will put pressure for obtaining a confession, sometimes going so far as to suggest it to be the more acceptable solution for the suspect (St-Yves & Meissner, 2014). As it has been explained in this chapter, the possibility of miscarriages of justice requires the adoption of measures to authenticate the confessions elicited from the suspects.

There are no "miracle recipes" that totally exclude the occurrence of false confessions from the justice system. However, Kassin et al. (2010) have been enthusiastically defending the obligation to proceed with the audiovisual recording of all interviews, as a powerful safeguard against false confessions.

Furthermore, it is essential that the existing evidence is analyzed in an integrated way with a view to confirming or not the robustness of the confession. The investigator should always attempt to verify and corroborate the details of the suspect's confession. The use of some questions about what motivated them to tell the truth allows us to conclude on the specific offender's motives, justifications, influencing factors that prompted them to commit the crime, and the voluntary nature of the confession.

Evaluation of the interview process

According to Walsh et al. (2016) investigators rarely benefit from training in the evaluation task and, consequently, assume that they rarely include this phase in their interviews (Walsh & Bull, 2010a, 2010b). Thus we can conclude that there is a relationship between the lack of training in this task and its actual implementation by investigators. On the other hand, Clarke and Milne (2001) report that feedback on the performance of investigators by their supervisors is residual.

It is essential that when an investigator conducts an investigative interview with a psychopath he receives feedback on his performance. Additionally, it is advisable to reflect on his performance, based on the feedback received and, equally, based on his own perceptions about the interview—the tendency to be a reflective practitioner is a vital element not only of professionalism but also in longer term skills maintenance too.

The inherent complexity of interviewing suspects, and especially those with psychopathic personality traits, demands that we draw on the lessons learned from these interviews and all their specificities. This learning must be integrated into the training curricula of law enforcement agencies.

Another aspect that should be considered at this phase is the psychological and emotional consequences that can result in investigators who repeatedly deal with traumatic or markedly violent narratives, or accounts that show disregard for the most basic principles of life in society such as those presented by psychopaths (e.g., Brady, 2017). Here, too, self-monitoring, peer support, and supervisor attention are important to allow the investigators to carry out adequate psychological debriefing.

Conclusions

Interviews with suspects of crime are an important element of police investigations. They can be crucial in helping establish what happened and may well provide evidence that enables the resolution of the criminal investigation.

However, interrogation methods do not have the same effectiveness with all suspects. Some personality profiles collaborate more easily and confess because they feel remorse and regret, while others are not at all concerned with these feelings. This is the case for psychopaths for whom the confession is seen an instrumental way. They calculate and seek their personal profit.

Experience and research have shown that these individuals do not behave like others during an interrogation and that these differences must be taken into account if the objectives of the investigative interview are to be achieved.

It is essential that investigators incorporate the scientific evidence that stems from a very relevant scientific production in the field of investigative interview. This is an area of psychological sciences that has benefited a lot from the collaboration between academics and practitioners, to ensure the applicability of science in police interviewing practices. The existence of a "psychopathy" label is no exception and, in the absence of a reasonable amount of research on the dynamics of interviewing suspects with this personality disorder, it is current best practices in interviewing suspects that should guide us. Likewise, with the psychopath, safeguards as to the nature of confessions by suspects must be guaranteed. The existence of a characteristic or a set of characteristics that makes our task more demanding should only increase the demand on ourselves to achieve the best results with a professional, fair, and human rights-respecting approach.

References

Abbe, A., & Brandon, S. E. (2013). Building and maintaining rapport in investigative interviews. *Police Practice and Research, 15*, 207–220.

Alison, L. J., Alison, E., Noone, G., Elntib, S., & Christiansen, P. (2013). Why tough tactics fail and rapport gets results: Observing rapport-based interpersonal techniques (ORBIT) to generate useful information from terrorists. *Psychology, Public Policy, and Law*, *19*(4), 411–431. https://doi.org/10.1037/a0034564.

Babiak, P., & Hare, R. D. (2006). *Snakes in suits: When psychopaths go to work.* New York: Harper Collins Publishers.

Baldwin, J. (1992). Video taping police interviews with suspects—An evaluation. In *Police research group—Police research series, paper 1.* Londres: Home Office.

Baldwin, J. (1993). Police interviewing techniques. Establishing the truth or proof? *The British Journal of Criminologie*, *33*, 325–352.

Brady, P. Q. (2017). Crimes against caring: Exploring the risk of secondary traumatic stress, burnout, and compassion satisfaction among child exploitation investigators. *Journal of Police and Criminal Psychology*, *32*(4), 305–318. https://doi.org/10.1007/s11896-016-9223-8.

Brimbal, L., Meissner, C. A., Kleinman, S. M., Phillips, E. L., Atkinson, D. J., Dianiska, R. E., et al. (2021). Evaluating the benefits of a rapport-based approach to investigative interviews: A training study with law enforcement investigators. *Law and Human Behavior*, *45*(1), 55–67. https://doi.org/10.1037/lhb0000437.

Bull, R. (2014). *Investigative interviewing*. New York, NY: Springer.

Bull, R., & Milne, R. (2004). Attempts to improve police interviewing of suspects. In G. D. Lassiter (Ed.), *Interrogations, confessions and entrapment*. New York: Plenum.

Bull, R., & Soukara, S. (2010). A set of studies of what really happens in police interviews with suspects. In G. D. Lassiter, & C. Meissner (Eds.), *Interrogations and confessions* (pp. 81–96). Washington: American Psychological Association.

Cassell, P., & Hayman, B. (1996). Police interrogation in the 1990s: An empirical study of the effects of Miranda. *UCLA Law Review*, *43*, 839–932.

Clarke, C., & Milne, R. (2001). *National Evaluation of the PEACE investigative interviewing course. Police research award scheme report no. PRAS/149*. London: Home Office.

Cleary, H. M. D., & Bull, R. (2019). Jail inmates' perspectives on police interrogation. *Psychology, Crime & Law*, *25*(2), 157–170.

Dando, C. J., Bull, R., Ormerod, T. C., & Sandham, L. S. (2015). Helping to sort the liars from the truth-tellers: The gradual revelation of information during investigative interviews. *Legal and Criminological Psychology*, *20*, 114–128.

Dawson, E., Hartwig, M., Brimbal, L., & Denisenkov, P. (2017). A room with a view: Setting influences information disclosure in investigative interviews. *Law and Human Behavior, 41*, 33.

Deeb, H., Vrij, A., Leal, S., & Burkhardt, J. (2021). The effects of sketching while narrating on information elicitation and deception detection in multiple interviews. *Acta Psychologica, 213*. https://doi.org/10.1016/j.actpsy.2020.103236.

Deslauriers-Varin, N., Lussier, P., & St-Yves, M. (2011). Confessing their crime: Factors influencing the offender's decision to confess to the police. *Justice Quarterly*, 1–33.

Deslauriers-Varin, N., & St-Yves, M. (2006). An empirical investigation of offenders' decision to confess their crime during police interrogation. In *Paper presented to the 2nd International Investigative Interviewing Conference, Portsmouth (UK), July 5–7.*

Dianiska, R. E., Swanner, J. K., Brimbal, L., & Meissner, C. A. (2019). Conceptual priming and context reinstatement: A test of direct and indirect interview techniques. *Law and Human Behavior, 43*(2), 131–143. https://doi.org/10.1037/lhb0000323.

Eastwood, J., Snook, B., & Luther, K. (2018). Measuring the effectiveness of the sketch procedure for recalling details of a live interactive event. *Applied Cognitive Psychology, 32*(6), 747–754. https://doi.org/10.1002/acp.3454.

Goodman-Delahunty, J., Martschuk, N., & Dhami, M. K. (2014). Interviewing high value detainees: Securing cooperation and disclosures. *Applied Cognitive Psychology, 28*, 883–897.

Granhag, P.-A., Strömwall, L., Willén, R., & Hartwig, M. (2012). Eliciting cues to deception by tactical disclosure of evidence: The first test of the evidence framing matrix. *Legal and Criminological Psychology, 18*, 341–355. https://doi.org/10.1111/j.2044-8333.2012.02047.x.

Griffiths, A., & Milne, R. (2006). Will it all end in tiers? Police interviews with suspects in Britain. In T. Williamson (Ed.), *Investigative interviewing: Rights, research and regulation* (pp. 167–189). Cullompton: Willan.

Gudjonsson, G. H. (2003). The psychology of interrogations and confessions. In *A handbook*. Chichester: England: John Wiley & Sons.

Gudjonsson, G. H. (2007). Investigative interviewing. In T. Newburn, T. Williamson, & A. Wright (Eds.), *Handbook of criminal investigation* (pp. 466–492). Devon, UK: Willan.

Gudjonsson, G. H. (2018). *The psychology of false confessions. Forty years of science and practice*. Chichester: Wiley Blackwell.

Gudjonsson, G. H. (2021). The science-based pathways to understanding false confessions and wrongful convictions. *Frontiers in Psychology, 12*, 633936. https://doi.org/10.3389/fpsyg.2021.633936.

Gudjonsson, G. H., & Bownes, I. (1992). The reasons why suspects confess during custodial interrogation: Data for Northern Ireland. *Medicine, Science and the Law, 32*, 204–212.

Gudjonsson, G. H., & Pearse, J. (2011). Suspect interviews and false confessions. *Current Directions in Psychological Science, 20*(1), 33–37. https://doi.org/10.1177/0963721410396824.

Gudjonsson, G. H., & Petursson, H. (1991). Custodial interrogation: Why do suspects confess and how does it relate to their crime, attitude and personality? *Personality and Individual Differences, 12*, 295–306.

Gudjonsson, G. H., Sigurdsson, J. F., Bragason, O. O., Einarsson, E., & Valdimarsdottir, E. B. (2004). Confessions and denials and the relationship with personality. *Legal and Criminological Psychology, 9*, 121–133. https://doi.org/10.1348/135532504322776898.

Gudjonsson, G. H., Sigurdsson, J. F., & Einarsson, E. (2004). The role of personality in relation to confessions and denials. *Psychology, Crime & Law, 10*(2), 125–135. https://doi.org/10.1080/10683160310001634296.

Hakkanen-Nyholm, H., & Hare, R. (2009). Psychopathy, homicide, and the courts: Working the system. *Criminal Justice and Behavior, 36*(8), 761–777.

Hare, R. D. (1991). *The Hare psychopathy checklist-revised.* Toronto, Ontario, Canada: Multi-Health Systems.

Hare, R. D. (1998). Psychopathy, affect, and behavior. In D. Cook, A. Forth, & R. Hare (Eds.), *Psychopathy: Theory, research, and implications for society* (pp. 105–137). The Netherlands: Kluwer.

Hartwig, M., Granhag, P. A., & Luke, T. (2014). Strategic use of evidence during investigative interviews: The state of the science. In *Credibility assessment* (pp. 1–36). Academic Press.

Hartwig, M., Granhag, P. A., Strömwall, L. A., & Kronkvist, O. (2006). Strategic use of evidence during police interviews: When training to detect deception works. *Law and Human Behavior, 30*, 603–619.

Hartwig, M., Granhag, P. A., Strömwall, L. A., & Vrij, A. (2005). Detecting deception via strategic disclosure of evidence. *Law and Human Behavior, 29*, 469–484. https://doi.org/10.1007/s10979-005-5521-x.

Herve, H., & Yuille, J. (2007). *The psychopath.* Lawrence Erlbaum Associates.

Holmberg, U., & Christianson, S. (2002). Murderers' and sexual offenders' experiences of police interviews and their inclination to admit or deny crimes. *Behavioral Sciences & the Law, 20*, 31–45.

Hoogesteyn, K., Meijer, E., & Vrij, A. (2019). The influence of room spaciousness on investigative interviews. *Legal and Criminological Psychology, 24*, 215–228.

Hoogesteyn, K., Meijer, E. H., & Vrij, A. (2020a). Detainee and layperson's expectations and preferences regarding police interview rooms. *PLoS One, 15*(11), e0241683. https://doi.org/10.1371/journal.pone.0241683.

Hoogesteyn, K., Meijer, E., & Vrij, A. (2020b). *Utility and effectiveness of the context manipulation.* Techniques: Police Investigators' Perspectives. *J Police Crim Psych.* https://doi.org/10.1007/s11896-020-09374-2.

Inbau, F. E., Reid, J. E., Buckley, J. P., & Jayne, B. C. (2013). *Criminal interrogation and confessions* (5th ed.). Burlington, MA: Jones and Bartlett Learning.

Jordan, S., Hartwig, M., Wallace, B., Dawson, E., & Xhihani, A. (2012). Early versus late disclosure of evidence: Effects on verbal cues to deception, confessions, and lie catchers accuracy. *Journal of Investigative Psychology and Offender Profiling, 9*, 1–12.

Kassin, S. M. (2014). False confessions: Causes, consequences, and implications for reform. *Policy Insights From the Behavioral and Brain Sciences, 1*(1), 112–121. https://doi.org/10.1177/2372732214548678.

Kassin, S. M., Drizin, S. A., Grisso, T., Gudjonsson, G. H., Leo, R. A., & Redlich, A. D. (2010). Police-induced confessions, risk factors, and recommendations: Looking ahead. *Law and Human Behavior, 34*(1), 49–52. https://doi.org/10.1007/s10979-010-9217-5.

Kassin, S. M., & Gudjonsson, G. H. (2004). The psychology of confessions: A review of the literature and issues. *Psychological Science in the Public Interest, 5*, 33–67. https://doi.org/10.1111/j.1529-1006.2004.00016.x.

Kebbell, M., Alison, L., Hurren, E., & Mazerolle, P. (2010). How do sex offenders think the police should interview to elicit confessions from sex offenders? *Psychology, Crime & Law, 16*(7), 567–584. https://doi.org/10.1080/10683160902971055.

Kebbell, M. R., Hurren, E. J., & Mazerolle, P. (2006). Sex offenders' perceptions of how they were interviewed. *Canadian Journal of Police & Security Services, 4*, 67–75.

Kebbell, M. R., Hurren, E., & Roberts, S. (2006). Mock-suspects' decisions to confess: The accuracy of eyewitness evidence is critical. *Applied Cognitive Psychology, 20*, 477–486.

Kelly, C. E., & Meissner, C. A. (2016). Interrogation and investigative interviewing in the United States: Research and practice. In D. W. Walsh, G. E. Oxburgh, A. D. Redlich, & T. Myklebust (Eds.), *International developments and practices in investigative interviewing and interrogation: Volume 2—Suspects* (pp. 255–266). Abingdon: Routledge.

Kelly, C. E., Miller, J. C., & Redlich, A. D. (2016). The dynamic nature of interrogation. *Law and Human Behavior*, *40*(3), 295–309.

Kelly, C. E., Miller, J. C., Redlich, A. D., & Kleinman, S. M. (2013). A taxonomy of interrogation methods. *Psychology, Public Policy, and Law*, *19*, 165–178. https://doi.org/10.1037/a0030310.

Kieckhaefer, J. M., Vallano, J. P., & Compo, N. S. (2013). Examining the effects of rapport building: When and why does rapport benefit adult witnesses. *Memory*.

Kim, J., Walsh, D., Bull, R., & Bergstrom, H. (2018). Planning ahead? Factors influencing investigators' attitudes towards planning for interviews with suspects. *Journal of Police and Criminal Psychology*, *33*, 158–174. https://doi.org/10.1007/s11896-017-9243-z.104.

King, L., & Snook, B. (2009). Peering inside a Canadian interrogation room: An examination of the Reid model of interrogation, influence tactics, and coercive strategies. *Criminal Justice and Behavior*, *36*, 674–694. https://doi.org/10.1177/0093854809335142.

Klaver, J. R., Lee, Z., & Hart, S. D. (2007). Psychopathy and nonverbal indicators of deception in offenders. *Law and Human Behaviour*, *31*, 337–351.

Larmour, S. R., Bergstrøm, H., Gillen, C. T. A., & Forth, A. E. (2015). Behind the confession: Relating false confession, interrogative compliance, personality traits, and psychopathy. *Journal of Police and Criminal Psychology*, *30*(2), 94–102. https://doi.org/10.1007/s11896-014-9144-3.

Leahy-Harland, S., & Bull, R. (2017). Police strategies and suspect responses in real-life serious crime interviews. *Journal of Police and Criminal Psychology*, *32*(2), 138–151.

Leo, R. A. (1996). Inside the interrogation room. *Journal of Criminal Law and Criminology*, *86*, 266–303.

Leo, R. A. (2008). *Police interrogation and American justice*. Cambridge: Harvard University Press.

Luke, T. J. (2021). A meta-analytic review of experimental tests of the interrogation technique of Hanns Joachim Scharff. *Applied Cognitive Psychology*, *35*, 360–373. https://doi.org/10.1002/acp.3771.

May, L., Gewehr, E., Zimmermann, J., Raible, Y., & Volbert, R. (2021). How guilty and innocent suspects perceive the police and themselves: Suspect interviews in Germany. *Legal and Criminological Psychology*, *26*, 42–61. https://doi.org/10.1111/lcrp.12184.

May, L., Granhag, P. A., & Tekin, S. (2017). Interviewing suspects in denial: On how different evidence disclosure modes affect the elicitation of new critical information. *Frontiers in Psychology*, *8*, 1154. https://doi.org/10.3389/fpsyg.2017.01154.

Meissner, C. A., Kelly, C. E., & Woestehoff, S. A. (2015). Improving the effectiveness of suspect interrogations. *Annual Review of Law & Social Sciences*, *11*, 211–233. https://doi.org/10.1146/annurev-lawsocsci-120814-121657.

Miller, J. C., Redlich, A. D., & Kelly, C. E. (2018). Accusatorial and information-gathering interview and interrogation methods: A multi-country comparison. *Psychology, Crime & Law*.

Miller, W. R., & Rollnick, S. (2002). *Motivational interviewing: Preparing people for change* (2nd ed.). New York, NY: The Guilford Press.

Milne, R., & Bull, R. (1999). *Investigative interviewing: Psychology and practice*. Chichester: Wiley.

Moston, S., Stephenson, G. M., & Williamson, T. M. (1992). The effects of case characteristics on suspect behaviour during police questioning. *British Journal of Criminology*, *32*(1), 23–40.

Neequaye, D. A., & Mac Giolla, E. (2021). *The use of the term rapport in the investigative interviewing literature—A critical examination of definitions*. https://doi.org/10.31234/osf.io/fmp8h.

Neumann, C. C., & Hare, R. D. (2008). Psychopathic traits in a large community sample: Links to violence, alcohol use, and intelligence. *Journal of Consulting and Clinical Psychology*, *76*, 893–899.

O'Toole, M. E., Logan, M., & Smith, S. (2012). Looking behind the mask: Implications for interviewing psychopaths. *FBI Law Enforcement Bulletin*, *81*(7), 14–19.

Oleszkiewicz, S., & Watson, S. J. (2021). A meta-analytic review of the timing for disclosing evidence when interviewing suspects. *Applied Cognitive Psychology*, *35*, 342–359. https://doi.org/10.1002/acp.3767.

Perri, F. S. (2010). The flawed interview of a psychopathic killer: What went wrong? *Journal of Investigative Psychology and Offender Profiling*, *8*(1), 41–57.

Perri, F. S., & Lichtenwald, T. G. (2008). The arrogant chameleons: Exposing fraud detection homicide. *The Forensic Examiner*, *17*(1), 26–34.

Porter, S., Woodworth, M., Earle, J., Drugge, J., & Boer, D. (2003). Characteristics of sexual homicides committed by psychopathic and nonpsychopathic offenders. *Law and Human Behavior*, *27*, 459–470.

Poyser, S., & Milne, R. (2021). The time in between a case of 'wrongful' and 'rightful' conviction in the UK: Miscarriages of justice and the contribution of psychology to reforming the police investigative process. *International Journal of Police Science & Management*, *23*(1), 5–16. https://doi.org/10.1177/14613557211006134.

Quayle, J. (2008). Interviewing a psychopathic suspect. *Journal of Investigative Psychology and Offender Profiling*, *5*, 79–91.

Redlich, A. D., Kelly, C. E., & Miller, J. C. (2014). The who, what, and why of human intelligence gathering: Self-reported measures of interrogation methods. *Applied Cognitive Psychology*, *28*(6), 817–828. https://doi.org/10.1002/acp.3040.

Russano, M. B., Kelly, C. E., & Meissner, C. A. (2019). From the ivory tower to the interrogation room: Training and field evaluation research on suspect interviewing. In R. Bull, & I. Blandón-Gitlin (Eds.), *The Routledge international handbook of legal and investigative psychology* (pp. 287–310). Routledge.

Russano, M., Narchet, F., Kleinman, S., & Meissner, C. (2014). Structured interviews of experienced HUMINT interrogators. *Applied Cognitive Psychology*, *28*, 847–859. https://doi.org/10.1002/acp.3069.

Schollum, M. (2005). *Investigative interviewing: The literature*. Wellington: New Zealand Police.

Sellers, S., & Kebbell, M. R. (2009). When should evidence be disclosed in an interview with a suspect? An experiment with mock-suspects. *Journal of Investigative Psychology and Offending Profiling*, *6*, 151–160.

Serin, R. C., Peters, R. D., & Barbaree, H. E. (1990). Predictors of psychopathy and release outcome in a criminal population. *Psychological Assessment: A Journal of Consulting and Clinical Psychology*, *2*(4), 419–422.

Sigurdsson, J. F., & Gudjonsson, G. H. (1994). Alcohol and drug intoxication during police interrogation and the reasons why suspects confess to the police. *Addiction*, *89*, 985–997.

Sigurdsson, J. F., & Gudjonsson, G. H. (1996). The psychological characteristics of 'false confessors'. A study among Icelandic prison inmates and juvenile offenders. *Personality and Individual Differences*, *20*(3), 321–329. https://doi.org/10.1016/0191-8869(95)00184-0.

Snook, B., Eastwood, J., Stinson, M., & Tedeschini, J. (2010). Reforming investigative interviewing in Canada. *Canadian Journal of Criminology and Criminal Justice*, *52*(2), 215–229.

Sorochinski, M., Hartwig, M., Osborne, J., Wilkins, E., Marsh, J., Kazakov, D., et al. (2014). Interviewing to detect deception: When to disclose the evidence? *Journal of Police and Criminal Psychology*, *29*, 87–94. https://doi.org/10.1007/s11896-013-9121-2.

Soukara, S., Bull, R., & Vrij, A. (2002). Police detectives' aims regarding their interviews with suspects: Any change at the turn of the millennium? *International Journal of Police Science and Management*, *4*(2), 101–114. https://doi.org/10.1177/146135570200400202.

Soukara, S., Bull, R., Vrij, A., Turner, M., & Cherryman, J. (2009). What really happens in police interviews with suspects? Tactics and confessions. *Psychology, Crime and Law*, *15*, 493–506.

St-Yves, M. (2002). *Interrogatoire de police et crime sexuel: profil du suspect collaborateur. Revue internationale de criminologie et de police technique et scientifique. Genève (Suisse)* (pp. 81–96).

St-Yves, M. (2004a). Les facteurs associés à la confession: la recherche empirique. In M. St-Yves, & J. Landry (Eds.), *Psychologie des entrevues d'enquête: de la recherche à la pratique* (pp. 53–71). Cowansville: Éditions Yvon Blais.

St-Yves, M. (2004b). La psychologie du suspect. In M. St-Yves, & J. Landry (Eds.), *Psychologie des entrevues d'enquête: de la recherche à la pratique* (pp. 73–84). Cowansville: Éditions Yvon Blais.

St-Yves, M. (2006). The psychology of rapport: Five basic rules. In *Investigative interviewing: Rights, research, regulation* (pp. 87–106). Willan: Publishing.

St-Yves, M. (2014). *Investigative interviewing: The essentials*. Toronto: Carswell Publisher.

St-Yves, M., & Kebbell, M. (2018). Investigative interviewing in suspected sexual homicides. In J. Proulx, et al. (Eds.), *Routledge international handbook of sexual homicide studies* (pp. 562–573). Routledge.

St-Yves, M., & Meissner, C. A. (2014). Interviewing suspects. In *Investigative interviewing: The essentials* (pp. 145–189). Toronto: Carswell Publisher.

Surmon-Böhr, F., Alison, L., Christiansen, P., & Alison, E. (2020). The right to silence and the permission to talk: Motivational interviewing and high-value detainees. *American Psychologist*, *75*(7), 1011–1021. https://doi.org/10.1037/amp0000588.

Tickle-Degnen, L., & Rosenthal, R. (1990). The nature of rapport and its nonverbal correlates. *Psychological Inquiry*, *4*, 285–293.

Vallano, J. P., & Schreiber Compo, N. (2015). Rapport-building with cooperative witnesses and criminal suspects: A theoretical and empirical review. *Psychology, Public Policy, and the Law*, *21*(1), 85–99.

Vanderhallen, M., Vervaeke, G., & Holmberg, U. (2011). Witness and suspect perceptions of working alliance and interviewing style. *Journal of Investigative Psychology and Offender Profiling*, *8*, 110–130.

Vrij, A., Meissner, C. A., Fisher, R. P., Kassin, S. M., Morgan, C. A., & Kleinman, S. M. (2017). Psychological perspectives on interrogation. *Perspectives on Psychological Science*, *12*(6), 927–955. https://doi.org/10.1177/1745691617706515.

Wachi, T., Kuraishi, H., Watanabe, K., Otsuka, Y., Yokota, K., & Lamb, M. E. (2018). Effects of rapport building on confessions in an experimental paradigm. *Psychology, Public Policy, and Law*, *24*(1), 36–47.

Walsh, D., & Bull, R. (2010a). Interviewing suspects of fraud: An in-depth analysis of interviewing skills. *Journal of Psychiatry and Law*, *38*, 99135.

Walsh, D., & Bull, R. (2010b). What really is effective in interviews with suspects? A study comparing interviewing skills against interviewing outcomes. *Legal and Criminological Psychology*, *15*, 305–321. https://doi.org/10.1348/135532509463356.

Walsh, D., & Bull, R. (2011). Benefit fraud investigative interviewing: A self-report study of investigation professionals' beliefs concerning practice. *Journal of Investigative Psychology and Offender Profiling*, *8*, 131–148.

Walsh, D., & Bull, R. (2012a). How do interviewers attempt to overcome suspects' denials? *Psychiatry, Psychology, and Law*, *19*, 151–168.

Walsh, D., & Bull, R. (2012b). Examining rapport in investigative interviews with suspects: Does its building and maintenance work? *Journal of Police and Criminal Psychology*, *27*, 73–84.

Walsh, D., & Bull, R. (2015). Interviewing suspects: Examining the association between skills, questioning, evidence disclosure, and interview outcomes. *Psychology, Crime & Law*, *21*(7), 661–680. https://doi.org/10.1080/1068316X.2015.1028544.

Walsh, D., & Marques, P. B. (2021). Is confession really necessary? The use of effective interviewing techniques to maximize disclosure from suspects. In P. B. Marques, & M. Paulino (Eds.), *Police psychology: New trends in forensic psychological science*. Amsterdam: Elsevier.

Walsh, D., & Milne, R. (2007). Perceptions of benefit fraud staff in the UK: Giving PEACE a chance? *Public Administration*, *85*(2), 525–540. https://doi.org/10.1111/j.1467-9299.2007.00645.x.

Walsh, D., Milne, R., & Bull, R. (2016). One way or another? Investigators' beliefs concerning evidence disclosure in interviews with suspects in England and Wales. *Journal of Police and Criminal Psychology*, *31*, 127–140. https://doi.org/10.1007/s11896-015-9174-5.

Williamson, T. M. (1990). *Strategic changes in police interrogation: An examination of police and suspect behaviour in the Metropolitan Police in order to determine the effects of new legislation, technology and organizational policies*. Unpublished Ph.D. Thesis, University of Kent.

Psychopathy evidence in legal proceedings

11

John F. Edens and Tiffany N. Truong

Introduction

Forensic mental health experts frequently provide evidence and testimony concerning psychopathic personality disorder (psychopathy) to address a wide range of questions that legal decision-makers (e.g., judges, juries) are tasked with adjudicating. The questions at issue for the courts may revolve around defendants' current or past mental health status, their ability to exercise volitional control over their actions, and/or whether they meet the definition of some particular legal classification, such as being a "dangerous offender" in Canada, a "sexually violent predator" in the United States, or having a "dangerous and severe personality disorder" in England (although this particular category now has been replaced; see Tyrer et al., 2015). Other types of questions addressed in courts of law may focus on defendants' likely future conduct, such as the potential for violent and other types of criminal acts or their likely responsiveness to rehabilitation efforts. The cases in which psychopathy evidence is used tend to be ones in which defendants face severe life-altering (e.g., indeterminate confinement, denial of release) or even life-ending (e.g., capital punishment) legal consequences (Cunningham & Reidy, 1998; Edens, Petrila, & Kelley, 2018).

In this chapter, we begin with a brief overview of legal admissibility issues concerning expert mental health evidence. Next, we detail some of the more common uses of psychopathy evidence based on reviews of published case law and surveys of legal and mental health professionals who work in forensic or correctional settings. Next, we review controversies related to the legal admissibility of expert evidence regarding psychopathy, focusing first on two broad concerns (e.g., whether the diagnosis is sufficiently reliable to warrant being admitted into legal proceedings and whether its potential to unduly prejudice judges and jurors against defendants outweighs its probative value). Next, we summarize debates related to more specific legal claims that have been made about ostensibly psychopathic defendants in court. Specifically, we review the scientific basis of debates concerning whether such individuals: (a) are unlikely to experience other (potentially legally salient) mental disorders, such as schizophrenia or intellectual disabilities; (b) have the capacity to control their criminal actions; and (c) are incapable of change and will be unresponsive to treatment and rehabilitation efforts. We conclude with a discussion of emerging issues in the classification, assessment, and diagnosis of this disorder (e.g., ICD-11 and DSM-5 alternative personality disorder model) and how these issues may impact the use of the concept of psychopathy in legal systems in the future.

Psychopathy and Criminal Behavior. https://doi.org/10.1016/B978-0-12-811419-3.00016-9

Psychopathy, expert evidence, and legal admissibility

What is the clinical basis for labeling someone as a "psychopath," "sociopath," or more generally "antisocial" or "dissocial" in a court of law? Before briefly discussing specific assessment methods and their uses in legal proceedings, it is important to note that over the years such terms seem to have been used interchangeably in many instances (Edens, Petrila, & Kelley, 2018), with expert witnesses relying on, for example, diagnoses of Antisocial Personality Disorder from the DSM (editions three through five) to diagnose and label a defendant as a psychopath. Separate from DSM-based diagnoses, support for a psychopathy diagnosis has been introduced into legal proceedings using numerous different types of structured and unstructured assessment methods, including professional rating scales (e.g., the Psychopathy Checklist-Revised [Hare, 2003]), self-report personality and psychopathology instruments (e.g., Minnesota Multiphasic Personality Inventory; Personality Assessment Inventory), and projective methods (e.g., Rorschach Inkblot Test). An extensive review of these different assessment approaches is not possible in this chapter, but it should be highlighted that extant research (Hare, 2003; Wood et al., 2010) suggests that there may not be a great deal of statistical overlap among the results of these approaches, especially those from different assessment domains (i.e., expert rating scale vs. self-report inventory vs. projective method). As such, one method may be suggestive of high levels of psychopathy (e.g., rating scale) whereas another approach might not (e.g., self-report inventory).

The diversity of assessment methods and instruments notwithstanding, during at least the last quarter century it seems that forensic mental health experts for the most part have diagnosed criminal defendants as psychopathic or sociopathic using either the Psychopathy Checklist-Revised (PCL-R; Hare, 1991, 2003) or the Antisocial Personality Disorder (APD) criteria from the DSM or ICD (Archer, Buffington-Vollum, Stredny, & Handel, 2006; Edens & Cox, 2012; Jackson & Hess, 2007; Singh et al., 2014; see also Viljoen, MacDougall, Gagnon, & Douglas, 2010; Viljoen, McLachlan, & Vincent, 2010). Although there are novel and promising alternative means of assessing psychopathic traits that eventually may work their way into court systems in the future (e.g., Cooke, Hart, Logan, & Michie, 2012), for the purposes of this review we will focus primarily on the scientific literature relevant to these two assessment methods.

Though not discussed specifically in reference to APD or psychopathy diagnoses, over the years psychology-law scholars have identified several recurrent problems with mental health evidence and testimony in courts of law. Grisso (1986, 2003), for example, detailed five common problems with such evidence, which he referred to as the five 'I's': *ignorance* and *irrelevance* in courtroom testimony, psychiatric or psychological *intrusion* into essentially legal matters, and *insufficiency* and *incredibility* of the information provided to the courts. *Ignorance* and *irrelevance* are reflected in an excessive reliance on "diagnostic testimony" that fails to link the mental health concept to the legal question at hand. *Intrusion* is evident when mental health examiners attempt to usurp the fact-finder's authority to determine the outcome by offering "ultimate opinions" concerning fundamentally legal questions (e.g., whether a defendant is/is not competent to proceed to adjudication). In regards to *insufficiency* and *incredibility*, Grisso (1986) argued that forensic mental health professionals are prone to provide testimony based on assessments that lack sufficient evidence to support their conclusions, which results in opinions that lack legal credibility.

Although originally described by Grisso (1986) primarily in the context of the assessment of legal competencies, these problems are germane to other types of psycholegal topics as well, such as evidence concerning personality disorders (Edens, DeMatteo, Kelley, & Arnold, 2018). For example, Edens, Petrila, and Kelley (2018) discussed the potential for mental health evidence such as a PCL-R score to be an intrusion into legal decision-making if a hypothetical expert witness were to conclude that the results of such an assessment definitively answered the legal question of whether a defendant met the criteria to be classified as a "sexual psychopath" or similar category. We will highlight other potential examples of Grisso's I's as they relate to psychopathy evidence in subsequent sections of this chapter.

The introduction of expert evidence relating to personality traits and diagnoses, like all expert evidence provided in any court, is governed by each jurisdiction's rules of admissibility. Such admissibility rules, as well as rules concerning who can be qualified as an "expert" on any given topic, vary across—and even within—different countries and an exhaustive review of them is not possible here (for general discussions, see *Daubert v. Merrell Dow Pharmaceuticals*, 1993; European Commission for the Efficiency of Justice, 2014; *Federal Rules of Evidence for United States Courts and Magistrates*, 1975; Matoba, 2003; Nuée, 2015). Generally speaking, many jurisdictions seem to consider some combination of whether the expert evidence is relevant to the case at hand, has the potential to assist the trier of fact, is based on valid and reliable science, and is not unduly prejudicial to the parties involved. In the United States, typically the proffered evidence first must be determined to be relevant to whatever psycholegal issue happens to be before the court. That is, does it provide the trier-of-fact with information that is helpful in the resolution of whatever legal issue is under consideration?

Historically, both clinicians and legal scholars have not consistently conceptualized personality disorders as being a form of "major" or "severe" mental disorder and they have therefore been construed as less relevant for sentencing, mitigation, or sanity determinations when compared to other disorders such as schizophrenia, bipolar disorder, or mental retardation/intellectual disabilities (Felthous & Sass, 2000; Johnson & Elbogen, 2013). For example, in *Foucha v. Louisiana* (1990), the United States Supreme Court admitted expert testimony that APD was not a mental illness for the purpose of detaining individuals after being found not guilty by reason of insanity. More generally, in the U.S. a diagnosis of APD typically does not support leniency or recommendations for treatment at the time of sentencing. As such, it is perhaps not surprising that it seems relatively rare for defense counsel to proactively introduce evidence that their client is psychopathic or antisocial in most criminal cases or civil commitment cases (DeMatteo et al., 2014a, 2014b; Edens & Cox, 2012), although there are anecdotal examples of such trial strategies being used (e.g., *Ex parte Cargill*, 2017).

That being said, there are certain areas in which personality disorders in general and psychopathy in particular clearly have been viewed by legal systems as highly relevant to adjudicating some types of cases. For example, the state of New York allows for a defense of "extreme emotional disturbance" that explicitly compels courts to consider the potential role of underlying personality disorders (Dyer & McCann, 2000). Similarly, in contrast to the aforementioned *Foucha* decision, the Supreme Court of the state of New Jersey held in *State v. Gallaway* (1993) that a defendant's diagnosis of Borderline Personality Disorder impaired cognitive functioning to the extent that the requisite mental state (i.e., purposeful action) necessary to classify it as murder was lacking. More specific to psychopathy, civil commitment cases in the U.S. frequently admit expert evidence concerning this disorder to aid in the determination as to whether a defendant (usually referred to as a "respondent" in such cases) is a "sexually violent predator" (SVP) who may warrant indeterminate detention (DeMatteo et al., 2014a; DeMatteo, Murphy, Galloway, & Krauss, 2015; Fitch & Ortega, 2000). The psychopathy evidence in such cases typically is introduced to support the claim that such individuals are likely to engage in sexual violence and perhaps that they also have a "behavioral abnormality" that causes some degree of impairment of their volitional control over their actions (*Kansas v. Crane*, 2002). The latter legal concept is intended to differentiate between essentially 'willful' criminal acts—typically not the focus of civil commitment in the U.S.—and acts that are ostensibly outside of the control of the defendant. We return to the issue of volitional control and psychopathy in a later section.

Because it is typically the prosecution that seeks to introduce it into evidence, some scholars have argued that a psychopathy diagnosis is primarily a "prosecution tool" (DeMatteo et al., 2014b, p. 96). The first edition of the PCL-R was commercially published in 1991 (Hare, 1991), with extended narrative critiques of its uses and abuses in legal settings first beginning to appear in the late 1990s/early 2000s (Edens, Petrila, & Buffington-Vollum, 2001; Fitch & Ortega, 2000; Hare, 1998; Kröber & Lau, 2000; Lyon & Ogloff, 2000; Ogloff & Lyon, 1998; Reed, 1996; Zinger & Forth, 1998). Since that time, various case law reviews and professional surveys have examined the increasing role of psychopathy evidence and the PCL-R in legal proceedings. Approximately 15 years after its commercial release, two case law reviews were published (DeMatteo & Edens, 2006; Walsh & Walsh, 2006) that investigated the use of the PCL-R in U.S. cases. Appearances were relatively infrequent over this time, with DeMatteo and Edens (2006) identifying 87 cases and Walsh and Walsh (2006) identifying 76 cases. Among these cases, the PCL-R was most often used as a risk assessment tool to predict future risk of sexual violence, general violence, or general offending in 91% (Walsh & Walsh, 2006) to 95% (DeMatteo & Edens, 2006) of the cases, which included SVP, capital sentencing, parole, civil commitment hearings, and juvenile transfer to adult court proceedings.

More recent reviews examining the frequency of the PCL-R being admitted into evidence in U.S. courts reported a dramatic increase in published cases during the period from 2005 through 2011 (DeMatteo et al., 2014a, 2014b): more than a 300% increase in half the time period examined by DeMatteo and Edens (2006) and Walsh and Walsh (2006). Among these 348 cases, most were from U.S. appellate courts (86%) with the remaining state cases primarily originating from the states of California (40%), Texas (11%), and Minnesota (11%). Similar to earlier reviews, the PCL-R was primarily used as a risk assessment tool in SVP cases (62%), parole hearings (24%), and, less commonly, in capital sentencing and (non-SVP) civil commitment. The predominance of SVP cases likely resulted from the controversial nature of these laws and the numerous appeals challenging the legality of applying new (or recently reenacted) civil commitment procedures to sex offenders.

Reviews also have examined how the instrument is being utilized in other countries. In Canada, evidence of psychopathy is frequently introduced to support a "Dangerous Offender" designation, which imposes indeterminate detention on offenders who, by reasons of violent sexual tendencies, are presumed to be a threat to others. Additionally, Canadian legislation provides a less severe designation of "Long-Term Offender," which classifies individuals who are deemed amenable for reintegration contingent on an extended period of community management following their sentences (Blais, 2015; Blais & Forth, 2014; Lloyd, Clark, & Forth, 2010; see also Viljoen, MacDougall, et al., 2010). Lloyd et al. (2010) found that, from 137 dangerous offender (or long-term offender) hearings, the PCL-R was used in 43% of these cases, with scores being related to expert ratings of treatment amenability. In various European countries (e.g., Great Britain, Germany, the Netherlands, Switzerland), psychopathy has been used to inform decisions about preventative and indeterminate detention and/or assess for potential difficulties in institutional adjustment (e.g., aggressive behaviors) among forensic inpatients and prison inmates (for more extensive reviews, see Ashworth & Zedner, 2014; Kröber & Lau, 2000; Leygraf & Elsner, 2007; Malsch & Duker, 2016; O'Loughlin, 2019). For the purpose of this chapter, we conducted a cursory review (as of 01/30/2020) of the case law database Nexis Uni using the following search terms: (psychopath OR psychopathy OR PCL-R OR PCLR) AND (checklist OR check-list OR diagnosis OR disorder). In addition to thousands of cases being identified in the U.S. (6119) and Canada (6069), these search terms identified hundreds of such cases in the following countries: Australia (822), New Zealand (228), United Kingdom (579).

The information detailed in the preceding paragraphs should be interpreted with certain caveats in mind. Case law databases represent a very small proportion of the actual cases in which psychopathy evidence is likely being introduced. Notably, Otto and Heilbrun (2002) reported anecdotal claims that the PCL-R may be used in as many as 60,000 to 80,000 mental health evaluations per year (in contrast to only a few thousand total case law citations), though the exact basis for this estimate was not provided. Furthermore, legal databases do not represent a random sampling of the broader population of cases. For example, in U.S. state cases, Nexis Uni provides coverage of all published and unpublished cases from state appellate courts. However, state trial court cases, which one would presume represent the bulk of cases involving psychopathy evidence, are not routinely published (DeMatteo et al., 2014b).

Concerns about how comprehensive case law reviews may be notwithstanding, it seems clear from the information reviewed before that psychopathy evidence makes its way into numerous forensic mental health assessments around the globe. Mental health professional survey data also suggest the widespread use of such evidence

(Archer et al., 2006; Edens & Cox, 2012; Jackson & Hess, 2007; Viljoen, McLachlan, & Vincent, 2010). For example, international survey data suggest that PCL-R scores are used in the context of forensic violence risk assessments around the world (see Singh et al., 2014, p. 200, Table 3).

Psychopathy evidence and inter-rater reliability

How accurate are diagnoses of psychopathy in court? That is, would multiple expert witnesses providing evidence about this disorder produce similar results and draw similar conclusions about the same defendant? Professional concerns about the accuracy of labeling criminal defendants as psychopathic, sociopathic, or antisocial go back decades in the U.S. (e.g., *Barefoot v. Estelle*, 1983) and are inextricably tied to testimony regarding the alleged "future dangerousness" of defendants in capital murder trials (Cunningham & Reidy, 1998, 2002; Ewing, 1983). Such early cases typically involved a diagnosis by a prosecution-retained mental health expert that was based primarily on a review of the case facts—often with no interview of the defendant having been conducted or other collateral information considered—and a conclusion by that expert that the defendant would be a continuing threat to society if not executed (Edens, Buffington-Vollum, Roskamp, & Anthony, 2005; Texas Defender Service, 2004). Over the years, changes to admissibility rules as well as precedent-setting legal cases seem to have mostly eliminated the introduction of such unstructured and unreliable diagnostic opinions (at least in U.S. capital murder trials) but evidence concerning psychopathy and violence risk that is ostensibly more scientifically grounded (e.g., the PCL-R) continues to be admitted in such cases in some jurisdictions (DeMatteo et al., 2014b, 2020; Edens et al., 2001).

The extent to which the psychometric properties reported in any assessment instrument's professional manual generalize to "field settings" (Edens & Boccaccini, 2017) is an area of increasing interest among forensic mental health professionals, perhaps reflecting the broader concerns within the forensic sciences about the reliability and validity of various forms of expert evidence (e.g., Kassin, Dror, & Kukucka, 2013; National Academy of Sciences, 2009). In regards to specific instruments typically used to operationalize psychopathy in legal cases, the PCL-R professional manual (Hare, 2003) indicates that the intra-class correlation (ICC) for the total score in various samples approximates .85 or higher (for a single rater). Additionally, numerous published studies (e.g., Kennealy, Hicks, & Patrick, 2007; McDermott et al., 2000; Poythress et al., 2010) have reported that well-trained evaluators in controlled research contexts can produce scores with high levels of inter-rater reliability.

Of course, there are numerous important differences between collecting rating scale data for research versus applied purposes (Edens & Boccaccini, 2017). For example, they may differ in regards to (a) the informed consent/disclosure process used, such as the right to refuse to participate and the privacy and confidentiality of any information collected; (b) the degree of access to relevant file/collateral information necessary to complete the assessment; and (c) the stakes of the outcome of the assessment for the examinee (i.e., few if any in research contexts, but potential major deprivations of liberty in the field). Additionally, from the perspective of the examinee, an interview performed for research purposes obviously diverges in important ways from a "forensic" interview. How such differences might, for example, influence the likely degree of self-disclosure and impression management evident in a real-world context seems to rarely be given much consideration in regards to its potential impact on the reliability (and validity) of the assessment process.

DeMatteo, Murrie, Edens, and Lankford (2019), Douglas, Nikolova, Kelley, and Edens (2015), and Edens, Petrila, and Kelley (2018) offer recent summaries of the field reliability of PCL-R evaluations. Here, we summarize and distill key findings from these earlier reviews. In regards to "applied reliability" findings, two early publications evaluated the inter-rater reliability of PCL-R scores obtained in forensic/correctional settings. Gacono and Hutton (1994) compared the scoring of one senior staff member to 31 doctoral trainees, who participated in an average of 5 PCL-R interviews/evaluations with this more experienced examiner. Typical inter-rater reliability statistics (intra-class correlations: ICCs) were not reported for the total sample, but all individual trainee scores correlated with the senior staff member scores between $r = .86$ and 1.00 for the 2 to 7 cases that they completed with this staff member (Table 1, p. 305). Correlational results are informative in terms of the relative ordering of examinees, but do not address absolute agreement in terms of score convergence/divergence. Fortunately, Gacono and Hutton reported some group-level data related to this issue, indicating that only about 8% of cases differed by greater than 2 points (see their Fig. 1). In a subsequent study, Kroner and Mills (2001) reported the ICC value for three practicing correctional psychologists who completed a total of 10 PCL-R assessments as part of routine inmate assessment procedures, obtaining an ICC value of .97.

In studies of practitioners, clinicians typically review the same collateral information and participate in or observe the same interview of the examinee. Though similar to research designs, such an approach is vastly different from typical adversarial legal cases, in which two (or more) examiners usually will independently review records and conduct separate interviews (Edens & Boccaccini, 2017). As well, there is no guarantee that examiners will have access to exactly the same file data in adversarial proceedings if they have been retained by opposing sides—although examiners obviously should strive as best they can to obtain any and all information relevant to scoring the PCL-R.

More recent studies in which separate evaluations were conducted have reported inconsistent inter-rater reliability in various field settings. Ismail and Looman (2018), for example, reported that reliability coefficients (e.g., total score ICC = .90) that were comparable to those reported in the PCL-R manual in a sample of 178 sex offenders evaluated at two separate Canadian forensic facilities (one of which happened to be the same facility in which the data reported by Kroner & Mills, 2001 were collected). One significant caveat concerning these results is that those who completed the second PCL-R were not purposefully blinded to the results of the first evaluation, leaving open the possibility of criterion contamination artificially inflating ICC statistics. In contrast to the encouraging results Ismail and Looman obtained, Jeandarme et al. (2017) reported a total score ICC of .42 in a Belgian offender sample ($N = 74$). Additionally, Sturup et al. (2014) reported a total score ICC value of only .70, even though their scores were derived by two separate three-person committees of trained mental health professionals.

In addition to the Ismail and Looman (2018) Canadian data, several field studies have examined the inter-rater reliability of PCL-R scores specifically for sex offenders, with most of these evaluations being conducted as part of adversarial SVP proceedings in the U.S. We describe these studies in greater detail later in relation to concerns about adversarial allegiance, but it is worth highlighting here that the total score ICC values have been quite low (Boccaccini, Turner, & Murrie, 2008; Edens, Cox, Smith, DeMatteo, & Sörman, 2015; Miller, Kimonis, Otto, Kline, & Wasserman, 2012; Murrie, Boccaccini, Johnson, & Janke, 2008). Moreover, the sample sizes reported in some of these studies have been quite large: Miller et al. (2012) reported a single-rater ICC of only .60 for a sample of 313 SVP cases with two scores, whereas Edens et al. (2015) reported a value of only .59 for a large sample of Canadian cases (N = 102 cases comparing a total of 225 pairs of PCL-R scores). In the latter study, the ICC was .66 for cases involving sex offenders and .46 for nonsex offender cases.

Also relevant to this review, a few published studies have compared PCL-R scores from the field with research-based scores (i.e., PCL-R results that were not obtained for the purpose of informing clinical or legal decision-making). Rufino, Boccaccini, Hawes, and Murrie (2012) compared the results of competing PCL-R evaluations for SVP cases (many of which had previously been reported by Murrie et al., 2009) to new scores provided by two trained raters who independently scored the cases (at a later date). The independent raters converged considerably in their assessment of the cases (N = 44), obtaining single-rater ICC values comparable to or higher than those reported in the PCL-R manual. When compared to the forensic examiners, however, the results were quite poor, ranging from .14 (defense expert vs. independent) to .63 (prosecution expert vs. independent). In contrast, Harris, Rice, and Cormier (2013) reported on 58 cases that compared PCL-R scores completed by a research assistant and by hospital clinicians in Canada, reporting a total score ICC_{A1} of .79. Although intriguing, the field data reported by Harris et al. (2013) were collected primarily from two specific mental health examiners (accounting for 42 of the 58 cases) and the generalizability of such findings to other contexts and examiners is unclear. Most recently, Tyrer et al. (2015) found that the ICC value across clinical and research staff involved in the Dangerous and Severe Personality Disorder program in England was a disappointing .50 for the total score for 33 cases.

Although much of the field reliability research has focused on total scores, there is generally clear evidence indicating that the two primary subscales of the PCL-R differ considerably in regards to inter-rater reliability. The interpersonal and affective traits (e.g., remorselessness, manipulativeness, grandiosity) characteristic of Factor 1 appear to be considerably less reliable than are Factor 2 items (Edens, Boccaccini, & Johnson, 2010; Harris et al., 2013; Ismail & Looman, 2018; Jeandarme et al., 2017; Miller et al., 2012; Rufino et al., 2012; Sturup et al., 2014; see also Tyrer et al., 2005). Even in studies in which the total score ICC is judged to be acceptable, the reliability of Factor 1 scores usually fall below .70 (Harris et al., 2013). In fact, some field results indicate that more than half the variance in Factor 1 scores is associated with some form of measurement error (e.g., Edens et al., 2010; Miller et al., 2012). Such results are particularly troubling given that these traits are considered by many mental health professionals and laypersons to be the most prototypical features of psychopathy (Kreis, Cooke, Michie, Hoff, & Logan, 2012; Smith, Edens, Clark, & Rulseh, 2014), even though they are actually the least relevant to predicting future crime and violence in most published research (see, e.g., Kennealy, Skeem, Walters, & Camp, 2010).

There are numerous potential causes for the modest level of inter-rater reliability reported in most of the studies summarized before. One such cause appears to be that examiners seem to differ appreciably in terms of the average PCL-R scores that they provide for the examinees that they are tasked with evaluating. That is, some mental health professionals appear to be more prone than others to rating the average examinee as much higher (or lower) on the PCL-R. For example, in a field study examining forensic experts retained by the same side in SVP cases, Boccaccini et al. (2008; p. 272) reported that two examiners who had conducted a combined total of 100 assessments provided PCL-R total scores that differed *on average* by almost 10 points. This indicates that the obtained scores are to no small extent a function of the expert conducting the assessment rather than simply being an objective assessment of the "true" level of psychopathy exhibited by the defendant. In fact, Boccaccini et al. (2008) estimated that over 30% of the variability in PCL-R scoring may be explained by the examiners who are conducting the evaluation rather than being a reflection of genuine differences in the defendants who are being assessed.

In addition to the individual examiner playing an important role in the PCL-R scores provided, the side of the case that retains the examiner also seems to have a pronounced impact on the results of these evaluations. In the first study to explore potential PCL-R adversarial allegiance, Murrie et al. (2008) collected PCL-R scores assigned by petitioner-retained (i.e., prosecution-retained) and defense-retained psychologists in 23 SVP cases in Texas. The difference between PCL-R scores was quite large (Cohen's $d = 1.03$) and reflective of a very low level of inter-rater agreement across raters (ICC = .39). In every case, the petitioner-retained evaluator assigned the higher score whereas the defense-retained evaluator assigned the lower score. When Murrie et al. (2009) updated this sample to include 35 SVP cases, they found similar allegiance effects in PCL-R scoring. Of some note, there was evidence of poor reliability even among evaluators on the same side of adversarial proceedings, but scores were systematically unreliable among opposing evaluators, with defense-retained evaluators usually assigning lower scores than those called by the prosecution.

More recently, DeMatteo et al. (2014a) reported on 29 sexually violent predator cases in which the same respondent was evaluated by two different examiners. The ICC in this sample was a modest .58, but of even greater concern was that scores produced by prosecutor experts were appreciably higher than the scores produced by defense experts. More specifically, prosecution experts reported scores of 30 or above in nearly 50% of the cases, whereas less than 10% of defense expert scores fell in that range. Noted earlier, a subsequent Canadian case law survey (Edens et al., 2015) examined a much larger number of criminal cases. Mean score differences across "Crown" (i.e., prosecution) and defense expert scores in this study again suggested adversarial allegiance, with mean scores differing by more than 4.5 points.

The aforementioned results suggest the possibility of allegiance effects, but do not definitively demonstrate that it is the cause of the prosecution vs. defense mean score differences on the PCL-R. To demonstrate the phenomenon of adversarial allegiance—as distinct from other potential forms of bias or selection effects—would require a research design in which attorneys are randomly assigned different forensic experts, experts are randomly assigned to attorneys, experts have access to exactly the same materials, and researchers have access to data from all experts who conducted an evaluation. Only in such a scenario would discrepant PCL-R scores from opposing evaluators be clearly attributable to adversarial allegiance rather than to selection effects or genuine differences in the data available to opposing evaluators.

To explore this possibility, Murrie, Boccaccini, Guarnera, and Rufino (2013) recruited over 100 practicing, doctoral-level forensic psychologists and psychiatrists and led them to believe that they were participating in a formal, large-scale forensic consultation. These individuals were randomly assigned to either a prosecution-allegiance or defense-allegiance condition. Participants briefly met with an attorney who posed as leading either a public defender service or a specialized prosecution unit, and the attorney then requested that the expert score the PCL-R and other instruments based on extensive offender records. Each participant scored the same four case files, which spanned from low risk to high risk. Each set of case materials was derived from an actual case and included extensive records and a transcript of a PCL-R interview.

In summary, the results showed a clear pattern of adversarial allegiance, with the scores assigned by those who believed they were working for prosecution experts being appreciably higher than the scores from those who believed they were working for the defense. For the PCL-R total score, prosecution evaluators assigned significantly higher scores for three of four cases, with effect sizes in the medium to large range (Cohen's d of .55 to .85) and similar in magnitude to effects (d = .63 to .83) documented in actual SVP proceedings (Murrie et al., 2009). The one case in which there was no significant evidence of an allegiance effect was selected by the research team to be unusually low in psychopathy. Examiners tended to converge on very low scores for this particular case, regardless of who they believed had retained them.

In summary, the inter-rater reliability of the PCL-R "in the field" seems to be much lower than what has been reported in the instrument's manual and in well-controlled research publications. Based on the results of these studies, Edens et al. (2015) argued that the field reliability of the PCL-R for an individual rater may be closer to .60 in applied forensic settings rather than the approximately .85 value reported in the professional manual. Although some statisticians have suggested that ICC estimates as low as .60 may represent "good" reliability for group-level research purposes, Nunnally and Bernstein (1994; p. 265) document how, as values drop below .90, using such instruments for individual case decision-making becomes increasingly problematic.

From the perspective of the PCL-R SEM, .60 would indicate that it is likely closer to 5 points rather than 3. As noted by Edens et al. (2015), for a typical male prisoner given a PCL-R score of approximately 22 (the average among male prisoners in the professional manual), an SEM of 5 indicates that there would be a 68% probability that his "true" raw score falls between 17 and 27. In terms of percentile ranks from the PCL-R manual (Hare, 2003, p. 164), these raw score values indicate a 68% likelihood of his true score falling somewhere between the 28th and 71st percentiles. Using a more conservative 95% confidence interval, there would be a 95% probability that the true score falls between 12 and 32, which corresponds to the 13th and 91st percentiles for male prisoners.

Although perhaps less extensively researched than the PCL-R, the history of the reliability of personality disorder diagnoses in general has been less than stellar in the mental health field. In fact, the most recent field trials for diagnostic reliability for DSM-5 (Freedman et al., 2013) indicated that APD diagnoses had very poor rates of agreement across independent examiners. Attempts to improve psychiatric diagnostic reliability over the years have focused on the development of various structured interviews in an attempt to standardize the assessment of psychiatric disorders, including personality disorders. Unfortunately, rates of diagnostic agreement across these different methods of assessing personality disorders such as APD generally have been relatively poor (Clark & Harrison, 2001; Clark, Livesley, & Morey, 1997; Cunningham & Reidy, 1998; Tyrer et al., 2015).

In summary, one would think that the potential unreliability of expert evidence should be a foundational issue that in practice raises challenges to the admissibility of any opinions based on such evidence. The published case law reviews discussed earlier for the most part have not suggested that *to date* attorneys are frequently challenging the reliability of such evidence and, when they do, it is relatively rare that judges exclude it. At least in the U.S., this may be because judges have considerable discretion in determining whether to admit expert evidence and may tend to prefer to allow jurors to decide how much weight to give to expert evidence of questionable reliability rather than exclude it outright. Rigorous cross-examination of expert witnesses and the presentation of rebuttal testimony are frequently described by U.S. courts as effective ways of challenging the probative value of controversial evidence (e.g., *Barefoot v. Estelle*, 1983; *Ford v. Wainwright*, 1986; *Panetti v. Quarterman*, 2007). Nevertheless, based on the published inter-rater reliability data, we would argue that attorneys facing the prospect of their clients being labeled as "psychopaths" should consider robust challenges to the admissibility of such evidence based on its *insufficiency* and *incredibility* (Grisso, 2003).

Psychopathy evidence and the potential for stigmatization

Given the socially undesirable nature of the traits associated with psychopathy, a legal controversy separate from its potential unreliability is whether it is likely to be unduly stigmatizing when used to label a defendant as being "a psychopath" in a court of law (O'Brien & Wayland, 2013). Community survey data indicates that, when asked to identify an example of a psychopath, laypersons in the U.S. most commonly mention famous American serial killers such as Ted Bundy and Jeffrey Dahmer. In fact, when asked to spontaneously identify the person they first thought of when hearing the term "psychopath," a sample of over 400 venirepersons from Texas most frequently listed Charles Manson (Edens, Clark, Smith, Cox, & Kelley, 2013; see also Helfgott, 1997; Smith et al., 2014).

Separate from research on prototypical exemplars of the psychopath label, research over the past 15 years also has investigated the perceived correlates of psychopathy among laypersons. This research, most of which involves the presentation of case vignettes to mock jurors, suggests that those who perceive defendants to be highly psychopathic tend to respond more negatively to them than do those jurors who do not view them as being particularly psychopathic (Edens, Davis, Fernandez, & Guy, 2013). A recent meta-analysis of this literature (Kelley, Edens, Mowle, Penson, & Rulseh, 2019) examined the association between perceived defendant psychopathy and legal outcomes in ten juror simulation studies. Those who rated hypothetical criminal defendants as more psychopathic supported more punitive legal consequences for them, such as longer sentences ($r_w = .27$) and death verdicts ($r_w = .22$), and viewed them as more dangerous ($r_w = .31$) and evil ($r_w = .44$). Interestingly, the prejudicial effect of perceived psychopathy in legal proceedings to date has appeared to be relatively specific to this disorder, in that juror ratings of other diagnoses investigated (e.g., schizophrenia, borderline personality disorder, depression) have resulted in weaker and nonsignificant associations with case outcomes (Cox, Edens, Rulseh, & Clark, 2016; Mowle, Edens, Clark, & Sörman, 2016).

Although there is relatively less research on the extent to which APD is stigmatizing in comparison to the psychopathy label, available research indicates that this diagnosis also is quite pejorative. In a study examining the prejudicial effects of 40 different diagnostic categories included in the DSM, APD was identified by laypersons as the most stigmatizing, even surpassing (albeit to a very modest degree) a diagnosis of "pedophilia" in terms of being socially rejected (Feldman & Crandall, 2007).

In addition to simulation studies, there is some evidence to suggest that when actual jurors support severe sanctions against criminal defendants, they tend to describe those defendants using terms very reminiscent of a prototypical psychopath. For example, Sundby (1998) published research from the Capital Jury Project indicating that jurors who had participated in capital trials described defendants whom they had sentenced to death with phrases such as "blasé," "cocky," "very unremorseful," "cocksure," "nonchalant," "no remorse—almost a cocky attitude," and "clever, smart, [and] calculating." More generally, the prototypically psychopathic trait of remorselessness plays a prominent role in the adjudication of defendants within the criminal justice system (Bandes, 2016; Morse, 2014; Zhong et al., 2014).

Collectively, the evidence cited before clearly suggests that *if* a juror believes a defendant to be psychopathic, that juror *then* tends to hold more negative attitudes toward that defendant and support more punitive sanctions. Such results do not, however, necessarily lead to the conclusion that expert evidence or testimony regarding psychopathy will change juror perceptions of a criminal defendant or lead them to judge him or her more severely in terms of potential legal sanctions. Since the early 2000s, research has investigated how laypersons respond to psychopathy evidence that is introduced by expert witnesses and whether such responses may result in more negative outcomes for defendants. This research typically involves simulation designs based on vignettes in which mock jurors review experimentally manipulated mental health evidence prior to providing opinions about their beliefs concerning appropriate outcomes (e.g., verdicts) and perceptions of the defendant (e.g., how dangerous they are). Of note, early mock jury studies found that experimental manipulations of psychopathy evidence did in fact cause mock jurors to perceive the defendant to be more psychopathic and resulted in greater support for more punitive sanctions (Edens, Colwell, Desforges, & Fernandez, 2005).

Berryessa and Wohlstetter (2019) recently published a meta-analysis that investigated the introduction of the label "psychopath" into evidence in jury simulation studies and examined its effects in relation to recommended sentences/sanctions, perceived dangerousness, and perceived treatment amenability. For studies experimentally comparing the effects of a psychopath label versus no diagnostic label, their study demonstrated significant differences in legal sentences/sanctions ($d = 0.17$), dangerousness ($d = 0.58$), and treatment amenability ($d = -0.30$), findings that generally were consistent with prior narrative reviews of this literature (e.g., Douglas et al., 2015; Edens, Petrila, & Kelley, 2018). However, their summary effect sizes for the three legally relevant outcomes in studies that compared a psychopathic label to another diagnostic label (e.g., schizophrenia) were weak and statistically nonsignificant (legal sentences/sanctions: $d = 0.09$; dangerousness: $d = 0.14$; treatment amenability: $d = 0.02$). The authors argued that their results suggested that there was a general negative labeling effect for psychopathy, but not a specific labeling effect for this disorder relative to other diagnostic conditions.

One of the most interesting findings reported by Berryessa and Wohlstetter (2019) was evidence of considerable heterogeneity among the effect sizes reported in the original research. This usually raises the concern that the individual studies being combined into a global effect size are not representative of the same underlying population. Given that mock juror investigations of the impact of diagnostic and other mental health information can differ in numerous important design features, it should not be surprising that heterogeneous effects would be found in this body of literature (Truong, Kelley, & Edens, 2021). Such studies can differ on, for example, the type of criminal case employed (e.g., murder, sexual offending, white collar crime) and the types of stimulus materials and experimental manipulations included in the case vignette (e.g., the number and/or severity of symptoms provided in support of a diagnostic conclusion). Notably, Berryessa and Wohlstetter (2019) investigated several potential moderators (e.g., type of sample, type of legal case) that might help to explain the disparate effect sizes identified in their meta-analysis and found some support for the idea that the methodological features of the studies included did influence the magnitude of the effect sizes that were reported.

Although informative, one potentially important design issue that Berryessa and Wohlstetter (2019) did not appear to systematically investigate was whether studies included some type of check to determine whether mock jurors were responsive to the experimental manipulations of mental health evidence (Truong et al., 2021). Of particular note, several of the research studies failing to identify a stigmatizing effect for psychopathy evidence relative to other diagnostic conditions did not include such checks to ascertain whether experimental manipulations had any effects on juror perceptions of the defendant's mental health status (i.e., whether the defendant actually was perceived to be more psychopathic in that condition compared to the others). Many of these studies focused on more distal case outcomes (e.g., support for death sentences) and did not examine the more proximal question of whether participants differ in their perceptions of the defendant's level of psychopathy across study conditions.

One such publication (Saks, Schweitzer, Aharoni, & Kiehl, 2014) manipulated the type of diagnostic evidence (Psychopathy, Schizophrenia, "Healthy") that was presented to participants, who then provided death verdict recommendations and rated the defendant on various other characteristics (e.g., perceived level of dangerousness, perceived control over their actions). Given the very large *N*s reported across the two samples investigated, this particular study likely had a pronounced effect on the Berryessa and Wohlstetter (2019) meta-analytic results. Notably, the results of Saks et al. suggested that psychopathy evidence had relatively little consistent impact on mock juror decision-making when compared to the schizophrenia condition and, somewhat oddly, there was evidence to suggest that both diagnostic labels had some mitigating impact on mock juror support for capital punishment relative to the "healthy" condition. That is, participants were less likely to vote for death when the defendant was labeled as psychopathic or schizophrenic than when labeled as not suffering from a mental disorder.

Recently, Truong et al. (2021) attempted to replicate the results of Saks et al. (2014) using identical stimulus materials and experimental manipulations but with the inclusion of a direct measure of how psychopathic participants perceived the defendant to be across all conditions. Perhaps the most salient finding reported by Truong et al. was that jurors did not differ in their ratings of the defendant's level of psychopathic traits across any conditions. Regardless of the expert testimony provided, mock jurors rated the defendant as highly psychopathic, even in a control condition in which no expert diagnostic evidence was presented. Because the case background materials provided to all participants had described the defendant as remorseless, manipulative, and superficial (among other personality traits), Truong et al. argued that this likely caused a ceiling effect (see their Table 1) that minimized any likely additional impact that the label "psychopath" would have on mock jurors in that experimental condition.

Similar to the results of Saks et al. (2014), Truong et al. (2021) also found support for the claim that jurors in the healthy condition showed *greater* support for death verdicts than in either the psychopathy or schizophrenia conditions, which did not differ from each other. It needs to be highlighted, however, that the healthy diagnostic condition differed from the other two diagnostic conditions not only in terms of the label presented to the study participants: within both disordered conditions, the defendant was explicitly described by expert witnesses as capable of controlling his behavior and acting in accordance with the law. In the psychopathic and schizophrenic conditions, however, these same experts asserted that, because of these diagnoses, the defendant was *incapable* of controlling his behavior. As such, the presence/absence of a mental disorder was confounded with expert claims concerning volitional control over criminal behavior.

Collectively, the findings of Saks et al. (2014) and Truong et al. (2021) could be argued to support the assertion that expert evidence claiming that a defendant is psychopathic (or schizophrenic) conceivably could have some mitigating effect on attitudes toward death verdicts, but with some very significant caveats. First, this may only apply to scenarios in which jurors *already believe* that a defendant is highly psychopathic. Second, it may only apply if defense experts are capable of convincing jurors that the psychopath label identifies a type of mental disorder that makes defendants *incapable* of controlling their criminal actions. Such an effect could be obtained in these two studies, but it should be reiterated that the psychopathy (as well as the schizophrenia) condition were being compared to one in which a psychologically healthy defendant was also described *by his own expert witnesses* as clearly capable of controlling his criminal actions (in stark contrast to the other two diagnostic conditions). The external validity of such a comparison condition is suspect, at least in an adversarial legal system such as the U.S. in which defense attorneys have considerable latitude over which expert witnesses they would choose to call to testify.

Additionally, neither study investigated whether such defense expert opinions would have any effect if followed by cross-examination and/or rebuttal evidence that makes the (very likely) prosecution argument that psychopathic criminals are fully capable of controlling their actions (DeMatteo et al., 2014a, 2014b; Edens, Petrila, & Kelley, 2018). It should also be noted that survey research suggests that community members attending jury duty in the U.S. generally endorse the position that psychopaths are responsible for their own actions and are capable of determining right from wrong (Smith et al., 2014). As such, defense claims to the contrary in real-world cases are likely to face an uphill battle to alter such initial attitudes and beliefs.

Although mock jury studies have greatly expanded our understanding of the effects of mental health evidence on laypersons, it seems critical to scrutinize thoroughly the design of experimental manipulations used to investigate the effects of psychopathy evidence in order to make sense of its impact on case decision-making. The results of Truong et al. (2021) also highlight the usefulness of considering intermediate constructs (e.g., juror perceptions of a defendant's diagnostic status) in addition to assessing more distal outcome variables in this type of research. Such quasi-manipulation checks would allow for a more precise interpretation of the effects of a study's stimulus materials and manipulations on these outcome variables. Additionally, further investigation of the effects of psychopathy evidence using other methodologies, such as observational data (see, e.g., Boccaccini, Murrie, & Turner, 2014), would be informative. Although such approaches suffer from their own limitations (e.g., inability to determine cause-and-effect relationships), they also likely improve upon the external validity and generalizability of the findings to other real-world legal settings.

In summary, although the bulk of the research suggests that psychopathy evidence is associated with negative attitudes toward a defendant and support for punitive legal outcomes, it does not necessarily support the argument that psychopathy evidence produces *undue* prejudice per se. In many contexts it may not be unreasonable to assume that a psychopathic defendant may pose a greater risk of violence compared with a nonpsychopathic defendant (Yang, Wong, & Coid, 2010). To the extent that legal outcomes are being influenced by psychopathy evidence beyond what is empirically justifiable, however, attributing such traits to a defendant could be unduly prejudicial. Concerns about stigmatization may be especially applicable to U.S. capital cases because, for example, psychopathy testimony predicts support for death verdicts even *after* accounting for juror ratings of perceived dangerousness (Edens, Colwell, et al.,

2005). As Kelley et al. (2019) noted, the strong association between ratings of psychopathy and ratings of being "evil" would seem to be evidence of undue prejudice, which highlights long-standing concerns that psychopathy may be a "moral judgement masquerading as a clinical diagnosis" (Blackburn, 1988, p. 511).

Other controversies regarding psychopathy evidence

Even if the inter-rater reliability and the potentially prejudicial effects of psychopathy evidence were not significant sources of general concern, the probative value of this type of evidence may be problematic when it is used to address certain specific legal questions. In this section, we address several such questions and highlight the extant scientific research relevant to each topic. More detailed discussions regarding several of these issues are available elsewhere and interested readers are encouraged to review these extensive critiques (DeMatteo et al., 2014a; DeMatteo et al., 2019; Douglas et al., 2015; Edens, DeMatteo, et al., 2018; Edens, Petrila, & Kelley, 2018; Jelicic, Merckelbach, & Bošković, 2018; O'Brien & Wayland, 2013; Polaschek & Skeem, 2018).

Psychopathy as a rebuttal to mental disorder evidence

As we noted in an earlier section, historically the legal system has taken a dim view of psychopathy and APD as potential exculpatory or mitigating factors in criminal proceedings. In fact, high PCL-R scores have been offered in court to rebut defense evidence that defendants suffer from some form of potentially mitigating or exculpatory mental disorder, such as schizophrenia or intellectual disabilities. In some regards, the PCL-R would seem to be particularly appealing to the prosecution as a rebuttal instrument when defense-retained experts argue that a defendant suffers from some form of serious mental illness because—unlike the DSM—the scoring of its items is independent of the presence of other psychopathological characteristics. Diagnosing APD, for example, is not appropriate if the antisocial conduct occurs in response to or in the context of certain other mental disorders (e.g., psychotic-spectrum disorders). The PCL-R, however, is essentially descriptive in its approach to item ratings and the "cause" of (for example) callousness, impulsivity, and/or irresponsible behavior is not particularly relevant to the score an examinee receives. Additionally, unlike APD diagnoses, crossing the quasi-diagnostic threshold on the PCL-R (score >/= 30) does not require any history of Conduct Disorder symptoms having been present as an adolescent.

In regards to the empirical relationship between psychotic-spectrum diagnoses and PCL-R scores and APD diagnoses, the extant evidence clearly indicates that highly psychopathic individuals can also suffer from major mental disorders (Darjee, Øfstegaard, & Thomson, 2017; De Page, Mercenier, & Titeca, 2018; Engelstad, Rund, Lau, Vaskinn, & Torgalsbøen, 2019; Sedgwick et al., 2018; Stratton, Brook, & Hanlon, 2017; Tengström, Hodgins, Grann, Långström, & Kullgren, 2004). In fact, there is evidence to suggest that an early precursor to the PCL-R actually misidentified an appreciable percentage of individuals with schizophrenia as being psychopathic

(Howard, Bailey, & Newman, 1984, cf. Hare & Harpur, 1986; more recently, see De Page, Matteucci, & Englebert, 2018). As such, attempting to rule out these types of disorders based only on an elevated PCL-R score has no real scientific support.

In relation to significant intellectual disabilities or deficits, guidelines have been published regarding how the standard PCL-R test administration procedures would need to be modified to assess individuals with intellectual disabilities (Morrissey, 2008), but relatively little scientific research has been published on whether this rating scale can adequately assess this disorder (simply for research purposes, rather than for applied settings such as criminal cases) when the person being assessed has very limited cognitive abilities. A few studies of European offenders have appeared in the literature over the years, however, and they suggest that this rating scale may not, in essence, "work" as well as an assessment of psychopathic traits when intellectual deficits are present (Morrissey et al., 2005, 2007, 2010). This in large part seems to reflect difficulties in determining how to score various specific PCL-R items (e.g., parasitic lifestyle, irresponsibility, many short-term marital relationships) that may overlap considerably with the types of adaptive behavior deficits that are commonly associated with significant intellectual deficits (e.g., poor academic performance, lack of independent living, impoverished employment history). It appears to be quite difficult to reliably differentiate between adaptive behavior deficits that are caused by limited intellectual abilities versus those that are associated more so with personality disorders such as psychopathy (Morrissey et al., 2010). It should also be highlighted here that the research conducted in this area to date has demonstrated that PCL-R scores *do not* predict any form of institutional violence or aggression among inmates with intellectual disabilities (Morrissey et al., 2007).

Finally, in addition to arguing for the absence of serious mental disorder, psychopathy evidence has on occasion been used to bolster prosecution claims that defendants are malingering severe mental disorder (DeMatteo & Edens, 2006; O'Brien & Wayland, 2013). Despite such assertions, and in contrast to the DSM-5 continuing to identify APD as a potential risk factor for malingering, the extant scientific literature does not provide particularly compelling evidence that highly psychopathic individuals are more likely than others to fabricate symptoms of severe mental disorder or are more adept at such dissimulation (DeMatteo & Edens, 2006; Jelicic et al., 2018; Resnick & Knoll IV, 2018; van Impelen et al., 2017; see also Pierson, Rosenfeld, Green, & Belfi, 2011). Using the PCL-R in such a capacity we would argue is a clear example of Grisso's (1986) *insufficiency* and *incredibility* problems in forensic mental health assessment. Moreover, given that there are well-validated assessment procedures designed to detect feigned mental disorder, forensic mental health examiners would be much better served by relying on those methods rather than an at best weak and indirect measure such as a personality disorder rating scale.

Psychopathy evidence and volitional impairment

Can individuals who are highly psychopathic control their behavior? If not, should they be held accountable for their criminal activities? Noted earlier, when rebutting defense claims regarding mental disorder the prosecution typically is using the psychopathy diagnosis to aid in the portrayal of defendants as having volitional control over their actions and as capable of understanding right from wrong. A lack of control—at least regarding how the legal concept of volitional impairment typically is construed in relation to criminal cases—is not a defining characteristic of psychopathy as it is commonly conceptualized by clinicians. Despite this, there are at least anecdotal examples of such claims being made in court, typically in SVP evaluations (DeMatteo et al., 2014a). For example, *In the Interest of J.M.* (2006), an expert witness provided testimony claiming that a defendant's elevated PCL-R Factor 1 score was indicative of impoverished volitional control, as it is legally defined. Describing research on psychopathy, this witness asserted that there exists "clear unequivocal laboratory evidence of a deficit in response modulation…the best operational you're going to get of diminishment of volitional capacity" (pp. 522–523; for a similar example, see *State v. Anderson*, 2007).

Despite its potential influence, most scholars seem to be of the opinion that testimony concerning neurological and psychophysiological correlates of psychopathy is of limited relevance to legal decisions (e.g., sentencing, culpability) because the extant research base suffers from numerous methodological limitations and has not been shown to add any incremental utility to standard assessment methods in predicting or explaining criminal behavior (e.g., Hare, Black, & Walsh, 2013; Patrick, Venables, & Skeem, 2012). Given the state of the science, one could reasonably argue that such mental health evidence suffers from the problems of *irrelevance*, *insufficiency*, and *incredibility* (Grisso, 1986, 2003). We should also note, however, that an increasing number of scholars and researchers seem to be warming to the idea that such evidence eventually should be considered as exculpatory (see, e.g., Kinscherff, 2010), or at least relevant to concepts such as diminished capacity. We return to this topic in the final section of this chapter.

The stability and treatment amenability of psychopathy

Although we have previously discussed the importance of psychometric reliability as it relates to assessments across different examiners, it is also important to consider reliability from a temporal perspective as well. In regards to psychopathy evidence, this comes up typically in relation to two inter-related questions: is psychopathy immutable over time, with diagnoses remaining stable over the course of the lifespan, and can psychopathy be successfully treated in forensic/correctional settings? Individuals designated as "psychopaths" are often viewed as a class of individuals who are unchanging and untreatable. Despite the presumption of immutability of this category of mental disorders, a wealth of scientific research on the long-term stability of personality disorder diagnoses actually indicates that they are neither intra-ctable nor untreatable (Clark, 2007; Loranger et al., 1991; Morey et al., 2007; Morey & Hopwood, 2013).

In relation to measuring potential change over time, it should be highlighted that the PCL-R was never intended to be particularly sensitive to such fluctuations, with the professional manual (Hare, 2003) stressing that it should not be used as an indicator of treatment responsiveness due to the "life course history" approach to scoring the items. That being said, examinations of the long-term stability of PCL-R scores have met with at best mixed results. Large-scale outcome studies investigating psychopathy among youth indicate some degree of stability across childhood and adolescence and through the transition to adulthood (Burke, Loeber, & Lahey, 2007; Loney, Taylor, Butler, & Iacono, 2007; Lynam et al., 2009; Lynam, Caspi, Moffitt, Loeber, & Stouthamer-Loeber, 2007). For example, Lynam et al. reported that correlation between the Childhood Psychopathy Scale (CPS) administered at age 12 and the screening version of the PCL-R at age 24 was .31 in a large sample of at-risk youths. The corresponding values for the CPS and the interpersonal and affective facets were only .19 and 15, respectively. Over a much shorter period of time, Burke et al. reported a PCL:YV stability coefficient of .66 from ages 18 to 19. The stability of Factor 1 scores was especially low (.43) but was appreciably stronger for Factor 2 (.73). In an older sample, Rutherford, Cacciola, Alterman, McKay, and Cook (1999) found a 2-year test-retest reliability value of .60 (ICC) for PCL-R total scores among 200 male patients receiving services in a methadone clinic.

The degree to which psychopathy is amenable to intervention remains an area of open inquiry and is subject to increasingly optimistic discussion and research (Larsen, Jalava, & Griffiths, 2020; Polaschek, 2014; Polaschek & Skeem, 2018). This is in sharp contrast to historical views and the results of some widely cited earlier treatment outcome research suggesting that rehabilitation efforts may make highly psychopathic individuals more dangerous (e.g., Harris, Rice, & Cormier, 1994 Rice, 1997). Among other questionable aspects of these early results, the Canadian rehabilitation program in question included mandatory "interventions" such as forced administration of psychotropic medication (e.g., stimulants), seclusion, and participation in marathon encounter groups *in the nude*. It is also important to highlight that, in response to civil litigation filed by former patients at this facility, the Canadian legal system recently held that such aspects of this treatment approach were in fact *torture*—not treatment (Fine, 2017; Polaschek & Skeem, 2018).

Despite such early claims, recent research offers some preliminary evidence of positive treatment effects for both adult and adolescent offenders (Caldwell, McCormick, Wolfe, & Umstead, 2012; D'Silva, Duggan, & McCarthy, 2004; Polaschek & Daly, 2013; Salekin, Worley, & Grimes, 2010; Skeem, Polaschek, & Manchak, 2009; Wong, Gordon, Gu, Lewis, & Olver, 2012). In regards to the treatment of psychopathic juvenile offenders, a growing body of research suggests that the likelihood of future violence can be appreciably reduced when appropriate intervention strategies are used (Caldwell, 2011; Caldwell et al., 2012; Caldwell, Skeem, Salekin, & Van Rybroek, 2006). For example, Caldwell (2011) found that psychopathic youth, particularly those with elevated interpersonal deficits, exhibited significant decreases in general and violent recidivism following an intensive treatment program based on social control theory and focused on interpersonal processes, social skill acquisition, and the development of conventional social bonds. Further, delinquent male adolescents who received the specialized treatment provided in this study self-reported changes in psychopathic characteristics throughout the program that was also correlated with improved institutional conduct and treatment compliance (Caldwell et al., 2012).

These encouraging results notwithstanding, available research does indicate that those who are highly psychopathic generally have been *relatively* less likely to benefit from the types of interventions that have been the focus of research and that they also are prone to exhibiting problematic behaviors such as difficulty in forming attachments, impulsive-disruptive behavior, and limited motivation (e.g., Langton, Barbaree, Harkins, & Peacock, 2006; Leygraf & Elsner, 2007; Looman, Abracen, Serin, & Marquis, 2005; Ogloff, Wong, & Greenwood, 1990). In comparison with other domains of psychopathy research, adult treatment strategies and outcomes have undergone relatively limited advancement, with emerging evidence based largely on case studies or recently initiated programs with preliminary results. But the relative absence of controlled studies examining treatment approaches that are known to decrease recidivism among adult correctional populations more generally should not be considered evidence to support the common assumption that any given highly psychopathic inmate or patient will not (or cannot) respond to interventions that have been demonstrated to work with other high-risk populations (see, generally, Andrews & Bonta, 2010).

Future directions

We end this chapter with a brief discussion of what we believe may be increasingly important issues and controversies concerning the role of psychopathy evidence in the courts over the next several years. Although we agree with the old Danish adage that "it is difficult to make predictions, particularly about the future," we offer the following as topics that we expect will become increasingly important for scholars, practitioners, and policy-makers to address moving forward.

First, whether the inter-rater reliability of PCL-R evaluations in adversarial settings can be improved is an important topic for further investigation. Noted earlier, at present one could reasonably argue that the level of reliability evident for the interpersonal and affective scales—which also are the most stigmatizing features of the disorder to attribute to a defendant—is so poor that such information should not be presented to legal decision-makers. Although the admissibility of expert evidence is ultimately determined by the judiciary, mental health experts bear considerable ethical responsibility in relation to selecting assessment instruments that are sufficiently reliable and valid to warrant their application in forensic settings. In relation to the conduct of psychological assessments, ethical standards in the U.S. mandate that "Psychologists' work is based upon established scientific and professional knowledge of the discipline" (APA, 2010; Standard 2.04) and that "Psychologists base the opinions contained in their recommendations, reports, and diagnostic or evaluative statements, including forensic testimony, on information and techniques sufficient to substantiate their findings" (APA, 2010; Standard 9.01). We would argue that, if 40-point rating scale truly does have an SEM of 5 or higher in adversarial settings (Edens et al., 2015), this falls well short of being "sufficient" for real-world applications (Nunnally & Bernstein, 1994).

That being said, there is some evidence to suggest that certain forensic mental health examiners can produce more reliable and valid results than others on instruments such as the PCL-R (Boccaccini, Rufino, Jeon, & Murrie, 2017), which raises the possibility of improving applied work in this area perhaps by some type of mandatory training or advanced certification. Although a review of this topic is beyond the scope of this chapter, how exactly one might create and implement such a system in any particular jurisdiction would seem to be fraught with numerous logistical problems. Additionally, advanced training in isolation may not be a panacea for poor reliability. Blais, Forth, and Hare (2017) recently examined inter-rater reliability among 280 raters who had completed formal PCL-R training and scored six practice cases. They reported low reliability for several individual items ($ICC_{A,1}$ values ranging from .14 to .82), at best marginal reliability (see Edens & Boccaccini, 2017; Nunnally & Bernstein, 1994) for total scores ($ICC_{A,1}$ = .75) and Factor 2 scores ($ICC_{A,1}$ = .78), and even lower reliability for Factor 1 scores ($ICC_{A,1}$ = .65). Particularly when one considers that the participants had just completed a multiday training workshop with the instrument developer, such results are not particularly encouraging. The authors of this research in fact bluntly concluded in their Public Significance Statement that the reliability achieved by these trained raters "did not meet the standard recommended for criminal cases" (p. 762).

Another area of potentially considerable consequence to the courts is the increasing role of neuroscience evidence regarding both the diagnosis and etiology of psychopathy (Umbach, Berryessa, & Raine, 2015). Although, as noted earlier, psychopathy evidence typically seems to be a "prosecution tool" used in an attempt to prejudice jurors against a defendant, there have been cases in which such evidence is proactively introduced by the defense. In these instances, the defense typically uses such evidence for exculpatory purposes (e.g., to claim that defendants are incapable of controlling their actions and should not be held criminally responsible for them) or as a mitigating factor suggesting that they are at least *less responsible* for whatever criminal acts they have committed. In recent years such defense claims have been bolstered in some cases by the introduction of neuroscience evidence (e.g., FMRI brain scans) arguing that psychopathic defendants essentially suffer from a form of brain dysfunction. It will be fascinating to observe how courts (and legislatures) will respond to neuroscientific research as it relates to legal concepts such as, for example, free will, volitional control, and legal responsibility. Additionally, although some mock jury simulations have examined how triers-of-fact may respond to neuroscience data, there remains much to be learned about the impact of such "brain evidence" on juror attitudes and outcomes in real-world cases.

Another area of uncertainty concerns how the assessment of psychopathy will evolve in mental health and forensic settings. The future of personality disorder classification systems seems to be dimensional models of dysfunction. This is evident in the current ICD-11 system as well as in the "Alternative Model" of personality disorders (see, e.g., Waugh et al., 2017) that was proposed for DSM-5 but ultimately relegated to its section of diagnoses and assessment methods in need of further research and investigation. The field reliability and validity of diagnostic information from such dimensional systems and how they will be received in the legal arena are open questions and will be important avenues of future applied research (cf. Filone, Strohmaier, Murphy, & DeMatteo, 2014).

Finally, in both DSM-5 and ICD-11, a new "Limited Prosocial Emotions" specifier was added to the diagnosis of Conduct Disorder that consists of four criteria that overlap considerably with the concept of psychopathy (lack of remorse or guilt, callousness/lack of empathy, lack of concern about performance in important activities, and shallow or deficient affect). Although evidence concerning psychopathy occasionally has been introduced in juvenile cases over the years (Viljoen, MacDougall, et al., 2010; Viljoen, McLachlan, & Vincent, 2010), it seems likely that the inclusion of this specifier in the official psychiatric nomenclature will lead to "juvenile psychopathy" evidence increasingly being introduced into juvenile justice settings. The preceding concerns we reviewed regarding the reliability of psychopathy evidence in adversarial settings and its potential for unduly stigmatizing defendants are even more salient in relation to the assessment of adolescents.

Conclusions

In conclusion, we would echo some of the concerns raised in other recent reviews of the role of psychopathy evidence in legal proceedings (DeMatteo et al., 2020, 2019; Edens, Petrila, & Kelley, 2018; O'Brien & Wayland, 2013). Courts should examine questions of admissibility more critically than they have in the past, particularly given extant findings that (a) cast doubt on the reliability of PCL-R ratings and APD diagnoses in applied (and particularly adversarial) settings and (b) raise significant concerns about the potentially unduly prejudicial effects of introducing such evidence in criminal and civil commitment cases. Although accumulated research findings suggest that those who are psychopathic—assuming a reliable assessment—are more likely to engage in various socially undesirable behaviors (e.g., criminal recidivism), it should not be assumed that a particular examiner's evaluation of any given defendant/respondent/prisoner is by definition "reliable and valid." Given these concerns, more analytic precision by the courts in assessing the question of admissibility would be welcome and would sharpen the inquiry into not only the strengths but the limitations of psychopathy evidence.

References

American Psychological Association. (2010). *Ethical principles of psychologists and code of conduct*. Retrieved from http://www.apa.org/ethics/code/index.aspx. (Accessed 25 September 2014).

Andrews, D. A., & Bonta, J. (2010). Rehabilitating criminal justice policy and practice. *Psychology, Public Policy, and Law*, *16*, 39–55. https://doi.org/10.1037/a0018362.

Archer, R. P., Buffington-Vollum, J. K., Stredny, R. V., & Handel, R. W. (2006). A survey of psychological test use patterns among forensic psychologists. *Journal of Personality Assessment*, *87*, 84–94. https://doi.org/10.1207/s15327752jpa8701_07.

Ashworth, A., & Zedner, L. (2014). *Preventive justice*. Oxford: Oxford University Press.

Bandes, S. A. (2016). Remorse and criminal justice. *Emotion Review*, *8*, 14–19. https://doi.org/10.1177/1754073915601222.

Barefoot v. Estelle. (1983). *463 U.S. 880*.

Berryessa, C. M., & Wohlstetter, B. (2019). The psychopathic "label" and effects on punishment outcomes: A meta-analysis. *Law and Human Behavior*, *43*, 9–25. https://doi.org/10.1037/lhb0000317.supp.

Blackburn, R. (1988). On moral judgements and personality disorders. The myth of psychopathic personality revisited. *The British Journal of Psychiatry*, *153*, 505–512. https://doi.org/10.1192/bjp.153.4.505.

Blais, J. (2015). Preventative detention decisions: Reliance on expert assessments and evidence of partisan allegiance within the Canadian context. *Behavioral Sciences & the Law*, *33*, 74–91. https://doi.org/10.1002/bsl.2155.

Blais, J., & Forth, A. E. (2014). Prosecution-retained versus court-appointed experts: Comparing and contrasting risk assessment reports in preventative detention hearings. *Law and Human Behavior*, *38*, 531–543. https://doi.org/10.1037/lhb0000082.

Blais, J., Forth, A. E., & Hare, R. D. (2017). Examining the interrater reliability of the Hare Psychopathy Checklist—Revised across a large sample of trained raters. *Psychological Assessment*, *29*, 762–775. https://doi.org/10.1037/pas0000455.

Boccaccini, M. T., Turner, D. T., & Murrie, D. C. (2008). Do some evaluators report consistently higher or lower scores on the PCL-R?: Findings from a statewide sample of sexually violent predator evaluations. *Psychology, Public Policy, and Law*, *14*, 262–283.

Boccaccini, M. T., Murrie, D. C., & Turner, D. B. (2014). Jurors' views on the value and objectivity of mental health experts testifying in sexually violent predator trials. *Behavioral Sciences & the Law*, *32*, 483–495. https://doi.org/10.1002/bsl.2129.

Boccaccini, M. T., Rufino, K. A., Jeon, H., & Murrie, D. C. (2017). Does the predictive validity of psychopathy ratings depend on the clinical experience of the raters? *The International Journal of Forensic Mental Health*, *16*, 130–138. https://doi.org/10.1080/14999013.2016.1266421.

Burke, J. D., Loeber, R., & Lahey, B. B. (2007). Adolescent conduct disorder and interpersonal callousness as predictors of psychopathy in young adults. *Journal of Clinical Child and Adolescent Psychology*, *36*, 334–346. https://doi.org/10.1080/15374410701444223.

Caldwell, M. F. (2011). Treatment-related changes in behavioral outcomes of psychopathy facets in adolescent offenders. *Law and Human Behavior*, *35*, 275–287. https://doi.org/10.1007/s10979-010-9239-z.

Caldwell, M., Skeem, J., Salekin, R., & Van Rybroek, G. (2006). Treatment response of adolescent offenders with psychopathy features: A 2-year follow-up. *Criminal Justice and Behavior*, *33*, 571–596. https://doi.org/10.1177/0093854806288176.

Caldwell, M. F., McCormick, D., Wolfe, J., & Umstead, D. (2012). Treatment-related changes in psychopathy features and behavior in adolescent offenders. *Criminal Justice and Behavior*, *39*, 144–155. https://doi.org/10.1177/0093854811429542.

Clark, L. A. (2007). Assessment and diagnosis of personality disorder: Perennial issues and an emerging reconceptualization. *Annual Review of Psychology*, *58*, 227–257.

Clark, L. A., & Harrison, J. A. (2001). Assessment instruments. In W. J. Livesley (Ed.), *Handbook of personality disorders* (pp. 277–306). New York: Guilford.

Clark, L. A., Livesley, W. J., & Morey, L. (1997). Personality disorder assessment: The challenge of construct validity. *Journal of Personality Disorders*, *11*, 205–231.

Cooke, D. J., Hart, S. D., Logan, C., & Michie, C. (2012). Explicating the construct of psychopathy: Development and validation of a conceptual model, the Comprehensive Assessment of Psychopathic Personality (CAPP). *International Journal of Forensic Mental Health*, *11*, 242–252. https://doi.org/10.1080/14999013.2012.746759.

Cox, J., Edens, J. F., Rulseh, A., & Clark, J. W. (2016). Juror perceptions of the interpersonal-affective traits of psychopathy predict sentence severity in a white-collar criminal case. *Psychology, Crime & Law*, *22*, 721–740. https://doi.org/10.1080/1068316X.2016.1174864.

Cunningham, M. D., & Reidy, T. J. (1998). Antisocial personality disorder and psychopathy: Diagnostic dilemmas in classifying patterns of antisocial behavior in sentencing evaluations. *Behavioral Sciences & the Law*, *16*, 333–351.

Cunningham, M. D., & Reidy, T. J. (2002). Violence risk assessment at federal capital sentencing: Individualization, generalization, relevance, and scientific standards. *Criminal Justice and Behavior*, *29*, 512–537. https://doi.org/10.1177/009385402236731.

D'Silva, K., Duggan, C., & McCarthy, L. (2004). Does treatment really make psychopaths worse? A review of the evidence. *Journal of Personality Disorders*, *18*, 163–177. https://doi.org/10.1521/pedi.18.2.163.32775.

Darjee, R., Øfstegaard, M., & Thomson, L. (2017). Schizophrenia in a high-security hospital: Long-term forensic, clinical, administrative & social outcomes. *Journal of Forensic Psychiatry & Psychology*, *28*, 525–547. https://doi.org/10.1080/14789949.2017.1308537.

Daubert v. Merrell Dow Pharmaceuticals. (1993). *509 U.S. 579*.

De Page, L., Matteucci, M., & Englebert, J. (2018). Les limites de la Psychopathy Checklist-Revised (PCL-R) dans une population médico-légale souffrant de schizophrénie [The shortcomings of the Psychopathy Checklist-Revised (PCL-R) in a forensic schizophrenic sample]. *Annales Médico-Psychologiques*, *176*, 954–958. https://doi.org/10.1016/j.amp.2017.10.011.

De Page, L., Mercenier, S., & Titeca, P. (2018). Assessing psychopathy in forensic schizophrenia spectrum disorders: Validating the Comprehensive Assessment of the Psychopathic Personality-Institutional Rating Scale (CAPP-IRS). *Psychiatry Research*, *265*, 303–308. https://doi.org/10.1016/j.psychres.2018.05.019.

DeMatteo, D., & Edens, J. F. (2006). The role and relevance of the Psychopathy Checklist-Revised in court: A case law survey of U.S. courts (1991-2004). *Psychology, Public Policy, and Law*, *12*, 214–241. https://doi.org/10.1037/1076-8971.12.2.214.

DeMatteo, D., Edens, J. F., Galloway, M., Cox, J., Smith, S. T., & Formon, D. (2014a). The role and reliability of the Psychopathy Checklist-Revised in U.S. sexually violent predator evaluations: A case law survey. *Law and Human Behavior*, *38*, 248–255. https://doi.org/10.1037/lhb0000059.

DeMatteo, D., Edens, J. F., Galloway, M., Cox, J., Smith, S. T., Koller, J. P., & Bersoff, B. (2014b). Investigating the role of the Psychopathy Checklist–Revised in United States case law. *Psychology, Public Policy, and Law*, *20*, 96–107. https://doi.org/10.1037/a0035452.

DeMatteo, D., Murphy, M., Galloway, M., & Krauss, D. (2015). A national survey of United States sexually violent person legislation: Policy, procedures, and practice. *The International Journal of Forensic Mental Health*, *14*, 245–266. https://doi.org/10.1080/14999013.2015.1110847.

DeMatteo, D., Murrie, D. C., Edens, J. F., & Lankford, C. (2019). Psychopathy in the courts. In M. DeLisi (Ed.), *Routledge international handbook of psychopathy and crime* (pp. 645–664). New York: Routledge.

DeMatteo, D., Hart, S. D., Heilbrun, K., Boccaccini, M. T., Cunningham, M. D., Douglas, K. S., … Reidy, T. J. (2020). Statement of concerned experts on the use of the Hare Psychopathy Checklist-Revised in capital sentencing to assess risk for institutional violence. *Psychology, Public Policy, and Law*, *26*(2), 133–144. https://doi.org/10.1037/law0000223.

Douglas, K. S., Nikolova, N. L., Kelley, S. E., & Edens, J. F. (2015). *Psychopathy* (pp. 257–323). Washington, DC, US: American Psychological Association. https://doi.org/10.1037/14461-009.

Dyer, F. J., & McCann, J. T. (2000). The Millon clinical inventories, research critical of their forensic application, and Daubert criteria. *Law and Human Behavior*, *24*, 487–497. https://doi.org/10.1023/A:1005500615111.

Edens, J. F., & Boccaccini, M. T. (2017). Taking forensic mental health assessment "out of the lab" and into "the real world": Introduction to the special issue on the field utility of forensic assessment instruments procedures. *Psychological Assessment*, *29*, 599–610. https://doi.org/10.1037/pas0000475.

Edens, J. F., & Cox, J. (2012). Examining the prevalence, role, and impact of evidence regarding antisocial personality, sociopathy, and psychopathy in capital cases: A survey of defense team members. *Behavioral Sciences & the Law*, *30*, 239–255.

Edens, J. F., Petrila, J., & Buffington-Vollum, J. K. (2001). Psychopathy and the death penalty: Can the Psychopathy Checklist—Revised identify offenders who represent "a continuing threat to society"? *Journal of Psychiatry and Law*, *29*, 433–481.

Edens, J. F., Buffington-Vollum, J. K., Roskamp, P., & Anthony, C. (2005). Predictions of future dangerousness in capital murder trials: Is it time to "disinvent the wheel"? *Law and Human Behavior*, *29*, 55–86.

Edens, J. F., Colwell, L. H., Desforges, D. M., & Fernandez, K. (2005). The impact of mental health evidence on support for capital punishment: Are defendants labeled psychopathic considered more deserving of death? *Behavioral Sciences & the Law*, *23*, 603–625.

Edens, J. F., Boccaccini, M. T., & Johnson, D. W. (2010). Inter-rater reliability of the PCL-R total and factor scores among psychopathic sex offenders: Are personality features more prone to disagreement than behavioral features? *Behavioral Sciences & the Law*, *28*, 106–119. https://doi.org/10.1002/bsl.918.

Edens, J. F., Clark, J., Smith, S. T., Cox, J., & Kelley, S. (2013). Bold, smart, dangerous and evil: Perceived correlates of core psychopathic traits among jury panel members. *Personality and Mental Health*, *7*, 143–153.

Edens, J. F., Davis, K. M., Fernandez, K., & Guy, L. S. (2013). No sympathy for the devil: Attributing psychopathic traits to capital murderers also predicts support for executing them. *Personality Disorders: Theory, Research, and Treatment*, *4*, 175–181.

Edens, J. F., Cox, J., Smith, S. T., DeMatteo, D., & Sörman, K. (2015). How reliable are Psychopathy Checklist-Revised scores in Canadian criminal trials? A case law review. *Psychological Assessment*, *27*, 447–456. https://doi.org/10.1037/pas0000048.

Edens, J. F., DeMatteo, D., Kelley, S. E., & Arnold, S. (2018). Personality assessment in forensic psychology. In V. Zeigler-Hill, & T. K. Shackelford (Eds.), *The SAGE handbook of personality and individual differences: The science of personality and individual differences* (pp. 548–572). Sage Reference. https://doi.org/10.4135/9781526451163.n26.

Edens, J. F., Petrila, J., & Kelley, S. E. (2018). In C. J. Patrick (Ed.), *Legal and ethical issues in the assessment and treatment of psychopathy* (pp. 732–751). New York, NY: Guilford.

Engelstad, K. N., Rund, B. R., Lau, B., Vaskinn, A., & Torgalsbøen, A.-K. (2019). Increased prevalence of psychopathy and childhood trauma in homicide offenders with schizophrenia compared to nonviolent individuals with schizophrenia. *Nordic Journal of Psychiatry*, *73*, 501–508. https://doi.org/10.1080/08039488.2019.1656777.

European Commission for the Efficiency of Justice. (2014). *Guidelines on the role of court-appointed experts in judicial proceedings of Council of Europe's Member States*. Retrieved from https://rm.coe.int/168074827a.

Ewing, C. P. (1983). "Dr. Death" and the case for an ethical ban on psychiatric and psychological predictions of dangerousness in capital sentencing proceedings. *American Journal of Law & Medicine*, *8*, 407–428.

Ex parte Cargill. (2017). *Tex. Crim. App. Unpub. LEXIS 323.* (Court of Criminal Appeals of Texas April 26, 2017, Filed).

Federal Rules of Evidence for United States Courts and Magistrates. (1975). *St. Paul, MN: West Publishing Company.*

Feldman, D. B., & Crandall, C. S. (2007). Dimensions of mental illness stigma: What about mental illness causes social rejection? *Journal of Social and Clinical Psychology, 26,* 137–154.

Felthous, A., & Sass, H. (2000). Introduction to this issue: International perspectives on psychopathic disorders. *Behavioral Sciences & the Law, 18,* 557–565. https://doi.org/10.1002/1099-0798(200010)18:5<557::AID-BSL412>3.0.CO;2-3.

Filone, S., Strohmaier, H., Murphy, M., & DeMatteo, D. (2014). The impact of DSM-5′s alternative model for personality disorders on criminal defendants. *Behavioral Sciences & the Law, 32,* 135–148. https://doi.org/10.1002/bsl.2097.

Fine, S. (June 7, 2017). Doctors tortured patients at Ontario mental-health centre, judge rules. *The Globe and Mail.* Retrieved from: https://www.theglobeandmail.com/news/national/doctors-at-ontario-mental-health-facility-tortured-patients-court-finds/article35246519/. (Accessed 26 January 2020).

Fitch, W. L., & Ortega, R. J. (2000). Law and the confinement of psychopaths. *Behavioral Sciences & the Law, 18,* 663–678. https://doi.org/10.1002/1099-0798(200010)18:5<663::AID-BSL408>3.0.CO;2-V.

Ford v. Wainwright. (1986). *477 U.S. 399.*

Foucha v. Louisiana. (1990). *504 U.S. 71.*

Freedman, R., Lewis, D. A., Michels, R., Pine, D. S., Schultz, S. K., Tamminga, C. A., … Yager, J. (2013). The initial field trials of DSM-5: New blooms and old thorns. *American Journal of Psychiatry, 170,* 1–5.

Gacono, C. B., & Hutton, H. E. (1994). Suggestions for the clinical and forensic use of the Hare Psychopathy Checklist-Revised (PCL-R). *International Journal of Law and Psychiatry, 17,* 303–317. https://doi.org/10.1016/0160-2527(94)90032-9.

Grisso, T. (1986). *Evaluating competencies: Forensic assessments and instruments.* New York: Kluwer.

Grisso, T. (2003). *Evaluating competencies: Forensic assessments and instruments* (2nd ed.). New York: Kluwer.

Hare, R. D. (1991). *The Psychopathy Checklist—Revised.* Toronto: Multi-Health Systems.

Hare, R. D. (1998). The Hare PCL-R: Some issues concerning its use and misuse. *Legal and Criminological Psychology, 3,* 99–119.

Hare, R. D. (2003). *Hare psychopathy Checklist—Revised (PCL–R): Technical manual* (2nd ed.). Toronto: Multi-Health Systems.

Hare, R. D., & Harpur, T. (1986). Weak data, strong conclusions: Some comments on Howard, Bailey, and Newman's use of the Psychopathy Checklist. *Personality & Individual Differences, 7,* 147–151.

Hare, R. D., Black, P., & Walsh, Z. (2013). The PCL-R: Forensic applications and limitations. In R. P. Archer, & E. M. Archer (Eds.), *Forensic uses of clinical assessment instruments* (2nd edition, pp. 266–290). New York, NY: Routledge.

Harris, G. T., Rice, M. E., & Cormier, C. A. (1994). Psychopaths: Is a therapeutic community therapeutic? *Therapeutic Communities, 15*(4), 283–299.

Harris, G. T., Rice, M. E., & Cormier, C. A. (2013). Research and clinical scoring of the Psychopathy Checklist can show good agreement. *Criminal Justice and Behavior, 40,* 1349–1362. https://doi.org/10.1177/0093854813492959.

Helfgott, J. B. (1997). The popular conception of the psychopath: Implications for criminal justice policy and practice. In *Paper presented at the 34th annual meeting of the academy of criminal justice sciences, Louisville, KY, March.*

Howard, R. C., Bailey, R., & Newman, A. (1984). A preliminary study of Hare's "Research Scale for the Assessment of Psychopathy" in mentally-abnormal offenders. *Personality & Individual Differences*, *5*, 389–396.

In the Interest of J.M. (2006). *713 N. W. 2d 518.*

Ismail, G., & Looman, J. (2018). Field inter-rater reliability of the Psychopathy Checklist–Revised. *International Journal of Offender Therapy and Comparative Criminology*, *62*, 468–481. https://doi.org/10.1177/0306624X16652452.

Jackson, R. L., & Hess, D. T. (2007). Evaluation for civil commitment of sex offenders: A survey of experts. *Sexual Abuse: Journal of Research and Treatment*, *19*, 425–448. https://doi.org/10.1177/107906320701900407.

Jeandarme, I., Edens, J. F., Habets, P., Bruckers, L., Oei, K., & Bogaerts, S. (2017). Psychopathy Checklist-Revised field validity in prison and hospital settings. *Law and Human Behavior*, *41*, 29–43.

Jelicic, M., Merckelbach, H., & Bošković, I. (2018). Seven myths about feigning. In H. Otgaar, & M. L. Howe (Eds.), *Finding the truth in the courtroom: Dealing with deception, lies, and memories* (pp. 227–242). New York, NY: Oxford University Press.

Johnson, S. C., & Elbogen, E. B. (2013). Personality disorders at the interface of psychiatry and the law: Legal use and clinical classification. *Dialogues in Clinical Neuroscience*, *15*, 203–211.

Kansas v. Crane. (2002). *534 U.S. 407.*

Kassin, S. M., Dror, I. E., & Kukucka, J. (2013). The forensic confirmation bias: Problems, perspectives, and proposed solutions. *Journal of Applied Research in Memory & Cognition*, *2*, 42–52. https://doi.org/10.1016/j.jarmac.2013.01.001.

Kelley, S. E., Edens, J. F., Mowle, E. N., Penson, B. N., & Rulseh, A. (2019). Dangerous, depraved, and death-worthy: A meta-analysis of the correlates of perceived psychopathy in jury simulation studies. *Journal of Clinical Psychology*, *75*, 627–643. https://doi.org/10.1002/jclp.22726.

Kennealy, P. J., Hicks, B. M., & Patrick, C. J. (2007). Validity of factors of the Psychopathy Checklist–Revised in female prisoners: Discriminant relations with antisocial behavior, substance abuse, and personality. *Assessment*, *14*, 323–340.

Kennealy, P. J., Skeem, J. L., Walters, G. D., & Camp, J. (2010). Do core interpersonal and affective traits of PCL-R psychopathy interact with antisocial behavior and disinhibition to predict violence? *Psychological Assessment*, *22*, 569–580. https://doi.org/10.1037/a0019618.

Kinscherff, R. (2010). Proposition: A personality disorder may nullify responsibility for a criminal act. *Journal of Law and Medical Ethics*, *38*, 745–759.

Kreis, M. K. F., Cooke, D. J., Michie, C., Hoff, H. A., & Logan, C. (2012). The Comprehensive Assessment of Psychopathic Personality (CAPP): Content validation using prototypical analysis. *Journal of Personality Disorders*, *26*, 402–413. https://doi.org/10.1521/pedi.2012.26.3.402.

Kröber, H. L., & Lau, S. (2000). Bad or mad? Personality disorders and legal responsibility—The German situation. *Behavioral Sciences & the Law*, *18*, 679–690.

Kroner, D. G., & Mills, J. F. (2001). The accuracy of five risk appraisal instruments in predicting institutional misconduct and new convictions. *Criminal Justice and Behavior*, *28*, 471–489. https://doi.org/10.1177/009385480102800405.

Langton, C., Barbaree, H., Harkins, L., & Peacock, E. (2006). Sex offenders' response to treatment and its association with recidivism as a function of psychopathy. *Sexual Abuse: A Journal of Research and Treatment, 18*, 99–120. https://doi.org/10.1177/107906320601800107.

Larsen, R. R., Jalava, J., & Griffiths, S. (2020). Are Psychopathy Checklist (PCL) psychopaths dangerous, untreatable, and without conscience? A systematic review of the empirical evidence. *Psychology, Public Policy, and Law, 26*, 297–311. https://doi.org/10.1037/law0000239.

Leygraf, N., & Elsner, K. (2007). Risks of diagnosing psychopathic disorders. In A. Felthous, & H. Sass (Eds.), *The international handbook of psychopathic disorders and the law* (pp. 135–146). New York, NY: Wiley.

Lloyd, C. D., Clark, H. J., & Forth, A. E. (2010). Psychopathy, expert testimony, and indeterminate sentences: Exploring the relationship between psychopathy checklist-revised testimony and trial outcome in Canada. *Legal and Criminological Psychology, 15*, 323–339. https://doi.org/10.1348/135532509X468432.

Loney, B. R., Taylor, J., Butler, M. A., & Iacono, W. G. (2007). Adolescent psychopathy features: 6-year temporal stability and the prediction of externalizing symptoms during the transition to adulthood. *Aggressive Behavior, 33*, 242–252. https://doi.org/10.1002/ab.20184.

Looman, J., Abracen, J., Serin, R., & Marquis, P. (2005). Psychopathy, treatment change, and recidivism in high-risk, high-need sexual offenders. *Journal of Interpersonal Violence, 20*, 549–568.

Loranger, A. W., Lenzenweger, M. F., Gartner, A. F., Susman, V. L., Herzig, J., Zammit, G. K., … Young, R. C. (1991). Trait-state artifacts and the diagnosis of personality disorders. *Archives of General Psychiatry, 48*, 720–728.

Lynam, D. R., Caspi, A., Moffitt, T. E., Loeber, R., & Stouthamer-Loeber, M. (2007). Longitudinal evidence that psychopathy scores in early adolescence predict adult psychopathy. *Journal of Abnormal Psychology, 116*, 155–165. https://doi.org/10.1037/0021-843X.116.1.155.

Lynam, D. R., Charnigo, R., Moffitt, T. E., Raine, A., Loeber, R., & Stouthamer-Loeber, M. (2009). The stability of psychopathy across adolescence. *Development and Psychopathology, 21*, 1133–1153. https://doi.org/10.1017/S0954579409990083.

Lyon, D. R., & Ogloff, J. R. P. (2000). Legal and ethical issues in psychopathy assessment. In C. Gacono (Ed.), *The clinical and forensic assessment of psychopathy* (pp. 139–173). Mahwah, NJ: Erlbaum.

Malsch, M., & Duker, M. J. A. (2016). *Incapacitation: Trends and new perspectives*. London: Routledge.

Matoba, R. (2003). Selection system for forensic expert witness and their qualification in Japan. *Legal Medicine, 5*, S58–S59. https://doi.org/10.1016/S1344-6223(02)00089-5.

McDermott, P. A., Alterman, A. I., Cacciola, J. S., Rutherford, M. J., Newman, J. P., & Mulholland, E. M. (2000). Generality of Psychopathy Checklist–Revised factors over prisoners and substance-dependent patients. *Journal of Consulting and Clinical Psychology, 68*, 181–186.

Miller, C. S., Kimonis, E. R., Otto, R. K., Kline, S. M., & Wasserman, A. L. (2012). Reliability of risk assessment measures used in sexually violent predator proceedings. *Psychological Assessment, 24*, 944–953. https://doi.org/10.1037/a0028411.

Morey, L. C., & Hopwood, C. J. (2013). Stability and change in personality disorders. *Annual Review of Clinical Psychology, 9*, 499–528.

Morey, L. C., Hopwood, C. J., Gunderson, J. G., Skodol, A. E., Shea, M. T., et al. (2007). Comparison of alternative models for personality disorders. *Psychological Medicine, 37*, 983–994.

Morrissey, C. (2008). *Guidelines for assessing psychopathy in offenders with intellectual disabilities using the PCL: R and PCL: SV*. Retrieved from http://mhinstitute.org.uk/-publications-/working-papers-41/item/28-guidelines-for-assessing-psychopathy-in-offenders-with-intellectual-disabilities-using-the-pclr-and-pclsv.html.

Morrissey, C., Hogue, T., Mooney, P., Lindsay, W. R., Steptoe, L., Taylor, J., et al. (2005). Applicability, reliability, and validity of the Psychopathy Checklist–Revised in offenders with intellectual disabilities: Some initial findings. *International Journal of Forensic Mental Health, 4*, 207–220.

Morrissey, C., Hogue, T., Mooney, P., Allen, C., Johnston, S., Hollin, C., et al. (2007). The predictive validity of the PCL-R in offenders with intellectual disability in a high secure hospital setting: Institutional aggression. *Journal of Forensic Psychiatry & Psychology, 18*, 1–15.

Morrissey, C., Cooke, D., Michie, C., Hollin, C., Hogue, T., Lindsay, W. R., & Taylor, J. L. (2010). Structural, item, and test generalizability of the Psychopathy Checklist-Revised to offenders with intellectual disabilities. *Assessment, 17*, 16–29.

Morse, S. J. (2014). Commentary: Reflections on remorse. *Journal of the American Academy of Psychiatry and the Law, 42*, 49–55.

Mowle, E. N., Edens, J. F., Clark, J. W., & Sörman, K. (2016). Effects of mental health and neuroscience evidence on juror perceptions of a criminal defendant: The moderating role of political orientation. *Behavioral Sciences & the Law, 34*, 726–741. https://doi.org/10.1002/bsl.2251.

Murrie, D. C., Boccaccini, M. T., Johnson, J. T., & Janke, C. (2008). Does interrater (dis)agreement on Psychopathy Checklist scores in sexually violent predator trials suggest partisan allegiance in forensic evaluations? *Law and Human Behavior, 32*, 352–362. https://doi.org/10.1007/s10979-007-9097-5.

Murrie, D. C., Boccaccini, M. T., Turner, D. B., Meeks, M., Woods, C., & Tussey, C. (2009). Rater (dis)agreement on risk assessment measures in sexually violent predator proceedings: Evidence of adversarial allegiance in forensic evaluation? *Psychology, Public Policy, and Law, 15*, 19–53.

Murrie, D. C., Boccaccini, M. T., Guarnera, L. A., & Rufino, K. A. (2013). Are forensic experts biased by the side that retained them? *Psychological Science, 24*, 1889–1897. https://doi.org/10.1177/0956797613481812.

National Academy of Sciences. (2009). *Strengthening forensic science in the United States: A path forward*. Washington, DC: National Academies Press.

Nuée, A. (2015). *Civil-law expert reports in the EU: National rules and practices*. Retrieved from: https://www.europarl.europa.eu/RegData/etudes/IDAN/2015/519211/IPOL_IDA(2015)519211_EN.pdf.

Nunnally, J., & Bernstein, I. (1994). *Psychometric theory* (3rd ed.). New York, NY: McGraw-Hill.

O'Brien, S., & Wayland, K. (2013). Deconstructing antisocial personality disorder and psychopathy: A guidelines-based approach to prejudicial psychiatric labels. *Hofstra Law Review, 42*, 519–588.

Ogloff, J. R. P., & Lyon, D. R. (1998). Legal issues associated with the concept of psychopathy. In D. J. Cooke, A. E. Forth, & R. D. Hare (Eds.), *Psychopathy: Theory, research, and implications for society* (pp. 401–422). Dordrecht, Netherlands: Kluwer.

Ogloff, J. R., Wong, S., & Greenwood, A. (1990). Treating criminal psychopaths in a therapeutic community program. *Behavioral Sciences & the Law, 8*, 181–190.

O'Loughlin, A. (2019). De-constructing risk, therapeutic needs and the dangerous personality disordered subject. *Punishment and Society, 21*, 616–638. https://doi.org/10.1177/1462474518811074.

Otto, R. K., & Heilbrun, K. (2002). The practice of forensic psychology: A look toward the future in light of the past. *American Psychologist, 57*, 5–18. https://doi.org/10.1037/0003-066X.57.1.5.

Panetti v. Quarterman. (2007). *551 U.S. 930.*

Patrick, C. J., Venables, N. C., & Skeem, J. L. (2012). Psychopathy and brain function: Empirical findings and legal implications. In H. Häkkänen-Nyholm, & J. Nyholm (Eds.), *Psychopathy and law: A practitioner's guide* (pp. 39–78). New York, NY: Wiley.

Pierson, A., Rosenfeld, B., Green, D., & Belfi, B. (2011). Investigating the relationship between antisocial personality disorder and malingering. *Criminal Justice & Behavior, 38*, 146–156.

Polaschek, D. L. (2014). Adult criminals with psychopathy: Common beliefs about treatability and change have little empirical support. *Current Directions in Psychological Science, 23*, 296–301.

Polaschek, D. L. L., & Daly, T. E. (2013). Treatment and psychopathy in forensic settings. *Aggression and Violent Behavior, 18*, 592–603. https://doi.org/10.1016/j.avb.2013.06.003.

Polaschek, D. L. L., & Skeem, J. L. (2018). Treatment of adults and juveniles with psychopathy. In C. J. Patrick (Ed.), *Handbook of psychopathy* (2nd ed., pp. 710–731). New York: Guilford.

Poythress, N. G., Lilienfeld, S. O., Skeem, J. L., Douglas, K. S., Edens, J. F., Epstein, M., & Patrick, C. J. (2010). Using the PCL-R to help estimate the validity of two self-report measures of psychopathy with offenders. *Assessment, 17*, 206–219.

Reed, J. (1996). Psychopathy—A clinical and legal dilemma. *British Journal of Psychiatry, 168*, 4–9.

Resnick, P. J., & Knoll, J. L., IV. (2018). Malingered psychosis. In R. Rogers, & S. D. Bender (Eds.), *Clinical assessment of malingering and deception* (4th ed., pp. 98–121). New York, NY: Guilford.

Rice, M. E. (1997). Violent offender research and implications for the criminal justice system. *American Psychologist, 52*, 414–423. https://doi.org/10.1037/0003-066X.52.4.414.

Rufino, K. A., Boccaccini, M. T., Hawes, S. W., & Murrie, D. C. (2012). When experts disagreed, who was correct? A comparison of PCL-R scores from independent raters and opposing forensic experts. *Law and Human Behavior, 36*, 527–537. https://doi.org/10.1037/h0093988.

Rutherford, M., Cacciola, J. S., Alterman, A. I., McKay, J. R., & Cook, T. G. (1999). The 2-year test-retest reliability of the Psychopathy Checklist-Revised in methadone patients. *Assessment, 6*, 285–291.

Saks, M. J., Schweitzer, N. J., Aharoni, E., & Kiehl, K. A. (2014). The impact of neuroimages in the sentencing phase of capital trials. *Journal of Empirical Legal Studies, 11*, 105–131. https://doi.org/10.1111/jells.12036.

Salekin, R. T., Worley, C., & Grimes, R. D. (2010). Treatment of psychopathy: A review and brief introduction to the mental model approach for psychopathy. *Behavioral Sciences & the Law, 28*, 235–266. https://doi.org/10.1002/bsl.928.

Sedgwick, O., Young, S., Greer, B., Arnold, J., Parsons, A., Puzzo, I., … Kumari, V. (2018). Sensorimotor gating characteristics of violent men with comorbid psychosis and dissocial personality disorder: Relationship with antisocial traits and psychosocial deprivation. *Schizophrenia Research, 198*, 21–27. https://doi.org/10.1016/j.schres.2017.06.045.

Singh, J. P., Desmarais, S. L., Hurducas, C., Arbach-Lucioni, K., Condemarin, C., Dean, K., … Otto, R. K. (2014). International perspectives on the practical application of violence risk assessment: A global survey of 44 countries. *The International Journal of Forensic Mental Health, 13*, 193–206. https://doi.org/10.1080/14999013.2014.922141.

Skeem, J. L., Polaschek, D. L. L., & Manchak, S. (2009). Appropriate treatment works, but how?: Rehabilitating general, psychopathic, and high-risk offenders. In J. L. Skeem, K. S. Douglas, & S. O. Lilienfeld (Eds.), *Psychological science in the courtroom: Consensus and controversy* (pp. 358–384). New York: Guilford.

Smith, S. T., Edens, J. F., Clark, J., & Rulseh, A. (2014). "So, what is a psychopath?" Venireperson perceptions, beliefs, and attitudes about psychopathic personality. *Law and Human Behavior*, *38*, 490–500. https://doi.org/10.1037/lhb0000091.

State v. Anderson. (2007). *730 N.W.2d 570.*

State v. Gallaway. (1993). *628 A.2d 735.*

Stratton, J., Brook, M., & Hanlon, R. E. (2017). Murder and psychosis: Neuropsychological profiles of homicide offenders with schizophrenia. *Criminal Behaviour and Mental Health*, *27*, 146–161. https://doi.org/10.1002/cbm.1990.

Sturup, J., Edens, J. F., Sörman, K., Karlberg, D., Fredriksson, B., & Kristiansson, M. (2014). Field reliability of the Psychopathy Checklist-Revised among life sentenced prisoners in Sweden. *Law and Human Behavior*, *38*, 315–324.

Sundby, S. E. (1998). The capital jury and absolution: The intersection of trial strategy, remorse, and the death penalty. *Cornell Law Review*, *83*, 1557–1598.

Tengström, A., Hodgins, S., Grann, M., Långström, N., & Kullgren, G. (2004). Schizophrenia and criminal offending: The role of psychopathy and substance use disorders. *Criminal Justice and Behavior*, *31*, 367–391. https://doi.org/10.1177/0093854804265173.

Texas Defender Service. (2004). *Deadly speculation: Misleading Texas capital juries with false predictions of future dangerousness*. Retrieved from http://texasdefender.org/wp-content/uploads/TDS_Deadly-Speculation.pdf.

Truong, T. N., Kelley, S. E., & Edens, J. F. (2021). Does psychopathy influence juror decision-making in capital murder trials? "The devil is in the (methodological) details." *Criminal Justice and Behavior*, *48*, 690–707.

Tyrer, P., Cooper, S., Seivewright, H., Duggan, C., Rao, B., & Hogue, T. (2005). Temporal reliability of psychological assessments for patients in a special hospital with severe personality disorder: A preliminary note. *Criminal Behaviour and Mental Health*, *15*, 87–92. https://doi.org/10.1002/cbm.40.

Tyrer, P., Duggan, C., Cooper, S., Tyrer, H., Swinson, N., & Rutter, D. (2015). The lessons and legacy of the programme for dangerous and severe personality disorders. *Personality and Mental Health*, *9*, 96–106. https://doi.org/10.1002/pmh.1293.

Umbach, R., Berryessa, C. M., & Raine, A. (2015). Brain imaging research on psychopathy: Implications for punishment, prediction, and treatment in youth and adults. *Journal of Criminal Justice*, *43*, 295–306.

van Impelen, A., Merckelbach, H., Niesten, I. J. M., Jelicic, M., Huhnt, B., & Campo, J.á. (2017). Biased symptom reporting and antisocial behaviour in forensic samples: A weak link. *Psychiatry, Psychology and Law*, *24*, 530–548. https://doi.org/10.1080/13218719.2016.1256017.

Viljoen, J. L., MacDougall, E. A. M., Gagnon, N. C., & Douglas, K. S. (2010). Psychopathy evidence in legal proceedings involving adolescent offenders. *Psychology, Public Policy, and Law*, *16*, 254–283. https://doi.org/10.1037/a0019649.

Viljoen, J. L., McLachlan, K., & Vincent, G. M. (2010). Assessing violence risk and psychopathy in juvenile and adult offenders: A survey of clinical practices. *Assessment*, *17*, 377–395. https://doi.org/10.1177/1073191109359587.

Walsh, T., & Walsh, Z. (2006). The evidentiary introduction of psychopathy checklist-revised assessed psychopathy in US courts: Extent and appropriateness. *Law and Human Behavior*, *30*, 493–507. https://doi.org/10.1007/s10979-006-9042-z.

Waugh, M. H., Hopwood, C. J., Krueger, R. F., Morey, L. C., Pincus, A. L., & Wright, A. G. C. (2017). Psychological assessment with the DSM–5 alternative model for personality disorders: Tradition and innovation. *Professional Psychology: Research and Practice*, *48*, 79–89. https://doi.org/10.1037/pro0000071.supp (Supplemental).

Wong, S. C. P., Gordon, A., Gu, D., Lewis, K., & Olver, M. E. (2012). The effectiveness of violence reduction treatment for psychopathic offenders: Empirical evidence and a treatment model. *The International Journal of Forensic Mental Health*, *11*, 336–349. https://doi.org/10.1080/14999013.2012.746760.

Wood, J. M., Lilienfeld, S. O., Nezworski, M. T., Garb, H. N., Allen, K. H., & Wildermuth, J. L. (2010). Validity of Rorschach Inkblot scores for discriminating psychopaths from non-psychopaths in forensic populations: A meta-analysis. *Psychological Assessment*, *22*, 336. https://doi.org/10.1037/a0018998.

Yang, M., Wong, S. C. P., & Coid, J. (2010). The efficacy of violence prediction: A meta-analytic comparison of nine risk assessment tools. *Psychological Bulletin*, *136*, 740–767. https://doi.org/10.1037/a0020473.

Zhong, R., Baranoski, M., Feigenson, N., Davidson, L., Buchanan, A., & Zonana, H. V. (2014). So you're sorry? The role of remorse in criminal law. *Journal of the American Academy of Psychiatry and the Law*, *42*, 39–48.

Zinger, I., & Forth, A. E. (1998). Psychopathy and Canadian criminal proceedings: The potential for human rights abuses. *Canadian Journal of Criminology*, *40*, 237–277.

Psychopathy, offending style and crime scene behavior

12

Sophia Tkazky, Donna Youngs, and David Rowlands

Introduction

Hare (1993) defined the psychopath as callous, remorseless, self-centered, lacking conscience, empathy, or the ability to form warm emotional relationships with others, and Meloy (1988) contended that psychopathic thought processes are well suited to predatory violence; however, the term "psychopath" represents a diverse group, with involvement in white-collar and organized crime receiving academic attention (e.g., Babiak & Hare, 2006; Häkkänen-Nyholm & Nyholm, 2012; Lesha & Lesha, 2012). Porter and Woodworth (2006) argued that intelligence serves as a moderator between psychopathy and violence, hence white-collar psychopathic offenders rarely use physical aggression, or use their intellectual abilities to avoid prosecution for similar violent crimes (Ishikawa, Raine, Lencz, Bihrle, & Lacasse, 2001). Although experts have long agreed that psychopaths appear to be "qualitatively" different from other criminals (e.g., Hare, 1996, 2006; Meloy, 1988; O'Toole & Häkkänen-Nyholm, 2012), the vast majority of studies on psychopathy and crime focus on offenders who are already in the system (e.g., interviewed by the police, treated by a psychologist, consulted or reviewed by specialists for court or parole hearings), with few exploring psychopathic personality correlates of offense style, or to be specific, the qualitative differences between psychopathic and nonpsychopathic offending.

Qualitative differences in violence

It has been estimated that more than half of violent crimes are committed by psychopaths (Hare, 1999). For example, studies consistently show that psychopaths commit from half to more than 80% of all sexual homicides (Häkkänen-Nyholm, Repo-Tiihonen, Lindberg, Salenius, & Weizmann-Henelius, 2009; Porter, Woodworth, Earle, Drugge, & Boer, 2003; Stone, 1998). Though previously this type of crime was considered to be rare (about 1%–4% of all homicides) (Meloy, 2000; Roberts & Grossman, 1993), Porter et al. (2003) suggest that 30% of homicides may be sexually motivated.

Using a dichotomous psychopathy coding classification (presence/absence), Hare and McPherson (1984) found that violent actions were a good predictor of psychopathy, observing a greater number of violent offenses in psychopathic than nonpsychopathic offenders. Accordingly, Gretton, McBride, Lewis, O'Shaughnessy, and Hare (1994) demonstrated that sexual offenses committed by psychopaths were characterized by

Psychopathy and Criminal Behavior. https://doi.org/10.1016/B978-0-12-811419-3.00018-2

higher levels of violence. Subsequently, the relationship between psychopathic traits and use of violence in achieving offense goals has been highlighted by many researchers (Cornell et al., 1996; Flight & Forth, 2007; Hutton & Woodworth, 2014; Vitacco, Neumann, Caldwell, Leistico, & Van Rybroek, 2006; Woodworth & Porter, 2002).

While Hare and McPherson's (1984) findings indicated that psychopaths more frequently used weapons during crime commission, these studies largely report quantitative differences. Though the findings represent important profile indicators, specific crime scene behaviors are neglected. Emphasis is on general offense style, level of violence, and motivation, rather than an examination of differences in deviant behaviors committed by psychopathic and nonpsychopathic offenders. Since psychopaths are not the only perpetrators of violent crime, the question arises whether it is possible to distinguish psychopaths from other violent criminals based on qualitative behavioral differences.

Indeed, the hypothesis that there are qualitative differences in violent behaviors between psychopathic and nonpsychopathic offenders is supported by a number of studies. For example, Forth and Kroner (1995) found that psychopathic rapists were more opportunistic than nonpsychopathic rapists, and Porter and Woodworth (2007) demonstrated that psychopaths were more likely to perpetrate primarily instrumental homicides which were cold-blooded and premeditated (Porter & Woodworth, 2007; Woodworth & Porter, 2002). Curiously, a comparison of these results suggests differences in psychopathic rapists and psychopathic murderers, the former evincing greater opportunism while the latter demonstrates offense premeditation. However, again, a detailed comparison of crime scene actions is absent from this data and the size of Porter and Woodworth's sample (9 psychopathic and 41 nonpsychopathic offenders) impedes generalization of results.

According to common definitions of instrumental and reactive violence, "instrumental violence" refers to violence that is employed as means to a secondary goal, while "reactive violence" involves a response to perceived threat or provocation (Shaw & Porter, 2012). Thus it can be said that analysis in terms of instrumental/reactive violence is focused on the motivation behind violence, and indirectly on the decision-making process before committing the violent crime. Though recent studies (e.g., Hutton & Woodworth, 2014) continue to focus on the relationship between psychopathic traits and motives for violence (e.g., instrumental/reactive), this latter point raises the question of victim choice, where research demonstrates certain qualitative differences between psychopathic and nonpsychopathic offenders.

In one of the first studies on the subject, Williamson, Hare, and Wong (1987) suggested that violent crimes committed by psychopathic offenders are more cold-blooded, and ruthless with little affective coloring, further arguing that the victims of such crimes were rarely family members or anyone close to the offender. In contrast, most of the homicides committed by nonpsychopathic offenders took place during extreme arousal (e.g., heated domestic dispute), and the victims, most frequently females, were known to the perpetrator. Homicides by psychopathic male offenders were usually motivated by revenge or retribution, and the victim was male and unknown to the murderer. Subsequent studies on both male (Wright & Wong, 1988) and female offenders (Weizmann-Henelius, Viemero, & Eronen, 2003) lend support to these findings, where targeting strangers and acquaintances, but not persons close to offender, was found to be common for homicides committed by psychopaths.

However, this association may be limited to homicides, as Brown and Forth (1997) demonstrated no significant difference between psychopathic and nonpsychopathic rapists in their tendency to target strangers. Porter et al. (2000) showed that in cases of sexual violence, psychopathic offenders tended to be more versatile in terms of age of their victims, and targeted both children and adults more frequently than nonpsychopathic offenders. Although no significant differences have been found between psychopathic and nonpsychopathic sexual offenders (rapists) in their choice of victim, other qualitative differences appear evident. For example, Kirsch and Becker (2007) observed a high incidence of psychopathy among sexual sadists (90% of all cases).

Certain types of homicide appear to be more associated with psychopathic personality traits. For example, in a study of Finnish offenders who committed a sexual homicide, Häkkänen-Nyholm et al. (2009) found that over half of all perpetrators were psychopaths, albeit using a lower cut-off score of 26 on the Psychopathy Checklist Revised (PCL-R; Hare, 2003). Correspondingly, a meta-analysis of 22 studies on data from 2603 homicide offenders by Fox and DeLisi (2019) showed a mean PCL-R score of 21.2 in homicide offenders generally—a score indicative of moderate psychopathy, which escalated in more severe manifestations of homicidal offending, including sexual homicide, sadistic homicide, serial homicide, and multioffender homicide, suggesting an important link between psychopathic personality and homicide typology.

Given the characteristic constellation of personality features, psychopathy has emerged as a theoretical framework with which to understand sexual homicide. In a recent study drawing on data from 616 adult male sex offenders, Beauregard and DeLisi (2018a) examined personality profiles of sexual homicide offenders (SHO) compared to a group of nonhomicidal sex offenders (NHSO) and violent nonhomicidal sex offenders (VNHSO). They found that SHO presented a background of abuse and behavioral problems, such as chronic lying, angry temperament, reckless behaviors, and a history of cruelty toward animals, illustrating hallmark psychopathic traits, whereas NHSO were more likely to report a rebellious attitude and neuropsychological deficits. The results appeared to support the idea that sexual homicide was more associated with psychopathic characteristics than other forms of sexual offense.

In a subsequent analysis (Beauregard & DeLisi, 2018b) drawing on the same data, the researchers examined personality profiles among the three groups in terms of personality disorder (PD) diagnosis and various crime characteristics. They discovered that compared to NHSO and VNHSO, the SHO had personality features characterized by Schizoid and Borderline PD. In terms of crime characteristics, SHO were significantly more likely to select a victim, use a weapon, and use drugs and alcohol before their offenses. However, they were less likely to force their victim to engage in sexual acts or humiliate them. Over 30% of SHO presented with Antisocial PD, evincing a pattern abusing the rights of others and rules of society. These results highlight comorbidity of Schizoid, Borderline, and Antisocial PD characteristic dysfunction that facilitates the lethal sexual violence of SHO compared with other nonhomicidal sex offenders. However, since only a third of SHO demonstrated Antisocial PD, with a higher comorbidity of exclusive Schizoid and Borderline Personality Disorder, the assumption that SHOs are psychopaths due to the nature of their crime should be considered with caution; though it is important to remember that while sharing certain symptoms, Antisocial PD and psychopathy represent different diagnoses and should not be conflated.

Interestingly, a more recent study by Chopin and Beauregard (2019) found differences in crime scene behavior between SHO and NHSO indicative of psychopathic traits, such as using a con approach and committing the crime in a residence—suggestive of premeditation and manipulation—as well as beating the victim, use of asphyxiation, and intentional use of a weapon, highlighting greater violence. However, though indicative, future studies need to include specific measures of psychopathy (e.g., PCL-R) to assess the extent to which different offense behaviors relate definitively to psychopathic personality.

Kirsch and Becker's (2007) analysis highlights another salient difference in crime scene activity between psychopathic and nonpsychopathic offending: sadistic behavior. As Knoll and Hazelwood (2009) relate: "When sexual sadism is comorbid with psychopathy, the offender's crimes may be particularly egregious" (p. 108). The detailed analysis of crime description conducted by Porter et al. (2003) revealed a significant difference between psychopaths and nonpsychopaths in sexual homicides, finding that psychopaths more frequently commit acts of both sadistic (i.e., offender obtained pleasure from homicide) and gratuitous violence. The coding criteria for gratuitous violence included evidence of torture/beating, mutilation or "overkill," and use of multiple weapons at the crime scene, while the criteria for sadistic violence were clear evidence that offenders took pleasure from violent actions rather than sexual assault. However, only types of violence were compared, not actual crime scene behaviors, though other prior studies suggest that psychopaths commit more severe and diverse forms of sexual violence (Porter, Campbell, Woodworth, & Birt, 2001; Porter et al., 2000), with certain researchers asserting a strong association between psychopathy and specifically sexual sadism (e.g., Dietz, Hazelwood, & Warren, 1990; Leaff, 1978).

More recently, Darjee (2019) examined the relationship between dimensional measures of sexual sadism and psychopathy among 51 male offenders, using the Sexual Sadism Scale (SeSaS) and the PCL-R. Over a third of participants were DSM-IV sexual sadists and a quarter were diagnostic psychopaths, scoring 30 or above on the PCL-R. Total PCL-R scores were compared, as well as specific Factor 1 traits (affective and interpersonal features—characterized by callousness, selfishness, manipulation, and lack of empathy or remorse) and Factor 2 traits (antisocial behavior and lifestyle features, characterized by instability and a chronically socially deviant lifestyle). Darjee found that sexual sadism and total PCL-R measures were moderately associated, and that sexual sadism predicted certain crime scene activity, such as control, sexual deviance, and unusual behaviors. Attempted homicide, having a coaccused, multiple sexual homicides, and previous sexual offending were also related to sexual sadism. Specifically, PCL-R Factor 1 predicted violent, exploitative, and detection-evading behaviors at the crime scene, as well as completed homicide and previous violent offending, while Factor 2 predicted impulsive behaviors at crime scenes, substance misuse, and previous general offending. Therefore it can be argued that, though complex, psychopathy and sexual sadism play key roles in violent crime, with Factor 1 being associated with more calculated and extreme crime scene violence. In this, the study suggests certain qualitative differences in crime scene actions between psychopaths relating to PCL-R Factor 1 and 2 scores.

Similarly, Rodre et al. (2019) examined homicides in Sweden from 2007 to 2009 among 72 offenders who had undergone PCL-R assessment, investigating whether psychopathic personality traits and behavioral styles affected the way in which homicides were committed. Homicide was categorized as instrumental or expressive, and the motive as belonging to one of five categories: (1) intimate-partner or family-related homicide, (2) homicide occurring during altercations, (3) robberies or burglaries, (4) criminal conflicts, or (5) sexual homicide. Results showed that offenders who committed homicide in an instrumental manner or with a sexual motive had higher scores on PCL-R Factor 1 (i.e., control, manipulation, lack of empathy) than offenders displaying an expressive manner or other motives, and that they were more likely to commit crimes against strangers, suggesting that Factor 1 personality traits influence crime scene behavior of the former type of offender more than Factor 2 behavioral styles. These findings build on previous research by Porter and Woodworth (2007) highlighting greater instrumentality in crimes committed by psychopaths, while reflecting Darjee's (2019) study revealing more calculated crime scene activity and extreme sexual violence in high scoring PCL-R Factor 1 offenders, compared to reactive and expressive actions relating to PCL-R Factor 2. The results suggest that PCL-R Factor 1 is a more powerful discriminator of differences in crime scene activity, in terms of levels of gratuitous violence, premeditation, and detection evasion, features previously shown to indicative of psychopathic personality (Porter & Woodworth, 2007; Rodre et al., 2019; Williamson et al., 1987). This notion raises the question of drawbacks to assessing psychopathy in prison populations, who are, by definition, presenting with antisocial lifestyles, and therefore likely to score high on Factor 2 traits, potentially affecting a diagnosis of psychopathy skewed too heavily toward behavioral rather than personality features.

From this literature, certain conclusions can be drawn suggesting qualitative differences in violence committed by psychopaths and nonpsychopaths:

(1) Differences in the manifestations of violence (i.e., level, style, and/or usage of violence). These include the following:
- Psychopaths are more sadistic than nonpsychopaths (Holt & Strack, 1999), especially when with respect to sexual sadism (Fox & DeLisi, 2019; Kirsch & Becker, 2007; Porter et al., 2003), demonstrating more exploitative, deviant, and unusual crime scene behaviors (Darjee, 2019).
- Psychopathic offenders commit more diverse and severe forms of violence, including sexual homicide and serial murder (e.g., Fox & DeLisi, 2019; Porter et al., 2001).
- Psychopathic offenders are more frequently involved in instrumental forms of violence (when violence is used as means to a goal) in comparison to nonpsychopathic offenders (Cornell et al., 1996; Flight & Forth, 2007; Rodre et al., 2019; Woodworth & Porter, 2002).
- Psychopathic offenders more frequently commit acts of not only sadistic, but also exploitative and excessive violence compared to nonpsychopathic offenders (Darjee, 2019; Fox & DeLisi, 2019; Porter et al., 2003).
- The violent crimes committed by psychopathic offenders are more callous, cold-blooded, and unemotional compared to those committed by nonpsychopathic offenders (Rodre et al., 2019; Williamson et al., 1987).

(2) Differences in the choice of victim.
- Victims of psychopathic offenders are more likely to be strangers than victims of nonpsychopathic offenders (Rodre et al., 2019; Williamson et al., 1987).
- When it comes to sexual violence, psychopathic offenders are more versatile in their choice of victims and more frequently target both adults and children compared to nonpsychopathic offenders (Porter et al., 2000).

(3) Some differences among psychopaths and nonpsychopaths were found to be "crime-specific" (i.e., manifested in certain crime types but not others):
- Premeditation was more typical for psychopathic perpetrators of homicide (Porter & Woodworth, 2007; Woodworth & Porter, 2002), while psychopathic rapists were more opportunistic in comparison to nonpsychopathic ones (Forth & Kroner, 1995).
- Targeting strangers and acquaintances, but not persons close to the offender was found to be common for both male and female psychopaths in homicides (Weizmann-Henelius et al., 2003; Wright & Wong, 1988), but not in rape (Brown & Forth, 1997).

These findings demonstrate that violent offenses committed by psychopaths are qualitatively different from those committed by nonpsychopaths in terms of level of sadism, levels and types of violence, as well as victim choice. Though, historically, few studies have examined specific crime scene actions, or address them in general way by proposing that psychopaths use weapons more frequently than nonpsychopaths (Hare & McPherson, 1984), several recent studies have examined crime scene actions in more depth. Of note is Darjee (2019), revealing more exploitative, sexually deviant, and unusual offense behaviors in sadistic psychopaths, and the distinction between PCL-R Factor 1 and 2 psychopathic traits in crime scene actions. Rodre et al. (2019) support a Factor 1 and 2 distinction, observing higher PCL-R Factor 1 scores in instrumental and sexual homicides. Fox and DeLisi (2019) research indicates a "homicide typology," in which psychopathic offenders were associated with more extreme offenses, such as sadistic, serial, and sexual murder. While Beauregard and DeLisi's (2018a, 2018b) studies revealed differences indicative of psychopathy and nonpsychopathy in SHO and NHSO, respectively, further studies specifically measuring differences in psychopathic traits are needed to corroborate such propositions.

Overall, the literature is progressing, with recent studies adding flesh to previous arguments. Research is beginning to reveal distinguishing features of psychopathic and nonpsychopathic offense patterns (Fox & DeLisi, 2019), as well as those discriminating differences among subtypes of psychopathy (e.g., Darjee, 2019; Rodre et al., 2019), with implications for investigation processes. Following from this, attempts to apply research on psychopathy and subtypes of psychopathy to practical aspects of law enforcement are being made. The systematization of psychopathy subtypes is the topic of the next part of this chapter.

Classification of psychopathy and application to offense behavior

Individuals meeting the criteria for psychopathy share common traits and features on four facets (interpersonal, affective, antisocial, lifestyle; Hare, 2003). These traits outline the "psychopathic group" and distinguish those who possess the disorder from nonpsychopaths, forming a basis for qualitative differences in offending behavior between psychopathic and nonpsychopathic offenders discussed in the previous part of this chapter. However, as indicated, differences are evident not only between psychopathic and nonpsychopathic "groups" but also within the psychopathic population, where subtypes of psychopathy can be distinguished in the various manifestations of the disorder (Arieti, 1963; Cleckley, 1941; Hare, 1970, 1999; Herve, 2007).

In his review of perspectives on psychopathic subtypes, Herve (2007) identified two groups of typologies: clinically derived (those based on clinical tradition—"intuition and observations"—p. 439) and empirically grounded (those derived from empirical evidence—e.g., Blackburn & Coid, 1998; Gretton, 1998; Ishikawa et al., 2001). Clinically derived typologies include classic psychopaths, explosive psychopaths, manipulative psychopaths, and pseudo-psychopaths. According to Henderson (1947), classic psychopaths are ruthless, insensitive to others, egotistical, and opportunistic sensation-seekers, whose aggression is impulsively goal-driven. Karpman (1946, 1955) defined the explosive psychopath as having poor behavioral control and a tendency to overreact, while maintaining emotions are shallower in comparison to other psychopaths. Manipulative psychopaths[a] are comparatively less aggressive and impulsive, preferring passive parasitic pursuits and deception/manipulation tactics to achieve their aims. Their needs and goals are less primitive and their emotions are less intense compared to other types (Arieti, 1963). Herve (2007) argues that, with a more sophisticated presentation, manipulative psychopaths are best suited to, and more prevalent in, white-collar criminal activities.

The three subtypes represent variations of idiopathic or primary psychopathy. Primary psychopathy is thought to derive from an innate deficit of emotional sensitivity and conscience, whereas an additional fourth type under the psychopathy "umbrella" is secondary or pseudo-psychopathy, referring to those acquiring psychopathy through environmental conditions, such as trauma, abuse, and parental rejection (Karpman, 1941). Unlike idiopathic psychopaths, pseudo-psychopaths are thought to have a conscience, experience internal conflicts, and complex emotions (Arieti, 1963).

Although the clinically derived classification system has existed for decades, little is known as to its empirical merit, since clinical impressions often lack reliability (e.g., Monahan, 1977). Indeed, a comparison of features assigned to various types reveals limited borders of distinction, with considerable overlap. For example, both explosive and classic psychopaths are characterized as vindictive, aggressive predators, and sensation-seekers with poor behavior control; both classic and manipulative psychopaths are described as callous, manipulative, irresponsible, grandiose, and remorseless.

Addressing this conceptual ambiguity, Herve (2007) endorsed use of the PCL-R (Hare, 2003), maintaining that in defining psychopathy facets (Factor 1—*affective* and *interpersonal* facets and Factor 2—*behavioral* and *lifestyle* facets), the measure

[a] Although labeled differently by various researchers (e.g., liers and swindlers, Kraepelin, 1907/1981; passive-parasitic, Karpman, 1946; unprincipled or covetous, Millon & Davis, 1998) they still represent one subtype, defined by Herve (2007) as manipulative psychopaths. For the reader's convenience the term "manipulative psychopath" will be used in the current chapter.

afforded investigation of psychopathy and psychopathy subtypes in a more precise manner (e.g., Darjee, 2019; Rodre et al., 2019). Interestingly, a growing body of literature using the PCL-R offers empirical support for the clinical typology, distinguishing idiopathic/primary and pseudo-/secondary psychopaths (e.g., Hick & Drislane, 2018; Skeem, Johansson, Andershed, Kerr, & Louden, 2007). Using the PCL-R, differences between psychopaths were found in aggressive versus manipulative deviant actions (Gretton, 1998), verbal intelligence (aggressive psychopaths = low verbal intelligence, manipulative psychopaths = high verbal intelligence), mapping on to differences in offense patterns. For example, Blackburn and Coid (1998) observed that primary psychopaths have less convictions for fraud and more for robbery and firearm offenses compared to secondary/pseudo-psychopaths. Psychopaths were also found to differ in terms of lifestyle manifestations of the disorder, highlighting successful, nonconvicted, psychopaths versus unsuccessful, convicted psychopaths (Ishikawa et al., 2001).

Henderson's (1947) classic psychopath appears to represent a pervasive high scoring psychopath, while the explosive/aggressive psychopath (Karpman, 1946) represents a more impulsive and volatile emphasis (PCL-R Factor 2 traits), with the manipulative psychopath perhaps (Arieti, 1963) a more callous and exploitative variant (PCL-R Factor 1 traits). Accordingly, Herve's own typology (2007) combined both clinical classification and an empirical approach. Based on data collected with the PCL-R from 202 male incarcerated offenders, Herve (2007) derived four subtypes, each differing in the display of affective, interpersonal, and lifestyle psychopathic features. The types were labeled after classical clinical typology: classic psychopaths, explosive psychopaths, manipulative psychopaths, and pseudo-psychopaths. Herve (2007) argues that subtype 1 is conceptually similar to the original clinical description of classic psychopaths, having the highest scores on all facets of the PCL-R, demonstrating the most conceited and manipulative interpersonal style, affective deficits, and antisocial lifestyle. Subtype 2—the explosive psychopath—shows the second highest PCL-R scores, and while demonstrating deceit, diminished affect, and irresponsible behavior, they score relatively low on the interpersonal facet. In contrast, subtype 3—the manipulative psychopath—scores low on lifestyle facets (less prone to risk-taking and impulsivity), but high on interpersonal and affective facets (deceitful interpersonal style and lack of empathy). The fourth subtype—secondary or pseudo-psychopaths—demonstrates interpersonal and lifestyle characteristics of the disorder but not the affective ones (Herve, 2007). This finding supports the clinical description of a pseudo-psychopath as someone who is not free of conscience, internal conflicts, and complex emotions (Arieti, 1963).

A recent study by Mokros et al. (2015) used latent profile analysis to test the hypothesis that homogenous classes existed among psychopaths in a sample of 1451 males with high PCL-R scores (> 27), where the four PCL-R facets served as dependent variables for clustering. The analysis revealed three classes, the first two of which were consistent with the "manipulative" versus "aggressive" typology (Herve, 2007; Hicks, Markon, Patrick, Krueger, & Newman, 2004). The third class reflected Herve's (2007) concept of the pseudo-psychopath, scoring almost as high on the PCL-R as other classes, but low on the affective facet, relating to lack of empathy, guilt, and remorse. Lacking this hallmark construct, the class was considered to fall short of true psychopathy. While no distinct representation of the classic psychopath emerged from Mokros et al. (2015) analysis, the results broadly supported Herve's (2007) typology, indicating that the framework may be useful in modeling offense behavior.

One effort to apply this typology to a classification of crime scene behaviors is given by O'Toole (2007), proposing that:

- Classic psychopaths' crime scene actions are characterized by careful planning brought together with risk-taking and impulsivity. O'Toole (2007) gives as an example a crime that occurs in the middle of the day in a low-risk environment. The crime committed by a classic psychopath is also characterized by excessive violence and hyperaggression.
- Explosive psychopaths are versatile in their crimes but impulsive. They are thrill-seekers and likely to use a blitz attack on their victims.
- Manipulative psychopaths are less versatile in their crimes than explosive or classic psychopaths, better blending in with law-abiding community. They are also less impulsive, which O'Toole (2007) suggested would be revealed in their crime scene actions, with crime scene behaviors indicating greater planning and control.

O'Toole's (2007) system lacks supportive empirical evidence, with the application of typology to crime scene actions being conducted on case examples and anecdotal evidence rather than meticulous data analysis. The framework maintains a certain dubiety, particularly with respect to classic and explosive types, both characterized as *criminal versatile*, *hyper-aggressive*, *impulsive* and *risk-taking*, especially when it comes to the choice of victim. O'Toole (2007) defends the distinction, arguing that "the classic psychopath's crimes are likely to manifest evidence of careful planning within a domain of impulsivity and risk taking, for example, occurring in the middle of the day in low risk environments (middle-class homes in low-crime neighborhood) and involving low-risk victims"[b] (p. 316). The classification was compared with a case study where "(...) the offender entered the home of a 12-year-old girl (...) The victim's mother and sister were asleep in the next room. This was a middle-class neighbourhood with a low incidence of crime (...) The offender entered the home and went almost immediately to the victim's bedroom. He talked briefly to the girls before leaving the residence with the victim. He wore no mask or disguise (...) If psychopathic, he would probably be explosive by nature" (O'Toole, 2007, pp. 321–322).

However, illustration of overlap is not necessarily contradictory, since O'Toole (2007) also highlights distinction in the classic psychopath's pervasive trait presentation, which should predict a balance of attributes and behaviors, whereas the explosive psychopathic demonstrates a less calculated, more emotionally reactive emphasis, reflecting our earlier discussion. Somewhat commensurate with this notion is the idea that psychopathy can be conceptualized as a continuum. Thus variations of psychopathic personality denote positions reflecting severity of presentation on different facets. Nevertheless, crossover of characteristics highlighted even with this brief analysis casts doubt on utility for distinguishing offending behavior.

Clearly, there is still ambiguity with respect to classifying psychopaths, suggesting need for a research methodology assuring more theoretical clarity. One issue with

[b] According to O'Toole (2007) low-risk victims are those whose lifestyle, habits, and general associates do not put them into environment/situation that enhances risk to become a victim of violent crime.

the current examination of psychopathic personality is reliance on the PCL-R, which assesses both underpinning personality facets (Factor 1) and lifestyle facets (Factor 2). Boduszek, Debowska, and Willmott (2017) argue that relying on the PCL-R, and specifically PCL-R total scores with a high inclusion threshold, could lead to the exclusion of participants scoring high on interpersonal/affective traits (Factor 1) but low on lifestyle indicators (Factor 2), maintaining that this weights outcomes toward behavioral features rather than underpinning personality traits. The argument resonates with recent studies (e.g., Darjee, 2019; Rodre et al., 2019) highlighting a greater significance of Factor 1 traits in distinguishing psychopathic offense patterns.

Addressing this discrepancy, Boduszek et al. (2017) employed the Psychopathic Personality Trait Scale (PPTS; Boduszek, Debowska, Dhingra, & DeLisi, 2016) with a sample of 1126 adult male prisoners. The PPTS consists of four dimensions: *affective responsiveness* (empathy and emotional depth), *cognitive responsiveness* (understanding others' emotions), *interpersonal manipulation* (glibness and deceit), and *egocentricity* (self-interest), eliminating the potentially confounding impact of behavioral items. Building on Mokros et al. (2015) findings, the study identified meaningful subtypes of psychopathy related to offending behavior, with latent profile analysis revealing five classes of psychopathic traits:

Class 1—(Low Psychopathy)—Baseline group, scoring low on all PPTS traits.
Class 2—Moderate Affective/Cognitive Responsiveness—Low Manipulation and Egocentricity.
Class 3—High Interpersonal Manipulation—Low Affective/Cognitive Responsiveness and Egocentricity.
Class 4—(Moderate Psychopathy)—High Interpersonal Manipulation—Moderate Affective/Cognitive and Egocentricity.
Class 5—(High Psychopathy)—Scoring high on all PPTS traits.

The results demonstrated that white-collar and property criminals were significantly more likely to fall into Class 2 or 3 (High Interpersonal Manipulation) than Class 1 (Low Psychopathy), and that the Class 5 (High Psychopathy) was significantly more represented by violent offenders than Class 2 (Moderate Affective), suggesting that violent crime is more reflected by the psychopathic traits of shallow affect and lack of empathy, whereas white-collar and property offenders may show greater depth of emotion and emotional responsiveness while being interpersonally manipulative. Outcomes broadly support a continuum concept of psychopathy with a class of highly psychopathic criminals, a class of manipulative psychopaths with less extreme affective unresponsiveness, a class of highly manipulative criminals with greater affective responsiveness, a class demonstrating moderate affective responsiveness and low manipulation, and finally, a low psychopathy class of criminals. In this formulation, Classes 2 and 3 represent a middle ground with contrasting psychopathic traits.

Relating findings to exiting models, Class 5 can be seen to represent Herve's (2007) classic psychopath, illustrating the spectrum of psychopathic traits, and being more likely to commit violent offenses, Class 4 may represent the manipulative psychopath (manipulative, emotionally unresponsive). The findings depart from Herve's (2007) typology with Class 3 (manipulative, emotionally responsive), though parallels may be drawn with aggressive psychopathy, whereas Class 2 may represent the pseudo-psychopath (Arieti, 1963).

Significantly, offenders were profiled exclusively on personality-derived psychopathy dimensions, eliminating the confounding impact of lifestyle features, and giving form to previous findings (e.g., Mokros et al., 2015) by revealing practically applicable classes, distinguishing psychopaths from nonpsychopaths and psychopathic personality traits according to different offense types. The research generally supports literature highlighting a proclivity toward violent offenses in psychopaths (Fox & DeLisi, 2019; Porter & Woodworth, 2007), while highlighting greater incidence of white-collar and property offenses where there is high manipulation without significant empathy or affect deficits. Primarily, Boduszek et al. (2017) suggest advantages in emphasizing personality traits over behavioral indictors for elucidating psychopathic traits that relate to offense patterns, thus offering some guidance to investigative processes. However, the study highlights only rudimentary offense differences, with more detailed analysis of specific crime scene actions and psychopathy being necessary to significantly enhance the investigative utility of the literature.

Investigative psychology: Avenues for future research

Other efforts to model crime scene behavior and psychopathy are discussed in LaBrode's (2007) examination of psychopathic serial killers. The purpose of their discussion was to, among other things, analyze the crimes and personality characteristics of psychopathic killers, highlighting the distinction between modus operandi (MO) and the signature aspect of offenses. It is argued that the practical instrumentality of the MO means that it may develop over time as the offender becomes more proficient, whereas the "signature" refers to specific, unique crime scene actions that reflect the offender's personality. These are actions that go beyond behaviors necessary to commit a crime, reflecting underlying personality factors, and from which the criminal derives gratification. While LaBrode's (2007) report pertains to psychopathic serial killers, the author raises an important point in highlighting the salience of specific deviant acts to effective offender profiling. As reported in this chapter, psychopathy research has been limited in this respect, with a commitment of empirical research examining such phenomena likely to provide practical insights.

For many years, the idea that offenders' crime scene actions reveal their personality traits has been an important factor in offender profiling practice. Offender profiling is based on the idea that people are guided by underlying psychological processes, therefore criminals will invariably leave unique clues at the crime scene. The broader investigative utility of offender profiling derives from the principle that through crime data analyses common patterns among types of offenders emerge which can aid investigators in focusing their suspect search. Crime scene actions concerning victimology, MO, signature behaviors, and crime classification provide information important in profiling a suspect. This perspective, especially signature behaviors, offers a research focus for distinguishing specific crime scene actions representative of psychopaths and subtypes of psychopaths.

With respect to early profiling research, Douglas, Burgess, Burgess, and Ressler (1992) discuss classification of serial killers into organized and disorganized offenders, purporting key crime scene actions indicative of certain offender profiles. In their formulation, organized criminals are socially competent and moderately intelligent, premeditate their crimes, restrain victims, and bring a weapon to the crime scene, whereas the disorganized offender is more opportunistic, sloppy, impulsive, below average intelligence, and socially inept. However, Canter, Alison, Alison, and Wentink (2004) discredit these arguments, highlighting propositional flaws such as an emphasis on investigator intuition rather than empirical evidence to support the typology.

Following early analyses of crime scene behavior and offender characteristics (Canter & Heritage, 1990), Canter developed the field of Investigative Psychology, an applied research area examining offense data, behavior patterns, and correlates in offender characteristics to develop empirical models of offending behavior and underpinning psychological phenomena that are useful to police investigations. The primary challenge of Investigative Psychology is to reveal the complex relationship between offending actions and offender characteristics. This endeavor relates directly to the subject of this chapter. The canonical form of offending actions and characteristics (as described by Canter, 1995) is the relationship of two domains: a combination of criterion variables (characteristics) that maps onto a combination of predictor variables (actions). Mental illnesses, personality disorders, and cognitive impairments play an important role in understanding offending behavior. Häkkänen and Laajasalo (2006) study demonstrated that crime scene behaviors can be specific not only to offenders' mental status (presence/absence of mental issues), but also to different psychiatric diagnoses. Thus psychotic offenders more frequently inflicted injuries to victims' faces, while offenders with a drug addiction typically stole something from the victim, and offenders with no mental issues were least likely to move the body.

Broadly, the focus of Investigative Psychology has been determining offender characteristics in terms of geography and interpersonal factors rather than psychopathology, serving expedience for police suspect focus. For example, in a study examining the relationship between personality facets and offending behavior in a cohort of 207 youth offenders, Youngs (2004) revealed differentiation between *person* and *property* offenses and between *expressive* and *instrumental* aspects of these offense styles. Examination of Fundamental Interpersonal Relations Orientation-Behavior (FIRO) Questionnaire (Schutz, 1992) data and crime scene details highlighted a relationship between interpersonal personality and offense style, with most of the variation in the dataset being related to aspects of "control": property offenses tended to be committed by individuals who reported higher levels of control from others, whereas *expressive-person* crime, incorporating violence and use of weapons was committed by offenders with a high need for control and dominance. The description of *expressive-person* offending style, in which the perpetrator targets others in order to fulfill incentives for control and exploitation, fits the description of psychopathy (Häkkänen-Nyholm & Nyholm, 2012). That this style was also characterized by violence and use of weapons reflects Hare and McPherson's (1984) and others' (e.g., Darjee, 2019) arguments that psychopathic offenders demonstrate such behaviors more frequently than nonpsychopathic ones.

While these attempts to extrapolate psychopathic personality correlates of offense style may appear somewhat tangential, the relatively rich data on violent crimes committed by psychopaths affords more penetrating speculation on the potential association between psychopathy and violent crime typology. Canter's (1994) Victim Role Model (VRM) may be useful in this respect. The VRM proceeds from an understanding that violent offending is an interpersonal activity, with interaction serving as the most psychologically significant factor. Thus interpersonal variations provide a basis for differentiating offending styles (Canter & Youngs, 2012). Canter and Youngs (2012) use a narrative perspective to understand individual differences through a range of destructive personal narratives that guide offending behavior. Arguing that violent offenders show an inability to self-story with others in central roles due to lack of empathy, Canter (1995) maintains that they assign nonagentic roles for their victims, and that these victim roles underpin offending behavior. It is contended that achievement of power along with a lack of empathy is at the heart of the offending interaction, mirroring focal psychopathic traits.

Canter (1994) describes three qualitatively different forms of control through which an offender can exert power over a victim and three corresponding manifestations of empathy deficits, forming a model for victim in the role of *object*, *vehicle*, or *person*. In the victim as *object*, control is expressed directly through possession and subjugation, allowing physical control. Here, there is a lack of awareness of any humanity. Where the victim assumes the role of *vehicle*, control takes the form of abuse, allowing emotional or psychological control, observing a lack of compassion for the victim's suffering manifest in exploitation, degradation, and/or torture. In the victim as a *person* role, control is achieved through manipulation, enabling power over the victim's actions, while an empathy deficit is revealed in undervaluing the victim with the decision to take advantage of them.

While all victim roles are underpinned by a motive to control and lack of empathy, specific roles allocated within the offender's narrative imply different forms of interpersonal treatment. For example, where emotional remove and control need is most pronounced (*victim as object*) violence may be typified by extreme crime scene actions, such as mutilation or dismemberment, while in the cases of *victim as person*, crime scene behaviors may reflect a lesser control incentive and higher emotional responsiveness (engaging in conversation, fondling) (Canter & Youngs, 2012).

The VRM has been successfully applied to various types of violent crimes, such as serial and single murders, rape, and behavior patterns specific to offending styles in each type of crime were shown (Canter et al., 2004; Canter & Heritage, 1990; Canter & Youngs, 2012; Fritzon & Ridgway, 2001). This research demonstrates the data richness of specific crime scene behaviors (stroking, binding, mutilation) in revealing different interpersonal qualities (control, callousness, lack of empathy) central to psychopathy research. Considering this application, Canter and Youngs (2012) propose hypotheses of specific relationships between psychiatric diagnoses and victim role assignment, citing the most obvious prediction of psychopathy relating to the *object* role assignment, since this illustrates the most extreme expression of control and empathy deficit. Certainly, considering research illustrating excessive violence committed by psychopaths (e.g., Fox & DeLisi, 2019), along with the centrality of affect and interpersonal features (manipulation, lack of empathy) to diagnosis (Hare, 1996), the VRM may be useful for examining relationships between specific crime scene details and features of psychopathic personality.

Focus on offender narratives by investigative psychologists has produced a wealth of applicable findings, revealing cognitive, affective, and identity differences by examining relationships between specific offender characteristics and offense behaviors (Youngs and Canter, 2012). Canter and colleagues use Multidimensional scaling procedures (MDS), a powerful form of analysis that examines the co-occurrence of variables to reveal patterns in complex behavior systems (Canter, 1985; Youngs & Canter, 2012). Moving beyond early offender profiling measures, this empirical approach to examination of offender and offense data has been instrumental in the development of predictive multivariate models, associating specific psychological characteristics with different patterns of offending behavior and providing direct applicability to police investigations (Ioannou, Canter, Youngs, & Synnott, 2015). The methodological and theoretic underpins of this approach offer guidance for further application in distinguishing differences in crime scene behaviors among psychopaths and nonpsychopaths, and different types of psychopaths.

Of further interest to this line of inquiry is a body of work distinguishing narrative roles among offenders. An emergent framework differentiates *revenger*, *professional*, *hero*, and *victim* offender roles according to degrees of power and intimacy in offense narratives. The roles map onto manifestations of control and ways of exploiting others (Canter & Youngs, 2009). According to the framework, the *revenger* sees himself as highly potent and other people as significant in a retribution quest. During crime commission, experiences of high negative arousal (anger and upset) are exemplary but the offender is powerful and in control, exhibiting high potency with high intimacy. The *professional*, likewise, illustrates power but others are insignificant and the experience of positive nonarousal (emotional calm) during crime commission is exemplary, showing high potency with low intimacy. In contrast, the *victim* offender role illustrates low potency with high intimacy, experiencing a lack of power and feeling alienated; negative arousal with a sense of helplessness is illustrated. Finally, the *hero* professes limited agency over his actions and no concern for others, experiencing offending as a brave and pleasurable activity, showcasing a low intimacy, low potency narrative (Ioannou, Canter, & Youngs, 2017; Youngs & Canter, 2012).

The predictive power of the framework was revealed in a subsequent study demonstrating how offender roles mapped onto crime type (Ioannou et al., 2015). In a study of 120 convicted criminals, offenses were classified into Property ($n=20$), Drug ($n=20$) Violent ($n=20$), Robbery ($n=20$), Sexual ($n=20$), and Murder ($n=20$). All cases were examined and assigned a narrative role, 97% of whom uniquely classified as either *revenger, professional, victim, hero*. For property, drug, and robbery offenses, *hero* and *professional* were the predominant roles, whereas for violent offenses and murders, the predominant role was *revenger*. Sex offenders most often fitted the *victim* role, followed by *revenger*. Interestingly, the researchers noted that almost half of offenders saw themselves in the *victim* role, arguing for an interpretation according to the VRM (Canter, 1994), *victim as person* role, where the offender attempts to achieve intimacy. Similarly, the *revenger* role aligned with the *victim as vehicle*, the offender using the subject to express anger and desires. Canter and Youngs (2012) postulate that psychopathy may be more prevalent where the victim is assigned the role of *object*, while *victim as vehicle* and *person* may represent less extreme offense patterns, symbolizing a lower control incentive and lesser empathy deficits. From a combining of the offender role's framework and VRM, a Narrative Action System (NAS) model emerged, accounting for both offender and victim narrative roles in the crime scene interaction.

Again, although these studies do not directly assess offending characteristics against psychopathy, they suggest future applications, revealing use in detailed comparative analysis of crime scene actions with personality characteristics for modeling offender typologies carrying investigative significance. Further, the examination of power and intimacy themes through personal narratives concerns control and empathy deficit mechanisms central to the study of psychopathy, narratives themselves a phenomenology of the interpersonal and affective (Factor 1 facets), and perhaps key correlates of dimensions of psychopathic personality. For example, the calm instrumentality of the *professional* relates a lack of emotionality and a callous task focus devoid of empathy, reflecting PCL-R Factor 1 features, while the *revenger* role combines callous potency with a more emotionally volatile offense style, perhaps more akin to PCL-R Factor 2 facets, or a combination of psychopathic features. With these considerations in mind, the NAS model may be useful in terms of relating intensity of roles' presentation (e.g., victim as *object* with *revenger* or *professional* offender role) with psychopathic traits and specific crime scene behaviors.

In a further study adopting this approach, Yaneva, Ioannnou, Hammond, and Synott (2018) attempted to distinguish characteristics of contract killers according to *professional*, *revenger*, *hero*, and *victim* themes. Identifying 56 crime scenes actions among 75 cases, analysis revealed four distinct aspects of contract killing commensurate with narrative roles. The *professional* role characterized criminally proficient cases, while the *victim* role was exemplified in a clumsier, amateur approach. *Revenger* and *hero* themes characterized a semiprofessional with a more aggressive murder style and, typically, were more experienced offenders. *Revenger* themes were affected by employee motives, often being related to gangland murders, while the *hero* role maintained a balance between personal desires and profit. The researchers posited that while not examined in the study, identification of psychopathic traits according to narrative themes could be possible, where the *professional* and *revenger* roles were perhaps most exemplary, demonstrating several key psychopathic features; the *professional* showing lack of emotionality, use of a gun, and capture evasion tactics (wearing mask, quick attack)—PCL-R Factor 1 traits, while the *revenger* illustrated extreme forms of violence, chronic offending history, and a greater level of emotionality, more exemplary of PCL-R Factor 2 facets. Although it should be stated that all roles among the sample showcased extreme violence with premeditation, such features central to contract killings.

Finally, a study by Goodlad, Ioannou, and Hunter (2019) attempted to directly apply offender roles to psychopathy. The researchers recruited a sample of 22 male offenders convicted of sexual or violent offenses, all of whom diagnosed with personality disorders and 18 diagnosed psychopaths (using PCL-R threshold of 25).

Analysis revealed that all cases could be classified according to the narrative themes (*professional*, *hero*, *victim*, *revenger*), or as a hybrid between two themes. The *professional* theme evinced control and calm in routine instrumental offending, illustrating hallmark psychopathic traits (Hare, 2003), though no significant relationship between the role and psychopathy was found. Interestingly, the association was close to significance, with the researchers arguing that since features fitting the *professional* theme relate to psychopathy, their result may reflect a limited sample size rather than an insignificant correlation. No relationship was shown between the *hero* theme and psychopathy, while the *victim* role related to borderline PD, unsurprisingly since theme attributes such as interpersonal instability, self-image, emotional dysregulation, and impulsivity are consistent with the diagnosis. However, again, no relationship with psychopathy was revealed. Likewise, no relationship was found between the *revenger* theme and psychopathy, or any other PD.

While the results may indicate an incongruity between the offender roles and psychopathic traits, sampling limitations may have confounded outcomes. Mindful of differences in offense types and PCL-R factor scores (Rodre et al., 2019), perhaps future studies with larger samples should analyze relationships between each PCL-R factor, since elements of the *professional* theme more directly map PCL-R Factor 1 features, while *revenger* attributes appear to reflect combined or Factor 2 features (Ioannou et al., 2015). Perhaps more beneficially, the PPTS could be employed to focus more directly on psychopathic personality at the exclusion of lifestyle features, following recent validation of the tool for classifying psychopaths in relation to offense types (Boduszek et al., 2017). Crucially, the study represents an attempt to apply the NAS model to psychopathy and opens the field for further studies heeding the sampling and analytic limitations of this inaugural endeavor.

Conclusions

Recognizing personality correlates of crime scene behaviors carries practical implications for police investigations, in terms of focusing the suspect search, tailoring interview processes, and subsequent treatment in the criminal justice system. Thus identifying offender characteristics that relate to specific offense patterns and crime scene actions is of paramount importance. Research examining differences between psychopathic and nonpsychopathic criminals is, therefore, of considerable significance, with many studies highlighting differences in offense patterns and crime scene behaviors between psychopaths and nonpsychopaths, and among psychopaths. These include greater instrumentality and premeditation, more extreme violence, exploitation and homicidal crimes, as well as higher levels of deviant, sexually sadistic, and unusual crime scene actions. In terms of differences between psychopaths, certain PCL-R Factor 1 and Factor 2 crime scene behaviors have been distinguished, with high Factor 1 scorers demonstrating more calculated, instrumental offending and extreme violence, while impulsivity, substance misuse, and a more expressive manner have been linked to higher PCL-R Factor 2 scorers (Darjee, 2019; Rodre et al., 2019). While these findings indicate specific, tangible crime scene actions differentiating types of psychopathic offender, PCL-R Factor 1 features appear to be associated with more recognized indicators of psychopathy (Porter & Woodworth, 2007). Further research revealed a more meaningful five-class typology using the PPTS, removing confounding PCL-R lifestyle facets, and accounting for nonpsychopathic and psychopathic personality traits in relation to specific offense patterns (Boduszek et al., 2017). The results are promising and advance the literature, though reveal only rudimentary offense type differences. Future research needs to build on these findings with a richer analysis of specific crime scene actions.

In this endeavor Investigative Psychology offers some guidance, with its focus on comparative empirical analysis of detailed offense and offender narrative data, revealing predictive relationships between crime scene actions and offender characteristics. The NAS model (Canter & Youngs, 2009) predicts crime commission according to offender (*professional*, *revenger*, *hero*, *victim*) and allocated victim roles (*object*, *vehicle*, *person*), which arise from underpinning control needs and empathy deficits manifesting as distortions to power and intimacy incentives. The model suggests parallels with affective and interpersonal traits of psychopaths. Canter (1994) offers a perspective on how needs for control through destruction and empathy deficits are operationalized through victim role allocation. It can be speculated that the NAS model may be useful for understanding a spectrum of psychopathic traits as they relate to specific crime scene actions, prospecting that the extremist presentation of control and empathy deficits (*professional*, *revenger*) with the victim as *object* reflects psychopathic crimes, and demonstrates the most destructive, callous crime scene behaviors (brutal murder, mutilation, dismemberment), while at the other extreme, a lower control incentive and affective responsivity (*victim*) with the victim as *person* may predict crime scene behaviors indicative of nonpsychopathy (engaging in conversation, fondling), further role permutations reflecting intermediate trait presentations and crime scene actions (e.g., smacking, restraining, groping, hair-pulling). Of course, such arguments are speculative, serving to illustrate potential advances, though with a platform of literature highlighting key differences between psychopaths and nonpsychopaths, the wealth of insights brought to law enforcement through Investigative Psychology research suggests that application to examination of psychopathy should prove fruitful.

References

Arieti, S. (1963). Psychopathic personality: Some views on its psychopathology and psychodynamics. *Comprehensive Psychiatry*, *4*(5), 301–312. https://doi.org/10.1016/S0010-440X(63)80056-5.

Babiak, P., & Hare, R. D. (2006). *Snakes in suits: When psychopaths go to work*. New York, NY, US: Regan Books/Harper Collins Publishers.

Beauregard, E., & DeLisi, M. (2018a). Stepping-stones to sexual murder: The role of developmental factors in the etiology of sexual homicide. *Journal of Criminal Psychology*, *8*(3), 199–214. https://doi.org/10.1108/JCP-02-2018-0010.

Beauregard, E., & DeLisi, M. (2018b). Unravelling the personality profile of the sexual murderer. *Journal of Interpersonal Violence*. https://doi.org/10.1177/0886260518777012.

Blackburn, R., & Coid, J. W. (1998). Psychopathy and the dimensions of personality disorder in violent offenders. *Personality and Individual Differences*, *25*(1), 129–145.

Boduszek, D., Debowska, A., Dhingra, K., & DeLisi, M. (2016). Introduction and validation of Psychopathic Personality Traits Scale (PPTS) in a large prison sample. *Journal of Criminal Justice*, *46*, 9–17.

Boduszek, D., Debowska, A., & Willmott, D. (2017). Latent profile analysis of psychopathic traits among homicide, general violent, and white-collar offenders. *Journal of Criminal Justice*, *51*, 17–23. https://doi.org/10.1016/j.jcrimjus.2017.06.001.

Brown, S. L., & Forth, A. E. (1997). Psychopathy and sexual assault: Static risk factors, emotional precursors, and rapist subtypes. *Journal of Consulting and Clinical Psychology*, *65*(5), 848.

Canter, D. (Ed.). (1985). *Facet theory: Approaches to social research* Springer Science & Business Media.

Canter, D. V. (1994). *Criminal shadows*. London: HarperCollins.

Canter, D. V. (1995). The psychology of offender profiling. In R. Bull, & D. Carson (Eds.), *Handbook of psychology in legal contexts* (pp. 343–355). Chichester: Wiley.

Canter, D. V., Alison, L. J., Alison, E., & Wentink, N. (2004). The organized/disorganized typology of serial murder: Myth or model? *Psychology, Public Policy, and Law*, *10*(3), 293–320. https://doi.org/10.1037/1076-8971.10.3.293.

Canter, D. V., & Heritage, R. (1990). A multivariate model of sexual offence behaviour: Developments in offender profiling. *Journal of Forensic Psychiatry*, *1*, 185–212. https://doi.org/10.1080/09585189008408469.

Canter, D. V., & Youngs, D. E. (2009). *Investigative psychology: Offender profiling and the analysis of criminal action*. John Wiley & Sons.

Canter, D. V., & Youngs, D. E. (2012). Sexual and violent offenders' victim role assignments: A general model of offending style. *The Journal of Forensic Psychiatry & Psychology*, *23*(3), 297–326. https://doi.org/10.1080/14789949.2012.690102.

Chopin, J., & Beauregard, E. (2019). The sexual murderer is a distinct type of offender. *International Journal of Offender Therapy and Comparative Criminology*, *63*(9), 1597–1620. https://doi.org/10.1177/0306624X18817445.

Cleckley, H. (1941). *The mask of sanity: An attempt to reinterpret the so-called psychopathic personality*. St. Louis: Mosby.

Cornell, D. J., Warren, J., Hawk, G., Stafford, E., Oram, G., & Pine, D. (1996). Psychopathy in instrumental and reactive violent offenders. *Journal of Consulting and Clinical Psychology*, *64*, 783–790. https://doi.org/10.1037//0022-006x.64.4.783.

Darjee, R. (2019). Sexual sadism and psychopathy in sexual homicide offenders: An exploration of their associates in a clinical sample. *International Journal of Offender Therapy and Comparative Criminology*, *63*(9), 1738–1765. https://doi.org/10.1177/0306624X19836872.

Dietz, P. E., Hazelwood, R. R., & Warren, J. (1990). The sexually sadistic criminal and his offenses. *The Journal of the American Academy of Psychiatry and the Law*, *18*(2), 163–178.

Douglas, J. E., Burgess, A. W., Burgess, A. G., & Ressler, R. K. (1992). *Crime classification manual: A standard system for investigating and classifying violent crime*. New York: Simon and Schuster.

Flight, J. I., & Forth, A. E. (2007). Instrumentally violent youths: The roles of psychopathic traits, empathy, and attachment. *Criminal Justice and Behavior*, *34*(6), 739–751. https://doi.org/10.1177/0093854807299462.

Forth, A. E., & Kroner, D. (1995). *The factor structure of the revised psychopathy checklist with incarcerated rapists and incest offenders*. Unpublished manuscript.

Fox, B., & DeLisi, M. (2019). Psychopathic killers: A meta-analytic review of the psychopathy-homicide nexus. *Aggression and Violent Behaviour*, *44*, 67–79. https://doi.org/10.1016/j.avb.2018.11.005.

Fritzon, K., & Ridgway, J. (2001). Near-death experience: The role of victim reaction in attempted homicide. *Journal of Interpersonal Violence*, *16*(7), 679–696. https://doi.org/10.1177/088626001016007004.

Goodlad, K., Ioannou, M., & Hunter, M. (2019). The criminal narrative experience of psychopathic and personality disordered offenders. *International Journal of Offender Therapy and Comparative Criminology*, *63*(4), 523–542. https://doi.org/10.1177/0306624X18808433.

Gretton, H. M. (1998). *Psychopathy and recidivism in adolescence: A ten-year retrospective follow-up* (Doctoral dissertation). University of British Columbia.

Gretton, H., McBride, M., Lewis, K., O'Shaughnessy, R., & Hare, R. D. (1994). Patterns of violence and victimization in adolescent sexual psychopaths. In *Paper presented at the biennial meeting of the American Psychology-Law Society (Div. 41 of the American Psychological Association), Santa Fe, New Mexico*.

Häkkänen, H., & Laajasalo, T. (2006). Homicide crime scene behaviors in a Finnish sample of mentally ill offenders. *Homicide Studies*, *10*(1), 33–54.

Häkkänen-Nyholm, H., & Nyholm, J.-O. (2012). Psychopathy in economical crime, organized crime, and war crimes. In H. Häkkänen-Nyholm, & J.-O. Nyholm (Eds.), *Psychopathy and law: A practioner's guide* (pp. 177–200). New York, NY: John Wiley & Sons Ltd. https://doi.org/10.1002/9781119944980.ch9.

Häkkänen-Nyholm, H., Repo-Tiihonen, E., Lindberg, N., Salenius, S., & Weizmann-Henelius, G. (2009). Finnish sexual homicides: Offence and offender characteristics. *Forensic Science International*, *188*(1–3), 125–130. https://doi.org/10.1016/j.forsciint.2009.03.030.

Hare, R. D. (1970). *Psychopathy: Theory and research*. New York: Wiley.

Hare, R. D. (1993). *Without conscience: The disturbing world of the psychopaths among us*. New York: Pocket Books.

Hare, R. D. (1996). Psychopathy: A clinical construct whose time has come. *Criminal Justice and Behavior*, *23*(1), 25–54. https://doi.org/10.1177/0093854896023001004.

Hare, R. D. (1999). Psychopathy as a risk factor for violence. *The Psychiatric Quarterly*, *70*, 181–197. https://doi.org/10.1023/A:1022094925150.

Hare, R. D. (2003). *The hare psychopathy checklist-revised*. Toronto, ON, Canada: Multi-Health Systems.

Hare, R. D. (2006). Psychopathy: A clinical and forensic overview. *Psychiatric Clinics of North America*, *29*(3), 709–724. https://doi.org/10.1016/j.psc.2006.04.007.

Hare, R. D., & McPherson, L. M. (1984). Violent and aggressive behaviour by criminal psychopaths. *International Journal of Law and Psychiatry*, *7*, 35–50. https://doi.org/10.1016/0160-2527(84)90005-0.

Henderson, D. K. (1947). *Psychopathic states* (2nd ed.). New York: W.W. Norton.

Herve, H. (2007). Psychopathic subtypes: Historical and contemporary perspectives. In H. Herve, & J. C. Yuille (Eds.), *The psychopath: Theory, research and practice* (pp. 431–460). Lawrence Erlbaum Associates Publishers.

Hick, B. M., & Drislane, L. E. (2018). Variants ("subtypes") of psychopathy. In C. J. Patrick (Ed.), *Handbook of psychopathy* (pp. 297–332). The Guildford Press.

Hicks, B. M., Markon, K. E., Patrick, C. J., Krueger, R. F., & Newman, J. P. (2004). Identifying psychopathy subtypes on the basis of personality structure. *Psychological Assessment*, *16*(3), 276–288. https://doi.org/10.1037/1040-3590.16.3.276.

Holt, S. E., & Strack, S. (1999). Sadism and psychopathy in violent and sexually violent offenders. *Journal of the American Academy of Psychiatry and the Law*, *27*(1), 23–32.

Hutton, E. L., & Woodworth, M. (2014). Violent female youth: An examination of instrumental violence, psychopathy, and offense characteristics. *Behavioral Sciences & the Law*, *32*(1), 121–134. https://doi.org/10.1002/bsl.2100.

Ioannou, M., Canter, D. V., & Youngs, D. E. (2017). Criminal narrative experience: Relating emotions to offence narrative roles during crime commission. *International Journal of Offender Therapy and Comparative Criminology*, *61*(14), 1531–1553. https://doi.org/10.1177/0306624X15625991.

Ioannou, M., Canter, D. V., Youngs, D. E., & Synnott, J. (2015). Offender crime narratives across different types of crimes. *Journal of Forensic Psychology Practice*, *15*(5), 383–400. https://doi.org/10.1080/15228932.2015.1065620.

Ishikawa, S. S., Raine, A., Lencz, T., Bihrle, S., & Lacasse, L. (2001). Autonomic stress reactivity and executive functions in successful and unsuccessful criminal psychopaths from the community. *Journal of Abnormal Psychology*, *110*(3), 423–432. https://doi.org/10.1037/0021-843X.110.3.423.

Karpman, B. (1941). On the need of separating psychopathy into two distinct clinical types: The symptomatic and the idiopathic. *Journal of Criminal Psychopathology*, *3*, 112–137.

Karpman, B. (1946). Psychopathy in the scheme of human typology. *Journal of Nervous and Mental Disease*, *103*, 276–288. https://doi.org/10.1097/00005053-194603000-00007.

Karpman, B. (1955). Criminal psychodynamics: A platform. *Archives of Criminal Psychodynamics*, *1*, 3–100.

Kirsch, L. G., & Becker, J. V. (2007). Emotional deficits in psychopathy and sexual sadism: Implications for violent and sadistic behaviour. *Clinical Psychology Review*, *27*(8), 904–922. https://doi.org/10.1016/j.cpr.2007.01.011.

Knoll, J. L., & Hazelwood, R. R. (2009). Becoming the victim: Beyond sadism in serial sexual murderers. *Aggression and Violent Behavior*, *14*(2), 106–114. https://doi.org/10.1016/j.avb.2008.12.003.

Kraepelin, E. (1981). *Clinical psychiatry* (2nd English ed.). New York: Scholars' Facsimiles & Reprints. A.R. Diefendorf, Trans. (Original work published in 1907).

LaBrode, R. T. (2007). Etiology of the psychopathic serial killer: An analysis of antisocial personality disorder, psychopathy, and serial killer personality and crime scene characteristics. *Brief Treatment and Crisis Intervention*, *7*(2), 151–160. https://doi.org/10.1093/brief-treatment/mhm004.

Leaff, L. A. (1978). The antisocial personality: Psychodynamic implications. In W. H. Reid (Ed.), *The psychopath: A comprehensive study of antisocial disorders and behaviors* (pp. 79–117). New York: Brunner/Mazel.

Lesha, J., & Lesha, D. (2012). Psychopathy and white-collar crime: A review of literature. *SEEU Review*, *8*(2), 57–74.

Meloy, J. R. (1988). *The psychopathic mind: Origins, dynamics, and treatment*. Rowman & Littlefield.

Meloy, J. R. (2000). The nature and dynamics of sexual homicide: An integrative review. *Aggression and Violent Behaviour*, *5*, 1–22. https://doi.org/10.1016/S1359-1789(99)00006-3.

Millon, T., & Davis, R. D. (1998). Ten subtypes of psychopathy. In T. Millon, E. Simonsen, M. Birket-Smith, & R. D. Davis (Eds.), *Psychopathy: Antisocial, criminal, and violent behavior* (pp. 161–170). The Guilford Press.

Mokros, A., Hare, R. D., Neumann, C. S., Santtila, P., Habermeyer, E., & Nitschke, J. (2015). Variants of psychopathy in adult male offenders: A latent profile analysis. *Journal of Abnormal Psychology*, *124*(2), 372–386. https://doi.org/10.1037/abn0000042.

Monahan, J. (1977). *Clinical prediction of violent behavior (the master work series)*. Jason Aronson, Incorporated.

O'Toole, M. E. (2007). Psychopathy as a behavior classification system for violent and serial crime scenes. In H. Herve, & J. C. Yuille (Eds.), *The psychopath: Theory, research and practice* (pp. 301–326). Mahwah, NJ: Lawrence Erlbaum Associates.

O'Toole, M. E., & Häkkänen-Nyholm, H. (2012). Psychopathy and violent crime. In H. Häkkänen-Nyholm, & J.-O. Nyholm (Eds.), *Psychopathy and law: A practioner's guide* (pp. 261–285). New York, NY: John Wiley & Sons Ltd. https://doi.org/10.1002/9781119944980.ch7.

Porter, S., Campbell, M. A., Woodworth, M., & Birt, A. R. (2001). A new psychological conceptualization of the sexual psychopath. In F. Columbus (Ed.), *Vol. 7. Advances in psychology research* (pp. 21–36). New York: Nova Science.

Porter, S., Fairweather, D., Drugge, J., Herve, H., Birt, A. R., & Boer, D. (2000). Profiles of psychopathy in incarcerated sexual offenders. *Criminal Justice and Behavior*, *27*(2), 216–233. https://doi.org/10.1177/0093854800027002005.

Porter, S., & Woodworth, M. (2006). Psychopathy and aggression. In C. Patrick (Ed.), *Handbook of psychopathy* (pp. 481–494). New York: Guilford.

Porter, S., & Woodworth, M. (2007). "I'm sorry I did it…but he started it": A comparison of the official and self-reported homicide descriptions of psychopaths and non-psychopaths. *Law and Human Behavior*, *31*(1), 91–107. https://doi.org/10.1007/s10979-006-9033-0.

Porter, S., Woodworth, M., Earle, J., Drugge, J., & Boer, D. (2003). Characteristics of sexual homicides committed by psychopathic and non-psychopathic offenders. *Law and Human Behavior*, *27*(5), 459–470. https://doi.org/10.1023/A:1025461421791.

Roberts, J. V., & Grossman, M. G. (1993). Sexual homicide in Canada: A descriptive analysis. *Annals of Sex Research*, *6*(1), 5–25. https://doi.org/10.1177/107906329300600101.

Rodre, S., Hedlund, J., Liljeberg, J., Kristiansson, M., Masterman, T., & Sturup, J. (2019). Psychopathy-associated personality traits influence crime-scene behaviour in male homicide offenders. *Nordic Journal of Psychiatry*, *73*(8), 471–474. https://doi.org/10.1080/08039488.2019.1626907.

Schutz, W. (1992). Beyond Firo-B—Three new theory-derived measures—Element. *B: Behavior, Element F: Feelings, Element S: Self. Psychological Reports*, *70*(3), 915–937.

Shaw, J., & Porter, S. (2012). Forever a psychopath? Psychopathy and the criminal career trajectory. In H. Häkkänen-Nyholm, & J.-O. Nyholm (Eds.), *Psychopathy and law: A practioner's guide* (pp. 261–285). New York, NY: John Wiley & Sons Ltd. https://doi.org/10.1002/9781119944980.ch10.

Skeem, J., Johansson, P., Andershed, H., Kerr, M., & Louden, J. E. (2007). Two subtypes of psychopathic violent offenders that parallel primary and secondary variants. *Journal of Abnormal Psychology*, *116*(2), 395–409. https://doi.org/10.1037/0021-843X.116.2.395.

Stone, M. H. (1998). Sadistic personality in murderers. In T. Millon, E. Simonsen, M. Birket-Smith, R. D. Davis, T. Millon, E. Simonsen, & R. D. Davis (Eds.), *Psychopathy: Antisocial, criminal, and violent behavior* (pp. 346–355). New York: Guilford Press.

Vitacco, M. J., Neumann, C. S., Caldwell, M. F., Leistico, A.-M., & Van Rybroek, G. J. (2006). Testing factor models of the psychopathy checklist: Youth version and their association with instrumental aggression. *Journal of Personality Assessment*, *87*, 74–83.

Weizmann-Henelius, G., Viemero, V., & Eronen, M. (2003). The violent female perpetrator and her victim. *Forensic Science International*, *133*(3), 197–203. https://doi.org/10.1016/S0379-0738(03)00068-9.

Williamson, S., Hare, R. D., & Wong, S. (1987). Violence: Criminal psychopaths and their victims. *Canadian Journal of Behavioural Science/Revue canadienne des sciences du comportement*, *19*(4), 454.

Woodworth, M., & Porter, S. (2002). In cold blood: Characteristics of criminal homicides as a function of psychopathy. *Journal of Abnormal Psychology*, *111*(3), 436–445. https://doi.org/10.1037/0021-843X.111.3.436.

Wright, S., & Wong, S. (1988). *Criminal psychopaths and their victims* (Unpublished thesis). Saskatoon, SK, Canada: Department of Psychology, University of Saskatchewan.

Yaneva, M., Ioannnou, M., Hammond, L., & Synott, J. (2018). Differentiating contract killers: A narrative-based approach. *The Howard Journal of Crime and Justice*, *57*(1), 107–123.

Youngs, D. (2004). Personality correlates of offence style. *Journal of Investigative Psychology and Offender Profiling*, *1*(2), 99–119. https://doi.org/10.1002/jip.8.

Youngs, D. E., & Canter, D. V. (2012). Narrative roles in criminal action: An integrative framework for differentiating offenders. *Legal and Criminological Psychology*, *17*(2), 233–249.

Psychopathy and drug-related crime and violence

13

Michael G. Vaughn, Katherine J. Holzer, and Jacob Eikenberry

Introduction

The use and abuse of illicit drugs and alcohol are widespread and constitute an important social and public health problem (Danaei et al., 2009; Rehm, Taylor, & Room, 2006). More than half of arrestees have one or more drugs in their system at the time of arrest, and drug users have some of the highest recidivism, or rearrest, rates for violent and nonviolent crime. According to the Federal Bureau of Investigation's Uniform Crime Reports (UCR), 11.2 million arrests were made in, 2014 (US Department of Justice, 2015). Of these, 1.56 million were for drug use violations. To further illustrate how pervasive substance use is among those involved in the criminal justice system, let's consider data from The US Arrestee Drug Abuse Monitoring (ADAM II) survey. ADAM includes urinalysis results collected from males within 48 h of arrest, thus shedding light on the prevalence of recent drug use among arrestees (Office of National Drug Control Policy, 2014). These data suggest that drug use is pervasive among arrestees: as many as 83% tested positive for at least one drug, and 50% tested positive for more than one drug (Office of National Drug Control Policy, 2014). Despite the breadth of literature now available on the drug-crime nexus, we have made little progress toward our understanding of the causal processes associated with the link. One important criminological construct, psychopathy, may be relevant with respect to elucidating the links between drugs, crime, and violence. Psychopathy is a syndrome comprised of a constellation of affective, interpersonal, and behavioral features and traits that result in a wide array of antisocial acts over the life course (Hare, 1999; Skeem, Polaschek, Patrick, & Lilienfeld, 2011; Vaughn & Howard, 2005). With respect to psychopathy and drug-related crime and violence, several key questions remain: are drugs of abuse an enhancer or a by-product of a criminal lifestyle of which psychopathy is part and parcel? Does the primary-secondary psychopathy construct provide clues to this relationship? Can convergent constructs such as the severe 5% facilitate understanding this link with large population-level data? What about sex differences? As one can readily see, there is much to learn about the role of psychopathy in drug-related crime and violence.

In this chapter, we provide an overview of theories of addiction and crime, delve into primary-secondary psychopathy, examine what is known about psychopathy and drug-related crime, examine the convergence with the severe 5% construct, and finally, discuss some future research and intervention implications.

Psychopathy and Criminal Behavior. https://doi.org/10.1016/B978-0-12-811419-3.00002-9

Theories of addiction and crime

Addiction is increasingly viewed as a chronic, relapsing brain disease caused by repeated exposures to drugs (Kalivas & Volkow, 2005). Salas-Wright, Vaughn, and Reingle Gonzalez (2016) proffered several principles related to addiction and crime that are important for background context when discussing psychopathy and drug-related crime and violence. First, there is no specific gene for drug use and crime, but there may be a genetic vulnerability that underlies both substance use disorder and antisocial behavior, including psychopathy. Second, drugs of abuse hijack the reward pathways in the brain, which results in compulsive drug-seeking and in many cases, crime. Drug misuse appears to alter the prefrontal cortex, the executive center for behavioral regulation and decision-making. Not all persons suffering from addiction will engage in crime, however, a large proportion do. Given what we know about psychopathy, we can see how these principles are applicable.

A prevailing theory used to explain the relationship between drug use and crime suggests that drug-related violence is largely a function of pharmacological (drug craving), economic (pursuit of money), or systemic (protection of distribution networks) reasons (Goldstein & Brownstein, 1987). This framework partially explains drug use among offenders, but psychosocial factors that drive drug use are left unexplained under this paradigm (Goldstein & Brownstein, 1987; Huebner & Cobbina, 2007). Psychopathic traits are in the mix for all of these explanations as the intoxicating effects of substances would likely encourage violence but also individuals who may be aggressive people (such as those scoring high on psychopathy measures) self-select into situations that encourage the consumption of substances such as alcohol linked to violence (Johnston, O'Malley, & Eveland, 1978). However, it is important to recognize that there may be meaningful variants of psychopathy that have implications for the drugs-crime link.

Primary and secondary psychopathy

The most widely accepted conceptualizations of psychopathy consist of the impulsive antisocial behavior and the affective-interpersonal features described by Cleckley in *The Mask of Sanity* (Brislin & Patrick, 2015; Cleckley, 1941; Fowles & Dindo, 2005). These features have also been used to distinguish between the conceptualization of primary and secondary psychopathy proposed by Karpman (1948). Primary psychopathy is characterized by callous/unemotional traits and lack of remorse, while secondary psychopathic features include impulsivity and violation of social norms (Ross, Bye, Wrobel, & Horton, 2008). Hare (1980) operationalized this conceptualization of psychopathy with the Psychopathy Checklist which measures two factors corresponding to primary psychopathic traits (Factor 1) and secondary psychopathic traits (Factor 2) (Hare et al., 1990).

Results of several earlier studies revealed the co-occurrence of antisocial personality disorder (ASPD) and substance use (for review: Glenn, Johnson, & Raine, 2013; Grande, Wolf, Schubert, Patterson, & Brocco, 1984). Notably, studies suggest that

ASPD more strongly correlates to Factor 2, or secondary, psychopathy traits which include the antisocial behavioral criteria rather than the Factor 1 affective traits associated with primary psychopathy (Hart & Hare, 1989; Hare & Neumann, 2008; Shine & Hobson, 1997). Given the co-occurrence of ASPD and substance use and studies indicating that ASPD correlates with Factor 2 psychopathy, it is not surprising that research examining the association between substance use and the two facets of psychopathy reveals that substance use disorders are more highly correlated with Factor 2 than Factor 1 (Hart, Forth, & Hare, 1991; Hart & Hare, 1989; Smith & Newman, 1990).

Hemphill, Hart, and Hare (1994) sought to replicate and extend research regarding the relationship between Factor 2 psychopathy and substance use in a study involving a variety of nonclinical substance use-related variables. In their correctional sample of 200 male inmates, Hemphill et al. (1994) found that total PCL-R scores were significantly correlated with drug abuse/dependence, number of substances tried, age at first alcohol intoxication (inversely associated), and number of charges for drug-related offenses. Additionally, age at first alcohol intoxication was inversely associated with psychopathy scores. PCL-R scores were not significantly associated with alcohol abuse/dependence. Analysis of the specific psychopathy factors indicated that Factor 2 scores were more strongly associated with drug abuse/dependence diagnoses and number of substances used than Factor 1 scores. Consistent with previous studies, their results revealed that substance use appears to be more strongly associated with the antisocial behaviors related to psychopathy rather than the interpersonal and affective characteristics. To further explore this relationship, Hemphill et al. (1994) conducted a meta-analysis with results from their study and three previous studies related to substance abuse and psychopathy. Results of this meta-analysis revealed a moderate association between psychopathy and drug abuse/dependence, and a weaker relationship with alcohol abuse/dependence.

More recent studies have extended the findings of the earlier studies through the examination of primary and secondary psychopathic subgroups of criminal offenders (Swogger & Kosson, 2007; Vassileva, Kosson, Abramowitz, & Conrod, 2005). Though the primary focus of these later studies was not specifically the relationship between psychopathy and substance use, their investigation into correlates of various subgroups of psychopathic criminals supports results from prior studies. For example, Vassileva et al. (2005) used the PCL-R and the Interpersonal Measure of Psychopathy, as well as diagnoses for substance use disorders and anxiety, to explore clusters of male criminal offenders. Their analyses revealed four subtypes, including two clusters with traits that resembled primary and secondary psychopathy. Participants in the nonpsychopathic groups either exhibited some antisocial and psychopathic features or did not exhibit any significant psychopathic behaviors. Individuals in the group consistent with secondary psychopathy (29% of the sample) were characterized by severe alcohol and drug dependence as well as higher anxiety. The primary psychopath group (17% of the sample) exhibited less severe substance use and lower anxiety than the other groups.

Swogger and Kosson (2007) sought to replicate and extend results from Vassileva et al.' (2005) study with an independent sample and three-factor model of psychopathy (interpersonal, affective, and behavioral) as well as measures of substance abuse/dependence and anxiety. Their analyses derived four distinct clusters, including two consistent with primary and secondary psychopathic traits. Approximately 20% of the sample were members of the secondary psychopathic group. These individuals exhibited higher rates of drug and alcohol dependence than any of the other three groups. Members of the primary psychopathy group (15.5% of the sample) exhibited mild drug and alcohol dependence.

Recent research has attempted to better understand the relationship between substance abuse and psychopathy by exploring the role the aggression may play (Onyedibe, Ifeagwazi, & Ugwu, 2018). A study with Nigerian prison inmates focused on the potential moderating role of aggression, finding that it differentially impacts the relationship between psychopathy and substance abuse depending on type of aggressive behavior and whether the individual has higher primary or secondary psychopathic traits. For example, scores on measures of verbal aggression and hostility were significantly higher among individuals with high primary psychopathy scores and low substance abuse compared to individuals with low primary psychopathy scores and low substance abuse. Such that, individuals with primary psychopathic traits and low substance abuse were more likely to engage in verbal aggression and hostility. Additionally, for individuals with low, moderate, and high rates of substance use, secondary psychopathy significantly predicted physical aggression. This finding suggests that individuals with secondary psychopathic traits are more likely to engage in physical aggression regardless of level of substance use. Another explanation involves an anxiolysis-disinhibition model, which posits that the influence of alcohol or drugs during a violent event may reduce the anxiety that would inhibit a violent response (Pihl, Peterson, & Lau, 1993). When alcohol or other drugs are used, social anxiety is suppressed, and an individual may act more aggressively, and by extension, use weapons.

What do we know about psychopathy and drug-related crime among juveniles?

Compared to nonpsychopathic youth, some studies have found higher rates of substance abuse among psychopathic youth (e.g., Mailloux, Forth, & Kroner, 1997; Murrie & Cornell, 2000) while other studies have found no correlation between substance use and psychopathy in this population (e.g., Campbell, Porter, & Santor, 2004; Corrado, Vincent, Hart, & Cohen, 2004).

These dissimilar findings, however, seem to change when examining primary and secondary forms of psychopathy. Juveniles that exhibit secondary forms of psychopathy are more stably linked to drug use and abuse. Additionally, these individuals have been shown to be less likely to benefit from treatment. For example, O'Neill, Lidz, and Heilbrun (2003) conducted a retrospective study with adjudicated adolescents that had been referred to a substance abuse program. The study found that psychopathic traits among the adolescents were negatively correlated with attendance, participation, substance use, and clinical improvement during the treatment period and positively associated to arrest rates following treatment. Psychopathy has been characterized as having two or more categories or subtypes (Falkenbach, Poythress, & Creevy, 2008; Hicks, Markon, Patrick, Krueger, & Newman, 2004; Poythress & Skeem, 2006; Skeem, Johansson, Andershed, Kerr, & Louden, 2007; Swogger & Kosson, 2007). These subtypes give rise to different levels of psychological distress and antisocial behaviors. Juveniles, too, have been researched through subtypologies and key differences among the designated groups have been found. For example, Vaughn, Edens, Howard, and Smith (2009) identified subtypes of psychopathic traits among juvenile offenders with high levels of psychopathy consistent with primary and secondary psychopathy. Consistent with theory and findings from the adult literature, the secondary subtype was characterized by higher levels of psychological distress (trauma, suicidal ideation, anxiety, phobic anxiety, depression, interpersonal sensitivity, obsessive-compulsive, paranoia, and somatization) and antisocial behaviors including past year drug use, violent and property offending, than the primary subgroup.

In a different sample of diversion program youths, latent class analysis revealed four subtypes of youth based on psychopathic features (Wareham, Dembo, Poythress, Childs, & Schmeidler, 2009). These classes were psychopath-like, impulsive, impulsive-anxious, and nonpsychopathic. The psychopath-like class was characterized by individuals exhibiting high psychopathic features and externalizing problems with low anxiety. The impulsive group had moderately high affective and behavioral psychopathic features and externalizing problems with low anxiety. The impulsive-anxious class had moderately high interpersonal and behavioral psychopathic features, externalizing problems, and anxiety and the final group, nonpsychopathic, had low scores on measures of psychopathy, anxiety, and externalizing problems. Of these classes, the impulsive-anxious class had significantly greater involvement in prior substance use than the psychopath-like and nonpsychopathic classes. While the psychopath-like group had characteristics indicative of primary psychopaths, the authors noted difficulty in identifying a group of secondary-psychopath-like adolescents. Similar to the Vaughn, Edens, et al. (2009) findings, this study found that the impulsive-anxious class had characteristics most similar to secondary psychopaths including high anxiety, externalizing problems, and socialization difficulties with lower levels of psychopathy.

Mirroring similar findings, Kimonis, Frick, Cauffman, Goldweber, and Skeem (2012) studied the relationship between psychopathic traits and substance-related disorders among juvenile offenders. Results were consistent with studies involving adults. Suggesting that compared to juvenile offenders with primary variants of psychopathy, those with secondary variants reported more frequent substance use, especially alcohol, prior to incarceration, were nearly twice as likely to abuse substances while incarcerated, and were more likely to be diagnosed with a substance use disorder.

Taking this line of research further, Montgomery, Vaughn, Thompson, and Howard (2013) investigated associations between past year substance use and various demographic and mental health factors in a sample of over 700 juvenile offenders. Results revealed that psychopathic traits, including impulsivity, fearlessness, callous-unemotionality, and narcissism, as well as psychiatric distress and frequency of antisocial behavior were related to higher levels of drug use. Results of a mixture regression model suggest that individuals in the lower substance-using class are more likely to be African-American, younger, from families receiving public aid and have fewer psychopathic traits. Individuals in the higher substance-using class are primarily Caucasian, older, and exhibit more psychopathic traits.

Many researchers have found that certain psychopathic characteristics among adolescents are predictive for several items through the life course. This provides sound justification for continuing to measure psychopathy among youth. Identifying and creating appropriate interventions so as to interrupt the extensive criminal acts that occur among adolescents is of paramount importance. Moffitt, Caspi, Harrington, and Milne (2002) compared the frequency of antisocial behaviors among 26-year-old male participants of the Dunedin longitudinal study considered either life-course-persistent or adolescent-limited offenders. The life-course-persistent offenders report higher levels of drug-related offenses than adolescent-limited offenders while they did not differ on engagement in property crimes or rule violations. In another study, Vaughn, Howard, and DeLisi (2008) examined correlates of psychopathy among juvenile offenders finding that higher psychopathy scores were associated with increases in delinquency, early criminal career onset, and hostile aggression. The authors found that factors of psychopathy including impulsivity, narcissism, and rebellious narcissism all predicted lifetime substance use and lifetime substance use was the strongest predictor of hostile aggression.

Research surrounding psychopathy and drug using juveniles has also looked at neural responses. Differences in neural responses related to drug craving were investigated among young offenders with history of stimulant and other drug abuse as a function of psychopathic traits (Vincent, Cope, King, Nyalakanti, & Kiehl, 2018). A drug-cue exposure task was administered to 54 high-risk male adolescent offenders with a history of stimulant use while their brain activity was monitored via fMRI. Results revealed a negative relationship between psychopathy scores and brain hemodynamic responses associated with drug craving in the amygdala and anterior cingulate cortex among youth with a history of drug use. Compared to adults, there were more negative associations between PCL scores and hemodynamic response among youth. The authors note that this finding was primarily due to callous-unemotional traits over the interpersonal and behavioral traits.

What do we know about psychopathy and drug-related crime with regard to gender?

The majority of research on psychopathy, in general, and its relationship with substance use specifically, involve male samples; however, recent studies have begun to look at potential gender differences in this association (Kennealy, Hicks, & Patrick, 2007; Schulz, Murphy, & Verona, 2016; Sellbom, Donnelly, Rock, Phillips, & Ben-Porath, 2017). Kennealy et al. (2007) explored the validity of the PCL-R among female inmates using Hare's four-facet model of the PCL-R and various antisocial and criminal behaviors, including substance use. The four-facet model separates Factor 1 into two factors: interpersonal (arrogant and deceitful interpersonal style) and affective (deficient affective experience), and Factor 2 is divided into lifestyle (impulsive and irresponsible behavioral style) and antisocial (antisocial deviance) factors. Within their female sample, results on the Short Drug Abuse Screening Test were significantly and positively correlated with PCL-R total scores. With regard to individual factors, drug use was positively correlated with Factor 2 scores; however, it was not significantly related to Factor 1 scores. Overall drug use and each drug class, except psychedelics, was positively associated with Factor 2 scores. Factor 1 scores were only positively associated with opiate use. In fact, Factor 1 scores were negatively associated with overall drug use, marijuana use, cocaine use, and nicotine use. Considering the four-facet model, lifestyle and antisocial scores were associated with scores on multiple drug use measures, while interpersonal and affective scores were not related with drug use scores, aside from opiate use with interpersonal scores. These results are consistent with those for male samples, suggesting that Factor 2 psychopathy scores are predictive of substance use, while Factor 1 scores are found to be protective against substance use.

Kennealy et al.' (2007) findings were supported by Schulz et al. (2016) in their examination of the relationship between psychopathic traits and drug use in a community sample of both males and females with histories of criminality and substance use. Results of this study indicated that traits associated with Factor 2 psychopathy—impulsivity and antisocial behaviors—were positively associated with drug use characteristics, including increased symptoms of abuse and dependence, earlier age of onset, and wider extent of experimentation. In particular, the lifestyle component of Factor 2 explained the majority of these relationships. Similar to results from Kennealy et al. (2007), the interpersonal-affective Factor 1 traits were negatively related to drug abuse symptoms and positively correlated with age of drug initiation. Schulz et al. (2016) also explored gender differences in the relationship between psychopathy and drug use, finding the strongest gender differences between the antisocial behavior facet of Factor 2 psychopathy and substance use variable. The antisocial dimension of psychopathy was associated with a greater number of drug use characteristics among females compared to males. These results suggested that the associations between antisocial behavior and drug abuse were stronger in women than men. Gender also served as a moderator of the relationship between Factor 1 scores and age of first drug use, with females exhibiting stronger relationships. Such that, Factor 1 traits predicted a later age of onset for drug use among females but not males. There were no gender differences, however, with regard to psychopathy and the more serious addictive behaviors reflected in the measurement of drug dependence. Additionally, interpersonal and affective psychopathic traits were negatively associated with drug abuse among both males and females. The authors concluded that the interpersonal-affective dimension of psychopathy may be a protective factor related to substance use in women as it is associated with later onset of drug use.

Results from studies exploring the relationship between illicit drug use and psychopathy among females are inconsistent. For example, alcohol and substance abuse were significantly and moderately correlated with psychopathy, primarily traits indicative of social deviance, in forensic, correctional, and university samples of males and females (Sellbom et al., 2017). An investigation into the possible moderating role of gender in this study, however, did not reveal any significant differences in the association between psychopathy and substance abuse between males and females.

Warren et al. (2005) compared scores for 132 female maximum-security prisoners on two risk assessments, the PCL-R and the Historical, Clinical, and Risk Management Scheme (HCR-20). Females convicted of drug crimes had lower Factor 1 (emotional detachment) scores on the PCL-R and lower Factor 2 scores (deficient affective experience) on the HCR-20. When comparing the mean total scores on either measure, however, results indicated no difference in scores between female offenders who committed a drug-related crime and those who committed nondrug-related crimes. More recently, Thomson (2017) explored whether female inmates convicted of a drug-related violent crime differed on a variety of characteristics, including psychopathic traits, compared to female inmates convicted of nondrug-related violent crime and nonviolent crimes. Psychopathic traits, including callousness, egocentricity, and antisociality, were measured using the Levenson Self-Report of Psychopathy scale. Results suggested female offenders in the drug-related violent crime group exhibited higher levels of antisocial psychopathic traits compared to those in the nonviolent crime group. Compared to females committing nondrug-related violence crimes, however, those convicted of drug-related violence crimes had lower levels of callous psychopathic traits.

Convergence based on severe 5% reasoning

There has been extensive study of constructs that are convergent with putative psychopathy and one of these recent developments is the severe 5% concept. Early birth cohort designs such as Wolfgang's chronic offenders study (Wolfgang, Figlio, & Sellin, 1972) were pathbreaking in their findings about a small number in a birth cohort accounting for the majority of crime. This finding being one of the most axiomatic of contributions that criminology has made. However, the study lacked generalizability and did not include important data on characteristics such as mental health and substance use. A 2009 study that examined subgroups among a cohort of young children was also important to the development of the severe 5% (Vaughn, DeLisi, Beaver, & Wright, 2009). This study employed data from a nationally representative sample of kindergarteners in the United States. Vaughn, DeLisi, et al. (2009) identified a severely impaired subgroup that comprised a relatively large 9.3% group of kindergarteners. One of the standout findings was that there was pronounced deficits in executive functioning and other factors that greatly diminished their ability to self-regulate. For instance, these children had poor fine and gross motor skills, greater externalizing behaviors, difficulty learning and difficulty with social interactions, and sadly received less affection and were punished more often based on parent reports. Two more studies using national data from the National Epidemiologic Survey of Alcohol and Related Conditions (NESARC) and the National Survey of Drug Use and Health (NSDUH) revealed adult and adolescent severe 5% subsets (Vaughn et al., 2011; Vaughn, Salas-Wright, DeLisi, & Maynard, 2014). Findings from the 2011 NESARC study, which is the largest comorbidity survey ever (diagnostic interviews of over 43,000 individuals), revealed that a severe 5.3% were diagnosed with coextensive mental health and substance use disorders. The, 2014 study using the NSDUH among a large sample (N=18,614) of 12–17 years old found evidence for a severe group (actual 4.7%) that was prolific across the externalizing antisocial spectrum, including a wide array of substance misuse.

The convergent validity of psychopathy and the severe 5% is based on the logic that psychopathic offenders account for a disproportionate amount of crime. Thus, although the NESARC and NSDUH did not contain well-established psychopathy measures it seems quite reasonable to surmise that a significant fraction of the severe 5% in those studies would have scored relatively high on such measures. Additional studies suggest that high cut scores on offending histories are associated with high psychopathy assessment results. Vaughn and DeLisi (2008) showed that high rate offending among institutionalized youth also had significantly higher psychopathy scores on eight specifications of psychopathy. Farrington, Ullrich, and Salekin (2010) examined the associations between psychopathy scores on the Psychopathy Checklist Screening Version (PCL: SV) and subsequent crime convictions in the Cambridge Study in Delinquent Development from the United Kingdom. Those who scored in the 90th percentile on Factor 1 (interpersonal and affective traits) were 20.8 times more likely to become a chronic offender. Those who scored in the 90th percentile on Factor 2 (antisocial features) were 25.8 times more likely to be a chronic offender. You might be wondering what the combined effect would be at the 90th percentiles on the total score? Those who scored in the 90th percentile on the PCL: SV total score were 44.2 times more likely to become a chronic offender. Other studies in Canada also show a similar pattern.

If indeed the severe 5% is composed of a large proportion of adults and adolescents who would score relatively high on measures of psychopathy had they been available in the data, then it seems reasonable to infer that the patterns on substance misuse presented in these studies provide a reasonable empirical portrait of psychopathy and drug use and the intertwined nature of crime and violence. Specifically, these studies found that among adults stealing, shoplifting, forgery, use of aliases, property destruction, fighting, weapon use, domestic violence, and several other antisocial behaviors were also part of the behavioral spectrum of drug use including cocaine, hallucinogens, tranquilizers, amphetamine, and opioids. Among juveniles, drugs such as alcohol, marijuana, inhalants, tobacco, and hallucinogens were part of a shared liability for severe 5% membership with truancy, theft, handgun carrying, drug selling, fighting, and attacks on persons. The prevalence of these behaviors was uniquely higher than other latent classes in the data.

In short, severe 5% individuals that account for an outsized proportion of crimes also have extensive mental health and substance use and are likely high scoring on a variety of psychopathy assessments. Of course, one of the ongoing major limitations of advancing research on psychopathy is its lack of a large-scale epidemiologic study of traits and co-occurring behaviors and disorders.

A role for intervention?

The formidable mix of traits associated with psychopathy coupled with the pessimism regarding the treatment of personality disorders in general, seems to point to a syndrome that cannot be effectively intervened upon. While these notions are understandable, the evidence-base on the treatment of psychopathy is relatively sparse especially with respect to well-designed studies capable of discerning a causal impact. Meanwhile, there are a bevy of relatively effective treatments for substance use disorders that have been implemented with difficult populations with some success. Our aim in this section is not to provide an exhaustive review of interventions but instead make the case that there are interventions that could be employed to possibly reduce crime and violence among psychopathic individuals via treating substance misuse.

Before discussing interventions for substance use disorders, we would be remiss in not mentioning a role for prevention. Prevention-based studies provide suggestive evidence of the interactions during pregnancy, birth, infancy, and early childhood on problem and criminal behavior (Raine, 2002). Home visiting and parent training programs have garnered attention as preventive interventions for later problem behavior. Outcome research on these programs has produced evidence of short- and long-term beneficial effects on antisocial and criminal behaviors of the focal child (Farrington & Welsh, 1999; Olds et al., 1998; Piquero, Farrington, Welsh, Tremblay, & Jennings, 2009). Home visiting programs generally focus attention on mothers prior to or immediately following birth. Home visiting programs utilize a trained nurse, doctor, or other professional visiting the mother in her home and providing useful parenting information on such factors as proper nutrition and health behaviors such as smoking, drinking, and drug use. Parent training programs provide training to parents to modify parenting behaviors to enhance their parenting skills, parent-child interaction, and improve emotional states and behaviors of the child. Overall, evidence suggests that early parent training can be effective in preventing later problematic and antisocial behavior (Barlow, Smailagic, Ferriter, Bennett, & Jones, 2010; Bernazzani, Cote, & Tremblay, 2001). However, it is not clear if these benefits are the same for the most recalcitrant of children—those that may have fledgling psychopathic features.

Several community, residential, and incarceration-based programs that include the most commonly employed behavioral, cognitive-behavioral, and motivational based interventions, therapeutic communities, and medication-assisted treatments have been shown to possess some degree of effectiveness. Contingency management and voucher-based reinforcement therapy are behavioral interventions that purport to reduce substance use and criminal behavior by rewarding attendance, abstinence, and other favorable outcomes with rewards such as vouchers or privileges (Prendergast, Podus, Finney, Greenwell, & Roll, 2006). Addressing triggers such as craving or cues and help with coping, avoidance, and self-monitoring are the realm of cognitive behavioral interventions. The deployment of behavioral and cognitive behavioral interventions for the treatment of substance use is supported (Bender, Tripodi, Sarteschi, & Vaughn, 2011; Dutra et al., 2008; Magill & Ray, 2009). As is evidence supporting motivational interventions in the treatment of substance use disorders with adults and adolescents (Jenson et al., 2011).

Within the context of long-term residential communities, the Therapeutic Communities (TC) paradigm has been extensively used. This approach, rooted in social learning theory, has demonstrated positive effects on reoffending and drug use with adults (Mitchell, Wilson, & MacKenzie, 2007). These programs house participants in units that are separated from the general population whereby staff and peers confront the attitudes that contribute to offending and substance misuse. Another useful approach that has suffered from being a pharmacotherapy and the stigma associated with providing medications for substance use disorders is medication-assisted therapy (MAT). This includes the use of medications such as buprenorphine or methadone and naltrexone. Positive effects on substance use and offending have been demonstrated (Amato et al., 2005). Despite the promise of the various approaches mentioned, it is unclear of the moderating role of psychopathic traits on outcomes, particularly those traits (i.e., callous-unemotionality) that are considered by many to be core features of the syndrome. Nonetheless, it would be hard to believe that given the ubiquity of many of these approaches in offender populations that those with psychopathic features have not benefitted to some degree.

Conclusions

While we know that psychoactive substance use likely has an enhancing impact on crime among those with psychopathic features, much remains to be known about the link. At this stage, the factors that are more pronounced among secondary psychopathy such as impulsivity seem to be drivers of the relationship. Indeed, the apparently stronger link between secondary traits and substance use compared to primary traits appears to be a consistent finding among juveniles, adults, and both males and females. It may also be that co-occurring illness such as anxiety and depression provides a pathway between psychopathy and substance misuse as evidenced from epidemiologic investigations of the severe 5%. However, what many believe are core affective features of psychopathy seem to be weakly related to drug use and resulting crime. This relative lack of drug use may have a crime-reducing effect on those afflicted with more pronounced primary features of the disorder. Longitudinal investigations and large-scale epidemiologic studies of psychopathic traits and co-occurring disorders are needed that can untangle the drug use and criminal career vis-à-vis psychopathy assessment. A better understanding of this relationship will allow for the development of interventions that may reduce both crime and substance use among individuals with psychopathy. Clearly, a significant proportion of what is known as drug-related crime and violence is committed by individuals who score relatively high on assessments of psychopathic features and this alone—given the enormous monetary and human costs—suggests greater investment into the mechanisms behind this finding is worthwhile.

References

Amato, L., Davoli, M., Perucci, C. A., Ferri, M., Faggiano, F., & Mattick, R. P. (2005). An overview of systematic reviews of the effectiveness of opiate maintenance therapies: Available evidence to inform clinical practice and research. *Journal of Substance Abuse Treatment, 28*, 321–329. https://doi.org/10.1016/j.jsat.2005.02.007.

Barlow, J., Smailagic, N., Ferriter, M., Bennett, C., & Jones, H. (2010). Group-based parent-training programmes for improving emotional and behavioural adjustment in children from birth to three years old. *The Cochrane Database of Systematic Reviews, 3*, 1–95. https://doi.org/10.1002/14651858.CD003680.

Bender, K., Tripodi, S. J., Sarteschi, C., & Vaughn, M. G. (2011). A meta-analysis of interventions to reduce adolescent cannabis use. *Research on Social Work Practice*, *21*, 153–164. https://doi.org/10.1177/1049731510380226.

Bernazzani, O., Cote, C., & Tremblay, R. E. (2001). Early parent training to prevent disruptive behavior problems and delinquency in children. *The Annals of the American Academy of Political and Social Science*, *578*, 90–103. https://doi.org/10.1177/000271620157800106.

Brislin, S. J., & Patrick, C. J. (2015). *Antisocial personality disorder and psychopathy in adults*. National Courts and Science Institute, Inc. Retrieved from http://ncsi.institute/uploads/3/4/8/7/3487753/brislin__patrick__antisocial_personality_disorder_and_psychopathy_in_adults.pdf. https://doi.org/10.1002/9781118625392.wbecp475.

Campbell, M. A., Porter, S., & Santor, D. (2004). Psychopathic traits in adolescent offenders: An evaluation of criminal history, clinical, and psychosocial correlates. *Behavioral Sciences & the Law*, *22*(1), 23–47. https://doi.org/10.1002/bsl.572.

Cleckley, H. (1941). *The mask of sanity; an attempt to reinterpret the so-called psychopathic personality*. St. Louis, MO: The C. V. Mosby Company.

Corrado, R. R., Vincent, G. M., Hart, S. D., & Cohen, I. M. (2004). Predictive validity of the psychopathy checklist: Youth version for general and violent recidivism. *Behavioral Sciences & the Law*, *22*(1), 5–22. https://doi.org/10.1002/bsl.574.

Danaei, G., Ding, E. L., Mozaffarian, D., Taylor, B., Rehm, J., Murray, C. J. L., et al. (2009). The preventable causes of death in the United States: Comparative risk assessment of dietary, lifestyle, and metabolic risk factors. *PLoS Medicine*, *6*(4). https://doi.org/10.1371/annotation/0ef47acd-9dcc-4296-a897-872d182cde57, e1000058.

Dutra, L., Stathopoulou, G., Basden, S., Leyro, T., Powers, M., & Otto, M. (2008). A meta-analytic review of psychosocial interventions for substance use disorders. *American Journal of Psychiatry*, *165*, 179–187. https://doi.org/10.1176/appi.ajp.2007.06111851.

Falkenbach, D., Poythress, N. G., & Creevy, C. (2008). The exploration of subclinical psychopathic subtypes and the relationship with types of aggression. *Personality and Individual Differences*, *44*(4), 821–832. https://doi.org/10.1016/j.paid.2007.10.012.

Farrington, D. P., Ullrich, S., & Salekin, R. T. (2010). Environmental influences on child and adolescent psychopathy. In R. T. Salekin, & D. R. Lynam (Eds.), *Handbook of child and adolescent psychopathy* (pp. 202–230). New York, NY: The Guilford Press.

Farrington, D. P., & Welsh, B. C. (1999). Delinquency prevention using family-based interventions. *Children and Society*, *13*, 287–303. https://doi.org/10.1002/CHI570.

Fowles, D. C., & Dindo, L. (2005). A dual-deficit model of psychopathy. In C. J. Patrick's (Ed.), *Handbook of psychopathy* (pp. 14–250). New York, NY: Guilford Press.

Glenn, A. L., Johnson, A. K., & Raine, A. (2013). Antisocial personality disorder: A current review. *Current Psychiatry Reports*, *15*. https://doi.org/10.1007/s11920-013-0427-7.

Goldstein, P. J., & Brownstein, H. (1987). *Drug related crime analysis-homicide: Narcotic & drug research incorporated*. Retrieved from https://www.ncjrs.gov/pdffiles1/Digitization/111509NCJRS.pdf.

Grande, T. P., Wolf, A. W., Schubert, D. S., Patterson, M. B., & Brocco, K. (1984). Associations among alcoholism, drug abuse, and antisocial personality: A review of literature. *Psychological Reports*, *55*(2), 455–474. https://doi.org/10.2466/pr0.1984.55.2.455.

Hare, R. D. (1980). A research scale for the assessment of psychopathy in criminal populations. *Personality and Individual Differences*, *1*, 111–119.

Hare, R. D. (1999). *Without conscience: The disturbing world of the psychopaths among us*. New York, NY: Guilford Press.

Hare, R. D., Harpur, T. J., Hakstian, A. R., Forth, A. E., Hart, S. D., & Newman, J. P. (1990). The revised psychopathy checklist: Descriptive statistics, reliability, and factor structure. *Psychological Assessment: A Journal of Consulting and Clinical Psychology*, *2*, 338–341.

Hare, R. D., & Neumann, C. S. (2008). Psychopathy as a clinical and empirical construct. *Annual Review of Clinical Psychology*, *4*, 217–246. https://doi.org/10.1146/annurev.clinpsy.3.022806.091452.

Hart, S. D., Forth, A. E., & Hare, R. D. (1991). The MCMI-II and psychopathy. *Journal of Personality Disorders*, *5*(4), 318–327. https://doi.org/10.1521/pedi.1991.5.4.318.

Hart, S. D., & Hare, R. D. (1989). Discriminant validity of the psychopathy checklist in a forensic psychiatric population. *Psychological Assessment: A Journal of Consulting and Clinical Psychology*, *1*, 211–218. https://doi.org/10.1037/1040-3590.1.3.211.

Hemphill, J. F., Hart, S. D., & Hare, R. D. (1994). Psychopathy and substance use. *Journal of Personality Disorders*, *8*(3), 169–180. https://doi.org/10.1521/pedi.1994.8.3.169.

Hicks, B. M., Markon, K. E., Patrick, C. J., Krueger, R. F., & Newman, J. P. (2004). Identifying psychopathy subtypes on the basis of personality structure. *Psychological Assessment*, *16*(3), 276. https://doi.org/10.1037/1040-3590.16.3.276.

Huebner, B. M., & Cobbina, J. (2007). The effect of drug use, drug treatment participation, and treatment completion on probationer recidivism. *Journal of Drug Issues*, *37*(3), 619–641. https://doi.org/10.1177/002204260703700307.

Jenson, C. D., Cushing, C. C., Aylward, B. S., Craig, J. T., Sorell, D. M., & Steele, R. G. (2011). Effectiveness of motivational interviewing for adolescent substance use behavior change: A meta-analytic review. *Journal of Consulting and Clinical Psychology*, *79*, 433–440. https://doi.org/10.1037/a0023992.

Johnston, L. D., O'Malley, P. M., & Eveland, L. K. (1978). Drugs and delinquency: A search for causal connections. In D. B. Kandel (Ed.), *Longitudinal research on drug use: Empirical findings and methodological issues* (pp. 137–156). Bristol, PA: Hemisphere Publishing Corp.

Kalivas, P. W., & Volkow, N. D. (2005). The neural basis of addiction: A pathology of motivation and choice. *American Journal of Psychiatry*, *162*(8), 1403–1413. https://doi.org/10.1176/appi.ajp.162.8.1403.

Karpman, B. (1948). The myth of the psychopathic personality. *The American Journal of Psychiatry*, *104*, 523–534. https://doi.org/10.1176/ajp.104.9.523.

Kennealy, P. J., Hicks, B. M., & Patrick, C. J. (2007). Validity of factors of the psychopathy checklist—Revised in female prisoners: Discriminant relations with antisocial behavior, substance abuse, and personality. *Assessment*, *14*(4), 323–340. https://doi.org/10.1177/1073191107305882.

Kimonis, E. R., Frick, P. J., Cauffman, E., Goldweber, A., & Skeem, J. (2012). Primary and secondary variants of juvenile psychopathy differ in emotional processing. *Development and Psychopathology*, *24*(3), 1091–1103. https://doi.org/10.1017/S0954579412000557.

Magill, M., & Ray, L. A. (2009). Cognitive-behavioral treatment with adult alcohol and illicit drug users: A meta-analysis of randomized controlled trials. *Journal of Studies on Alcohol and Drugs*, *70*, 516–527. https://doi.org/10.15288/jsad.2009.70.516.

Mailloux, D. L., Forth, A. E., & Kroner, D. G. (1997). Psychopathy and substance abuse in adolescent male offenders. *Psychological Reports*, *80*, 529–530.

Mitchell, O., Wilson, D. B., & MacKenzie, D. L. (2007). Does incarceration-based drug treatment reduce recidivism? A meta-analytic synthesis of the research. *Journal of Experimental Criminology*, *3*, 353–375. https://doi.org/10.1007/s11292-007-9040-2.

Moffitt, T. E., Caspi, A., Harrington, H., & Milne, B. J. (2002). Males on the life-course-persistent and adolescence-limited antisocial pathways: Follow-up at age 26 years. *Development and Psychopathology*, *14*(1), 179–207.

Montgomery, K. L., Vaughn, M. G., Thompson, S. J., & Howard, M. O. (2013). Heterogeneity in drug abuse among juvenile offenders: Is mixture regression more informative than standard regression? *International Journal of Offender Therapy and Comparative Criminology*, *57*(11), 1326–1346. https://doi.org/10.1177/0306624X12459185.

Murrie, D. C., & Cornell, D. G. (2000). The Millon adolescent clinical inventory and psychopathy. *Journal of Personality Assessment*, *75*(1), 110–125. https://doi.org/10.1207/S15327752JPA7501_8.

Office of National Drug Control Policy. (2014). *2013 annual report, arrestee drug abuse monitoring program II*. Washington, DC. Retrieved from https://obamawhitehouse.archives.gov/sites/default/files/ondcp/policy-and-research/adam_ii_2013_annual_report.pdf.

Olds, D., Henderson, C. R., Jr., Cole, R., Eckenrode, J., Kitzman, H., Luckey, D., et al. (1998). Long-term effects of nurse home visitation on children's criminal and antisocial behavior: 15-year follow-up of a randomized controlled trial. *Journal of the American Medical Association*, *280*, 1238–1244. https://doi.org/10.1001/jama.280.14.1238.

O'Neill, M. L., Lidz, V., & Heilbrun, K. (2003). Adolescents with psychopathic characteristics in a substance abusing cohort: Treatment process and outcomes. *Law and Human Behavior*, *27*(3), 299–313. https://doi.org/10.1023/A:1023435924569.

Onyedibe, M. C. C., Ifeagwazi, C. M., & Ugwu, D. I. (2018). Psychopathy and aggressive behavior among Nigerian male prison inmates: The moderating role of substance abuse. *Journal of Psychology in Africa*, *28*(5), 365–370. https://doi.org/10.1080/14330237.2018.1523342.

Pihl, R. O., Peterson, J. B., & Lau, M. A. (1993). A biosocial model of the alcohol-aggression relationship. *Journal of Studies on Alcohol, supplement*(11), 128–139. https://doi.org/10.15288/jsas.1993.s11.128.

Piquero, A. R., Farrington, D. P., Welsh, B. C., Tremblay, R., & Jennings, W. G. (2009). Effects of early family/parent training programs on antisocial behavior and delinquency. *Journal of Experimental Criminology*, *5*, 83–120. https://doi.org/10.1007/s11292-009-9072-x.

Poythress, N. G., & Skeem, J. L. (2006). Disaggregating psychopathy: Where and how to look for subtypes. In C. Patrick (Ed.), *Handbook of psychopathy* (pp. 172–192). New York: Guilford Press.

Prendergast, M., Podus, D., Finney, J., Greenwell, L., & Roll, J. (2006). Contingency management for treatment of substance use disorders: A meta-analysis. *Addiction*, *101*, 1546–1560. https://doi.org/10.1111/j.1360-0443.2006.01581.x.

Raine, A. (2002). Annotation: The role of prefrontal deficits, low autonomic arousal, and early health factors in the development of antisocial and aggressive behavior in children. *Journal of Child Psychology and Psychiatry*, *43*, 417–434. https://doi.org/10.1111/1469-7610.00034.

Rehm, J., Taylor, B., & Room, R. (2006). Global burden of disease from alcohol, illicit drugs and tobacco. *Drug and Alcohol Review*, *25*, 503–513. https://doi.org/10.1080/09595230600944453.

Ross, S. R., Bye, K., Wrobel, T. A., & Horton, R. S. (2008). Primary and secondary psychopathic characteristics and the schedule for non-adaptive and adaptive personality (SNAP). *Personality and Individual Differences*, *45*, 249–254. https://doi.org/10.1016/j.paid.2008.04.007.

Salas-Wright, C. P., Vaughn, M. G., & Reingle Gonzalez, J. M. (2016). *Drug abuse and antisocial behavior: A biosocial life-course approach*. New York, NY: Palgrave Macmillan.

Schulz, N., Murphy, B., & Verona, E. (2016). Gender differences in psychopathy links to drug use. *Law and Human Behavior*, *40*(2), 159. https://doi.org/10.1037/lhb0000165.

Sellbom, M., Donnelly, K. M., Rock, R. C., Phillips, T. R., & Ben-Porath, Y. S. (2017). Examining gender as moderating the association between psychopathy and substance abuse. *Psychology, Crime & Law*, *23*(4), 376–390. https://doi.org/10.1080/1068316X.2016.1258466.

Shine, J., & Hobson, J. (1997). Construct validity of the hare psychopathy checklist, revised, on a UK prison population. *Journal of Forensic Psychiatry*, *8*, 546–561. https://doi.org/10.1080/09585189708412275.

Skeem, J., Johansson, P., Andershed, H., Kerr, M., & Louden, J. E. (2007). Two subtypes of psychopathic violent offenders that parallel primary and secondary variants. *Journal of Abnormal Psychology*, *116*(2), 395. https://doi.org/10.1037/0021-843X.116.2.395.

Skeem, J. L., Polaschek, D. L., Patrick, C. J., & Lilienfeld, S. O. (2011). Psychopathic personality: Bridging the gap between scientific evidence and public policy. *Psychological Science in the Public Interest*, *12*(3), 95–162. https://doi.org/10.1177/1529100611426706.

Smith, S. S., & Newman, J. P. (1990). Alcohol and drug abuse-dependence disorders in psychopathic and nonpsychopathic criminal offenders. *Journal of Abnormal Psychology*, *99*(4), 430. https://doi.org/10.1037/0021-843X.99.4.430.

Swogger, M. T., & Kosson, D. S. (2007). Identifying subtypes of criminal psychopaths: A replication and extension. *Criminal Justice and Behavior*, *34*(8), 953–970. https://doi.org/10.1177/0093854807300758.

Thomson, N. D. (2017). An exploratory study of female psychopathy and drug-related violent crime. *Journal of Interpersonal Violence*. https://doi.org/10.1177/0886260517690876.

US Department of Justice. (2015). *Crime in the United States, 2014*. Washington, DC. Retrieved from https://ucr.fbi.gov/crime-in-the-u.s/2014/crime-in-the-u.s.-2014/resource-pages/fbi-releases-2014-crime-statistics.

Vassileva, J., Kosson, D. S., Abramowitz, C., & Conrod, P. (2005). Psychopathy versus psychopathies in classifying criminal offenders. *Legal and Criminological Psychology*, *10*(1), 27–43. https://doi.org/10.1348/135532504X15376.

Vaughn, M. G., & DeLisi, M. (2008). Were Wolfgang's chronic offenders psychopaths? On the convergent validity between psychopathy and career criminality. *Journal of Criminal Justice*, *36*, 33–42. https://doi.org/10.1016/j.jcrimjus.2007.12.008.

Vaughn, M. G., DeLisi, M., Beaver, K. M., & Wright, J. P. (2009). Identifying latent classes of behavioral risk based on early childhood manifestations of self-control. *Youth Violence and Juvenile Justice*, *7*, 16–31. https://doi.org/10.1177/1541204008324911.

Vaughn, M. G., DeLisi, M., Gunter, T., Fu, Q., Beaver, K. M., Perron, B. E., et al. (2011). The severe 5%: A latent class analysis of the externalizing spectrum in the United States. *Journal of Criminal Justice*, *39*, 75–80. https://doi.org/10.1016/j.jcrimjus.2010.12.001.

Vaughn, M. G., Edens, J. F., Howard, M. O., & Smith, S. T. (2009). An investigation of primary and secondary psychopathy in a statewide sample of incarcerated youth. *Youth Violence and Juvenile Justice*, *7*(3), 172–188. https://doi.org/10.1177/1541204009333792.

Vaughn, M. G., & Howard, M. O. (2005). The construct of psychopathy and its potential contribution to the study of serious, violent, and chronic youth offending. *Youth Violence and Juvenile Justice*, *3*(3), 235–252. https://doi.org/10.1177/1541204005276320.

Vaughn, M. G., Howard, M. O., & DeLisi, M. (2008). Psychopathic personality traits and delinquent careers: An empirical examination. *International Journal of Law and Psychiatry*, *31*(5), 407–416. https://doi.org/10.1016/j.ijlp.2008.08.001.

Vaughn, M. G., Salas-Wright, C. P., DeLisi, M., & Maynard, B. R. (2014). Examining violence and externalizing behavior among youth in the United States: Is there a severe 5%? *Youth Violence and Juvenile Justice*, *12*, 3–21. https://doi.org/10.1177/1541204013478973.

Vincent, G. M., Cope, L. M., King, J., Nyalakanti, P., & Kiehl, K. A. (2018). Callous-unemotional traits modulate brain drug craving response in high-risk young offenders. *Journal of Abnormal Child Psychology*, *46*(5), 993–1009. https://doi.org/10.1007/s10802-017-0364-8.

Wareham, J., Dembo, R., Poythress, N. G., Childs, K., & Schmeidler, J. (2009). A latent class factor approach to identifying subtypes of juvenile diversion youths based on psychopathic features. *Behavioral Sciences & the Law*, *27*(1), 71–95. https://doi.org/10.1002/bsl.844.

Warren, J. I., South, S. C., Burnette, M. L., Rogers, A., Friend, R., Bale, R., et al. (2005). Understanding the risk factors for violence and criminality in women: The concurrent validity of the PCL-R and HCR-20. *International Journal of Law and Psychiatry*, *28*(3), 269–289. https://doi.org/10.1016/j.ijlp.2003.09.012.

Wolfgang, M. E., Figlio, R. M., & Sellin, T. (1972). *Delinquency in a birth cohort*. Chicago, IL: University of Chicago Press.

Are gang members psychopaths? 14

Jennifer J. Tostlebe and David C. Pyrooz

Introduction

> The most sociopathic youths of the type described [having traits of criminality, lack of empathy, egocentrism, manipulative, and impulsivity] find that *the violent gang provides for them a vehicle* through which they can acquire and achieve gratifications consistent with their personality ability and needs.
>
> *Yablonsky (1962, p. 242, emphasis added)*

> Gang members...have, to varying degrees, developed what I shall call a *defiant individualist* character....The defiant individualist character is composed of seven attributes [competitiveness, mistrust or wariness, self-reliance, social isolation, survival instinct, Social Darwinist worldview, and defiant air]....Gang members will more generally display nearly all of these traits and to a much more intense degree.... What is most important to understand is that *this is not because they have joined gangs* but because of their particular experiences before they joined.
>
> *Sanchez-Jankowski (1991, pp. 23–26, 28, emphasis added)*

The issue of psychopathology among gang populations is a controversial one. Some gang researchers, like the authors of the prominent works cited earlier, point to psychopathic traits as characteristic of the individuals who ultimately join gangs, particularly with regard to gang leaders, but also, more generally, gang members. In other words, the gang membership/psychopathy link is a consequence of selective mixing, or homophily. Other researchers point to the gang context as a source of a broader range of problematic traits and behaviors, of which psychopathy could be included. In this case, group influences are the mechanisms of psychopathic onset, continuity, and, perhaps, change. Still others outright reject these notions altogether, arguing that the variety of individuals—leaders and regular members alike—found within a gang is remarkably similar to the general population (Klein, 1968; Short, 1997). In fact, Klein (1968, p. 54) stated matter-of-factly: "most gang leaders are *not* sociopaths or psychopaths." Given this controversy, it is important to know the extent to which the concept of psychopathy matters to the explanation of gang membership, and vice versa. To be sure, the jury is still out with regard to the gang membership/psychopathy link. But as we describe later, the way the empirical evidence shakes out will have enormous implications for how we think about and respond to the 30,000 gangs and over 1 million gang members in the United States (Egley, Howell, & Harris, 2014; Pyrooz & Sweeten, 2015).

This chapter explores the relationship between gang membership and psychopathy. Our aim is to take stock—theoretically and empirically—of the gang membership/psychopathy link. We begin by describing psychopathy in criminology. Second, we apply the concept of psychopathy to gang membership. Here, we review the small

Psychopathy and Criminal Behavior. https://doi.org/10.1016/B978-0-12-811419-3.00007-8

body of evidence of psychopathy among gang members. Third, we specify the theoretical basis for an association between gang membership and psychopathy. We do this through the adaptation of Thornberry, Krohn, Lizotte, and Chard-Wierschem's (1993) tripartite theoretical model on the gang membership/offending link—selection, facilitation, and enhancement—to capture the antipodal and mixed positions on the relationship we described earlier. Psychopathy, as it is defined today, has been an object of scientific investigation for over 50 years. However, social and environmental factors—such as gang membership—are largely missing from theory and research on the topic. Gang membership has been an object of scientific inquiry for nearly a century, but psychology and individual differences more generally are largely missing from theory and research on gangs (Alleyne & Wood, 2010). We attempt to bridge these two lines of inquiry. The implications of this research are not subtle for the psychopathy and gang literatures. If the sources of psychopathy are sociological or if the sources of gang membership are psychopathological, it would bring new meaning to these respective literatures, as well as the policies and practices that extend from the research.

A brief overview of psychopathy in criminology

Psychopathy is classified as a personality disorder, and generally defined by a constellation of *interpersonal* (e.g., lying, superficial charm, and manipulative), *affective* (e.g., lack of remorse, callous, and unemotional), *lifestyle* (e.g., thrill-seeking, impulsive, and sexual promiscuity), and *antisocial* (e.g., criminal versatility, poor behavioral control, and conduct disorder) characteristics that manifest in a wide range of criminal behaviors (Cleckley, 1941; Hare, 2003). As such, the construct of psychopathy maintains an established and well-developed standing in the criminological, psychological, and psychiatry literatures. This is due, in part, to its moderate to strong association with crime and problem behaviors (see Asscher et al., 2011; Beaver, Boutwell, Barnes, Vaughn, & DeLisi, 2017; Longman, Hawes, & Kohlhoff, 2016; Olver & Wong, 2015), particularly among violent offenders (Fox & Delisi, 2019). The results of meta-analyses indicate that the relationship between psychopathy and various criminal outcomes has an overall effect size between 0.23 and 0.68 (Asscher et al., 2011; Blais, Solodukhin, & Forth, 2014; Fox & Delisi, 2019; Geerlings, Asscher, Stams, & Assink, 2020), with stronger effect sizes related to violent behavior. These effect sizes compare to other leading explanations of crime, such as self-control, which has a mean effect size between 0.35 and 0.42 (Vazsonyi, Mikuška, & Kelley, 2017).

The empirical evidence on psychopathy is so robust that it has attracted the superlatives of criminologists. Leading experts in this area of research have remarked that "of all the known correlates to crime, especially violent predatory crimes, psychopathy and psychopathic personality traits are among the most consistent and robust predictors" (Beaver, Rowland, Schwartz, & Nedelec, 2011, p. 430) and that psychopathy is "the unified theory of delinquency and crime and the purest explanation of antisocial behavior" (DeLisi, 2009, p. 256). These are major statements about the psychopathy/offending link, particularly in a field of study where most of the variance in the outcome of interest—that is, criminal offending—goes unexplained when testing leading criminological theories (Weisburd, Cave, & Piquero, 2015).

Of course, it is important to recognize that not all offenders have psychopathic personality traits. Much like Wolfgang, Figlio, and Sellin (1972) identified that 6% of delinquents accounted for the majority, but not all, of offenses in their seminal study on criminal careers, Hart and Hare (1997) specified that:

> many psychopaths engage in chronic criminal conduct and do so at a high rate, whereas *only a small minority* of those who engage in criminal conduct are psychopaths. This means that psychopaths are responsible for a disproportionate amount of crime in our society.
>
> *(p. 22, emphasis added)*

It is thus an overstatement to claim psychopathy as a general theory of crime, that is, the singular source of crime across demographic and cultural groups, although psychopathy may nonetheless rank as one of the most robust predictors, both in terms of its reliability and effect size.

This naturally raises questions about the origins of psychopathy, an area of study where less is known. In other words, why do some individuals exhibit a constellation of psychopathic tendencies while others do not? In the pages to come, we will describe the theoretical and empirical basis for biological *and* sociological origins of psychopathy (Hare, 1999), weaving together this etiology and its relation to the onset and continuity of gang membership. Based on the roots of the etiology of psychopathy, we find it surprising that most attention has been aimed toward understanding the biology sources of psychopathy, with little consideration of social and environmental sources. Few social groups have come to capture the attention of the general public, criminal justice agencies, and researchers due to displays of aggression and brutality (which are characteristic of psychopathy) like gangs have. What remains to be determined, however, is whether these various audiences are interested not in gangs per se, but in a collection of young people with psychopathic personality traits. We aim to extend the understanding of the etiology of psychopathy to the context of gang membership.

The gang membership/psychopathy link

It is not uncommon to see individuals with psychopathic traits or gang members present in television (e.g., *You*, *Dexter*, *Mindhunter*, *Sons of Anarchy*, and *Gangland Undercover*), in films (e.g., *Silence of the Lambs*, *Seven Psychopaths*, *American History X*, and *End of Watch*), and the news due to their violence and criminal behaviors. It is also not unusual to hear individuals refer to people who commit murder as psychopaths due to their displays of callousness, aggression, and lack of empathy. Given that gangs are associated with approximately 16% of homicides in the United States (Egley et al., 2014) and that psychopathic traits are "a significant risk factor for various forms of lethal violence" (Fox & Delisi, 2019, p. 76), it would not require an article of faith to attach a psychopathic label to gang members. But is such a label also an article of truth?

In 2012, national estimates indicate that there were approximately 850,000 gang members in the United States (Egley et al., 2014). However, this number may be conservative as these estimates are gathered from surveys of law enforcement. About 2% of youth between ages 5 and 17 are actively involved in gangs, and 8% of young people have been in gangs by their early twenties (Pyrooz, 2014; Pyrooz & Sweeten, 2015). Gang members are also overrepresented in incarcerated settings, where they compose between 13% and 47% of the juvenile, county jail, and prison populations (Morris et al., 1995; Pyrooz & Mitchell, 2020; Ruddell, Decker, & Egley, 2006; Winterdyk & Ruddell, 2010).

Psychopathic personality traits are estimated to be prevalent within 0.3%–12% of the general population (Colins, Fanti, Salekin, & Andershed, 2016; Neumann & Hare, 2008; Patrick & Drislane, 2015). Approximately 10%–60% of incarcerated youth and adults display psychopathic personality traits (Assadi et al., 2006; Cale, Lussier, McCuish, & Corrado, 2015; Campbell, Porter, & Santor, 2004; Dåderman & Kristiansson, 2003; Fox & Delisi, 2019). However, this estimate is imprecise, both in range and quality, as it is derived primarily from studies with small sample sizes, and in different geographical contexts, that utilized different psychopathy scales, varying psychopathy cut-off scores, and offenders of varying risk levels.

There are several parallels between gang membership and psychopathy. Both groups constitute a small minority of the general population. Studies repeatedly demonstrate that both gang membership and psychopathic personality traits place individuals at a heightened risk of criminal offending, including homicide and other violent crimes (Blais et al., 2014; Fox & Delisi, 2019; Melde & Esbensen, 2013; Pyrooz & Decker, 2013; Woodworth & Porter, 2002). An equally important, but smaller group of studies demonstrate that both gang members and psychopaths are overrepresented in incarcerated populations.

We highlighted the works of Sanchez-Jankowski (1991) and Yablonsky (1962) in the introduction not only because they distinguished gang members by their psychopathic qualities, including impulsive behavior, moral disengagement, and lack of empathy, but also because these are two of the most impactful works in research on gangs. Indeed, these books are two of the most cited works in gang research (Pyrooz & Mitchell, 2015). Yet it is important to contrast these statements against other prominent works claiming that while some gang members likely have traits characteristic of psychopathy, the overall rate of psychopathy among all gang members is minimal (Klein, 1971; Short, 1997). Still, the gang and psychopathy literatures have advanced in significant ways since these early observations.

Table 1 contains a summary of studies on the gang membership/psychopathy link. Before we elaborate theoretically on this relationship, detailing how such a relationship may manifest, we reach several observations about this literature. First, there are few studies examining the psychopathy/gang membership link—we identified only nine studies that focused on this relationship. Second, the research design for nearly all of these studies is cross-sectional rather than longitudinal—having only one snapshot of information challenges the ability to reach firm conclusions, as we describe later. Finally, evidence of a psychopathy/gang membership link is mixed—some research reveals a positive association, while other work reveals no association at all.

Table 1 Summary of studies on the gang membership/psychopathy link.

Study	Sample	Study design	Psychopathy measure	Finding(s)
Ang, Huan, Chan, Cheong, and Leaw (2015) Singapore	- Student sample - 1027 adolescents - 5% gang	Cross-sectional design with a questionnaire	- Antisocial Process Screening Device (APSD) - General psychopathy	- No association - Psychopathy was not a significant predictor of self-reported gang membership.
Carson and Ray (2019) Philadelphia and Phoenix, United States	- Offender sample - 1264 adolescents - 17.3% gang	Prospective longitudinal design with interviews every 6 months (years 1–4) and then annually (years 4–7)	- Psychopathy Checklist: Youth Version (PCL:YV) - General psychology + the two factors of psychopathy	- + Association - − Compared with non-gang members, the adult joiner, persister group had lower scores on Factor 1 and higher scores on Factor 2. Compared with the adolescent desister group, the adult joiner, persister group scored lower on Factor 1.
Chu, Daffern, Thomas, Ang, and Long (2014) Singapore	- Offender sample - 168 adolescent males - 64% gang	Cross-sectional design with questionnaires and a semistructured interview	- Youth Psychopathic Traits Inventory (YPI) - General psychopath + the three dimensions of psychopathy	- No association - The impulsive-irresponsible dimension significantly predicted gang membership. After controlling for covariates, that could be endogenous to psychopathy, this difference disappeared.
Dmitrieva, Gibson, Steinberg, Piquero, and Fagan (2014) Philadelphia and Phoenix, United States	- Offender sample - 1170 adolescents - 26% gang; 11% gang leadership over the last 7 pooled-period years	Prospective longitudinal design with interviews every 6 months (years 1–4) and then annually (years 4–7)	- Youth Psychopathic Traits Inventory (YPI) - The three dimensions of psychopathy	- + Association - Psychopathy was not predictive of low-level gang membership. The GM dimension was predictive of gang leadership, which changed from a negative to a positive relationship over age. Over the course of membership, gang members and leaders developed GM and II traits. Years spent as a low-level member increased CU traits.
Dupéré, Lacourse, Willms, Vitaro, and Tremblay (2007) Canada (nationally representative sample)	- Community sample - 3522 adolescents - 6% gang	Prospective longitudinal design with interviews every 2 years	- Parent reported scales (hyperactivity, low-anxiety, and low prosociality) - General psychopathy	- + Association - Adolescents with preexisting psychopathic tendencies had 1.75 times greater odds of joining a gang than their peers without such tendencies.

Continued

Table 1 Continued

Study	Sample	Study design	Psychopathy measure	Finding(s)
Mallion and Wood (2018) United Kingdom (Category C public sector training prison)	- Offender sample - 73 male adults - 60% gang	Cross-sectional within-participants design with an interview	- Inventory of Callous-Unemotional Traits (ICU) - The callous-unemotional (CU) dimension of psychopathy	- No association - Callous-unemotional traits could not differentiate between street gang and nonprisoners.
Thornton et al. (2015) Jefferson Parish, LA; Orange County, CA; Philadelphia, PA	- Offender sample - 1216 adolescent boys - 5% gang during the past 6 months; 5% gang during life	Cross-sectional design with an interview	- Inventory of Callous-Unemotional Traits (ICU) - The callous-unemotional (CU) dimension of psychopathy	- + Association - Callous-unemotional traits were associated with gang membership.
Valdez, Kaplan, and Codina (2000) Texas, United States	- Community sample - 75 adolescent boys - 67% gang	Cross-sectional design with an interview	- Psychopathy Checklist—Screening Version (PCL-SV) - General psychopathy + the two factors of psychopathy	- + Association - Gang members demonstrated higher levels of overall psychopathy and higher levels on the affective and behavioral psychopathy factors than nongang members. More than half of both the gang (52%) and nongang (76%) samples were categorized as nonpsychopathic.
Vaughn, Edens, Howard, and Smith (2009) Missouri, United States	- Offender sample - 267 adolescents - 46% gang	Cross-sectional design with an interview	- APSD + modified Psychopathic Personality Inventory Short-Form (PPI-SF) - General psychopathy, used to construct subgroups	- + Association - Secondary psychopaths, characterized by traits within the affective and lifestyle facets, were more likely to join a gang (59.8%) than primary psychopaths, characterized by traits within the interpersonal facet (50.0%) and individuals without psychopathic traits (37.8%).

A tripartite theoretical model

Fig. 1 contains a graphical representation of our theoretical model of the gang membership/psychopathy link. This figure captures both between- and within-individual differences in psychopathy relative to onset, continuity, and change in gang membership. There are three trajectories reported, which represent the selection, facilitation, and enhancement models. The vertical lines refer to the onset and termination of gang membership. The *x*-axis refers to time in years, where movement from the left to the right equals more time passed. The *y*-axis refers to psychopathic personality traits, where movement from the bottom to the top equals a higher prevalence or exhibition of psychopathic traits.

If gang members exhibit a constellation of psychopathic personality traits, why is this the case? We answer this question by situating this relationship in an organizing theoretical model. We adapt Thornberry et al.'s (1993) selection, facilitation, and enhancement models to establish a theoretical foundation for understanding the gang membership/psychopathy link. The utility of this model is that it incorporates both between- and within-individual differences, while also accounting for temporality. These are important theoretical advances, as it is established that there is intra-individual variability in psychopathy and that the contours of gang membership—onset, continuity, and change—are largely anchored to periods of the life course (Pyrooz, 2014). In presenting this theoretical model, we discuss the accompanying explanation of the etiology of psychopathy as it relates to gang membership and review the empirical evidence that supports each model. In more specific terms, the question we aim to map out is, do gangs *attract* people who have underlying psychopathic personality characteristics (selection), *create* psychopathic traits among those who join gangs (facilitation), or some combination of the two (enhancement)?

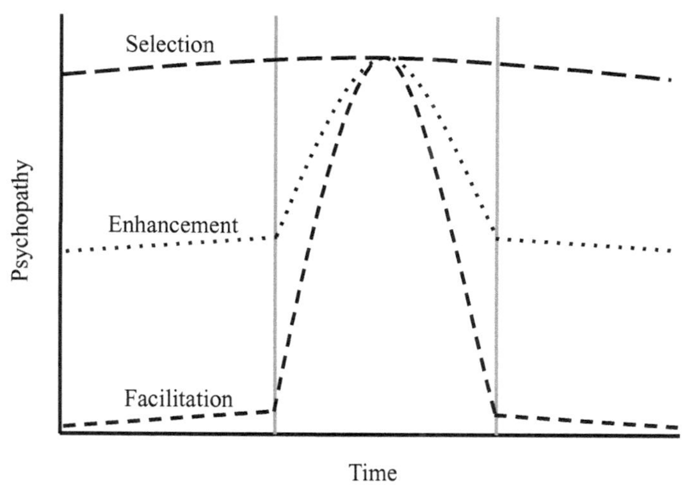

Fig. 1 Tripartite model of gang membership and psychopathy.

Selection

The *selection hypothesis* contends that the sources of psychopathy are found before the onset of gang membership. This is consistent with a "kind of persons" model, as it implies that individuals who have preexisting psychopathic personality traits are the ones who decide to join gangs. It suggests that a gang is simply a group of people who share common individual deficits such as poor self-control, conduct disorders, personality deficits, or, in our case, psychopathy. This is consistent not only with theories that explain gang membership as the product of relatively stable differences in criminal propensity between individuals, but also with biological perspectives on the etiology of psychopathic personality traits, which emphasize that various biological factors impact brain function and personality structure resulting in the exhibition of psychopathic personality characteristics.

For example, Moore, Blair, Hettema, and Roberson-Nay (2019) reviewed 39 genetic studies, 24 of which were heritability and 16 were molecular genetics. The former group of studies revealed that the heritability of callous-unemotional traits is between 36% and 67% among the general population. The latter group of studies have mixed results, and lack replication, though candidate gene studies have implicated several genes, primarily those belonging to the serotonin and oxytocin systems (e.g., BDNF, COMT, HRT1B, HTR2A, MAOA, OXTR, and SLC6A4), as having a role in the development of callous-unemotional traits. Regarding gang membership, studies point to genetic factors as an explanation for a large amount of the variance in gang membership (Connolly & Beaver, 2015), as well as the candidate gene, MAOA, as a predictor of gang joining (Beaver, Delisi, Vaughn, & Barnes, 2010), although it is premature to reach any sound conclusions on the topic. Alternative biological explanations for the etiology of psychopathy include brain abnormalities, in particular among emotion-relevant brain areas (Pujol, Harrison, Contreras-Rodriguez, & Cardoner, 2018), and brain injury (Vaughn, Salas-Wright, DeLisi, & Perron, 2014), although this relationship too is less empirically sound. Given that head injury is prevalent in offender populations (Durand et al., 2017; Ray & Richardson, 2017; Shiroma, Ferguson, & Pickelsimer, 2010) and there is a link between gang membership and victimization (Pyrooz, Moule, & Decker, 2014), it is also possible that brain injury could play a role in gang joining and continuity, and there is some evidence in support of this (Fahmy, Jackson, Pyrooz, & Decker, 2020).

How do individuals with biological or personality deficits end up together? In this theoretical dynamic, individuals with these shared characteristics end up together, "select" each other, or "flock together" due to social rejection and homophily. Prosocial others view the callousness, unreliability, shallow affect, and pathological lying (i.e., Factor 1, emotion and relationships) of psychopathic youth as untenable. Likewise, fellow youth who share these characteristics may be attracted to one another due to outward displays of common psychopathic traits, such as dangerous and exciting lifestyle choices or criminal actions (i.e., Factor 2, behavior). A pure interpretation of the selection model, as outlined in Fig. 1, posits that gangs have no causal influence on psychopathy; instead, individual factors such as psychopathy are the source, not the consequence, of gang membership, and as such, psychopathic personality traits remain prevalent before, during, and after gang membership. There would be between-individual differences in psychopathic traits, where future, current, and former gang members would score higher on psychopathy than their nongang counterparts. However, we would not expect to observe intra-individual changes in psychopathy with the onset or termination of gang membership.

This continuity is rooted in psychological theory and empirical evidence. According to the DSM-V (American Psychiatric Association, 2013), a personality disorder (e.g., psychopathy) is:

> a persistent pattern of inner experience and behavior that deviates markedly from the expectations of the individual's culture, is diffuse and inflexible, *begins in adolescence or early adulthood*, it is *stable over time* and leads to suffering or injury.
>
> *(p. 645, emphasis added)*

Furthermore, researchers have reported moderate-to-high rank-order stability ($\rho = 0.31$–0.76), as well as individual-level stability from mid adolescence to early adulthood (Forsman, Lichtenstein, Andershed, & Larsson, 2008; Hemphälä, Kosson, Westerman, & Hodgins, 2015; Lynam, Caspi, Moffitt, Loeber, & Stouthamer-Loeber, 2007). While personality features are not fully developed during childhood (McCuish & Lussier, 2018; Waller, Gardner, & Hyde, 2013), it is notable that children with psychopathic features display similar personality traits and neurological indicators as adults with psychopathy (Lynam & Gudonis, 2005; Viding & McCrory, 2018). In fact, research has suggested that antecedents of psychopathic traits may be identified as early as age 3 (Fanti & Kimonis, 2017). Therefore even though it has been reported that some individuals join gangs as early as 5 years old (Augustyn, Ward, & Krohn, 2017; Pyrooz & Sweeten, 2015), we would still expect to see this continuity trend in psychopathic personality traits before, during, and after their gang membership.

Evidence for the selection explanation of gang membership begins by acknowledging that individuals with psychopathic personality traits may be particularly attracted to the gang life because of the opportunities provided by the gang context, as Robert Hare (1999) writes:

> *Gangs have always provided greater opportunities for young psychopaths. Their impulsive, selfish, callous, egocentric, and aggressive tendencies easily blend in with—and may even set the tone for—many of the gang's activities.*
>
> *(p. 176)*

What Hare is describing is what gang researchers call "pulls" (for a review see, Densley, 2015), which represent positive attractions to the gang. This is distinguishable from "pushes," which are negative forces, or "risk factors," that propel individuals toward the gang. Of course, selection into gangs is a reflection of both pushes and pulls. Gangs may be attractive to those high in psychopathy, a pull factor, but also represent a "last resort" since they are cut-off from other prosocial groups.

Gang members often report joining a gang for "pull" reasons, such as fun or excitement, getting money, opportunities to meet girls, and status or prestige. There appears to be something "seductive" about the gang image (Katz, 1988), as individuals describe their motivation to join a gang as the "quest for a new experience" (Thrasher, 1927, p. 82) or a way "to fill unsupervised time and spice up otherwise mundane lives" (Densley, 2018, p. 10). A less common, but still mentioned, reason for joining a gang is the promise of making money, primarily through drug sales (Decker & Van Winkle, 1996; Descormiers & Corrado, 2016; Sanchez-Jankowski, 1991). Selling drugs or partaking in other criminal activities can produce quick profits, which is consistent with Factor 2 traits of psychopathy, including poor impulse control and sensation and thrill-seeking. Money also provides secondary attractions such as the ability to impress girls. "Getting girls" has been named as a motivation for joining a gang (Decker & Curry, 2000; Decker & Van Winkle, 1996) and risky sex is common among gang members (Little, Gonzalez, Snell, & Molidor, 1999; Quinn, Dickson-Gomez, Broaddus, & Pacella, 2019; Sanders, Thomas, & Deeds, 2012; Voisin et al., 2004). As impersonal sexual promiscuity is a behavior believed to represent psychopathy, risky sexual activity and the desire to get girls among gang members could point toward evidence for a selection explanation of the gang membership/psychopathy link.

While Factor 2 traits may be especially likely to appear among gang populations, the interpersonal and affective facets (i.e., Factor 1 of psychopathy) also include traits that have been linked to gang membership. Individuals cite prestige, power, and status as reasons for joining the gang life. Grandiosity (i.e., an unrealistic sense of superiority) has been shown to be higher among gang members, particularly among gang leaders (Thornton et al., 2015). While this study is limited due to its cross-sectional analysis, it seems reasonable that individuals with psychopathic interpersonal traits may choose to select into a gang, as status and prestige accompanies leadership. Other Factor 1 traits, such as neutrality toward lying and a lack of guilt and sympathy for others, have been labeled as risk factors for selecting into a gang (Dupéré et al., 2007; Peterson & Morgan, 2014).

Those high in psychopathy may have difficulty making and keeping friends due to traits within the interpersonal and affective facets (e.g., manipulative, frequent lying, callousness, lack of remorse, or caring for others). The difficulties experienced due to psychopathic personality traits may push individuals to select into delinquent peer groups, such as gangs. After all, what prosocial children (and for that matter, the parents of these children) want to associate with self-absorbed youth who cheat, lie, and steal? This line of reasoning for joining gangs has been theorized within control theory (Gottfredson & Hirschi, 1990; Kissner & Pyrooz, 2009). If gangs are composed of young people with psychopathic traits, we would expect these relationships to be "cold and brittle," as Hirschi termed it, lack cooperation and trust, and ephemeral over time.

We would also expect that the gang membership/offending link is a consequence of the extraneous influences of psychopathy. This means that gang researchers have been mistaken in their theoretical emphasis on group processes of gangs. Policymakers and practitioners are interested in gangs because of psychopathy, not group process, and thus should reorient their efforts by responding to the individual traits of psychopathy rather than group identity.

Facilitation

The *facilitation hypothesis* holds that the sources of psychopathy are found in the gang. This is referred to as a "kinds of groups" or "kinds of contexts" model and implies that gangs have a causal influence on psychopathy. In other words, if it were not for gang membership, an individual would not display prominent psychopathic personality characteristics. Facilitation is consistent with a social environmental explanation of the etiology of psychopathy, which describes the etiology of psychopathy occurring at multiple stages of the life course, including early negative environmental and socialization experiences and later social interactions. Unlike biological explanations of the development of psychopathy, which place emphasis on innate genetics and neurological deficits, social environmental factors describe psychopathy as emerging through antisocial experiences, such as adverse upbringing environments or exposure to traumatic events, and social interactions, particularly with deviant peers and partners. The literature supports this explanation finding that negative environments, such as a low family SES and exposure to violence, as well as social experiences with deviant peers and antisocial romantic partners, perceiving a lack of parental warmth, and physical punishment by the parent or guardian contribute to the development and enhancement of psychopathic personality traits (Backman, Laajasalo, Jokela, & Aronen, 2018; Lynam, Loeber, & Stouthamer-Loeber, 2008; Ray, 2018).

While the empirical evidence documents the stability of psychopathy, more recently studies have demonstrated evidence of within-individual change in psychopathy. This has been observed generally, as well as within the individual facets of psychopathy, highlighting developmental malleability in this construct (Blonigen, Hicks, Krueger, Patrick, & Iacono, 2006; Hawes et al., 2018; McCuish & Lussier, 2018; Salihovic, Özdemir, & Kerr, 2014). For example, McCuish and Lussier (2018) concluded that 35%–50% of youth in their sample with a psychopathy score in the 90th percentile or above (who were those that demonstrated the largest decreases in psychopathy) experienced a reliable decrease in their test score over the short term. This number increased to 75% of youth in these percentiles when looking at long-term effects. As such, psychopathy may not be as fixed as once thought, which raises continued questions about the etiology of psychopathic personality traits, including social-environmental influences.

Can gang membership facilitate changes in psychopathy? The facilitation hypothesis on this relationship points to the group processes of the gang that influence attitudes, norms, and behaviors, which therefore create psychopathic personality traits within individuals. Group processes refer to influences of the gang that encourage individuals to act in ways they otherwise would not. McGloin and Collins (2015) describe the types of intragang micro-level processes including, for example, *normative influence*, which is the way gangs establish and enforce commitment to the group, as well as the display of acceptable norms and values. Individuals who select into the group may engage in "group think," that is, people only consider behaviors, actions, or decisions that are acceptable to other members (Janis, 1982). Through this process, gangs influence the belief systems, risky behaviors, and entitativity and commitment to the ingroup (and aggression to the outgroup) of gang members, who establish identities consistent with gang norms (i.e., traits consistent with psychopathy). Fig. 1 posits that for the facilitation hypothesis, there are no between-individual differences in levels of psychopathy before and after gang membership, which is what we expect as these individuals are no different from their nongang peers. Young people are not attracted to gangs due to social rejection or homophily on psychopathic traits, instead it is sociological explanations—peer associations, neighborhood characteristics—that explain selection into gangs. However, a host of gang-related group processes elevate levels of psychopathy within gang members, producing intra-individual changes associated with the contours of gang membership.

It is well established that gang membership has a facilitation effect on offending behavior. However, it is unclear whether gangs may also facilitate the acquisition of psychopathological traits. Gang membership is strongly age graded, with most individuals joining between the ages of 12 and 15 (Pyrooz & Sweeten, 2015), an age range when individuals are most susceptible to peer influence (Steinberg & Monahan, 2007). Socialization to gangs involves establishing a new identity for themselves and internalizing antisocial traits consistent with psychopathic characteristics (e.g., recklessness, lack of remorse for their actions, sexual promiscuity, delinquency, and criminal versatility). Additionally, adolescence to emerging adulthood is the period when psychopathic traits are said to emerge (American Psychiatric Association, 2013), which highlights a potential overlap between gang influences and psychopathic trait development.

Individuals who assume the role of a gang member may derive a sense of group identity from involvement in the gang life and illegal activity (Goldman, Giles, & Hogg, 2014), which reflects antisocial traits (e.g., psychopathic traits) and is reinforced by the gang's dynamics, attitudes, and activities. For example, Dmitrieva et al. (2014) found that psychopathy was not predictive of low-level gang membership. However, over the course of gang membership, both low-level members and gang leaders developed a higher prevalence of grandiose-manipulative and impulsive-irresponsible traits, as well as lower temperance; years spent as a low-level member was found to increase callous-unemotional traits. Densley, Cai, and Hilal (2014) found that gang members with longer durations in the gang and higher positions display higher social dominance orientation (Factor 1 trait of psychopathy) than members with shorter durations in the gang and lower positions. This supports the notion that attitudes and behaviors that reflect social dominance orientation are likely developed and reinforced within the gang context. While limited by cross-sectional designs, studies by Alleyne and Wood (2010), Alleyne, Fernandes, and Pritchard (2014) and Dhingra, Debowska, Sharratt, Hyland, and Kola-Palmer (2015) demonstrate that gang youth enact techniques of neutralization and moral disengagement to justify and displace responsibility for their actions (i.e., interpersonal and affective facets of psychopathy), which is unsurprising as participating in group crime facilitates feelings of reduced guilt and shame (McGloin & Collins, 2015).

While there is minimal research on this topic with regard to gang membership, there is evidence that deviant peers may reinforce the development of callousness and tolerant beliefs regarding criminal and other antisocial behavior. Lynam et al. (2008) examined moderators of the relationship between psychopathy at age 13 and psychopathy at age 24. Findings suggest that, among boys who were not showing psychopathic personality traits at age 13, delinquent peers were found to be possible contributors to adult psychopathy. In fact, peer delinquency interacted with psychopathy at age 13 to predict total psychopathy at age 24, particularly on the interpersonal and antisocial facets of psychopathy. Ray (2018) examined trajectories of the grandiose-manipulative, callous-unemotional, and impulsive-irresponsible dimensions from the Youth Psychopathic Traits Inventory (YPI) among a sample of serious juvenile offenders. Findings indicated that delinquent peer associations were associated with a small increase in the callous-unemotional dimension over time. Backman et al. (2018) were interested in how within-individual changes in relationships with peers and romantic partners influence psychopathic traits. Their findings suggest that both types of interpersonal relationships, depending on the quality of the relationship and level of antisocial behavior within the relationship, can produce changes in individual-level psychopathic traits across time.

Enhancement

Hare (1999) recognized that the "pure" biological (i.e., selection) or social/environment (i.e., facilitation) explanations of the etiology of psychopathy are likely untenable. He noted:

> *as with most controversies, the 'truth' no doubt lies somewhere in between. That is, psychopathic attitudes and behaviors very likely are the result of a* combination *of biological factors and environmental forces.*
>
> *(p. 165)*

Twin studies have supported this proclamation with findings pointing to genetic, as well as nonshared environmental factors, as contributors to the variation in psychopathic personality traits. This evidence has been found in samples of children (e.g., Bezdjian, Raine, Baker, & Lynam, 2011; Tuvblad, Fanti, Andershed, Colins, & Larsson, 2017), adolescents (e.g., Beaver, Vaughn, & Delisi, 2013), and adults (e.g., Blonigen et al., 2006; Brook et al., 2010). Thus the empirical evidence supports both "pure" biological and social environmental explanations of the development of psychopathic personality traits, as well as a combined biological and social environmental factors etiology.

The *enhancement hypothesis* can be thought of as just that, a mixture of selection (i.e., biological/developmental) and facilitation (i.e., social/environmental). In this hypothesis, individuals with elevated individual deficits (e.g., psychopathy) select into gangs. Upon joining, affiliation with deviant peers and groups reinforce, maintain, and enhance preexisting tolerant beliefs regarding antisocial attitudes and behaviors, techniques of neutralization, and psychopathic tendencies more generally, assuming such attitudes and behaviors are consistent with the normative orientations of the peer group. In this sense, psychopathy is both a source and consequence of gang membership, and we can therefore refer to this model as a "kinds of persons and contexts" explanation (Curry, Decker, & Pyrooz, 2014). As shown in Fig. 1, the enhancement hypothesis is supported so long as the kinds of persons who end up in gangs display psychopathic traits before and/or after gang membership (i.e., between-individual differences) and the kinds of contexts associated with gangs combine to produce an even higher exhibition of psychopathic characteristics during gang membership than prior or after to gang membership (i.e., intraindividual differences).

An example of the enhancement model can be seen within Melde and Esbensen's (2011) work. They found that at-risk youth are more likely to join gangs than youth who exhibit more prosocial characteristics. Over time, these at-risk youth experience significant antisocial changes in their emotions, attitudes, and behavior. As deviant behavior is rewarded and reinforced by the gang, youth with preexisting psychopathic traits relish in the rewards of their gang status and, as such, we expect to find continuity in their gang membership and an increase in antisocial traits. This finding is further supported by other research showing that the high-risk gang youth remaining in gangs for longer periods than low-risk youth (for example, see Sweeten, Pyrooz, & Piquero, 2013).

Despite this argument, it is possible that those high in psychopathic personality traits at gang onset maintain shorter durations of involvement in gangs. Individuals high on Factor 1 (e.g., manipulative and pathological lying) and/or Factor 2 (e.g., impulsivity, criminality, unreliable) psychopathic traits may be less attractive to the gang. Research indicates that gangs are active in the selection process, reading "between the signs" to avoid adverse selection, an evolving process that continues throughout gang membership, and limit their interaction with individuals they deem as untrustworthy or impetuous (Pyrooz & Densley, 2016). As such, gangs may push individuals with these traits out of the gang, resulting in isolation from both gang peers, as well as prosocial peers.

Conclusions

This chapter reviewed the state of the literature on the linkages between gang membership and psychopathy. We began by offering a brief overview of psychopathy in criminology—its history and relevance for criminal offending. Next, we turned our attention to the small body of research on the link between psychopathy and gang membership. Missing from this line of research is a theoretical foundation. We addressed this void by extending Thornberry et al.'s (1993) tripartite theoretical model—selection, facilitation, and enhancement—to psychopathy and gang membership, where we outlined multiple perspectives on how this relationship could unfold temporally between- and within-individuals. A core conclusion of ours is that the state of the evidence is premature to afford empirical primacy to either perspective. Although if we had to speculate, we would expect an enhancement model to best represent the relationship between gang membership and psychopathy.

In the end, the theoretical and empirical study of psychopathy and gangs constitute two large bodies of research that have intersected only on rare occasions. Both areas of research have been crucial for extending theory and methodology across a range of substantive areas, but altogether we know very little about how psychopathy influences gang membership and how gang membership influences psychopathy. This is despite the fact that there are mixed positions in the gang literature about the relevance of psychopathy—and seemingly time-stable traits more generally—to the understanding of gang membership. This chapter has taken a step forward in extending our understanding of this interaction by modifying an established theoretical model into a new—and untested—model. Future research that offers empirical tests of our theoretical model will contribute significantly to our understanding of the gang membership/psychopathy relationship and likely influence research on the intersection of this relationship and criminal offending, not to mention shape the policies and practices for responding to gangs.

References

Alleyne, E., Fernandes, I., & Pritchard, E. (2014). Denying humanness to victims: How gang members justify violent behavior. *Group Processes & Intergroup Relations*, *17*(6), 750–762. https://doi.org/10.1177/1368430214536064.

Alleyne, E., & Wood, J. L. (2010). Gang involvement: Psychological and behavioral characteristics of gang members, peripheral youth, and nongang youth. *Aggressive Behavior*, *36*(6), 423–436. https://doi.org/10.1002/ab.20360.

American Psychiatric Association. (2013). *Diagnostic and statistical manual of mental disorders* (5th ed.). Washington, DC: American Psychiatric Association.

Ang, R. P., Huan, V. S., Chan, W. T., Cheong, S. A., & Leaw, J. N. (2015). The role of delinquency, proactive aggression, psychopathy and behavioral school engagement in reported youth gang membership. *Journal of Adolescence*, *41*, 148–156. https://doi.org/10.1016/j.adolescence.2015.03.010.

Assadi, S. M., Noroozian, M., Pakravannejad, M., Yahyazadeh, O., Aghayan, S., Shariat, S. V., & Fazel, S. (2006). Psychiatric morbidity among sentenced prisoners: Prevalence study in Iran. *British Journal of Psychiatry*, *188*, 159–164. https://doi.org/10.1192/bjp.188.2.159.

Asscher, J. J., Van Vugt, E. S., Stams, G. J. J. M., Deković, M., Eichelsheim, V. I., & Yousfi, S. (2011). The relationship between juvenile psychopathic traits, delinquency and (violent) recidivism: A meta-analysis. *Journal of Child Psychology and Psychiatry, and Allied Disciplines*, *52*(11), 1134–1143. https://doi.org/10.1111/j.1469-7610.2011.02412.x.

Augustyn, M. B., Ward, J. T., & Krohn, M. D. (2017). Exploring intergenerational continuity in gang membership. *Journal of Crime and Justice*, *40*(3), 252–274. https://doi.org/10.1080/0735648X.2017.1337556.

Backman, H., Laajasalo, T., Jokela, M., & Aronen, E. T. (2018). Interpersonal relationships as protective and risk factors for psychopathy: A follow-up study in adolescent offenders. *Journal of Youth and Adolescence*, *47*, 1022–1036. https://doi.org/10.1007/s10964-017-0745-x.

Beaver, K. M., Boutwell, B. B., Barnes, J. C., Vaughn, M. G., & DeLisi, M. (2017). The association between psychopathic personality traits and criminal justice outcomes: Results from a nationally representative sample of males and females. *Crime and Delinquency*, *63*(6), 708–730. https://doi.org/10.1177/0011128715573617.

Beaver, K. M., Delisi, M., Vaughn, M. G., & Barnes, J. C. (2010). Monoamine oxidase A genotype is associated with gang membership and weapon use. *Comprehensive Psychiatry*, *51*(2), 130–134. https://doi.org/10.1016/j.comppsych.2009.03.010.

Beaver, K. M., Rowland, M. W., Schwartz, J. A., & Nedelec, J. L. (2011). The genetic origins of psychopathic personality traits in adult males and females: Results from an adoption-based study. *Journal of Criminal Justice*, *39*(5), 426–432. https://doi.org/10.1016/j.jcrimjus.2011.07.002.

Beaver, K. M., Vaughn, M. G., & Delisi, M. (2013). Nonshared environmental effects on adulthood psychopathic personality traits: Results from a monozygotic twin difference scores analysis. *Psychiatric Quarterly*, *84*, 381–393. https://doi.org/10.1007/s11126-013-9255-5.

Bezdjian, S., Raine, A., Baker, L. A., & Lynam, D. R. (2011). Psychopathic personality in children: Genetic and environmental contributions. *Psychological Medicine*, *41*(3), 589–600. https://doi.org/10.1017/S0033291710000966.

Blais, J., Solodukhin, E., & Forth, A. E. (2014). A meta-analysis exploring the relationship between psychopathy and instrumental versus reactive violence. *Criminal Justice and Behavior*, *41*(7), 797–821. https://doi.org/10.1177/0093854813519629.

Blonigen, D. M., Hicks, B. M., Krueger, R. F., Patrick, C. J., & Iacono, W. G. (2006). Continuity and change in psychopathic traits as measured via normal-range personality: A longitudinal-biometric study. *Journal of Abnormal Psychology*, *115*(1), 85–95. https://doi.org/10.1037/0021-843X.115.1.85.

Brook, M., Panizzon, M. S., Kosson, D. S., Sullivan, E. A., Lyons, M. J., Franz, C. E., … Kremen, W. S. (2010). Psychopathic personality traits in middle-aged male twins: A behavior genetic investigation. *Journal of Personality Disorders*, *24*(4), 473–486. https://doi.org/10.1521/pedi.2010.24.4.473.

Cale, J., Lussier, P., McCuish, E., & Corrado, R. (2015). The prevalence of psychopathic personality disturbances among incarcerated youth: Comparing serious, chronic, violent and sex offenders. *Journal of Criminal Justice*, *43*(4), 337–344. https://doi.org/10.1016/j.jcrimjus.2015.04.005.

Campbell, M. A., Porter, S., & Santor, D. (2004). Psychopathic traits in adolescent offenders: An evaluation of criminal history, clinical, and psychosocial correlates. *Behavioral Sciences & the Law*, *22*, 23–47. https://doi.org/10.1002/bsl.572.

Carson, D. C., & Ray, J. V. (2019). Do psychopathic traits distinguish trajectories of gang membership? *Criminal Justice and Behavior*, *46*(9), 1337–1355. https://doi.org/10.1177/0093854819867388.

Chu, C. M., Daffern, M., Thomas, S. D. M., Ang, Y., & Long, M. (2014). Criminal attitudes and psychopathic personality attributes of youth gang offenders in Singapore. *Psychology, Crime and Law*, *20*(3), 284–301. https://doi.org/10.1080/1068316X.2013.772182.

Cleckley, H. M. (1941). *The mask of sanity: An attempt to reinterpret the so-called psychopathic personality*. St. Louis: Mosby Company.

Colins, O. F., Fanti, K. A., Salekin, R. T., & Andershed, H. (2016). Psychopathic personality in the general population: Differences and similarities across gender. *Journal of Personality Disorders*, *31*(1), 49–74. https://doi.org/10.1521/pedi_2016_30_237.

Connolly, E. J., & Beaver, K. M. (2015). Guns, gangs, and genes: Evidence of an underlying genetic influence on gang involvement and carrying a handgun. *Youth Violence and Juvenile Justice*, *13*(3), 228–242. https://doi.org/10.1177/1541204014539522.

Curry, G. D., Decker, S. H., & Pyrooz, D. C. (2014). *Confronting gangs: Crime and community*. Oxford: Oxford University Press.

Dåderman, A. M., & Kristiansson, M. (2003). Degree of psychopathy—Implications for treatment in male juvenile delinquents. *International Journal of Law and Psychiatry*, *26*, 301–315. https://doi.org/10.1016/S0160-2527(03)00040-2.

Decker, S. H., & Curry, G. D. (2000). Addressing key features of gang membership: Measuring the involvement of young members. *Journal of Criminal Justice*, *28*(6), 473–482. https://doi.org/10.1016/S0047-2352(00)00063-5.

Decker, S. H., & Van Winkle, B. (1996). *Life in the gang: Family, friends, and violence*. Cambridge, UK: Cambridge University Press.

DeLisi, M. (2009). Psychopathy is the unified theory of crime. *Youth Violence and Juvenile Justice*, *7*(3), 256–273. https://doi.org/10.1177/1541204009333834.

Densley, J. A. (2015). Joining the gang: A process of supply and demand. In S. H. Decker, & D. C. Pyrooz (Eds.), *The handbook of gangs* (pp. 235–256). Chichester, West Sussex: Wiley-Blackwell.

Densley, J. A. (2018). Gang joining. In *Oxford research encyclopedia of criminology and criminal justice*. New York, NY: Oxford University Press. https://doi.org/10.1093/acrefore/9780190264079.013.437.

Densley, J. A., Cai, T., & Hilal, S. (2014). Social dominance orientation and trust propensity in street gangs. *Group Processes & Intergroup Relations, 17*(6), 763–779. https://doi.org/10.1177/1368430214533161.

Descormiers, K., & Corrado, R. R. (2016). The right to belong: Individual motives and youth gang initiation rites. *Deviant Behavior, 37*(11), 1341–1359. https://doi.org/10.1080/01639625.2016.1177390.

Dhingra, K., Debowska, A., Sharratt, K., Hyland, P., & Kola-Palmer, S. (2015). Psychopathy, Gang membership, and moral disengagement among juvenile offenders. *Journal of Criminal Psychology, 5*(1), 13–24. https://doi.org/10.1108/JCP-11-2014-0016.

Dmitrieva, J., Gibson, L., Steinberg, L., Piquero, A., & Fagan, J. (2014). Predictors and consequences of gang membership: Comparing gang members, gang leaders, and non-gang-affiliated adjudicated youth. *Journal of Research on Adolescence, 24*(2), 220–234. https://doi.org/10.1111/jora.12111.

Dupéré, V., Lacourse, É., Willms, J. D., Vitaro, F., & Tremblay, R. E. (2007). Affiliation to youth gangs during adolescence: The interaction between childhood psychopathic tendencies and neighborhood disadvantage. *Journal of Abnormal Child Psychology, 35*(6), 1035–1045. https://doi.org/10.1007/s10802-007-9153-0.

Durand, E., Chevignard, M., Ruet, A., Dereix, A., Jourdan, C., & Pradat-Diehl, P. (2017). History of traumatic brain injury in prison populations: A systematic review. *Annals of Physical and Rehabilitation Medicine, 60*(2), 95–101. https://doi.org/10.1016/j.rehab.2017.02.003.

Egley, A., Howell, J. C., & Harris, M. (2014). *Highlights of the 2012 national youth gang survey. Juvenile justice fact sheet*.

Fahmy, C., Jackson, D. B., Pyrooz, D. C., & Decker, S. H. (2020). Head injury in prison: Gang membership and the role of prison violence. *Journal of Criminal Justice*. https://doi.org/10.1016/j.jcrimjus.2020.101658.

Fanti, K. A., & Kimonis, E. (2017). Heterogeneity in externalizing problems at age 3: Association with age 15 biological and environmental outcomes. *Developmental Psychology, 53*(7), 1230–1241. https://doi.org/10.1037/dev0000317.

Forsman, M., Lichtenstein, P., Andershed, H., & Larsson, H. (2008). Genetic effects explain the stability of psychopathic personality from mid- to late adolescence. *Journal of Abnormal Psychology, 117*(3), 606–617. https://doi.org/10.1037/0021-843X.117.3.606.

Fox, B., & Delisi, M. (2019). Psychopathic killers: A meta-analytic review of the psychopathy-homicide nexus. *Aggression and Violent Behavior, 44*, 67–79. https://doi.org/10.1016/j.avb.2018.11.005 Received.

Geerlings, Y., Asscher, J. J., Stams, G. J. J. M., & Assink, M. (2020). The association between psychopathy and delinquency in juveniles: A three-level meta-analysis. *Aggression and Violent Behavior, 50*. https://doi.org/10.1016/j.avb.2019.101342.

Goldman, L., Giles, H., & Hogg, M. A. (2014). Going to extremes: Social identity and communication processes associated with gang membership. *Group Processes & Intergroup Relations, 17*(6), 813–832. https://doi.org/10.1177/1368430214524289.

Gottfredson, M. R., & Hirschi, T. (1990). *A general theory of crime*. Stanford University Press.

Hare, R. D. (1999). *Without conscience: The disturbing world of the psychopaths among us*. Guilford Press.

Hare, R. D. (2003). *The Hare PCL-R*. Toronto, ON: Multi-Health Systems.

Hart, S. D., & Hare, R. D. (1997). Psychopathy: Assessment and association with criminal conduct. In D. Stoff, J. Breiling, & J. D. Maser (Eds.), *Handbook of antisocial behavior* (pp. 22–35). Hoboken, NJ: John Wiley & Sons Inc.

Hawes, S. W., Byrd, A. L., Gonzalez, R., Cavanaugh, C., Bechtold, J., Lynam, D. R., & Pardini, D. A. (2018). The developmental course of psychopathic features: Investigating stability, change, and long-term outcomes. *Journal of Research in Personality*, *77*, 83–89. https://doi.org/10.1016/j.jrp.2018.09.009.

Hemphälä, M., Kosson, D., Westerman, J., & Hodgins, S. (2015). Stability and predictors of psychopathic traits from mid-adolescence through early adulthood. *Scandinavian Journal of Psychology*, *56*(6), 649–658. https://doi.org/10.1111/sjop.12257.

Janis, I. L. (1982). *Groupthink: Psychological studies of policy decisions and fiascoes*. Boston: Houghton Mifflin.

Katz, J. (1988). *Seductions of crime: Moral and sensual attractions in doing evil*. New York, NY: Basic Books.

Kissner, J., & Pyrooz, D. C. (2009). Self-control, differential association, and gang membership: A theoretical and empirical extension of the literature. *Journal of Criminal Justice*, *37*(5), 478–487. https://doi.org/10.1016/j.jcrimjus.2009.07.008.

Klein, M. W. (1968). Impressions of juvenile gang members. *Adolescence*, *3*(9), 53.

Klein, M. W. (1971). *Street Gangs and street workers*. Englewood Cliffs, NJ: Prentice-Hall.

Little, B. B., Gonzalez, J., Snell, L., & Molidor, C. (1999). Risk behaviors for sexually transmitted diseases among gangs in dallas, texas. *Journal of Gang Research*, *6*(3), 33–47.

Longman, T., Hawes, D. J., & Kohlhoff, J. (2016). Callous–unemotional traits as markers for conduct problem severity in early childhood: A meta-analysis. *Child Psychiatry & Human Development*, *47*(2), 326–334. https://doi.org/10.1007/s10578-015-0564-9.

Lynam, D. R., Caspi, A., Moffitt, T. E., Loeber, R., & Stouthamer-Loeber, M. (2007). Longitudinal evidence that psychology scores in early adolescence predict adult psychopathy. *Journal of Abnormal Psychology*, *116*(1), 155–165. https://doi.org/10.1037/0021-843X.116.1.155.

Lynam, D. R., & Gudonis, L. (2005). The development of psychopathy. *Annual Review of Clinical Psychology*, *1*, 381–407. https://doi.org/10.1146/annurev.clinpsy.1.102803.144019.

Lynam, D. R., Loeber, R., & Stouthamer-Loeber, M. (2008). The stability of psychopathy from adolescence into adulthood: The search for moderators. *Criminal Justice and Behavior*, *35*(2), 228–243. https://doi.org/10.1177/0093854807310153.

Mallion, J. S., & Wood, J. L. (2018). Comparison of emotional dispositions between street gang and non-gang prisoners. *Journal of Interpersonal Violence*, 1–21. https://doi.org/10.1177/0886260518789147.

McCuish, E. C., & Lussier, P. (2018). A developmental perspective on the stability and change of psychopathic personality traits across the adolescence–adulthood transition. *Criminal Justice and Behavior*, *45*(5), 666–692. https://doi.org/10.1177/0093854818761992.

McGloin, J. M., & Collins, M. E. (2015). Micro-level processes of the gang. In S. H. Decker, & D. C. Pyrooz (Eds.), *The Handbook of Gangs* (pp. 276–293). Chichester, West Sussex: Wiley-Blackwell.

Melde, C., & Esbensen, F.-A. (2011). Gang membership as a turning point in the life course. *Criminology*, *49*(2), 513–552. https://doi.org/10.1111/j.1745-9125.2011.00227.x.

Melde, C., & Esbensen, F.-A. (2013). Gangs and violence: Disentangling the impact of gang membership on the level and nature of offending. *Journal of Quantitative Criminology*, *29*, 143–166. https://doi.org/10.1007/s10940-012-9164-z.

Moore, A. A., Blair, R. J., Hettema, J. M., & Roberson-Nay, R. (2019). The genetic underpinnings of callous-unemotional traits: A systematic research review. *Neuroscience & Biobehavioral Reviews*, *100*, 85–97. https://doi.org/10.1016/j.neubiorev.2019.02.018.

Morris, R. E., Harrison, E. A., Knox, G. W., Tromanhauser, E., Marquis, D. K., & Watts, L. L. (1995). Health risk behavioral survey from 39 juvenile correctional facilities in the United States. *Journal of Adolescent Health, 17*(6), 334–344. https://doi.org/10.1016/1054-139X(95)00098-D.

Neumann, C. S., & Hare, R. D. (2008). Psychopathic traits in a large community sample: Links to violence, alcohol use, and intelligence. *Journal of Consulting and Clinical Psychology, 76*(5), 893. https://doi.org/10.1037/0022-006X.76.5.893.

Olver, M. E., & Wong, S. (2015). Short- and long-term recidivism prediction of the PCL-R and the effects of age: A 24-year follow-up. *Personality Disorders, Theory, Research, and Treatment, 6*(1), 97. https://doi.org/10.1037/per0000095.

Patrick, C. J., & Drislane, L. E. (2015). Antisocial personality disorder and psychopathy. In P. H. Blaney, R. F. Krueger, & T. Millon (Eds.), *Oxford textbook of psychopathology* (pp. 681–706). New York, NY: Oxford University Press.

Peterson, D., & Morgan, K. A. (2014). Sex differences and the overlap in youths' risk factors for onset of violence and gang involvement. *Journal of Crime and Justice, 37*(1), 129–154. https://doi.org/10.1080/0735648X.2013.830393.

Pujol, J., Harrison, B. J., Contreras-Rodriguez, O., & Cardoner, N. (2018). The contribution of brain imaging to the understanding of psychopathy. *Psychological Medicine, 49*(01), 20–31. https://doi.org/10.1017/S0033291718002507.

Pyrooz, D. C. (2014). From your first cigarette to your last dyin day: The patterning of gang membership in the life-course. *Journal of Quantitative Criminology, 30*(2), 349–372. https://doi.org/10.1007/s10940-013-9206-1.

Pyrooz, D. C., & Decker, S. H. (2013). Delinquent behavior, violence, and gang involvement in China. *Journal of Quantitative Criminology, 29*, 251–272. https://doi.org/10.1007/s10940-012-9178-6.

Pyrooz, D. C., & Densley, J. A. (2016). Selection into street gangs: Signaling theory, gang membership, and criminal offending. *Journal of Research in Crime and Delinquency, 53*(4), 447–481. https://doi.org/10.1177/0022427815619462.

Pyrooz, D. C., & Mitchell, M. M. (2015). Little gang research, big gang research. In S. H. Decker, & D. C. Pyrooz (Eds.), *The handbook of gangs* (pp. 28–58). John Wiley & Sons Inc.

Pyrooz, D. C., & Mitchell, M. M. (2020). The use of restrictive housing on gang and non-gang affiliates in U.S. prisons: Findings from a national survey of correctional agencies. *Justice Quarterly, 37*(4), 590–615. https://doi.org/10.1080/07418825.2019.1574019.

Pyrooz, D. C., Moule, R. K., Jr., & Decker, S. H. (2014). The contribution of gang membership to the victim–offender overlap. *Journal of Research in Crime and Delinquency, 51*(3), 315–348. https://doi.org/10.1177/0022427813516128.

Pyrooz, D. C., & Sweeten, G. (2015). Gang membership between ages 5 and 17 years in the United States. *Journal of Adolescent Health*, 1–6. https://doi.org/10.1016/j.jadohealth.2014.11.018.

Quinn, K., Dickson-Gomez, J., Broaddus, M., & Pacella, M. (2019). "Running trains" and "sexing-in": The functions of sex within adolescent gangs. *Youth & Society, 51*(2), 151–169. https://doi.org/10.1177/0044118X16667375.

Ray, B., & Richardson, N. J. (2017). Traumatic brain injury and recidivism among returning inmates. *Criminal Justice and Behavior, 44*(3), 472–486. https://doi.org/10.1177/0093854816686631.

Ray, J. V. (2018). Developmental patterns of psychopathic personality traits and the influence of social factors among a sample of serious juvenile offenders. *Journal of Criminal Justice, 58*, 67–77. https://doi.org/10.1016/j.jcrimjus.2018.07.004.

Ruddell, R., Decker, S. H., & Egley, A., Jr. (2006). Gang interventions in jails: A national analysis. *Criminal Justice Review*, *31*(1), 33–46. https://doi.org/10.1177/0734016806288263.

Salihovic, S., Özdemir, M., & Kerr, M. (2014). Trajectories of adolescent psychopathic traits. *Journal of Psychopathology and Behavioral Assessment*, *36*(1), 47–59. https://doi.org/10.1007/s10862-013-9375-0.

Sanchez-Jankowski, M. (1991). *Islands in the street: Gangs and american urban society*. Berkeley: University of California Press.

Sanders, B., Thomas, Y. F., & Deeds, B. G. (Eds.). (2012). *Crime, HIV and health: Intersections of criminal justice and public health concerns* Springer Science & Business Media.

Shiroma, E. J., Ferguson, P. L., & Pickelsimer, E. E. (2010). Prevalence of traumatic brain injury in an offender population: A meta-analysis. *Journal of Correctional Health Care*, *16*(2), 147–159. https://doi.org/10.1177/1078345809356538.

Short, J. F., Jr. (1997). *Poverty, ethnicity, and violent crime*. Boulder, CO: Westview Press.

Steinberg, L., & Monahan, K. C. (2007). Age differences in resistance to peer pressure. *Developmental Psychology*, *43*(6), 1531–1543. https://doi.org/10.1037/0012-1649.43.6.1531.

Sweeten, G., Pyrooz, D. C., & Piquero, A. R. (2013). Disengaging from gangs and desistance from crime. *Justice Quarterly*, *30*(3), 469–500. https://doi.org/10.1080/07418825.2012.723033.

Thornberry, T. P., Krohn, M. D., Lizotte, A. J., & Chard-Wierschem, D. (1993). The role of juvenile gangs in facilitating delinquent behavior. *Journal of Research in Crime and Deliquency*, *30*(1), 55–87. https://doi.org/10.1177/0022427893030001005.

Thornton, L. C., Frick, P. J., Shulman, E. P., Ray, J. V., Steinberg, L., & Cauffman, E. (2015). Callous-unemotional traits and adolescents' role in group crime. *Law and Human Behavior*, *39*(4), 368–377. https://doi.org/10.1037/lhb0000124.

Thrasher, F. M. (1927). *The gang: A study of 1, 313 gangs in Chicago*. Chicago: University of Chicago Press.

Tuvblad, C., Fanti, K. A., Andershed, H., Colins, O. F., & Larsson, H. (2017). Psychopathic personality traits in 5 year old twins: The importance of genetic and shared environmental influences. *European Child & Adolescent Psychiatry*, *26*(4), 469–479. https://doi.org/10.1007/s00787-016-0899-1.

Valdez, A., Kaplan, C. D., & Codina, E. (2000). Psychopathy among Mexican American gang members: A comparative study. *International Journal of Offender Therapy and Comparative Criminology*, *44*(1), 46–58.

Vaughn, M. G., Edens, J. F., Howard, M. O., & Smith, S. T. (2009). An investigation of primary and secondary psychopathy in a statewide sample of incarcerated youth. *Youth Violence and Juvenile Justice*, *7*(3), 172–188. https://doi.org/10.1177/1541204009333792.

Vaughn, M. G., Salas-Wright, C. P., DeLisi, M., & Perron, B. (2014). Correlates of traumatic brain injury among juvenile offenders: A multi-site study. *Criminal Behaviour and Mental Health*, *24*, 188–203. https://doi.org/10.1002/cbm.1900.

Vazsonyi, A. T., Mikuška, J., & Kelley, E. L. (2017). It's time: A meta-analysis on the self-control-deviance link. *Journal of Criminal Justice*, *48*, 48–63. https://doi.org/10.1016/j.jcrimjus.2016.10.001.

Viding, E., & McCrory, E. J. (2018). Understanding the development of psychopathy: Progress and challenges. *Psychological Medicine*, *48*(4), 566–577. https://doi.org/10.1017/S0033291717002847.

Voisin, D. R., Salazar, L. F., Crosby, R., DiClemente, R. J., Yarber, W. L., & Staples-Horne, M. (2004). The association between gang involvement and sexual behaviours among detained adolescent males. *Sexually Transmitted Infections*, *80*(6), 440–442. https://doi.org/10.1136/sti.2004.010926.

Waller, R., Gardner, F., & Hyde, L. W. (2013). Clinical psychology review What are the associations between parenting, callous—Unemotional traits, and antisocial behavior in youth? A systematic review of evidence. *Clinical Psychology Review*, *33*(4), 593–608. https://doi.org/10.1016/j.cpr.2013.03.001.

Weisburd, D., Cave, B., & Piquero, A. R. (2015). How do criminologists interpret statistical explanation of crime? A review of quantitative modeling in published studies. In A. R. Piquero (Ed.), *The handbook of criminological theory* (pp. 395–414). Wiley-Blackwell.

Winterdyk, J., & Ruddell, R. (2010). Managing prison gangs: Results from a survey of U.S. prison systems. *Journal of Criminal Justice*, *38*(4), 730–736. https://doi.org/10.1016/j.jcrimjus.2010.04.047.

Wolfgang, M. E., Figlio, R. M., & Sellin, T. (1972). *Delinquency in a birth cohort*. Chicago, IL: University of Chicago Press.

Woodworth, M., & Porter, S. (2002). In cold blood: Characteristics of criminal homicides as a function of psychopathy. *Journal of Abnormal Psychology*, *111*(3), 436–445. https://doi.org/10.1037//0021-843X.111.3.436.

Yablonsky, L. (1962). *The violent gang* (1970th ed.). New York, NY: Macmillan.

Psychopathy and sexual offending over the life course: An exploratory longitudinal investigation

15

Evan McCuish, Patrick Lussier, and Raymond Corrado

Introduction

Empirical studies identified psychopathy as one of the most important risk factors for sexual offending (Cale, Lussier, McCuish, & Corrado, 2015; Caputo, Frick, & Brodsky, 1999; Lalumière & Quinsey, 1996), including sexual recidivism (Parks & Bard, 2006; Quinsey, Rice, & Harris, 1995). However, less attention has been given to the relationship between psychopathy and the timing and continuity of sexual offending, including whether early symptoms of psychopathy are informative of a specific proclivity for long-term and repetitive involvement in sex crimes and whether such crimes are disproportionately more common compared to other types of offenses. Two major theoretical perspectives have presented somewhat competing assertions about the mechanisms by which psychopathy influences sexual offending. One perspective, rooted in forensic psychology, focuses on a psychopathy-as-pathology explanation of the link between psychopathy and sexual offending (e.g., Knight & Sims-Knight, 2004; Malamuth, 2003). The other is rooted in evolutionary psychology and focuses on psychopathy-as-adaptive-strategy to explain this link (e.g., Glenn, Kurzban, & Raine, 2011; Lalumière, Harris, Quinsey, & Rice, 2005). Although this chapter does not directly test these two theoretical models, it does introduce how the developmental criminology approach, which examines the relationship between key risk factors and offending sequences (see Loeber & Le Blanc, 1990), can be used to draw implications regarding the validity of each perspective.

The chapter is organized into three sections. First, historical viewpoints on the relationship between psychopathy and sexual offending are discussed to illustrate the evolution of research and theorizing on this relationship. Specific attention is given to clinical and evolutionary perspectives on the relationship between psychopathy and sexual offending. The principles of these two perspectives are described and developmental criminology is introduced to provide a framework for examining offending patterns of individuals with features of psychopathy. Second, a developmental criminology approach is used to more clearly understand the specific relationship between psychopathy and sexual offending. This was done by using data on males from the Incarcerated Serious and Violent Young Offender Study (ISVYOS) to examine whether psychopathy was associated with repeated adjudications for sexual

Psychopathy and Criminal Behavior. https://doi.org/10.1016/B978-0-12-811419-3.00003-0

offenses between adolescence and adulthood, whether psychopathy was associated with the timing of a person's sexual offense, and whether individuals with strong features of psychopathy were primarily involved in the justice system due to their sexual offending. Addressing these questions has implications for clinical theoretical perspectives asserting that features of psychopathy, such as impulsivity, boldness, narcissism, arrogance, and limited prosocial emotions, will be associated with early and prolonged involvement in sexual offending (e.g., Knight & Sims-Knight, 2004). Addressing these questions also has implications for evolutionary perspectives that hypothesize that psychopathy will be linked to a specific type of mating effort defined by coercive behavior (Jonason, Li, Webster, & Schmitt, 2009) and therefore such individuals will be disproportionately involved in sexual offenses compared to other crimes. Finally, the results of these analyses are interpreted beyond simply asserting that a relationship between psychopathy and sexual offending exists. Greater attention to the causal mechanisms linking psychopathy to sexual offending is needed. As one step forward, we recommend closer attention to the situational dynamics that give rise to opportunities for sexual offenses, as individuals with features of psychopathy may be more likely to engage in sexual offenses as a response to partner rejection or in the context of dating and other relationships where manipulation and deceit are used.

Historical perspectives

Although psychopathy has been linked to sexual offending for at least a century, the description and explanation of this relationship has been inconsistent over this time. Initially, and especially in the United States, perpetrators of sexual offenses were described as sexual psychopaths due to the often seemingly irrational, impulsive, and violent nature of their offending (Jenkins, 1998). In fact, concerns over individuals considered psychologically abnormal, but not legally insane, who had perpetrated serious sex offenses were directly responsible for the first wave of sexual offender laws. Socially ostracized and considered prime candidates for physical castration by some (e.g., Le Maire, 1956), these individuals influenced the enactment of Sexual Psychopathy Laws in North America. Sexual Psychopathy Laws emerged in the 1930s and provided the courts with new legal dispositions to confine individuals considered sexual psychopaths (also referred as "criminal sexual psychopaths" or "sexually dangerous persons" in some US States; e.g., Sutherland, 1950). Such legal dispositions allowed judges to indefinitely confine sexual psychopaths in maximum-security institutions to receive some form of therapy until they no longer posed a threat to the community. Sexual Psychopathy Laws were generally aimed at perpetrators of various sexual offenses who were characterized by a disregard for their victims' feelings, the malicious intent and motive for their crime, and their uncontrollable sexual urges (e.g., Karpman, 1951). However, some individuals received similar sanctions for more minor forms of sexual offenses on the basis that these offenses were stepping-stones to what was presumed to be an inevitable escalation into serious and violent sexual offenses (Jenkins, 1998).

While "sexual psychopath" and "sexual psychopathy" were legal terms, they were not recognized by psychiatrists and clinical researchers, who were very critical of the vagueness and ambiguity of the criteria for psychopathy, to the point that some in these fields completely rejected the idea of sexual psychopathy (e.g., Gebhard, Gagnon, Pomeroy, & Christenson, 1965; Hacker & Frym, 1955). Because it was a legal term rather than a medical one, the definition and understanding of it varied from one jurisdiction to another. Among other things, psychiatrists who made recommendations to the court in sexual psychopathy cases were confused between the legal term of sexual psychopathy and the medical term of psychopathic personality (e.g., Cohen, 1956). In that regard, inspection of the clinical profile of individuals recognized by the courts as sexual psychopaths and the relative absence of "genuine psychopaths" among them called into question Sexual Psychopath Laws (e.g., Abrahamsen, 1950). Paradoxically, while these laws served the purpose of identifying sex offenders more amenable to therapy, individuals associated with Cleckley's (1955) description of features of psychopathy as a personality disorder were possibly excluded from the legal designation of a sexual psychopath due to the belief among practitioners that individuals with such features were not amenable to change. As a result, these laws were regularly amended to address various problems and issues and then eventually abandoned altogether.

Although terms like sexual psychopath and sexual psychopathy were gradually abandoned as legal concepts, the term psychopathy reemerged, but this time as a meaningful clinical concept for the description, explanation, and prediction of sexual offending (e.g., Seto & Barbaree, 1999). Attitudes about the relevance of this construct did not emerge overnight. In fact, early clinical writings about psychopathy made little mention of sexual behavior and sexual lifestyle, including sexual offending. Debates over the concept of psychopathy and its diagnostic criteria (e.g., Karpman, 1948) limited research on the psychopathy-sexual offending link. Cleckley (1955) suggested that psychopathy was not associated with deviant sexual urges and deviant sexual preferences but could occasionally relate to abnormal sexual acts. Consensual sex provided individuals labeled at the time as "psychopaths" with little pleasure as they gave little thought to their sexual partner's feelings. Rather, clinical observations on such individuals in custody suggested that sex was merely a means by which they asserted their power over someone else. As opposed to sexual gratification, pleasure emerged from the experience of winning over another person through deception, manipulation, coercion, and/or violence (e.g., Samenow, 1984). In other words, sexual activity was another way in which the individual exerted their dominance over others. However, clinical researchers began to acknowledge that rape and sexual assault were pseudosexual acts (e.g., Groth & Burgess, 1977) that were first and foremost antisocial and violent rather than sexually deviant (e.g., Alder, 1984; Seto & Barbaree, 1997). This growing recognition favored attention to the clinical concept of psychopathy as a potential risk factor for sexual offenses. Such recognition was supported by clinical research suggesting the presence of an "antisocial, psychopathic type" among subgroups of rapists and sexual aggressors (e.g., Knight, Rosenberg, & Schneider, 1985; Kopp, 1962). It was not until the emergence of the Hare Psychopathy Checklist (PCL; Hare, 1985) in the 1980s, however, that the concept of psychopathy was systematically measured with individuals convicted for a sex crime, especially those in maximum-security institutions. Consequently, its role and importance in the etiology of sexual offending became less anecdotal and more scientifically notable.

The prevalence of psychopathy among individuals convicted for a sex crime has been determined mainly using the PCL-Revised (PCL-R) and its variants (PCL:YV; PCL:SV). These studies produced inconsistent findings, casting doubts about its clinical importance in the prediction of sexual offending and sexual recidivism. However, the interpretation of such inconsistencies should be contextualized. Indeed, across studies the estimated prevalence of psychopathy, based on PCL-R scores, for convicted sex offenders ranged from about 1 of 10 to 2 of 3 (e.g., Porter et al., 2000; Serin, Malcolm, Khanna, & Barbaree, 1994). There are two important sampling issues that may explain the varying prevalence of psychopathy. First, research conducted in psychiatric settings as opposed to with inmates in prison or with college students in the community has produced contrasting results. In Canada, the prevalence of psychopathy in sex offenders in maximum-security psychiatric institutions is expected to be significantly higher than those sampled in a prison setting or a probation service given that the presence of a personality disorder may be a requirement for admission in a psychiatric hospital. Furthermore, while the rates of rape, sexual assault, and sexual coercion on college and university campuses are significant and well documented (e.g., Koss, Gidycz, & Wisniewski, 1987), the prevalence of psychopathy among students approximates that of the general population (e.g., Forth, Brown, Hart, & Hare, 1996), which is quite low (Skeem & Mulvey, 2001). Second, the estimated prevalence of psychopathy varies across sex offender groups. Types of sexual offenses that also involve violence appear to be associated with a higher prevalence of psychopathic traits. For example, perpetrators of rape and sexual assault against an adult victim, as well as sexual murderers, are more likely to present with psychopathic personality traits than individuals having perpetrated a sex crime against a child (e.g., Porter et al., 2000; Porter, Woodworth, Earle, Drugge, & Boer, 2003; Quinsey et al., 1995). Thus the prevalence of psychopathy may vary across studies according to an individual study's composition of sexual offenders. It remains unclear, however, whether a particular subtype of perpetrators of violent sexual offenses (e.g., sadistic, opportunistic, angry) is more inclined to present a psychopathic personality profile (Barbaree, Seto, Serin, Amos, & Preston, 1994). More recent research seems to suggest a psychopathy-sexual sadism connection, as the two concepts share common grounds (e.g., emotional detachment; O'Connell & Marcus, 2019). That said, such discrepancies may have little to do with sexual offending per se but rather the differential proclivity for psychopathic sex offenders to be involved in nonsexual antisocial and criminal behavior.

The importance of psychopathy to the issue of sexual offending was more clearly established in the context of risk assessment and risk prediction in a maximum-security psychiatric institution. Pioneering work conducted in Penetanguishene, Ontario by a team of Canadian researchers contributed to the development of an actuarial risk assessment instrument for violent and sexual offenders soon to be released back into the community (Quinsey, Harris, Rice, & Cormier, 1998). Their research not only demonstrated that the probabilities of violent and sexual recidivism could be informed by using a series of individual characteristics, such as a person's age and criminal history features, but also by psychopathy, as measured by the PCL-R (Quinsey et al., 1995). In fact, their findings showed that for sex offenders in a maximum-security psychiatric institution, psychopathy was among the most important factors to consider for the prediction of violence and sexual recidivism. Many others followed this work by reexamining the psychopathy-sexual recidivism link among juvenile and adult offenders (e.g., Hill, Habermann, Klusmann, Berner, & Briken, 2008; Långström & Grann, 2000). Although there were contrasting findings across individual studies, Hawes, Boccaccini, and Murrie's (2013) meta-analysis of 20 studies showed that the statistical association between psychopathy as measured by the PCL-R and sexual recidivism was more important than previously reported (see Hanson & Morton-Bourgon, 2005). Their findings also showed that the predictive value of the PCL-R was strongly attributable to the Factor 2 of the PCL-R, and more specifically its antisocial facet. This was especially true for the prediction of sexual recidivism among perpetrators of rape. A subset of these studies also showed that offenders with evidence of psychopathy and sexual deviance were at a significantly higher risk of sexual recidivism. These findings reiterate the importance of acknowledging the role of antisociality in sexual offending and sexual recidivism (Lussier, Proulx, & LeBlanc, 2005).

Theoretical perspectives

The abovementioned interest in investigating the link between psychopathy as a personality disorder rather than legal distinction was strongly influenced by the availability of instruments like the PCL-R. In turn, this renewed interest gave rise to clinical theories regarding the relationship between psychopathy and sexual offending. The psychopathy-as-pathology perspective implies that the symptoms of this disorder are directly responsible for sexual offending. Knight and Sims-Knight (2004) outlined the causal nexus between abuse experiences, features of psychopathy, and cognitive distortions about sexual behavior, all of which converge to increase the likelihood of later involvement in sexual offending (also see Malamuth, 2003). In the context of dating, relationships, and other encounters, an individual's sense of entitlement may influence their attempt to overcome initial resistance to consensual sexual behavior. Overcoming resistance may be brought about by interpersonal symptoms of psychopathy (e.g., deception, manipulation, and coercion) that in turn result in their involvement in a sexual offense. Moreover, individuals may be less likely to feel deterred from harming others due to low levels of empathy and a lack of attachment to victims. Symptoms of psychopathy may disinhibit individuals by increasing the likelihood and intensity of negative emotional states such as anger and frustration when faced with perceived or actual adversities (e.g., being ignored, turned down, asked to stop; Proulx, McKibben, & Lusignan, 1996). Psychopathy may promote the use of coercion and violence after experiencing rejection given that such individuals are at an increased likelihood of having deviant sexual interests (Serin et al., 1994) and have a sense of entitlement and a rigid thinking style that discounts the opinions of others (Cooke, Hart, Logan, & Michie, 2004). Symptoms such as a lack of impulse control allow individuals to act on criminal opportunities (Morselli & Tremblay, 2004) and this may be true specifically for opportunities for sexual offenses even if the initial intent was not to commit a sexual offense (e.g., robbery, burglary; Pedneault, Harris, & Knight, 2012).

Clinical theories, although certainly receiving more attention given the prevalence of the assessment of psychopathy as part of clinical risk assessment, were not the only perspective on the link between psychopathy and sexual offending. In evolutionary theories concerning the relationship between psychopathy and sexual offending, instead of viewing psychopathy-as-pathology, psychopathy is viewed as an adaptive mating strategy (see Glenn et al., 2011). Rather than sexually offending because of specific symptoms or because of the accumulation of disadvantage that limits opportunity for consensual experiences (Seto & Barbaree, 1997), individuals with strong features of psychopathy will sexually offend as part of a distinct relational strategy that reflects an alternative lifestyle (e.g., Yochelson & Samenow, 1976). The evolutionary perspective suggests that individuals with psychopathic features engage in what is referred to as a fast life history mating strategy, which involves short-term partnerships, a high number of sexual partners, low investment in relationships, a neglectful parenting style, increased risk-taking, and selfish attitudes and behaviors (Glenn et al., 2011; Jonason et al., 2009). This mating strategy can also involve the use of coercion, deception, and other manipulation tactics consistent with the perpetration of a sex crime, especially when encountering sexual contexts (e.g., dates) involving an unwilling partner (Lalumière et al., 2005). In fact, contrary to the idea that sexual offenses are perpetrated by individuals with low social and heterosexual competence and few conventional sexual experiences, adult males adjudicated for a sexual offense report a number of noncoercive sexual experiences and sexual partners (e.g., Cortoni & Marshall, 2001). Prospective longitudinal studies have shown that one developmental feature predictive of juvenile sexual offending is an early onset of consensual sexual intercourse (Lussier, Blokland, Mathesius, Pardini, & Loeber, 2015).

The association between psychopathy and sexual offending rarely has been approached from a developmental perspective (but see Lawing, Frick, & Cruise, 2010). This perspective is concerned with the dynamic processes by which a phenotype emerges and evolves over time. At the intersection of psychopathy and sexual offending is a branch of developmental research referred to as developmental criminology (Loeber & Le Blanc, 1990). Developmental criminology is interested in the continuity and discontinuity of antisocial and criminal behavior across different age stages (e.g., Robins, 1978). Developmental criminologists argued that antisocial and criminal behavior develop in a hierarchical and predictable way along various pathways, with the earliest manifestations of such behavior occurring in early childhood (Loeber & Le Blanc, 1990). This is not to say that children's attitudinal, emotional, and behavioral adjustment problems are solely the result of features of psychopathy, nor is it to say that children will maintain features of psychopathy over the life course and therefore demonstrate a lifelong pattern of serious and violent offending. In fact, the expectation is that there will be more discontinuity than continuity of antisocial and criminal behavior over different age stages (Robins, 1978) and the same can be said about features of psychopathy (McCuish & Lussier, 2018). It is this point that underscores one of the key challenges of developmental criminology: identifying the factors responsible for the continuity and discontinuity of antisocial and criminal behavior as the child ages and is exposed to changing environments and settings. Until recently, this body of research has neglected the study of the development of psychopathy and sexual offending from the earliest age stages (e.g., McCuish & Lussier, 2018) despite suggestions that such personality traits do not emerge de novo in adulthood.

The limited body of developmental criminology research on sexual offending indicated that this behavior rarely continues across different age stages (e.g., Lussier & Blokland, 2014; Zimring, Piquero, & Jennings, 2007). As well, such crimes tend to occur against the backdrop of a criminal career primarily defined by involvement in nonsexual offenses. Moreover, offending trajectories of adolescents adjudicated for sexual offenses resemble those of adolescents adjudicated for nonsexual offenses (McCuish, Lussier, & Corrado, 2016). Developmental criminology therefore supports the viewpoint that sexual offenses are not a distinct phenomenon. On its own, involvement in a specific crime-type may not be informative of a person's broader criminal career or require specific explanation (Capaldi & Patterson, 1996). Thus, instead of looking at specific crime-types in isolation, developmental criminology is interested in timing, sequences, versatility, and aggravation of criminal behavior (Loeber & Le Blanc, 1990), all of which have been asserted to be associated with psychopathy. Features of psychopathy are an important indicator of an earlier onset of offending and greater offending versatility (McCuish, Corrado, Hart, & DeLisi, 2015; McCuish, Corrado, Lussier, & Hart, 2014). If individuals with features of psychopathy are involved in more frequent and versatile offending, it increases the probability that they will also be more likely to perpetrate sexual offenses. Similarly, the earlier onset of offending for such individuals implies that their sexual offenses will also emerge earlier in the life course compared to others. Such possibilities were directly examined in the current study.

The incarcerated serious and violent young offender study

From clinical, evolutionary, and developmental perspectives, psychopathy is expected to influence an earlier onset of sexual offending. However, in contrast with developmental criminology, clinical and evolutionary perspectives also assert that psychopathy is associated with continued sexual offending over the life course and, especially from evolutionary perspectives, is also associated with disproportionate involvement in sexual offenses relative to other crimes. This chapter used data from the Incarcerated Serious and Violent Young Offender Study (ISVYOS) to address four questions from these different perspectives. The four questions concerned whether individuals with strong features of psychopathy were more likely to (1) engage in sexual offenses,

(2) be involved in multiple sexual offenses, (3) demonstrate a specific proclivity for involvement in sexual offenses compared to other crimes, and (4) begin sexual offending at an earlier age.

The ISVYOS is an ongoing longitudinal study of males and females interviewed in youth custody facilities throughout British Columbia (BC), Canada. Participants were recruited between 1998 and 2011 with a data collection hiatus between 2003 and 2005. Participants are thus divided into Cohort 1 (1998–2003) and Cohort 2 (2005–11). Both cohorts were used in the current study. The BC Ministry of Child and Family Development is the caregiver to incarcerated youth and consented to the ISVYOS' recruitment of participants from custody centers throughout BC. Research assistants (RAs) approached youth while on their custody center unit to invite them to participate in the study. Approximately 5% of youth declined to participate. Participating youth were interviewed in a private room to ensure confidentiality. To obtain assent, participants were read and given a copy of an information sheet explaining the purpose of the study, how information would be collected (e.g., interview and file information), and that all information would be kept confidential unless the participant made a direct threat against themselves or someone else. Participants signed a form acknowledging that they understood the details of the study and that they could withdraw at any time.

The current study began with the subsample of ISVYOS participants who received a PCL:YV assessment (n=538). Females (n=97) were excluded because only 1% of this group were involved in sexual offenses. Participants were also excluded if their criminal record had been sealed (n=23) or if they were under age 20 at the time their criminal history was coded during the most recent wave of data collection (n=5). These exclusions led to a final sample of 413 males with a PCL:YV assessment. In terms of ethnicity, 59.1% of the sample was White (n=244). Compared to the general population of British Columbia (Statistics Canada, 2013), a disproportionate number of participants self-reported an Indigenous ethnic background (n=107; 25.9%). This overrepresentation was in line with the overrepresentation of Indigenous youth in custody in Canada (Malakieh, 2017). The remainder of the sample were of a non-Indigenous minority (e.g., Chinese, Indian, Black; n=59; 14.3%) or did not self-report their ethnic background (n=3; 0.7%).

Offending and psychopathy in the ISVYOS

Offending was measured using data from British Columbia Corrections' computerized system, Corrections Network (CORNET), which contained information on participants' movement in and out of custody as well as the exact criminal offense, date of conviction, and type of sentence received. Offending was measured for the entire sample from age 12 until their age at the most recent wave of data collection (M=30.69, SD=5.51; Range=20–39). The start of the follow-up period represented the minimum age of criminal responsibility in Canada. From that point on, every criminal charge (and crime-type) that resulted in a conviction was coded at each person-period observation (i.e., frequency of convictions at age 12, at age 13, etc.). The current study also looked at lifetime adjudications for sexual offenses. Individuals adjudicated for sexual offenses ($n=63$) were involved in crimes such as sexual assault, sexual interference (sexual-based offense against individuals under 14 years of age), and indecent exposure. Sixteen of these individuals (25.4% of the sample) were adjudicated for sexual offenses involving multiple victims, 11 of these individuals (17.5% of the sample) incurred separate charges for sexual offenses, and five individuals (7.9% of the sample) incurred charges for sexual offenses during both adolescence (ages 12–17) and adulthood (age 18 and older).

Features of psychopathy were measured using the PCL:YV, which is an expert-rating tool created to capture interpersonal, affective, and behavioral symptoms of psychopathy in adolescence (Forth, Kosson, & Hare, 2003). The 20 items of the PCL:YV are scored on a 0–2 scale (0 = item does not apply; 1 = item applies somewhat; 2 = item definitely applies) using information from a 60–90-min semistructured interview with the participant and a review of file information. PCL:YV assessments were completed when the participant was an average of 16.59 ($SD=1.34$) years of age. The average total score on the PCL:YV was 21.69 ($SD=6.68$). Although empirical evidence favors representing psychopathy as a dimensional construct (Edens, Marcus, Lilienfeld, & Poythress, 2006), there is also a history of examining individuals scoring high on a measure of psychopathy to all others. In the current study, consistent with previous literature examining the relationship between psychopathy and sexual offending (e.g., Declercq, Willemsen, Audenaert, & Verhaeghe, 2012), a score of at least 30 was used to denote a high score on the PCL:YV ($n=53$; 12.8% of the sample). Additional details regarding the scoring of the PCL:YV are provided by McCuish, Mathesius, Lussier, and Corrado (2018).

The relationship between psychopathy and sexual offending in the ISVYOS

The relationship between psychopathy and sexual offending was investigated in two stages. The first concerned between-group comparisons and involved inspecting whether features of psychopathy were more common among those adjudicated for sexual offenses compared to those adjudicated for nonsexual offenses. This line of analysis included an examination of whether specific features of psychopathy were responsible for any differences across these groups. The second stage of the analytic strategy focused on within-group differences in the relationship between features of psychopathy and sexual offending. Three questions were addressed that concerned whether features of psychopathy were associated with (1) adjudications for multiple sexual offenses, (2) a specific proclivity for sexual offending compared to other types of criminal behavior, and (3) the timing of a person's sexual offense.

Comparing features of psychopathy between offender groups from the ISVYOS

As shown in Table 1, individuals adjudicated for a sexual offense averaged significantly higher scores on the PCL:YV. The difference in total test scores was primarily

Table 1 PCL:YV item means and standard deviation for the full sample and across offending types.

	Full sample ($n=413$)		Adjudicated for sexual offenses ($n=63$)		Adjudicated for nonsexual offenses ($n=353$)		
	M	*SD*	*M*	*SD*	*M*	*SD*	Comparisons
PCL:YV items							
Glib/superficial charm	0.74	0.74	0.89	0.84	0.71	0.72	$t(402)=1.66$, *ns*
Grandiose sense of self worth[a]	0.81	0.76	0.94	0.72	0.78	0.77	$t(89.80)=1.56$, *ns*
Pathological lying	0.62	0.70	0.83	0.73	0.59	0.68	$t(408)=2.54$, $P<.05$
Conning/manipulative	1.02	0.74	1.17	0.76	1.00	0.73	$t(402)=1.65$, *ns*
Lack of remorse or guilt	1.37	0.68	1.49	0.60	1.35	0.69	$t(408)=1.48$, *ns*
Shallow affect	0.84	0.76	0.90	0.80	0.83	0.76	$t(410)=0.71$, *ns*
Callous/lack of empathy	1.20	0.70	1.41	0.64	1.16	0.70	$t(409)=2.68$, $P<.01$
Failure to accept responsibility	1.20	0.73	1.37	0.63	1.18	0.74	$t(408)=1.95$, *ns*
Stimulation seeking	1.26	0.66	1.24	0.74	1.27	0.65	$t(407)=0.29$, *ns*
Parasitic lifestyle	0.61	0.66	0.66	0.70	0.60	0.65	$t(392)=0.57$, *ns*
Lacks long-term goals	0.86	0.74	0.90	0.78	0.86	0.74	$t(402)=0.38$, *ns*
Impulsivity	1.14	0.69	1.15	0.70	1.14	0.68	$t(400)=0.02$, *ns*
Irresponsibility	1.19	0.66	1.15	0.69	1.19	0.65	$t(397)=0.42$, *ns*
Poor behavioral control[a]	1.43	0.68	1.52	0.59	1.41	0.69	$t(95.42)=1.39$, *ns*
Early behavioral problems	1.09	0.80	1.26	0.79	1.06	0.79	$t(377)=1.76$, *ns*
Juvenile delinquency[a]	1.75	0.44	1.83	0.38	1.74	0.45	$t(95.14)=1.60$, *ns*
Revocation of conditional release	1.37	0.77	1.33	0.85	1.38	0.76	$t(374)=0.48$, *ns*
Criminal versatility	1.56	0.70	1.65	0.68	1.54	0.70	$t(410)=1.10$, *ns*
Promiscuous sexual behavior	0.84	0.79	1.21	0.81	0.77	0.77	$t(372)=4.07$, $P<.001$
Short-term relationships[a]	0.70	0.76	0.98	0.82	0.65	0.74	$t(66.96)=2.76$, $P<.01$
PCL:YV score							
Total score	21.69	6.68	23.86	7.47	21.30	6.46	$t(411)=2.82$, $P<.01$
Interpersonal facet	3.20	2.16	3.81	2.25	3.09	2.13	$t(410)=2.48$, $P<.05$
Affective facet	4.61	2.15	5.16	2.08	4.51	2.15	$t(411)=2.22$, $P<.05$
Lifestyle facet	5.08	2.04	5.06	2.32	5.09	1.99	$t(411)=0.08$, *ns*
Antisocial facet	7.25	2.17	7.64	2.20	7.18	2.16	$t(411)=1.54$, *ns*

[a] Violated Levene's test for equality of variances; equal variances not assumed.

due to interpersonal and affective deficits, as those adjudicated for a sexual offense averaged higher scores on these facets but not the lifestyle and antisocial facets of the PCL:YV. The only items from the interpersonal and affective facets that were significantly higher for those adjudicated for a sex offense were the pathological lying and callousness/lack of empathy items. Short-term relationships and impersonal sexual behavior were also significantly higher for those adjudicated for a sexual offense. Based on a chi-square analysis, there was a significant association between having a high PCL:YV score and adjudication for a sexual offense (χ^2 [1] = 10.49, $P < .01$). The percentage of such individuals with a high PCL:YV score was more than double that for perpetrators of nonsexual offenses (25.4% versus 10.6%). The same substantive finding was observed using slightly lower test score thresholds (e.g., ≥ 27; ≥ 28).

Comparing psychopathy among perpetrators of sexual offenses from the ISVYOS

First, we examined whether features of psychopathy were significantly associated with any of three measures of repeat sexual offending: (1) having multiple victims (not necessarily multiple charges), (2) having multiple charges for a sex crime, and (3) being adjudicated for a sexual offense in both adolescence and adulthood. Regardless of how repeat sexual offending was measured, across those with and without repeat sexual offenses, there were no significant differences in average PCL:YV total scores and scores on each of the four facets ($P \geq .05$). Scoring high on the PCL:YV was also unrelated to the three measures of repeat sexual offending ($P \geq .05$). In other words, PCL:YV scores were not informative of whether an individual was involved in repeat or nonrepeat sexual offending, at least based on official criminal history.

Psychopathy and the crime-mix of perpetrators of sex offenses from the ISVYOS

Although repeat sexual offending was not more common among individuals with features of psychopathy, it was possible that such individuals showed a greater proclivity for sexual offending. This would be evidenced by a criminal career that consisted of a greater proportion of sexual offenses compared to other crime-types. To evaluate this, the aggregate crime-mix was examined through age 23. Over 90% of those adjudicated for a sexual offense were this age at the time of data collection; however, not all individuals were adjudicated for a sexual offense by this age. Fig. 1 displays the average crime-mix for those scoring high on the PCL:YV (Fig. 1A) and those whose score was lower than 30 (Fig. 1B).

These figures indicate that sexual offending constituted a very small proportion of the crime-mix for incarcerated adolescent males followed into adulthood, and this was true regardless of their score on the PCL:YV. A quarter of individuals scoring high on the PCL:YV incurred charges for more than one sexual offense. Over the same time-period, 56.3% of this group were convicted of multiple violent offenses, 81.3% were convicted of multiple property offenses, 87.5% were convicted

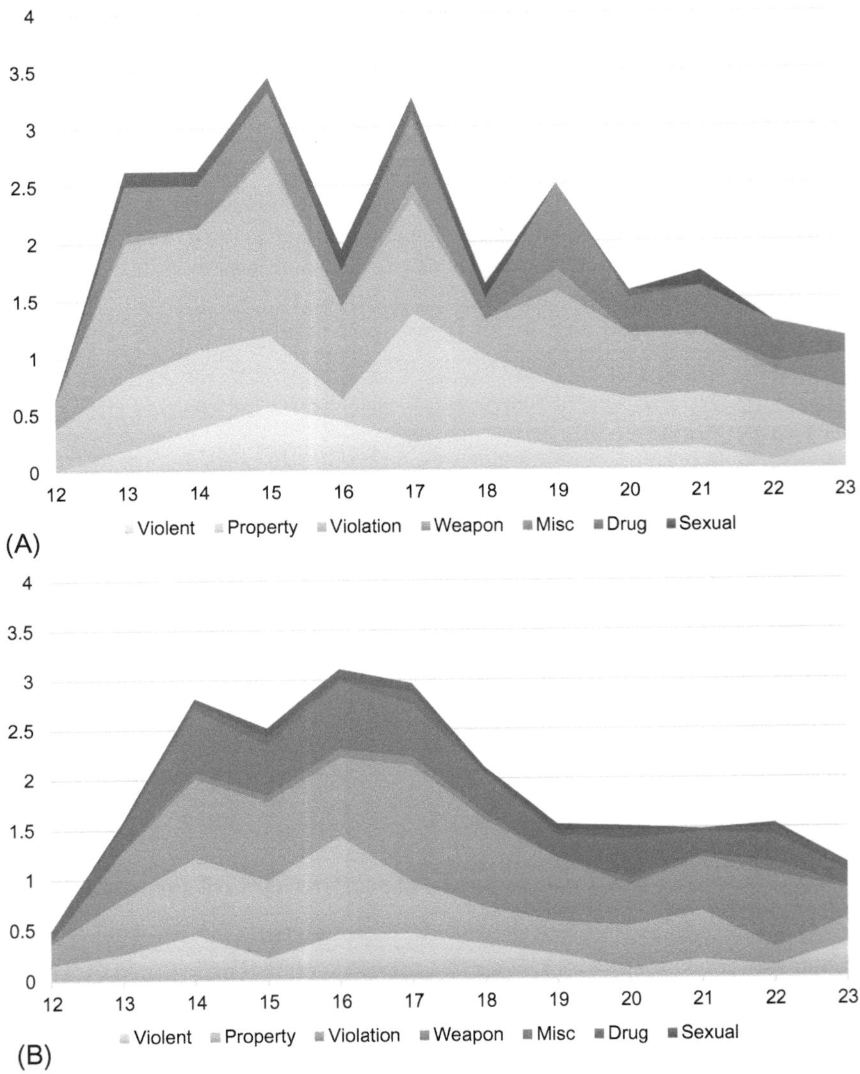

Fig. 1 (A) The crime-mix of persons with a HIGH score on the PCL:YV. A high score defined as 30 or higher on the PCL:YV. (B) The crime-mix of persons with a LOW score on the PCL:YV. A low score defined as below 30 on the PCL:YV. Each figure focuses solely on individuals adjudicated for a sexual offense.

of multiple violations of court orders, and 62.5% were convicted of multiple offenses falling under the miscellaneous category. The prevalence of having multiple convictions for weapons (25.0%) and drug (18.8%) convictions was similar when compared to the prevalence of multiple convictions for sexual offenses. In sum, for individuals scoring high on the PCL:YV, sexual offenses were among the rarest crime-types committed.

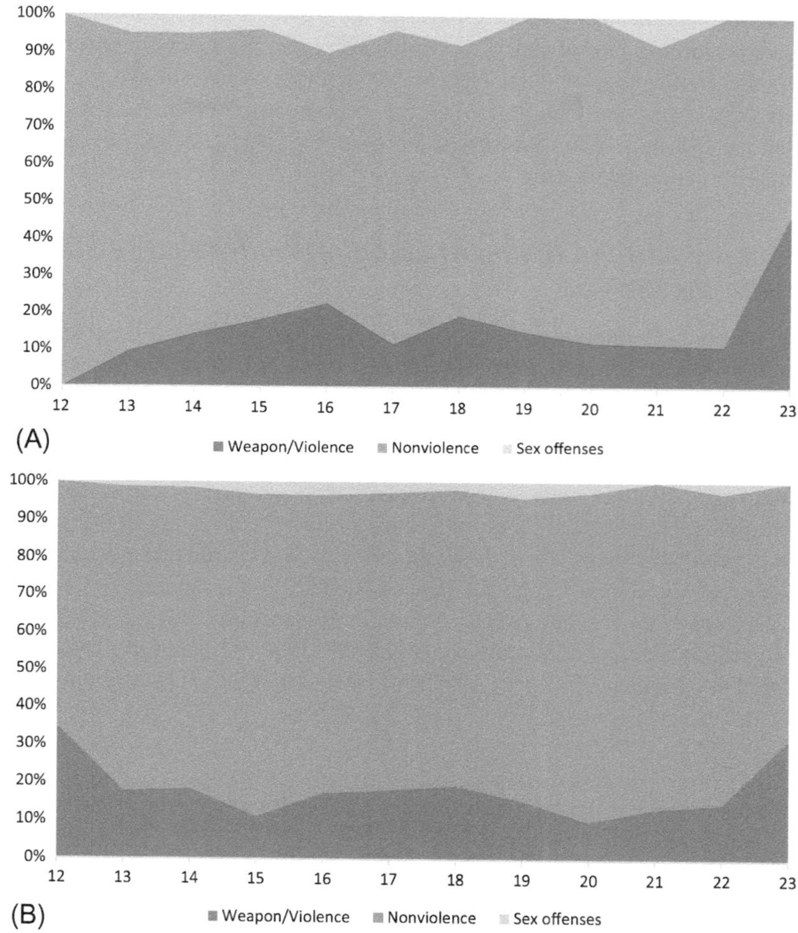

Fig. 2 (A) Proportion of an individual's total crime accounted for by weapon/violent crimes, nonviolent crimes, and sexual offenses (HIGH scores on the PCL:YV). A high score defined as 30 or higher on the PCL:YV. (B) Proportion of an individual's total crime accounted for by weapon/violent crimes, nonviolent crimes, and sexual offenses (LOW scores on the PCL:YV). A low score defined as below 30 on the PCL:YV. Each figure Each figure focuses solely on individuals adjudicated for a sexual offense.

Fig. 2 examines, for those scoring high on the PCL:YV (Fig. 2A) and those whose score was lower than 30 (Fig. 2B), the proportion of all convictions that were either (a) weapons or violent offenses, (b) nonviolent offenses, and (c) sexual offenses. Both these figures illustrate that convictions for sexual offenses comprise a small proportion of offenders' total criminal behavior. For those scoring high on the PCL:YV, sexual offenses never comprised more than 0.10 of the total proportion of all their convictions. For those with a score of less than 30, the proportion of their convictions that were sexual offenses never eclipsed 0.05. For both groups, nonviolent offenses (e.g., property, drug, violations, and miscellaneous offenses) formed the greatest proportion of their total offending. While those scoring high on the PCL:YV might not be specifically seeking opportunities for perpetrating sexual offenses, their continued involvement in criminal activities that includes targeting vulnerable populations (e.g., drug users, homeless persons, sexually exploited youths, persons involved in the sex trade) may make them at-risk of perpetrating sexual offenses that go undetected and therefore are not captured by the current data.

Psychopathy and the timing of adjudication for first sexual offense in the ISVYOS

Looking at Fig. 1A, individuals who scored high on the PCL:YV appeared more likely to have sexual offenses form part of their crime-mix at an earlier period of the life course. To directly examine this, an ANOVA analysis (Table 2) compared mean PCL:YV scores across individuals who were adjudicated for a sexual offense during adolescence (ages 12–17), individuals who were adjudicated for a sexual offense in adulthood (ages 18 and older), and individuals who were adjudicated for nonsexual offenses only.

Table 2 shows that those whose first adjudication for a sexual offense was in adolescence averaged significantly higher scores on the PCL:YV compared to the other two groups of offenders. The adolescence-onset individuals also averaged significantly higher scores on the interpersonal facet of the PCL:YV compared to those who were adjudicated for a sexual offense in adulthood. Average PCL:YV total scores and facet

Table 2 Timing of the sexual offense and features of psychopathy.

	Perpetrators of nonsexual offenses ($n=353$)	Adjudication for a sexual offense in adolescence ($n=40$)	Adjudication for a sexual offense in adulthood ($n=23$)	Comparisons
PCL:YV scores	*M* (*SD*)	*M* (*SD*)	*M* (*SD*)	
PCL:YV total	21.30 (6.46)[b]	25.60 (6.95)[a,c]	20.12 (7.32)[b]	$F(2, 410)=8.83$, $P<.001$
Interpersonal facet	3.09 (2.13)[b]	4.47 (2.07)[a,c]	2.42 (2.00)[b]	$F(2, 409)=9.53$, $P<.001$
Affective facet	4.51 (2.15)[b]	5.60 (1.96)[a]	4.23 (2.09)	$F(2, 410)=5.30$, $P<.01$
Lifestyle facet	5.09 (1.99)	5.36 (2.25)	4.43 (2.41)	$F(2, 410)=1.45$, *ns*
Antisocial facet	7.18 (2.16)	7.77 (2.13)	7.35 (2.37)	$F(2, 410)=1.45$, *ns*

Adolescents were first adjudicated for a sexual offense between ages 12 and 17. Adults were first adjudicated for a sexual offense at age 18 or older. Posthoc differences determined via Bonferroni correction.
[a] Significantly different from perpetrators of nonsexual offenses only.
[b] Significantly different from individuals adjudicated for a sexual offense in adolescence.
[c] Significantly different from individuals adjudicated for a sexual offense in adulthood.

scores did not vary when compared across those adjudicated for a sexual offense in adulthood and those who perpetrated nonsexual offenses. In other words, the relationship between features of psychopathy and adjudication for a sexual offense appeared specific to adjudications for sexual offenses early in the life course.

Fig. 3 was used to inspect the age of onset of adjudication for a sexual offense within an individual's broader criminal career. For example, did those with an adjudication for a sex crime in adolescence begin their criminal career with this offense? To inspect this in regards to features of psychopathy, the data were examined separately

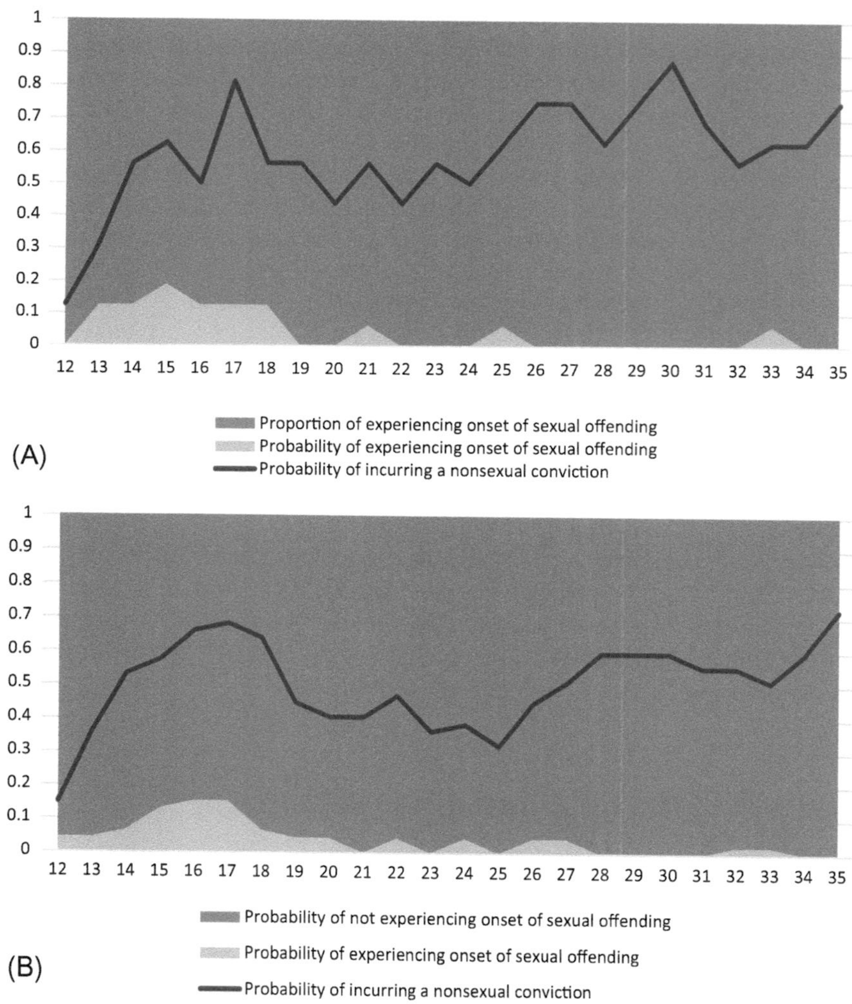

Fig. 3 (A) Proportion of individuals with a HIGH score on the PCL:YV that experienced their onset of sexual offending across each year of age. A high score defined as 30 or higher on the PCL:YV. (B) Proportion of individuals with a LOW score on the PCL:YV that experienced their onset of sexual offending across each year of age. A low score defined as below 30 on the PCL:YV. Each figure focuses solely on individuals adjudicated for a sexual offense.

for individuals with high (Fig. 3A) and low (Fig. 3B) PCL:YV scores. The shaded area represents the probability that an individual experienced the onset of adjudication for a sexual offense at each year of age. The line through the figure represents the probability that an individual incurred a nonsexual conviction at each year of age. Just over two-thirds of those who scored high on the PCL:YV were adjudicated for a sexual offense before age 18 compared to 58.7% of individuals with a score less than 30. For the former, the probability of first adjudication for a sexual offense peaked at age 15 and remained relatively stable during adolescence. In other words, it is not only a matter of being repeatedly involved in criminal activities and then using such offenses as opportunities to perpetrate sexual offenses against vulnerable victims. Rather, the findings suggest that psychopathic features may prompt someone to take advantage of someone sexually at first opportunity. For adolescent males with features of psychopathy, a diverse criminal repertoire was not required to first engage in a sexual offense. For those with a score less than 30, the probability of first adjudication for a sexual offense peaked at age 17. For both groups, the probability of incurring convictions for nonsexual offenses remained relatively high and stable throughout the life course. Those adjudicated for sexual offenses were active in nonsexual offenses before, at the time of, and after their adjudication for a sexual offense.

Although PCL:YV test scores were associated with an earlier onset of adjudication for a sexual offense, it may be the case that the stigmatization of being known to have committed a sexual offense influenced a higher rating on the PCL:YV. To examine this assertion, participants were split into three groups: males that perpetrated nonsexual offenses, males that were adjudicated for sexual offenses before their PCL:YV assessment, and males that were adjudicated for sexual offenses after their PCL:YV assessment. A series of ANOVA analyses (available from the first author) indicated that only the group that was adjudicated for a sexual offense prior to their PCL:YV rating averaged higher scores compared to males adjudicated for nonsexual offenses only. Thus a rival plausible explanation for the finding that PCL:YV scores were associated with an earlier adjudication for a sexual offense is that the ratings on at least some items (e.g., callous/lack of empathy, promiscuous sexual behavior, short-term relationships) were biased against persons with a history of sexual offending.

Summarizing the relationship of psychopathy and sexual offending

Both theoretical and empirical attention has been given to the relationship between psychopathy and sexual offending. These prior studies focused on lifetime involvement in sexual offenses (Lalumière & Quinsey, 1996), sexual offenses during a specific age range (Cale et al., 2015), and sexual recidivism (Quinsey et al., 1995) and observed that features of psychopathy were associated with an increased likelihood of sexual offending. The current study expanded on this research by addressing questions relevant to clinical, evolutionary, and developmental theories regarding psychopathy and sexual offending that pertained to (1) the relationship between psychopathy and repeated adjudication for sexual offenses, (2) whether features of psychopathy were related to a specific proclivity for sexual offending compared to other types of criminal behavior, and (3) whether features of psychopathy were associated with an earlier adjudication for sexual offenses. These questions were addressed using a sample of incarcerated male adolescents who received a PCL:YV rating and were followed into adulthood (n=413). The current study design is distinct from prior research on sexual offending in that it includes a large comparison group of individuals who were only adjudicated for nonsexual offenses. It also departs from most recidivism studies by following adolescents well beyond a 3-year period and examining sexual offending in both adolescence and adulthood. In line with prior research, although features of psychopathy were associated with a history of sexual offending (Cale et al., 2015), features of psychopathy were unrelated to sexual recidivism (Edens, Campbell, & Weir, 2007). This also resembled Lawing et al.'s (2010) finding that callous-unemotional (CU) traits were not associated with the duration of an adolescent's sexual offending. However, unlike the current study, Lawing et al. (2010) found that individuals with high CU traits averaged a greater number of victims. These differences may be related to the current study's focus on the broader psychopathy construct rather than specific traits.

Prior studies on adult sexual recidivism showed that psychopathy, typically measured using the PCL-R, was a significant but modest risk factor for sexual recidivism (e.g., Hawes et al., 2013; Quinsey et al., 1995), which justified its inclusion in some risk assessment tools (e.g., Quinsey et al., 1998). Like the current study, these adult studies were almost exclusively based on official data about sexual offending, which therefore eliminates the current study's use of official data as a possible explanation for why the current study's findings were inconsistent with prior research on the relationship between psychopathy and sexual recidivism. One reasonable explanation for these inconsistencies is that features of psychopathy, as measured in the current study, were more dynamic than initially believed (McCuish & Lussier, 2018). Those with high scores on the PCL:YV may present a clinical profile that can be misconstrued as stable psychopathic features when in reality such features represent a developing youth with emotional and behavioral difficulties that may improve with increased maturity. In other words, before concluding that adolescent features of psychopathy are not associated with continued sexual offending over the life course it is necessary to distinguish between individuals who score high on instruments in adolescence but not in adulthood and adolescents that continue to score high on such instruments across the life course. This research indicates that it is hazardous to make long-term predictions about the sexual offending patterns of youth, even when using well-known and validated tools like the PCL:YV.

Those adjudicated for a sexual offense were primarily involved in nonsexual offenses, which was consistent with research focusing solely on adults (Serin, Mailloux, & Malcolm, 2001). By inspecting the aggregate crime-mix, the current study also found that individuals who scored high on the PCL:YV typically did not show a specific proclivity for being adjudicated for sexual offenses. These individuals tended to engage in a wide range of nonsexual offenses that emerged before, during, and after their involvement in a sexual offense. In effect, although having a high score on the PCL:YV was associated with involvement in sexual offending, sexual offending was atypical when looking at the broader offending patterns of such individuals. This was in line with suggestions that sexual offending would be a part of a broader repertoire of criminal behavior (Knight & Sims-Knight, 2004; Lussier, 2005; Malamuth, 2003). Findings were also in line with developmental criminology perspectives concerning the importance of examining the timing and sequencing of offenses rather than focusing on a specific type of crime. Regarding offense timing, the current study also that the relationship between features of psychopathy and sexual offending appeared specific to sexual offenses that emerged in adolescence (ages 12–17) rather than adulthood (ages 18–35 in the current study).

Explicating the psychopathy-sexual offending relationship

Historical viewpoints on the psychopathy-sexual offending relationship began with an emphasis on legal distinctions of certain offenders as "psychopaths" that justified their indeterminate detention in custody centers, psychiatric hospitals, and treatment centers (Jenkins, 1998). This initial viewpoint was tautological in that it was a common belief that all dangerous sex offenders were "psychopaths" simply because of the nature of the offense. More contemporary theories focused on clinical and evolutionary perspectives to explain the link between psychopathy and sexual offending (Hawes et al., 2013). However, there is still room for theoretical refinement. Such refinement should give consideration to two principles: sensitivity and specificity. Sensitivity requires the identification of an outcome that is highly probable for individuals with strong features of psychopathy and specificity requires that the outcome being explained is not also common among individuals that do not present with strong features of psychopathy. Sexual offending is too common (Koss et al., 1987) and strong features of psychopathy too rare (Skeem & Mulvey, 2001) for the latter to adequately account for the former.

Thinking about the sensitivity component, we argue that greater attention should be given to the situational dynamics that come prior to the sexual offense. In line with situational action theory (Wikström & Treiber, 2009), an individual's propensity, when interacting with an appropriate environmental context, increases the probability of an offense. With respect to psychopathy and sexual offending, certain symptoms can help create an increased propensity for sexual offending via both a disinhibiting role (e.g., lack of control, impulsivity, callous and selfish) but also as a powerful motivational factor (e.g., hostility toward women, desire to dominate or demonstrate power) for perpetrating a sexual offense. This assertion balances early perspectives on the asexual nature of the sexual offenses perpetrated by individuals with features of psychopathy (Cleckley, 1955) with more contemporary perspectives on features of psychopathy increasing the likelihood of adhering to an antisocial lifestyle to increase the availability of opportunities for sexual gratification (Samenow, 1984). As shown in the current study, there is a tendency for individuals with features of psychopathy to engage in a wide range of offenses, the vast majority of which are nonsexual. Future research (but also see Pedneault et al., 2012) should examine whether the tendency to engage in many different types of nonsexual offenses exposes offenders to opportunities for sexual offenses. Features of psychopathy may create environmental contexts conducive to involvement in a sexual offense and may influence individuals to act on this opportunity because of their low levels of self-control or their inability to develop appropriate emotional responses to their victim's distress. In sum, although speculative at this point, it is possible that features of psychopathy directly influence sexual offending through a disregard for the feelings of others and a heightened tendency for deviant sexual interests (Serin et al., 1994), but it is also possible that features of psychopathy increase the likelihood of early and serious involvement in antisocial and criminal behavior (e.g., gang-related activities, robberies, burglaries, drug dealing, sexual exploitation) and that such behaviors create various opportunities to perpetrate sexual offenses (e.g., Lussier, Proulx, & LeBlanc, 2005; Pedneault et al., 2012).

Specificity, on the other hand, requires accounting for the observation that the prevalence of sex offending is greater than the prevalence of persons with strong features of psychopathy (Koss et al., 1987; Skeem & Mulvey, 2001). Unlike historical perspectives (Jenkins, 1998), most individuals involved in sexual offenses will not present with strong features of psychopathy. We recommend giving greater attention to specific features of the sexual offense event that may be more specific to individuals with features of psychopathy. Although the lack of consent (e.g., the victim is coerced into sex, the victim is too young to consent, the victim is intoxicated) is a core feature of sexual offenses, those with strong features of psychopathy may be particularly likely to act on opportunities where the victim is vulnerable (e.g., intoxication, involvement in the sex trade, dating context). Indeed, it may not be the "sexual offense" that matters, but rather the nature of the interaction between offender and victim that can trigger the perpetration of a sexual offense. Individuals with features of psychopathy may have a specific tendency to engage in sexual behaviors, criminal or otherwise, that involve aspects of deception, manipulativeness, boldness, and coercion. Research would therefore involve linking psychopathy to specific forms of sexual deviancy that (a) emerge in contexts associated with manipulativeness, deceit, dominance, and a callous disregard for the well-being of others and (b) occur in situational contexts where there may be a vulnerable victim during the commission of a nonsexual offense or where traits like low self-control and sensation seeking behaviors increase the likelihood that the perpetrator act on opportunities to sexually offend.

Conclusions

The current study observed a relationship between psychopathy and sexual offending, but not for repeated adjudications for sexual offenses and not in terms of a specific proclivity for sexual offending compared to other types of criminal behavior. It appeared that features of psychopathy were associated with an earlier adjudication for sexual offenses. Among those adjudicated for a sexual offense, the current study did not distinguish according to victim-type. The importance of psychopathy to explanations of sexual offending may vary across studies simply because of differences in the composition of types of sexual offenses (e.g., Porter et al., 2000; Quinsey et al., 1995) and thus comparing the current study to others should be done with caution. Theoretical descriptions should consider whether the relationship between psychopathy and sexual offending varies according to which of three dimensions of sexual offending (i.e., sexual violence and abuse, sexual misconduct, and sexual exploitation; Lussier & Mathesius, 2018) the behavior falls under. Future research should also consider the interactions between victim and offender that preceded the sexual offense. Features of psychopathy may be more informative of the nature of this interaction than they are of involvement in sexual offending more broadly.

Although the current study measured sexual offending across multiple developmental periods, the same was not true for the PCL:YV. The argument that psychopathy will be associated with continued sexual offending over the life course is dependent on the assumption that features of the disorder remain stable over time. This assumption has not always received empirical support; features of psychopathy in adolescence are not necessarily informative of features of psychopathy in adulthood (McCuish & Lussier, 2018). Future research is needed that accounts for the instability of features of psychopathy. This instability may help explain the lack of a relationship between features of psychopathy in adolescence and continued involvement in sexual offenses through adulthood.

The current study also introduced the possibility that the timing of the PCL:YV assessment in relation to the timing of a person's adjudication for a sexual offense is important for their PCL:YV score. It is possible that individuals who engage in sexual offenses earlier in the life course are expected to demonstrate a higher prevalence of neuropsychological perturbations (Moffitt, 1993). Early onset sexual offenders may be more likely to be characterized by features of psychopathy given that other risk factors may be less relevant to this age stage (e.g., unemployment, substance use, marital problems, loneliness, hostility toward women). A rival explanation is that although persons responsible for scoring the PCL:YV should consider the extent to which the instrument's items manifest over different periods of time and different social contexts, it is possible that raters placed too much emphasis on a person's adjudication for a sexual offense when scoring certain items. Future research could address this question by conducting interrater reliability analyses of raters who are, or are not, exposed to information about a person's sexual offense.

Acknowledgments

This work was supported by the Social Sciences and Humanities Research Council of Canada [410-2004-1875]. In addition, the authors gratefully acknowledge the assistance of the British Columbia Ministry of Children and Family Development (MCFD). The views expressed herein are those of the authors and do not necessarily reflect the views or policies of the agencies that funded or supported the research.

Conflict of interest

The authors declare that they have no conflict of interest.

Ethical approval

The authors attest that they have complied with ethical standards, including, but not limited to, oversight by the Simon Fraser University Research Ethics Board and the Ministry of Child and Family Development.

References

Abrahamsen, D. (1950). Study of 102 sex offenders at Sing Sing. *Federal Probation*, *14*, 26–32.

Alder, C. (1984). The convicted rapist: A sexual or a violent offender? *Criminal Justice and Behavior*, *11*(2), 157–177.

Barbaree, H. E., Seto, M. C., Serin, R. C., Amos, N. L., & Preston, D. L. (1994). Comparisons between sexual and nonsexual rapist subtypes: Sexual arousal to rape, offense precursors, and offense characteristics. *Criminal Justice and Behavior*, *21*(1), 95–114.

Cale, J., Lussier, P., McCuish, E., & Corrado, R. (2015). The prevalence of psychopathic personality disturbances among incarcerated youth: Comparing serious, chronic, violent and sex offenders. *Journal of Criminal Justice*, *43*, 337–344.

Capaldi, D. M., & Patterson, G. R. (1996). Can violent offenders be distinguished from frequent offenders: Prediction from childhood to adolescence. *Journal of Research in Crime and Delinquency*, *33*, 206–231.

Caputo, A. A., Frick, P. J., & Brodsky, S. L. (1999). Family violence and juvenile sex offending: The potential mediating role of psychopathic traits and negative attitudes toward women. *Criminal Justice and Behavior*, *26*, 338–356.

Cleckley, H. M. (1955). *The mask of sanity: An attempt to clarify some issues about the so-called psychopathic personality*. St-Louis, MI: Mosby.

Cohen, E. S. (1956). Administration of the criminal sexual psychopath statute in Indiana. *Indiana Law Journal*, *32*, 450–467.

Cooke, D. J., Hart, S. D., Logan, C., & Michie, C. (2004). *Comprehensive assessment of psychopathic personality—Institutional rating scale (CAPP-IRS)*. Glasgow, UK: Department of Psychology, Glasgow Caledonian University.

Cortoni, F., & Marshall, W. L. (2001). Sex as a coping strategy and its relationship to juvenile sexual history and intimacy in sexual offenders. *Sexual Abuse*, *13*, 27–43.

Declercq, F., Willemsen, J., Audenaert, K., & Verhaeghe, P. (2012). Psychopathy and predatory violence in homicide, violent, and sexual offences: Factor and facet relations. *Legal and Criminological Psychology*, *17*, 59–74.

Edens, J. F., Campbell, J. S., & Weir, J. M. (2007). Youth psychopathy and criminal recidivism: A meta-analysis of the psychopathy checklist measures. *Law and Human Behavior*, *31*, 53–75.

Edens, J. F., Marcus, D. K., Lilienfeld, S. O., & Poythress, N. G., Jr. (2006). Psychopathic, not psychopath: Taxometric evidence for the dimensional structure of psychopathy. *Journal of Abnormal Psychology*, *115*, 131–144.

Forth, A. E., Brown, S. L., Hart, S. D., & Hare, R. D. (1996). The assessment of psychopathy in male and female noncriminals: Reliability and validity. *Personality and Individual Differences*, *20*(5), 531–543.

Forth, A. E., Kosson, D. S., & Hare, R. (2003). *The hare psychopathy checklist: Youth version*. New York, NY: Multi-Health Systems.

Gebhard, P. H., Gagnon, J. H., Pomeroy, W. B., & Christenson, C. V. (1965). *Sex offenders: An analysis of types*. London: Heinemann.

Glenn, A. L., Kurzban, R., & Raine, A. (2011). Evolutionary theory and psychopathy. *Aggression and Violent Behavior*, *16*, 371–380.

Groth, A. N., & Burgess, A. W. (1977). Rape: A sexual deviation. *American Journal of Orthopsychiatry*, *47*(3), 400–406.

Hacker, F. J., & Frym, M. (1955). The sexual psychopath act in practice: A critical discussion. *California Law Review*, *43*, 766–779.

Hanson, R. K., & Morton-Bourgon, K. E. (2005). The characteristics of persistent sexual offenders: A meta-analysis of recidivism studies. *Journal of Consulting and Clinical Psychology*, *73*(6), 1154.

Hare, R. D. (1985). *The psychopathy checklist*. Psychology Department, University of British Columbia.

Hawes, S. W., Boccaccini, M. T., & Murrie, D. C. (2013). Psychopathy and the combination of psychopathy and sexual deviance as predictors of sexual recidivism: Meta-analytic findings using the psychopathy checklist—Revised. *Psychological Assessment*, *25*, 233.

Hill, A., Habermann, N., Klusmann, D., Berner, W., & Briken, P. (2008). Criminal recidivism in sexual homicide perpetrators. *International Journal of Offender Therapy and Comparative Criminology*, *52*(1), 5–20.

Jenkins, P. (1998). *Moral panic: Changing concepts of the child molester in modern America*. New Haven, CT: Yale University Press.

Jonason, P. K., Li, N. P., Webster, G. D., & Schmitt, D. P. (2009). The dark triad: Facilitating a short-term mating strategy in men. *European Journal of Personality*, *23*(1), 5–18.

Karpman, B. (1948). The myth of the psychopathic personality. *American Journal of Psychiatry*, *104*(9), 523–534.

Karpman, B. (1951). The sexual psychopath. *The Journal of Criminal Law and Criminology*, *42*, 184–198.

Knight, R. A., Rosenberg, R., & Schneider, B. A. (1985). Classification of sexual offenders: Perspectives, methods, and validation. In *Rape and sexual assault: A research handbook* (pp. 222–293).

Knight, R. A., & Sims-Knight, J. E. (2004). Testing an etiological model for male juvenile sex offending against females. *Journal of Child Sexual Abuse*, *13*, 33–55.

Kopp, S. B. (1962). The character structure of sex offenders. *American Journal of Psychotherapy*, *16*(1), 64–70.

Koss, M. P., Gidycz, C. A., & Wisniewski, N. (1987). The scope of rape: Incidence and prevalence of sexual aggression and victimization in a national sample of higher education students. *Journal of Consulting and Clinical Psychology*, *55*, 162–170.

Lalumière, M. L., Harris, G. T., Quinsey, V. L., & Rice, M. E. (2005). *The causes of rape: Understanding individual differences in male propensity for sexual aggression*. Washington, DC: American Psychological Association.

Lalumière, M. L., & Quinsey, V. L. (1996). Sexual deviance, antisociality, mating effort, and the use of sexually coercive behaviors. *Personality and Individual Differences*, *21*, 33–48.

Långström, N., & Grann, M. (2000). Risk for criminal recidivism among young sex offenders. *Journal of Interpersonal Violence*, *15*(8), 855–871.

Lawing, K., Frick, P., & Cruise, K. (2010). Differences in offending patterns between adolescent sex offenders high or low in callous—Unemotional traits. *Psychological Assessment*, *22*, 298–305.
Le Maire, L. (1956). Danish experiences regarding the castration of sexual offenders. *The Journal of Criminal Law and Criminology*, *47*, 294–310.
Loeber, R., & Le Blanc, M. (1990). Toward a developmental criminology. In M. Tonry, & N. Morris (Eds.), *Crime and justice* (pp. 375–473). Chicago, IL: University of Chicago Press.
Lussier, P. (2005). The criminal activity of sexual offenders in adulthood: Revisiting the specialization debate. *Sexual Abuse*, *17*, 269–292.
Lussier, P., & Blokland, A. (2014). The adolescence-adulthood transition and Robins's continuity paradox: Criminal career patterns of juvenile and adult sex offenders in a prospective longitudinal birth cohort study. *Journal of Criminal Justice*, *42*, 153–163.
Lussier, P., Blokland, A., Mathesius, J., Pardini, D., & Loeber, R. (2015). The childhood risk factors of adolescent-onset and adult-onset of sex offending: Evidence from a prospective longitudinal study. In A. Blokland, & P. Lussier (Eds.), *Sex offenders: A criminal career approach* (pp. 53–70). John Wiley & Sons.
Lussier, P., & Mathesius, J. (2018). Not in my backyard: Public sex offender registries and public notification laws. *Canadian Journal of Criminology and Criminal Justice*, *61*, 105–116.
Lussier, P., Proulx, J., & LeBlanc, M. (2005). Criminal propensity, deviant sexual interests and criminal activity of sexual aggressors against women: A comparison of explanatory models. *Criminology*, *43*(1), 249–282.
Malakieh, J. (2017). Youth correctional statistics in Canada, 2015/2016. *Statistics Canada*.
Malamuth, N. M. (2003). Criminal and non-criminal sexual aggressors: Integrating psychopathy in a hierarchical-mediational confluence model. In R. A. Prentky, E. Janus, & M. Seto (Eds.), *Understanding and managing sexually coercive behavior* (pp. 33–58). New York, NY: New York Academy of Sciences.
McCuish, E. C., Corrado, R. R., Hart, S. D., & DeLisi, M. (2015). The role of symptoms of psychopathy in persistent violence over the criminal career into full adulthood. *Journal of Criminal Justice*, *43*, 345–356.
McCuish, E. C., Corrado, R., Lussier, P., & Hart, S. D. (2014). Psychopathic traits and offending trajectories from early adolescence to adulthood. *Journal of Criminal Justice*, *42*, 66–76.
McCuish, E. C., & Lussier, P. (2018). A developmental perspective on the stability and change of psychopathic personality traits across the adolescence–adulthood transition. *Criminal Justice and Behavior*, *45*, 666–692.
McCuish, E., Lussier, P., & Corrado, R. (2016). Criminal careers of juvenile sex and nonsex offenders: Evidence from a prospective longitudinal study. *Youth Violence and Juvenile Justice*, *14*, 199–224.
McCuish, E. C., Mathesius, J. R., Lussier, P., & Corrado, R. R. (2018). The cross-cultural generalizability of the psychopathy checklist: Youth version for adjudicated indigenous youth. *Psychological Assessment*, *30*, 192–203.
Moffitt, T. E. (1993). Adolescence-limited and life-course-persistent antisocial behavior: A developmental taxonomy. *Psychological Review*, *100*, 674–701.
Morselli, C., & Tremblay, P. (2004). Criminal achievement, offender networks and the benefits of low self-control. *Criminology*, *42*, 773–804.
O'Connell, D., & Marcus, D. K. (2019). A meta-analysis of the association between psychopathy and sadism in forensic samples. *Aggression and Violent Behavior*, *46*, 109–115.
Parks, G. A., & Bard, D. E. (2006). Risk factors for adolescent sex offender recidivism: Evaluation of predictive factors and comparison of three groups based upon victim type. *Sexual Abuse: A Journal of Research and Treatment*, *18*, 319–342.

Pedneault, A., Harris, D. A., & Knight, R. A. (2012). Toward a typology of sexual burglary: Latent class findings. *Journal of Criminal Justice*, *40*, 278–284.

Porter, S., Fairweather, D., Drugge, J., Herve, H., Birt, A., & Boer, D. P. (2000). Profiles of psychopathy in incarcerated sexual offenders. *Criminal Justice and Behavior*, *27*(2), 216–233.

Porter, S., Woodworth, M., Earle, J., Drugge, J., & Boer, D. (2003). Characteristics of sexual homicides committed by psychopathic and nonpsychopathic offenders. *Law and Human Behavior*, *27*(5), 459–470.

Proulx, J., McKibben, A., & Lusignan, R. (1996). Relationships between affective components and sexual behaviors in sexual aggressors. *Sexual Abuse*, *8*, 279–289.

Quinsey, V. L., Harris, G. T., Rice, M. E., & Cormier, C. A. (1998). *Violent offenders: Appraising and managing risk*. American Psychological Association.

Quinsey, V. L., Rice, M. E., & Harris, G. T. (1995). Actuarial prediction of sexual recidivism. *Journal of Interpersonal Violence*, *10*, 85–105.

Robins, L. N. (1978). Sturdy childhood predictors of adult antisocial behaviour: Replications from longitudinal studies. *Psychological Medicine*, *8*(4), 611–622.

Samenow, S. E. (1984). *Inside the criminal mind*. Times Book.

Serin, R. C., Mailloux, D. L., & Malcolm, P. B. (2001). Psychopathy, deviant sexual arousal, and recidivism among sexual offenders. *Journal of Interpersonal Violence*, *16*, 234–246.

Serin, R. C., Malcolm, P. B., Khanna, A., & Barbaree, H. E. (1994). Psychopathy and deviant sexual arousal in incarcerated sexual offenders. *Journal of Interpersonal Violence*, *9*, 3–11.

Seto, M. C., & Barbaree, H. E. (1997). Sexual aggression as antisocial behavior: A developmental model. In D. M. Stoff, J. Breiling, & J. D. Maser (Eds.), *Handbook of antisocial behavior* (pp. 524–533). Hoboken, NJ: John Wiley & Sons Inc.

Seto, M. C., & Barbaree, H. E. (1999). Psychopathy, treatment behavior, and sex offender recidivism. *Journal of Interpersonal Violence*, *14*, 1235–1248.

Skeem, J. L., & Mulvey, E. P. (2001). Psychopathy and community violence among civil psychiatric patients: Results from the MacArthur violence risk assessment study. *Journal of Consulting and Clinical Psychology*, *69*, 358–374.

Statistics Canada. (2013). British Columbia (Code 59) (table). National Household Survey (NHS) Aboriginal Population Profile. 2011 National Household Survey. Statistics Canada Catalogue no. 99-011-X2011007. Ottawa. Released November 13, 2013. http://www12.statcan.gc.ca/nhs-enm/2011/dp-pd/aprof/index.cfm?Lang=E (accessed April 6, 2014).

Sutherland, E. H. (1950). The diffusion of sexual psychopath laws. *American Journal of Sociology*, *56*(2), 142–148.

Wikström, P.-O. H., & Treiber, K. H. (2009). Violence as situational action. *International Journal of Conflict and Violence*, *3*(1), 75–96.

Yochelson, S., & Samenow, S. (1976). *The criminal personality*. New York, NY: Aronson.

Zimring, F. E., Piquero, A. R., & Jennings, W. G. (2007). Sexual delinquency in racine: Does early sex offending predict later sex offending in youth and young adulthood? *Criminology & Public Policy*, *6*, 507–534.

Psychopathy is integral to understanding homicide and violence

16

Matt DeLisi and Bryanna Fox

Introduction

A versatile offender and intravenous methamphetamine user, one man from our clinical experiences sat in his vehicle after police stopped him for a traffic violation. On parole and carrying a loaded firearm, the prior felon politely conversed with the officer upon first contact. The officer went back to his car to run the vehicle's tags, and as he returned, the offender shot the officer in the mouth. The officer fell to the ground and was grievously wounded. With an alarming sense of insouciance, the suspect frisked the officer—searching in vain for his driver's license—then stole the officer's firearm and, shortly thereafter, his vehicle. The dying officer's body worn camera captured all of this interaction. While in custody, the forensic examiner showed the offender this video. With no display of affect, the offender acknowledged to the forensic examiner, "That is going to look bad in court." The court convicted the defendant of capital murder and sentenced him to death.

Those dealing with the most violent criminal offenders will likely recognize the interpersonal, behavioral, and affective traits from this anecdote. The reason is that this constellation of traits and behaviors—coalescing in a condition known as psychopathy—appears consistently among the most violent and severe offenders in the criminal population. Indeed, the current authors have more than four decades of experiences interacting with serious criminal offenders in a variety of roles including law enforcement, pretrial services, clinical assessment, and research. These experiences and interaction with thousands of criminal defendants are consistent with DeLisi's (2009, 2016) thesis that psychopathy is the unified theory of crime because features of the disorder are congruent with antisocial conduct from early childhood through adulthood and across multitudinous forms of deviance (for other explorations of its generality, see, Bergstrøm, Larmour, & Farrington, 2018; Fox, Jennings, & Farrington, 2015; Hare, 1993, 1996). The association between psychopathy and criminal violence is so resounding that it is as if psychopathy was a sinister blueprint to create a prototypical antisocial person. Here, we briefly highlight recent research on psychopathy and homicide, sexual, and general violent offending. Space limitations preclude an exhaustive review of these topics, but we profile particularly insightful studies and meta-analyses to provide the reader with a comprehensive view of their empirical associations. Last, we offer insights from our assorted experiences to refine, advance, and extend the psychopathy construct.

Psychopathy and Criminal Behavior. https://doi.org/10.1016/B978-0-12-811419-3.00012-1

Psychopathy and homicide offending

The nightly news is replete with examples of homicide offenders who kill their victims usually for banal circumstances and where the criminal conduct reveals profound characterological deficits. A closer inspection of many homicides reveals that the offender is pathologically self-centered and thoroughly indifferent not only to the victim's feelings, but also to their victim's very existence. For instance, sexual homicide involves the killing of a victim to facilitate, heighten, or punctuate sexual gratification. In most cases—sexual homicides constitute a fraction of all murders—a homicide reflects the offender's desire to end an argument, to silence a perceived annoyance, or to eliminate a potential witness. Lethal violence is a by-product of a personality style dominated by entitlement and callousness. It should be no surprise that psychopathy permeates homicide offending.

The evidence for an empirical linkage between homicide and psychopathy is abundant and diverse. Jolliffe, Loeber, Farrington, and Cotter (2011) compared youth who had been convicted of homicide to other violent offenders in the Pittsburgh Youth Study, and found that homicidal youth were significantly more psychopathic than other delinquents. Homicide offenders scored nearly four times higher than controls on arrogance and deceitfulness, more than 26 times higher on deficient affective experience, over 54 times higher on impulsive and irresponsible lifestyle, and nearly 38 times higher on juvenile delinquency and criminal versatility. These are gargantuan differences. Although fewer than 15% of delinquent controls were clinically psychopathic, nearly 70% of the homicide offenders were clinical psychopaths. In addition, the predominant emotional reaction during the commission of their homicide was no emotional reaction, with 30% of homicide offenders reported feeling absolutely nothing emotionally while murdering their victim. Furthermore, over 40% reported feeling nothing or a general sense of numbness after their offense.

Deficits in emotional life and conscience are nearly comical in their absurdity among criminal psychopaths. During a forensic interview with a chronic offender, one of us asked the defendant how many people he had shot during his criminal career (records indicated he had shot four people). With a nonchalant shrug of the shoulders, the defendant stated, "Just three." Another interviewee described perpetrating homicides while in prison confinement and even simulated the areas on one victim's body where he had stabbed. When asked if the attack resulted in the other inmate's death, the defendant quietly laughed and reported, "No, I guess I must not have got him in the heart." Affective deficits are so complete that psychopathic offenders routinely describe their violent acts in a deliberative, detached, almost clinical manner.

Psychopathy also affects the manner and qualitative nature of homicide. Woodworth and Porter (2002) studied the homicides of 125 Canadian offenders, some of whom were psychopathic and others who were not. They found that more than 93% of the homicides by psychopaths were instrumental in nature. Comparatively, about 48% of homicides by nonpsychopaths were instrumental. Less than 7% of homicides by psychopaths were reactive compared to 52% among nonpsychopathic offenders. In a related study, Porter, Woodworth, Earle, Drugge, and Boer (2003) reported that nearly

85% of sexual murderers scored in the moderate to high range on psychopathy. The psychopaths' sexual homicides were also more violent, sadistic, and gratuitous than their nonpsychopathic homicidal peers.

Despite these studies, criminologists have only recently quantified the association between homicide and psychopathy. In a landmark work, Fox and DeLisi (2019) employed data from 29 unique samples from 22 studies that included 2603 homicide offenders in the first meta-analysis of the psychopathy-homicide linkage. They found that the mean Psychopathy Checklist—Revised (PCL-R) score for all homicide offenders was 21.2 indicating moderate psychopathy, and the overall effect size $r=0.68$ was large. Importantly, the effect sizes were even larger for more violent and severe expressions of homicide, such as sexual homicide ($r=0.71$), serial homicide ($r=0.74$), sadistic homicide ($r=0.78$), and multioffender perpetrated homicide ($r=0.80$) (Fox & DeLisi, 2019). This study showed empirically what many researchers and clinicians had witnessed anecdotally: the more violent, extreme, or horrific the homicide, the more likely it was to have been committed by a higher scoring psychopathic offender.

The linkage between homicide and psychopathy works both ways, thus, psychopaths are also more likely to be killed than nonpsychopathic individuals. A recent study, for example, reported that psychopaths exhibited a mortality risk that was five times greater than the general population, and when psychopaths died their manner of death was more likely to involve criminal violence, such as homicide (Vaurio, Repo-Tiihonen, Kautiainen, & Tiihonen, 2018). Historical evidence for this research finding is seen in the 2018 murder of Whitey Bulger—a notorious career criminal and brutal mob boss who murdered nearly 20 victims (Lehr & O'Neill, 2013). The psychopath's lifestyle and social interaction patterns are so substantially pervaded with violence and generalized criminal offending that murder is a common by-product.

Psychopathy and sexual offending

Although there is considerable complexity to the psychopathy-sexual offending nexus in terms of features of the disorder and variants of sexual crime (e.g., rape, child molestation, mixed-victim offending, and others), psychopathy is nevertheless a common risk factor for sexual aggression. In their recent systematic review of the literature, Cale and Burton (2019, p. 346) concluded, "when the affective, interpersonal, and antisocial dimensions of psychopathy coincide with persistent and harmful deviant sexual fantasies and/or paraphilia, the outcome tends to be the most serious and violent sexual crimes." Ample research supports their advisement. In a study of 302 treated sexual offenders followed in the community up to nearly 18 years, the prevalence of noncompletion of treatment among men who were highly psychopathic was five times greater than noncompletion of treatment prevalence among low psychopathy offenders (Sewall & Olver, 2019). Based on a variety of measures, scholars linked psychopathy to a range of maladaptive behaviors. These include various forms of recidivism, noncompliance with supervision, and deviant/antisocial thinking regarding sexual behavior among a host of offenders including juvenile sexual offenders

(Cale, Lussier, McCuish, & Corrado, 2015; Wijetunga, Nijdam-Jones, Rosenfeld, Martinez, & Cruise, 2018), adult sex offenders and general offenders (Cardona, Berman, Sims-Knight, & Knight, 2018; Garofalo, Bogaerts, & Denissen, 2018), and adult prisoners (Debowska, Boduszek, & Willmott, 2018). Linkages between psychopathy and deviant sexual interests and behaviors also exist in community samples (van Bommel, Uzieblo, Bogaerts, & Garofalo, 2018).

Quantitative summary reviews of sexual aggression illustrate the salience of psychopathy. Hanson and Morton-Bourgon (2005) performed a meta-analysis of 82 sexual recidivism studies that included 1620 research findings from 29,450 sexual offenders. Among the many findings from their study, it was striking how strong the association between psychopathy and sexual offending was even when compared with other sexually oriented risk factors. For example, sexual deviancy had the following effects for sexual recidivism ($d=0.30$), violent nonsexual recidivism ($d=-0.05$), violent recidivism ($d=0.19$), and any recidivism ($d=0.04$). The respective effect sizes for antisocial orientation in which many of the items were derived from psychopathy measures were $d=0.23$, $d=0.51$, $d=0.54$, and $d=0.52$. Thus psychopathy was moderately to strongly associated with all forms of recidivism and its association with sexual recidivism was on par with sexual deviancy. In other models, psychopathy had a significant ($d=0.29$) correlation with sexual recidivism that was again comparable with any deviant sexual interest ($d=0.31$) and sexual preoccupation ($d=0.39$).

More recently, Hawes, Boccaccini, and Murrie (2013) reviewed 20 studies spanning 5239 participants and reported significant results with an average effect size for the PCL-R and sexual recidivism. They also found that high psychopathy scores coupled with high sexual deviance was a particularly dangerous combination in terms of likelihood of sexual reoffending. Across seven studies in their meta-analysis, the high psychopathy-high sexual deviance offenders were upwards of 15 times more likely to sexually reoffend. Importantly, psychopathy was also significantly predictive of violent recidivism not including sexual recidivism and a total recidivism measure. In other words, psychopathy is on par with domain-specific features of sexual deviancy and interests in the prediction of sexual aggression, violence, and recidivism, which attests to its potency as an omnibus risk factor for crime.

Psychopathy and other violent offending

Psychopathic offenders often go the extra mile to inflict pain, suffering, and humiliation on their victims, even in circumstances where the abuse is incidental to the perpetration of the crime. For instance, we are familiar with psychopaths that during armed robberies placed their firearm in or on the face of victims to the crime even though the victim was completely compliant with the offender's demands. In some cases, psychopathic offenders will place the barrel of their firearm in the mouth of the victim just to see the distress that the behavior causes the victims. Evidenced by victim impact statements in some of these cases, the robber's behavior creates an appalling psychological toll on the victim even years after the event.

The aforementioned incidents reveal the association between psychopathy and various manifestations of violence, including violent acts that are purposive or instrumental and those that are gratuitous, emotional, or expressive (recall the Woodworth and Porter study). Our experiences with psychopathic offenders are not unique in this regard. To illustrate, Blais, Solodukhin, and Forth (2014) performed a meta-analysis of 53 studies spanning 55 unique samples and including 8753 participants to assess the relation between psychopathy, instrumental violence, and reactive violence. Psychopathy was significantly associated with both variants of violence. The overall effect size between psychopathy and instrumental violence was $r=0.36$ and the respective effect sizes for the interpersonal factor ($r=0.44$), affective factor ($r=0.38$), lifestyle factor ($r=0.41$), and antisocial factor ($r=0.28$) were moderate. For reactive violence, the overall effect size was $r=0.35$ and the respective effect sizes for the interpersonal factor ($r=0.42$), affective factor ($r=0.31$), lifestyle factor ($r=0.49$), and antisocial factor ($r=0.30$) were also moderate.

Psychopathy is also in the foreground of criminal careers. Several studies have shown that offenders with the earliest criminal debut who offend at the highest rates and who perpetrate a broader mix of violence usually exhibit more psychopathic features (McCuish, Corrado, Hart, & DeLisi, 2015; Vaughn, Howard, & DeLisi, 2008). A meta-analysis of 53 studies containing 60 samples and 10,073 participants found that psychopathy was significantly associated with violent delinquency and general delinquency (Asscher et al., 2011). Indeed, a central recommendation from this review was that early screening and identification of psychopathic features among young delinquents is one of the most important targets for intervention and treatment.

Psychopathy drives violent offending and other institutional misconduct within correctional institutions (Shaffer, McCuish, Corrado, Behnken, & DeLisi, 2015) as supported by meta-analytic work (Guy, Edens, Anthony, & Douglas, 2005; Walters, 2003). Psychopathic inmates are overrepresented among those engaged in the most challenging and violent forms of misconduct. For instance, a recent study found that various features of psychopathy were significantly associated with violent misconduct and instigating a violent encounter with another inmate (Thomson et al., 2019). In various interviews with correctional clients that were involved in security threat groups, psychopathic features were common. These offenders admitted that they always possessed weapons and that a willingness to stab or physically assault other inmates, correctional officers, and correctional staff was simply a requisite part of being in confinement. In their words, stabbing other inmates and guards "was part of the business of being in prison."

Interacting with psychopathic offenders: Familiar insights and novel recommendations

Even the most skeptical critic of the psychopathy construct would blush at its significant empirical associations with various forms of violent crime. We have had the advantage—as perverse as that sounds—of interacting with thousands of criminal offenders in a variety of contexts to further underscore this point. The following are insights about psychopathy and novel recommendations for researchers to further its forensic and social science usefulness.

First, superficial charm is a characteristic feature of the disorder, but as we have addressed previously (DeLisi, 2016), this charm often comes off as so insincere, and frankly absurd, that it is not effective as a manipulation strategy (at least among those trained on the features of psychopathy). As an example, one offender we recently interviewed, arrested in his trailer home for sexual battery of his step-daughter, detailed colorful stories of cruising in the Caribbean on a yacht borrowed from a high-level New York mafia boss and his experiences as the CEO of no less than seven different companies. These stories were so patently fabricated, it bordered on the surreal.

While we have certainly conversed with psychopathic offenders who were charming and glib, many psychopathic offenders also employ a conversational style that goes in the opposite direction: toward brutal straightforwardness. While most psychopaths in our experience commit tons of lies of omission and avoid providing incriminating or prejudicial information voluntarily, when asked about events that they know the interviewer is already aware of, psychopaths tend to be direct and provide substantive information (though they often shift blame for their horrific acts to others, including the victims). Interestingly, the straightforward manner in which offenders report about their crimes, and particularly the manner in which they committed their crimes, paradoxically represents elements of conscientiousness. In our experiences, offenders that are less grandiose, and even who display some glimpses of humility, tend to be more straightforward in providing information about their criminal careers. However, even straightforward accounts of their offending nevertheless are permeated with antisocial features in terms of conversation style and affective displays. To illustrate, a violent offender once responded to our directions about the purpose of a forensic interview by interrupting and sternly advising, "I'll tell you whatever the fuck you need to know."

Second, we harken back to a word from the prior point—absurd—that is useful for understanding psychopath's criminal careers. Psychopathy is a core variable for understanding heterogeneity in criminal careers (Vaughn & DeLisi, 2008), and we suggest that the most psychopathic offenders evince criminal histories that are implausibly extensive and violent almost to an absurd degree, but that we have had personal experiences of validating with official records. Psychopathic offenders that are the worst of the worst are useful guides for law enforcement and correctional practitioners. These offenders stand out in terms of the prevalence and gratuity of violence they engage in, committing a disproportionate share of the most serious, heinous, and violent types of crime (Blais et al., 2014; Corrado, McCuish, Hart, & DeLisi, 2015; DeLisi, 2016; Fox et al., 2015). It has been estimated that up to 85% of sexual murderers show moderate to strong psychopathy (Porter et al., 2003), and that upwards of 40% of homicide offenders in general score a 27 or higher on the PCL-R (Laurell & Daderman, 2007).

For most psychopathic offenders, violence and criminal behavior are practically inherent to their being. For instance, many offenders we have interviewed report that they are always armed, that they continuously engage in violent offending, and that a violent response (e.g., shooting or stabbing a victim) is the preferred way to respond to an adversarial encounter. These offenders commonly have multiple charges for attempted murder of a law enforcement officer, tend to respond with violence during arrest, and often have multiple violence indicators, such as being the perpetrator or victim of serious violent crimes on their official rap sheet. It is obvious that psychopathy is a powerful driver of offending frequency, chronicity, and severity, but it also serves as insight for understanding offenders that seemingly exist to engage in deviant behavior.

A third and related issue relates to criminal propensity and the constructs that constitute it. When psychopathology is severe, it nearly always illustrates comorbidity (Caspi et al., 2014). When psychopathy is very acute among an offender, for instance PCL-R scores of 35+, it likely coincides with other pernicious antisocial features including but not limited to sadism, sexual sadism, pedophilia, hypersexual and paraphilic sexual activity, hostile attribution bias, pathological anger, and severe emotional regulation disorder (e.g., Intermittent Explosive Disorder). Several offenders divulged to us that they experienced a powerful urge or instinct that they believed drove their antisocial behavior. This urge or instinct emerged in early childhood and only started to dissipate when offenders were relatively old, for instance, age 70 years or older. Although offenders are not terribly insightful in describing the nosology of their antisocial features, they nevertheless at times use evocative and almost brilliant terms (e.g., urge, rage, life force, darkness, machine, blindness) to typify what is likely criminal propensity. The notorious serial murderer Dennis Rader, for example, referred to his homicidal and sexually sadistic drives as "factor X." A pressing research need is to obtain qualitative data from highly psychopathic violent offenders to better understand allied conditions that inform their criminal propensity.

Psychopathy is integral to understanding violent offenders

In short, our research and personal experiences interacting with countless psychopathic offenders yield two broad takeaway points. First, that despite the variations in the name given to the constellation of traits and behaviors consistently shown to be most predictive of serious crime and violent offending, psychopathy appears to be the single unifying theme throughout. For example, the well-known "general theory of crime" proposed by Gottfredson and Hirschi (1990) posits that low self-control, a core element of psychopathy, is the fundamental trait underlying the propensity to commit crime and violence. This theory has received wide empirical support and gained wide acceptance in the field of criminology. However, research has shown that much of the variance accounted for by self-control was in fact subsumed by other major psychopathic traits, such as narcissism (Vaughn, DeLisi, Beaver, Wright, & Howard, 2007). This finding suggests that self-control (as outlined by the general theory of crime) is actually just a "watered down, less specified form of psychopathy" (DeLisi, 2009, p. 257).

Indeed, many of the core elements of psychopathy, including callousness/lack of empathy and remorse, narcissism, impulsivity, shallow affect, poor behavioral controls, conning and manipulativeness, and more, have been identified as key risk factors for extreme violence and criminality, psychopathy arguably provides a "parsimonious and valid theoretical framework for all forms of serious antisocial and criminal behavior" (Fox et al., 2015, p. 275). In fact, the psychopathic construct has been shown to predict violent behavior better than actuarial instruments specifically designed to predict future violence (Edens, Campbell, & Weir, 2007; Hemphill, Templeman, Wong, & Hare, 1998). As summarized by DeLisi and Vaughn (2008), it appears that there is "a synergy between the violent criminals' personality traits, lifestyle, and observed behavior that dovetails so exquisitely it is as if their criminality is wrapped up in a box. That box is psychopathy" (p. 164). Consequently, it is imperative for researchers across disciplines to begin drawing specifically upon the features and body of literature associated with psychopathy to better understand, predict, and prevent violence and serious criminal behavior.

The second and final takeaway is that psychopathy is extraordinarily prevalent among the "worst of the worst" offenders, with up to 40% of murderers and 85% of sexual and sadistic homicide offenders scoring highly on psychopathic traits. Given the approximately 1% prevalence of psychopathy in the general population (Coid, Yang, Ullrich, Roberts, & Hare, 2009; DeLisi, 2016), it is estimated that there are currently over 3.2 million psychopaths in the United States, with as many as 82,000 in New York City and over 170,000 living in Los Angeles alone. Considering the propensity for these people to violate the law and cause significant distress for others, it is extremely likely for law enforcement and clinicians to come in contact with a psychopath at some point during their career. In fact, one study of nearly 600 mental health and criminal justice practitioners in the United States found that over 77% had personally interviewed a psychopath (Meloy & Meloy, 2003). Even more striking, this study also found that the vast majority of those who interacted with psychopathic offenders experienced significant physiological symptoms such as an upset stomach, the chills, increased heart rate, and having their hair stand on end during the experience (Meloy & Meloy, 2003).

Conclusions

Psychopathy is inextricably bound to antisocial behavior and its downstream consequences, namely criminal justice system involvement. Therefore it is critical for practitioners most likely to come in contact with these offenders to arm themselves with knowledge on psychopathy to be most prepared and have a deeper understanding of those they are dealing with, as psychopathy is integral to understanding violent offending.

References

Asscher, J. J., van Vugt, E. S., Stams, G. J. J., Deković, M., Eichelsheim, V. I., & Yousfi, S. (2011). The relationship between juvenile psychopathic traits, delinquency and (violent) recidivism: A meta-analysis. *Journal of Child Psychology and Psychiatry*, *52*(11), 1134–1143.

Bergstrøm, H., Larmour, S. R., & Farrington, D. P. (2018). The usefulness of psychopathy in explaining and predicting violence: Discussing the utility of competing perspectives. *Aggression and Violent Behavior*, *42*, 84–95.

Blais, J., Solodukhin, E., & Forth, A. E. (2014). A meta-analysis exploring the relationship between psychopathy and instrumental versus reactive violence. *Criminal Justice and Behavior*, *41*(7), 797–821.

Cale, J., & Burton, M. (2019). Psychopathy and sexual aggression: A review of empirical research. In M. DeLisi (Ed.), *Routledge international handbook of psychopathy and crime* (pp. 334–350). New York, NY: Routledge.

Cale, J., Lussier, P., McCuish, E., & Corrado, R. (2015). The prevalence of psychopathic personality disturbances among incarcerated youth: Comparing serious, chronic, violent and sex offenders. *Journal of Criminal Justice*, *43*(4), 337–344.

Cardona, N., Berman, A. K., Sims-Knight, J. E., & Knight, R. A. (2018). Covariates of the severity of aggression in sexual crimes: Psychopathy and borderline characteristics. *Sexual Abuse*. https://doi.org/10.1177/1079063218807485.

Caspi, A., Houts, R. M., Belsky, D. W., Goldman-Mellor, S. J., Harrington, H., Israel, S., … Moffitt, T. E. (2014). The p factor: One general psychopathology factor in the structure of psychiatric disorders? *Clinical Psychological Science*, *2*(2), 119–137.

Coid, J., Yang, M., Ullrich, S., Roberts, A., & Hare, R. D. (2009). Prevalence and correlates of psychopathic traits in the household population of Great Britain. *International Journal of Law and Psychiatry*, *32*(2), 65–73.

Corrado, R. R., McCuish, E. C., Hart, S. D., & DeLisi, M. (2015). The role of psychopathic traits and developmental risk factors on offending trajectories from early adolescence to adulthood: A prospective study of incarcerated youth. *Journal of Criminal Justice*, *43*(4), 357–368.

Debowska, A., Boduszek, D., & Willmott, D. (2018). Psychosocial correlates of attitudes toward male sexual violence in a sample of financial crime, property crime, general violent, and homicide offenders. *Sexual Abuse*, *30*(6), 705–727.

DeLisi, M. (2009). Psychopathy is the unified theory of crime. *Youth Violence and Juvenile Justice*, *7*(3), 256–273.

DeLisi, M. (2016). *Psychopathy as unified theory of crime*. New York, NY: Palgrave Macmillan.

DeLisi, M., & Vaughn, M. G. (2008). The Gottfredson-Hirschi critiques revisited: Reconciling self-control theory, criminal careers, and career criminals. *International Journal of Offender Therapy and Comparative Criminology*, *52*, 520–537.

Edens, J. F., Campbell, J. S., & Weir, J. M. (2007). Youth psychopathy and criminal recidivism: A meta-analysis of the psychopathy checklist measures. *Law and Human Behavior*, *31*(1), 53–75.

Fox, B., & DeLisi, M. (2019). Psychopathic killers: A meta-analytic review of the psychopathy-homicide nexus. *Aggression and Violent Behavior*, *44*, 67–79.

Fox, B. H., Jennings, W. G., & Farrington, D. P. (2015). Bringing psychopathy into developmental and life-course criminology theories and research. *Journal of Criminal Justice*, *43*(4), 274–289.

Garofalo, C., Bogaerts, S., & Denissen, J. J. (2018). Personality functioning and psychopathic traits in child molesters and violent offenders. *Journal of Criminal Justice*, *55*, 80–87.

Gottfredson, M., & Hirschi, T. (1990). *A general theory of crime*. Stanford, CA: Stanford University Press.

Guy, L. S., Edens, J. F., Anthony, C., & Douglas, K. S. (2005). Does psychopathy predict institutional misconduct among adults? A meta-analytic investigation. *Journal of Consulting and Clinical Psychology*, *73*(6), 1056–1064.

Hanson, R. K., & Morton-Bourgon, K. E. (2005). The characteristics of persistent sexual offenders: A meta-analysis of recidivism studies. *Journal of Consulting and Clinical Psychology*, *73*(6), 1154–1163.

Hare, R. D. (1993). *Without conscience: The disturbing world of the psychopaths among us*. New York, NY: The Guilford Press.

Hare, R. D. (1996). Psychopathy: A clinical construct whose time has come. *Criminal Justice and Behavior*, *23*(1), 25–54.

Hawes, S. W., Boccaccini, M. T., & Murrie, D. C. (2013). Psychopathy and the combination of psychopathy and sexual deviance as predictors of sexual recidivism: Meta-analytic findings using the psychopathy checklist—Revised. *Psychological Assessment*, *25*(1), 233–243.

Hemphill, J. F., Templeman, R., Wong, S., & Hare, R. D. (1998). Psychopathy and crime: Recidivism and criminal careers. In D. J. Cooke, A. E. Forth, & R. D. Hare (Eds.), *Psychopathy: Theory, research and implications for society* (pp. 375–399). Dordrecht, Netherlands: Kluwer Academic.

Jolliffe, D., Loeber, R., Farrington, D. P., & Cotter, R. B. (2011). Homicide offenders speak. In R. Loeber, & D. P. Farrington (Eds.), *Young homicide offenders and victims* (pp. 115–121). Boston, MA: Springer.

Laurell, J., & Daderman, A. M. (2007). Psychopathy (PCL-R) in a forensic psychiatric sample of homicide offenders: Some reliability issues. *International Journal of Law and Psychiatry*, *30*, 127–135.

Lehr, D., & O'Neill, G. (2013). *Whitey: The life of America's most notorious mob boss*. New York, NY: Broadway Books.

McCuish, E. C., Corrado, R. R., Hart, S. D., & DeLisi, M. (2015). The role of symptoms of psychopathy in persistent violence over the criminal career into full adulthood. *Journal of Criminal Justice*, *43*(4), 345–356.

Meloy, J. R., & Meloy, M. J. (2003). Autonomic arousal in the presence of psychopathy: A survey of mental health and criminal justice professionals. *Journal of Threat Assessment*, *2*(2), 21–33.

Porter, S., Woodworth, M., Earle, J., Drugge, J., & Boer, D. (2003). Characteristics of sexual homicides committed by psychopathic and nonpsychopathic offenders. *Law and Human Behavior*, *27*(5), 459–470.

Sewall, L. A., & Olver, M. E. (2019). Psychopathy and treatment outcome: Results from a sexual violence reduction program. *Personality Disorders, Theory, Research, and Treatment*, *10*(1), 59–69.

Shaffer, C., McCuish, E., Corrado, R. R., Behnken, M. P., & DeLisi, M. (2015). Psychopathy and violent misconduct in a sample of violent young offenders. *Journal of Criminal Justice*, *43*(4), 321–326.

Thomson, N. D., Vassileva, J., Kiehl, K. A., Reidy, D., Aboutanos, M., McDougle, R., & DeLisi, M. (2019). Which features of psychopathy and impulsivity matter most for prison violence? New evidence among female prisoners. *International Journal of Law and Psychiatry*, *64*, 26–33.

van Bommel, R., Uzieblo, K., Bogaerts, S., & Garofalo, C. (2018). Psychopathic traits and deviant sexual interests: The moderating role of gender. *International Journal of Forensic Mental Health*, *17*(3), 256–271.

Vaughn, M. G., & DeLisi, M. (2008). Were Wolfgang's chronic offenders psychopaths? On the convergent validity between psychopathy and career criminality. *Journal of Criminal Justice*, *36*(1), 33–42.

Vaughn, M. G., DeLisi, M., Beaver, K., Wright, J. P., & Howard, M. O. (2007). Toward a psychopathology of self-control theory: The importance of narcissistic traits. *Behavioral Sciences & the Law*, *25*, 803–821.

Vaughn, M. G., Howard, M. O., & DeLisi, M. (2008). Psychopathic personality traits and delinquent careers: An empirical examination. *International Journal of Law and Psychiatry*, *31*(5), 407–416.

Vaurio, O., Repo-Tiihonen, E., Kautiainen, H., & Tiihonen, J. (2018). Psychopathy and mortality. *Journal of Forensic Sciences*, *63*(2), 474–477.

Walters, G. D. (2003). Predicting institutional adjustment and recidivism with the psychopathy checklist factor scores: A meta-analysis. *Law and Human Behavior*, *27*(5), 541–558.

Wijetunga, C., Nijdam-Jones, A., Rosenfeld, B., Martinez, R., & Cruise, K. R. (2018). Using the juvenile sex offender assessment protocol–revised to assess psychopathy: A preliminary investigation. *Criminal Justice and Behavior*, *45*(4), 483–502.

Woodworth, M., & Porter, S. (2002). In cold blood: Characteristics of criminal homicides as a function of psychopathy. *Journal of Abnormal Psychology*, *111*(3), 436–445.

Psychopathy in human trafficking offenders: Current trends and challenges

17

Holly Hargreaves-Cormany, James Beasley, Terri Patterson, Kara Meadows, Princess-Kasharáe Middleton, Ellen Wood, Jonathan Alicchio, and Nathanael Gaspar

Introduction

Psychopathic offenders engaging in human trafficking offenses systematically target and take advantage of vulnerable individuals through complex and convoluted phases of identifying, recruiting, and maintaining control over their victims (Spidel et al., 2007). The stories of the many victims and survivors of these offenses shed light on the darkest motives and practices of these extremely dangerous offenders and offer valuable insights into their methodologies for carrying out such deeply personal, targeted abuse. As explored in this chapter, the knowledge gained through a careful examination of trafficking behaviors and offenses from both victims' and offenders' perspectives can be used to assist in the investigation of future offenses and to develop more effective prevention and intervention techniques (Gotch, 2016; Hargreaves-Cormany, Patterson, & Muirhead, 2016; Serie et al., 2018).

As a survivor and advocate, Holly Austin Smith depicts her experience as a victim of child sex trafficking and many examples of these offenders' methodologies in her novel *Walking Prey*. She describes how she was lured into child sex trafficking at a particularly vulnerable time in her life, which was influenced by her strong desire to escape her dysfunctional family home, feel loved, seek an alternative lifestyle, and the illusory promises of love, attention, and power presented to her by her trafficker (Smith, 2014). Holly has overcome her experiences and the numerous obstacles associated with being a victim of child sex trafficking and now speaks out against all forms of human trafficking and exploitation. She has served as a consultant with several renowned agencies and organizations across the country to combat these crimes, including the National Center for Missing and Exploited Children and the Office for Victims of Crime (Smith, 2014). As demonstrated in the following quotes, Smith and other victim advocates offer detailed descriptions and case examples illuminating key patterns of offending as well as common characteristics of victims and offenders, which are helpful in improving our knowledge and understanding of these complex sex trafficking offenses.

- "It was an instant friendship without any pressure or pause. I realize now that this was a tactic. Teens can be socially awkward; if a person or conversation feels uncomfortable, then

Psychopathy and Criminal Behavior. https://doi.org/10.1016/B978-0-12-811419-3.00021-2

a teen may shy away. Child traffickers are charismatic; they make it their business to be sympathetic and relatable to teen's troubles" (Smith, 2014, p. 153).

- "Through the mirage of genuine conversation and compliments, he tapped into my interests, and he constructed glamorous opportunities for a better life" (Smith, 2014, p. 185).
- "It became the family I never had until I realized how violent pimps could be" (Smith, 2014, p. 116).
- "I understood two things in this moment: (1) I understood that I was not in control of what was happening to me after all, and (2) I believed that I had brought all of this on myself. Because I had chosen to run away with this man, I believed that I deserved what was happening to me. Did I cry? Crying would imply the presence of an emotion, of which I had none. I had only skin and teeth and bones" (Smith, 2014, p. 107).

Another example found in Kimberly Mehlman-Orozco's novel *Hidden in Plain Sight: America's Slaves of the New Millennium* is a quote from a victim of international sex trafficking obtained in an interview with an ICE agent in the United States. The victim states, "It's not just easy for me to leave because I was kept. You know, 12 hours a day, at the same place, over and over again, it was terrible. It was just the, the nastiest place I ever been. I felt miserable every single day. When I was going to shower, I was hating myself. I was even thinking about suicide many times because I didn't have a choice to get out. My life was in danger the whole time, and they knew where my mom is living. It was not about me; it was about her!" (Mehlman-Orozco, 2017, p. 96). This shows how the offender was able to gain and maintain control over the victim through the use of threats and other psychological manipulation. These and similar methods are commonly described in accounts provided by many other trafficking victims. For example, Wendy Barnes shares her story in her novel, *And Life Continues: Sex Trafficking and My Journey to Freedom*, which also involves the offender's use of threats to control the victim. She writes, "Whenever I would attempt to break up with him…, the threats toward my family would begin..." (Barnes & Foster, 2015).

The traits and behaviors of these psychopathic offenders become evident and palpable through these victims' quotes and the depictions of their experiences with their offenders. It becomes clear how these offenders' deviant personalities and lifestyles are projected and forced onto their victims in many ways. They exhibit key characteristics of psychopathy, which include but are not limited to manipulation, deception, superficial charm, a lack of remorse and empathy, poor behavioral controls, violent attitudes and behaviors, and criminal versatility (Hare, 1999; Hargreaves-Cormany, Patterson, & Muirhead, 2016). Further evidence of the overlap in the characteristics of psychopathy and the characteristics of perpetrators of human trafficking will be demonstrated throughout the chapter. Lastly, these stories and insights shared by these victims and survivors of sex trafficking can inform crucial changes needed to more effectively carry out prevention strategies for these offenses. In order to stop future sex trafficking offenders, awareness, research, training, and collaboration are all necessary components to any approach (Shared Hope International, 2019).

Research to date suggests that only a small group of individuals consistently engage in high rates of antisocial behavior across time and contexts, such individuals are likely classified as psychopaths (Moffitt, 1993). Studies exploring this population of likely psychopaths have extremely important implications for society (Moffitt, 1993). Although psychopaths make up a small percentage of the population, they engage in a disproportionately large percentage of crimes. According to Hare (1999), 20% of prison inmates—including both males and females—could be diagnosed as psychopaths. This is a stark contrast to the rest of the world's population, which is estimated to be closer to 1%.

With respect to specific offenses, psychopaths commit 50% of all serious crimes and are responsible for 44% of law enforcement deaths on duty. In comparison to other offenders, psychopaths commit almost twice as many acts of violence, both in and out of prison. Furthermore, their recidivism rates are much higher than their non-psychopathic counterparts, as they are nearly double for crime in general and triple for violent crime. Perhaps the most chilling data, however, proposes that psychopathy is a stable construct. This indicates that once a person has met enough criteria for diagnosis, they are extremely unlikely to ever dip below the threshold toward normalcy ever again. It is concerning to recognize that not only is psychopathy a consistent predictor of violence, but the callousness and lack of empathy displayed by these offenders make them highly resistant to any therapeutic intervention. Numerous studies have indicated that psychopaths engage in criminal behavior more often, are more likely to be violent, and demonstrate greater criminal versatility when compared to their non-psychopathic offender counterparts (Hare & Neumann, 2009; Hargreaves-Cormany, Patterson, & Muirhead, 2016). Future research into this personality disorder is imperative as psychopathy has been shown to significantly predict recidivism rates, treatment outcomes, and successful reintegration into the community (Gotch, 2016; Hare, 1999; Olver & Wong, 2006; Spidel et al., 2007).

The overlap in the characteristics of psychopathy and the characteristics of perpetrators of human trafficking is of particular interest to researchers because examining these commonalities may be the key to improving the current understanding of these patterns of offending (Spidel et al., 2007). Both human traffickers and psychopaths exhibit a propensity for violence and the use of various other tactics involving coercion, control, and inflicting harm on others to achieve their goals (Cima, Tonnaer, & Hauser, 2010; Hoppenbrouwers et al., 2013). The existing research suggests that the reason for these shared features may be that many psychopaths are drawn to engaging in the activities surrounding human trafficking since this enables them to maintain a feeling of being in control of others (Spidel et al., 2007). While these offenders' behaviors may change in accordance with shifts in their perceived opportunities, their underlying personality and instrumental goals remain consistent across their lifespans (Moffitt, 1993).

Although the crime of human trafficking can be traced back to the early origins of human society, it has only recently gained widespread recognition and awareness as a major international criminal enterprise (Busch-Armendariz, Nsonwu, & Cook Heffron, 2009; Gotch, 2016). According to the Federal Bureau of Investigation (2016), human trafficking is the third most prevalent criminal activity in the world. In order to help combat the problem of human trafficking, in 2000, the United Nations adopted the Protocol to Prevent, Suppress and Punish Trafficking in Persons, Especially Women and Children (Palermo Protocol), which supplemented the previous protocols established by the United Nations Convention Against Transnational Organized Crime (Organization for Security and Co-operation in Europe [OSCE], 2018).

The Palermo Protocol defines human trafficking by using the three specific elements of *action*, *means*, and *purpose*, which must all be carried out by the trafficker (U.S. Department of State, 2019). Therefore the traffickers' *actions* must be taken by *means* of force, fraud, or coercion for the intended *purpose* of exploiting a victim (U.S. Department of State, 2019). The Palermo Protocol (2000) goes on to further define "trafficking in persons" as the following:

> *"Trafficking in persons" shall mean the recruitment, transportation, transfer, harboring or receipt of persons, by means of the threat or use of force or other forms of coercion, of abduction, of fraud, of deception, of the abuse of power or of a position of vulnerability or of the giving or receiving of payments or benefits to achieve the consent of a person having control over another person, for the purpose of exploitation. Exploitation shall include, at a minimum, the exploitation of the prostitution of others or other forms of sexual exploitation, forced labour or services, slavery or practices similar to slavery, servitude or the removal of organs.*

Furthermore, the Palermo Protocol (2000) defines juvenile human trafficking as any event in which a child under the age of 18 is taken advantage of by being recruited, transported, transferred, harbored, or received, regardless of whether the juvenile victims have given their consent or not. Moreover, the Palermo Protocol not only includes definitions, but also it provides provisions intended to help and support trafficking victims by offering rehabilitative and recovery services, which include, but are not limited to, housing, medical assistance, and employment opportunities (OSCE, 2018).

The Palermo Protocol created the basic foundation for international government authorities to develop and expand upon (U.S. Department of State, 2019). The goal is that the Palermo Protocol will help governments establish their own policies and legislations addressing the best way to criminalize human trafficking offenders, while protecting and helping the victims (U.S. Department of State, 2019). As of March 2019, the Palermo Protocol had been ratified by 173 parties and has been largely accepted and used around the world since its adoption in 2000, regardless of it being the first global attempt to address the problem of trafficking in human beings (U.S. Department of State, 2019).

Yet, even with the Palermo Protocol being recognized nationally, the most recent *Global Report on Trafficking in Persons 2018* indicates that the rate in which human trafficking is taking place is continuing to rise (United Nations Office on Drugs and Crime [UNODC], 2018). In fact, there have been exorbitant human trafficking increases reported in countries in Asia and the Americas (UNODC, 2018). However, the increase in the number of reported sex trafficking victims can be viewed somewhat positively, because the number of sex trafficking convictions has also continued to rise (UNODC, 2018). Nevertheless, countries in North America, Central America, Central and South-Eastern Europe, and the Caribbean continue to have problems with convicting sex trafficking offenders despite their number of victims continuing to rise (UNODC, 2018).

Consequently, there are still an estimated 4.8 million victims of human sex trafficking worldwide, with women and girls accounting for the majority of sexual exploitation cases (International Labour Organization, 2017). With the preceding data in mind, it is clear to see how human sex trafficking is a highly prevalent criminal enterprise that has an international impact spanning across the world.

Literature review

Research on psychopathy in human trafficking offenders

There is a scarcity of research on human trafficking offenders, and the majority of existing studies have relied on victims' experiences to inform our understanding of the perpetrators of this crime (Gotch, 2016; Spidel et al., 2007). An extensive literature review revealed that the recent study conducted by this author and her colleagues (Hargreaves-Cormany, Patterson, & Muirhead, 2016; Hargreaves-Cormany & Patterson, 2016) is the only such empirical research conducted on offenders engaging in the sex trafficking of juveniles. Hargreaves-Cormany and Patterson's research is groundbreaking because it not only incorporates the perspectives of offenders, victims, and law enforcement, but also it analyzes the data with advanced statistical analyses utilizing a mixed methods design and best practices in the development of risk scales by adhering strictly to well-respected models from the field.

The studies conducted by Hargreaves-Cormany, Patterson, & Muirhead, 2016 examined the sex trafficking of juveniles (STJ) with one article focusing on examination of psychopathy in STJ Offenders and the development of a typology of STJ Offenders along with STJ Offender Risk Scales and the other article focusing on victimology and development of a spectrum of characteristics in STJ Survivors/Victims. Four scales were developed to examine the STJ Offender typology as well as to generate the STJ Risk Scales.

The participants of the study included 117 offenders and 179 victims involved in cases of juvenile sex trafficking between the years of 1990 and 2011. The most sophisticated analyses that could be conducted with this type of data, latent class analyses (LCA), were completed as well as logistic regression analyses and qualitative analyses in the STJ Survivor/Victim article. All data was derived from specialized research protocols created for this study which included demographics of the offenders and victims and various aspects of the nature of the criminal act(s) perpetrated by the offender focused upon the STJ Offense (Hargreaves-Cormany, Patterson, & Muirhead, 2016; Hargreaves-Cormany & Patterson, 2016). The LCA indicators were the STJ Scales measuring Criminal History Severity, Violence Severity, Criminal Sophistication, and Charismatic Offender Behavioral Style (Hargreaves-Cormany, Patterson, & Muirhead, 2016). This comprehensive examination of offenders engaging in the sex trafficking of juveniles was conducted to contribute to the limited research on this offender population and to devise a typology of these offenders.

The main findings of this study were the high rate of psychopathy among offenders who had engaged in the sex trafficking of juveniles and the development of a STJ Offender Typology and Risk Scale (STJ; Hargreaves-Cormany, Patterson, & Muirhead, 2016). The results indicated that 75% (n=27) of the offenders in the sample (n=36) scored 30 or higher (n = 24) on the Hare Psychopathy Checklist-Revised (PCL-R) and met the criteria for psychopathy or came very close to meeting the criteria by scoring 29.5 (n=3). Two overarching typologies emerged, the Charismatic/Manipulative STJ offenders and Aggressive/Antisocial STJ offenders. Additional subtypes were also used to further characterize these offenders, including: Violent and Nonviolent Charismatic/Manipulative Offenders (VCM, NVCM) and Aggressive/Antisocial Offenders with Minor or No Charismatic/Manipulative Characteristics (AAMCM, AANCM) (Hargreaves-Cormany, Patterson, & Muirhead, 2016).

A thorough risk assessment comparing the level of dangerousness of each of the aforementioned typologies revealed that the offenders who utilize tactics involving both violence and coercion or manipulation, known as the Violent Charismatic/Manipulative Offenders (VCM), pose the greatest risk to society. The rationale for their heightened dangerousness stems from the increased intelligence, social competence, and criminal sophistication exhibited by these offenders in their perpetration of their crimes (Hargreaves-Cormany, Patterson, & Muirhead, 2016). In combination with their charismatic and manipulative personalities, these characteristics enable them to avoid detection and criminal sanctions, which may account for minimal prior involvement in the criminal justice system in highly sophisticated offenders. Both Spidel et al. (2007) and Hargreaves-Cormany, Patterson, & Muirhead, 2016 found that the majority of the sex trafficking offenders that they examined had criminal histories, including convictions for past violent offenses. Violent Charismatic/Manipulative STJ Offenders were also the most prevalent of the offender typologies in the sample, which has important applications for practices in the field (Hargreaves-Cormany, Patterson, & Muirhead, 2016).

The prevalence of psychopathy and psychopathic traits among human traffickers remains unclear, as limited research involving small samples has been conducted to date (Gotch, 2016; Spidel et al., 2007). According to the National Human Trafficking Resource Center, those involved in human trafficking for sexual exploitation are interchangeably referred to as "pimps" or "traffickers" (Gotch, 2016). This is true in the research on these offenders as well, so the terms will be used interchangeably in this text.

The categorization of offenders and the development of specific typologies of human traffickers are useful when examining the many types of human trafficking crimes and their diverse impacts on the victims (Busch-Armendariz et al., 2009). The increased rates of psychopathy among human trafficking offenders demonstrate the increased danger that these offenders pose to society (Hargreaves-Cormany, Patterson, & Muirhead, 2016). This research can be highly informative for a diverse population of professionals who come into contact with these victims and offenders, including law enforcement officials, victim advocates, corrections officers, as well as psychologists and other treatment providers (Gotch, 2016). Preventing and intervening in these crimes in the future depends on the development of methods that are empirically informed and data-driven.

Links between psychopathy & human trafficking offenders

While minimal research has been conducted on this particular class of offenders, the existing findings indicate a link between psychopathy and those who are involved in pimping and human trafficking (Spidel et al., 2007). Spidel et al. (2007) investigated the psychopathic characteristics exhibited by a sample of 22 offenders who were charged, convicted, or had admitted to obtaining an income from prostitution and had existing PCL-R scores on file. The PCL-R scores were significantly higher for the offenders who had engaged in pimping than the comparison sample of offenders. These findings suggest consistent overlap in the psychological and physical abuse inflicted by psychopaths and human traffickers.

For example, the tactics of coercion, superficial charm, manipulation, and deception are commonly implemented by both psychopaths and perpetrators of human trafficking. A common strategy employed by these offenders is to lure victims under the guise of a genuine emotional attachment or connection. They then gradually increase their manipulative, coercive, and predatory behaviors to maintain their sense of control (Gotch, 2016; Spidel et al., 2007). It is extremely difficult for victims of human trafficking to escape these controlling psychopathic offenders due to the use of strategies that prey on their psychological and emotional attachments, as well as the very real fear that these criminals will seek physical retaliation given that they have threatened to do so and have likely done so in many instances in the past (Polaris Project, 2006).

Spidel et al. (2007) also found that many of the offenders in their study had additional shared characteristics indicative of higher levels of psychopathy. The majority had a high school education, a history of substance abuse, additional psychiatric diagnoses, and a criminal record that included previously violent offenses. Furthermore, a parasitic lifestyle is another characteristic associated with psychopathy and is included in Hare's PCL-R (Hare, 1999). The act of engaging in human trafficking is evidence of a parasitic lifestyle, as it involves intentionally manipulating and exploiting others for financial gain. The higher rates of psychopathy among pimps and traffickers are significant with its implication that victims of human trafficking will encounter psychopaths and are at greater risk of physical and emotional harm (Spidel et al., 2007).

Gotch (2016) investigated a sample of 28 adult male offenders who had been arrested, charged, or convicted of domestic trafficking for sexual exploitation and specifically examined the psychological, environmental, and criminogenic factors of these offenders. The data was collected from the offenders' pretreatment psychosexual evaluation reports, which included a clinical interview, assessment data including scores on the PCL-R, and official documents such as police reports, criminal records, presentence investigation reports, court records, and treatment records. The PCL-R scores of this sample of trafficking offenders were highly significant. The majority of offenders (79%) scored in the high or very high range of psychopathic traits (Gotch, 2016). These findings indicate the necessity of developing and maintaining an extensive database of references for professionals who work with this highly specialized population of offenders. Gotch's (2016) exploration and findings emphasize the heterogeneous nature of these offenders given their divergent motivations, tactics, and values that ultimately contribute to their commission of human trafficking offenses.

Offenders' motives

In order to develop effective policies and prevention and intervention methods against perpetrators engaging in human trafficking, it is necessary to understand these offenders' underlying motivations and reasoning, especially why they perceive it to be lucrative and beneficial (Gotch, 2016). This population of offenders is unique in that it consists of violent offenders, sexual offenders, and mixed (both violent and sexual) offenders (Hargreaves-Cormany, Patterson, & Muirhead, 2016). The motivation of these offenders is different than that of many nonpsychopathic sex offenders, who are typically driven by sexual gratification and/or fantasy. Rather, human trafficking offenders' motivations are largely predatory and instrumental with their main goal being the achievement of financial profits and in some cases sexual gratification as well (Hargreaves-Cormany, Patterson, & Muirhead, 2016).

This is well aligned with the findings of previous studies, given the inflated levels of psychopathy present among these offenders. These results also demonstrate the wide range of motivations that frequently overlap among human trafficking offenders. These include all of the following: financial benefits, sexual motives, power and control, antisocial or psychopathic personality traits, involvement in general criminality, and propensity for violence or domestic violence (Gotch, 2016; Olver & Wong, 2006). While the present chapter primarily focuses on the presence of psychopathic traits among these offenders, the frequent overlap in motivations indicates that all of these factors remain particularly relevant to an in-depth exploration of human trafficking perpetrators.

Human trafficking offenders' enhanced ability to manipulate victims through "tactical empathy"

The study of empathy is important to the field of forensic psychology and can help in better understanding the mechanisms as to how psychopathic human trafficking offenders think and act to better perpetrate their crimes (Hoffer, Hargreaves-Cormany, Muirhead, & Meloy, 2018). Research by de Waal (2008, 2009) and Preston and de Waal (2002) led to the development of the evolutionary interpretation and evaluation of the construct of empathy. This definition contended that empathy developed from mammalian maternal care of mothers and was transmitted to offspring (de Waal, 2008, as cited in Bubandt & Willerslev, 2015; Hoffer et al., 2018). This concept was further developed through the model of empathy, which depicted it as a "Russian Doll Model" that consisted of multiple layers of different types of empathy and empathic responses based on its previously mentioned evolution (Bubandt & Willerslev, 2015; Hoffer et al., 2018; Preston & de Waal, 2002).

There are two types of empathy that stem from this evolutionary model. Cognitive empathy is defined as "understanding another's feelings and knowing what they are thinking, whether by means of simple associations or more complex perspective-taking processes" (de Wied et al., 2007, p. 99 as cited in Hargreaves-Cormany, Patterson, & Muirhead, 2016). Cognitive empathy or perspective taking was defined by de Waal (2006) as the ability to "assess the situation and reasons for other's emotions" (p. 39).

Conversely, affective empathy is defined as concerning, "...the vicarious experience of emotions consistent with those of others, that is, feeling *with* others" (de Wied et al., 2007, p. 99 as cited in Hargreaves-Cormany, Patterson, & Muirhead, 2016). Thus, from a scientific perspective, empathy is a neutral capacity. It is neither morally "good" or "bad" instead it should be viewed as a tool that can be used for antisocial and/or prosocial behavior. Empathy is often confounded with terms like "mutual understanding, altruism, consolation, intersubjective compassion, care or social cohesion-goals" (Bubandt & Willerslev, 2015). While these are aspects of empathy; there is a dual nature to empathy which includes use of empathy for antisocial and predatory purposes. This type of empathy is referred to as "tactical empathy" (Hoffer et al., 2018).

Empathy, specifically cognitive empathy is elevated in predatory and psychopathic offenders. Studies have shown that offenders with elevated levels of psychopathic traits tend to have lower levels of emotional empathy, which is believed to be caused by deficits in emotional processing (Brook & Kosson, 2013; Wai & Tiliopoulos, 2012). Due to lower levels of being able to feel what others are feeling, it is theorized that cognitive empathy becomes far more developed in order to hide this emotional empathy deficit (Dadds et al., 2009). This ability to devise what others are feeling or their emotional state cognitively allows for the identification for those at risk or susceptible to influence due to cognitive analysis of facial cues and observable emotional states (Brook & Kosson, 2013). Thus, given the high levels of psychopathy in STJ Offenders demonstrated in the existing research, it is likely that human trafficking offenders have high levels of cognitive empathy which enable them to better perpetrate their crimes through this detached cognitive analysis of emotional states and risk profile (Hargreaves-Cormany, Patterson, & Muirhead, 2016).

Offenders' methodologies

These offenders' extensive manipulation methods are evidenced by the multiphase processes by which they con, habituate, and control their victims (Hargreaves-Cormany, Patterson, & Muirhead, 2016; Serie et al., 2018). Spidel et al. (2007) emphasized the maladaptive nature of the victim-offender relationship among perpetrators of sex trafficking and their victims. Psychopathic pimps often consider and treat their victims as property and demonstrate convincing but ultimately insincere emotional attachments in order to manipulate and coerce their victims' cooperation with their demands. Their interpersonal tactics involve interchanging attention and affection with violence and intimidation often leaving their victims in a deeply confused and distressed state (Serie et al., 2018; Spidel et al., 2007). They may recruit their victims with or without the initial use of some form of coercion or manipulation. Their techniques are varied and evolve over time while frequently increasing in the presence and severity of violence. The diversity of these offenders' behaviors, wavering back and forth between providing attention, protection, and affection to utilizing intimidation and violence as a means of control, contributes to the ongoing, cyclical, and complicated nature of these relationships (Serie et al., 2018).

A 2018 study by Serie et al. aimed to answer the call for further research on sex trafficking offenders by conducting and analyzing interviews with the offenders themselves. The authors' goal was to gain insight into the sex trafficking offenders' perspectives of the victim-offender relationship and their methods of operation. Interviews were conducted with 12 male offenders, ages 21 to 71, who were either already convicted of or charged with sex trafficking offenses. The majority of the victims of the offenders in this sample were females under the age of 18, and most of the offenders interviewed had between one and four known victims, with one exception being one offender who was convicted of trafficking 17 victims (Serie et al., 2018).

In the Serie et al. (2018) study, a grounded theory approach was used to analyze the interviews. Four key themes were found to be significant, including the offenders' perceptions of all of the following: the initiation of contact with the victims, the victim-offender relationship, the offenders' roles and methodologies, and the victims' reports to the police. According to the traffickers, contact was primarily initiated as a request or offer for help with a problematic situation and as a request or offer for a job. In some cases, contact was initiated by the trafficker, and in other cases, the victims had initiated the contact.

The initiation interactions illustrated in this study offer more evidence of the increased vulnerability exhibited by victims of human trafficking, as detailed in the research of Hargreaves-Cormany & Patterson, 2016. Vulnerable juveniles are frequently targeted by these psychopathic offenders due to the victims' financial strain or lack of social support. Victims may initially be attracted to a perceived ability of trafficking offenders to "fill the void" in their lives by providing for their basic survival needs, including both financial and emotional support, ultimately leading to their recruitment and participation in sex trafficking operations (Hargreaves-Cormany & Patterson, 2016). For example, an offender in the Serie et al. (2018) study explained how he sought out and selected vulnerable victims, "These girls were vulnerable and already experienced something alike or had been sexually abused… I knew that and would pick them out" (Respondent 6, p. 8). Another offender interviewed in the study explained how he was able to get girls to work for him and stay with him, "I have the space and the means, and the means are my control, and the agreements I make" (Respondent 16, p. 8).

Based on the same interview data, four types of victim-offender relationships were described: a helping relationship, in which the offender initially provides the victim with a place to stay or protection; an emotional bond, in which the relationship started as a perceived friendship or intimate relationship; an agreement relationship, in which the relationship was based on a business agreement from which both parties wanted to make money; and controlling relationships, in which the victim was viewed as an object that could be manipulated and controlled to serve the offenders' needs (Serie et al., 2018). The victim-offender relationship patterns appeared to be dynamic, as they often changed frequently over time and across individual victims and offenders.

The majority of the sex trafficking offenders in this sample reported that they simply acted as facilitators, and the victims were acting of their own free will in choosing to participate in the illicit activities. Evidence of this means of operation was seen in the helping, emotional, and agreement relationships. The methods used in the controlling relationships differed greatly with the involvement of emotional and/or physical manipulation of the victims. More specifically, emotional manipulation was exhibited by the offenders by showing love and affection to the victim prior to gradually resetting their expectations and the use of threats or false promises. The offenders reported that as time went on, they often increasingly shifted to more physical violence in an effort to ensure that their victims would continue to work for them (Serie et al., 2018). One offender explained, "One time I noticed she did not want to work for me anymore, and I would wait for her, put her in the car and she had to work; you have girls who say they are going to report you… who get beaten up" (Serie et al., 2018, Respondent 6, p. 9). These detailed accounts of the tactics employed by these offenders, as described in their own words, indicate not only the type and extent of manipulation and control exercised over the victims, but also the offenders' keen awareness and intentionality in detecting and exploiting vulnerable victims. Thus this serves as additional evidence of their psychopathic traits and behaviors.

Lastly, many of the offenders reported that the victims who had turned them in to the police had made false accusations or were often seeking the sympathy and attention that is commonly received by victims, or revenge for the dissolution of their romantic relationships. The findings indicate the complex nature of human trafficking offenses, as differences exist across individual sex traffickers and over time within the same victim-offender relationship. It is important to note that a limitation of the Serie et al.'s (2018) study is that it reflects the offenders' perceptions of their relationships with their victims, which may or may not be an accurate representation of reality and the veracity of their statements is unknown.

Societal context and its facilitating role

Qualitative research conducted by the National Center for Missing & Exploited Children (NCMEC) has emphasized the role of the glamorization of pimp culture by mainstream media (music lyrics and music videos, movies, etc.) in the rapid expansion of human trafficking operations (NCMEC, 2017). In the attempt to gain a more complete understanding of these offenders' methods, it is of interest to consider the role of technological advancement as well (Hargreaves-Cormany, Patterson, & Muirhead, 2016). In recent years, the development of online platforms has led to an increasing number of sex trafficking crimes being initiated via the Internet. The nature of the online environment assists these offenders in many ways, by providing increased accessibility, anonymity, and opportunities to network with other criminals participating in similar criminal activities (Owens, Eakin, Hoffer, Muirhead, & Shelton, 2016).

Victimology

While sex traffickers may be friends, family members, or intimate partners of their victims, they can also be strangers or acquaintances (Serie et al., 2018). The most relevant victim selection characteristics for human trafficking offenders are vulnerability and accessibility (Hargreaves-Cormany, Patterson, & Muirhead, 2016). These highly predatory and psychopathic offenders typically target vulnerable victims, as they are highly skilled in recognizing and exploiting others' weaknesses (Spidel et al., 2007; Williamson & Cluse-Tolar, 2002). They are keenly aware of individuals who appear to be afflicted by multiple stressors and more inclined to participate in recruitment and victimization practices, which are often presented as an escape from or better alternative to their existing, problematic lives. The juvenile victims that are targeted by these offenders are often experiencing one or more of the following stressors: a dissolution or interruption in their home life, such as removal from their home and placement in foster care or Child Protective Services intervention; dysfunctional family environment involving increased conflict and/or financial difficulties; or living in neighborhoods plagued by low socioeconomic status and high crime rates (Hargreaves-Cormany, Patterson, & Muirhead, 2016). Victims are frequently lured by promises of a loving relationship or a better life. Unfortunately for many victims, any perceived improvement in their life may appear to be a better option than what they are currently enduring in their lives as they are often in already abusive home environments when recruited into sex trafficking.

While it seems obvious that one's environment and past experiences can influence future behavior, there may be a biological component involved as well (Nelson, Kendall, & Shields, 2014). In fact, there is evidence to suggest that the events of a person's life actually impact biological development—a concept known as "biological embedding" (Nelson et al., 2014). Along with this idea of biological embedding comes the discussion of epigenetics, in which it is believed that genes themselves can change without a blatant alteration of the genetic sequence (Gonzalez, 2013). If this is true, then, one's genome is constantly interacting with his surroundings. With respect to victims of juvenile sex trafficking, this idea of biological embedding can help explain the true depth of their vulnerability. If they are already living in situations that put them at risk for seeking attention and affirmation, then those voids can further be ingrained through impairments in cognitive functioning and decision-making abilities (Nelson et al., 2014). Similarly, environmental stressors may also manifest as mental health issues and physical illness, which both increase the likelihood of falling prey to addiction (Hargreaves-Cormany & Patterson, 2016). In essence, the interaction of extremely psychopathic STJ Offenders with highly vulnerable STJ Victims is the perfect storm based upon all of the aforementioned contentions discussed thus far within this chapter and as supported within the literature.

Implications and future directions for research and practice

Research on human trafficking is lacking for various reasons including variations in the ways that this crime is defined within the criminal justice system and subsequent research (Gotch, 2016; National Institute of Justice, 2012). Human trafficking can include both the sexual exploitation and sex trafficking behaviors of these offenders. Differences in the situational characteristics of human trafficking offenses—such as whether the crime is perpetrated international or domestically, among adult and minor victims and offenders, on the streets or online, by family or nonfamily members, by strangers or acquaintances, or by those involved with gang activity—can also further complicate this crime. In addition, there is frequent intersection between the smuggling and trafficking trades, so differentiating between these two offenses can be difficult at times.

The ways in which human trafficking offenders are classified as a result of court proceedings vary across cases and jurisdictions as well. In some instances, they are considered sexual offenders, and in others, they are considered domestic violence offenders (Gotch, 2016). These circumstances can create confusion and conflict as to how investigations should be handled, how pimps should be charged, and how the prosecutions that ensue should ultimately be adjudicated. The ideal, or course, would be to aim for greater consistency in these areas, across and within individual jurisdictions.

The specificity of the criminal subculture involved in human trafficking networks also further complicates the research, as well as the resulting recommended practical strategies for dealing with this unique population of offenders (Gotch, 2016). The human trafficking and sex trade industry utilizes its own language, cultural values and aspects, and means of operation. Therefore knowledge of the idiosyncrasies of this criminal population is vital to working with the offenders and victims who are involved (National Institute of Justice, 2012; Polaris Project, 2006).

In their efforts to combat labor trafficking, governments and other entities encounter some of the same barriers that exist in the fight against sex trafficking. There is a dearth of research on labor trafficking, making it difficult to create and implement effective intervention and prevention strategies. Moreover, the covert nature of this form of trafficking poses challenges in estimating the extent of this type of criminal activity. It is noted that children are commonly the victims of labor trafficking, due to the fact that they comprise a vulnerable population. While adults are much more likely to be exploited through labor trafficking than through sex trafficking, there are instances in which entire families, including children, are exploited by labor traffickers. Though mechanisms for victims to earn money for their traffickers may differ between these two forms of exploitation, methods of recruitment may appear similar. In both cases, traffickers prey on the weaknesses of potential victims. Whether a victim is in search of better economic stability within a work setting, or is attracted to the presumed protection and security offered by a pimp, the trafficker often represents him/herself as the person best able to fulfill that need or desire. Indeed, some labor traffickers may even take on the role of a love interest when preying on young women, mirroring common tactics used by sex traffickers.

There is no available research on the psychopathic tendencies of labor traffickers but reports as to how their methodologies resemble those of sex traffickers suggest a strong possibility of higher levels of psychopathy in that population. These offenders commonly view others as pawns to be manipulated for their own benefit, exhibit charisma that they use to attract and maintain control of their victims, and show little or no remorse for their actions. Perhaps the main difference between the two categories of traffickers is that labor traffickers often take advantage of individuals who are extremely desperate and seeking work in any venue they can find, despite obvious hardships and the risk of arrest and incarceration. Recruiting such victims may not require the same type or degree of manipulation as sex trafficking victims, since potential victims of labor trafficking may be already residing illegally in a country or jurisdiction, and/or are otherwise in dire financial straits. Nonetheless, a tentative assumption can be made that labor traffickers display some of the same psychopathic traits as sex traffickers. More research is necessary in order for more conclusive comparisons to be made.

Existing research further demonstrates that human trafficking cases remain difficult to identify and investigate not only due to local criminal justice officials' lack of knowledge and experience with these types of cases, but also due to the lack of effective policies and protocols to guide their investigations and management of human trafficking cases (National Institute of Justice, 2012). Finally, development and generation of reliable as well as accurate statistics on the prevalence, frequency, and geographic distribution of human trafficking continues to be a significant challenge due to the covert nature of these offenses (Clawson, Layne & Small, 2006, as cited in research by Roe-Sepowitz et al., 2017).

Examining the characteristics and behaviors of offenders who engage in human trafficking can provide a better understanding of the underlying causes and motivations behind this crime. This knowledge can then be used to inform future investigation, risk assessment, and prevention and intervention methods in an effort to address this widespread criminal enterprise (Busch-Armendariz et al., 2009). Analyzing the role that psychopathy plays in human trafficking offenses and other offenses can provide important insights into these offenders' risk for future violence, potential intervention and treatment methodologies, and their prognosis (Hare & Neumann, 2005).

The present review of the existing literature highlights the importance of fostering a working knowledge, understanding, and awareness of the construct of psychopathy in professionals dealing with sex trafficking offenders (Spidel et al., 2007). These offenders are known to minimize their offenses and the damaging effects of their criminal behaviors on their victims and society as a whole. They often deny the extent of their involvement or refuse to accept responsibility for their crimes in favor of transferring the blame to their victims or other individuals that may be entwined in their web of criminal activities. These offenders may even go so far as to reframe their actions by offering the interpretation that they are providing a service to those involved in sex trafficking, including the buyers, their criminal associates, and their victims (Spidel et al., 2007). This methodology further highlights the psychopathic traits and behaviors exhibited by sex trafficking offenders and demonstrates the magnitude of their ruthless, callous, and predatory nature.

Research demonstrates that pimps are a unique population of offenders in need of specialized prevention and intervention strategies (Porter, ten Brinke, & Wilson, 2009). The antisocial nature and behaviors of psychopaths lead to additional problematic features among these offenders, such as their decreased motivation for change (Moffitt, 1993; Olver, Lewis, & Wong, 2013). Olver et al. (2013) found that higher psychopathic traits, as measured using Hare's PCL-R, were associated with reduced progress in therapy and level of risk posed to society. In particular, psychopaths with greater callous-unemotional (CU) traits, or higher scores on Factor 1 of the PCL-R, Interpersonal and Affective Characteristics, have been found to be particularly resistant to realizing notable progress in therapeutic treatments. These severely personality-disordered offenders present with the additional challenges of increased difficulty in building rapport and genuine relationships with their therapists, accepting responsibility for their behaviors, recognizing the harm or damage they have caused, and accepting challenges to their disordered thought processes (Olver et al., 2013).

In severe cases of psychopathy, it is contended that psychotherapy actually exacerbates the condition of the patient and instead of providing the objective of treatment and particularly in group therapy programs it instead provides a training ground for how to better manipulate victims (Kosson, Gacono, & Bodholdt, 2000; Vitale, 2018). More specifically, within the dynamics of therapy sessions, for example, psychopaths can observe and learn from the interactions around them which types of verbal, facial, and bodily expressions have the greatest impact toward influencing and convincing therapists of their sincerity in progressing in their treatment (Lee, 1999). Then, upon release, these individuals are better equipped to use those same techniques on their intended or actual victims (Lee, 1999).

Porter et al. (2009) found that highly psychopathic incarcerated offenders were able to utilize their abilities to charm, manipulate, and con parole boards into authorizing their conditional release and allowing them to return to the community. This knowledge has important implications, such as promoting the awareness of the extreme danger that these offenders pose to our society. Psychopaths currently pose a threat to society based on their abilities to manipulate the authorities, the criminal justice system, and deny chargers. It was found that psychopathic sex offenders are 2.43 times more likely to be released than nonpsychopathic offenders and are 2.79 times more likely to be released from general crimes (Babiak et al., 2012). Psychopaths have the ability to imitate emotions that will deter the court system with granting punishment. Babiak et al. (2012) found in their research that psychopaths are 2.5 times faster than other offenders in being released by the parole board. It is for these reasons psychopaths not only pose a threat to society but the criminal justice system as well.

Future research efforts should focus on understanding and addressing the demand associated with commercial sexual exploitation and trafficking, exploring the complex and criminally sophisticated nature of human trafficking offenders, and developing long-term, empirically validated prevention and intervention methods to combat this extremely dangerous and far-reaching criminal enterprise (Gotch, 2016). Such endeavors might include gathering more detailed information about and from the buyers (johns), including their relationships and interactions with the sellers (pimps) and the trafficked victims, especially in those instances wherein the buyers have repeated sexual interactions with the same victims over time.

Gender and the associated variations in levels of psychopathy and motivations among these offenders should also be explored since females are often excluded from the research due to a limited sample size. Differences among perpetrators of domestic trafficking across geographic regions should also be investigated given that there may be different strategies and tactics used in various locations in order to evade detection and to adapt to the different sentencing practices in different states and/or countries (Gotch, 2016). Data could be derived not only from the participants in the criminal activity, but also from law enforcement practitioners and managers, as well as prosecutors, to determine what lessons can be learned from the changing tactics of the offenders that might better inform how those changes can be addressed through more creative and progressive investigative techniques.

The variations in the classification and sentencing of these offenders make it increasingly difficult to conduct research on the recidivism rates of sex trafficking offenders. Therefore research exploring the recidivism and criminal offense patterns of these offenders across the lifespan is needed to further inform the means of intervention that would be best suited for sex trafficking offenders (Hargreaves-Cormany, Patterson, & Muirhead, 2016). In this approach, there likely is much information that can be obtained not only from prosecutors, but also from the therapeutic community, as well as correctional systems throughout the country.

Conclusions

Human trafficking is the third largest criminal enterprise in the world and is not localized to specific geographic areas, thus it is imperative to recognize its global impact and work toward effectively combatting this immensely far-reaching issue. As discussed throughout this chapter, the limited existing research has found that significantly higher rates of psychopathy are exhibited by human trafficking offenders. This further indicates the need for interdisciplinary teams of professionals in the field to conduct additional studies exploring these highly relevant and increasingly problematic areas of study in our society today in order to address the dearth of empirical research on human trafficking, as well as the intersection of psychopathy and this crime. Calls for such research and practice initiatives are found in various task force reports such as the Resolution on Human Trafficking in the United States adopted as American Psychological Association (2017) Policy by the APA Council of Representatives in 2017.

While the research conducted by Hargreaves-Cormany, Patterson, & Muirhead, 2016, as well as other authors discussed in this chapter, serves as a good foundation upon which to build further research, more studies are needed to further elucidate the intricate nature of the crime of human trafficking and the role of psychopathy in this crime. Further research could provide a more comprehensive understanding of this important societal issue and could thereby encourage and attract additional stakeholders to become involved in combatting human trafficking.

The recent passing of bills in the U.S. House of Representatives, such as the "Allow States and Victims to Fight Online Sex Trafficking Act" and the "Put Trafficking Victims First Act of 2019," is promising as this demonstrates increased awareness and support for antitrafficking initiatives that advocate for survivors of sex trafficking. Furthermore, initiatives such as the American Bar Association's Survivor Reentry Project, which offers resources to educate attorneys about the crime of human trafficking and the importance of advocating for survivors, can serve as model programs to be implemented by various stakeholders invested in this important issue internationally. In summary, providing advanced education to professionals in the various fields dealing with human trafficking, increasing the empowerment of survivors, and more comprehensive interdisciplinary collaboration on initiatives to combat human trafficking are the keys to having the most effective strategic interdiction of human trafficking enterprises.

References

American Psychological Association. (2017). *Resolution on human trafficking in the United States especially of women and girls*. Washington, DC: American Psychological Association. Retrieved from http://www.apa.org/about/policy/trafficking-women-girls.aspx.

Babiak, P., Folino, J., Hancock, J., Hare, R. D., Logan, M., Mayer, E. L., ... Woodworth, M. (2012). *Psychopathy: An important forensic concept for the 21st century*. July 01. Retrieved from https://leb.fbi.gov/articles/featured-articles/psychopathy-an-important-forensic-concept-for-the-21st-century.

Barnes, W., & Foster, S. D. J. (Eds.). (2015). *And life continues: Sex trafficking and my journey to freedom*. Scotts Valley, CA: CreateSpace Independent Publishing.

Brook, M., & Kosson, D. S. (2013). Impaired cognitive empathy in criminal psychopathy: Evidence from a laboratory measure of empathic accuracy. *Journal of Abnormal Psychology*, *122*(1), 156–166.

Bubandt, N., & Willerslev, R. (2015). The dark side of empathy: Mimesis, deception, and the magic of alterity. *Comparative Studies in Society and History*, *57*(1), 5–34.

Busch-Armendariz, N., Nsonwu, M., & Cook Heffron, L. (2009). Understanding human trafficking: Development of typologies of traffickers PHASE II. In *Paper presented at the first annual interdisciplinary conference on human trafficking, Lincoln, NE, October*. Retrieved from https://www.researchgate.net/profile/Noel_Busch-Armendariz/publication/266448254_Understanding_Human_Trafficking_Development_of_Typologies_of_Traffickers_PHASE_II/links/551eaafc0cf29dcabb05d8a3.pdf.

Cima, M., Tonnaer, F., & Hauser, M. D. (2010). Psychopaths know right from wrong but don't care. *Social Cognitive and Affective Neuroscience*, *5*(1), 59–67.

Dadds, M., Hawes, D., Frost, A., Vassallo, S., Bunn, P., Hunter, K., & Merz, S. (2009). Learning to "talk the talk": The relationship of psychopathic traits to deficits in empathy across childhood. *Journal of Child Psychology and Psychiatry*, *50*, 599–606.

de Waal, F. (2008). Putting the altruism back into altruism: The evolution of empathy. *Annual Review of Psychology*, *59*, 279–300.

de Waal, F. (2009). The age of empathy. In *Nature's lessons for a kinder society*. New York, NY: Harmony Books.

Federal Bureau of Investigation. (2016). *Human trafficking and involuntary servitude*. May 03. Retrieved from: https://www.fbi.gov/investigate/civil-rights/human-trafficking. (Accessed 15 April 2019).

Gonzalez, A. (2013). The impact of childhood maltreatment on biological systems: Implications for clinical interventions. *Paediatrics & Child Health*, *18*(8), 415–418.

Gotch, K. (2016). Preliminary data on a sample of perpetrators of domestic trafficking for sexual exploitation: Suggestions for research and practice. *Journal of Human Trafficking*, *2*(1), 99–109.

Hare, R. D. (1999). *Without conscience: The disturbing world of the psychopaths among us*. New York, NY: Guilford Press.

Hare, R. D., & Neumann, C. S. (2005). Structural models of psychopathy. *Current Psychiatry Reports*, *7*(1), 57–64.

Hare, R. D., & Neumann, C. S. (2009). Psychopathy: Assessment and forensic implications. *The Canadian Journal of Psychiatry*, *54*(12), 791–802.

Hargreaves-Cormany, H. A., & Patterson, T. D. (2016). Characteristics of survivors of juvenile sex trafficking: Implications for treatment and intervention initiatives. *Aggression and Violent Behavior*, *30*, 32–39.

Hargreaves-Cormany, H. A., Patterson, T. D., & Muirhead, Y. E. (2016). A typology of offenders engaging in the sex trafficking of juveniles (STJ): Implications for risk assessment. *Aggression and Violent Behavior, 30*, 40–47.

Hoffer, T., Hargreaves-Cormany, H., Muirhead, Y., & Meloy, J. R. (2018). *Violence in animal cruelty offenders*. Cham: Springer International Publishing.

Hoppenbrouwers, S., Nazeri, A., de Jesus, D., Stirpe, T., Felsky, D., Daskalakis, Z., & Voineskos, A. (2013). White matter deficits in psychopathic offenders and correlation with factor structure. *PLoS One, 8*(8), e72375.

International Labour Organization. (2017). *Forced labour, modern slavery, and human trafficking*. International Labour Organization. Retrieved from: https://www.ilo.org/global/topics/forced-labour/lang- -en/index.htm.

Kosson, D. S., Gacono, C. B., & Bodholdt, R. H. (2000). Assessing psychopathy: Interpersonal aspects and clinical interviewing. In C. B. Gacono (Ed.), *The LEA series in personality and clinical psychology. The clinical and forensic assessment of psychopathy: A practitioner's guide* (pp. 203–229). Mahwah, NJ, US: Lawrence Erlbaum Associates Publishers.

Lee, J. H. (1999). The treatment of psychopathic and antisocial personality disorders: A review. In *Clinical decision making support unit* (pp. 1–33). Berkshire: Broadmoor Hospital.

Mehlman-Orozco, K. (2017). *Hidden in plain sight: America's slaves of the new millennium*. Santa Barbara, CA: Praeger.

Moffitt, T. E. (1993). Adolescence-limited and life-course-persistent antisocial behavior: A developmental taxonomy. *Psychological Review, 100*, 674–701.

National Center for Missing & Exploited Children (NCMEC). (2017). *Child sex trafficking in America: A guide for parents and guardians [PDF document]*. Retrieved from http://www.missingkids.org/content/dam/pdfs/NCMEC%20CST%20fact%20sheet_ParentGuardian.pdf.

National Institute of Justice. (2012). *Identifying challenges to improve the investigation and prosecution of state and local human trafficking cases [PDF document]*. Retrieved from http://www.urban.org/UploadedPDF/412593-State-and-Local-Human-TraffickingCases.pdf.

Nelson, H., Kendall, G., & Shields, L. (2014). Neurological and biological foundations of children's social and emotional development: An integrated literature review. *The Journal of School Nursing, 30*(4), 240–250.

Olver, M. E., Lewis, K., & Wong, S. C. (2013). Risk reduction treatment of high-risk psychopathic offenders: The relationship of psychopathy and treatment change to violent recidivism. *Personality Disorders: Theory, Research, and Treatment, 4*(2), 160.

Olver, M. E., & Wong, S. C. (2006). Psychopathy, sexual deviance, and recidivism among sex offenders. *Sexual Abuse: A Journal of Research and Treatment, 18*(1), 65.

Organization for Security and Co-operation in Europe (OSCE). OSCE Office of the Special Representative and Co-ordinator for Combating Trafficking in Human Beings. (2018). *The critical role of civil society in combating trafficking in human beings*. (Occasional paper no. 8). Retrieved from https://www.osce.org/secretariat/405197?download=true.

Owens, J. N., Eakin, J. D., Hoffer, T., Muirhead, Y., & Shelton, J. L. E. (2016). Investigative aspects of crossover offending from a sample of FBI online child sexual exploitation cases. *Aggression and Violent Behavior, 30*, 3–14.

Palermo Protocol. (2000). *Protocol to prevent, suppress and punish trafficking in persons, especially women and children, supplementing the United Nations Convention against transnational organized crime*. Nov. 15, 2237 U.N.T.S. 319.

Polaris Project. (2006). *Domestic sex trafficking: The criminal operations of the American pimp [PDF document]*. Retrieved from http://www.dcjs.virginia.gov/victims/humantrafficking/vs/documents/Domestic_Sex_Trafficking_Guide.pdf.

Porter, S., ten Brinke, L., & Wilson, K. (2009). Crime profiles and conditional release performance of psychopathic and non-psychopathic sexual offenders. *Legal and Criminological Psychology*, *14*(1), 109–118.

Preston, S., & de Waal, F. (2002). Empathy: Its ultimate and proximate bases. *Behavioral and Brain Sciences*, *25*, 1–72.

Roe-Sepowitz, D., Gallagher, J., Hogan, K., Ward, T., Denecour, N., Bracy, K., & Arizona State University Office of Sex Trafficking Intervention Research. (2017). *A six-year analysis of sex traffickers of minors: Exploring characteristics and sex trafficking patterns*. November 09. Retrieved from https://www.mccaininstitute.org/six-year-analysis-of-sex-traffickers/.

Serie, C. M., Krumeich, A., van Dijke, A., de Ruiter, E., Terpstra, L., & de Ruiter, C. (2018). Sex traffickers' views: A qualitative study into their perceptions of the victim–offender relationship. *Journal of Human Trafficking*, *4*(2), 169–184.

Shared Hope International. (2019). *What we do: Prevent*. Retrieved from https://sharedhope.org/what-we-do/prevent/.

Smith, H. A. (2014). *Walking prey: How America's youth are vulnerable to sex slavery*. New York, NY: Palgrave Macmillan.

Spidel, A., Greaves, C., Cooper, B. S., Hervé, H. F., Hare, R. D., & Yuille, J. C. (2007). The psychopath as pimp. *Canadian Journal of Police and Security Services*, *4*(4), 193–199.

U.S. Department of State. (2019, June). *2019 Trafficking in persons report [PDF file]*. Retrieved from https://www.state.gov/wp-content/uploads/2019/06/2019-Trafficking-in-Persons-Report.pdf.

United Nations Office on Drugs and Crime (UNODC). (2018). *Global report on trafficking in persons 2018 [E-book]* (4th ed., pp. 21–24). New York: UNODC. Retrieved from https://www.unodc.org/documents/data-and-analysis/glotip/2018/GLOTiP_2018_BOOK_web_small.pdf.

Vitale, J. (2018). Assessing and treating psychopaths. In M. Ternes, P. R. Magaletta, & M. W. Patry (Eds.), *The practice of correctional psychology* (pp. 173–196). Springer.

Wai, M., & Tiliopoulos, N. (2012). The affective and cognitive empathic nature of the dark triad personality. *Personality and Individual Differences*, *52*(7), 794–799.

Williamson, C., & Cluse-Tolar, T. (2002). Pimp-controlled prostitution: Still an integral part of street life. *Violence Against Women*, *8*(9), 1074–1092.

Psychopathy and terrorist involvement

18

Emily Corner and Paul Gill

Introduction

Psychopathological theories are very common in investigations seeking to identify causality across multiple types of nonpolitical violent behavior (Leistedt, 2013). The application of psychopathological theories to explain terrorist behavior is therefore unsurprising. The terrorist suffering from a mental disorder is initially an attractive concept; the callous, destructive actions, and behaviors involved in terrorism invite a stigmatizing label. The academic investigation of mental disorders' association with being a terrorist has experienced four paradigms of conceptual and empirical development. These four paradigms differed from one another in terms of their empirical evidence, the specific mental disorders studied, and their conceptualizations of terrorist involvement. Initially, psychopathy sat at the forefront of such explanations. Lacking in empirical evidence, this paradigm offered psychopathy as a *cause* of terrorist involvement. It focused upon individual drives, and characterized terrorist involvement as a yes/no dichotomy (e.g., a subject was either a terrorist or not). The second paradigm instead turned the psychopathological focus away from "pure" psychopathy toward personality traits.

Multiple seminal reviews conducted within the third paradigm synthesized the existing evidence base and rightly questioned the causative nature and prevalence of psychopathy and personality traits. Misinterpretations of these reviews led to some commonly held, yet false, generalizations within the literature. Many subsequent studies not only rejected the explanatory power of mental disorders as concluded within the reviews, but also likely downplayed the presence of any mental health problems among terrorists in the first place (Abrahms, 2011; Post, 2005, 2007; Sher & Rice, 2015).

Empirical analyses have flourished in the past decade and encapsulate the fourth paradigm. The studies within this paradigm are starting to carve a middle ground between the hardcore line adopted by paradigms one and two and the mistaken assumptions that followed seminal reviews of paradigm three. This latest paradigm is characterized by its empiricism, and understanding that terrorist involvement is a complex process (e.g., terrorist involvement is usually the outcome of a pathway involvement of multiple push/pull factors and that the meaning of terrorist involvement may differ across roles within the group; Gill, 2012; Horgan, 2005), and the understanding of the role of mental health within this process is still in its infancy.

Psychopathy and Criminal Behavior. https://doi.org/10.1016/B978-0-12-811419-3.00017-0

Paradigm one—Psychopathy as key

The earliest academic research which sought to explain terrorist behavior looked to the most commonly attributed cause of extreme behavior in society—psychopathy. Most early published analyses placed psychopathy as the core explanatory variable for terrorist behavior. This speculative opinion was derived mainly from popular culture, and the desire to attribute mental disorders to those committing such heinous, violent acts (Victoroff, 2005). Morf (1970) cites Dr. André Lussier, one of the first psychiatrists to give opinion on the cause of terrorist behavior. Lussier describes individuals who were not able to hold a positive role in society, who crave glamor and revolt, and have a misplaced assumption that their actions carry greatness. Lussier concluded that terrorists are in a state of "mental urgency," craving an "illusion of power," which is satiated through attacking the strongest perceived enemy (Morf, 1970, p. 15). The earliest form of analysis examining the role of psychopathy in terrorists we are aware of is Pearce (1977). It is a simple paper, constituting five pages, and is targeted at police negotiators. The paper articulates three types of hostage takers: the criminal psychopath, the mentally ill, and the political terrorist. The political terrorist, Pearce posits, "may show some evidence of psychopathy, paranoia, or other psychiatric illness but most frequently and predominantly there is evidence of superego lacunae" (1977). Pearce continues: The political terrorist "may be an aggressive psychopath, who has espoused some particular cause because extremist causes can provide an external focal point for all the things that have gone wrong in his life" (1977). The paper offers no case studies, confirming literature nor data of any sort. It is primarily oriented toward promoting how, and in what circumstances, psychiatrists can aid police negotiators. Despite its scientific limitations, the paper had an unintended lasting effect on how subsequent studies depicted terrorist motivations.

The same year Cooper (1977) suggested psychopaths could make ideal terrorists because they are free of the moral constraints that might hinder others to conduct violence. In this way, the analysis mirrors Pearce's focus on the superego lacunae. Cooper further argues that psychopaths are more likely lone actors because "few... terrorist organizations would purposefully recruit them to their ranks" (1977, p. 188). In a separate paper, Cooper (1978) goes much further in his position in a number of statements:

> *Terrorism has an innate 'self-righteousness' about it that is remarkably similar to the attitudes displayed by the psychopath... The terrorist like the psychopath is distinguished by the peculiar slant of his morality. It is not he who is out of step, it is the others, however numerous they might be. It is, perhaps, in this development of, and adherence to, a distinctively personal code of conduct, substantially out of tune with that of the rest of society, that the psychopath and the terrorist are seen at their closest.... an indifference to the rights of others at best and an active, festering hostility at worst... It is small wonder that, on occasion at least, the distinction between them seems scarcely worth making... Despite their conduct and the repugnant side of their personalities, both the psychopath and the terrorist are capable of exciting sympathy even from those whom such a reaction might hardly have been expected.* (p. 256)

Other pragmatic and theoretical accounts noted the equifinality of psychopathy and terrorist engagement, highlighting that they emerge from similar traits and states. For example, Martens (2004) suggests terrorists and ASPD[a] patients share characteristics such as social alienation, disturbed early socialization processes, aggressive narcissistic attitudes, impulsivity and hostility, poor self-esteem, defensive attitudes, arrogance and disdain, deep trauma and moral disengagement.

Cooper (1978) additionally argues that psychopathy might indeed drive terrorist behavior, but often badly, leading to the development of poor-quality terrorists: "Terrorism, like any other serious undertaking, requires dedication, perseverance, and a certain selflessness. These are the very qualities that are lacking in the psychopath. They make for mediocrity in performance" (1978, p. 261). He refers to Andreas Baader as "the failure" and "rather pathetic" (1978, p. 259). Cooper also suggests "the concomitants of the psychopathic personality probably worked more effectively against the prospects for success" for Baader (1978, p. 259). Cooper argues that if it were not for engaging in terrorism, many would find another outlet for their violent impulses. Almost a decade later, Tanay (1987) agreed with Cooper, arguing that terrorist acts are merely psychopathic tendencies hidden behind political rhetoric to provide the terrorist with an excuse to aggress.

Later analyses became more sophisticated and empirical in nature, but the focus on psychopathy was never far away. For example, Ferracuti and Bruno (1981) assert nine commonalities among their sample of 908 right-wing Italian terrorists. These are (1) ambivalence toward authority, (2) defective insight, (3) adherence to convention, (4) emotional detachment from the consequences of their actions, (5) sexual role uncertainties, (6) magical thinking, (7) destructiveness, (8) low education, and (9) adherence to violent subculture norms and weapons fetishes. The study also concludes that right-wing terrorists were more likely than their left-wing counterparts to possess psychopathic personalities. Strenz's (1988) investigation of left-wing terrorists in the 1960s and 1970s defined (1) leaders, (2) activist-operators, and (3) idealists. Although Strenz defines the activist-operators to present with a psychopathic personality structure, it is the description of the leaders given by the author that fits closer to the diagnostic criteria of psychopathy.[b] Much later, Hamden's (2002) typology of terrorists included the ideal type named "Psychopathic."

The impression of a terrorist as a psychopath holds "intuitive appeal," until one delves further into the underlying construct of psychopathy (Borum, 2004, p. 31). Clinical diagnostic criteria are clear that those diagnosed with psychopathy present with a lack or remorse, persistent disregard for, and violation of, the rights of others, disrespect toward the feelings of others, patterns of irresponsibility in many aspects of their life, and indifference and a lack of remorse for their negative actions (American

[a] Although currently there exists a distinction between the diagnosis of ASPD and that of psychopathy, it is considered that ASPD diagnoses focus on observable behaviors, whereas the diagnosis of psychopathy also requires interrogation of personality traits.

[b] Strenz (1988) defines leaders to cloak their paranoia through charismatic self-confidence and commanding presence, whereas the activist-operators are defined by a history of criminal activity and desire for violence and hedonism.

Psychiatric Association, 2013; Hare, 1985). The discord between the conclusions in the above-mentioned studies and clinical diagnostics spans from the labeling of psychopathy in the absence of rigorous clinical diagnostic procedures. Standard clinical procedures require direct access to individuals in clinical settings for prolonged periods. These protocols were not followed in terrorism studies. Pearce (1977) utilized autobiographies, biographies, and media interviews as determinants for diagnosis. In one case, he diagnosed psychopathy following the analysis of tattoos found on one terrorist's body. Kellen (1982) also used secondary source material, basing his conclusions on behavior during media interviews.

Alongside an absence of rigorous clinical procedures, the studies in this paradigm also failed to consider that much like many other mental health conditions, traits of psychopathy fall on a continuum. Robert Hare commented that most people would likely score a 3 or 4 on the Psychopathy Checklist (PCL-R) (Hare, 2007). Therefore terrorists are likely to exhibit at least some of the traits included on the PCL-R. Although terrorists may have been included in forensic population studies that have critically examined the PCL-R, there is currently no empirical study on clinical psychopathy scores for terrorists.

In the absence of rigorous clinical and empirical procedures, the reductionist conclusions, where terrorists are characterized as abnormal purely on the nature of the attack behavior, ignore the highly complex neurological, psychological, and sociological processes that move an individual toward terrorist behavior (Horgan, 2003). Silke (1998) likens the attempts to apply psychological dispositions to terrorists to the circular thinking of the Cheshire Cat from Alice in Wonderland. The Cat thinks that only mad people can inhabit Wonderland, so therefore anyone he met in Wonderland must be mad. We support Silke's argument that empirical support for psychopathy remains elusive. The lack of valid concepts and objective empirical research, alongside advancement of psychological research concerning psychopathy, and development of the widely accepted validated measure (PCL-R; Hare, 1985) aided the gradual demise of the psychopath-as-terrorist theory. This permitted other psychological theories to come to the fore.

Paradigm two—Personality as key

In a continuing attempt to identify fundamental psychological qualities of terrorists, researchers turned to psychoanalytical theories. Early work in this paradigm ran concurrently to work attributing psychopathy to terrorist behavior, but following the 1980s, psychoanalysis largely replaced the studies of paradigm one. Psychoanalysis examines the relationship between conscious and unconscious thought and focuses upon psychological development from childhood. The findings from this paradigm are reasonably similar to the previous, in that they hold assumptions of the terrorist being essentially abnormal. However, the abnormality is determined by unconscious motives and impulses spanning from childhood maltreatment, and has theoretical roots in Freud's Oedipus complex (Borum, 2004).

One of the earliest, and most complete, empirical studies into the terrorist personality was carried out on German terrorist movements in the 1970s. The *Analysen zum*

Terrorismus included comprehensive interviews and analyses of 250 terrorist careers (Jäger, Schmidtchen, & Süllwold, 1981). The results demonstrated 25% of interviewees had lost one or both parents in early life and 33% reported severe conflict with their parents (Post, 1984). As influential as the findings of the *Analysen zum Terrorismus* were, many citing studies failed to report methodological issues, which severely affected both the validity and replicability of the results. There were issues in arranging interviews, which reduced the subject pool, hostility, and poor cooperation during interviews, little effort to stratify the findings across the roles held during engagement, no control group, and most importantly, interviewees were suspected terrorists, who were not yet convicted of any terrorist offense (Crenshaw, 1986; Horgan, 2003).

Many studies in this paradigm highlighted various aspects of personality, with narcissism being the most common. Narcissists possess an overinflated sense of self to the effect that they profess to be superior to others, have volatile self-esteem, interpersonal problems, and are prone to aggression in response to ego threats (Hogg and Vaughan, 2005). Narcissistic injuries, caused by early emotional injuries, lead to a damaged sense of self in adulthood. Incapable of overcoming these early emotional experiences, the individual directs his/her anger toward other targets held to be responsible. Much like paradigm one, narcissism offers an intuitive explanation for why individuals choose to fight for a terrorist cause. The theorized relationship between narcissism and aggression was readily attributed to terrorist behavior (Johnson & Feldman, 1992; Lasch, 1979; Pearlstein, 1991; Post, 1984, 1986). This research area heavily cited the results of the *Analysen zum Terrorismus*. Studies in this paradigm that championed narcissism highlighted issues such as parental abuse (Akhtar, 1999; Baruch, 2003; DeMause, 2002; Kent & Nicholls, 1977), deviance within the family system (Berko, 2007; Böllinger, 1985), the inability to identify with a father figure (Billig, 1985), and the experience of conflict with parents (de Cataldo Neuberger, Valentini, & Campling, 1996; Kellen, 1982).

Others moved beyond descriptive profiles, and toward explaining how and why such narcissistic individuals become involved in terrorism (Johnson & Feldman, 1992; Lasch, 1979; Pearlstein, 1991; Post, 1984, 1986). For example, Crayton (1983; cited by Borum, 2004) explained that charismatic group leaders draw narcissistically vulnerable individuals to the group, and "narcissistic rage" prompts aggressive responses to perceived injustices during involvement. Crayton went further, asserting that group processes drive narcissism, enhancing collective self-image. These early studies assessed narcissism as the fundamental reason for terrorist behavior. But this work was often highly descriptive, simplistic, and held a focus on early life trauma. There is evidence, however, that more modern studies are moving to include narcissism as one distal facet of the causal chain, which is evaluated in conjunction with other more proximate factors occurring in an individual's life prior to their engagement in terrorism. The most prominent example is that of the case of Anders Brievik. Psychiatrists concluded that Breivik, who killed 77 in Norway in 2011, had a narcissistic personality, and the negative symptoms of this were exacerbated by delusions and extreme right-wing attitudes toward "cultural Marxism" in Europe (Jacobsen & Maier-Katkin, 2015; Tørrissen & Aspaas, 2012). In their work spanning from the evaluation of terrorist prisoners in the United Kingdom, Lloyd and Kleinot (2017) also note the importance of political grievance formation stemming from early life "narcissistic wounds," and satisfaction in inflicting pain on others.

As evidenced by the volume of academic interest over time, the intuitive plausibility of narcissism has often led to it being cited as a fundamental explanation for terrorist behavior. Much like the concepts in paradigm one, these arguments held sway over time. Twelve years apart, both Lasch (1979) and Pearlstein (1991) asserted that narcissism was key to understanding the terrorist personality. For Pearlstein (1991), terrorists utilize their narcissistic rage in undertaking their duties. However, despite such assertions, there was a definitive lack of empirical rigor in literature published following Analysen zum Terrorismus. Studies made many persuasive arguments concerning the personality of terrorists, consistently citing the German study, yet failed to provide further valid or reliable evidence to support their claims. Added to this is the lack of comparative analysis interrogating the prevalence rates in narcissistic traits between terrorists and general population samples. Despite the popularity of the notion that terrorists were often reticent, psychologically damaged youths, the theory, much like the work of paradigm one, lacked empirical strength: No statistical data, no standardized psychological instruments, and no control group (Victoroff, 2005).

Paradigm three—Synthesizing the evidence

At the end of the 1990s and into the early years of the new Millennium, a series of scholarly outputs synthesized the existing evidence surrounding psychopathological or personality-driven explanations of terrorist involvement (Borum, 2004; Horgan, 2003, 2005; Silke, 1998, 2003; Victoroff, 2005). These reviews largely agreed with one another. Collectively, they questioned the "empirical, theoretical and conceptual foundations" of earlier studies (Horgan, 2003, p. 23). The reviews argued that poor research designs and a lack of empiricism ultimately undermined the arguments in favor of terrorism being rooted in disorders of personality, including psychopathy. Many of the studies supporting psychopathy and personality-level explanations were conducted in the absence of rigorous clinical diagnostic procedures conducted on an individual in a clinical setting for prolonged periods. Instead, they relied on autobiographies, biographies, secondhand case studies, media interviews, and willful misreadings of actual empirical work (Horgan, 2005).

On theoretical grounds, they argued investigations centering on psychopathy and/or personality traits or disorders clearly suffer from the fundamental attribution error (Hogg & Vaughan, 2005). This error is a basic human tendency to use dispositions as an explanatory variable for behavior while underestimating the powerful impact of the situational context within which the individual behaves. The reviews argued that the early research focused too much on the actions of the terrorist rather than the processes through which the individual became a terrorist. The reviews did not conclude that there are no terrorists who are psychopaths or narcissists but rather it is too simple (and unsupported) to suggest these factors caused the initial engagement with terrorism alone.

On empirical grounds, the reviews consistently found little support for the argument that psychopathy drives terrorist behavior. For Horgan (2003, p. 6), "there remains little to support the argument that terrorists can or should be necessarily regarded as psychopathic owing to the nature of the offences committed." Similarly, the reviews questioned the empirical foundations of the personality strand of research. Horgan (2003, p. 10) highlights that "attempts to assert the presence of a terrorist personality, or profile, are pitiful." Silke (2003, p. 32) similarly outlines, "quite simply, the best of the empirical work does not suggest, and never has suggested, that terrorists possess a distinct personality or that their psychology is somehow deviant from that of 'normal' people." Victoroff (2005, p. 12) notes that "the conclusion, at least on the basis of uncontrolled empirical psychological studies...has been that terrorists do not usually exhibit what we refer to as Axis I or even Axis II psychiatric disorders." Victoroff (2005, p. 3) further characterizes the research in paradigms one and two as "theoretical speculation based on subjective interpretation of anecdotal observations." It is important to carefully reread these conclusions. Psychopathy and personality disorders were found to be unsupported empirically. Later, we show that many citations of these studies largely misinterpreted these conclusions and instead generalized to psychopathology in general.

Despite a commonly held belief in subsequent studies, these reviews did not argue people with pathological disorders do not join terrorist groups. For example, Horgan (2003, p. 7) outlines that "perhaps, if the opportunity ever arose to examine actual terrorists in clinical settings, there might be some evidence to link at least a few of the 'sore thumbs' with pathological disorders." Instead, they argue that the prevalence rates of various mental disorders are no different to those found in general society. Horgan (2003, p. 17) cites McCauley (1991, p. 132) as being "precise" in his assertion that "[this] is not to say that there is no pathology among terrorists, but the rate of diagnosable pathology, at least, does not differ significantly from control groups of the same age and background." Silke (2003, p. 32) agrees by asserting he "is not saying that mentally unbalanced or pathological personalities are *never* present in terrorist organizations." Victoroff (2005, p. 14) outlines that "sociopaths may sometimes be among the terrorists." On a related note, the reviews largely agree that when psychopathic members are present they are either likely to take up specific roles within the movement (Victoroff, 2005), or be on the fringes (Silke, 2003).

The reviews regularly cite studies that affirm the lack of difference between terrorist and control groups in terms of disorder prevalence. Horgan (2003, p. 18) notes a "persistence of evidence to suggest terrorist normality." Silke also utilizes the word "normal" on a couple of occasions. For example, "most serious researchers in the field at least nominally agree with the position that terrorists are essentially *normal* individuals" (1998, p. 53). By "normal," these reviews mean that terrorists were no more or less likely to experience particular mental disorders than the average person on the street. They did not mean that terrorists never suffer from mental disorders, yet that is frequently the way subsequent citations understood these particular sentences (we return to this in the next section). Indeed, a couple of the reviews even cite the Lyons and Harbinson (1986) study of Northern Irish terrorists where 16% suffered from a form of mental illness.

These reviews became very influential within the literature that followed. They also coincided in time with a large growth in the number of published terrorism-related articles (Silke & Schmidt-Petersen, 2015). However, many of these citations misunderstood the finer points. Whereas the reviews often used very specific language, the citations generalized to a higher level of abstraction and overlooked many of the nuances. In turn, this led to the false assumption that there was no relationship whatsoever between mental disorders and terrorist involvement. This had major implications for both government practice and media portrayal of terrorist and mass casualty events. The point of the reviews was not to firmly put an end to studies of mental disorder and terrorist involvement. Rather, they intended to highlight the problems with existing studies and to argue for less simplistic linear assumptions between experiencing particular mental disorders and terrorist engagement.

Many citations assumed that because of the flaws inherent in the early studies, there is no mental disorder prevalence whatsoever and that it cannot be linked to why (alongside many other factors) some individuals in some groups engage in terrorism. What the reviews show is the lack of scientific rigor behind these studies. They generally do not point toward scientific evidence to the contrary. The studies that are regularly cited as confirming the absence of mental disorders are potentially not as scientific or rigorously examined to the same degree as those confirming a relationship. Merari (2010, pp. 253–254) eloquently sums up this misconception:

> *By and large, the opinion that terrorists do not have a common psychological profile rests on the absence of research rather than on direct findings. A scientifically sound conclusion that terrorists have no common personality traits must be based on many comparative studies of terrorists from different countries and functions, using standard psychological tests and clinical interviews. As such studies have not been published, the only scientifically sound conclusion for now is that we do not know whether terrorists share common traits, but we cannot be sure that such traits do not exist.*

Paradigm four—The empirical turn

Although still in its infancy, the field of study has undoubtedly improved in terms of its theoretical, conceptual, and empirical rigor since the publication of the seminal literature reviews. Horgan (2014) notes an increase in "solid, quality research output" aided by a growth in full-time dedicated researchers and, relatedly, research funding from a variety of government sources. Many of these improvements led to some changes in thought surrounding mental disorder and terrorism. There is a consensus that there is no single variable that can explain these phenomena. Instead, it has repeatedly been demonstrated that radicalization and terrorist engagement should be viewed as a process. The multiple pathways toward terrorism have been eloquently depicted in both theoretical frameworks and empirical (qualitative and quantitative) approaches.

Empirical studies typically reflect the diversity in backgrounds and experiences within a single sample. No terrorist profile exists. For example, studies have measured the prevalence rate of diagnosed mental disorders at 4.54% in a sample of European jihadists ($n = 242$; Bakker, 2006); 7.6% US far-right inspired group members who had committed at least one murder ($n=92$; Gruenewald, Chermak, & Freilich, 2013), 8% of US group terrorists from an array of ideological backgrounds ($n=136$; Hewitt, 2003), 11.9% in a diverse ideological sample of terrorist group members ($n=97$; Corner & Gill, 2019), 12.9% of Palestinian lone-actor terrorists ($n=62$; Perry, Hasisi, & Perry, 2018), 22% of US lone-actors from an array of ideological backgrounds ($n=136$; Hewitt, 2003), 25.6% of US ideological active shooters ($n=40$; Capellan, 2015), 31.9% of lone-actor terrorists ($n=119$; Gill, Horgan, & Deckert, 2014), 32.7% of lone-actor terrorists ($n=49$; Gill, Corner, McKee, Hitchen, & Betley, 2020), 40.4% of far-right inspired lone-actors who had committed at least one murder ($n=47$; Gruenewald et al., 2013), 43.7% of US extremists ($n=284$; LaFree, Jensen, James, & Safer-Lichtenstein, 2018), and 57% of white supremacists ($n=44$; Bubolz & Simi, 2019).

Even in those studies reporting relatively high mental disorder diagnoses, the diagnoses themselves vary greatly. Weenink (2015) studied police files of 140 Dutch individuals who became foreign fighters. Six percent had diagnosed disorders. These included psychotic, narcissistic, attention-deficit/hyperactivity (ADD/HD), schizophrenia, autism spectrum, and posttraumatic stress disorder (PTSD). In Corner, Gill, and Mason's (2016) sample of 153 lone-actor terrorists, 1.3% experienced traumatic brain injury, 0.7% drug dependence, 8.5% schizophrenia, 0.7% schizoaffective disorder, 2.0% delusional disorder, 0.7% psychotic disorder, 7.2% depression, 3.9% bipolar disorder, 1.3% unspecified anxiety disorder, 0.7% dissociative disorder, 1.3% obsessive compulsive disorder (OCD), 3.3% PTSD, 0.7% unspecified sleep disorder, 6.5% unspecified personality disorder, and 3.3% autism spectrum disorder. In Gill, Corner, McKee, Hitchen, & Betley, 2020 closed source study of 49 UK lone-actor terrorists, 12.2% experienced a mood disorder, 10.2% schizophrenia, 4.1% intellectual disabilities, and 2% an assortment of personality disorders. Knight et al. (2017) study of 24 UK violent extremists showed single cases of individuals had Asperger syndrome, personality disorders, and schizophrenia. van Leyenhorst and Andreas's (2017) closed source study of 26 Dutch terrorist suspects demonstrated single cases with attention deficit hyperactivity disorder (ADHD), psychotic disorder, borderline personality disorder, or PTSD.

Some studies find elevated rates of certain diagnoses compared to the societal base rate. These studies include schizophrenia and psychosis in Dutch foreign fighters (Weenink, 2015); schizophrenia, autism, and delusional disorder in lone-actor terrorists (Corner et al., 2016); subscale measures of psychopathic deviate, paranoid, depressive, schizophrenic, and hypomanic tendencies in Palestinian and Israeli terrorists (Gottschalk & Gottschalk, 2004). In a survey of over 400 Hezbollah fighters, Schbley (2003, pp. 115–116) found a strong statistical relationship between "some self-reported criteria of intermittent explosive, psychotic, and oppositional personality disorders and a person's absolutist tendency, affinity for martyrdom, susceptibility to the culting process, psychotic depression, and acts of terrorism and self-immolation."

Other studies find lower rates of personality disorders, and psychiatric illness compared to nonideologically inspired murderers (Lyons & Harbinson, 1986). Merari and colleagues carried out various psychological tests on a sample of would-be suicide bombers and compared the results with various control groups (e.g., other terrorists and nonpolitical criminals) (Merari, 2010; Merari, Diamant, et al., 2009; Merari, Fighel, et al., 2009). These studies employed a range of techniques including clinical interviews and personality tests. Compared to the nonpolitical criminals, the would-be suicide bomber group received significantly more diagnoses of avoidant-dependent personality disorder (60% vs 17%), depressive symptoms (53% vs 8%), and more readily displayed suicidal tendencies (40% vs 0%). On the other hand, the nonpolitical criminal group was more likely to contain members with psychopathic tendencies (25% vs 0%) and impulsive-unstable tendencies (67% vs 27%). Suicide bomber organizers scored higher in ego-strength, impulsivity, and emotional instability than would-be suicide bombers.

These studies are a substantial proportion of all current empirical works which have endeavored to gauge the prevalence rates of a wide range of mental disorders in terrorist offenders. The results validate the conclusions of the seminal reviews of paradigm three. Contrary to the conclusions within paradigm one, psychopathy (and associated traits) is rarely identified across multiple samples of terrorist offenders. This is not to say that terrorists are never psychopaths, but it is likely a function of diagnostics. Unlike other psychiatric diagnostic procedures, the process for diagnosis of psychopathy is arduous and requires further formal training for those carrying out assessments. There is also a lack of evidence of specific personality traits, including narcissism. This again is likely due to the assessment of personality. Much of the work in paradigm four has relied on distance diagnostic procedures, or interrogation of formal psychiatric assessments focusing on disorders, not personality traits. Further investigation, where specific diagnostic procedures for psychopathy are included during analysis, and systematic assessment of personality using established measures is likely to go some way to help solve this problem.

Conclusions

The empirical studies outlined before suggest psychopathy will happen from time to time within terrorist samples. Both emerge from similar contexts. Psychopathy and related personality disorders may increase individual vulnerabilities. They may, in certain circumstances, have other impacts. For example, sequence analyses of lone-actor terrorist data demonstrate that during radicalization "mental health problems appear to be a precursor to, and consequence of, criminal behaviours, which are themselves markers of lack of commitment to prosocial moral rules (moral susceptibility) and/or markers of selection into criminogenic settings, some of which may be radicalising (including prison)" (Corner, Bouhana, & Gill, 2019, p. 120). In other contexts, research shows how extremist propaganda provided extremists with an explanation for their negative personal experiences including experiences of trauma and mental health problems (Bubolz & Simi, 2019). Certain mental health problems (or markers thereof), in certain circumstances, may also be attractive to particular recruiters for particular tasks and functions within an extremist network (Bubolz & Simi, 2019).

The vast majority of empirical research on personality and mental disorders and violent extremism takes the nomothetic route. Typically, the route taken has been to count the prevalence of such disorders within large(ish) samples of terrorists and those with attitudinal affinity with a terrorist cause. Such approaches leave us with various "counts," within-group comparisons, and across-group comparisons. They leave us with a sense of how present disorders are. In some cases, they identify common relationships between variables within the whole sample. Such studies, however, are to a large degree difficult to apply to a single case which needs assessing and managing in the here and now. We need more than an understanding of "presence," we need an understanding of "relevance." For a risk factor to be meaningful, we need to understand the mechanisms through which it impacts upon violent extremism, and why the risk factor does not impact each individual equally. To this end, much more work is needed from the idiographic perspective. This could help untangle the *relevance* of disorders in particular individuals who became violent extremists at particular moments in their life. There are cases out there worthy of much greater study with this case in mind. Antisocial personality disorder was confirmed in the cases of Anders Breivik, Keith Luke, and Amedy Coulibaly among others. There are additional suggestions it may have been present in cases like David Copeland, Franz Fuchs, Roger Stockham, Ryan Gibson, Volkert Van Der Graaf among others. Comparative analyses would be worthwhile if sufficient documents become available. Control groups of individuals who presented with similar problems but did not engage in violent extremism may help us understand the mechanisms and mediators through which a distal risk factor like psychopathy, may be linked to terrorist engagement.

References

Abrahms, M. (2011). Does terrorism really work? Evolution in the conventional wisdom since 9/11. *Defence and Peace Economics*, *22*(6), 583–594.

Akhtar, S. (1999). The psychodynamic dimension of terrorism. *Psychiatric Annals*, *29*(6), 350–355. https://doi.org/10.3928/0048-5713-19990601-09.

American Psychiatric Association. (2013). *Diagnostic and statistical manual of mental disorders* (5th ed.). Arlington, VA: American Psychiatric Publishing.

Bakker, E. (2006). *Jihadi terrorists in Europe: Their characteristics and the circumstances in which they joined the jihad: An exploratory study*. Netherlands Institute of International Relations Clingendael.

Baruch, E. H. (2003). Psychoanalysis and terrorism: The need for a global talking cure. *Psychoanalytic Psychology*, *20*(4), 698–700. https://doi.org/10.1037/0736-9735.20.4.698.

Berko, A. (2007). *The path to paradise: The inner world of suicide bombers and their dispatches*. Westport, CT: Praeger Publishers.

Billig, O. (1985). The lawyer terrorist and his comrades. *Political Psychology*, *6*, 29–46.

Böllinger, L. (1985). Terrorist conduct as a result of a psychological process. In P. Pichot, P. Berner, & K. Thau (Eds.), *6. Psychiatry the state of the art* (pp. 387–389). New York, NY: Plenum Press.

Borum, R. (2004). *Psychology of terrorism*. University of South Florida Tampa Dept of Mental Health Law and Policy.

Bubolz, B. F., & Simi, P. (2019). The problem of overgeneralization: The case of mental health problems and US violent white supremacists. *American Behavioral Scientist*. https://doi.org/10.1177/0002764219831746.

Capellan, J. A. (2015). Lone wolf terrorist or deranged shooter? A study of ideological active shooter events in the United States, 1970–2014. *Studies in Conflict and Terrorism, 38*(6), 395–413.

Cooper, H. H. A. (1977). Whither now-terrorism on the brink. *Chitty's Law Journal, 25*, 181.

Cooper, H. H. A. (1978). Psychopath as terrorist. *Legal Medical Quarterly, 2*, 253.

Corner, E., Bouhana, N., & Gill, P. (2019). The multifinality of vulnerability indicators in lone-actor terrorism. *Psychology, Crime & Law, 25*(2), 111–132.

Corner, E., & Gill, P. (2019). Psychological distress, terrorist involvement and disengagement from terrorism: A sequence analysis approach. *Journal of Quantitative Criminology*, 1–28.

Corner, E., Gill, P., & Mason, O. (2016). Mental health disorders and the terrorist: A research note probing selection effects and disorder prevalence. *Studies in Conflict and Terrorism, 39*(6), 560–568.

Crenshaw, M. (1986). The psychology of political terrorism. In M. G. Hermann (Ed.), *Political psychology* Jossey-Bass Inc.

de Cataldo Neuberger, L., Valentini, T., & Campling, J. (1996). *Women and terrorism.* London: Macmillan.

DeMause, L. (2002). The childhood origins of terrorism. *The Journal of Psychohistory, 29*(4), 340–348.

Ferracuti, F., & Bruno, F. (1981). Psychiatric aspects of terrorism in Italy. In *The mad, the bad and the different: Essays in honor of Simon Dinhz* (pp. 199–213). Lexington, MA: Lexington Books.

Gill, P. (2012). Terrorist violence and the contextual, facilitative and causal qualities of group-based behaviors. *Aggression and Violent Behavior, 17*(6), 565–574.

Gill, P., Corner, E., McKee, A., Hitchen, P., & Betley, P. (2020). What do closed source data tell us about lone actor terrorist behaviour? The preliminary findings from project regulus. *Terrorism and Political Violence*, 1–18. https://doi.org/10.1080/09546553.2019.1668781.

Gill, P., Horgan, J., & Deckert, P. (2014). Bombing alone: Tracing the motivations and antecedent behaviors of lone-actor terrorists. *Journal of Forensic Sciences, 59*(2), 425–435.

Gottschalk, M., & Gottschalk, S. (2004). Authoritarianism and pathological hatred: A social psychological profile of the Middle Eastern terrorist. *The American Sociologist, 35*(2), 38–59.

Gruenewald, J., Chermak, S., & Freilich, J. D. (2013). Distinguishing "loner" attacks from other domestic extremist violence. *Criminology & Public Policy, 12*(1), 65–91.

Hamden, R. H. (2002). The retributional terrorist: Type 4. In C. E. Stout (Ed.), *1. The psychology of terrorism: A public understanding* (pp. 166–192). Westport, CT: Praeger Publishers.

Hare, R. D. (1985). Comparison procedures for the assessment of psychopathy. *Journal of Consulting and Clinical Psychology, 53*(1), 7–16.

Hare, R. D. (2007). Psychological instruments in the assessment of psychopathy. In A. R. Felthous, & H. Saβ (Eds.), *International handbook on psychopathic disorders and the law* (pp. 41–67). John Wiley & Sons Ltd.

Hewitt, C. (2003). *Understanding terrorism in America.* New York, NY: Routledge.

Hogg, M. A., & Vaughan, G. M. (2005). *Social psychology.* London: Prentice Hall.

Horgan, J. (2003). The search for the terrorist. In *Terrorists, victims and society: Psychological perspectives on terrorism and its consequences* (pp. 3–27).

Horgan, J. (2005). *The psychology of terrorism.* London: Routledge.

Horgan, J. (2014). *The psychology of terrorism* (2nd ed.). London: Routledge.

Jacobsen, C., & Maier-Katkin, D. (2015). Breivik's Sanity: Terrorism, Mass Murder, and the Insanity Defense. *Human Rights Quarterly, 37*, 137.

Jäger, H., Schmidtchen, G., & Süllwold, L. (1981). In L. Böllinger (Ed.), *2. Lebenslaufanalysen*. Opladen: Westdeutscher Verlag.

Johnson, P. W., & Feldman, T. B. (1992). Personality types and terrorism: Self psychology and perspectives. *Forensic Reports*, *5*(4), 293–303.

Kellen, K. (1982). *On terrorists and terrorism: A RAND note*. Santa Monica, CA: RAND.

Kent, I., & Nicholls, W. (1977). The psychodynamics of terrorism. *Mental Health and Society*, *1*(2), 1–8.

Knight, S., Woodward, K., & Lancaster, G. L. J. (2017). Violent versus nonviolent actors: An empirical study of different types of extremism. *Journal of Threat Assessment and Management*, *4*(4), 230–248. https://doi.org/10.1037/tam0000086.

LaFree, G., Jensen, M. A., James, P. A., & Safer-Lichtenstein, A. (2018). Correlates of violent political extremism in the United States. *Criminology*, *56*(2), 233–268.

Lasch, C. (1979). *The culture of narcissism: American life in an age of diminishing expectations*. New York: Warner.

Leistedt, S. J. (2013). Behavioural aspects of terrorism. *Forensic Science International*, *228*(1–3), 21–27. https://doi.org/10.1016/j.forsciint.2013.02.004.

Lloyd, M., & Kleinot, P. (2017). Pathways into terrorism: The good, the bad and the ugly. *Psychoanalytic Psychotherapy*, *31*(4), 367–377. https://doi.org/10.1080/02668734.2017.1360380.

Lyons, H. A., & Harbinson, H. J. (1986). A comparison of political and non-political murderers in Northern Ireland, 1974–84. *Medicine, Science and the Law*, *26*(3), 193–198.

Martens, W. H. (2004). The terrorist with antisocial personality disorder. *Journal of Forensic Psychology Practice*, *4*(1), 45–56.

McCauley, C. (1991). Terrorism, research and public policy: An overview. *Terrorism and Political Violence*, *3*(1), 126–144.

Merari, A. (2010). *Driven to death: Psychological and social aspects of suicide terrorism*. Oxford: Oxford University Press.

Merari, A., Diamant, I., Bibi, A., Broshi, Y., & Zakin, G. (2009). Personality characteristics of "self martyrs"/"suicide bombers" and organizers of suicide attacks. *Terrorism and Political Violence*, *22*(1), 87–101.

Merari, A., Fighel, J., Ganor, B., Lavie, E., Tzoreff, Y., & Livne, A. (2009). Making Palestinian "martyrdom operations"/"suicide attacks": Interviews with would-be perpetrators and organizers. *Terrorism and Political Violence*, *22*(1), 102–119.

Morf, G. (1970). *Terror in Quebec: Case studies of the FLQ. Vol. 4074*. Toronto: Clarke.

Pearce, K. I. (1977). Police negotiations: A new role for the community psychiatrist. *Canadian Psychiatric Association Journal*, *22*(4), 171–175.

Pearlstein, R. M. (1991). *The mind of the political terrorist*. Washington, DC: Scholarly Resources.

Perry, S., Hasisi, B., & Perry, G. (2018). Who is the lone terrorist? A study of vehicle-borne attackers in Israel and the West Bank. *Studies in Conflict and Terrorism*, *41*(11), 899–913.

Post, J. M. (1984). Notes on a psychodynamic theory of terrorist behavior. *Terrorism*, *7*(2), 241–256. https://doi.org/10.1080/10576108408435577.

Post, J. M. (1986). Narcissism and the charismatic leader-follower relationship. *Political Psychology*, *7*(4), 675–688.

Post, J. M. (2005). When hatred is bred in the bone: Psycho-cultural foundations of contemporary terrorism. *Political Psychology*, *26*(4), 615–636.

Post, J. M. (2007). *The mind of the terrorist: The psychology of terrorism from the IRA to al-Qaeda*. Palgrave Macmillan.

Schbley, A. (2003). Defining religious terrorism: A causal and anthological profile. *Studies in Conflict and Terrorism*, *26*(2), 105–134.

Sher, L., & Rice, T. (2015). Prevention of homicidal behavior in men with psychiatric disorders. *The World Journal of Biological Psychiatry*, 1–18.

Silke, A. (1998). Cheshire-cat logic: The recurring theme of terrorist abnormality in psychological research. *Psychology Crime and Law*, *4*(1), 51–69.

Silke, A. (2003). *Terrorists, victims and society: Psychological perspectives on terrorism and its consequences*. London: Wiley.

Silke, A., & Schmidt-Petersen, J. (2015). The golden age? What the 100 most cited articles in terrorism studies tell us. *Terrorism and Political Violence*, 1–21.

Strenz, T. (1988). A terrorist psychosocial profile: Past and present. *FBI Law Enforcement Bulletin*, *57*, 13–19.

Tanay, E. (1987). Pseudo-political terrorism. *Journal of Forensic Sciences*, *32*(1), 192–200.

Tørrissen, T., Aspaas, A. (2012). Court Psychiatric Report by Dr. Terje Tørrissen and Dr. Agnar Aspaas (English Translation).

van Leyenhorst, M., & Andreas, A. (2017). Dutch suspects of terrorist activity: A study of their biographical backgrounds based on primary sources. *Journal for Deradicalization*, (12), 309–344.

Victoroff, J. (2005). The mind of the terrorist a review and critique of psychological approaches. *Journal of Conflict Resolution*, *49*(1), 3–42.

Weenink, A. W. (2015). Behavioral problems and disorders among radicals in police files. *Perspectives on Terrorism*, *9*(2), 17–33.

Psychopathy and corporate crime

19

Cynthia Mathieu

> *A criminal is a person with predatory instincts without sufficient capital to form a corporation.*
>
> **Clarence Darrow**

Introduction

In the context of this chapter, I would rephrase the above quote as such: A corporate psychopath is a person with predatory instincts, an uncanny ability to manipulate and a good formal education, which allows him or her to operate within corporations. I might also add… when they don't have the means to form corporations, *they join them.*

In 2002, Dr. Robert Hare, considered the father of modern psychopathy, mentioned "not all psychopaths are in prison. Some are in the Boardroom." This quote created a shock wave through the fields of psychology and business. Since the release of *Snakes in Suits* (Babiak & Hare, 2006), one of the first books on corporate psychopathy, research on the subject has been burgeoning. However, most of the studies address leadership and counterproductive work behavior and few, if any, have looked into the links between psychopathy and corporate crime. The present chapter will address how psychopathic individuals operate within organizational contexts and how psychopathic traits may be at the root of corporate crime.

Psychopathy: From clinical and correctional settings to corporation

> *But vague as the concept of schizophrenia remains and various as its manifestations are, the schizophrenic, when recognized, is promptly called a patient with mental illness and treated as such. The psychopath, however, continues to be treated as a petty criminal at one moment, as a mentally ill person at the next, and again as a well and normal human being-all without the slightest change in his condition having occurred.*
>
> *(Cleckley, 1988, p. 188)*

Hervey Cleckley was the first to define the concept of psychopathy. Right from the first edition of his book, *The Mask of Sanity*, in 1941, he did not limit his study of these individuals to incarcerated criminals or forensic/clinical setting. In his book, Cleckley presents a section that he entitled "The disorder in full clinical manifestations" as well as a second section entitled "Incomplete manifestations or suggestions of the disorder" in which he discusses the psychopath as a physician, a psychiatrist, a man of the world, a gentleman, a scientist and a business man.

Psychopathy and Criminal Behavior. https://doi.org/10.1016/B978-0-12-811419-3.00010-8

What distinguishes the "full clinical manifestation" psychopaths from the ones who present "incomplete manifestations of the disorder"? Cleckley offers this explanation: "The true difference between them [the psychopaths who present an incomplete manifestation of the disorder] and the psychopaths who continually go to jails or to psychiatric hospitals is that they keep up a far better and more consistent outward appearance of being normal. This outward appearance may include business or professional careers that continue in a sense successful, and which are truly successful when measured by financial reward or by the casual observer's opinion of real accomplishment. It must be remembered that even the most severely and obviously disabled psychopath presents a technical appearance of sanity, often one of high intellectual capacities, and not infrequently succeeds in business or professional activities for short periods, sometimes for considerable periods." (Cleckley, 1988, p. 191). Cleckley's book on psychopathy is entitled "The mask of sanity." It refers to the fact that psychopathic individuals are able to keep up appearances so that, to the layperson, they seem to be "normal" and functional individuals.

Some psychopathic individuals are able to not only "keep up appearances"; they manage to build such a persona that people actually admire them and view them as successful. In fact, one important element of Cleckley's explanation of subclinical psychopathy relates to the notion of success. He mentions that, when success is measured by financial rewards or by the casual observer's opinion, psychopaths can manage to appear successful. As mentioned in an article I wrote in 2016 for *Aftermath: Surviving psychopathy* (a non-for-profit organization helping victims of psychopaths), "I believe that the corporate psychopath's greatest success is making everyone believe that he is successful." This image of success allows the psychopath to thrive during selection interviews and climb the corporate ladder (Mathieu, 2016).

What differentiates corporate psychopaths from psychopaths found in prison settings?

Babiak, Neumann, and Hare (2010) have conducted a study of 203 managers and executives selected as part of a management development program by their companies. The authors collected information on each of the managers and were able to assess psychopathy using the Psychopathy Checklist—Revised (Hare, 2003), considered to be the gold-standard measure of psychopathy. They found that 3.9% of the managers in their sample had a score of 30 or higher which is the common research threshold for psychopathy using the PCL-R. The prevalence of psychopathy in the general population is thought to be less than 1% (Coid, Yang, Ullrich, Roberts, & Hare, 2009; Hare, 2003; Neumann & Hare, 2008). The authors found that psychopathy was associated with positive assessment of communication skills, creativity, and strategic thinking while being negatively associated with management style, job performance, and being a team player. Interestingly, they were able to prove that the Hare Four-Factor model of psychopathy was valid in the workplace and consistent with offender, psychiatric, and community samples. Although they found that the Interpersonal Factor of the PCL-R was significantly higher than the other three factors, the model composed of Interpersonal, Affective, Lifestyle, and Antisocial Factors was valid. In fact, they found that the Antisocial factor predicted increase ratings on charisma/presentation style (along with the Interpersonal factor). They also found that the only factor that predicted significant lower ratings on the responsibility/performance composite was the Interpersonal factor.

A relatively new approach to studying psychopathy consists of using latent profile analysis to identify subgroups of psychopathic individuals (Hare, 2016; Mokros et al., 2015). In essence, as hypothesized by Cleckley, there are subgroups within psychopathic individuals. As mentioned earlier, the Four Factor model of psychopathy proposed by Hare and tested with the PCL-R includes these four factors: *Interpersonal, Affective, Lifestyle*, and *Antisocial*. The pattern of correlations among these factors is consistent with the presence of two second-order factors, commonly known as Factor 1 (Interpersonal/Affective) and Factor 2 (Lifestyle/Antisocial) (Hare, 2016; Neumann, Hare, & Pardini, 2014; Neumann, Vitacco, & Mokros, 2016). However, individuals scoring above the threshold for psychopathy on the PCL-R (a score of 30) can differ in how they score on each of the factors, exhibiting different traits and behaviors. For instance, an individual above the threshold for psychopathy but scoring high on Factor 1 (Interpersonal/Affective) and low on Factor 2 (Lifestyle/Antisocial) would differ from an individual obtaining the same high general score on the PCL-R with a high score on Factor 2 and a low score on Factor 1.

The sample of 203 managers and executives from the Babiak et al. (2010) study was used to run a latent profile analysis by the same authors. The authors found subgroups of psychopathy within their corporate sample that were very similar to the subgroups found in offender samples by Mokros et al. in 2015 (see Mathieu, Babiak, & Hare, 2020 for more details on the results). The difference between the subgroups from the offender sample and the corporate sample was that, for the corporate sample, all subgroups scored high on Factor 1 (Interpersonal/Affective). Hence, the fourth subgroup for the offender sample (high scores on Factor 2 and low scores on Factor 1) named the *Sociopathic group* (Mokros et al., 2015) was not present in the corporate sample. This is not an indication that corporate psychopathy is not associated with antisocial behavior; in fact, some of the corporate psychopathy subgroups present high scores on Factor 2. Rather, this indicates that, as predicted by Cleckley, psychopaths who are able to thrive in a corporate setting are the ones who are better equipped at putting on a mask. In other words, psychopaths who make it in the corporate world present good manipulative skills, hence their high scores on Factor 1. Factor 2, as measured by the PCL-R is associated with gang-related violence and sexual violence. While these types of antisocial behaviors may be common in criminal populations, in corporate samples, it is very likely that individuals would score low on these types of violence due, in part on having been subjected to more positive environmental factors that gave corporate psychopaths tools and advantages that the common criminal does not have. These factors may include a better education, higher socioeconomic status, and/or being introduced to a business network. These environmental advantages give the corporate psychopath access to more lucrative forms of crime.

In discussing environmental versus genetic factors explaining psychopathy, Hare, Neumann, and Widiger (2012) indicate that Factor 2 (Lifestyle/Antisocial) is more strongly accounted for by a common genetic factor than Factor 1 (Interpersonal/Affective). This means that environmental and personal factors may have a stronger influence on Factor 1. Such environmental and personal factors may be associated with lifestyle and personal attributes (e.g., socioeconomic status, physical appearance, social skills and connections, intelligence, education), opportunities available (e.g., family or political connections, business associates, economic events), and the financial and legal resources available to defend them. These resources available to them would also have an influence on the type of crime they chose to commit. Psychopaths with the means and resources to climb the corporate ladder have access to more lucrative criminal opportunities and, if caught, they have access to excellent legal resources and face more lenient punishment. These elements make corporate crime very attractive for psychopaths.

Financial crime

"Financial crime threatens people in every aspect of their lives: at home, at work, online and offline" (Interpol, 2020). Baker (2005) reports that the estimates of global flows of illicit money varies between $ 1061 US billion and $ 1599 US billion. Both INTERPOL and EUROPOL identify financial crime as a priority in their fight against crime. EUROPOL describes financial crime as "illegal acts committed by an individual or a group of individuals to obtain a financial or professional advantage. The principal motive of such crimes is economic gain" (Europol, 2020). Money laundering is the act of converting criminal incomes to legal form that allows the offender to enjoy the fruit of his crime (Levi & Reuter, 2006). These crimes can take various forms such as drug distribution, white-collar crime, corruption, terrorism, cybercrime, and bribery. Levi and Reuter (2006) present three phases to the process of money laundering: (a) placement (cash is deposited into accounts), (b) layering (funds are moved to other institutions to obscure origin), and (c) integration (funds are used to acquire legitimate assets). To date, it is difficult to find empirical research with a focus on profiling fraudsters who commit money laundering crimes. However, as mentioned by Levi and Reuter (2006), money laundering is often perpetrated with the help of someone like employees of financial institutions, auto dealers, real estate agents, accountants, and lawyers. Thus the fraudster manages to coerce or bribe employees in order to get what they want. Although, to date, research into the profile of money laundering perpetrators is nonexistent, it appears clear that perpetrators need a certain set of skills to manipulate employees and other professionals into getting what they want, at the risk of hurting employees' careers. While law enforcement has put a lot of effort into mechanisms assisting in money laundering detection and intervention (prosecuting), it would be useful to identify a criminal profile of money laundering perpetrators. Since these individuals need to manipulate and coerce corporate employees or professionals, their profile may very well be close to the profile of fraudsters who operate within organizations. The following section including red flags for corporate fraudsters could be used to track and identify money laundering perpetrators. Prevention measures could include presenting these red flags to employees within corporations such as financial institutions who are at risk of coming in contact with money laundering perpetrators.

Corporate fraud

The Association of Certified Fraud Examiners (2018) reports that about 5% of annual revenues is lost to occupational fraud; if we apply this 5% to the Gross World Product, it would amount to USD 4 trillion dollars annual loss in organizations world-wide. The total loss caused by occupational frauds included in the Association of Fraud examiner study was USD 7.1 billion in 2018. The median loss due to fraud for an organization was USD 130,000; however, while 55% of occupational frauds cost less than USD 200,000, 22% cost more than USD 1 million.

Didier Lavio from Price Waterhouse Cooper (2018) warns organizations: "The time is therefore right for them [organisations] to adopt a new, more holistic view of fraud. One that recognises the true shape of the threat: not merely a cost of doing business, but a shadow industry which can impact every territory, every sector and every function." To view occupational fraud as a "shadow industry" goes against popular conceptions that occupational fraud is committed by frustrated employees or employees in need of additional financial resources. If we are to consider occupational fraud as an industry, these questions need to be answered: Who runs that industry, how do they do it and how can organizations protect themselves? Barnard (2008, p. 201) responds to the first question with this statement:

> *In short, con men, especially those involved in face-to-face schemes, are manipulative actors with superior cognitive and interpersonal skills. It is little wonder that they are thought to be the elite of the criminal underworld, revered for their artistry, sharpness, and guile.*

Profiles of fraudsters

According to the Association of Certified Fraud Examiners's (2018) report on corporate fraud, 70% of corruption cases were perpetrated by someone in a position of authority (32% owner/managers and 38% managers). Twenty-four percent of fraudsters had a high school graduate degree or less (average loss $75,000), 15% had some university (average loss $130,000), 47% had a university degree (average loss $160,000), and 14% had a postgraduate degree (average loss $230,000). Sixty-nine percent of fraudsters were men (average loss $156,000) and 31% female (average loss $89,000). Ninety-six percent of fraudsters had no prior history of criminal fraud convictions. However, this does not mean that fraudsters did not commit previous crimes, it simply indicates that they were not convicted of previous crimes.

The Association of Certified Fraud Examiners (2020) mention that 85% of all frauds displayed at least one of these 6 behavioral red flags while committing their crimes:

1. Living beyond means
2. Financial difficulties
3. Unusually close association with vendor/customer
4. Control issues, unwillingness to share duties
5. Irritability, suspiciousness, or defensiveness
6. "Wheeler-dealer" attitude

While these are Red Flags identified for all perpetrators, it seems that these Red Flags differ according to the perpetrator's position in the organization (see Fig. 1).

As mentioned by Barnard (2008), fraudsters are more than just thieves since their work involves both theft and deception. Similar to what was presented earlier in the section differentiating psychopaths in prison settings to corporate psychopaths, fraudsters share the same traits as common thieves; however, fraudsters present interpersonal and manipulative skills that allow them to commit a different type of crime: one that is much, much more lucrative. As Barnard (2008, p. 201) presents: fraudsters "need to have highly refined interpersonal skills-the ability to persuade, cajole, shame, excite, calm, and continually re-focus their victims during the course of the fraud."

Traits associated with corporate fraudsters are low behavioral self-control, high hedonism, and high narcissism (Blickle, Schlegel, Fassbender, & Klein, 2006). Cohen, Ding, Lesage, and Stolowy (2012) conducted a study on corporate fraudsters by analyzing corporate fraud cases. They found that fraudsters have been identified by others as tyrannical/autocratic, narcissistic, encouraging hero worship of executives, and alcoholic. Among the prizes received by corporate fraudsters during the course of their career, Cohen et al. (2012) found: Youngest chief executive, marketing genius, admired head of a fast-growing company, very rich and very young manager, highest-paid CEO, worldwide recognition, and financial wizard. There is no doubt that these individuals possess a set of skills that allows them to project an image of success. In fact, white-collar criminals are pathological liars and exhibit highly refined interpersonal skills in order to manipulate their victims (Perri, 2011). A study comparing common offenders and white-collar offenders showed that white-collar offenders were older and more qualified than common offenders (Ribeiro, Guedes, & Cruz, 2019). However, the same authors did not find significant differences between common and white-collar criminals on recidivism risks, self-control, risk seeking, impulsivity, or self-centrism (Ribeiro et al., 2019). Furthermore, in terms of personality traits, the authors compared common criminals to White-Collar criminals on the FFM of personality and the only significant difference they found between the two groups was that white-collar criminals scored higher on Openness to experience. These results seem to indicate that common criminals and white-collar criminals share many resemblances, despite popular belief.

Barnard (2008) describes white-collar fraudsters as presenting these eight characteristics that she calls "The con man's toolkit": (a) intellectual agility, (b) skills in deception, (c) skills in building trust, (d) "heart" and "larceny sense," (e) business

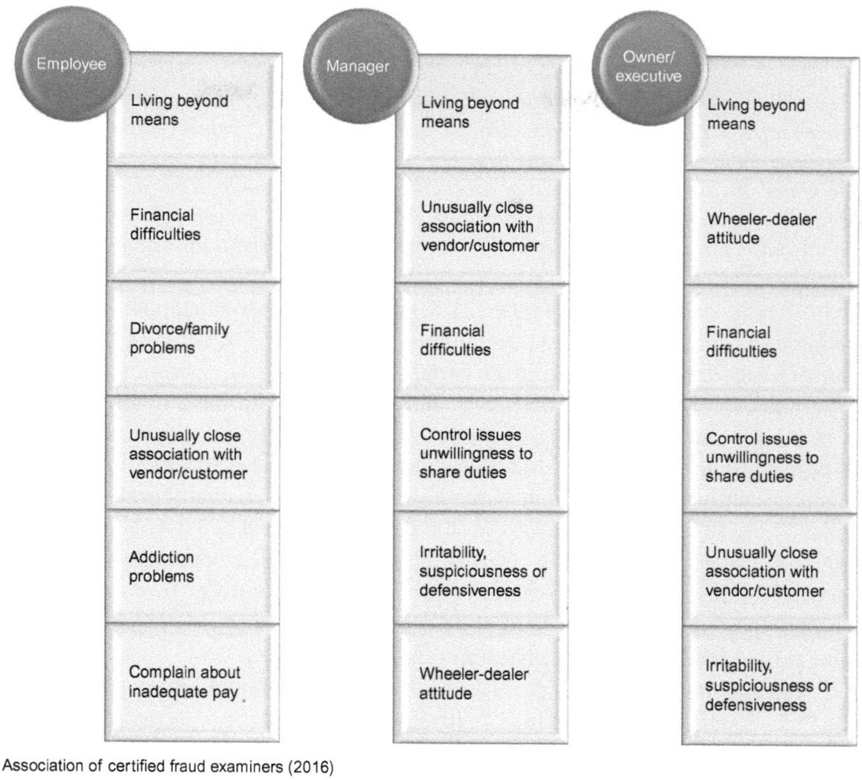

Fig. 1 Characteristics "Red flags" of financial crime perpetrators (Association of Certified Fraud Examiners, 2016).

savvy, (f) the ability to "read" one's victims, (g) lack of empathy, and (h) lack of remorse. Barnard (2008, p. 205) mentions that fraudsters "must create and then sustain an attractive, often charismatic character around which to construct their stories." The traits presented by Barnard and the allusion to building a character bear a striking resemblance to Cleckley's affirmation that psychopaths create a persona that others admire and view as successful.

Few studies have empirically investigated the link between psychopathy and corporate fraud. One of the deterrents may be that, for a long time, the white-collar criminal has been viewed as a one-time nonviolent criminal. However, Perri (2011, p. 222) reports that "With Collar Criminals display behavioural traits as diverse as those of street level offenders, possess the same cold, self-serving ends, and, at times, adopt violent tactics." In fact, Perri (2011) presents cases in which white-collar criminals resorted to murder to ensure that their schemes would not be discovered. He calls these white-collar criminals who resort to violence "red collar criminals." In an article published in 2016, Perri identifies psychopathic traits in red collar criminals based on case studies of white-collar criminals who resorted to murder, thus reinforcing their previous claim that personality traits can act as predictors or risk factors of red collar criminality. Perri and Lichtenwald (2007, p. 21) noted that:

> *Red-collar criminals feed upon this misconception to create smoke screens about their motives. A background investigation of the red-collar criminals identified on the Perri-RCM [Perri-Red-Collar Crime Matrix] does not support the suggestion that these persons somehow acted out of character when they committed murder. In fact, quite the opposite holds true: the capacity to kill without remorse was a seed inherent in the red-collar criminal that germinated when the proper conditions surfaced.*

Lingnau, Fuchs, and Dehne-Niemann (2017) report that individuals presenting psychopathic traits are more likely to score higher on acceptance of white-collar crime in the form of accounting fraud and insider-trading fraud. Ragatz, Fremouw, and Baker (2012) found that white-collar offenders and offenders who have committed other types of crimes did not differ significantly on psychopathy scores and although the white-collar criminals were less likely to adhere to a criminal lifestyle, they did not differ significantly from other non-white-collar offenders on their level of criminal thinking. These first empirical results on the relationship between psychopathic traits and white-collar crime lead to the conclusion that white-collar criminals may present psychopathic traits and although white-collar criminals may differ from street criminals in how these traits are expressed, the fact remains that they do present such traits and thus pose a real threat to organizations and its employees.

Perri and Lichtenwald (2007, p. 29) recommend that criminal investigators should use the PCL-R (Hare, 2003) to help in "exposing the red collar psychopath." However, since the PCL-R relies on informant report, it could not be used for employee selection purposes. Furthermore, PCL-R items pertaining to antisocial and/or violent activities or perceived dysfunctional lifestyle, also included in most self-report measures of psychopathy, would not be appropriate for business settings. Therefore Paul Babiak and Robert Hare began working several years ago on the development of an instrument for rating psychopathic features in corporate and organizational settings. The result was the *B-Scan Self* and the *B-Scan 360*, designed as rating scales in which various members of an organization complete the assessment as a self-report or rate others, including supervisors, peers, and subordinates (For more information see Mathieu & Babiak, 2016a and Mathieu, Hare, Jones, Babiak, & Neumann, 2013). The items were selected to tap into workplace traits and behaviors consistent with the four-factor model of the Hare psychopathy construct. The B-Scan follows the same four-factor structure as the PCL-R family of instrument (including the Psychopathy Checklist-Revised (PCL-R; Hare, 2003), the Psychopathy Checklist-Screening Version (PCL-SV; Hart, Cox, & Hare, 1995), and the Self-Report Psychopathy Scale-Fourth Edition (SRP-IV; Paulhus, Neumann, & Hare, 2016) with the main difference being in the definition of Factor 4 (Antisocial Factor). Factor 4, in the PCL-R and SRP-4, includes violent or gang-related acts and sexual misconduct, elements that would likely be absent in corporate psychopaths' profiles. Rather, the antisocial factor of the B-Scan includes workplace misconduct (see Table 1 for a description of the B-Scan facets).

Using the B-Scan, we found that psychopathy was an underlying factor to another type of crime which falls into a category of negative behavior called "counterproductive work behavior." Much like corporate fraud, some of the behaviors we have studied such as workplace incivility, harassment, and abusive leadership are not considered as "violent crimes" when, in fact, the consequences on victims, although not visible, can be quite detrimental not only for their careers but for their life and general health. As stated by Hare (1999, p. 2) "The most obvious expressions of psychopathy—but by no means the only ones—involve flagrant criminal violation of society's rules. Not surprisingly, many psychopaths are criminals, but many others remain out of prison, using their charm and chameleon-like abilities to cut a wide swath through society and leaving a wake of ruined lives behind them." Not unlike war crimes, the crimes committed by corporate psychopaths result in collateral damage.

Introducing the concept of antipersonnel crime: The hidden face of corporate crime

The Cambridge dictionary defines antipersonnel weapons as such: "Anti-personnel weapons are weapons that are intended to kill or injure people rather than damage weapons or buildings." Nevertheless, Prokosch (1995) reports that more soldiers and civilians have died as a result of the indiscriminate use of landmines and other anti-personnel weapons than from any other type of modern armament. The "International Campain to can Landmines" (1997 Nobel Peace Prize Co-Laureate) describes landmines (antipersonnel mines) as such: "A key characteristic of the weapon is that it is designed to maim rather than kill an enemy soldier. This follows the 'logic' that

Table 1 PCL-R and B-Scan facets.

PCL-R/B-Scan factors	PCL-R facets	B-Scan facets
Interpersonal	Glibness/superficial charm	Insincere
	Grandiose sense of self worth	Arrogant
	Pathological lying	Untrustworthy
	Conning/manipulative	Manipulative/unethical
Affective	Lack of remorse or guilt	Remorseless
	Shallow affect	Shallow
	Callous/lack of empathy	Insensitive
	Failure to accept responsibility	Blaming
Lifestyle	Need for stimulation/proneness to boredom	Impatient
	Parasitic lifestyle	Selfish
	Lack of realistic long-term goals	Unfocused
	Impulsivity	Erratic
	Irresponsibility	Unreliable
Antisocial	Poor behavior controls	Dramatic
		Bullying

more resources are taken up caring for an injured soldier on the battlefield than dealing with a soldier who has been killed. Over time, antipersonnel landmines began to be deployed on a wider scale, often in internal conflicts and specifically targeting civilians. They were used to terrorize communities, deny access to farming land, and restrict population movement." I believe that some tactics used in the workplace have similar processes: they aim at frightening employees, deny access to information and/or resources, and restrict their possibility to move within the organization. These tactics are used to provide power and control over others in the workplace and include workplace harassment, incivility and abusive, and tyrannical behavior toward colleagues or employees. These behaviors have been known to have a significant negative impact on employees and the workplace.

Furthermore, these behaviors may be indicators of other types of crimes. In fact, according to the 2018 report of the Association of Fraud Examiners, 62% of owners/executive fraudsters engaged in non-fraud-related misconduct, the most common was bullying or intimidation. Furthermore, 41% of non-owners/executives also had non-fraud-related misconduct. It thus seems that individuals who commit organizational fraud are also responsible for other problems in the workplace (see Table 2 for Misbehaviors and HR red flags identified by the Association of Fraud Examiners). Many of these misbehaviors and HR red flags have been associated with psychopathy.

Corporate psychopathy and antipersonnel crime

Psychopathic individuals are not afraid to use and abuse others to obtain what they want. Babiak and Hare (2006, p. 140) describe the modus operandi of corporate psychopaths as follows: "They take advantage of communication weaknesses, organizational systems and processes, interpersonal conflicts, and general stressors that plague all companies. They abuse coworkers and, by lowering morale and stirring up conflict, the company itself. Some may even steal and defraud" (Babiak & Hare, 2006, pp. 139–140).

Studies using the B-Scan have found that leaders presenting psychopathic traits are more prone to using negative leadership styles (Laissez-Faire leadership) and less likely to use positive leadership styles (Transactional and Transformational leadership) (Mathieu, Neumann, Babiak, & Hare, 2015). Moreover, psychopathic traits

Table 2 Misbehaviors and HR Red flags perpetrated by fraudsters.

Misbehaviors	HR Red flags
Bullying or intimidation (21%)	Poor performance evaluation 14%
Excessive absenteeism (14%)	Fear of job loss 13%
Excessive tardiness (10%)	Actual job loss 5%
Excessive internet browsing (7%)	Cut in pay 3%
Sexual harassment (4%)	Demotion 3%
Visiting inappropriate websites (4%)	

Information taken from the Report to the Nation (2018) Association of Certified Fraud Examiners.

in leaders predicted abusive leadership and had a negative impact on employee job satisfaction and turnover intentions (Mathieu & Babiak, 2016b). Finally, psychopathy traits in leaders predict higher psychological distress and work–family conflict for employees (Mathieu et al., 2015). In fact psychopathic traits seem to predict employee attitudes better than leadership style (Mathieu & Babiak, 2015). Indeed, psychopathic traits in leaders predicted employees' work motivation, job satisfaction, turnover intentions, and job neglect even when controlling for leadership style (Mathieu & Babiak, 2016b).

As far as workplace harassment, a study by Mathieu and Babiak (2016c) indicated that psychopathy is a stronger predictor of harassment in the workplace than personality traits included in the HEXACO model of personality (Honesty/humility, Emotionality, Extraversion, Agreeableness, Conscientiousness, Openness). It is thus clear that psychopathic individuals are not only likely to be associated with corporate fraud, but they also seem to cause a lot of damage to employees within the organization.

How corporate psychopaths operate

Babiak (2016) presents the Psychopathic Process Model in which he proposes five career phases observed in corporate psychopaths' careers:

Phase 1: Organizational entry. Two factors facilitate entry for psychopathic candidates: the fact that most organizations use unstructured interviews in which psychopaths thrive by manipulating their image. Furthermore, the fact that credentials are rarely verified makes it easy for psychopaths to lie on their resume and during the interview.

Phase 2: Assessment. Psychopaths "scan" the organization to identify key players and who would be useful to the psychopath; they identify pawns and patrons. They begin creating a network and an image that will form the basis for future manipulation.

Phase 3: Manipulation. Psychopaths use communication networks to create their image and to create conflicts and spread disinformation to further their career. They spend a lot of time one on one with their targets. They use pawns to do their work, patrons to protect them, and they discredit any detractors or rivals. They use the "divide and conquer" philosophy, making sure that others do not share information by creating conflict and distrust among coworkers.

Phase 4: Confrontation. During this phase, the psychopaths' manipulation, violence, and abuse is discovered usually by pawns who realize that they are being played. It is during this phase that pawns realize that the "closer than usual" business relationship that they thought genuine with the psychopath is, in fact, all an act. However, as Babiak mentions, when the pawns try to talk to management or coworkers, they realize that their reputation has been tampered with by the psychopath and they find themselves isolated. This situation creates a feeling of shame for having trusted and having developed a deeper and more emotional relationship with the psychopath.

Phase 5: Ascension. Babiak (2016) mentions that, at this point, the psychopath has built a strong network of powerful individuals and is able to manipulate the power structure of the organization. At this point, some patrons become no longer indispensable for the psychopath and are moved aside. "The patron has now become the patsy" (Babiak, 2016, p. 18).

How corporate fraudsters operate

Albrecht (2003) proposed a model presenting three factors that can predict the occurrence of fraud. This model includes: (a) Perceived pressure (financial need, debts, and greed), (b) Perceived opportunity (access to resources, absence of or weak internal control), and (c) Rationalization (rationalizing their actions as acceptable). Cohen et al. (2012) proposed a model including Albrecht's factors and adding elements from the extended "theory of planned behavior" (Ajzen, 1991). Indeed, Cohen et al. (2012) add four factors to the traditional fraud model: (a) Attitude toward fraud (a person's belief that fraud will have a positive outcome), (b) subjective norms (a person's perception that significant people in their life could agree with the behavior), (c) perceived behavioral control (ease of performing the behavior as well as anticipated obstacles), and (d) moral obligation (derived from a person's moral belief or sense of ethics or derived by the law). The Association of Certified Fraud Examiners presents case studies of fraud schemes. In each case, it is easy to see that fraudsters manipulate to get what they want. In some cases the individuals being manipulated were the victims, in other cases, the fraudster manipulated others into "helping" them achieve their goal oftentimes without the other person realizing that they were acting as facilitators in fraud schemes. Not surprisingly, owners/executives are more likely to collude with others to commit their fraud (Association of Certified Fraud Examiners, 2018).

As for internet frauds, the profile and modus operandi may not be as different form the one that has been presented for face-to-face corporate fraud: "Perpetrators of Internet frauds, like perpetrators of face-to-face schemes, must be ruthless-willing and able to steal the money of faceless victims with no empathy and no remorse. The people who do this work well are often some of the smartest, most cunning and most heartless of offenders. And, they-like perpetrators of face-to-face frauds-may suffer from a chronic personality disorder." (Barnard, 2008, p. 214)

Comparing the traits and behavioral processes of corporate psychopaths and fraudsters provides a clear image of how fraud can occur within organizations and of who is susceptible to commit it. Indeed, the red flag behaviors associated with fraudsters are very similar to psychopathic traits and behaviors. The same manipulation skills that serve psychopaths in committing corporate crime also help them enter organizations and climb the corporate ladder.

What can be done to prevent corporate crime?

Aside from the financial costs, fraud and economic crimes also have an impact on the following business elements: Employee morale (48%), business relations (38%), reputation/brand strength (36%) (PWC report, 2018), it is thus crucial to find solutions and act to prevent corporate crime from happening.

Benson and Simpson (2009) explain that, in order to prevent white-collar crime from happening, we need to understand the features that allow crime to occur in organizational settings. The authors use three theories to explain opportunity to commit white-collar crime. The first theory is the Routine Activity Theory stating that three elements must be in place in order to allow crime to be committed: (a) a target (victim), (b) a motivated offender, and (c) a common place where the offender can gain access to the target (organizational features that facilitate contact between the victim and the offender). The second theory put forward by Benson and Simpson (2009) to explain opportunity structure in white-collar crime is the Crime Pattern Theory. This theory states that offenders become aware of crime opportunities in familiar settings where they can easily find victims and navigate the system and procedures they know well. The third theory used to explain opportunity perspective in white-collar crime is the Situational Crime Prevention Theory which states that criminals chose to commit a crime based on their evaluation of costs and benefits on these five dimensions: (a) the efforts necessary to commit the crime, (b) the risks of getting detected, (c) the rewards associated with the crime, (d) the conditions that may support the crime, (e) excuses that the offender can use to justify their actions (Benson & Simpson, 2009). Based on the psychopathic process model presented earlier, it is clear that opportunity perspective explained by these three theories applies to corporate psychopaths and their modus operandi.

One of the elements facilitating psychopaths' entrance within organizations according to Babiak (2016) is the fact that many organizations do not invest in a thorough and structured selection process. Furthermore, the fact that organizations are afraid of bad publicity and thus tend to try to deal with corporate fraud by keeping it secret puts these organizations at increased risk of being victims of corporate crime. The same fear of bad publicity is true when it comes to dealing with antipersonnel crime in the form of abusive behavior and harassment. Companies tend to try to avoid dealing with the problem by either ignoring it or transferring the problematic employee or leader to another team or work unit, thus creating chaos elsewhere in the company. Although there is no full-proof solution to avoid corporate crime, following are recommendations that should help reduce the risk for organizations to become victims of such crimes.

1. Reporting corporate crime

   The first step in stopping corporate crime is the same step used to stop other types of crimes: reporting the crime to authorities. Unfortunately, between 2008 and 2018, rates of referral for occupational fraud to law enforcement went from 69% to 58% (Association of Certified Fraud Examiners, 2018). The reasons for not referring to law enforcement are fear of bad publicity (38%), internal discipline sufficient (33%), too costly (24%), private settlement (21%). Another deterrent may be that, in some organizational fraud cases, organizations who report the crime receive fines from authorities for having inadequate controls or allowing fraud to occur. These fines may range anywhere between $10,000 and more than $1,000,000 depending on the amount of the fraud, with a median fine of $100,000 for the frauds included in the Association of Fraud Examiners' 2018 report. Since higher management and executives tend to commit the most costly frauds, this is yet another disposition that protects them from being brought to justice. Furthermore, in a keynote address to the Canadian Bar Association in 2011, David Johnston, former Governor-General of Canada, a former Dean of Law, said that judges and lawyers "must act with 'urgency' to break through what criminologists have called a 'court culture' of complacency….How many lawyers 'papered the deals' that involved fraudulent statements of assets, liabilities, income and valuations?". Hansen (2009, p. 33) adds that "The problem with occupational crime is that it is committed within the confines of positions of trust and in organizations, which prohibits surveillance and accountability."

2. Punishing corporate crime

   The criminal justice system is not the only place where corporate criminals can enjoy laxity in terms of repercussions they receive for their crime. The Association of Fraud Examiners reports that, of the fraudsters studied, 44% faced termination, 18% received a settlement agreement, 16% were permitted or required to resign, and 12% received *no punishment* or negative consequences. Organizations may be afraid of the bad publicity if they decide to take action against one of their employees, especially if the fraudster is among higher managers. An organization that fails to report fraud sends a message that crime will not be punished… opening the door for dark individuals, such as psychopaths, to enter and commit crimes.

3. Competency-based structured interviews

   Prevention is always the best method of dealing with any type of crime. Since psychopathy traits are associated with corporate crime, one way to prevent corporate crime would be to prevent psychopathic individuals from entering the organization. In order to make good hiring/promotion decisions, competency-based recruitment is key. Building a competency profile for each position that needs to be filled and making sure that the profile takes into account both task-oriented and people-oriented skills such as empathy, humility, and honesty constitutes the foundation of a good selection process. Structured competency-based recruitment and promotion interviews should then be conducted based on the competency profile that was built. Professionals in charge of hiring or promotion processes should be aware of impression management biases and try, as much as possible, to rate the candidates according to the elements composing the competency profile for the position. Extraversion, although a competency that would no doubt be rated highly for a sales representative profile, may not be as important for a librarian or an engineer position. Although individuals high on extraversion may have an advantage during the interview process as they are able to sell themselves very well, they may not be the best candidate for a position. Just as hiring a manager based on their task-oriented skills without taking into consideration their interpersonal abilities could lead to disastrous results for his/her team.

4. Background checks

   Candidates with dark personalities would be very likely to lie about their credentials, it is thus recommended to run a thorough background check on candidates (references, education, previous work experience). In the cases that were studied in the Association of Certified Fraud Examiners' report to the nation (2016), 49.1% of fraudsters were hired without a background check. For the 50.9% that had a background check, 11.2% had red flag(s). Employment background of perpetrator revealed that 82.5% were never punished or terminated, 8.7% were previously punished, and 8.3% were previously terminated. While background checks and competence-based interviews for selection are good, adding psychometric testing to these methods is even better.

5. Psychometric testing

   Psychometric tests help in decision-making by adding more information on the candidate either for selection or promotion purposes. Valid psychometric measures for employee selection and promotion are varied, some measure personality traits, others are structured to measure specific workplace behaviors and skills. Ideally, to prevent from hiring or promoting a psychopathic individual, organizations could use a measure built specifically to assess all four facets of psychopathy such as the B-Scan Self (Mathieu & Babiak, 2016a) or the B-Scan 360 (measuring psychopathy in others) (Mathieu et al., 2013). However, if, for some reason, it is not possible to use a measure of corporate psychopathy, professionals in charge of employee selection and promotion could use standard industrial-organizational measures to assess the candidate's scores on some of the traits associated with corporate psychopathy (i.e., low scores on teamwork, low scores on humility, low scores on conscientiousness and empathy). However, while these traits are part of what makes dark personalities, they are by no means sufficient to get a portrait of the individual on the four factors composing psychopathy. They may however, serve as "red flags" during the selection and/or promotion process.

6. Annual performance appraisals

   In terms of promotion or performance appraisal, when the candidates are already within the organizations, multirater evaluations such as 360 degree-type evaluations are very helpful. These multirater evaluations are built to acquire feedback on the candidate from all angles (self-report, employee-reports, colleague-reports, and report from direct supervisor). While time consuming, 360 degree evaluations allow decision-makers to get a full picture of the candidate or the manager. Regardless of the fact that sometimes employees are afraid to rate their supervisor, 360 degree evaluations are still a good way of getting the clearest picture possible. In order to increase participation and avoid possible negative impacts on employees completing a 360 degree feedback evaluation of their superior, ensuring confidentiality is essential.

If an organization suspects that they are dealing with corporate fraud committed by an individual with psychopathic traits, outside assistance and professional advice may be needed. The Federal Bureau of Investigations (FBI) has offered tips on how to confront psychopathic individuals if the organization suspects criminal activities (Babiak & O'Toole, 2012). These tips include:

- Investigators should familiarize themselves with the typical traits and characteristics of psychopaths.
- Understand the manipulation techniques used to create and manage the psychopathic bonds established with victim organizations.
- The psychopath's reputation, as judged by those in power with whom they have bonded, known as patrons, often provide added protection from closer investigation. As a result, the investigator may need to build a case with management for the use and broad application of more sophisticated techniques.

Finally, on the organizational level, it is important for organizations to build a culture based on transparency and have clear rules on occupational fraud, harassment, and abusive behaviors. Employees need to feel safe to come forward with information on fraud and on antipersonnel behavior; protecting the employee's identity is key (some organizations have confidential hotlines for employees who wish to come forward with sensitive information). When corporate fraud or abusive behavior is brought forward, actions must be taken as soon as possible since the impact of both corporate fraud and abusive leadership will inflict greater damage if ignored. Taking a stance against corporate crime will send a clear message throughout the organization and in the general population and act as a deterrent when psychopathic individuals are looking for their next "prey organization."

Research linking corporate crime and psychopathy

In an article explaining the link between white-collar crime and psychopathy, Perri, Lichtenwald, and Mieczkowska (2014, p. 84) conclude "Over seventy years have passed since the publications of Sutherland's and Cleckley's scholarship and to date scholarship on white-collar offenders is still woefully languishing despite the tremendous costs: financial, emotional and reputational to society. The authors conclude that a plausible partial explanation for this dearth in scholarship is due to the neglect by the behavioral sciences to focus some of their attention to white-collar crime and the legacy Sutherland left behind that discouraged an inter-disciplinary collaborative environment to collectively try to come up with explanations to crime causations and individual susceptibilities." With the use of instruments that allow to effectively measure psychopathy within corporations, it is now possible to attain the goal set by Perri and his colleagues and test the theory that psychopathy is an underlying factor that could explain different forms of corporate crime.

Conclusions

Whether or not we consider psychopaths as successful depends on our definition of success. If, as mentioned by Cleckley, success is defined by money, power, or social status, then we might be inclined to consider some psychopathic individuals in the corporate world as successful. This perception of success has an influence on how organizations, society, and the legal system deal with these individuals and their crimes. Unfortunately, this outward assessment of success does not take into consideration the damages or the actions that these individuals have executed to get to where they are or to get what they want. There is a saying "happiness is not about the destination, it is about the journey." I believe that the same is true for success. The means taken by individuals to get to where they are defines who they are as a person/employee/leader and should matter when we assess whether this individual is successful or not. One of the reasons why corporate crime is on the rise is no doubt associated with the fact that the criminal justice system is lenient when it comes to punishment for corporate crimes, making it the "perfect type of crime" for psychopaths. In essence, not only is it easier for an individual with psychopathic traits to be hired, but once in place, organizational structures as well as the criminal justice system make it easy for these individuals to use their power to abuse others or commit corporate crime without having to fear or face consequences.

References

Ajzen, I. (1991). The theory of planned behavior. *Organizational Behavior and Human Decision Processes*, *50*(2), 179–211. https://doi.org/10.1016/0749-5978(91)90020-T.

Albrecht, W. S. (2003). *Fraud examination*. Southwestern/Thomson.

Association of Certified Fraud Examiners. (2016). Report to the nations 2016 global study on occupational fraud and abuse. https://www.acfe.com/report-to-the-nations/2016/ (Accessed September 2017).

Association of Certified Fraud Examiners. (2018). *Report to the nations 2018 global study on occupational fraud and abuse*. Retrieved from https://www.acfe.com/report-to-the-nations/2018/.

Association of Certified Fraud Examiners. (2020). Report to the nations 2020 global study on occupational fraud and abuse. https://www.acfe.com/report-to-the-nations/2018/ (Accessed July 2020).
Babiak, P. (2016). Psychopathic manipulation at work. In C. B. Gacono (Ed.), *Personality and clinical psychology series. The clinical and forensic assessment of psychopathy: A practitioner's guide* (pp. 353–373). New York, NY: Routledge/Taylor & Francis Group.
Babiak, P., & Hare, R. D. (2006). *Snakes in suits: When psychopaths go to work.* New York, NY: Regan Books/Harper Collins Publishers.
Babiak, P., Neumann, C. S., & Hare, R. D. (2010). Corporate psychopathy: Talking the walk. *Behavioral Sciences & the Law*, *28*(2), 174–193. https://doi.org/10.1002/bsl.925.
Babiak, P., & O'Toole, M. E. (2012). The corporate psychopath. *FBI Law Enforcement Bulletin*, *81*, 7.
Baker, R. (2005). *Capitalism's Achilles Heel—Dirty money and how to renew the free-market system.* Hoboken, NJ: John Wiley & Sons.
Barnard, J. W. (2008). Securities fraud, recidivism, and deterrence. *Faculty Publications*, *161*, 189–227.
Benson, M. L., & Simpson, S. S. (2009). *White collar crime: An opportunity perspective.* Routledge.
Blickle, G., Schlegel, A., Fassbender, P., & Klein, U. (2006). Some personality correlates of business white-collar crime. *Applied Psychology*, *55*(2), 220–233. https://doi.org/10.1111/j.1464-0597.2006.00226.x.
Cleckley, H. (1988). *The mask of sanity* (5th ed.). St. Louis, MO: Mosby.
Cohen, J., Ding, Y., Lesage, C., & Stolowy, H. (2012). Corporate fraud and managers' behavior: Evidence from the press. In *Entrepreneurship, governance and ethics* (pp. 271–315). Dordrecht: Springer.
Coid, J., Yang, M., Ullrich, S., Roberts, A., & Hare, R. D. (2009). Prevalence and correlates of psychopathic traits in the household population of Great Britain. *International Journal of Law and Psychiatry*, *32*(2), 65–73. https://doi.org/10.1016/j.ijlp.2009.01.002.
Europol. (2020). https://www.europol.europa.eu/crime-areas-and-trends/crime-areas/economic-crime (Accessed 18 July 2020).
Hansen, L. L. (2009). Corporate financial crime: Social diagnosis and treatment. *Journal of Financial Crime*, *16*(1), 28–40. https://doi.org/10.1108/13590790910924948.
Hare, R. D. (1999). Psychopathy as a risk factor for violence. *The Psychiatric Quarterly*, *70*, 181–197. https://doi.org/10.1023/A:1022094925150.
Hare, R. D. (2003). *Hare psychopathy checklist revised (PCL-R): Technical manual.* North Tonawanda, NY: Multi-Health Systems.
Hare, R. D. (2016). Psychopathy, the PCL-R, and criminal justice: Some new findings and current issues. *Canadian Psychology/Psychologie Canadienne*, *57*(1), 21–34. https://doi.org/10.1037/cap0000041.
Hare, R. D., Neumann, C. S., & Widiger, T. A. (2012). Psychopathy. In T. A. Widiger (Ed.), *The Oxford handbook of personality disorders* (pp. 478–504). New York, NY: Oxford University Press.
Hart, S. D., Cox, D. N., & Hare, R. D. (1995). *Manual for the Psychopathy Checklist: Screening Version (PCL: SV).* Toronto, ON: Multi-Health Systems.
Interpol. (2020). https://www.interpol.int/en/Crimes/Financial-crime (Accessed 18 July 2020).
Johnston, D. (2011). *Keynote address, Canadian Bar Association meeting.* Halifax, Canada.
Levi, M., & Reuter, P. (2006). Money laundering. *Crime and Justice*, *34*(1), 289–375.
Lingnau, V., Fuchs, F., & Dehne-Niemann, T. E. (2017). The influence of psychopathic traits on the acceptance of white-collar crime: Do corporate psychopaths cook the books and misuse the news? *Journal of Business Economics*, *87*(9), 1193–1227.

Mathieu, C. (2016). *The devil lurks in the suit*. Retrieved from http://aftermath-surviving-psychopathy.org/index.php/the-devil-lurks-in-the-suit/.

Mathieu, C., & Babiak, P. (2015). Tell me who you are, I'll tell you how you lead: Beyond the full-range leadership model, the role of corporate psychopathy on employee attitudes. *Personality and Individual Differences*, *87*, 8–12. https://doi.org/10.1016/j.paid.2015.07.016.

Mathieu, C., & Babiak, P. (2016a). Validating the B-Scan Self: A self-report measure of psychopathy in the workplace. *International Journal of Selection and Assessment*, *24*(3), 272–284. https://doi.org/10.1111/ijsa.12146.

Mathieu, C., & Babiak, P. (2016b). Corporate psychopathy and abusive supervision: Their influence on employees' job satisfaction and turnover intentions. *Personality and Individual Differences*, *91*, 102–106. https://doi.org/10.1016/j.paid.2015.07.016.

Mathieu, C., & Babiak, P. (2016c). Workplace harassment: The influence of corporate psychopathy and the HEXACO model of personality. *Personality and Individual Differences*, *101*, 298.

Mathieu, C., Babiak, P., & Hare, R. D. (2020). Psychopathy in the workplace. In A. Felthous, & H. Sass (Eds.), *The international handbook on psychopathic disorders and the law*. New Jersey: Wiley.

Mathieu, C., Hare, R. D., Jones, D. N., Babiak, P., & Neumann, C. S. (2013). Factor structure of the B-Scan 360: A measure of corporate psychopathy. *Psychological Assessment*, *25*(1), 288–293. https://doi.org/10.1037/a0029262.

Mathieu, C., Neumann, C., Babiak, P., & Hare, R. D. (2015). Corporate psychopathy and the full-range leadership model. *Assessment*, *22*(3), 267–278. https://doi.org/10.1177/1073191114545490.

Mokros, A., Hare, R. D., Neumann, C. S., Santtila, P., Habermeyer, E., & Nitschke, J. (2015). Variants of psychopathy in adult male offenders: A latent profile analysis. *Journal of Abnormal Psychology*, *124*, 372–386. https://doi.org/10.1037/abn0000042.

Neumann, C. S., & Hare, R. D. (2008). Psychopathic traits in a large community sample: Links to violence, alcohol use, and intelligence. *Journal of Consulting and Clinical Psychology*, *76*(5), 893–899. https://doi.org/10.1037/0022-006x.76.5.893.

Neumann, C. S., Hare, R. D., & Pardini, D. A. (2014). Antisociality and the construct of psychopathy: Data from across the globe. *Journal of Personality*, *83*(6), 678–692. https://doi.org/10.1111/jopy.12127.

Neumann, C. S., Vitacco, M. J., & Mokros, A. S. (2016). Using both variable-centered and person-centered approaches to understanding psychopathic personality. In C. B. Gacono (Ed.), *The clinical and forensic assessment of psychopathy: A Practitioner's guide* (2nd ed., pp. 14–31). New York, NY: Routledge.

Paulhus, D. L., Neumann, C. S., & Hare, R. D. (2016). Self-Report Psychopathy Scale – Fourth edition (SRP 4).

Perri, F. S. (2011). White-collar criminals: The 'kinder, gentler' offender? *Journal of Investigative Psychology and Offender Profiling*, *8*(3), 217–241.

Perri, F. S. (2016). Red collar crime. *International Journal of Psychological Studies*, *8*(1), 61–84. https://doi.org/10.5539/ijps.v8n1p61.

Perri, F., & Lichtenwald, T. (2007). A proposed addition to the FBI criminal classification manual. *The Forensic Examiner*, *16*(4), 18–29. https://doi.org/10.1002/jip.140.

Perri, F. S., Lichtenwald, T. G., & Mieczkowska, E. M. (2014). Sutherland, Cleckley and beyond: White-collar crime and psychopathy. *International Journal of Psychological Studies*, *6*(4), 71.

Price Waterhouse Cooper. (2018). *Pulling fraud out of the shadows: Global economic crime fraud survey* (p. 2018). Retrieved from https://www.pwc.com/gx/en/forensics/global-economic-crime-and-fraud-survey-2018.pdf.
Prokosch, E. (1995). *The technology of killing: A military and political history of antipersonnel weapons*. Zed Books.
Ragatz, L. L., Fremouw, W., & Baker, E. (2012). The psychological profile of white-collar offenders: Demographics, criminal thinking, psychopathic traits, and psychopathology. *Criminal Justice and Behavior*, *39*(7), 978–997.
Ribeiro, R., Guedes, I. S., & Cruz, J. N. (2019). White-collar offenders vs. common offenders: A comparative study on personality traits and self-control. *Crime, Law and Social Change*, *72*(5), 607–622.

Psychopathy: Cybercrime and cyber abuse

20

Evita March

Introduction

In contemporary society, the Internet plays a fundamental role in interpersonal relationships (Sindermann, Sariyska, Lachmann, Brand, & Montag, 2018). The Internet has changed human connection in profound ways (Bogolyubova, Panicheva, Tikhonov, Ivanov, & Ledovaya, 2018), facilitating a range of diverse and new social connections and interactions (Lim & Richardson, 2016). Although these online connections are associated with positive social benefits (Bogolyubova et al., 2018) enabling quick and easy social interaction (Loos, Haddon, & Mante-Meijer, 2016), the Internet also promotes a sense of anonymity and decreased accountability, self-awareness, and inhibition (Morrissey, 2010), which in turn can promote deindividuation.

Online deindividuation may foster the manifestation of negative, online antisocial behavior (Hardaker, 2010), including cyberbullying, trolling, cyberstalking, and online aggression (collectively referred to as cyber abuse; March & Marrington, 2019). Further, some online antisocial behaviors may be illegal, criminal activity, such as cyber fraud and child pornography use, and thus approximate the definition of cybercrime (see Wall, 2007). The online antisocial behaviors that characterize cyber abuse and cybercrime are not specific to a single culture and are considered a global issue (Erdur-Baker, 2010).

Cyber abuse and cybercrime are rightfully a global issue, as both are associated with significant negative impact. Experiencing online antisocial behaviors has similar psychopathological outcomes as experiencing traditional harassment, including depression, anxiety, and low self-esteem (Nicol, 2012). Unlike more traditional, face-to-face antisocial behaviors, victims of online antisocial behavior are often targeted in the perceived safety of their own home, aggravating the victim's perceived vulnerability and wellbeing (Del Rey et al., 2016). Online antisocial behaviors are considered to be more pervasive than traditional antisocial behaviors, and have a longer lasting impact on the victim (Park, Na, & Kim, 2014).

In an effort to understand how to respond to and manage online antisocial behavior, research has focused on predictors of this behavior, and psychopathy has emerged as a subclinical trait strongly related to both cyber abuse and cybercrime. A systematic review (see Moor & Anderson, 2019) synthesizing the research on the Dark Triad personality traits (i.e., Machiavellianism, psychopathy, and narcissism; Paulhus & Williams, 2002) and the Dark Tetrad traits (the inclusion of sadism; Chabrol, Van Leeuwen, Rodgers, & Sejourne, 2009) concluded that of all the traits, psychopathy

Psychopathy and Criminal Behavior. https://doi.org/10.1016/B978-0-12-811419-3.00015-7

shared the strongest relationship with a range of antisocial online behavior. This relationship is considered to be largely due to the characteristics of trait psychology; specifically, high impulsivity and low empathy (Moor & Anderson, 2019). In this chapter, I present findings of a body of research that has explored psychopathy as a correlate and predictor of a range of online antisocial behaviors.

Psychopathy and disordered internet use

To begin, I discuss the role of psychopathy in disordered Internet use, which includes Internet and social media addiction, selfies and self-presentation, and online gaming.

Psychopathy and internet/social media addiction

People with higher levels to psychopathy tend to exhibit greater addiction to the Internet and social media. Sindermann et al. (2018) describe Internet Use Disorder (IUD) as synonymous with Internet addiction—the over usage of the Internet. Internet addiction has a prevalence rate of 6% across 31 nations from seven world regions (Cheng & Li, 2014) and is associated with significant aversive individual outcomes (Andreassen, 2015). Compared to people with low levels, those with higher levels of psychopathy spend more time online and on social media (Fox & Rooney, 2015).

Given dysfunctional impulsivity is a key characteristic of trait psychopathy, and addiction is strongly associated with impulsivity, Sindermann et al. (2018) hypothesized that trait psychopathy would be a significant predictor of IUD. This prediction was tested across two studies: In study one, participants were recruited online ($N = 468$; 338 women, *M*age = 29.64, $SD = 14.15$), and in study two, participants were university students recruited on campus ($N = 472$; 329 women, *M*age = 23.19, $SD = 8.42$). All participants in study one and two completed an online questionnaire, which included a measure of psychopathy (the Short Dark Triad Scale; Jones & Paulhus, 2014) and the Short Internet Addiction Test (s-IAT; Pawlikowski, Altstötter-Gleich, & Brand, 2013) to measure IUD. The s-IAT measures unspecified IUD, and includes additional questions to measure specific forms of IUD (e.g., internet gaming, internet gambling).

For both men and women, there were significant positive correlations between psychopathy and tendencies toward IUD, particularly unspecified IUD. The authors surmised that individuals with high levels of psychopathy might be attracted to and even form an addiction to the anonymous online environment, as this environment provides greater opportunity to successfully cheat and deceive other people (behavior characteristic of psychopathy; Halevy, Shalvi, and Verschuere, 2014). This anonymous environment, and opportunity to cheat and deceive others, may perpetuate and reinforce their use of the Internet, thus increasing the possibility of disordered usage.

Demircioğlu and Köse (2018) examined the relationship between trait psychopathy and social media addiction. More specific than Internet addiction, social media addiction is the inability to control social media use, and this excessive use of social media impairs individual functioning (Ryan, Chester, Reece, & Xenos, 2014). Demircioğlu and Köse (2018) assessed 237 university students (161 women, *M*age = 21.51 years, *SD* = 1.80) who completed the Short Dark Triad measure and a Turkish Social Media Addiction Scale (Tutgun-Ünal & Deniz, 2015), and positive associations were found between psychopathy and social media addiction. Akin to Sindermann et al. (2018), Demircioğlu and Köse (2018) attributed this relationship to characteristics of social media that are attractive to individuals with high psychopathy. Specifically, social media may be an attractive platform to these individuals, as they can use this platform to (perhaps anonymously) express their hostile and aversive attitudes without fear of punishment. Chung, Morshidi, Yoong, and Thian (2019) and Lee (2019) further corroborated these results, reporting positive relationships between psychopathy and social media addiction and Social Networking Sites addiction, respectively.

Psychopathy, selfies, and online self-presentation

Recent research has documented the rise in popularity of "selfies", defined as pictures taken of oneself and shared on social media (McCain et al., 2016). In an initial study exploring selfies, Fox and Rooney (2015) assessed personality as predictors of posting and editing selfies in a sample of men (*N* = 800, *M*age = 29.29, *SD* = 6.52). Participants completed the Dirty Dozen (Jonason & Webster, 2010) and estimated their selfie posting frequency and editing behavior. Although psychopathy was related to both increased posting and editing of selfies, it only emerged as a significant predictor of posting selfies. The authors attributed the utility of psychopathy to predict posting selfies, not editing selfies, to impulsivity, a key characteristic of psychopathy.

Further exploring the relationship between psychopathy and selfie posting, McCain et al. (2016) recruited participants via MTurk (*N* = 348; 49% women; *M*age = 31.85[a]) and undergraduate students (*N* = 491; 78.6% women; *M*age = 18.87, *SD* = 1.29). All participants completed the Short Dark Triad scale and responded to a series of questions regarding selfie behaviors (e.g., frequency of taking selfies, aspects of selfies taken, and emotional responses to posting selfies). People with higher levels of psychopathy posted more selfies each day, and were less likely to experience negative emotions during the selfie process (i.e., the process of posting a selfie, and gaining likes and comments on a selfie). Specifically, the higher an individual's level of psychopathy, the less likely they are to experience negative emotions in reaction to likes, comments, etc. Perhaps this lack of negative affect experienced in relation to selfie feedback is due to the callous, unemotional nature of trait psychopathy (e.g., Frick & Ray, 2015).

[a] *SD* not available.

Adler (2017) also reported a positive relationship between psychopathy and frequency of posting selfies for both men and women, and surmised that individuals with high psychopathy seek excitement, and combined with characteristic impulsivity they may post selfies in an effort to create excitement when bored.

Beyond selfies, research has also explored how individuals with higher levels of psychopathy generally present themselves online. Using Latent Semantic Analysis, Garcia and Sikström (2014) predicted personality by exploring semantic representations of Facebook status updates. Participants ($N=304$; 172 women; *M*age=26.40, $SD=7.52$) were recruited online and psychopathy was measured with the Eysenck Personality Questionnaire Revised psychoticism subscale (EPQR-S; Eysenck, Eysenck, & Barrett, 1985). Participants were also asked to provide their 15 most recent Facebook status updates by downloading the software Mystatus. Results showed utility for semantic content of Facebook statuses in predicting psychopathy, and the authors posited that individuals with higher psychopathy may use Facebook to increase their social status and monitor/manipulate social groups. Further, the Facebook statuses of these individuals appeared to lack appropriate social and verbal filters.

Psychopathy and online gaming

Finally, research has also considered the role of psychopathy in online gaming behaviors. Although research has not demonstrated utility for psychopathy to predict problematic (i.e., addictive) online gaming behavior (see Kircaburun & Griffiths, 2018; Kircaburun, Jonason, and Griffiths, 2018a), there is evidence that psychopathy is related to other problematic behavior when gaming, such as disruption and aggression. Ladanyi and Doyle-Portillo (2017) sought to explore predictors of antisocial online gaming behavior; specifically, disruptive online gamers (known as *grief trolls*, or *griefers*), who disrupt the online experience of others (Foo, 2008) and enjoy eliciting negative reactions from other online gamers. Ladanyi and Doyle-Portillo (2017) explored predictors of grief trolls in massively multiplayer online role-playing games (MMOPRGs; e.g., World of Warcraft), hypothesizing that characteristics that predict Internet trolling would also predict grief trolling.

Participants ($N=285$) completed the Short Dark Triad and the established Grief Play Scale (Ladanyi & Doyle-Portillo, 2017), which measures the frequency individuals engage in disruptive activities in MMORPGs. Results showed a positive correlation between psychopathy and the Grief Play Scale. Further, results supported the Grief Play Scale as a measure of a construct (i.e., grief trolling) meaningfully distinct from online trolling in the larger, online environment. The authors suggest that the utility of psychopathy to predict disruptive online gaming can be attributed to the key psychopathy characteristics of aggression and being self-centered.

Psychopathy and cyber aggression

I now present research that has explored the role of psychopathy in cyber aggression. Cyber aggression is a general term given to socially undesirable online behaviors

(Bogolyubova et al., 2018), and encompasses behaviors such as cyber harassment, cyberbullying, and other forms of online aggression (Pabian, De Backer, & Vandebosch, 2015). To assess the relationship between psychopathy and generalized cyber aggression, Bogolyubova et al. (2018) recruited a total of 6724 individuals (77.9% women; *M*age = 44.96 years, *SD* = 11.58). Participants completed an online survey which assessed psychopathy (with the Short Dark Triad scale) and engagement in harmful online behaviors. Three types of harmful online behavior were selected for assessment in this study: Sending threats or insults, dissemination of personal information, and posting inflammatory messages or derogatory remarks on social media. Psychopathy was found to be a unique predictor of engagement in all harmful, cyber aggressive behaviors.

The relationship between psychopathy and cyber aggression has also been explored in younger populations. Pabian et al. (2015) investigated the relationship between psychopathy and cyber aggression among adolescents. Participants aged 14–18 years (*N* = 324; 63% women; *M*age = 16.05, *SD* = 1.31) completed a measure of psychopathy (the Short Dark Triad scale) the Facebook Intensity Scale (Ellison, Steinfield, & Lampe, 2007), and a measure of cyber aggression. Structural Equation Modeling indicated that when controlling for age and gender, Facebook intensity and psychopathy significantly predict cyber aggression. Kurek, Jose, and Stuart (2019) assessed personality and technology behaviors in a sample of 709 high school student from New Zealand (*M*age = 15.56 years), and found the best predictors of cyber aggression were psychopathy, online disinhibition, and nonclinical (i.e., everyday) sadism.

In addition to exploring cyber aggressive behaviors, such as harassment and bullying, researchers have also explored predictors of milder forms of antisocial online behavior, such as generalizing statements, nonspecific insults, and provocative and impolite comments. Koban, Stein, Eckhardt, and Ohler (2018) recruited 256 participants (190 women; *M*age = 24.38 years, *SD* = 5.57) who completed a measure of psychopathy (the Dirty Dozen) and a measure developed for the study to assess uncivil online behavior. Results showed psychopathy was not a significant predictor of less extreme forms of uncivil online behavior. Although the authors suggested future research use a more comprehensive measure of psychopathy, and differentiate between primary and secondary psychopathy, it is possible that psychopathy is a better predictor of cyber aggression and abuse in comparison to milder uncivil online behavior. I now turn my attention to more specific cyber aggressive (i.e., cyber abuse) behaviors, including cyberbullying, trolling, and cyberstalking.

Psychopathy and cyberbullying

Cyberbullying is commonly defined as the repeated use of technology in an attempt to harass and cause distress to others (Slonje, Smith, & Frisén, 2013). Cyberbullying can include a range of behaviors, such as harassing, impersonating, slandering, and excluding the victim (Willard, 2007). There are a range of reasons why someone might perpetrate cyberbullying behaviors, including revenge, jealousy, boredom, and seeking approval (Varjas, Talley, Meyers, Parris, & Cutts, 2010). Due to the extremely detrimental psychological, physical, and emotional consequences of cyberbullying (Van Geel, Goemans, Toprak, & Vedder, 2017), a significant amount of research has explored predictors in an attempt to manage and prevent cyberbullying. Psychopathy has been found to be a significant, reliable predictor of perpetrating cyberbullying.

Gibb and Devereux (2014) explored psychopathy and cyberbullying in a college sample. Although rates of cyberbullying are expected to decrease after adolescence, college samples still report high rates of experiencing cyberbullying. Gibb and Devereux (2014) hypothesized psychopathy would predict perpetrating cyberbullying behaviors, as this trait is characterized by high impulsivity, thrill seeking behavior, and low levels of empathy (Paulhus & Williams, 2002), and has previously been associated with traditional bullying behavior (Baughman, Dearing, Giammarco, & Vernon, 2012). Participants (University students; $N = 297$; 61% women; Mage = 22.70, $SD = 7.02$) completed the Short Dark Triad and a modified version of the Cyberbullying Questionnaire (CBQ; Calvete, Orue, Estevez, Villardon, & Padilla, 2010), and a positive relationship was found between psychopathy and perpetrating cyberbullying behaviors.

This relationship has been replicated in other studies. Goodboy and Martin (2015) explored the utility of psychopathy in predicting cyberbullying. In their study, 227 undergraduate students (112 women; Mage = 20.97, $SD = 2.32$) completed a measure of psychopathy (Dirty Dozen) and a measure of visual and text cyberbullying. Visual cyberbullying was measured with items such as *In the past year at this school, I used a mobile phone to send other students a video of a student I knew would embarrass them* and text cyberbullying was measured with items such as *In the past year at this school, I wrote nasty things about a student on a profile page*. Positive correlations were found between psychopathy and both visual and text cyberbullying. Of the dark personality traits (i.e., narcissism, Machiavellianism, and psychopathy), psychopathy was the only significant predictor of the two forms of cyberbullying. The authors recommended that when exploring cyberbullying, researchers should pay particular attention to psychopathy as there appears to be a unique relationship between psychopathy and aggression.

Gibb (2016) found psychopathy to be a significant, positive predictor of cyberbullying, with each 1-point increase in the psychopathy mean score approximately tripling the likelihood of perpetrating cyberbullying. In another particularly novel study, Balakrishnan, Khan, Fernandez, and Arabnia (2019) built a cyberbullying detection model based on personality traits (Big 5 and Dark Triad), and researchers found that factoring user's personality greatly improves cyberbullying detection mechanisms. Specifically, extraversion, agreeableness, and neuroticism (Big 5), and psychopathy (Dark Triad) were significant traits when detecting bullies, achieving up to 96% (precision) and 95% (recall). The authors suggested that unlike other dark personality traits, the predatory nature of psychopathy may motivate these individuals to seek online victims to bully in an attempt to inflict emotional and psychological harm. Further, the individual with higher levels of psychopathy feels little remorse in doing so, as they often disregard the distress they cause others.

In addition to the research conducted exploring psychopathy and cyberbullying in adults, this relationship has also been explored in younger populations. Van Geel et al. (2017) explored the utility of psychopathy to predict cyberbullying in a sample of high school students. A total of 17 senior vocational high schools participated in the study (N = 1568; 61.9% women; Mage = 17.58, SD = 1.39), and participants completed a measure of psychopathy (the Short Dark Triad scale) and a measure of cyberbullying (the European Cyberbullying Intervention Project Questionnaire; Del Rey et al., 2015). Interestingly, psychopathy was only a significant, positive predictor of cyberbullying until nonclinical sadism was included in the predictive model. Upon the inclusion of sadism, psychopathy was only marginally significant. The authors acknowledge that this result conflicts with previous research on psychopathy and cyberbullying, but note that previous research did not include sadism in the predictive model. The authors posit that perhaps cyberbullies are better motivated by sadistic pleasure instead of callousness, strategic considerations, or a threatened ego (i.e., psychopathy).

Lastly, Orue and Andershed (2015) explored the relationship between three dimensions of psychopathy (interpersonal, affective, and behavioral) and cyberbullying. Participants were 993 (58.9% women; Mage = 15.38; SD = 1.12) high school students. Schools were selected via a cluster sampling procedure, where schools were stratified according to school type (public vs. private) and urbanity. Participants completed the Youth Psychopathic Inventory-Short Form (YPI-S) which includes 18 items drawn from the original 50 item YPI (Andershed, Kerr, Stattin, & Levander, 2002), and the perpetration subscale of a Cyberbullying Questionnaire (CBQ). Results showed that for the total sample, all dimensions of the YPI-S were significantly, positively correlated with cyberbullying.

Psychopathy and trolling

Psychopathy has also been related to the online antisocial behavior of Internet trolling (i.e., "trolling"). Buckels, Trapnell, and Paulhus (2014) define trolling as behaving in a deceptive, destructive, or disruptive manner in an online social environment. Trolling includes instigating arguments and posting provocative, malicious messages in an attempt to deliberately provoke, disrupt, and upset others (Craker & March, 2016). Previous research has noted four characteristics of trolling: Aggression, deception, disruption, and success (Hardaker, 2010). The deceptive and apparently pointless disruptive characteristics of trolling differentiate this behavior from other online antisocial behaviors, such as cyberbullying, where perpetrator identities are usually clear (Hardaker, 2010). Experiencing trolling can have serious consequences, with victims reporting increases in suicidal ideation and self-harm (Coles & West, 2016).

In the first empirical research study to assess the relationship between psychopathy and trolling, Buckels et al. (2014) recruited two large samples: 188 Canadian psychology students (55% women, Mage = 21.15, SD = 3.63) and 609 United States residents (43% women, Mage = 35.04, SD = 12.98). The authors hypothesized that psychopathy would be related to the aggressive online behavior of trolling, as psychopathy predicts other aggressive behaviors such as bullying. Participants completed the Short Dark Triad and the Global Assessment of Internet trolling (GAIT; Buckels et al., 2014), which includes items such as "I have sent people to shock websites for the lulz" "I like to troll people in forums or the comments section of websites." Results showed that when controlling for other dark traits (e.g., Machiavellianism and narcissism), psychopathy was a significant positive predictor of trolling behaviors.

Craker and March (2016) replicated and extended these results, exploring trolling specifically on the social media site Facebook. The sample comprised of 396 adults (75.9% women, *M*age = 34.41, *SD* = 1.70). Participants completed the Dirty Dozen and a modified version of the GAIT which assessed trolling specifically on Facebook. Results provided support for Buckels et al. (2014), showing psychopathy as a significant, positive predictor of Facebook trolling behavior. Craker and March (2016) concluded that people who troll on Facebook are likely driven by the need to satisfy predatory impulses and display a lack of guilt for the distress they cause others.

Psychopathy has also been found to predict trolling on other online platforms; Seigfried-Spellar and Lankford (2018) explored trolling behaviors on the app Yik Yak. Yik Yak [now discontinued] facilitated anonymous communication between users who are geographically located within a 10 mile radius. One hundred and thirty-three current Yik Yak users (47% women; *M*age = 19.9, *SD* = 1.09; 57% men, *M*age = 20.3, *SD* = 1.66) completed a measure of psychopathy (the Short Dark Triad scale) and a questionnaire developed for the study that measures different commenting styles on Yik Yak (e.g., posting, lurking, confessing, trolling). Results showed psychopathy to be a significant, positive predictor of trolling behaviors on Yik Yak.

The relationship between psychopathy and trolling behaviors has also been explored on Location Based Real-Time dating apps. March, Grieve, Marrington, and Jonason (2017) recruited participants (N = 357; 71% women; *M*age = 22.50, *SD* = 6.55) to complete an anonymous, online survey including a measure of psychopathy (the Short Dark Triad scale) and a modified version of the GAIT, modified to assess trolling behaviors on dating apps (e.g., "I like to troll people in forums or the comments section of websites" was changed to "I like to troll people on the app"). People with higher levels of psychopathy were more likely to troll other people on LBRTD apps (specifically, Tinder). The authors attributed this behavior to satisfying predatory impulses and a lack of regard for the distress this causes others - possibly due to a lack of empathy.

To explore the premise that the relationship between psychopathy and trolling could be attributed to empathy deficits, Sest and March (2017) explored the utility of cognitive empathy and affective empathy in predicting trolling. Cognitive empathy is a more deliberate, reasoning form of empathy, and affective empathy is a more spontaneous, emotional form (Sest & March, 2017). Participants (N = 415; 63% women; *M*age = 23.37, *SD* = 7.19) completed an online questionnaire comprising a measure of psychopathy (the Short Dark Triad scale), a measure of empathy (Empathy Quotient; Baron-Cohen & Wheelwright, 2004) and a revised version of the GAIT (GAIT-Revised; Sest & March, 2017). Higher levels of psychopathy and lower levels of affective empathy were found to predict greater perpetration of trolling. Interestingly, the relationship between cognitive empathy and trolling was moderated by psychopathy. Specifically, cognitive empathy was significantly, positively related to trolling, but only if the individual had average to high levels of psychopathy. Sest and March (2017) posited that this higher cognitive empathy would enable Internet "trolls" to select content that would maximize chances of inflicting psychological harm on their victim, and that such individuals are likely to be experts at inflicting emotional suffering.

Lopes and Yu (2017) conducted a unique study exploring the relationship between psychopathy and trolling. Given that people with high levels of psychopathy choose their targets carefully (e.g., Book, Costello, & Camilleri, 2013), Lopes and Yu (2017) sought to explore the relationship between psychopathy and trolling individuals of different social status (e.g., popular vs. less popular). Participants ($N = 135$; 113 women; *M*age 20.45, $SD = 3.55$) were university students who completed an online questionnaire comprising a measure of psychopathy (the Short Dark Triad scale) and mock Facebook profiles. These mock profiles were created on student opinion regarding what one would expect to find on a "popular" students' Facebook profile compared to a less popular student. Participants then indicated their agreement with trolling comments toward different Facebook profiles. For example, both the popular and less popular Facebook profile would contain a status about educational attainment. Participants were able to view comments that had been posted by other students, including trolling comments. An example of a trolling comment to the less popular profile is "No matter how hard you try, you'll never get a good grade coz you're an idiot!", and an example of a trolling comment to the popular profile is, "Which lecturer did you sleep with to get that grade?". Participants were then asked to respond with how much they agreed with the comments on a 5-point Likert scale from 1 (strongly disagree) to 5 (strongly agree). Results showed that psychopathy was significantly, positively related to overall trolling. Further, people with higher levels of psychopathy were more likely to agree with trolling comments targeted at popular (compared to less popular) profiles. This finding challenges previous ideas that individuals with high psychopathy prey on victims they perceive to be weaker; they may actually prefer individuals of higher social status to exploit for their own benefit.

Lastly, March (2019) explored the relationship between the primary and secondary dimensions of psychopathy and perpetration of trolling. Participants ($N = 733$; 70.5% women; *M*age = 23.53, $SD = 7.98$) completed an online questionnaire comprising the GAIT-Revised and the Levenson Self-Report Psychopathy Scale (LSRP; Levenson, Kiehl, & Fitzpatrick, 1995). Results indicated primary psychopathy, not secondary psychopathy, was a significant positive predictor of trolling. Based on these results, the Internet troll may be is less impulsive, neurotic, and emotionally reactive (traits associated with secondary psychopathy), and more callous, manipulative, and lacking in remorse (traits associated with primary psychopathy). In addition, March (2019) also replicated results of Sest and March (2017), finding psychopathy to moderate the relationship between cognitive empathy and trolling. Specifically, cognitive empathy shares a positive relationship with trolling, but only when an individual's level of psychopathy is average to high.

Psychopathy and cyberstalking

In addition to cyberbullying and trolling, psychopathy has also been related to the cyber abuse behavior of cyberstalking. Cyberstalking is defined as stalking via technology, such as the use of hidden webcams, GPS devices, and SpyWare to another's behavior (Sheridan & Grant, 2007). Smoker and March (2017) explored the utility of psychopathy to predict intimate partner cyberstalking, which refers to cyberstalking behavior toward current, former, or potential intimate partners. A total sample of 689 participants (70% women; *M*age = 26, *SD* = 10.21) completed a measure of psychopathy (the Short Dark Triad scale) and the Intimate Partner Cyberstalking Scale (IPCS-scale; Smoker & March, 2017). Psychopathy was found to be a significant positive predictor of intimate partner cyberstalking. Smoker and March (2017) explained that individuals with high psychopathy often engage in psychological game-playing in intimate relationships, and cyberstalking provides an opportunity for these individuals to participate in such romantic game-playing. March, Litten, Sullivan, and Ward (2020) explored the utility of primary psychopathy and secondary psychopathy to predict perpetration of intimate partner cyberstalking, and found only secondary psychopathy was a significant predictor. The utility of secondary psychopathy to predict intimate partner cyberstalking suggests impulsivity and poor self-control are central characteristics in this behavior, and also hints at the possible addictiveness of cyberstalking (March et al., 2020).

Contrary to the results of Smoker and March (2017), and March et al. (2020), Kircaburun, Jonason, and Griffiths (2018b) did not find psychopathy to predict cyberstalking. However, this could be attributed to the authors not directly measuring intimate partner cyberstalking (only cyberstalking in general), and the measure of psychopathy. To measure psychopathy Smoker and March (2017) used the Short Dark Triad scale, and March et al. (2020) used the Hare Self-Report Psychopathy Scale 4 (SRP-4; Paulhus, Neumann, Hare, Williams, and Hemphill, 2017); both established, validated measures of psychopathy. Comparatively, Kircaburun et al. (2018b) assessed psychopathy with the Dirty Dozen, which has previously been criticized for comparatively lower validity (Jones & Paulhus, 2014).

Stiff (2019) explored Facebook surveillance, defined as when Facebook users look at their friends Facebook "profiles" in an attempt to collect information, in a manner that is not intended to benefit the target (i.e., the user whose profile is being surveyed). Stiff (2019) differentiated Facebook surveillance from typical Facebook use by noting it is "deliberate, covert, and targeted" (p. 63), and hypothesized that given individuals with high psychopathy dislike feelings of uncertainty (Sabouri et al., 2016), they may be motivated to reduce such discomfort by engaging in a behavior that reduces it (i.e., cyberstalking). To assess the relationship between trait psychopathy and Facebook surveillance, 259 (150 women; *M*age = 20.49, *SD* = 19.16) participants recruited via Prolific.ac completed a measure of psychopathy (the Short Dark Triad scale) and a measure of Facebook surveillance. A factor analysis of the Facebook surveillance measure revealed two factors that were labeled "Facebook tracking" (e.g., I like to "stalk" some people's Facebook profiles) and "Facebook investigating" (e.g., I have waited for a specific person to post on Facebook so I can read what they have written). Results showed a significant direct effect of psychopathy on Facebook tracking, but not for Facebook investigating. Stiff (2019) posited that as Facebook tracking is more recreational in nature, individuals with high levels of psychopathy may enjoy engaging in this behavior to satisfy their voyeuristic tendencies and need for power and control.

Psychopathy and online sexual behavior

The research presented in the previous section highlight the role of psychopathy in perpetrating a range of cyber abuse behaviors, including online aggression, cyberbullying, trolling, and cyberstalking. In this next section, we turn our attention to the role of psychopathy in online sexual behavior, including consumption of online pornography, sending unsolicited sexual images, online infidelity, and antisocial behavior on Tinder.

Shim, Lee, and Paul (2007) conducted one of the first research studies to explore reactions upon being exposed to unsolicited sexual content online. Compared to solicited sexual content, unsolicited is when an individual receives sexual content online that they have not asked for. Shim et al. (2007) hypothesized that due to psychopathy characteristics of seeking high arousal and stimulation, individuals with high levels of psychopathy would likely seek more sexually bizarre, aggressive, and potentially violent pornography, and would likely respond favorably to unsolicited Internet pornography. Participants ($N = 337$; 179 women; *M*age = 20, $SD = 1.81$) completed the Self Report Psychopathy Scale III (SRP-III; Hare, 1982), and responses were categorized as low psychopathy, medium psychopathy, and high psychopathy. To assess responses to unsolicited Internet pornography respondents answered the question on a 7-point scale (1 = never, and 7 = all the time): "Did you ever open a message or a link in a message that showed you actual pictures of naked people or of people having sex that you did not want?" Results indicated that people with higher levels of psychopathy were more willing to be exposed to unsolicited Internet pornography. Shim et al. (2007) posited that given the novelty and sensation seeking characteristics of psychopathy, this potentially leads such individuals to pursue unsolicited sexual content online. It is likely they will experience some level of affective satisfaction from experiencing unsolicited Internet pornography (e.g., typing a web address incorrectly and arriving at a pornography website).

Paul (2009) conducted a follow-up study exploring psychopathy and online pornography use and arousal, hypothesizing that individuals with high psychopathy will rely more on Internet pornography for higher levels of arousal. Participants ($N = 337$; 179 women; *M*age = 20, $SD = 1.81$) completed the SRP-III scale and a measure of perceived arousal to various genres of Internet pornography. Participants were asked to consider how *sexually arousing* they found each of 15 different genres of pornographic content. To measure Internet pornography use, respondents were asked the following question: "Thinking about an average week during the last several months, please describe how often you look at each of the following types of pornographic content on the Internet" (all 15 genres were repeatedly considered for this question). Results of a regression analysis indicated that, for both men and women, individuals with higher levels of psychopathy were more likely to use all forms of online pornographic content; however, they were only more likely to be aroused if the content was perceived as intense or even socially inappropriate. The author posited that this result aligns with characteristic psychopathy, where individuals require more intense stimuli to experience arousal and are less concerned with societal norms.

March and Wagstaff (2017) examined the relationship between psychopathy and enjoyment of sending/receiving unsolicited pictures of one's own genitals, which the authors termed "explicit image orientation." Receiving unsolicited images of genitals is increasingly common when online dating, and March and Wagstaff (2017) hypothesized trait psychopathy would be positively related to explicit image orientation as this behavior is considered sexually deviant (see Döring, 2014). Two hundred and forty participants (72% women; *M*age = 25.96, *SD* = 9.79) were recruited online via social media and completed an anonymous questionnaire. Psychopathy was measured with the LSRP scale and explicit image orientation was assessed using the Explicit Image Scale (EIS; March & Wagstaff, 2017), with higher scores indicating higher enjoyment of sending and receiving unsolicited explicit images. A significant, positive correlation between psychopathy and explicit image orientation was found; however, psychopathy was not a significant predictor. Machiavellianism (as measured with the MACH-IV; Christie & Geis, 1970) significantly mediated the relationship between psychopathy and EIS. The authors suggest that based on the significant, predictive utility of Machiavellianism, combined with the mediating nature of Machiavellianism, explicit images may better be conceptualized as an aggressive mating strategy, rather than a sexually deviant behavior. Explicit image orientation may be better associated with strategic exploitation (i.e., Machiavellianism) compared to a callous, impulsive nature (i.e., psychopathy).

Psychopathy has also been explored in relation to online infidelity. Timmermans, De Caluwé, and Alexopoulos (2018) examined the relationship between psychopathy and (1) Tinder use when in a committed relationship, (2) Tinder use when single, or (3) no use of Tinder. The authors compared nonsingle Tinder users' motives and behavioral outcomes to single Tinder users and non-Tinder users, and if levels of psychopathy, narcissism, and Machiavellianism would differ among these as previous research has found narcissism and trait psychopathy to relate to infidelity (e.g., Brewer, Hunt, James, & Abell, 2015). Participants (*N* = 471, 72.8% women, *M*age = 22.89, *SD* = 4.57) completed a measure of psychopathy (the Short Dark Triad scale) and a measure of infidelity, which assessed individuals who were in a relationship and using Tinder and their motives for using Tinder. Results showed nonsingle Tinder users had higher levels of psychopathy compared to nonsingle nonusers. Further, for nonsingle Tinder users there was a positive relationship between psychopathy and the motivation to use Tinder for sexual experience. The authors suggested this result is consistent with previous research on trait psychopathy and short-term mating strategies (e.g., Jonason, Valentine, Li, & Harbeson, 2011); specifically, individuals with high psychopathy seek out multiple, potential partners to satisfy their own unrestricted sexuality and self-interest. As such, the more opportunity on Tinder for sexual encounters, the more likely individuals high on psychopathy (nonsingle or single) are to use this app.

Lastly, Duncan and March (2019) explored psychopathy and a variety of antisocial behaviors that occur on Tinder (e.g., being mean to others, using Tinder to show off). Participants (*N* = 587; 79% women; *M*age = 23.75, *SD* = 6.05) completed a measure of psychopathy (the Short Dark Triad scale) and the Antisocial Uses of Tinder Scale. A factor analysis of the Antisocial Uses of Tinder Scale indicated the presence of three independent factors; *general* (e.g., "I use Tinder to be mean to people"), *esteem* (e.g., "I use Tinder to get an ego boost from quality matches"), and *sexual* ("I use Tinder to meet my own sexual needs, disregarding the benefit of others") antisocial behavior. People with higher levels of psychopathy were more likely to engage in general antisocial behavior and sexual antisocial behavior on Tinder, but not esteem antisocial behavior on Tinder. Those higher levels of trait psychopathy may be attracted to Tinder as the app offers potential for opportunistic predatory behavior, and to satisfy their desire for short-term, impulsive relationships (see Furnham, Richards, & Paulhus, 2013).

Psychopathy and online child pornography

Internet child pornography is a particularly prolific criminal and social concern. Offenders of Internet child pornography download, collect, and circulate child pornography online (Webb, Craissati, & Keen, 2007). In comparison to contact (i.e., face-to-face) child sex offenders, little research has explored Internet child sex offenders. Some research has reported internet child pornography offenders are generally aged 25–50 years, with no prior criminal background (Burke, Sowerbutts, Blundell, & Sherry, 2001). Compared to contact child sex offenders, Internet child sex offenders are more likely to be educated, intelligent, employed, and in a relationship (Burke et al., 2001). However, other research (e.g., Galbreath, Berlin, & Sawyer, 2002; Seto & Eke, 2005) have found that some Internet child pornography offenders did have a criminal history.

Webb et al. (2007) aimed to build a psychological profile of Internet child pornography offenders. Further, the authors performed a comparison of Internet offenders with contact sex offenders in an effort to determine similarities and differences in their psychological profile. The sample comprised 210 male participants. Of these 210 participants, 90 (43%) had a previous internet child pornography offense (Mage = 38, SD = 10), and 120 (57%) had a previous offense of sexually assaulting a child under the age of 16 (Mage = 45, SD = 14). Psychopathy was assessed with The Psychopathy Checklist: Screening Version (PCL: SV; Hart, Cox, & Hare, 1995). Results showed significant differences between Internet offenders and contact offenders; specifically, contact offenders had significantly higher psychopathy compared to Internet offenders.

Despite psychopathy being associated with deviant sexual behavior such as sexual coercion (Figueredo, Gladden, Sisco, Patch, & Jones, 2015), repeated sexual advances (Zeigler-Hill, Besser, Morag, & Campbell, 2016), and more positive attitudes toward rape (Jonason, Girgis, & Milne-Home, 2017), there is a distinct paucity in research exploring psychopathy, and even other personality traits, as predictors of Internet child pornography consumption and offenses. Given the potential for individual differences to both manage and prevent behavior (e.g., March, 2019), such studies could provide vital information regarding management of Internet child pornography offenses. However, there are particularly difficult hurdles present when assessing consumption of Internet child pornography, including mandatory reporting and socially biased responses. One suggestion is that researchers could adopt an "attitudes" framework to assess consumption of Internet child pornography (for example, the assessment of rape enabling attitudes; see Jonason et al., 2017). Further, as an alternative to directly assessing child pornography, researchers could assess consumption of "barely legal" online pornography (i.e., pornography where actors are of legal age but presented as underage). Although such studies are not directly assessing consumption of Internet child pornography, results could potentially be extrapolated to this behavior.

Psychopathy and cyber deceit and fraud

We now turn our attention to psychopathy and online deception. In one of the earliest studies of deception online, four types were outlined: Trolling, category deception, impersonation, and identity concealment (Donath, 1998). The deception considered in this section is not the form of deception adopted in trolling (i.e., deception as a means to provoke and derail social proceedings). In this section, we consider the other forms of online deception; in particular, impersonation, which is a key element of cyber fraud. Online impersonation includes behaviors such as catfishing and scamming (Drouin, Miller, Wehle, & Hernandez, 2016), which may both approach cyber fraud. Other more subtle forms of impersonation include category deception (e.g., assuming a different social role online, such as gender or age), and identity concealment (e.g., parts or all of their true identity are hidden or misrepresented). Drouin et al. (2016) note these more subtle forms are more common than outright cyber fraud.

To explore the relationship between psychopathy and online deception, Drouin et al. (2016) recruited 272 participants (131 women; Mage = 32.22, SD = 8.32) online. Participants completed a measure of psychopathy (the Dirty Dozen), and answered questions regarding their perception of their own honesty online (e.g., "How often do you think that YOU are [or would be, if you don't use social media] completely honest about who you are on social media sites") and others' honesty online (e.g., "How often do you think that OTHERS are completely honest about who they are on social media sites?"). Four different online platforms were presented: Social media, anonymous chat rooms, dating websites, sexual communication websites. Higher levels of psychopathy was related to lower perceptions of own honesty online, but was not related to perceptions of others' honesty.

Beyond psychopathy, it is important to note that correlations for self and others' honesty were strongest *within* platforms; for example, self-honesty on social media was most strongly related to others' honesty on social media. The authors suggested that perception of others' honesty may be more important than personal characteristics. Specifically, the relationship between self- and others' honesty may be more context-specific than global; you are more likely to be honest if you believe others are being honest.

Modic, Palomäki, Drosinou, and Laakasuo (2018) explored the relationship between psychopathy and cyber fraud; specifically, the willingness to deceive during an online insurance claim. In study 1344 participants (191 women; *M*age = 40; *SD* = 12.4) completed a measure of psychopathy (the Short Dark Triad scale) and an insurance claim task. The insurance claim tasks were realistic online insurance claims, and participants were instructed to file a claim for an insured household item they had broken. The researchers measured whether the participant overclaimed the item value, terming this behavior "fibbing." Results showed no significant relationship between psychopathy and fibbing.

In study 2, 699 participants (334 women; *M*age = 32.2; *SD* = 10.2) completed a measure of psychopathy (the Short Dark Triad scale) and the insurance claim task; however, this time the task included monetary incentives for fibbing. Further, the task now also included information regarding whether the items were broken in anger, while drunk, or by accident. This time, results showed positive correlations between psychopathy and fibbing when the items were broken in anger or while drunk, but not by accident.

Modic et al. (2018) highlight that the monetary incentives may explain the different results between psychopathy and fibbing in study 1 and study 2. Given that individuals with high psychopathy are not particularly interested in scenarios that are not beneficial and do not directly apply to them (e.g., Miller & Lynam, 2001), they may not have responded to the insurance claim task in study 1. In study 2 however, when there was an incentive to fib, individuals with high psychopathy would have found this far more attractive. As such, these individuals may be more inclined to commit cyber fraud if there is a clear, personal incentive. The authors also suggested that for individuals with high psychopathy, situations that elicit anger or frustration may increase the chance of fraudulent cyber behavior.

Conclusions

In this chapter, we have considered research that has explored the role of psychopathy in a range of online behaviors, such as cyber abuse (e.g., cyberbullying, trolling) and cyber crime (e.g., online child pornography, cyber fraud). Interpretations and explanations of these relationships are dependent on the online behavior being considered. For example, the relationship between disordered Internet use (i.e., Internet addiction) and psychopathy may be attributed to the anonymity that exists online, which in turn facilitates successful lying and cheating (Sindermann et al., 2018). Meanwhile, engagement in online self-promotional behavior, such as selfies, could be attributed to the impulsive, sensation seeking characteristics of psychopathy (Adler, 2017; Fox & Rooney, 2015).

When considering online antisocial behaviors such as aggression, cyberbullying, trolling, and cyberstalking, perpetration of these behaviors is largely attributed to the callous, aggressive, opportunistic nature of psychopathy (e.g., Balakrishnan et al., 2019). People with higher levels of psychopathy may perpetrate such online antisocial behaviors in an attempt to satisfy predictor impulses (Craker & March, 2016). Due to low levels of empathy that are typically associated with high psychopathy (e.g., Sest & March, 2017), these individuals will display a brazen disregard for the distress their behavior causes others (March et al., 2017).

Despite trait psychopathy being associated with deviant sexual behavior (Figueredo et al., 2015; Jonason et al., 2017; Zeigler-Hill et al., 2016), there is a significant paucity in research exploring the role of psychopathy (and largely, other personality traits) in predicting consumption of Internet child pornography. Although significant hurdles are present in exploring such behavior and offenses, research exploring the role of personality in Internet child pornography consumption could provide vital information regarding management and prevention. As such, it is recommended future research endeavor to explore the potential for psychopathy to predict Internet child pornography consumption and offenses.

Lastly, it is recommended that future research exploring psychopathy and online behavior endeavor to explore psychopathy as a multidimensional trait, as researchers have cautioned against treating psychopathy as unidimensional (e.g., Koban et al., 2018; March, 2019). Further, research differentiating between psychopathy dimensions has found utility for different dimensions predicting online behavior (see March, 2019). As discussed throughout this chapter, different characteristics of psychopathy have been associated with different online behavior. For example, the characteristics of callousness and empathy deficits (i.e., primary psychopathy) are associated with trolling, whereas the characteristics of impulsivity and risk taking (i.e., secondary psychopathy) are associated with intimate partner cyberstalking. Future research exploring psychopathy and online behavior should implement a more comprehensive measure of psychopathy to explore the multidimensional nature of this trait and its role in perpetrating cyber abuse and cyber crime.

References

Adler, N. (2017). *Who posts selfies and why? Personality, attachment style, and mentalization as predictors of selfie posting on social media*. (DDoctoral DDissertation). Retrieved from City of New York (CUNY) Academic Works https://academicwords.cuny.edu/gc_etds/2301.

Andershed, H., Kerr, M., Stattin, H., & Levander, S. (2002). Psychopathic traits in non-referred youths: Initial test of a new assessment tool. In E. Blaauw, & L. Sheridan (Eds.), *Psychopaths: Current international perspectives* (pp. 131–158). The Hague: Elsevier.

Andreassen, C. S. (2015). Online social network site addiction: A comprehensive review. *Current Addiction Reports*, *2*, 175–184. https://doi.org/10.1007/s40429-015-0056-9.

Balakrishnan, V., Khan, S., Fernandez, T., & Arabnia, H. R. (2019). Cyberbullying detection on twitter using Big Five and Dark Triad features. *Personality and Individual Differences*, *141*, 252–257. https://doi.org/10.1016/j.paid.2019.01.024.

Baron-Cohen, S., & Wheelwright, S. (2004). The empathy quotient: An investigation of adults with Asperger syndrome or high functioning autism, and normal sex differences. *Journal of Autism and Developmental Disorders*, *34*(2), 163–175. https://doi.org/10.1023/B.JADD.0000022607.19833.00.

Baughman, H. M., Dearing, S., Giammarco, E., & Vernon, P. A. (2012). Relationships between bullying behaviours and the Dark Triad: A study with adults. *Personality and Individual Differences*, *52*, 571–575. https://doi.org/10.1016/j.paid.2011.11.020.

Bogolyubova, O., Panicheva, P., Tikhonov, R., Ivanov, V., & Ledovaya, Y. (2018). Dark personalities on Facebook: Harmful online behaviors and language. *Computers in Human Behavior*, *78*, 151–159. https://doi.org/10.1016/j.chb.2017.09.032.

Book, A., Costello, K., & Camilleri, J. (2013). Psychopathy and victim selection: The use of gait as cue vulnerability. *Journal of Interpersonal Violence*, *28*, 8–14. https://doi.org/10.1177/0886260512475315.

Brewer, G., Hunt, D., James, G., & Abell, L. (2015). Dark triad traits, infidelity and romantic revenge. *Personality and Individual Differences*, *83*, 122–127. https://doi.org/10.1016/j.paid.2015.04.007.

Buckels, E. E., Trapnell, P. D., & Paulhus, D. L. (2014). Trolls just want to have fun. *Personality and Individual Differences*, *67*, 97–102. https://doi.org/10.1016/j.paid.2014.01.016.

Burke, A., Sowerbutts, S., Blundell, S., & Sherry, M. (2001). Child pornography and the internet: Policing and treatment issues. *Psychiatry, Psychology and Law*, *9*(1), 79–84. https://doi.org/10.1375/132187102760196925.

Calvete, E., Orue, I., Estevez, A., Villardon, L., & Padilla, P. (2010). Cyberbullying in adolescents: Modalities and aggressors' profile. *Computers in Human Behavior*, *26*, 1128–1135. https://doi.org/10.1016/j.chb.2010.03.017.

Chabrol, H., Van Leeuwen, N., Rodgers, R., & Séjourné, N. (2009). Contributions of psychopathic, narcissistic, Machiavellian, and sadistic personality traits to juvenile delinquency. *Personality and Individual Differences*, *47*, 734–739. https://doi.org/10.1016/j.paid.2009.06.020.

Cheng, C., & Li, A. Y. L. (2014). Internet addiction prevalence and quality of (real) life: A meta-analysis of 31 nations across seven world regions. *Cyberpsychology, Behavior, and Social Networking*, *17*(12), 755–760. https://doi.org/10.1089/cyber.2014.0317.

Christie, R., & Geis, F. L. (1970). *Studies in machiavellianism*. New York, NY: Academic.

Chung, K. L., Morshidi, I., Yoong, L. C., & Thian, K. N. (2019). The role of the dark tetrad and impulsivity in social media addiction: Findings from Malaysia. *Personality and Individual Differences*, *143*, 62–67. https://doi.org/10.1016/j.paid.2019.02.016.

Coles, B. A., & West, M. (2016). Trolling the trolls: Online forum users' constructions of the nature and properties of trolling. *Computers in Human Behavior*, *60*, 233–244. https://doi.org/10.1016/j.chb.2016.02.070.

Craker, N., & March, E. (2016). The dark side of Facebook®: The Dark Tetrad, negative social potency, and trolling behaviours. *Personality and Individual Differences*, *102*, 79–84. https://doi.org/10.1016/j.paid.2016.06.043.

Del Rey, R., Casas, J. A., Ortega-Ruiz, R., Schultze-Krumbholz, A., Scheithauer, H., Smith, P., et al. (2015). Structural validation and cross-cultural robustness of the European Cyberbullying Intervention Project Questionnaire. *Computers in Human Behavior*, *50*, 141–147. https://doi.org/10.1016/j.chb.2015.03.065.

Del Rey, R., Lazuras, L., Casas, J. A., Barkoukis, V., Ortega-Ruiz, R., & Tsorbatzoudis, H. (2016). Does empathy predict (cyber) bullying perpetration, and how do age, gender and nationality affect this relationship? *Learning and Individual Differences*, *45*, 275–281. https://doi.org/10.1016/j.lindif.2015.11.021.

Demircioğlu, Z. I., & Köse, A. G. (2018). Effects of attachment styles, dark triad, rejection sensitivity, and relationship satisfaction on social media addiction: A mediated model. *Current Psychology*, 1–15. https://doi.org/10.1007/s12144-018-9956-x.

Donath, J. S. (1998). Identity and deception in the virtual community. In M. A. Smith, & P. Kollock (Eds.), *Communities in cyberspace* (pp. 29–59). New York, MA: Routledge.

Döring, N. (2014). Consensual sexting among adolescents: Risk prevention through abstinence education or safer sexting? *Cyberpsychology*, *8*, 9. https://doi.org/10.5817/CP2014-1-9.

Drouin, M., Miller, D., Wehle, S. M., & Hernandez, E. (2016). Why do people lie online? "Because everyone lies on the internet". *Computers in Human Behavior*, *64*, 134–142. https://doi.org/10.1016/j.chb.2016.06.052.

Duncan, Z., & March, E. (2019). Using Tinder® to start a fire: Predicting antisocial use of Tinder® with gender and the Dark Tetrad. *Personality and Individual Differences*, *145*, 9–14. https://doi.org/10.1016/j.paid.2019.03.014.

Ellison, N. B., Steinfield, C., & Lampe, C. (2007). The benefits of Facebook "'friends:" Social capital and college students' use of online social network sites. *Journal of Computer-Mediated Communication*, *12*, 1143–1168. https://doi.org/10.1111/j.1083-6101.2007.00367.x.

Erdur-Baker, O. (2010). Cyberbullying and its correlation to traditional bullying, gender and frequent and risky usage of internet-mediated communication tools. *New Media & Society*, *12*, 109–125. https://doi.org/10.1177/1461444809341260.

Eysenck, S. B., Eysenck, H. J., & Barrett, P. (1985). A revised version of the psychoticism scale. *Personality and Individual Differences*, *6*, 21–29. https://doi.org/10.1016/0191-8869(85)90026-1.

Figueredo, A. J., Gladden, P. R., Sisco, M. M., Patch, E. A., & Jones, D. N. (2015). The unholy trinity: The dark triad, coercion, and Brunswik-symmetry. *Evolutionary Psychology*, *13*, 435–454. https://doi.org/10.1177/147470491501300208.

Foo, C. Y. (2008). *Grief play management: A qualitative study of grief play management in MMORPGs*. Saarbrücken, Germany: VDM Verlag.

Fox, J., & Rooney, M. C. (2015). The Dark Triad and trait self-objectification as predictors of men's use and self-presentation behaviors on social networking sites. *Personality and Individual Differences*, *76*, 161–165. https://doi.org/10.1016/j.paid.2014.12.017.

Frick, P. J., & Ray, J. V. (2015). Evaluating callous-unemotional traits as a personality construct. *Journal of Personality*, *83*, 710–722. https://doi.org/10.1111/jopy.12114.

Furnham, A., Richards, S. C., & Paulhus, D. L. (2013). The Dark Triad of personality: A 10 year review. *Social and Personality Psychology Compass*, *7*(3), 199–216. https://doi.org/10.1111/spc3.12018.

Galbreath, N., Berlin, F., & Sawyer, D. (2002). Paraphilias and the internet. In A. Cooper (Ed.), *Sex and the internet: A guidebook for clinicians* (pp. 187–205). Philadelphia, PA: Brunner-Routledge.

Garcia, D., & Sikström, S. (2014). The dark side of Facebook: Semantic representations of status updates predict the Dark Triad of personality. *Personality and Individual Differences*, *67*, 92–96. https://doi.org/10.1016/j.paid.2013.10.001.

Gibb, Z. G. (2016). *Individual, cultural and behavioral correlates of cyberbullying behaviors in college students*. (Doctoral Dissertation). Retrieved from the University of Nevada, Reno, ProQuest Dissertations Publishing Database (Accession No. 10246630).

Gibb, Z. G., & Devereux, P. G. (2014). Who does that anyway? Predictors and personality correlates of cyberbullying in college. *Computers in Human Behavior*, *38*, 8–16. https://doi.org/10.1016/j.chb.2014.05.009.

Goodboy, A. K., & Martin, M. M. (2015). The personality profile of a cyberbully: Examining the Dark Triad. *Computers in Human Behavior*, *49*, 1–4. https://doi.org/10.1016/j.chb.2015.02.052.

Halevy, R., Shalvi, S., & Verschuere, B. (2014). Being honest about dishonesty: Correlating self-reports and actual lying. *Human Communication Research*, *40*(1), 54–72. https://doi.org/10.1111/hcre.12019.

Hardaker, C. (2010). Trolling in asynchronous computer-mediated communication: From user discussions to academic definitions. *Journal of Politeness Research*, *6*, 215–242. https://doi.org/10.1515/JPLR.2010.011.

Hare, R. D. (1982). Psychopathy and the personality dimensions of psychoticism, extraversion and neuroticism. *Personality and Individual Differences*, *3*, 35–42. https://doi.org/10.1016/0191-8869(82)90072-1.

Hart, S. D., Cox, D. N., & Hare, R. D. (1995). *Manual for the Hare psychopathy checklist—revised: Screening version (PCL: SV)*. Toronto: Multi-Health Systems.

Jonason, P. K., Girgis, M., & Milne-Home, J. (2017). The exploitive mating strategy of the dark triad traits: Tests of rape-enabling attitudes. *Archives of Sexual Behavior*, *46*, 697–706. https://doi.org/10.1007/s10508-017-0937-1.

Jonason, P. K., Valentine, K. A., Li, N. P., & Harbeson, C. L. (2011). Mate-selection and the Dark Triad: Facilitating a short-term mating strategy and creating a volatile environment. *Personality and Individual Differences*, *51*, 759–763. https://doi.org/10.1016/j.paid.2011.06.025.

Jonason, P. K., & Webster, G. D. (2010). The Dirty Dozen: A concise measure of the Dark Triad. *Psychological Assessment*, *22*, 420–432. https://doi.org/10.1037/a0019265.

Jones, D. N., & Paulhus, D. L. (2014). Introducing the short dark triad (SD3): A brief measure of dark personality traits. *Assessment*, *21*, 28–41. https://doi.org/10.1177/1073191113514105.

Kircaburun, K., & Griffiths, M. D. (2018). The dark side of internet: Preliminary evidence for the associations of dark personality traits with specific online activities and problematic internet use. *Journal of Behavioral Addictions*, *7*(4), 993–1003.

Kircaburun, K., Jonason, P. K., & Griffiths, M. D. (2018a). The Dark Tetrad traits and problematic online gaming: The mediating role of online gaming motives and moderating role of game types. *Personality and Individual Differences*, *135*, 298–303.

Kircaburun, K., Jonason, P. K., & Griffiths, M. D. (2018b). The Dark Tetrad traits and problematic social media use: The mediating role of cyberbullying and cyberstalking. *Personality and Individual Differences*, *135*, 264–269. https://doi.org/10.1016/j.paid.2018.07.034.

Koban, K., Stein, J.-P., Eckhardt, V., & Ohler, P. (2018). Quid pro quo in Web 2.0. Connecting personality traits and Facebook usage intensity to uncivil commenting intentions in public online discussions. *Computers in Human Behavior*, *79*, 9–18. https://doi.org/10.1016/j.chb.2017.10.015.

Kurek, A., Jose, P., & Stuart, J. (2019). 'I did it for the LULZ': How the dark personality predictors online disinhibition and aggressive online behavior in adolescence. *Computers in Human Behavior*, *98*, 31–40. https://doi.org/10.1016/j.chb.2019.03.027.

Ladanyi, J., & Doyle-Portillo, S. (2017). The development and validation of the Grief Play Scale (GPS) in MMORPGs. *Personality and Individual Differences*, *114*, 125–133. https://doi.org/10.1016/j.paid.2017.03.062.

Lee, S.-L. (2019). Predicting SNS addiction with the Big Five and the Dark Triad. *Cyberpsychology: Journal of Psychosocial Research on Cyberspace*, *13*(1). https://doi.org/10.5817/CP2019-1-3.

Levenson, M. R., Kiehl, K. A., & Fitzpatrick, C. M. (1995). Assessing psychopathic attributes in a noninstitutionalized population. *Journal of Personality and Social Psychology*, *68*, 151–158. https://doi.org/10.1037/0022-3514.68.1.151.

Lim, J., & Richardson, J. (2016). Exploring the effects of students' social networking experience on social presence and perceptions of using SNSs for educational purposes. *The Internet and Higher Education*, *29*, 31–39. https://doi.org/10.1016/j.iheduc.2015.12.001.

Loos, W., Haddon, L., & Mante-Meijer, E. (2016). *The social dynamics of information and communication technology*. New York, MA: Routledge.

Lopes, B., & Yu, H. (2017). Who do you troll and why: An investigation into the relationship between the Dark Triad Personalities and online trolling behaviours towards popular and less popular Facebook profiles. *Computers in Human Behavior, 77*, 69–76. https://doi.org/10.1016/j.chb.2017.08.036.

March, E. (2019). Psychopathy, sadism, empathy, and the motivation to cause harm: New evidence confirms malevolent nature of the internet troll. *Personality and Individual Differences, 141*, 133–137. https://doi.org/10.1016/j.paid.2019.01.001.

March, E., Grieve, R., Marrington, J., & Jonason, P. K. (2017). Trolling on Tinder®(and other dating apps): Examining the role of the Dark Tetrad and impulsivity. *Personality and Individual Differences, 110*, 139–143. https://doi.org/10.1016/j.paid.2017.01.025.

March, E., Litten, V., Sullivan, D. H., & Ward, L. (2020). Somebody that I (used to) know: Gender and dimensions of dark personality traits as predictors of intimate partner cyberstalking. *Personality and Individual Differences, 163*, 110084.

March, E., & Marrington, J. (2019). A qualitative analysis of internet trolling. *Cyberpsychology, Behavior, and Social Networking, 22*(3), 192–197. https://doi.org/10.1089/cyber.2018.0210.

March, E., & Wagstaff, D. L. (2017). Sending nudes: Sex, self-rated mate value, and trait Machiavellianism predict sending unsolicited explicit images. *Frontiers in Psychology, 8*. https://doi.org/10.3389/fpsyg.2017.02210.

McCain, J. L., Borg, Z. G., Rothenberg, A. H., Churillo, K. M., Weiler, P., & Campbell, W. K. (2016). Personality and selfies: Narcissism and the Dark Triad. *Computers in Human Behavior, 64*, 126–133. https://doi.org/10.1016/j.chb.2016.06.050.

Miller, J. D., & Lynam, D. (2001). Structural models of personality and their relation to antisocial behavior: A meta-analytic review. *Criminology, 39*, 765–798. https://doi.org/10.1111/j.1745-9125.2001.tb00940.x.

Modic, D., Palomäki, J., Drosinou, M., & Laakasuo, M. (2018). The dark triad and willingness to commit insurance fraud. *Cogent Psychology, 5*. https://doi.org/10.1080/23311908.2018.1469579.

Moor, L., & Anderson, J. R. (2019). A systematic literature review of the relationship between dark personality traits and antisocial online behaviours. *Personality and Individual Differences, 144*, 40–55. https://doi.org/10.1016/j.paid.2019.02.027.

Morrissey, L. (2010). Trolling is an art: Towards a schematic classification of intention in Internet trolling. *Griffith Working Papers in Pragmatics and Intercultural Communications, 3*(2), 75–82. Retrieved from https://www.griffith.edu.au/__data/assets/pdf_file/0005/270419/2.-Morrisey-Trolling.pdf.

Nicol, S. (2012). Cyber-bullying and trolling. *Youth Studies Australia, 31*, 3–4. Retrieved from http://journals.sfu.ca/ysa/index.php/YSA/article/viewFile/78r/98.

Orue, I., & Andershed, H. (2015). The youth psychopathic traits inventory-short version in Spanish adolescents: Factor structure, reliability, and relation with aggression, bullying, and cyber bullying. *Journal of Psychopathology and Behavioral Assessment, 37*, 563–575. https://doi.org/10.1007/s10862-015-9489-7.

Pabian, S., De Backer, C. J., & Vandebosch, H. (2015). Dark Triad personality traits and adolescent cyber-aggression. *Personality and Individual Differences, 75*, 41–46. https://doi.org/10.1016/j.paid.2014.11.015.

Park, S., Na, E.-Y., & Kim, E. (2014). The relationship between online activities, netiquette and cyberbullying. *Children and Youth Services Review, 42*, 74–81. https://doi.org/10.1016/j.childyouth.2014.04.002.

Paul, B. (2009). Predicting Internet pornography use and arousal: The role of individual difference variables. *Journal of Sex Research, 46*, 344–357. https://doi.org/10.1080/00224490902754152.

Paulhus, D. L., Neumann, C. S., Hare, R., Williams, K. M., & Hemphill, J. F. (2017). *Selfreport psychopathy scale (4th edition (SRP 4) manual)*. Toronto, Canada: Multi-Health Systems Incorporated.

Paulhus, D. L., & Williams, K. M. (2002). The Dark Triad of personality: Narcissism, Machiavellianism, and psychopathy. *Journal of Research in Personality, 36*, 556–563. https://doi.org/10.1016/S0092-6566(02)00505-6.

Pawlikowski, M., Altstötter-Gleich, C., & Brand, M. (2013). Validation and psychometric properties of a short version of Young's Internet Addiction Test. *Computers in Human Behavior, 29*, 1212–1223. https://doi.org/10.1016/j.chb.2012.10.014.

Ryan, T., Chester, A., Reece, J., & Xenos, S. (2014). The uses and abuses of Facebook: A review of Facebook addiction. *Journal of Behavioral Addictions, 3*, 133–140. https://doi.org/10.1556/JBA.3.2014.016.

Sabouri, S., Gerber, M., Bahmani, D. S., Lemola, S., Clough, P. J., Kalak, N., et al. (2016). Examining Dark Triad traits in relation to mental toughness and physical activity in young adults. *Neuropsychiatric Disease and Treatment, 12*, 229–235. https://doi.org/10.2147/NDT.S97267.

Seigfried-Spellar, K. C., & Lankford, C. M. (2018). Personality and online environment factors differ for posters, trolls, lurkers, and confessors on Yik Yak. *Personality and Individual Differences, 124*, 54–56. https://doi.org/10.1016/j.paid.2017.11.047.

Sest, N., & March, E. (2017). Constructing the cyber-troll: Psychopathy, sadism, and empathy. *Personality and Individual Differences, 119*, 69–72. https://doi.org/10.1016/j.paid.2017.06.038.

Seto, M., & Eke, A. (2005). The criminal histories and later offending of child pornography offenders. *Sexual Abuse: A Journal of Research and Treatment, 17*, 201–210. https://doi.org/10.1007/sll194-005-4605-y.

Sheridan, L. P., & Grant, T. (2007). Is cyberstalking different? *Psychology, Crime & Law, 13*, 627–640. https://doi.org/10.1080/10683160701340528.

Shim, J. W., Lee, S., & Paul, B. (2007). Who responds to unsolicited sexually explicit materials on the internet? The role of individual differences. *Cyberpsychology & Behavior, 10*, 71–79. https://doi.org/10.1089/cpb.2006.9990.

Sindermann, C., Sariyska, R., Lachmann, B., Brand, M., & Montag, C. (2018). Assocaitions between the dark triad of personality and unspecific/specific forms of Internet-use disorder. *Journal of Behavioral Addictions, 7*, 985–992. https://doi.org/10.1556/2006.7.2018.114.

Slonje, R., Smith, P. K., & Frisén, A. (2013). The nature of cyberbullying, and strategies for prevention. *Computers in Human Behavior, 29*, 26–32. https://doi.org/10.1016/j.chb.2012.05.024.

Smoker, M., & March, E. (2017). Predicting perpetration of intimate partner cyberstalking: Gender and the Dark Tetrad. *Computers in Human Behavior, 72*, 390–396. https://doi.org/10.1016/j.chb.2017.03.012.

Stiff, C. (2019). The Dark Triad and Facebook surveillance: How Machiavellianism, psychopathy, but not narcissism predict using Facebook to spy on others. *Computers in Human Behavior, 94*, 62–69. https://doi.org/10.1016/j.chb.2018.12.044.

Timmermans, E., De Caluwé, E., & Alexopoulos, C. (2018). Why are you cheating on tinder? Exploring users' motives and (dark) personality traits. *Computers in Human Behavior, 89*, 129–139. https://doi.org/10.1016/j.chb.2018.07.040.

Tutgun-Ünal, A., & Deniz, L. (2015). Development of the social media addiction scale. *AJIT-e: Online Academic Journal of Information Technology*, *6*, 52–70. https://doi.org/10.5824/1309-1581.2015.4.004.x.

Van Geel, M., Goemans, A., Toprak, F., & Vedder, P. (2017). Which personality traits are related to traditional bullying and cyberbullying? A study with the Big Five, Dark Triad, and Sadism. *Personality and Individual Differences*, *106*, 231–235. https://doi.org/10.1016/j.paid.2016.10.063.

Varjas, K., Talley, J., Meyers, J., Parris, L., & Cutts, H. (2010). High school students' perceptions of motivations for cyberbullying: An exploratory study. *The Western Journal of Emergency Medicine*, *11*, 269–273. Retrieved from https://escholarship.org/uc/uciem_westjem.

Wall, D. (2007). *Cybercrime: The transformation of crime in the information age*. Cambridge, UK: Polity Press.

Webb, L., Craissati, J., & Keen, S. (2007). Characteristics of internet child pornography offenders: A comparison with child molesters. *Sexual Abuse: A Journal of Research and Treatment*, *19*, 449–465. https://doi.org/10.1007/s11194-007-9063-2.

Willard, N. E. (2007). *Cyberbullying and cyberthreats: Responding to the challenge of online social aggression, threats, and distress*. Champaign, IL: Research Press.

Zeigler-Hill, V., Besser, A., Morag, J., & Campbell, W. K. (2016). The dark triad and sexual harassment proclivity. *Personality and Individual Differences*, *89*, 47–54. https://doi.org/10.1016/j.paid.2015.09.048.

Psychopathy and animal cruelty offenders

21

Sara C. Haden, Shelby E. McDonald, and Wyatt D'Emilia

Introduction

Animal cruelty (AC) is related to adult violence, intimate partner violence, child abuse, and elder abuse (see Petersen & Farrington, 2007). AC offenders include those who intentionally victimize animals by performing malicious acts of abuse toward animals. This group of offenders also includes individuals who engage in hoarding behavior and subject animals to severe forms of neglect. Organized forms of AC (e.g., dogfighting, cockfighting) are also considered offenses in some states. According to the Humane Society of the United States (HSUS), the most common victims of AC offenses are companion animals (dogs and cats), along with horses and livestock (Animal Cruelty Facts and Stats, 2019).

In the United States, the definition of what constitutes an AC crime varies greatly by state in addition to the nature of the behavior committed by the perpetrator. The Animal Legal Defense Fund helps legal cases involving AC in multiple domains—animals used in research, captive animals (i.e., zoos), companion animals, farmed animals, and even wildlife (About Us, 2019). Contrary to other countries (e.g., France, Germany), the US considers animals to be "property" or "legal things" rather than "legal persons." This limits the legal status of animals and has implications for what is considered to be a crime against a nonhuman animal. However, although they are considered "property," animals are afforded some protections by criminal anticruelty laws, and they can even be beneficiaries of legally enforceable trusts. Companion animals are also allowed to be involved in domestic violence protection orders in some states. Just recently in Alaska, Illinois, and California, joint custody was assigned to pets marking a different perspective on animals as property (Monyak, 2018). Notably, other countries consider animals to be "sentient beings" determined by the European Union Article in the Treaty of Lisbon (2009), as well as the French National Assembly, New Zealand, and Quebec all in 2015 (as cited in Monyak, 2018).

The HSUS defines AC as "intentional, malicious acts of harm and less clear-cut situations where the needs of an animal are neglected." (Fighting Animal Cruelty and Neglect, 2019). In the US, all 50 states have enacted felony AC laws since 2014. Unfortunately, animals are abused and killed every day; furthermore, the perpetrators rarely face consequences, as most cases are never reported. As behavioral profiling became more popular in the 1970s, it was discovered that many serial killers and rapists had a history of AC, especially during their childhood (Coleman, 1991). These perpetrators were characterized by psychopathic traits such as a lack of remorse and empathy, selfishness, impulsivity, and sensation seeking behaviors.

Psychopathy and Criminal Behavior. https://doi.org/10.1016/B978-0-12-811419-3.00013-3

At one point the presence of the "Homicidal Triad" (also known as the "Macdonald Triad") during childhood was posited to increase the risk of homicidal behavior in adulthood (Macdonald, 1963). This triad included AC, fire setting, and enuresis (bed wetting after age five). Relatedly, Paulhus and Williams (2002) coined the "Dark Triad" personality traits (i.e., Machiavellianism, narcissism, and psychopathy) and this was strongly linked to animal torture and cruelty (Kavanagh, Signal, & Taylor, 2013).

The purpose of this chapter is to describe what is known about people who commit AC. The chapter first discusses different conceptualizations of AC behavior and reviews legal protections afforded to nonhuman animals in the US. After presenting the epidemiology of AC offenders, different theories of AC, and their links to psychopathy, are detailed. The last section focuses on existing research on the role of psychopathic traits in our understanding of who perpetrates AC behavior.

Conceptualizations of animal cruelty

Since relationships between humans and nonhuman animals are complex, it is difficult to clearly define AC. In fact, many of our socially and culturally sanctioned activities involve regularly harming nonhuman animals. Speciesism is the idea and practice of treating one species, usually human animals, as more important and deserving of rights. This justification is used as a defense for many of the cruel behaviors carried out toward nonhuman animals (Singer, 1975). However, we cannot clearly draw a line between human and nonhuman animal species, as humans tend to privilege certain nonhumans over others (Caviola, Everett, & Faber, 2019). For example, in Western cultures, humans are more likely to accept some animals as companions (e.g., dogs, cats), while others are used for our consumption, experimentation, sport, equipment, and entertainment (e.g., cows, pigs, horses, rats). Speciesism impacts how we understand what is cruel toward another species.

There is also a continuum defining what acts are considered animal torture and cruelty. Kellert and Felthous (1985) describe substantial cruelty to animals as engaging in a pattern of behaviors that deliberately, repeatedly, and unnecessarily cause hurt to vertebrate animals and potential serious injury. Brown (1988) defined it as unnecessary physical suffering knowingly inflicted on a living sentient being. Ascione (1993) understood AC to be "socially unacceptable behavior that intentionally causes unnecessary pain, suffering, or distress to and/or the death of an animal" (p. 51). Note that this definition excludes "humane" killing of farm animals, animals used in hunting practices, and those subjected to research, since these behaviors are considered to be acceptable in most cultures. Rowan (1999) went on to differentiate between cruelty (characterized by the perpetrator's enjoyment of the animal's suffering) and abuse (characterized by using an inappropriate level of force). More recently Dadds, Turner, and McAloon (2002) included acts of deliberate omission (not due to ignorance) as forms of cruelty that bring physical or psychological harm to an animal.

Given these different definitions, this chapter adopts a conceptualization of AC similar to that of Gullone (2014) that is also based on these former definitions:

> *Animal cruelty is behavior performed [repetitively and] proactively by an individual with the deliberate intention of causing physical and/or psychological harm (i.e., pain, suffering, distress, and/or death) to a non-human animal with the understanding that the non-human animal is motivated to avoid the harm (p. 38).*

It is important to note that this definition encompasses any type of nonhuman animal as potential victims (i.e., companion, wildlife, livestock). Unfortunately, what defines an AC offender depends on laws in the state in which the individual may have been arrested or charged. An offender of AC has generally committed the most heinous acts of cruelty.

Animal cruelty and the legal system

Classifying AC as a crime and documenting the behavior is necessary in order to understand who commits these crimes. The nature of the charge, their likelihood of being found guilty, along with the potential sentence a guilty charge carries, depends on the state where the crime was committed. All of the perpetrators of AC described following were charged with a crime.

- Jacob Bushkin, a 27-year-old man from Arizona stabbed his golden retriever service dog 100 times. The dog was later found in a garbage can (Musumeci, 2019).
- Michael Wenzel, a 22-year-old male boat pilot of Florida, dragged a shark from a speeding boat with his friends while they laughed. He and his friends were pictured pouring beer in the mouths of groupers and forcibly grabbing pelicans and seagulls from the sky (Salo, 2019).
- Jose Manuel Pantoja, a 28-year-old man, found a 13-year-old Chihuahua in his neighborhood and used him as a soccer ball, placing a bungee cord around the dog's throat and chest along with electrical wires around his legs (Woods, 2019).

While there are indeed several federal animal protection laws, most of our knowledge of animal cruelty offenders is based on offenders of state laws. Prior to discussing state animal protection laws, a brief review of federal laws is described.

Federal laws

In 1873 the first law related to nonhuman animals was enacted (Animal Welfare Institute, 2019). Called the "28 Hour Law," vehicles transporting animals are required to stop every 28 h to allow animals to have exercise, food, and water, unless these are provided in the vehicle (this does not apply to birds including chicken and turkeys). Early laws even recognized that nonhuman animals could experience pain. For example, The Humane Slaughter Act (1958, later revised in 1978) requires that animals used for slaughter (not birds) be stunned prior in order to minimize pain and prevent "needless suffering" (United States Congress, 1958). The Animal Welfare Act of 1966 is enforced by the Department of Agriculture and sets minimum standards regarding zoo and laboratory animals, as well as commercially bred animals. Organized AC (e.g., dog fighting, cockfighting) would also fall under the Animal Welfare Act if it crosses state lines (United States Congress, 1966).

Unfortunately, the enforcement of these federal animal protection laws is lacking. In a report by the Animal Welfare Institute, Jones (2008) provided the first comprehensive review of enforcement of humane slaughter standards from 2002 through 2007, entitled "Crimes without Consequences." While the treatment of animals that fall in the purview of these laws is more appreciated now, in large part due to undercover investigations by animal advocates (i.e., whistleblowers), many argue that these animals are the most abused and most often ignored (Jones, 2008). As such, we know little about the perpetrators of these crimes. However, social media has given rise to an increase of "whistleblower" videos of pigs being transported in excessive heat, cows crying when their calves are taken from them, and emaciated chickens lying in their waste. Advocates argue that they are exposing animal protection violations; however, ag-gag bills (i.e., antiwhistleblower) are being passed in some states in order to prevent the investigation of slaughterhouses and factory farms. In fact, violators of ag-gag laws stand to endure a much harsher sentence than violators of animal protection laws in these contexts (Solotaroff, 2013).

Some of these undercover investigations do show vicious acts of AC committed by humans. For example, in 2012, footage at a Butterball turkey semen collection facility in North Carolina was exposed showing workers throwing, kicking, dragging, and repeatedly beating turkeys' heads with metal prods (Platt, 2012). The turkeys were shown with severe lacerations and broken or missing limbs and eyes. They were unable to move. Six workers were arrested on AC charges and eventually convicted. One worker pled guilty and was convicted of one of the first felony cruelty to animal charges against birds in the food industry. Brian Douglass served 30 days in jail and several years of supervised probation in addition to a $550 fine.

State laws

Unlike the case of Brian Douglass, most AC offenders are not charged with federal crimes related to animal protection laws. For this reason, knowledge about who makes up the population of AC offenders comes from offenders of state animal protection laws in the US. These laws are primarily concerned with companion animals while some also include wildlife protection laws. Currently there are varying forms of felony provisions in all 50 states. The Animal Legal Defense Fund lists the 2018 US Animal Protection Laws State Rankings (Animal Legal Defense Fund, 2019). The rankings depend on the number of provisions that each state has regarding animal protections. For example, Illinois is ranked number one and includes acts of AC, neglect, fighting, abandonment, and sexual assault as felony penalties. Kentucky has been consistently ranked as the worst state for animal protections as it only includes felony penalties for cruelty and fighting for select species. Other provisions such as having adequate definitions of what is basic animal care, increased penalties for repeat abusers/hoarders, and mandatory reporting of suspected cruelty by veterinarians are also considered in this ranking. Notably, veterinarians in Kentucky are actually prohibited from reporting suspected animal abuse.

In 2016, our understanding of who commits AC offenses was expanded, as details about AC crimes were included in the National Incident-Based Reporting System (NIBRS) (Federal Bureau of Investigation, 2016). This change allows law enforcement, researchers, and policy makers to obtain information about the nature of these crimes and their perpetrators. The inclusion of AC crimes in the NIBRS was driven in large part due by evidence that AC is often related to other violent crime. In this system, although animals are defined as "property" in the US, AC crimes are considered a type of "crime against society" (compared to other categories—"crimes against persons" and "crimes against property"). Crimes against society also include drug/narcotic offenses, gambling, pornography/obscene material, prostitution, and weapon law violations. Using the NIBRS, more data regarding the circumstances of the AC offense are also collected. At the end of the first year of this addition to the NIBRS, 1126 instances of AC were reported and 21% of people were arrested (Federal Bureau of Investigation, 2019a, 2019b). Most of these crimes occurred at home (75%). In the 2017 NIBRS report, 3228 AC offenses were recorded, nearly triple what was reported in 2016.

Animal cruelty offenders

The bulk of what is known about the population of AC offenders is from retrospective accounts given by men incarcerated for other criminal offenses. Some more recent studies have been able to focus specifically on AC offenders. In fact, a large study by the FBI's Behavioral Analysis Unit examined criminal histories of AC offenders between 2004 and 2009. This included 259 active AC cases across 41 states (Hoffer, Hargreaves-Cormany, Muirhead, & Meloy, 2018). This is the most extensive study of AC offenders. The all-male offenders ranged from 17 to 82 years old (with an average age of 34 years). The most common victim was a dog (64%), with pit bull or pit bull mixes representing the largest proportion (26.5%) who was usually a puppy and less than one year of age (46%). A majority of AC offenders (73%) had a history of other arrests and 60% had a history of interpersonal violence. Levitt, Hoffer, and Loper (2016) reported on an analysis of a subset ($n = 150$) of these perpetrators. They found that most of these men had been arrested for abusing their own pet (46%) and were in their 30s (average age 37 years), Caucasian (68%), US citizens (85%), employed (45%), and unmarried at the time of their offense (76%). Sixty-one percent of perpetrators had children. Nearly all of them (96%) had another documented criminal offense, most frequently a drug possession followed by an assault charge and parole/probation violation. Moreover, 60% had been arrested for interpersonal violence in the past and 18% specifically for a sex offense (with an adult or child victim). Data regarding the nature of the crime were also gathered. Using the premeditated/proactive and impulsive/reactive distinction often applied to violent behavior, these AC offenders were grouped into one of two categories: (1) "Affective offenders"—AC was characterized by anger, impulsivity, fear of threat; (2) "Predatory offenders"—AC was characterized by a lack of emotion and greater planning behavior. Affective AC offenders more likely beat, threw, kicked, or choked their victims, while predatory AC offenders tended to shoot, stab, mutilate, torture, or burn their victims. While a heterogeneous group, the picture of the typical AC offender gleaned from this pioneering work is of an adult man with a criminal history who has likely been violent toward humans as well.

A few separate studies of AC offenders have also been conducted. Burchfield (2018) reported on 1990 animal crimes between 2009 and 2012 using the Chicago Police Department data. In most cases, when their primary offense was an animal crime it was for animal abuse/neglect (97%) compared to animal fighting, and 92% of these were classified as misdemeanors. The majority of these offenders in this sample were male (88%), Black (73%), and between the ages of 18 and 34 (56%). Another recent study conducted in the Netherlands reported on a sample of animal abuse offenders specifically (N=97 offenders with 90 cases of abuse) (van Wijk, Hardeman, & Endenburg, 2018). Offenders were predominantly men (89%), ranging in age from 7 to 78 years (average 35 years), unemployed (40%), and single (34%). Notably, 51% were first-time offenders. Regarding the actual offense, most cases involved their own companion animals (47%) who were tortured in the offender's home. When able to determine the cause of death, most veterinarians identified death by being hit/kicked/thrown to death (31%), notably in most cases the cause was unclear (39%).

Sociodemographic, behavioral, and psychiatric correlates of cruelty to animals were examined in the 2001–2002 National Epidemiologic Survey on Alcohol and Related Conditions (N=43,093) (Vaughn et al., 2009). The lifetime prevalence of AC was assessed by one question: "In your entire life, did you ever hurt or be cruel to an animal or pet on purpose?". Those endorsing yes to this question constituted 1.8% of the sample (about 775 perpetrators). Perpetrator characteristics most strongly associated with AC behavior included being male, African-American (notably only African-American and White were reported), non-Hispanic, with lower income, less education, widowed/separated/divorced, and living in the western region of the US. Levels of cruelty to animals were positively related to a number of psychological disorders including alcohol use, conduct disorder (CD), personality disorder symptoms (specifically antisocial, obsessive-compulsive, histrionic personality disorders), pathological gambling, as well as a family history of antisocial behavior. Furthermore, perpetrators of AC were significantly likely to have a history of other antisocial behaviors: 17 times more likely to have robbed/mugged another person, 12 times more likely to have set fires, and also 12 times more likely to have harassed/threatened people. The findings from this work highlight the history of violence and presence of personality pathology that is present among these perpetrators. Notably, these 775 individuals had not been charged with a crime, let alone a crime against an animal. It is therefore possible that offender populations that are typically studied are different. This next section reviews several common models of AC and highlights how psychopathy may play a role in each theory.

Theories of animal cruelty

Cultural model

A very broad context for understanding how human and nonhuman animals interact is the cultural model. Essentially, culture is argued to distally influence how humans interact with nonhuman animals. Contexts that value the well-being of nonhuman animals, in turn, influence norms and standards that surround their treatment. Societal norms and religious belief influence how humans value and interact with nonhumans. Buddhism as a religion and a philosophy describes how Buddha was born as different nonhuman animals; therefore killing nonhuman animals is essentially equated as killing humans (Szűcs, Geers, Jezierski, Sossidou, & Broom, 2012). The daily life of a Buddhist is, therefore, influenced by this belief: not farming animals, not seeking their companionship (dogs and cats, for example, are not viewed as pets), animals are not hunted, etc. Under the Judeo-Christian faith, animals are considered to be dominated by humans, having no souls, but treated if they are hurt and rescued if they are trapped (Gatward, 2001). Islamic religions also give humans power over nonhumans but killing animals is generally considered a sin unless it is out of necessity.

Cultural norms also affect how humans understand nonhumans. For example, bullfighting is considered a national sport and cultural tradition in Spain in which a bullfighter kills a wild bull with a sword in a larger outdoor arena (Mitchell, 1991). This practice was introduced to Spain in the 11th century. The Festival of Sacrifice or Eid al-Adha is considered an Islamic holiday commemorating Prophet Abraham in which Muslims slaughter sheep, camels, and goats to remind them that life is sacred (Brooke, 1987). The meat is consumed by the families or shared with others and is considered a blessing. The Pakistan Tanners' Association reported that in 2017, 10 million animals were slaughtered in Pakistan alone (The New York Times, 2017). It could be argued that these cultural traditions are indeed AC and perhaps even desensitize humans (including children) to violence. These contexts can affect more proximal, individual differences that influence our treatment of nonhumans.

Most conceptualizations of psychopathy are not culturally based and view psychopathic traits as individual personality characteristics (Hare, 1991; Lykken, 1995). However, psychopathic traits of perpetrators may be filtered through a cultural lens to explain AC. If cultures are more accepting of animal aggression or use acts of aggression as religious traditions, individuals with psychopathic traits may also be more likely to engage in this type of violence. Oftentimes violence toward animals has been excused by claiming it is culturally appropriate (Block, 2013).

Interestingly, a recent study by Verschuere et al. (2018) that used network analysis to identify core characteristics of psychological constructs in samples of North American and Dutch offenders found that certain symptoms of psychopathy are culturally specific. For example, while callousness was the primary psychopathy symptom found among US-based offenders, symptoms of irresponsibility and parasitic lifestyle were most common among Dutch offenders. In other words, certain features of psychopathy were more central for each culture. Other research has supported a cultural influence on psychopathy. Oshukova et al. (2016) reported that Finnish and Dutch adolescents presented with distinct psychopathic traits and this was also differentiated by sex. In the only cross-national comparison of psychopathy across Saudi Arabia, Egypt, and the US, Latzman et al. (2015) found that psychopathy traits were validated in the Arabic-speaking Middle East compared to Western culture. However, the symptom, cold-heartedness/openness, was less associated with psychopathy in the Middle-Eastern samples than the US. This particular personality feature was also dropped in a measurement study of the Personality Inventory for DSM-5 (Krueger, Derringer, Markon, Watson, & Skodol, 2012) in Arabic-speaking Middle Eastern countries (Bahrain, Kuwait, and Qatar) (Al-Attiyah, Megreya, Alrashidi, Dominguez-Lara, & Al-Sheerawi, 2017). The authors argue that perhaps this construct is less relevant in non-Western samples. It is unclear if certain psychopathic traits may be culturally specific for AC. Therefore while a cultural theory of AC can certainly contribute to our understanding of rates of aggression toward animals, an individual, through their proximal experiences, personality structure, and acute cognitive processing, must translate these systemic beliefs and ideals. The remaining theories consider more direct variables.

Childhood animal cruelty and "dirty play"

Perhaps the one theory that would not support a strong connection between AC and psychopathy is Arluke's (2002) "dirty play" hypothesis. Arluke argues that AC inflicted by children is a form of play that allows them to practice acting independently or exerting control. In this sense, "dirty play" is considered to be normal behavior in a child's development. This perspective relies on the symbolic interactionist view of AC that appreciates how children have a need to construct their own behavior and this construction is ordered and rational. Contrary to some of the later theories covered in this chapter, the "dirty play" theory emphasizes the value of dealing with anger and aggressing toward animals (beyond simply pent up frustration). Arluke (2002) interviewed White, male middle-class students who averaged 19 years of age about their cruelty toward animals. The research showed that there was a period in their lives when they did indeed harm animals and most of them felt guilty about it. Arluke (2002) compared this period to a "cultural 'time out' [rather] than a lasting sign of incivility or antisocial personality" (p. 424), likened to the Amish "rumspringa" that allows Amish girls and boys between age 18 and 21 to leave home and experience "immoral" behavior and return to the community still "morally intact."

Arluke (2002) argues that childhood AC behaviors should not necessarily be considered a warning sign for later adult violence since it is relatively common perhaps even developmentally normal. The distinction may be necessary when more "up close" acts of AC are present. For example, when examining retrospective reports of animal abuse behaviors from school shooters (Arluke & Madfis, 2014), the AC behaviors were considerably more severe—strangling, bludgeoning, burning, mutilating, and also similar to serial killers' histories of AC (perhaps similar to the "predatory" AC offenders labeled by Hoffer et al. (2018)). Psychopathic traits are more present in these individuals and therefore may be used to differentiate between "dirty play" and more problematic forms of animal abuse.

Frustration and displacement theory

This theory is based on Berkowitz's (1989) work that posited human discomfort can result in frustration and ultimately aggressive impulses. When applying this theory to acts of AC, individuals may act on these impulses and take out their frustration on nonhuman animals. This could be a direct consequence of frustration due to an animal's behavior (e.g., bitten by a cat) or a displaced response (e.g., the original target of frustration). One possible scenario illustrating the indirect consequence is a child who has just been abused by a parent and then kicks the family dog, displacing their frustration on the nonhuman animal, a less powerful target.

An important piece of this theory is that the aggression toward the animal is considered to be reactive or impulsive rather than proactive or planned. In other words, the individual acts out aggressively because the person has been directly provoked in some way. This distinction is important as psychopathy is characterized by poor behavioral controls (Hare, 1991) and a recent meta-analysis of 53 studies supported a positive relationship between reactive violence (compared to proactive) and psychopathy. On the same hand, aggression is complex, and this dichotomy between reactive and proactive functions of aggression is not always as clear-cut. In fact, while psychopathy has been primarily linked to reactive functions of aggression, there is evidence that both reactive and proactive aggression are related to callous and unemotional traits (e.g., Cima & Raine, 2009; Lehmann & Ittel, 2012). The evidence becomes even more ambiguous when the core components of psychopathy are examined (typically psychopathy is comprised of two factors—[1] affective/interpersonal and [2] antisocial/behavioral) in relation to the reactive/proactive dichotomy. Specifically, Factor 1 (composed of affective and interpersonal traits) of psychopathy has been linked to increased proactive aggression compared to Factor 2 (composed of antisocial and behavioral) (e.g., Cornell et al., 1996; Fite, Stoppelbein, & Greening, 2009; Jambroes et al., 2018).

As previously reviewed, Hoffer et al. (2018) applied this dichotomy to animal crime offenders—affective and predatory. Predatory AC offenders may indeed be ones with psychopathic traits characterized by having better impulsive control—waiting to aggress until it is more appropriate, beneficial, and perhaps more satisfying for the individual. The behavior is calculated. However, consistent with the affective AC offender (and much of the research on psychopathy) it could also be argued that a history of feeling frustrated and controlled may lead individuals to, in turn, become more controlling and purposeful in their own aggression. Both interpretations could be correct—moreover some reactive children who abuse animals may indeed later become proactive aggressors. In domestic violence situations, the perpetrator may proactively use AC to control their partner (Adams, 1995). In this way, the abuse serves an instrumental function, demonstrating power over an animal in an effort to control another person. Clearly appreciating the roles that emotion, frustration, and cognitive complexity play during violent behavior is central to understanding how psychopathy contributes to our conceptualization of the AC offender.

Social cognitive model

This large theory can be applied to nearly any human social behavior. Based largely on Bandura's (1973) social learning theory, along with the social information processing (SIP) model of aggression (Crick & Dodge, 1994; Dodge, 1980; Dodge, 1986), the social cognitive model of AC posits that a history of observing violence, coupled with a lens that primes and emphasizes hostile cues and aggressive responses, predicts AC behavior (Henry, 2018). This model is comprehensive, focusing on the interaction between individual proximal and distal factors. Observing a behavior affects one's beliefs and way of processing social information (cognitive schemas) which then, in turn, influences how one thinks about and reacts to social events. In this way, cultural context and experiences with nonhuman animals are filtered through more specific individual experiences, knowledge, and belief structures. According to Crick and Dodge's (1994) SIP model, individuals proceed through five stages of processing social information before acting out aggressively: (1) selectively attending to cues that prime aggression, (2) attributing hostile intent to cues that are ambiguous (hostile attribution bias), (3) favoring social goals that are aggressive, (4) frequently and easily accessing aggressive scripts, and (5) evaluating the aggressive response more favorably than a nonaggressive response.

Henry (2018) details how mechanisms from social cognitive theory are indeed applied to AC behavior. They argue how attributional biases related to AC may underlie motivations for animal abuse. Schemas associated with hostility and mistrust are common among people who engage in violent behavior. Arguably, these same schemas can be applied to AC. Moreover, AC may be more easily accessible given past observations of violence toward animals and then evaluated favorably due to these experiences. Their beliefs about aggressing toward animals are more acceptable because it is supported by their past experiences. In essence, their repertoire of potential responses, and their affinity for a particular response, is affected by what they know about the world. Behaving aggressively toward animals is perhaps chosen based on limited responses and a lack of appreciation for other methods of handling hostile attributions.

Psychopathic traits have consistently been tied directly to hostile cognitive schemas. A core feature of psychopaths is that they demonstrate extreme hostility because they view the world as hostile and unpredictable (Hare, 1991). Similarly to how the hostile attribution bias influences decisions to behave aggressively, hostile distortions contribute to psychopaths' antisocial behaviors (Newman & Wallace, 1993). In one of the first studies of hostile attributions, Serin (1991) found that psychopathic individuals did indeed attribute more hostile intent to other's behaviors. Specifically, when psychopaths were presented with vignettes that asked them to imagine themselves as the victim of a negative action by another individual (e.g., a person bumps into you at a bar and spills their drink in your lap), they readily attributed a hostile bias to the perpetrator (e.g., the person deliberately bumped into me and spilled my drink). Vitale, Newman, Serin, and Bolt (2005) built on this work and found the presence of psychopathic traits was indeed one pathway predicting hostile attribution biases for male offenders.

Nentjes, Bernstein, Arntz, van Breukelen, and Slaats (2015) examined psychopathy and theory of mind, among three groups: nonoffenders, psychopathic male criminal offenders, and nonpsychopathic male criminal offenders. Participants completed the

Reading the Mind in the Eyes Task (RMET; Baron-Cohen, Wheelwright, Hill, Raste, & Plumb, 2001) under timed and untimed conditions in which they were presented with a series of different pictures of the eye region and asked what word best represents what the picture is feeling or thinking. As expected, they found that psychopaths attributed more hostile interpretations of other's intentions on the RMET task. Interestingly, psychopathic offenders correctly attributed hostility when they had more time to process the information (not under the timed condition) compared to nonpsychopathic offenders and nonoffender controls. In other words, psychopaths showed an increased sensitivity to actual hostile states. This implies that this "bias" is actually more accurate when the cues are subtle and when they have time to process the information. One interpretation stems from Rusting's (1998) work and argues that the hostile social information from the RMET was processed more accurately because it was in fact congruent with their own personality. It could also be interpreted that psychopaths have a history of repeated exposures to hostile environments (including exposure to AC) and as such, it has become adaptive to be able to accurately read hostile motives (Leist & Dadds, 2009). The social cognitive model certainly contributes to our understanding of violence behavior and can be applied to violence behavior toward animals. Moreover, the influence of psychopathy in this model is well supported.

Violence graduation hypothesis

The violence graduation hypothesis (VGH) stems from empirical work that has consistently demonstrated the strong positive relationship between childhood AC and human-directed violence in adulthood (e.g., Hensley, Tallichet, & Dutkiewicz, 2009; Kellert & Felthous, 1985; Merz-Perez, Heide, & Silverman, 2001). Compared to Arluke's (2002) "dirty play" hypothesis, VGH posits that AC during childhood is essentially a way for children to rehearse later violence toward humans. In fact, rates of childhood AC are consistently very high among violent offenders: 48% of rapists and 30% of pedophiles (Tingle, Barnard, Robbins, Newman, & Hutchinson, 1986); 21% of serial murders (Wright & Hensley, 2003); 45% of school shooters (Verlinden, Hersen, & Thomas, 2000); 36% (childhood) and 46% (adolescent) sexual homicide offenders (Ressler, Burgess, & Douglas, 1988); 63% of incarcerated South African men with violent crimes (Schiff, Louw, & Ascione, 1999); and 26% of violent inmates compared to 7% of nonviolent offenders (Merz-Perez et al., 2001).

Unfortunately, focusing on retrospective accounts of violent offenders, employing only self-report data, and lacking a control group have limited this research. Ascione (2005) highlights how employing more prospective or longitudinal designs can strengthen this line of research. By following children who have been cruel to animals, the VGH can actually be studied. Arguably, when retrospective accounts of childhood AC by offenders is the focus, the support for VGH is biased. Certainly, it is possible that childhood AC could be related to less violent or perhaps no presence of human-directed violence in adulthood (Arluke, 2002). Many of the violent offenders did not report a history of childhood AC. In a recent meta-analysis of 15 studies, Patterson-Kane (2016) reported a weak link between AC and human-directed violence. Walters (2013) conducted a meta-analysis of 19 studies and found that the link between childhood AC to later criminal offending was not specific as childhood AC also correlated with nonviolent offending.

Despite these methodological limitations, it is noteworthy that, consistent with theories of aggression (e.g., Farrington & Hawkins, 1991; Moffitt, 1993), acts of violence during childhood tend to be predictive of more severe forms of adult antisocial behavior. According to these models, childhood-onset antisocial behavior is more likely to persist through middle adulthood than later adolescent-onset antisocial behavior. Moreover, this childhood-onset group also tends to have more callous and unemotional traits (as discussed by Gullone, 2014) which is a key feature of psychopathy. Fontaine, McCrory, Boivin, Moffitt, and Viding (2011) reported on callous-unemotional traits in children as related to adult psychopathy. They found that in their large twin sample ($N=9578$), the trajectory of children at age four that were characterized by callous-unemotional traits and conduct problems had the most negative outcomes including peer problems, emotional difficulties, and hyperactivity at 12 years of age. Frick, Ray, Thornton, and Kahn (2014) conducted the most exhaustive review of studies examining relations between these traits and conduct problems in children. Frick et al. (2014) concluded that the presence of callous-unemotional traits during childhood is a stronger predictor of antisocial outcomes compared to the number and severity of conduct problems, and their age of onset (also beyond symptoms of ADHD and impulsivity). This conclusion underscores the need to treat children who show elevated levels of these traits in order to prevent such outcomes. Research has also supported the progression of childhood callous-unemotional traits to specific psychopathic traits in adulthood, above and beyond childhood conduct problems (e.g., Burke, Loeber, & Lahey, 2007). Therefore the VGH hypothesis would perhaps lend support to the relationship between AC and psychopathy, especially for those offenders who have a history of childhood AC.

Deviance generalization hypothesis

Another popular framework from which to understand AC behavior is the deviance generalization hypothesis (DGH), which understands AC as an aggressive behavior that occurs in the context of other aggressive behaviors (Arluke, Levin, Luke, & Ascione, 1999; Hartup, 2005). The idea is that antisocial behavior likely stems from an underlying source. Arluke et al. (1999) work with offenders and nonoffenders supported this hypothesis. They found that while animal abusers were more likely to be involved in criminal behavior compared to the nonoffender control group, and over five times more likely to have a violent versus nonviolent criminal record, these abusers also had a significantly greater likelihood of all other antisocial acts (property, drug-related, and disorderly conduct). Most importantly, when studying the chronological order to antisocial behaviors reported in criminal records, AC was not more likely to precede than follow violent offenses (in fact it was in the opposite direction, albeit nonsignificant: 58% follow interpersonal violence, while 42% preceded it). In another study, Febres et al. (2014) found that while men who had been arrested for interpersonal violence had a high prevalence of animal abuse (41%), this did not predict their interpersonal violence beyond traits for antisocial personality disorders and alcohol abuse.

The role that psychopathy plays under this hypothesis is clear as psychopathic traits underlie many different antisocial acts. In fact, psychopathic individuals are characterized by their criminal versatility (Hare, 1991). Using a sample of male county jail inmates, Swogger and Kosson (2007) cluster analyzed symptoms of psychopathy. Similar to findings from Vassileva, Kosson, Abramowitz, and Conrod' (2005) cluster analysis of male inmates, primary and secondary psychopaths were distinguished by greater nonviolent and violent criminal versatility compared to criminals with low psychopathic traits and those criminals with negative affect.

Research on psychopathic traits and animal cruelty

Surprisingly, there is little research specifically on the AC and psychopathy link. However, we are able to appreciate this relationship when we explore the association between symptoms of psychopathy and AC. Most of this work has focused the relationship between (childhood) AC with adult interpersonal violence, criminal offending, conduct disorder, and empathy.

Interpersonal violence

There is a plethora of research examining the association between *childhood* AC with adult interpersonal violence (e.g., domestic violence, violent criminal behavior). In fact, this association is often referred to as "the Link" in the literature (Gullone, 2012). Certainly the "triad" theories emphasized how AC (along with other child behavior) predicted later violence (Macdonald, 1963; Paulhus & Williams, 2002). Empirical work has also supported this connection. Decades ago, Felthous (1979) interviewed male inpatients in a psychiatric hospital about their childhood behaviors. This study found that those who were considered "aggressive" as defined by a history of assaultive behaviors, threatening serious harm, or carrying a weapon to harm others, were significantly more likely to have purposeful killed animals (23%) or tortured them (18%), compared to nonaggressive patients (10% versus 5%). Aggressive attitudes are also more common among individuals from the community who endorse a history of animal abuse. Flynn (1999) examined attitudes toward violence among a sample of mostly White young adults from a university in the southern region of the US. The sample was divided based on those who had endorsed some form of AC ($n=47$) and those who had not ($n=227$). They found that the former group had more favorable attitudes toward corporal punishment and husbands slapping their wives.

In a recent review of the literature on "the Link," Monsalve, Ferreira, and Garcia (2017) reviewed nearly 100 articles published between 2015 and 2017. Though these studies were fraught with methodological limitations (e.g., small sample sizes, lack of a control group), 98% found a significant positive relationship between AC and interpersonal violence. They found weaker support for "the Link" in studies that used a prospective design, predicting adult violence from childhood AC.

Antisocial behavior

There is also support for the link between antisocial adult behavior (i.e., criminal behavior) and childhood AC, especially violent antisocial acts. Merz-Perez et al. (2001) found that a history of AC was more common among violent versus nonviolent criminal behavior. In their qualitative analysis of the inmates' AC behaviors, the groups also differed in their methods of aggression, response to the cruelty, and the type of animal victim. Hensley and Tallichet (2009) focused on the method of AC and its relationship to the number of violent crimes committed as an adult. They found that repeated acts of criminal violence were linked to more "hands on" approaches to AC including drowning and having sex with animals during childhood and adolescence.

Recent research on mass shooters supports this as well. Arluke and Madfis (2014) reviewed 23 cases of mass shooters who were under 20 years of age and who had killed multiple victims to determine if they had a history of animal abuse and, if so, the circumstances surrounding it. They found that animal abuse was common (43%) and "up close" (e.g., decapitating cats, dissecting squirrels). Arluke, Lankford, and Madfis (2018) later compared 20 mass/active shooters with and without a history of childhood AC. They found that the majority who had an animal abuse history had been cruel to animals during their childhood (75%) and majority of the violence (75%) was considered "at close range" compared to more "detached" ways of abusing animals. Interestingly, those offenders who had a history of animal abuse also tended to be younger at the time of their offense than those without a history (about 12 years younger). Notably, the most common place where the murders occurred was at a school. With regards to the nature of the AC, the authors discuss how sadistic serial killers are more commonly described as psychopaths than mass/active shooters. However, their analysis suggested that given the nature of the animal abuse committed by active/mass shooters, they are likely higher in psychopathic traits than those without such a history of AC.

Conduct disorder

Conduct disorder (CD) is defined as a "repetitive and persistent patterns of behavior in which the basic rights of others or major age-appropriate societal norms or rules are violated" (DSM-5; American Psychiatric Association, 2013, p. 33). AC during childhood is considered one of the core symptoms of CD. Children who have a diagnosis of CD are very likely to develop Antisocial Personality Disorder in adulthood (75% go on to meet criteria) (Gelhorn, Sakai, Price, & Crowley, 2007). Animal abuse is considered to be one of the earliest indicators of CD. However, not all children who have a CD diagnosis are cruel to animals. In fact, only about 25% of children with the diagnosis report hurting animals on purpose (Gelhorn et al., 2007). Notably, this subgroup tends to be associated with more severe behavioral problems and a distinct background. Luk, Staiger, Wong, and Mathai (1999) reported that children with CD who abused animals were more likely to have poorer family functioning and elevated self-perceptions compared to those without a history of AC.

However, while being cruel to animals during childhood is a strong predictor of adult antisocial features, it does not necessarily predict later violence toward adults (e.g., Arluke, 2002). Some researchers have argued that other factors play a role in determining the prognostic value of childhood AC. Schwartz, Fremouw, Schenk, and Ragatz (2012) reported that AC during childhood was linked to greater criminal thinking, bullying, and power orientation, and perhaps these variables are more predictive of psychopathic traits in adulthood than AC.

Using Mulvey's (2013) Pathways to Desistance study, Walters (2014) prospectively analyzed how AC behavior at baseline (aged 14–18) predicted aggressive and nonaggressive offending (up to 84 months later). While AC behavior at baseline was directly predictive of future offending, hostility and callousness/unemotionality significantly helped to explain the link. In other words, these cognitive-personality indicators mediated the relationship. Hostility and callousness/unemotionality are indeed core traits of psychopathy (Hare, 1991).

A lack of empathy

Many researchers posit children who lack empathy, a key feature of psychopathy, are ones who commit repetitive acts of violence toward animals (e.g., Grisso, 1998; Miller, 2009). Some have even argued that engaging in AC is a hallmark of psychopathy (Kaufman, Hilliker, & Daleiden, 1996). Dadds, Whiting, and Hawes (2006) studied children aged 6–13 years to determine if childhood AC was indeed a marker of an early manifestation of psychopathy. They examined the different pathways to AC including family environment, other externalizing behaviors, and psychopathic traits in childhood (operationalized as callous-unemotional traits on the Antisocial Process Screening Device [Frick & Hare, 2001]). They found that childhood AC was significantly related to callous-unemotional traits and other externalizing behaviors for male children only. While family conflict was associated with child behavior problems, it was not uniquely related to childhood AC. They argued that perhaps cruelty to animals during childhood is a behavioral manifestation of psychopathic traits.

Henderson, Hensley, and Tallichet (2011) studied methods of AC used during childhood by adult violent offenders. They proposed that the animals were used as "training objects" for children with psychopathic traits, allowing them to practice more sadistic acts of violence on nonhuman victims that they later were able to carry out on human victims during adulthood. In support of this, Stupperich and Strack (2016) found that childhood animal abuse helped to significantly explain the relationship between adult psychopathy and sadistic behavior in a sample of German forensic male adult patients. While psychopathic traits were not specifically measured during childhood, given the presence of it in adulthood, perhaps these children were showing symptoms of callous-unemotional traits and acted out aggression on animals during their development prior to perpetrating violence against humans in adulthood. In other words, part of the reason why there is this link is due to perpetration of AC during childhood.

It is tough to know what comes first, the AC or disruptions in empathy development. Most researchers acknowledge that empathy is indeed something that a child develops and it is generally fostered in the social (e.g., caregiving) environment. Feshbach

(1989), when discussing empathy in families who abuse their child(ren), emphasized how empathy is a developed behavior and when parents abuse their children, they are lacking adequate empathy and this will essentially transfer to their abused child(ren). Although compromised empathy may be a contributing factor in the development of AC behaviors (e.g., Grisso, 1998), Flynn (1999) argued that abusing animals during childhood actually leads to interferences with their empathy development. Of course, this relationship may actually be recursive—characterized by a reduced capacity for empathy leading to AC and these cruel behaviors further compromising empathy development. The research reviewed in this section supports that cruelty toward animals is indeed linked to traits of psychopathy. As Gullone (2012) suggests, AC during childhood can be viewed as a moral impairment that gives us the ability to learn more about violence in adulthood.

Conclusions

In this chapter, we define AC, describe the implications of AC laws for understanding AC offenders, and provide an overview of several theoretical conceptualizations of AC. Although models of AC are abundant and offer insight into the development of AC and psychopathy in adulthood, there is relatively little research in this area. Conceptual models of AC highlight the dynamic interplay between developmental processes (e.g., empathy, cognitive schemas, emotion regulation), socialization (e.g., family environment, peer group), and environment (e.g., culture), and how these factors may interact to shape AC. However, there is significant need for longitudinal research to test these models and identify developmental precursors to psychopathy-related AC behavior. Furthermore, a significant gap in our knowledge about AC concerns the heritability of this behavior as well as the role of gene–environment interactions.

A notable body of research highlights the role of genetic contributions to the development of antisocial behavior and psychopathic traits (see Fontaine, McCrory, & Viding, 2018 for a review). One issue that is of particular importance to advancing knowledge of links between AC and psychopathy concerns the link between childhood *exposure* to AC and AC behavior in childhood and adulthood. Children living in adverse family environments where child maltreatment and/or intimate partner violence occur are at increased risk for exposure to AC as well as engaging in AC behaviors and interpersonal violence. Psychopathic traits play a significant role in family violence, and are robust predictors of male-to female violence in particular (Fernández-Suárez, Pérez, Herrero, Juarros-Basterretxea, & Rodríguez-Díaz, 2018). The heritability of callous and unemotional traits (which are predictive of psychopathy) is between 36% and 67% (Moore et al., 2019). Recent research suggests that callous/unemotional traits may play a critical role in mediating the effects of childhood exposure to AC and maladjustment among children living in households experiencing family violence (McDonald et al., 2018). However, more research is needed to examine these relations over time and in the context of genetic factors. Once the impact of genetic influences and/or differential susceptibility is established, scholars in this area will have a better understanding of the developmental processes and environmental factors that lead to an individual's disregard for the welfare of nonhuman and human animals and concomitant acts of cruelty. Such information is needed to effectively intervene in populations at risk for or exhibiting this behavior. Although this chapter addresses links between AC and psychopathy, it is important to note that Patterson-Kane's (2016) recent meta-analysis of studies examining AC among violent offenders reported a weak link between AC and violence against humans. This study did not specifically focus on AC offenders meeting criteria for psychopathy; still, the finding underscores that most individuals who have engaged in AC do not go on to perpetrate violence against other humans and/or meet clinical criteria for psychopathy. AC should be viewed as a risk factor for aggressive antisocial and criminal behavior, as well as a public health concern impacting the welfare of both human and nonhuman animals.

References

About Us. (2019). *The animal legal defense fund*. Retrieved from: https://aldf.org/about-us/.

Adams, C. J. (1995). Woman-battering and harm to animals. In C. J. Adams, & J. Donovan (Eds.), *Animals and women: Feminist theoretical explorations* (pp. 55–84). Durham, NC: Duke University Press.

Al-Attiyah, A. A., Megreya, A. M., Alrashidi, M., Dominguez-Lara, S. A., & Al-Sheerawi, A. (2017). The psychometric properties of an Arabic version of the personality inventory for DSM-5 (PID-5) across three Arabic-speaking Middle Eastern countries. *International Journal of Culture and Mental Health, 10*(2), 197–205. https://doi.org/10.1080/17542863.2017.1290125.

American Psychiatric Association. (2013). *Diagnostic and statistical manual of mental disorders (DSM-5®)*. Washington, DC: American Psychiatric Association Publishing.

Animal Cruelty Facts and Stats. (2019). *The Humane Society of the United States*. https://www.humanesociety.org/resources/animal-cruelty-facts-and-stats.

Animal Legal Defense Fund. (2019). *2018 U.S. animal protection laws state rankings [Data file]*. https://aldf.org/project/2018-us-state-rankings/.

Animal Welfare Institute. (2019). *Legal Protections for Farm Animals During Transport*. https://awionline.org/sites/default/files/uploads/documents/fa-legalprotectionsduring-transport-12262013.pdf.

Arluke, A. (2002). Animal abuse as dirty play. *Symbolic Interaction, 25*(4), 405–430. https://www.jstor.org/stable/10.1525/si.2002.25.4.405.

Arluke, A., Lankford, A., & Madfis, E. (2018). Harming animals and massacring humans: Characteristics of public mass and active shooters who abused animals. *Behavioral Sciences & the Law, 36*(6), 739–751. https://doi.org/10.1002/bsl.2385.

Arluke, A., Levin, J., Luke, C., & Ascione, F. (1999). The relationship of animal abuse to violence and other forms of antisocial behavior. *Journal of Interpersonal Violence, 14*(9), 963–975. https://journals.sagepub.com/doi/pdf/10.1177/088626099014009004.

Arluke, A., & Madfis, E. (2014). Animal abuse as a warning sign of school massacres: A critique and refinement. *Homicide Studies, 18*(1), 7–22. https://doi.org/10.1177/1088767913511459.

Ascione, F. R. (1993). Children who are cruel to animals: A review of research and implications for developmental psychopathology. *Anthrozoös*, *6*(4), 226–247. https://www.tandfonline.com/doi/abs/10.2752/089279393787002105.

Ascione, F. R. (2005). Children, animal abuse and family violence—The multiple intersection of animal abuse, child victimization and domestic violence. In K. A. Kendall-Tackett, & S. M. Giacomoni (Eds.), *Child victimisation: Maltreatment, bullying and dating violence; prevention and intervention* (pp. 3.1–3.36). Kingston, NJ: Civic Research Institute Inc.

Bandura, A. (1973). *Aggression: A social learning analysis*. Englewood Cliffs, NJ: Prentice-Hall.

Baron-Cohen, S., Wheelwright, S., Hill, J., Raste, Y., & Plumb, I. (2001). The "Reading the Mind in the Eyes" test revised version: A study with normal adults, and adults with Asperger syndrome or high-functioning autism. *The Journal of Child Psychology and Psychiatry and Allied Disciplines*, *42*(2), 241–251. https://doi.org/10.1017/S0021963001006643.

Berkowitz, L. (1989). Frustration-aggression hypothesis: Examination and reformulation. *Psychological Bulletin*, *106*(1), 59–73. https://doi.org/10.1037/0033-2909.106.1.59.

Block, K. (2013, May 23). *Culture is never an excuse for animal cruelty*. Humane Society International. https://www.hsi.org/news-media/bullfighting_cruelty_052113/.

Brooke, C. (1987). Sacred slaughter: The sacrificing of animals at the Hajj and Id al Adha. *Journal of Cultural Geography*, *7*(2), 67–88. https://doi.org/10.1080/08873638709478508.

Brown, L. (1988). *Cruelty to animals: The moral debt*. Berlin, GE: Springer.

Burchfield, K. B. (2018). The nature of animal crime: Scope and severity in Chicago. *Crime & Delinquency*, *64*(14), 1904–1924. https://doi.org/10.1177/0011128717719515.

Burke, J. D., Loeber, R., & Lahey, B. B. (2007). Adolescent conduct disorder and interpersonal callousness as predictors of psychopathy in young adults. *Journal of Clinical Child and Adolescent Psychology*, *36*(3), 334–346. https://www.tandfonline.com/doi/full/10.1080/15374410701444223.

Caviola, L., Everett, J. A., & Faber, N. S. (2019). The moral standing of animals: Towards a psychology of speciesism. *Journal of Personality and Social Psychology*, *116*(6), 1011–1029. https://doi.org/10.1037/pspp0000182.

Cima, M., & Raine, A. (2009). Distinct characteristics of psychopathy relate to different subtypes of aggression. *Personality and Individual Differences*, *47*(8), 835–840. https://www.sciencedirect.com/science/article/pii/S0191886909003067.

Coleman, V. (1991). *Why animal experiments must stop*. London, UK: Green Print—Merlin Press.

Cornell, D. G., Warren, J., Hawk, G., Stafford, E., Oram, G., & Pine, D. (1996). Psychopathy in instrumental and reactive violent offenders. *Journal of Consulting and Clinical Psychology*, *64*(4), 783–790. https://www.ncbi.nlm.nih.gov/pubmed/8803369.

Crick, N. R., & Dodge, K. A. (1994). A review and reformulation of social information processing mechanisms in children's social adjustment. *Psychological Bulletin*, *115*(1), 74–101. https://doi.org/10.1037/0033-2909.115.1.74.

Dadds, M. R., Turner, C. M., & McAloon, J. (2002). Developmental links between cruelty to animals and human violence. *Australian & New Zealand Journal of Criminology*, *35*(3), 363–382. https://journals.sagepub.com/doi/pdf/10.1375/acri.35.3.363?casa_token=qE4jgqLh29oAAAAA:Jf3UV8OeGwseUwgHfsq5Lq6vdKeu6yDQnaGDJHk-L0SRQVNEz49KykiQ0mUDFiRHfg-qzT6oaA.

Dadds, M. R., Whiting, C., & Hawes, D. J. (2006). Associations among cruelty to animals, family conflict, and psychopathic traits in childhood. *Journal of Interpersonal Violence*, *21*(3), 411–429. https://journals.sagepub.com/doi/pdf/10.1177/0886260505283341.

Dodge, K. A. (1980). Social cognition and children's aggressive behavior. *Child Development*, *51*, 162–170. https://www.jstor.org/stable/1129603.

Dodge, K. A. (1986). A social information processing model of social competence in children. In M. Perlmutter (Ed.), *Vol. 18. Minnesota symposium in child psychology* (pp. 85–134). Hillsdale, NJ: Erlbaum.

Farrington, D. P., & Hawkins, J. D. (1991). Predicting participation, early onset and later persistence in officially recorded offending. *Criminal Behaviour and Mental Health, 1*(1), 1–33. https://onlinelibrary.wiley.com/doi/abs/10.1002/cbm.1991.1.1.1.

Febres, J., Brasfield, H., Shorey, R. C., Elmquist, J., Ninnemann, A., Schonbrun, Y. C., … Stuart, G. L. (2014). Adulthood animal abuse among men arrested for domestic violence. *Violence Against Women, 20*(9), 1059–1077. https://journals.sagepub.com/doi/pdf/10.1177/1077801214549641.

Federal Bureau of Investigation. (2016, February 1). *Tracking animal cruelty*. Federal Bureau of Investigation. https://www.fbi.gov/news/stories/-tracking-animal-cruelty.

Federal Bureau of Investigation. (2019a). *2016 national incident-based reporting system [Data file]*. https://ucr.fbi.gov/nibrs/2016.

Federal Bureau of Investigation. (2019b). *2017 national incident-based reporting system [Data file]*. https://ucr.fbi.gov/nibrs/2017.

Felthous, A. R. (1979). Childhood antecedents of aggressive behaviors in male psychiatric patients. *The Bulletin of the American Academy of Psychiatry and the Law, 8*(1979), 104–110.

Fernández-Suárez, A., Pérez, B., Herrero, J., Juarros-Basterretxea, J., & Rodríguez-Díaz, F. J. (2018). The role of psychopathic traits among intimate partner-violent men: A systematic review. *Revista Iberoamericana de Psicologia y Salud, 9*(2), 84. https://doi.org/10.23923/j.rips.2018.02.017.

Feshbach, N. D. (1989). The construct of empathy and the phenomenon of physical maltreatment of children. In D. Cicchetti, & V. Carlson (Eds.), *Child maltreatment: Theory and research on the causes and of child abuse and neglect* (pp. 349–373). Cambridge, UK: Cambridge University Press.

Fighting Animal Cruelty and Neglect. (2019). *The Humane Society of the United States*. https://www.humanesociety.org/all-our-fights/fighting-animal-cruelty-and-neglect.

Fite, P. J., Stoppelbein, L., & Greening, L. (2009). Proactive and reactive aggression in a child psychiatric inpatient population: Relations to psychopathic characteristics. *Criminal Justice and Behavior, 36*(5), 481–493. https://journals.sagepub.com/doi/pdf/10.1177/0093854809332706.

Flynn, C. P. (1999). Animal abuse in childhood and later support for interpersonal violence in families. *Society & Animals: Journal of Human-Animal Studies, 7*(2), 161–172. https://s3.amazonaws.com/academia.edu.documents/32347335/flynn_society_and_animals_1999.pdf?AWSAccessKeyId=AKIAIWOWYYGZ2Y53UL3A&Expires=1554333103&Signature=RvOUlNZrgsum7bsib0YHPaD4Hn0%3D&response-content-disposition=inline%3B%20filename%3DAnimal_Abuse_in_Childhood_and_Later_Supp.pdf.

Fontaine, N. M., McCrory, E. J., Boivin, M., Moffitt, T. E., & Viding, E. (2011). Predictors and outcomes of joint trajectories of callous–unemotional traits and conduct problems in childhood. *Journal of Abnormal Psychology, 120*(3), 730–742. https://doi.org/10.1037/a0022620.

Fontaine, N. M., McCrory, E. J., & Viding, E. (2018). Genetic contributions to the development of psychopathic traits and antisocial behavior inyouths. In A. R. Beech, A. J. Carter, R. E. Mann, & P. Rotshtein (Eds.), *The Wiley Blackwell handbook of forensic neuroscience*. https://doi.org/10.1002/9781118650868.ch18.

Frick, P. J., & Hare, R. D. (2001). *Antisocial process screening device: APSD*. Toronto: Multi Health Systems.

Frick, P. J., Ray, J. V., Thornton, L. C., & Kahn, R. E. (2014). Can callous-unemotional traits enhance the understanding, diagnosis, and treatment of serious conduct problems in children and adolescents? A comprehensive review. *Psychological Bulletin*, *140*(1), 1–57. https://doi.org/10.1037/a0033076.

Gatward, G. J. (2001). *Livestock ethics: Respect and our duty of care for farm animals*. Lincoln, UK: Chalcombe Publications.

Gelhorn, H. L., Sakai, J. T., Price, R. K., & Crowley, T. J. (2007). DSM-IV conduct disorder criteria as predictors of antisocial personality disorder. *Comprehensive Psychiatry*, *48*(6), 529–538. https://www.sciencedirect.com/science/article/pii/S0010440X07000806.

Grisso, T. (1998). *Forensic evaluation of juveniles*. Sarasota, FL: Professional Resource Press. ISBN 156887037X, 9781568870373.

Gullone, E. (2012). *Animal cruelty, antisocial behaviour, and aggression: More than a link*. Basingstoke, UK: Palgrave Macmillan.

Gullone, E. (2014). An evaluative review of theories related to animal cruelty. *Journal of Animal Ethics*, *4*(1), 37–57. https://doi.org/10.5406/janimalethics.4.1.0037. https://link.springer.com/book/10.1057%2F9781137284549.

Hare, R. D. (1991). *The Hare psychopathy checklist-revised: Manual*. Toronto, ON: Multi Health Systems, Incorporated.

Hartup, W. W. (2005). Peer interaction: What causes what? *Journal of Abnormal Child Psychology*, *33*(3), 387–394. https://doi.org/10.1007/s10802-005-3578-0.

Henderson, B. B., Hensley, C., & Tallichet, S. E. (2011). Childhood animal cruelty methods and their link to adult interpersonal violence. *Journal of Interpersonal Violence*, *26*(11), 2211–2227. https://journals.sagepub.com/doi/pdf/10.1177/0886260510383038.

Henry, B. (2018). A social-cognitive model of animal cruelty. *Psychology, Crime & Law*, *24*(5), 458–478. https://doi.org/10.1080/1068316X.2017.1371306.

Hensley, C., & Tallichet, S. E. (2009). Childhood and adolescent animal cruelty methods and their possible link to adult violent crimes. *Journal of Interpersonal Violence*, *24*(1), 147–158. https://journals.sagepub.com/doi/pdf/10.1177/0886260508315779.

Hensley, C., Tallichet, S. E., & Dutkiewicz, E. L. (2009). Recurrent childhood animal cruelty: Is there a relationship to adult recurrent interpersonal violence? *Criminal Justice Review*, *34*(2), 248–257. https://doi.org/10.1177/0734016808325062.

Hoffer, T., Hargreaves-Cormany, H., Muirhead, Y., & Meloy, J. R. (2018). Meloy's biopsychosocial model of violence. In *Violence in animal cruelty offenders* (pp. 17–19). Berlin, GE: Springer.

Jambroes, T., Jansen, L. M., vd Ven, P. M., Claassen, T., Glennon, J. C., Vermeiren, R. R., … Popma, A. (2018). Dimensions of psychopathy in relation to proactive and reactive aggression: Does intelligence matter? *Personality and Individual Differences*, *129*, 76–82. https://doi.org/10.1016/j.paid.2018.03.001.

Jones, D. (2008). *Crimes without consequences: The enforcement of humane slaughter laws in the United States*. Washington, DC: Animal Welfare Institute.

Kaufman, K. L., Hilliker, D. R., & Daleiden, E. L. (1996). Subgroup differences in the modus operandi of adolescent sexual offenders. *Child Maltreatment*, *1*(1), 17–24. https://doi.org/10.1177/1077559596001001003.

Kavanagh, P., Signal, T., & Taylor, N. (2013). The Dark Triad and animal cruelty: Dark personalities, dark attitudes, and dark behaviors. *Personality and Individual Differences*, *55*, 666–670. https://doi.org/10.1016/j.paid.2013.05.019.

Kellert, S. R., & Felthous, A. R. (1985). Childhood cruelty toward animals among criminals and noncriminals. *Human Relations; Studies Towards the Integration of the Social Sciences*, *38*(12), 1113–1129. https://journals.sagepub.com/doi/pdf/10.1177/001872678503801202.

Krueger, R. F., Derringer, J., Markon, K. E., Watson, D., & Skodol, A. E. (2012). Initial construction of a maladaptive personality trait model and inventory for DSM 5. *Psychological Medicine*, *42*(9), 1879–1890. https://doi.org/10.1017/S0033291711002674.

Latzman, R. D., Megreya, A. M., Hecht, L. K., Miller, J. D., Winiarski, D. A., & Lilienfeld, S. O. (2015). Self-reported psychopathy in the Middle East: A cross-national comparison across Egypt, Saudi Arabia, and the United States. *BMC Psychology*, *3*(1), 37–50. https://bmcpsychology.biomedcentral.com/track/pdf/10.1186/s40359-015-0095-y.

Lehmann, A., & Ittel, A. (2012). Aggressive behavior and measurement of psychopathy in female inmates of German prisons—A preliminary study. *International Journal of Law and Psychiatry*, *35*(3), 190–197. https://www.sciencedirect.com/science/article/pii/S0160252712000222.

Leist, T., & Dadds, M. R. (2009). Adolescents' ability to read different emotional faces relates to their history of maltreatment and type of psychopathology. *Clinical Child Psychology and Psychiatry*, *14*(2), 237–250. https://doi.org/10.1177/1359104508100887.

Levitt, L., Hoffer, T. A., & Loper, A. B. (2016). Criminal histories of a subsample of animal cruelty offenders. *Aggression and Violent Behavior*, *30*, 48–58. https://www.sciencedirect.com/science/article/pii/S135917891630043X.

Luk, E. S., Staiger, P. K., Wong, L., & Mathai, J. (1999). Children who are cruel to animals: A revisit. *Australian and New Zealand Journal of Psychiatry*, *33*(1), 29–36. https://doi.org/10.1046/j.1440-1614.1999.00528.x.

Lykken, D. T. (1995). *The antisocial personalities*. Mahwah, NJ: Erlbaum.

Macdonald, J. M. (1963). The threat to kill. *American Journal of Psychiatry*, *120*(2), 125–130. https://ajp.psychiatryonline.org/doi/pdfplus/10.1176/ajp.120.2.125?casa_token=drik_XU7fioAAAAA%3A65NN94mUv_MIZCdJHREihNOWeZRvWGbPCI0wgDI-T7fd3jq88rKAMnGozS-1RqeXINDt0uHp&.

McDonald, S. E., Cody, A. M., Booth, L. J., Peers, J. R., Luce, C. O. C., Williams, J. H., & Ascione, F. R. (2018). Animal cruelty among children in violent households: Children's explanations of their behavior. *Journal of Family Violence*, *33*(7), 469–480. https://doi.org/10.1007/s10896-018-9970-7.

Merz-Perez, L., Heide, K. M., & Silverman, I. J. (2001). Childhood cruelty to animals and subsequent violence against humans. *International Journal of Offender Therapy and Comparative Criminology*, *45*(5), 556–573. https://journals.sagepub.com/doi/pdf/10.1177/0306624X01455003.

Miller, C. B. (2009). Empathy, social psychology, and global helping traits. *Philosophical Studies*, *142*(2), 247–275. https://doi.org/10.1007/s11098-007-9185-x.

Mitchell, T. (1991). *Blood sport: A social history of Spanish bullfighting*. Philadelphia, PA: University of Pennsylvania Press.

Moffitt, T. E. (1993). Adolescence-limited and life-course-persistent antisocial behavior: A developmental taxonomy. *Psychological Review*, *100*(4), 674–701. https://doi.org/10.1037/0033-295X.100.4.674.

Monsalve, S., Ferreira, F., & Garcia, R. (2017). The connection between animal abuse and interpersonal violence: A review from the veterinary perspective. *Research in Veterinary Science*, *114*, 18–26. https://doi.org/10.1016/j.rvsc.2017.02.025.

Monyak, S. (2018, February 2). *When the law recognizes animals as people*. The New Republic. https://newrepublic.com/article/146870/law-recognizes-animals-people.

Moore, A. A., Rappaport, L. M., Blair, R. J., Pine, D. S., Leibenluft, E., Brotman, M. A., … Roberson-Nay, R. (2019). Genetic underpinnings of callous-unemotional traits and emotion recognition in children, adolescents, and emerging adults. *Journal of Child Psychology and Psychiatry*, *60*(6), 638–645. https://doi.org/10.1111/jcpp.13018.

Mulvey, E. P. (2013). *Research on pathways to desistance [Maricopa County, AZ and Philadelphia County, PA]: Subject measures, 2000-2010 (ICPSR29961-v2) [Data file]*. Ann Arbor, MI: Inter-university Consortium for Political and Social Research [Distributor]. 01-07.

Musumeci, N. (2019, March 1). *Cruel creep busted in savage killing of golden retriever service dog*. The New York Post. https://nypost.com/2019/03/01/cruel-creep-busted-in-savage-killing-of-golden-retriever-service-dog/.

Nentjes, L., Bernstein, D., Arntz, A., van Breukelen, G., & Slaats, M. (2015). Examining the influence of psychopathy, hostility biases, and automatic processing on criminal offenders' theory of mind. *International Journal of Law and Psychiatry*, *38*, 92–99. https://www.sciencedirect.com/science/article/pii/S0160252715000138.

Newman, J. P., & Wallace, J. F. (1993). Diverse pathways to deficient self-regulation: Implications for disinhibitory psychopathology in children. *Clinical Psychology Review*, *13*(8), 699–720. https://pdfs.semanticscholar.org/1922/b83dfc9ac44ceb4511dd6438e-36d0a86c211.pdf.

Oshukova, S., Kaltiala-Heino, R., Hillege, S., de Ruiter, C., Joffe, G., Miettunen, J., … Lindberg, N. (2016). Self-reported psychopathic traits in Finnish and Dutch samples of non-referred adolescents: Exploration of cultural differences. *Child and Adolescent Psychiatry and Mental Health*, *10*(1), 3–8. https://doi.org/10.1186/s13034-015-0090-3.

Patterson-Kane, E. (2016). The relation of animal maltreatment to aggression. In L. Levitt, G. Patronek, & T. Grisso (Eds.), *Animal maltreatment: Forensic mental health issues and evaluations* (pp. 140–158). Oxford, UK: Oxford University Press.

Paulhus, D. L., & Williams, K. M. (2002). The dark triad of personality: Narcissism, Machiavellianism, and psychopathy. *Journal of Research in Personality*, *36*(2002), 556–563. https://www.sciencedirect.com/science/article/pii/S0092656602005056.

Petersen, M. L., & Farrington, D. P. (2007). Cruelty to animals and violence to people. *Victims and Offenders*, *2*(1), 21–43. https://www.tandfonline.com/doi/full/10.1080/15564880600934187.

Platt, J. (2012, November 16). *Undercover videor depicts abuse at Butternall turkey farms*. Mother Nature Network. https://www.mnn.com/earth-matters/animals/stories/undercover-video-depicts-abuse-at-butterball-turkey-farms.

Ressler, R. K., Burgess, A. W., & Douglas, J. E. (1988). *Sexual homicide: Patterns and motives*. New York, NY: Simon and Schuster.

Rowan, A. N. (1999). Cruelty and abuse to animals: A typology. In F. R. Ascione, & P. Arkow (Eds.), *Child abuse, domestic violence, and animal abuse: Linking the circles of compassion for prevention and intervention* (pp. 328–334). West Lafayette, IN: Purdue University Press.

Rusting, C. L. (1998). Personality, mood, and cognitive processing of emotional information: Three conceptual frameworks. *Psychological Bulletin*, *124*(2), 165–196. https://psycnet.apa.org/fulltext/1998-10661-002.pdf.

Salo, J. (2019, February 28). *Boat captain pleads guilty in shark-dragging video case*. The New York Post. https://nypost.com/2019/02/28/boat-captain-pleads-guilty-in-shark-dragging-video-case/.

Schiff, K. G., Louw, D. A., & Ascione, F. R. (1999). The link between cruelty to animals and later violent behaviour against humans: A theoretical foundation. *Acta Criminologica*, *12*(2), 25–33.

Schwartz, R. L., Fremouw, W., Schenk, A., & Ragatz, L. L. (2012). Psychological profile of male and female animal abusers. *Journal of Interpersonal Violence*, *27*(5), 846–861. https://journals.sagepub.com/doi/pdf/10.1177/0886260511423254.

Serin, R. C. (1991). Psychopathy and violence in criminals. *Journal of Interpersonal Violence*, *6*(4), 423–431. https://journals.sagepub.com/doi/pdf/10.1177/088626091006004002.

Singer, P. (1975). *Animal liberation: A new ethics for our treatment of animals*. New York, NY: HarperCollins Publishers.

Solotaroff, P. (2013, December 10). *In the belly of the beast. Rolling Stone*. https://www.rollingstone.com/interactive/feature-belly-beast-meat-factory-farms-animal-activists/.

Stupperich, A., & Strack, M. (2016). Among a German sample of forensic patients, previous animal abuse mediates between psychopathy and sadistic actions. *Journal of Forensic Sciences*, *61*(3), 699–705. https://doi.org/10.1111/1556-4029.13057.

Swogger, M. T., & Kosson, D. S. (2007). Identifying subtypes of criminal psychopaths: A replication and extension. *Criminal Justice and Behavior*, *34*(8), 953–970. https://journals.sagepub.com/doi/pdf/10.1177/0093854807300758.

Szűcs, E., Geers, R., Jezierski, T., Sossidou, E. N., & Broom, D. M. (2012). Animal welfare in different human cultures, traditions and religious faiths. *Asian-Australasian Journal of Animal Sciences*, *25*(11), 1499–1506. https://www.ncbi.nlm.nih.gov/pmc/articles/PMC4093044/.

The New York Times. (2017, September 2). *Eid al-Adha: Muslims around the world celebrate holy festival*. The New York Times. https://www.nytimes.com/2017/09/02/world/eid-al-adha-muslims.html.

Tingle, D., Barnard, G. W., Robbins, L., Newman, G., & Hutchinson, D. (1986). Childhood and adolescent characteristics of pedophiles and rapists. *International Journal of Law and Psychiatry*, *9*(1), 103–116. https://www.safetylit.org/citations/index.php?fuseaction=citations.viewdetails&citationIds=citjournalarticle_131539_24.

United States Congress. (1958). *The humane slaughter act (P.L. 85–765)*. Washington, DC: U.S. Government Printing Office.

United States Congress. (1966). *The animal welfare act (P.L. 89–544)*. Washington, DC: U.S. Government Printing Office.

van Wijk, A., Hardeman, M., & Endenburg, N. (2018). Animal abuse: Offender and offence characteristics. A descriptive study. *Journal of Investigative Psychology and Offender Profiling*, *15*(2), 175–186. https://doi.org/10.1002/jip.1499.

Vassileva, J., Kosson, D. S., Abramowitz, C., & Conrod, P. (2005). Psychopathy versus psychopathies in classifying criminal offenders. *Legal and Criminological Psychology*, *10*(1), 27–43. https://doi.org/10.1348/135532504X15376.

Vaughn, M. G., Fu, Q., DeLisi, M., Beaver, K. M., Perron, B. E., Terrell, K., & Howard, M. O. (2009). Correlates of cruelty to animals in the United States: Results from the National Epidemiologic Survey on alcohol and related conditions. *Journal of Psychiatric Research*, *43*(15), 1213–1218. https://www.sciencedirect.com/science/article/pii/S0022395609000909.

Verlinden, S., Hersen, M., & Thomas, J. (2000). Risk factors in school shootings. *Clinical Psychology Review*, *20*(1), 3–56. https://doi.org/10.1016/S0272-7358(99)00055-0.

Verschuere, B., van Ghesel Grothe, S., Waldorp, L., Watts, A. L., Lilienfeld, S. O., Edens, J. F., … Noordhof, A. (2018). What features of psychopathy might be central? A network analysis of the Psychopathy Checklist-Revised (PCL-R) in three large samples. *Journal of Abnormal Psychology*, *127*(1), 51–65. https://doi.org/10.1037/abn0000315.

Vitale, J. E., Newman, J. P., Serin, R. C., & Bolt, D. M. (2005). Hostile attributions in incarcerated adult male offenders: An exploration of diverse pathways. *Aggressive Behavior: Official Journal of the International Society for Research on Aggression*, *31*(2), 99–115. https://onlinelibrary.wiley.com/doi/pdf/10.1002/ab.20050.

Walters, G. D. (2013). Testing the specificity postulate of the violence graduation hypothesis: Meta-analyses of the animal cruelty–offending relationship. *Aggression and Violent Behavior*, *18*(6), 797–802. https://doi.org/10.1016/j.avb.2013.10.002.

Walters, G. D. (2014). Pathways to early delinquency: Exploring the individual and collective contributions of difficult temperament, low maternal involvement, and externalizing behavior. *Journal of Criminal Justice*, *42*(4), 321–326. https://doi.org/10.1016/j.jcrimjus.2014.04.003.

Woods, A. (2019, March 7). *Man tortured dog by using it as a 'soccer ball': Cops*. The New York Post. https://nypost.com/2019/03/07/man-tortured-dog-by-using-it-as-a-soccer-ball-cops/.

Wright, J., & Hensley, C. (2003). From animal cruelty to serial murder: Applying the graduation hypothesis. *International Journal of Offender Therapy and Comparative Criminology*, *47*(1), 71–88. https://doi.org/10.1177/0306624X02239276.

Treatment of psychopathic offenders: A review of research, past, and current practice

22

Mark E. Olver

Introduction

The treatment of psychopathy is a clinical conundrum that has long been the focus of debate and controversy (Hare, 1996). Individuals with prominent psychopathic traits, and thus those who might most readily be the focus of intervention and risk management services tend to be most highly represented in criminal justice and forensic clinical settings. Even among offender populations, high scores on the tool most frequently used to assess psychopathy, the Hare Psychopathy Checklist-Revised (PCL-R; Hare, 1991, 2003) or its derivatives, are associated with myriad negative criminal justice correlates including violent (Campbell, French, & Gendreau, 2009) and general (Leistico, Salekin, DeCoster, & Rogers, 2008) recidivism, failure on conditional release (Hart, Kropp, & Hare, 1988), institutional misconducts (Guy, Edens, Anthony, & Douglas, 2005), and lengthier c

The people who bear the moniker "psychopath" have frequently been dubbed untreatable. But is this a fair or accurate portrayal, given the available evidence to date? This chapter provides an overview of issues, challenges, and evidence in the treatment of psychopathy. The focus specifically is on adult male offender populations, a broad group among whom psychopathy tends to be most heavily represented. The chapter begins with a review of findings on the response of psychopathic offenders to treatment services, and what aspects of the syndrome seem to have greatest bearing on outcome. The chapter proceeds with a discussion of core themes and findings from aggregate reviews of the psychopathy treatment literature, and then unpacks the features of programs that plainly appear not to work, with supporting evidence, juxtaposed with promising approaches that might work. The chapter then turns to a discussion of Wong's (2015) two-component model for the treatment of psychopathy as an illustrative example of a promising treatment framework, which conceptualizes intervention approaches through the lens of Andrews and Bonta's (2010) risk-need-responsivity model. The chapter concludes with a synopsis of psychopathy treatment studies within the last 20 years that feature programs with elements of the two-component model that examine associations between treatment participation with recidivism outcome. A core argument woven throughout the chapter, as others have similarly argued (Polaschek, 2014; Skeem, Monahan, & Mulvey, 2002), is that psychopathic men are no less treatable than other high-risk offenders, and with well coordinated,

Psychopathy and Criminal Behavior. https://doi.org/10.1016/B978-0-12-811419-3.00001-7

high intensity, responsive programs and follow-up, that these men can make positive changes and move on to lives characterized by less crime and violence.

In this chapter, the PCL-R and its Screening Version (PCL: SV; Hart, Cox, & Hare, 1995) are employed as the operational definition of psychopathy. The PCL-R is a 20-item symptom construct rating scale designed to assess psychopathy. With items scored on a three-point (0,1,2) scale and possible scores ranging from 0 to 40, scores ranging from 25 (often from file review alone) to 30 (file plus interview) have been used to characterize psychopathy. Essential to this operationalization is the PCL-R factor structure. Factor 1 represents the interpersonal and affective features of psychopathy and is subdivided into the Interpersonal (i.e., superficial, grandiose, deceitful, manipulative) and Affective (i.e., lack of remorse, callous, shallow affect, fail to accept responsibility) facets, while Factor 2 represents the chronic antisocial lifestyle of psychopathy and can be subdivided into the Lifestyle (i.e., need for stimulation, parasitic, lacks goals, impulsive, irresponsible) and Antisocial (i.e., poor behavior controls, early behavior problems, juvenile delinquency, release failure, criminal versatility) facets (Hare & Neumann, 2008). With this operationalization in mind, the chapter now turns to a review of treatment responses of high PCL-R scoring men in correctional and forensic contexts.

Psychopathy and response to treatment

Psychopathic individuals are notoriously recalcitrant to treatment and positive behavior change. Even in his early writings, Cleckely (1941) voiced pessimism about the potential for psychopathic offenders to effect positive change from treatment, a sentiment that was further echoed by psychiatrist Benjamin Karpman (1946) who dubbed one subtype (the primary or idiopathic variant) a "virtually incurable case, requiring indefinite institutionalization" (p. 285). Subsequent reviews over the years have voiced similar pessimism, with Suedfeld and Landon (1978) stating that a chapter on effective treatments of psychopathy would be the "shortest" in any psychopathy book. Several years later, Harris and Rice (2006) offered similar remarks about the lack of evidence for effective interventions and noted further that inappropriate services run the risk of even increasing the risk posed to public safety by psychopathic persons.

Some of these concerns have been borne out by evidence, with a few caveats. First, treatment research has demonstrated that high psychopathy men do tend to demonstrate less progress from intervention (Olver, Lewis, & Wong, 2013), engage in disruptive treatment behaviors (Ogloff, Wong, & Greenwood, 1990), form weaker working alliances (DeSorcy, Olver, & Wormith, 2017), and have higher rates of treatment dropout (Olver, Stockdale, & Wormith, 2011). Indeed, a meta-analysis of correctional treatment attrition (Olver et al., 2011) found that dimensional PCL-R score and psychopathy diagnosis, more specifically, were among the strongest predictors of noncompletion of correctional programming.

Deeper examination of the psychopathy treatment literature demonstrates a more nuanced association between psychopathy and treatment response. Various lines of research from a high intensity sexual violence reduction program (the Clearwater

Program) operated by Correctional Service Canada (CSC) has shown that PCL-R Factor 1, and the affective facet specifically, to be uniquely associated with treatment noncompletion (Olver & Wong, 2011), decreased therapeutic progress toward sexual violence risk reduction (Sewall & Olver, 2019), treatment interfering behaviors (Hobson, Shine, & Roberts, 2000), and weaker working alliances, particularly the therapeutic bond or emotional connection with the therapist (DeSorcy et al., 2017). Parallel findings have been obtained from a high intensity violence reduction program (Aggressive Behavioral Control or ABC Program) operated within the same agency, where PCL-R affective facet scores were uniquely associated with decreased therapeutic progress toward violence risk reduction. These findings have therapeutic implications and will be revisited later in this chapter, but identify important strands in the nexus of psychopathy and treatment response.

Psychopathy treatment reviews

There have been some efforts at aggregate reviews of the psychopathy treatment literature, which have generated some important leads. Salekin (2002) conducted an initial review through a meta-analysis of 42 psychopathy treatment studies spanning approximately 60 years of research. Several themes were evident from this heterogeneous literature. For one, there was a staggering range of treatment approaches utilized that included psychoanalytic, therapeutic communities (TCs), and cognitive behavioral treatment (CBT) approaches as the most common, followed by less common approaches that included psychodrama, electroconvulsive shock therapy, rational emotive therapy, actional approaches, personal construct therapy, and even unspecified interventions, among others. A large number of the works featured case studies, there were very few controlled outcome designs, and there was an enormous miscellany of definitions of treatment success (e.g., increased anxiety and capacity for guilt, reduced criminal charges and convictions, improved institutional functioning, improved employment possibilities). Very few of these studies operationalized psychopathy using a PCL measure (in part because most of these studies predated its development), which is a concern, as this raises ambiguity about whether the targeted population was actually being treated. Moreover, very few studies examined criminal recidivism as an outcome variable, which is also concerning, as reduced criminal behavior would seem to be a quite essential benchmark of treatment success. These limitations notwithstanding, Salekin (2002) noted that approximately 60% of studies noted some form of treatment effect and that the notion that psychopathy was untreatable was in his view, not scientifically supported.

Salekin, Worley, and Grimes (2010) later conducted an updated review of studies that were more methodologically rigorous given that they featured contemporary programs, used a PCL-based measure of psychopathy, examined criminal recidivism as a treatment outcome variable, and included a comparison group or a pre-post measure of treatment change that was linked to postprogram criminal outcomes. Of the four studies that Salekin et al. (2010) identified as the strongest methodologically, two studies featuring CBT programs demonstrated evidence for recidivism reduction

(Olver & Wong, 2009; Skeem et al., 2002), although the two studies featuring TC approaches did not (Richards, Casey, & Lucente, 2003; Van Stelle, Bulmer, & Moberg, 2004).

Ineffective treatment approaches: What doesn't work

The aforementioned reviews may give cautious optimism for the treatability of high psychopathy men from correctional or forensic treatment programs; however, not all programs are equal in their content, staffing, and implementation and there is much variability in potential effects. One prominent example of this was a TC operated by the Penetanguishene Mental Health Centre in Ontario Canada in the 1960s and 1970s by psychiatrist Elliott Barker. The men attending services were either remanded awaiting sentencing or trial or found not criminally responsible on account of mental disorder (at the time referred to as Lieutenant Governor's Warrant), and thus had significant mental health as well as criminogenic needs. This was a high intensity and controversial program—the men were locked in small rooms for days on end, often handcuffed in pairs, and left to confront one another on their issues. As needed, hallucinogenic substances (often prescribed by the patients!) were administered to reduce defensiveness, and the men were subjected to group pressures, and sleep deprivation. There was little direct staff involvement, as the patients directed the flow of treatment services.

An evaluation several years after the closure of the program by Rice, Harris, and Cormier (1992) examined 176 men who had attended the program a minimum of 2 years and released to the community, compared to 146 men those who had not attended the program. The men were rated on the PCL-R on the basis of available file information to generate high (PCL-R 25+) and low (PCL-R < 25) psychopathy groups who were either treated or untreated. Low psychopathy men who attended the program had lower rates of return to custody for a new violent offense (22%) compared to those men who did not (39%); however, 77% of high PCL-R scoring men who participated in the TC were convicted for a new violent offense in contrast to 55% of those who did not, a statistically significant difference. The TC seemed to make the high psychopathy men worse! What went wrong?

The brief description of this TC reveals several obvious antitherapeutic elements. One issue that may be less obvious is that the men were overtreated. The risk principle (Andrews & Bonta, 2010) of effective correctional treatment posits that treatment dosage should be matched to the risk level of the individual, such that higher risk cases receive more services while lower risk cases receive few or no services. The risk principle is most effective when baseline risk is accurately assessed and then cases are assigned to the appropriate treatment intensity. In this TC, there is no evidence that the men's level of risk was even assessed initially, let alone that they were assigned to the suitable dosage of treatment. Further, the TC was approximately 80 hours per week—even the highest intensity programs tend to involve 10–15 service hours per week over the course of 6–8 months to enable participants to digest the material, retain concepts, and to practice and generalize new skills (Olver & Wong, 2013). At the rate the TC operated, it would have exceeded the dosage of a high intensity correctional program in the matter of weeks. A related issue is that the TC would have intermixed low- and high-risk offenders—this can undermine treatment effectiveness as lower risk vulnerable men are exposed to negative high role models as well as being at risk for victimization (especially with a lack of staff supervision).

A second set of issues is with respect to the treatment foci of the program. The need principle (Andrews & Bonta, 2010) stipulates that social and psychological characteristics linked to the origin and maintenance of criminal behavior, known as criminogenic needs, should be targeted for intervention. Relevant examples include antisocial attitudes, negative peers, family/marital problems, substance abuse, problems with anger or emotional regulation, unemployment, poor cognitive problem solving, and so on. The targets in the TC tended to focus on honesty of disclosure, authenticity, fostering insight, reducing defensiveness, and increasing accountability; but these domains tend not to be criminogenic. These domains also tend to overlap with the personality and emotional issues, or Factor 1, of PCL-R measured psychopathy. While much confrontation may have occurred, the men would have spent little time developing new prosocial behavior skills and abilities as alternatives to crime and violence. And at the end, their personalities likely also remain unchanged.

A third set of issues was that the interventions were unresponsive, unstructured, and ethically dubious. The responsivity principle (Andrews & Bonta, 2010) stipulates that effective correctional treatment should: (i) employ cognitive behavioral methods of change within the context of a warm, empathic, humane, firm but fair relationship (termed general responsivity), and (ii) be tailored to the unique characteristics of clientele to promote engagement such as individual differences in levels of motivation, learning style, literacy, cognitive ability, personality, culture, and so on (termed specific responsivity). Administration of psychoactive substances to a group of men who may have had fragile mental health and/or a history of substance misuse presents as many ethical challenges as it could be countertherapeutic; the same arguably applies to other coercive properties of the program. The lack of staff oversight and direct involvement, however, in addition to generating possible safety and security risks also represented many missed opportunities for prosocial role modeling, reinforcement of positive behaviors, and direct teaching of prosocial skills, or what have been termed core correctional practices (Andrews & Dowden, 2006).

Promising treatment approaches: What might work

Simourd and Hoge (2000) aptly summarized the psychopathy treatment landscape as one that was "short on quantity and long on lore," with a high representation of programs that did not follow the risk-need-responsivity (or RNR) principles of effective correctional intervention (p. 270). Unfortunately, much of the therapeutic pessimism that remains today is anchored in the Penetanguishene TC program evaluation previously reviewed. The Salekin (2002) and Salekin et al. (2010) reviews also identified candidate interventions and program that might work, which is where we now turn.

Wong (2015) and colleagues (Wong, Gordon, Gu, Lewis, & Olver, 2012; Wong & Hare, 2005) have proposed a two-component model for the treatment of psychopathy grounded in the RNR principles and the two-factor/four-facet PCL-R structural model of psychopathy. Component 1, termed the "interpersonal component" identifies Factor 1 as a set of responsivity issues to be managed, rather than a direct target of intervention. As reviewed earlier, Factor 1, in particular the callous and unemotional features of psychopathy as measured by the affective facet, is associated with a number of negative therapeutic outcomes (e.g., attrition, reduced progress, weaker therapeutic bonds) which provide evidence for its responsivity relevance. That is, there are adaptations that can be made in terms of program delivery and responses by frontline institutional staff to promote client retention in treatment, to maximize gains, and to maintain treatment integrity.

However, given that the extant literature has demonstrated that Factor 1 tends to change little over the lifespan (Harpur & Hare, 1994) and tends to be a weak (or at least inconsistent) predictor of violence (Yang, Wong, & Coid, 2010), this renders Factor 1 a less than viable treatment target. Rather, treatment should target something that is both changeable and predictive of important outcomes. As such, Component 2, termed the "criminogenic component," asserts that Factor 2, that is, lifestyle instability and antisociality should be the focus of risk reduction interventions and targeted directly per the risk and need principles. Extant research shows that Factor 2 by contrast tends to show age-related declines (Harpur & Hare, 1994), is robustly predictive of violence and other correctional outcomes (Yang et al., 2010), and is highly correlated with measures of criminogenic need (e.g., Douglas, Yeomans, & Boer, 2005; Olver & Wong, 2009; Wong & Gordon, 2006).

Implementation of the two-component model: Component 1

How is the two-component model, based in RNR, executed? Component 1, managing Factor 1 as a responsivity issue is not easy, and it is a responsivity issue for good reason. Psychopathic men are frequently disruptive in group; they may play games and pit staff against each other, antagonize staff and copatients, violate institutional rules, lie and deceive throughout therapy, or simply fail to display desired markers of progress. They may violate boundaries, respond with anger and abuse if confronted or challenged, or engage in manipulative tactics to subvert authority and meet their needs. Psychopathic clients can be intimidating to work with, and their engagement in what at times seem to be relentless therapy interfering behaviors can conjure up a variety of emotional reactions: (i) staff may feel angry and lash out in unprofessional ways, (ii) they may feel hopeless and helpless and feel victimized by lies and deceit, or (iii) some may be vulnerable to boundary interfering and manipulative tactics of psychopathic men and prone to develop personal or romantic feelings for them. All these taken in tandem make Factor 1 an essential set of responsivity issues to manage, but also make psychopathic men at risk for the negative therapeutic outcomes discussed earlier.

One critical element is staff training and to learn and understand the nature of psychopathy per the two-component model and the PCL-R operationalization. In this manner, staff learn to expect therapy interfering behaviors and are less likely to be caught off guard when they encounter them (i.e., to be forewarned is to be forearmed). This also means that they are likely to respond in a professional, effective, safe, and ethical manner. In addition to changing the mind-set, this involves exercising a good deal of patience, having realistic expectations ("Rome wasn't built in a day"), having open lines of communication, as well as mutual support among staff to create an environment that is conducive to open disclosure and honesty about client interactions and the clinicians' personal reactions. Communication and routine documentation are also quite critical for patients to know that staff talk to each other and support one another.

Second, staff education can promote the formation of effective boundaries such that staff take care to not share personal information (or at least very minimal), are cognizant of patient overtures that may involve boundary or rule violations, and for staff to respond appropriately when they do occur (e.g., refusing to keep secrets or do special favors). Third, staff learn to manage their countertransference, that is, their emotional reactions to the patient. Staff have a critical opportunity as professional role models for these men and to lead by example in the ways that interact with them—remaining calm, professional, nondefensive, and avoiding being lured into power and control battles. Fourth, staff may also focus on different elements of the working alliance. Bordin's (1979) model conceptualizes the alliance in terms of tasks (mutually agreed upon activities in therapy), bond (emotional connection with the therapist), and goals (mutually agreed outcomes of therapy). Extant research (DeSorcy et al., 2017) demonstrates that psychopathic men tend to struggle more with the emotional bond of therapy; however, the same work demonstrates that there may be greater hope in terms of tasks and goals. As such, rather than trying to foster empathy or a deep emotional connection with one's client, focusing on the tasks of targeting criminogenic needs and the goals of violence reduction and remaining out of prison likely have greater promise. A final consideration for Component 1 discussed here is use of motivational interviewing or MI (Miller & Rollnick, 2002), which can be summed up in five succinct principles: express empathy (i.e., provide validation), develop discrepancy (i.e., point out how treatment interfering behaviors are sabotaging one's own goals and interests), rolling with resistance (i.e., constructively work with resistance to use it as momentum for change), support self-efficacy (i.e., point out and reinforce positive changes), and avoid argumentation (i.e., refrain from getting caught up in power and control battles). MI can help increase motivation to change, but it also represents a constructive and clinically effective means of responding to challenging or resistant clients.

In short, managing Factor 1 is as much a therapeutic attitude as it is a set of clinically helpful behaviors. Men should not be discharged for displaying the very issues that got them referred for services to begin with; such treatment interfering behaviors and challenges are a direct expression of problems that require intervention, and the potential for change can only occur when difficult clients are retained in treatment despite the challenges they bring.

Implementation of the two-component model: Component 2

The implementation of Component 2 per the risk and need principles involves adherence to standard CBT correctional approaches. Per the risk principle, most psychopathic offenders will be high risk, at least for general reoffending and often for violence as well (i.e., otherwise the PCL-R would not predict these outcomes so well), and as such, they will likely require a high intensity programming (e.g., violence or sexual violence reduction, depending on the offense history and treatment needs), as well as transition services to the community. Per the need principle, psychopathic offenders also tend to have the same set of criminogenic needs as other offenders; the only difference is that the needs may be more severe and are likely greater in number (Simourd & Hoge, 2000). Negative peers, substance problems, relationship issues, poor anger control, overreliance on aggression, poor problem solving, and lack of marketable employment skills abound and are no less relevant for psychopathic offenders than they are for other justice involved men. As such, large scale, comprehensive, multimodal treatment programs that are residential, high intensity, well staffed, and target a range of criminogenic needs are ideal, but other more focused groups or interventions (e.g., substance abuse programming, educational upgrading) can also be helpful and appropriate.

Critical to the implementation of Component 2 per the risk and need principles is a comprehensive risk assessment to assess level of risk and potential for recidivism, to identify criminogenic needs to be targeted for correctional programming, and to evaluate changes in risk and potential for conditional release or follow-up services postintervention. Use of dynamic risk tools such as the Violence Risk Scale (Wong & Gordon, 1999–2003), Level of Service Inventory-Revised (Andrews & Bonta, 1995), or the Historical Clinical Risk-20 Version 3 (Douglas, Hart, Webster, & Belfrage, 2011) among other evidence informed dynamic tools are viable candidates.

This naturally begs the question as to how does one know when a psychopathic client has changed? When is a client merely talking the talk as opposed to walking the walk? Gordon and Wong (2010) use the term offense analogue behaviors (OABs) and offense replacement behaviors (ORBs) to denote risk-relevant behaviors displayed in an institutional setting that could signal when criminogenic issues remain or when they might be improving. In short, OABs are manifestations of criminogenic needs in a secure environment where opportunities to offend might be less present and security is tighter. Examples such as violating unit rules, dealing in contraband, physical altercations or verbal abuse of staff or inmates, failure to cooperate with correctional or release planning, or associating with notorious negative influences within the institution are examples of OABs. By contrast, maintaining prosocial and assertive interactions, avoiding conflict or deleterious influences in the institution, maintaining institutional school or work, cooperating with correctional programming and release planning, and abiding by institutional rules are all examples of ORBs and indicators of risk reduction. Treatment is intended to target and reduce the frequency of OABs, and to increase the frequency of ORBs, which in essence are prosocial skills and strategies indicative of reduced risk. The Violence Risk Scale (VRS) and the Violence Risk Scale-Sexual Offense version (VRS-SO; Wong, Olver, Nicholaichuk, & Gordon, 2003/2017), in addition to tracking and measuring change from treatment or other change agents, also have OAB/ORB guides to aid in the detection of positive changes or maintenance of negative behaviors. Such considerations have equal relevance for high psychopathy men with the targeting and monitoring of OABs and ORBs being an important component of a risk reduction regime for this population per Component 2.

Empirical support for promising treatment approaches

Although the treatment of psychopathic offenders has long been steeped in controversy and shrouded in mystery, correctional systems have been treating, releasing, and managing psychopathic offenders in the community since antiquity (irrespective of whether they were assessed as such). Not all psychopathic offenders inexorably reoffend, violently or otherwise (Burt, Olver, & Wong, 2016). And tentative evidence does exist from programs implementing something akin to the two-component model that there may be promise to these efforts.

Many developments have occurred within the sex offender treatment field. For instance, Olver and Wong (2009), in a sample of 156 men who attended a high intensity sexual violence reduction program (the Clearwater Program referenced earlier), found that while high PCL-R scoring men did evince higher rates of program noncompletion, that most (73.3%) of these men actually successfully completed the program. In other words, many, if not most, high psychopathy men if given the appropriate response and structure are capable of completing a correctional program. The men were also assessed for their risk of sexual violence from file information using a dynamic risk-need tool—the VRS-SO—and followed up in the community an average of 10 years postrelease. Changes in sexual violence risk, as measured by the VRS-SO were significantly associated with decreased sexual and violent recidivism after accounting for baseline pretreatment risk and controlling for PCL-R total score. In addition, VRS-SO change scores were significantly associated with decreased violence among high psychopathy men (i.e., PCL-R 25+), and those men who completed treatment had lower rates of violent recidivism than those high psychopathy men who did not.

Sewall and Olver (2019) expanded this line of research to almost double the sample size ($N=296$) of men rated on the PCL-R and VRS-SO who attended the Clearwater Program and extended the follow-up time to 18 years postrelease. VRS-SO change scores remained significantly associated with decreased sexual and violent recidivism upon follow-up after controlling for psychopathy (PCL-R total score) and baseline pretreatment risk (VRS-SO pretreatment score and Sex Offender Risk Appraisal Guide score). A further interesting finding was that the PCL-R total score was not significantly associated with change—that is, high psychopathy men registered no less change than lower psychopathy men—even though scores on the affective facet specifically were associated with less change and hence decreased therapeutic gain.

Elsewhere two other sexual violence programs in CSC have examined the association between psychopathy, treatment response, and subsequent recidivism. Langton, Barbaree, Harkins, and Peacock (2006) examined the association of PCL-R measured psychopathy and treatment behavior with sexual and violent recidivism in a sample of 418 federal sex offenders through the Warkworth Sexual Behavior Clinic in Ontario, Canada. A psychopathy-treatment interaction was found such that high psychopathy men (PCL-R 25+) who displayed poor treatment behavior had a significantly higher and faster rate of sexual recidivism over an average 5 years follow-up than high psychopathy men who displayed positive treatment behavior. (There was no difference among the low psychopathy groups.) Further, in Ontario's Regional Treatment Centre Sex Offender Treatment Program, Looman, Abracen, Serin, and Marquis (2005) examined the association between PCL-R measured psychopathy, risk reduction, and recidivism in a sample of 99 high risk-high need federal sex offenders. High psychopathy men (PCL-R 25+) who were also evaluated in their posttreatment reports to have reduced their risk had lower (although not statistically significant) rates of general violent recidivism (30%) in the community postrelease, than those high psychopathy men who were appraised as not having lowered their risk (50%) after treatment.

The violent offender and psychiatric treatment literature also suggest some potential for optimism. In one of the earliest psychopathy treatment outcome studies, in a sample of 871 civil psychiatric outpatients, Skeem et al. (2002) found that attendance in a CBT-based program was significantly associated with decreased violent recidivism over the ensuing follow-up after controlling for PCL: SV score. Some years later, Olver et al. (2013) examined psychopathy and treatment response in a Canadian sample of 152 violent federal offenders who attended a high intensity CBT-based violence reduction program (the ABC program as referenced earlier) and followed up an average of 5 years in the community postrelease. Changes in risk, measured from pre to posttreatment on the VRS, were significantly associated with decreased violent recidivism in the community upon follow-up after controlling for PCL-R score.

Finally, Wong et al. (2012) examined a series of recidivism outcomes in a matched sample of 32 high psychopathy men (*M* PCL-R = 28.6, *SD* = 2.0) who attended the ABC Program compared to an untreated control group of 32 men (*M* PCL-R = 28.0, *SD* = 2.3) matched on PCL-R score, risk level, demographic, and offense history variables. Although the treated group did not differ significantly from the controls in terms of their likelihood of returning to prison, number of new offenses, or even time to new offense, treated men had significantly shorter cumulative and aggregate sentences; in fact, treated men overall served approximately half the total amount of time in prison for new offense than the untreated men. The results are consistent with a harm reduction perspective; that is, rather than eradicating recidivism altogether, violence reduction treatment was associated with a reduction in the severity of new offenses as evidenced by shorter sentence lengths for subsequent cumulative new offenses.

Conclusions

The treatment of psychopathic offenders has been the focus of pessimism and debate. Psychopathic offenders do evidence higher rates of most recidivism outcomes, can be challenging to engage therapeutically, and are often resistant to change. The pessimism is only exacerbated unfortunately against a backdrop of inappropriate interventions and antiquated programs, which may foster little change in their clientele at best or increase the severity of the problem at worst. Recent developments in the past 20 years has given some room for cautious optimism, prompting a shift from the notion that "nothing works" to one of "what might work?" Psychopathic offenders have routinely been treated, released, and managed in the community by correctional systems, and treatment advocates assert that there is little evidence to suggest that psychopathic offenders are any less treatable than other high risk-high need offenders. Wong's (2015) two-component model conceptualizes the treatment of psychopathy through the lens of the RNR model, where Factor 1 is managed as a responsivity issue while Factor 2 and risk-relevant criminogenic needs are targeted though CBT-based services as usual with high-risk offenders per the risk and need principles. The emerging literature to date suggests that the RNR principles appear no less relevant for high psychopathy individuals, and that completion of evidence informed programs has associations with reductions in sexual and violent recidivism for correctional and psychiatric populations. These advances, notwithstanding, the debate regarding the treatability of this challenging population wages on, underscoring the need for continued quality services and rigorous evaluation.

References

Andrews, D. A., & Bonta, J. (1995). *Level of service inventory-revised (LSI-R): An offender assessment system. User's guide*. Toronto, ON: Multi-Health Systems.

Andrews, D. A., & Bonta, J. (2010). Rehabilitating criminal justice policy and practice. *Psychology, Public Policy, and Law*, *16*, 39–55.

Andrews, D. A., & Dowden, C. (2006). Risk principle of case classification in correctional treatment. *International Journal of Offender Therapy and Comparative Criminology*, *50*, 88–100.

Bordin, E. S. (1979). The generalizability of the psychoanalytic concept of the working alliance. *Psychotherapy: Theory, Research, and Practice*, *16*, 252–260.

Burt, G. N., Olver, M. E., & Wong, S. C. P. (2016). Investigating characteristics of the nonrecidivating psychopathic offender. *Criminal Justice and Behavior*, *43*, 1741–1760.

Campbell, M. A., French, S., & Gendreau, P. (2009). The prediction of violence in adult offenders: A meta-analytic comparison of instruments and methods of assessment. *Criminal Justice and Behavior*, *36*, 567–590.

Cleckely, H. (1941). *The mask of sanity*. St. Louis, MO: Mosby.

DeSorcy, D. R., Olver, M. E., & Wormith, J. S. (2017). Working alliance and psychopathy: Linkages to treatment outcome in a sample of treated sexual offenders. *Journal of Interpersonal Violence*, *35*(7–8), 1739–1760.

Douglas, K. S., Hart, S. D., Webster, C. D., & Belfrage, H. (2011). *Historical clinical risk management (Version 3): Professional guidelines for evaluating risk of violence [Draft 2.1]*. Vancouver, BC: Mental Health, Law, and Policy Institute, Simon Fraser University.

Douglas, K. S., Yeomans, M., & Boer, D. P. (2005). Comparative validity analysis of multiple measures of violence risk in a sample of criminal offenders. *Criminal Justice and Behavior*, *32*, 479–510.

Gordon, A., & Wong, S. C. P. (2010). Offense analogue behaviours as indicator of criminogenic need and treatment progress in custodial settings. In M. Daffern, L. Jones, & J. Shine (Eds.), *Offence paralleling behaviour: A case formulation approach to offender assessment and intervention* (pp. 171–183). West Sussex, UK: Wiley–Blackwell.

Guy, L. S., Edens, J. F., Anthony, C., & Douglas, K. S. (2005). Does psychopathy predict institutional misconduct among adults? A meta-analytic investigation. *Journal of Consulting and Clinical Psychology*, *73*, 1056–1064.

Hare, R. D. (1991). *The Hare psychopathy checklist-revised*. Toronto, ON: Multi-Health Systems.

Hare, R. D. (1996). Psychopathy, a clinical construct whose time has come. *Criminal Justice and Behavior*, *23*, 25–54.

Hare, R. D. (2003). *Manual for the revised psychopathy checklist* (2nd ed.). Toronto, ON: Multi-Health Systems.

Hare, R. D., & Neumann, C. S. (2008). Psychopathy as a clinical and empirical construct. *Annual Review of Clinical Psychology*, *4*, 217–246.

Harpur, T. J., & Hare, R. D. (1994). Assessment of psychopathy as a function of age. *Journal of Abnormal Psychology*, *103*, 604–609.

Harris, G., & Rice, M. (2006). Treatment of psychopathy: A review of empirical findings. In C. Patrick (Ed.), *Handbook of psychopathy* (pp. 555–572). New York, NY: Guilford.

Hart, S. D., Cox, D. N., & Hare, R. D. (1995). *The Hare psychopathy checklist: Screening version (PCL: SV)*. Toronto, ON: Multi-Health Systems.

Hart, S. D., Kropp, P. R., & Hare, R. D. (1988). Performance of psychopaths following conditional release from prison. *Journal of Consulting and Clinical Psychology*, *56*, 227–232.

Hobson, J., Shine, J., & Roberts, R. (2000). How do psychopaths behave in a prison therapeutic community? *Psychology Crime and Law*, *6*, 139–154.

Karpman, B. (1946). Psychopathy in the scheme of human typology. *Journal of Nervous and Mental Disease*, *103*, 276–288.

Langton, C. M., Barbaree, H. E., Harkins, L., & Peacock, E. J. (2006). Sex offenders' response to treatment and its association with recidivism as a function of psychopathy. *Sexual Abuse: A Journal of Research and Treatment*, *18*, 99–120.

Leistico, A. R., Salekin, R. T., DeCoster, J., & Rogers, R. (2008). A large-scale meta-analysis relating the Hare measures of psychopathy to antisocial conduct. *Law and Human Behavior*, *32*, 28–45.

Looman, J., Abracen, J., Serin, R., & Marquis, P. (2005). Psychopathy, treatment change, and recidivism in high-risk, high-need sexual offenders. *Journal of Interpersonal Violence*, *20*, 549–568.

Miller, W. R., & Rollnick, S. (2002). *Motivational interviewing: Preparing people for change* (2nd ed.). New York, NY: The Guilford Press.

Ogloff, J. D., Wong, S., & Greenwood, M. A. (1990). Treating criminal psychopaths in a therapeutic community program. *Behavioral Sciences & the Law*, *8*, 181–190.

Olver, M. E., Lewis, K., & Wong, S. C. P. (2013). Risk reduction treatment of high risk psychopathic offenders: The relationship of psychopathy and treatment change to violent recidivism. *Personality Disorders, Theory, Research, and Treatment*, *4*, 160–167.

Olver, M. E., Stockdale, K. C., & Wormith, J. C. (2011). A meta-analysis of predictors of offender treatment attrition and its relationship to recidivism. *Journal of Consulting and Clinical Psychology*, 6–21.

Olver, M. E., & Wong, S. C. (2009). Therapeutic responses of psychopathic sexual offenders: Treatment attrition, therapeutic change, and long-term recidivism. *Journal of Consulting and Clinical Psychology*, *77*, 328.

Olver, M. E., & Wong, S. C. P. (2011). Predictors of sex offender treatment dropout: Psychopathy, sex offender risk, and responsivity implications. *Psychology Crime and Law*, *17*, 457–471.

Olver, M. E., & Wong, S. C. P. (2013). Treatment programs for high risk sexual offenders: Program and offender characteristics, attrition, treatment change, and recidivism. *Aggression and Violent Behavior, 18*, 579–591.

Olver, M. E., & Wong, S. C. P. (2015). Short and long-term recidivism prediction of the PCL-R and the effects of age: A 24-year follow-up. *Personality Disorders, Theory, Research, and Treatment, 6*, 97–105.

Polaschek, D. L. L. (2014). Adult criminals with psychopathy: Common beliefs about treatability and change have little empirical support. *Current Directions in Psychological Science, 23*, 296–301.

Rice, M. E., Harris, G. T., & Cormier, C. A. (1992). An evaluation of a maximum security therapeutic community for psychopaths and other mentally disordered offenders. *Law and Human Behavior, 16*, 399–412.

Richards, H. J., Casey, J. O., & Lucente, S. W. (2003). Psychopathy and treatment response in incarcerated female substance abusers. *Criminal Justice and Behavior, 30*, 251–276.

Salekin, R. (2002). Psychopathy and therapeutic pessimism: Clinical lore or clinical reality? *Clinical Psychology Review, 22*, 79–112.

Salekin, R., Worley, C., & Grimes, R. (2010). Treatment of psychopathy: A review and brief introduction to the mental model approach for psychopathy. *Behavioral Sciences & the Law, 28*, 235–266.

Sewall, L. A., & Olver, M. E. (2019). Psychopathy and treatment outcome: Results from a sexual violence reduction program. *Personality Disorders, Theory, Research, and Treatment, 10*, 59–69.

Simourd, D. J., & Hoge, R. D. (2000). Criminal psychopathy: A risk-and-need perspective. *Criminal Justice and Behavior, 27*, 256–272.

Skeem, J. L., Monahan, J., & Mulvey, E. P. (2002). Psychopathy, treatment involvement, and subsequent violence among civil psychiatric patients. *Law and Human Behavior, 26*, 577–603.

Suedfeld, P., & Landon, P. B. (1978). Approaches to treatment. In R. D. Hare, & D. Schalling (Eds.), *Psychopathic behavior: Approaches to research* (pp. 347–376). Chichester: Wiley.

Van Stelle, K. R., Bulmer, C., & Moberg, D. P. (2004). Treatment retention of dually diagnosed offenders in an institutional therapeutic community. *Behavioral Sciences & the Law, 22*, 585–597.

Wong, S. C. P. (2015). Treatment of violence prone individuals with psychopathic personality traits. In J. Livesley, G. Dimaggio, & J. Clarkin (Eds.), *Integrated treatment of personality disorder: A modular approach* (pp. 345–376). New York, NY: Guilford Press.

Wong, S., & Gordon, A. (1999–2003). *The violence risk scale*. Saskatoon, SK: Regional Psychiatric Centre and University of Saskatchewan.

Wong, S. C. P., & Gordon, A. (2006). The validity and reliability of the violence risk scale: A treatment-friendly violence risk assessment tool. *Psychology, Public Policy, and Law, 12*, 279–309.

Wong, S. C. P., Gordon, A., Gu, D., Lewis, K., & Olver, M. E. (2012). The effectiveness of violence reduction treatment for psychopathic offenders: Empirical evidence and a treatment model. *International Journal of Forensic Mental Health, 11*, 336–349.

Wong, S., & Hare, R. D. (2005). *Guidelines for a psychopathy treatment program*. Toronto, ON: Multi-Health Systems.

Wong, S., Olver, M., Nicholaichuk, T., & Gordon, A. (2003/2017). *The violence risk scale: Sexual offense version (VRS-SO)*. Saskatoon, SK: Regional Psychiatric Centre and University of Saskatchewan.

Yang, M., Wong, S. C. P., & Coid, J. (2010). The efficacy of violence prediction: A meta-analytic comparison of nine risk assessment instruments. *Psychological Bulletin, 136*, 740–767.

Afterword—Psychopathy: Key unresolved questions

Scott O. Lilienfeld

As the chapters in this stimulating and wide-ranging volume demonstrate, the construct of psychopathy is alive and well. As recently as the 1970s, Hervey Cleckley, whom we might regard as the grandfather of the contemporary psychopathy field, told Robert Hare, whom many would consider the father of the contemporary psychopathy field, that he felt like a "lone voice crying in the wilderness" in the waning years of his career (Lilienfeld, Watts, Smith, Patrick, & Hare, 2018). Despite the success of his seminal book, *The Mask of Sanity* (Cleckley, 1941/1982), Cleckley was deeply disappointed that the concept he had helped to promulgate had received so little attention from psychologists, psychiatrists, criminologists, and the general public.

Yet were Cleckley alive today and able to read this book, he would surely feel vindicated. This book's chapters are remarkably diverse, illustrating the penetration of the psychopathy construct into basic and applied domains as multifarious as clinical assessment, emotional functioning, neural correlates, development, hostage taking, crime scene evidence, gang membership, cybercrime, animal cruelty, terrorism, and human trafficking. To the extent that one indicator of the health of a scientific construct or theory is its fruitfulness (Kuhn, 1970) or deductive fertility (Meehl, 2002), that is, the extent to which it leads researchers into productive new territory, the psychopathy construct would appear to be in good scientific shape. As I will soon argue, however, a number of pressing questions regarding this construct remain.

What have we learned?

So, what have we learned about psychopathy in the more than two and half decades since Cleckley's death in 1984? We have learned a number of useful things, although perhaps fewer than we might have hoped given the more than six decades that have elapsed since the seminal laboratory study of Lykken (1957), which launched the systematic research investigation of psychopathy. I will briefly highlight three of them here (see also Lilienfeld, in press, for a list of the major knowns and unknowns in psychopathy research).

First, we have learned that whatever psychopathy is, it shades imperceptibly into normality. The results of numerous taxometric studies (Meehl & Golden, 1982) of both interview-based and self-report psychopathy measures (e.g., Edens, Marcus,

Lilienfeld, & Poythress Jr, 2006; Edens, Marcus, & Vaughn, 2011; Guay, Ruscio, Knight, & Hare, 2007; Marcus, John, & Edens, 2004; Murrie et al., 2007; Walters, Brinkley, Magaletta, & Diamond, 2008; Walters, Duncan, & Mitchell-Perez, 2007) and even of paralimbic brain regions ostensibly linked to psychopathy (Walters, Ermer, Knight, & Kiehl, 2015) demonstrate that psychopathy is underpinned by one or more dimensions rather than by a taxon, that is, a category in nature. Seara-Cardoso and colleagues (Chapter 3) similarly observe that the functional brain imaging correlates of psychopathy are similar in offender and community samples, again broadly consistent with a dimensional perspective on this condition. The finding that psychopathy is dimensional rather than taxonic probably strikes many readers as counterintuitive, and understandably so: The psychopaths who come readily to our minds, whether they be serial killers, ruthless corporate executives, or brutal dictators, are typically the most extreme or outlandish. It should perhaps be noted that, contrary to the assertion of Smith and colleagues (Chapter 1), a condition cannot be simultaneously a dimension and a taxon; one precludes the other. Furthermore, the finding that psychopathy is dimensional vitiates these authors' argument that "A designation of psychopathy is appropriate only when enough individual traits are fully present." The data are now clear that this categorical designation is arbitrary from a scientific standpoint. The use of cut-off scores on the PCL-R and other psychopathy measures has scant scientific justification, and is likely to diminish statistical power given the well-known psychometric costs of dichotomization of continuous distributions (Rucker, McShane, & Preacher, 2015; Streiner, 2002).

Second, we have learned that psychopathy is not merely dimensional, but multidimensional (Lilienfeld, 2018; Patrick, Fowles, & Krueger, 2009). Many authors (e.g., Deming & Koenigs, 2020; Poeppl et al., 2019) continue to treat psychopathy as a unidimensional, monolithic entity. But growing data demonstrate that the subdimensions of psychopathy not only differ in their external correlates, but sometimes fractionate in opposing directions with them (Lilienfeld et al., 2019). As Netjes and colleagues note (Chapter 4), the interpersonal-affective and antisocial-lifestyle features of psychopathy tend to display markedly different implications for emotional processing. For example, the former subdimensions are often tied to diminished reactivity to fear-related stimuli and to diminished activity in brain regions (e.g., amygdala) linked to fear processing, whereas the latter subdimensions often display the reverse pattern of results (e.g., Hyde, Byrd, Votruba-Drzal, Hariri, & Manuck, 2014). The lessons for assessment and research are clear. Practitioners and researchers should be certain to measure and account for psychopathy subdimensions and to avoid exclusive reliance on psychopathy total scores, a practice that risks diluting or obscuring differential relations between these subdimensions and psychologically important external correlates. Further, the multidimensionality of psychopathy may raise questions concerning the hypothesis that psychopathy provides a unified theory of crime (see DeLisi and Fox, Chapter 16): Can psychopathy constitute a unified theory of crime if it itself is not uniform?

Third, we have learned that psychopathy is not independent of the general personality realm. Psychopathy appears be a constellation or configuration of several well-established personality dimensions, especially reversed conscientiousness and reversed agreeableness (Lilienfeld, Watts, Smith, Berg, & Latzman, 2015; Lynam & Derefinko, 2006; Miller, Sleep, Crowe, & Lynam, 2020). Nevertheless, the relevance of other personality dimensions, especially those ostensibly tied to largely adaptive psychological functioning, such as surgent (agentic) extraversion and reversed neuroticism, remains a lightning rod of active scientific debate (Lilienfeld et al., 2012; Lynam & Miller, 2012; Miller et al., 2020; Sörman et al., 2016). As Farrington and Bergstrom (Chapter 4) point out, the discipline of psychopathy remains largely disconnected from the study of general personality, and relatively few researchers administer indices of normal personality traits in conjunction with measures of psychopathy. I agree with Farrington and Bergstrom that "It is unfortunate that the study of psychopathy tends to have been divorced from the study of normative personality" (see also Veal and Ogloff, Chapter 7). As a consequence of this state of neglect, it is often difficult or impossible to ascertain the extent to which findings in the psychopathy literature, including those linking psychopathy to one or more variants of criminal behavior, are attributable to one or more general personality dimensions as opposed to psychopathy per se.

Psychopathy: Three key unresolved questions

The chapters of this book, rich and informative as they are, leave us with at least three unresolved questions. These questions, which perhaps are not asked frequently enough, pose broader challenges for the field of psychopathy.

First, consistent with this book's title, many of the chapters underscore the vast reach of the psychopathy construct into the domain of criminal behavior. Indeed, it is difficult to think of a single major category of crime that is untouched by psychopathy or its constituent traits. Still, the extent to which measures of psychopathy predict and explain criminal behavior above and beyond criminal behavior itself remains a vexing point of contention. As Veal and Ogloff (Chapter 7) observe, psychopathy is a consistent and robust predictor of criminal risk (see also Leistico, Salekin, DeCoster, & Rogers, 2008). Yet, as these authors also note, the incremental validity of the Psychopathy Checklist-Revised (PCL-R; Hare, 2003), the most extensively validated psychopathy measure in forensic contexts, for predicting criminological risk above and beyond actuarial risk indices (which largely comprise indices of past criminal behavior) may be less pronounced than assumed by many authors (see also Walters, 2012). Early assertions (see Gendreau, Goggin, & Smith, 2002, for a discussion) that the PCL-R is an "unparalleled" predictor of offender risk have not stood the test of time. Some of the difficulty here surely stems from criterion contamination given that a number of items on the PCL-R and some other widely used psychopathy indices themselves reflect antisocial and in some cases criminal behavior (Carre, Mueller, Schleicher, & Jones, 2018). A key challenge for future psychopathy researchers will should be to demonstrate that psychopathy and its component traits are not superfluous in predicting and understanding deviant behaviors above and beyond alternative measures of these behaviors themselves. For example, meta-analytic evidence suggests that the PCL-R's affective and antisocial behavior facets may possess validity in predicting sexual deviance (Hawes, Boccaccini, & Murrie, 2013), and future research should examine the extent to which these facets afford helpful information not provided by general criminal risk measures.

Second, it perhaps goes without saying that the etiology (causation) of psychopathy remains elusive. At the risk of overstatement, is debatable whether we are any closer to an understanding of the causes of psychopathy than we were at the time of Cleckley's death in 1984. This has not been for want of trying. Over the past half century or more, the psychopathy field has witnessed a parade of initially promising etiological models: low empathy, low fear, cortical immaturity, inadequate cortical arousal, deficient response modulation, deficient violence inhibition mechanism, left-hemisphere dysfunction, afferent inhibition of cues to aversive stimuli, abnormalities in specific amygdala nuclei, paralimbic dysfunction, and so on (see Patrick, 2016, for a comprehensive overview). Most or all of these models may capture a kernel of the truth, but none has emerged as a comprehensive model of psychopathy. Perhaps the time has come to question whether such etiological endeavors are likely to pay off given the multifactorial nature of psychopathy (Lilienfeld, Smith, & Watts, 2016). With precious few historical exceptions, such as general paresis (Maj, 2013), efforts to link unitary etiological agents to any given mental disorder have had a decidedly poor track record (Kendler, 2012). Rather than continue the search for a unifying cause underlying a multidimensional entity, it may be more fruitful to deconstruct psychopathy into its subcomponents (e.g., Patrick et al., 2009) and to instead focus our etiological efforts on these subcomponents.

Third and finally, the burgeoning evidence of close empirical linkages between psychopathy and general personality (e.g., Farrington and Bergstrom, Chapter 4) raises the important question of whether psychopathy is as distinctive an entity as many of us, myself included, have long assumed. Rather than a unique condition warranting unique etiological models, evolutionary models, laboratory paradigms, treatment approaches, and the like, might psychopathy instead be better conceptualized as a constellation or configuration of traits (e.g., reversed conscientiousness, reversed agreeableness, high surgent extraversion) that have long been familiar to personality psychologists (Lilienfeld et al., 2019)? And if so, should the discipline of psychopathy be merged into the broader discipline of trait psychology?

Psychopathy scholars must be wary of committing what I term the *sui generis fallacy*: the error of assuming that any given mental disorder should be approached separately from all others, as well as from personality psychology at large. Once we devote a substantial chunk of our careers to investigating or treating Disorder X, we want to believe that this disorder is somehow unique. Furthermore, we may bristle at the implication that this disorder is "merely" one composite among others of well-established personality trait dimensions. This suggestion may seem to undermine our identity as research experts or clinical specialists in this disorder.

My own view, which is probably shared by few of my colleagues in the psychopathy field, is that psychopathy is indeed unique, but not in the way we have typically assumed. Instead, my colleagues and I have proposed that psychopathy is distinctive not in its etiology, but in its *interpersonal impact on us*. That is, psychopathy is a unique configuration of attributes comprising (a) superficial charm and a propensity to make an initial positive impression on others conjoined with (b) profound affective deficits and poor impulse control (Lilienfeld et al., 2019). This paradoxical combination of traits, underscored by Cleckley (1941/1982) and others (e.g., Patrick, 2006), is especially interpersonally impactful because it heightens the risk of deception, manipulation, seduction, and the like. We are especially likely to be fooled by people with this combination of traits because they present us with a misleading façade of psychological health, one that conceals a deeply pathological interior (Ten Brinke et al., 2017). In short, psychopaths are the quintessential social chameleons.

It remains to be seen whether this interpersonal model of psychopathy is correct. Still, it seems likely that a better understanding of how psychopathic behaviors play out in the context of everyday social interactions will be essential in helping us to solve the puzzle of how psychopathy increases risk for criminal behavior in its manifold forms. With its broad coverage of the varied intersections between psychopathy and crime across differing levels of analysis, this book offers a valuable roadmap for future scholarly inquiry in this regard.

References

Carre, J. R., Mueller, S. M., Schleicher, K. M., & Jones, D. N. (2018). Psychopathy and deviant workplace behavior: A comparison of two psychopathy models. *Journal of Personality Disorders*, *32*, 242–261. https://doi.org/10.1521/pedi_2017_31_296.

Cleckley, H. (1941/1982). *The mask of sanity*. Augusta, GA: Emily Cleckley Publishers.

Deming, P., & Koenigs, M. (2020). Functional neural correlates of psychopathy: A meta-analysis of MRI data. *Translational Psychiatry*, *10*, 1–8. https://doi.org/10.1038/s41398-020-0816-8.

Edens, J. F., Marcus, D. K., Lilienfeld, S. O., & Poythress, N. G., Jr. (2006). Psychopathic, not psychopath: Taxometric evidence for the dimensional structure of psychopathy. *Journal of Abnormal Psychology*, *115*, 131–144. https://doi.org/10.1037/0021-843x.115.1.131.

Edens, J. F., Marcus, D. K., & Vaughn, M. G. (2011). Exploring the taxometric status of psychopathy among youthful offenders: Is there a juvenile psychopath taxon? *Law and Human Behavior*, *35*, 13–24. https://doi.org/10.1007/s10979-010-9230-8.

Gendreau, P., Goggin, C., & Smith, P. (2002). Is the PCL-R really the "unparalleled" measure of offender risk? A lesson in knowledge cumulation. *Criminal Justice and Behavior*, *29*, 397–426. https://doi.org/10.1177/0093854802029004004.

Guay, J.-P., Ruscio, J., Knight, R. A., & Hare, R. D. (2007). A taxometric analysis of the latent structure of psychopathy: Evidence for dimensionality. *Journal of Abnormal Psychology*, *116*, 701–716. https://doi.org/10.1037/0021-843X.116.4.701.

Hare, R. D. (2003). *The Hare Psychopathy Checklist-Revised (PCL-R)*. Toronto, CA: Multihealth Systems.

Hawes, S. W., Boccaccini, M. T., & Murrie, D. C. (2013). Psychopathy and the combination of psychopathy and sexual deviance as predictors of sexual recidivism: Meta-analytic findings using the psychopathy checklist—Revised. *Psychological Assessment*, *25*, 233–243. https://doi.org/10.1037/a0030391.

Hyde, L. W., Byrd, A. L., Votruba-Drzal, E., Hariri, A. R., & Manuck, S. B. (2014). Amygdala reactivity and negative emotionality: Divergent correlates of antisocial personality and psychopathy traits in a community sample. *Journal of Abnormal Psychology*, *123*, 214–224. https://doi.org/10.1037/a0035467.

Kendler, K. S. (2012). The dappled nature of causes of psychiatric illness: Replacing the organic–functional/hardware–software dichotomy with empirically based pluralism. *Molecular Psychiatry*, *17*, 377–388. https://doi.org/10.1038/mp.2011.182.

Kuhn, T. S. (1970). *The structure of scientific revolutions* (2nd ed.). Chicago: University of Chicago Press.

Leistico, A. M. R., Salekin, R. T., DeCoster, J., & Rogers, R. (2008). A large-scale meta-analysis relating the Hare measures of psychopathy to antisocial conduct. *Law and Human Behavior*, *32*, 28–45. https://doi.org/10.1007/s10979-007-9096-6.

Lilienfeld, S. O. (2018). The multidimensional nature of psychopathy: Five recommendations for research. *Journal of Psychopathology and Behavioral Assessment*, *40*, 79–85. https://doi.org/10.1007/s10862-018-9657-7.

Lilienfeld, S.O. (in press). Psychopathy: The knowns and the unknowns. In T.A. Widiger (Ed.), Oxford handbook of personality disorders. New York: Oxford University Press.

Lilienfeld, S. O., Patrick, C. J., Benning, S. D., Berg, J., Sellbom, M., & Edens, J. F. (2012). The role of fearless dominance in psychopathy: Confusions, controversies, and clarifications. *Personality Disorders, Theory, Research, and Treatment*, *3*, 327–340. https://doi.org/10.1037/a0026987.

Lilienfeld, S. O., Smith, S. F., & Watts, A. L. (2016). The perils of unitary models of the etiology of mental disorders—The response modulation hypothesis of psychopathy as a case example: Rejoinder to Newman and Baskin-Sommers. *Psychological Bulletin*, *142*, 1394–1403.

Lilienfeld, S. O., Watts, A. L., Murphy, B., Costello, T. H., Bowes, S. M., Smith, S. F., … Tabb, K. (2019). Personality disorders as emergent interpersonal syndromes: Psychopathic personality as a case example. *Journal of Personality Disorders*, *33*, 577–622. https://doi.org/10.1521/pedi.2019.33.5.577.

Lilienfeld, S. O., Watts, A. L., Smith, S. F., Berg, J. M., & Latzman, R. D. (2015). Psychopathy deconstructed and reconstructed: Identifying and assembling the personality building blocks of Cleckley's chimera. *Journal of Personality*, *83*, 593–610. https://doi.org/10.1111/jopy.12118.

Lilienfeld, S. O., Watts, A. L., Smith, S. F., Patrick, C. J., & Hare, R. D. (2018). Hervey Cleckley (1903–1984): Contributions to the study of psychopathy. *Personality Disorders, Theory, Research, and Treatment*, *9*, 510–520. https://doi.org/10.1037/per0000306.

Lykken, D. T. (1957). A study of anxiety in the sociopathic personality. *The Journal of Abnormal and Social Psychology*, *55*, 6–10. https://doi.org/10.1037/h0047232.

Lynam, D. R., & Derefinko, K. J. (2006). Psychopathy and personality. In C. J. Patrick (Ed.), *Handbook of psychopathy* (pp. 133–155). New York, NY: Guilford Press.

Lynam, D. R., & Miller, J. D. (2012). Fearless dominance and psychopathy: A response to Lilienfeld et al. *Personality Disorders, Theory, Research, and Treatment*, *3*, 341–353.

Maj, M. (2013). Mental disorders as "brain diseases" and Jaspers' legacy. *World Psychiatry*, *12*, 1–3. https://doi.org/10.1002/wps.20000.

Marcus, D. K., John, S. L., & Edens, J. F. (2004). A taxometric analysis of psychopathic personality. *Journal of Abnormal Psychology*, *113*, 626–635.

Meehl, P. E. (2002). Cliometric metatheory: II. Criteria scientists use in theory appraisal and why it is rational to do so. *Psychological Reports*, *91*, 339–404. https://doi.org/10.2466/pr0.2002.91.2.339.

Meehl, P. E., & Golden, R. (1982). Taxometric methods. In P. Kendall, & J. Butcher (Eds.), *Handbook of research methods in clinical psychology* (pp. 127–181). New York: Wiley.

Miller, J. D., Sleep, C. E., Crowe, M. L., & Lynam, D. R. (2020). Psychopathic boldness: Narcissism, self-esteem, or something in between? *Personality and Individual Differences, 155*. https://doi.org/10.1016/j.paid.2019.109761.

Murrie, D. C., Marcus, D. K., Douglas, K. S., Lee, Z., Salekin, R. T., & Vincent, G. (2007). Youth with psychopathy features are not a discrete class: A taxometric analysis. *Journal of Child Psychology and Psychiatry, 48*, 714–723. https://doi.org/10.1111/j.1469-7610.2007.01734.x.

Patrick, C. J. (2006). Back to the future: Cleckley as a guide to the next generation of psychopathy research. In C. J. Patrick (Ed.), *Handbook of psychopathy*. New York, NY: Guilford Press.

Patrick, C. J. (2016). *Handbook of psychopathy* (2nd ed.). New York: Guilford Press.

Patrick, C. J., Fowles, D. C., & Krueger, R. F. (2009). Triarchic conceptualization of psychopathy: Developmental origins of disinhibition, boldness, and meanness. *Development and Psychopathology, 21*, 913–938. https://doi.org/10.1017/S0954579409000492.

Poeppl, T. B., Donges, M. R., Mokros, A., Rupprecht, R., Fox, P. T., Laird, A. R., … Eickhoff, S. B. (2019). A view behind the mask of sanity: Meta-analysis of aberrant brain activity in psychopaths. *Molecular Psychiatry, 24*, 463–470. https://doi.org/10.1038/s41380-018-0122-5.

Rucker, D. D., McShane, B. B., & Preacher, K. J. (2015). A researcher's guide to regression, discretization, and median splits of continuous variables. *Journal of Consumer Psychology, 25*, 666–678. https://doi.org/10.1016/j.jcps.2015.04.004.

Sörman, K., Edens, J. F., Toney Smith, S., Clark, J. W., Kristiansson, M., & Svensson, O. (2016). Boldness and its relation to psychopathic personality: Prototypicality analyses among forensic mental health, criminal justice, and layperson raters. *Law and Human Behavior, 40*(3), 337–349. https://doi.org/10.1037/lhb0000176.

Streiner, D. L. (2002). Breaking up is hard to do: The heartbreak of dichotomizing continuous data. *The Canadian Journal of Psychiatry, 47*, 262–266. https://doi.org/10.1177/070674370204700307.

Ten Brinke, L., Porter, S., Korva, N., Fowler, K., Lilienfeld, S. O., & Patrick, C. J. (2017). An examination of the communication styles associated with psychopathy and their influence on observer impressions. *Journal of Nonverbal Behavior, 41*, 269–287. https://doi.org/10.1007/s10919-017-0252-5.

Walters, G. D. (2012). Psychopathy and crime: Testing the incremental validity of PCL-R-measured psychopathy as a predictor of general and violent recidivism. *Law and Human Behavior, 36*, 404–412. https://doi.org/10.1037/h0093928.

Walters, G. D., Brinkley, C. A., Magaletta, P. R., & Diamond, P. M. (2008). Taxometric analysis of the Levenson self-report psychopathy scale. *Journal of Personality Assessment, 90*, 491–498. https://doi.org/10.1080/00223890802248828.

Walters, G. D., Duncan, S. A., & Mitchell-Perez, K. (2007). The latent structure of psychopathy: A taxometric investigation of the Psychopathy Checklist–Revised in a heterogeneous sample of male prison inmates *Assessment, 14*, 270–278.

Walters, G. D., Ermer, E., Knight, R. A., & Kiehl, K. A. (2015). Paralimbic biomarkers in taxometric analyses of psychopathy: Does changing the indicators change the conclusion? *Personality Disorders, Theory, Research, and Treatment, 6*, 41–52. https://doi.org/10.1037/per0000097.

Index

Note: Page numbers followed by *f* indicate figures and *t* indicate tables.

R